A HANDY DICTIONARY OF SPORTING TERMS

THE LANGUAGE OF
SPORT

BY TIM CONSIDINE

ANGUS
& ROBERTSON
PUBLISHERS

This book is dedicated to the late Bob Considine, whose kindness
and hospitality I'm afraid I tested at the beginning of my professional involvement
with sports, and to all the other great writers and broadcasters,
past and present, who have added so much to our
enjoyment and understanding of athletics by enriching,
popularizing, and, in many cases, creating the language of sport.

For Willie and Chris

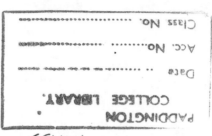

ANGUS & ROBERTSON PUBLISHERS

*Unit 4, Eden Park, 31 Waterloo Road,
North Ryde, NSW, Australia 2113, and
16 Golden Square, London W1R 4BN,
United Kingdom*

*This book is copyright.
Apart from any fair dealing for the
purposes of private study, research,
criticism or review, as permitted
under the Copyright Act, no part may
be reproduced by any process without
written permission. Inquiries should
be addressed to the publishers.*

*First published in paperback
in the United States of America by
World Almanac Publications in 1983
This revised edition first published
in paperback in Australia by Angus &
Robertson Publishers and in the
United Kingdom by Angus & Robertson
(UK) Ltd in 1986*

*Copyright © Tim Considine 1982
Published by arrangement with
World Almanac Publications*

*National Library of Australia
Cataloguing-in-publication data.*

*Considine, Tim.
  The language of sport.
  ISBN 0 207 15010 9.
  1. Sports — Dictionaries. I. Title.
796'.03'21*

*Illustrations by Ed Murawinski
Printed in Shenzhen, China*

CONTENTS

PREFACE

When man first conceived the notion of sports, that is the codifying of contests into repeatable games and competitions, a new language was born. This volume is a dictionary of that language some three thousand years later in this, the age of sports medicine, sports law, sports science, and twenty-four-hour satellite coverage by sports-only cable television networks. In the 1980s, more people than ever before participate in, watch, follow, and talk sports.

Sports language is so universal and its imagery so strong that some of it finds its way into non-sports use. Something is said to have come "out of left field" or a good looking person is called a "knockout." "Heavyweight," "can't get to first base," and "throw in the towel," are other popular examples. The expression "to start from scratch" dates back to 776 B.C. and the first Olympic Games, where the starting point for a jumping contest or a footrace was a line scratched in the sand. There are more obscure examples as well. The word "agony" is derived from the Greek word *agon,* which means athletic contest. "Ascetic" is also Greek derived, meaning an athlete in full training. Even the Bible contains sports language and imagery. In the Authorized Version of the New Testament, Acts 20:24, St. Paul sums up his life, "I have fought the good fight. I have finished my course. I have kept the faith. Henceforth there is laid up for me a crown of righteousness." Mostly, though, the language is used to enhance the enjoyment of the sports it describes—whether accurately, colorfully, passionately, or humorously.

Because of the constant state of flux of all languages, even as this work is being prepared, new words and expressions are being formed which will eventually find acceptance and popular use. The over-5,000 entries defined herein represent a comprehensive collection of traditional and contemporary terminology, jargon, and slang from nine of the most popular sports.

Each chapter begins with a history tracing the growth and development of the sport from its origins to the present day, with emphasis on the formulation of rules, important firsts, and famous or noteworthy players and contributors. An alphabetical listing of terms follows, using the most common spelling. Whenever possible, specific origins, anecdotes, and related records accompany the term definitions. Broadened or secondary uses, and those removed from the original sports usage, are also included.

i

ACKNOWLEDGMENTS

The author would like to thank the many people who have helped to make this book possible, including Editorial Assistant and Research Coordinator Ellen Baskin; Researchers David Aust, Bob Borgen, Roger Cossack, Tom Craig, Geoffrey Dean-Smith, LeeAn Lowe, Joe McDonnell, Bob Rodgers, and Carl Wilson; Patricia Fisher, Assistant Editor, World Almanac Publications; and the coaches, athletes, officials, administrators, writers, broadcasters, and sports afficianados who provided invaluable assistance, information, and encouragement in the preparation of this volume, among them Joe Axelson (General Manager and President, Kansas City Kings), Jim Campbell (Research Editor, NFL Properties), Sam Foulds (USSF Historian), Hadassa Gilbert (USSF referee), Herbert Goldman (Managing Editor, *The Ring*), Gail Goodrich (former Los Angeles Laker All-Star player), Stephen Green (Curator, Marylebone Cricket Club), Richard D. Haskell (Executive Director, Massachusetts Golf Association), Tommy Higson (Lancashire Cricket Club), C.J. Hoddell (co-founder Hoddell Stotesbury Rugby Society), Toros Kibritjian (FIFA and senior NASL referee), Patrick Leahy (USGA Press Relations Manager), Mario Machado (radio and television broadcaster), Prof. Julio Mazzei (coach, New York Cosmos), Pete Newell (Basketball Hall of Fame coach and general manager), Nick Newman (Chairman, Olympic Limo Cricket Club), Carlos Palomino (former World Welterweight Champion), Don Sawyer (international amateur, college, and high school basketball referee), Norm Schacter (NFL Rule Book Co-editor and League Observer), Bob Sibbald (NASL player and coach), Walter Dean-Smith (Wilmslow Golf Club), Dr. Edward S. Steitz (President ABAUSA, Editor USA rules, member FIBA Technical Committee), June Steitz (Librarian, Basketball Hall of Fame), Dennis F. Storer (sports historian and former coach, United States National Rugby Team), Burt Randolph Suger (Editor and Publisher, *The Ring*), and Gary Wiren (PGA Director of Club Relations).

The author would also like to thank the following organizations for information and materials provided: the Amateur Athletic Union (AAU), the Amateur Basketball Association of the United States of America (ABAUSA), the American League (AL), the American Soccer League (ASL), the American Youth Soccer Organization (AYSO), the Association of Tennis Professionals (ATP), the Basketball Hall of Fame, the Canadian Football League (CFL), the Consulate General of the People's Republic of China in San Francisco, the International Tennis Federation (ITF), the Ladies Professional Golf Association (LPGA), Lancashire Cricket Club, the Major Indoor Soccer League (MISL), Marylebone Cricket Club, the National Collegiate Athletic Association (NCAA), the National Football League (NFL), the National Football League Players Association (NFLPA), the National Golf Foundation, the National League (NL), the North American Soccer League (NASL), Pop Warner Football, the Professional Golfer's Association (PGA), the Rugby Football League (RFL), the Rugby Football Union (RFU), *Soccer America* Team Tennis, *The Ring*, the United States Golf Association (USGA), the United States of America Rugby Football Union (USARFU), the United States Soccer Federation (USSF), the United States Tennis Association (USTA), the Women's Sports Foundation, and the Women's Tennis Association (WTA).

BASEBALL

Bat and ball games have been played throughout history by many different cultures, but baseball is most closely related to cricket, the earliest form of which dates back to England in 1300 and the reign of Edward I, and another English sport, rounders. In 1744, the first published reference to rounders, a woodcut of children playing the game with an accompanying verse titled, "Base Ball", appeared in *A Little Pretty Pocket Book*.

It was rounders, a more impromptu game than cricket, that the sons of early American settlers most frequently played. Numerous variations emerged, but all drew on the basic ideas and equipment of rounders. Two teams of nine players took turns hitting a thrown ball with a bat in order to score by running around a set of four posts without being put out by fielders catching the ball or touching it to a post before the batter arrived. Eventually, the posts became bases, the bowler (thrower) a pitcher, and the bowler's square a pitcher's mound. By the 1840s, a new game was evolving that resembled rounders and utilized much of its terminology, but reflected the active, freewheeling American personality. The oblong bat was made round and lengthened, allowing more powerful hits, and it became necessary to anchor the bases to withstand the headlong lunges of runners trying to avoid being "plugged" (a popular innovation which allowed a base runner to be put out between bases by being hit with a thrown ball). Exact rules and playing field configurations varied from town to town, and the game was known by a variety of names including "one old cat" and "two old cat", or simply "town ball".

Though a once popular legend held that Abner Doubleday, a US Army general, laid out the first baseball diamond in 1839 at Cooperstown, New York (present site of the Baseball Hall of Fame and Museum), most historians now agree that the first real baseball game took place at the Elysian Fields in Hoboken, New Jersey on June 19, 1846. In that historic contest, played under rules established by Alexander Cartwright, who umpired the game, the New York Nine defeated the Knickerbockers by a score of 23–1. Soon amateur teams throughout the East and Midwest were playing versions of Cartwright's "New York Game". In 1859, Amherst played Williams in the first US college-level game, with Amherst winning 66–32.

After the American Civil War, during which Southerners picked up the game from Union prisoners, baseball's popularity spread rapidly. Amateur teams representing cities went on barnstorming tours to play the local favorites. As a result of a humiliating defeat admin-

1

istered by one of these traveling teams, the Washington Nationals, some angry citizens of Cincinnati decided to do something radical. In 1869, the Cincinnati Red Stockings became the first professional baseball team. That year on an 11,000-mile tour of their own, the Red Stockings compiled a record of fifty-six wins and one tie, attracting interest wherever they played.

The economic potential of the sport was becoming more and more evident. In 1871, the National Association of Professional Baseball Players, the first attempt at a professional league, was formed with nine teams competing. The Philadelphia Athletics won the first championship. Though plagued by erratic scheduling and a lack of strong leadership, the league continued on, managing to struggle through the 1875 season before the taint of gambling and bribery finally caused its failure.

In February of 1876, a group of businessmen and club representatives led by Chicago White Stockings owner, William Hulbert, drew up a constitution for a new federation, and on April 22, 1876, with the strongest organizations and the best players of the old Association in tow, the National League opened its first season with a game in Philadelphia. On that day, Boston defeated the home team 6–5 in front of 3,000 spectators.

By 1881, the National League had demonstrated enough success to inspire a new rival league, the American Association. Armed with players lured away from National League teams and with innovations like Sunday baseball games, an admission price of twenty-five cents (as opposed to fifty cents in the National League), and the sale of beer in the ballparks, the American Association soon became a formidable competitor. In 1883, the two leagues signed a mutually protective document, called the National Agreement, to prevent further harm to either from player raids. The uneasy truce lasted until 1890 when a number of the best players from both leagues, frustrated at being treated as chattel by the owners and united since 1885 in the Brotherhood of Professional Ballplayers, broke off and started their own league, the Players' League. Their venture lasted only one season and ultimately few concessions were won, but the added competition had managed to deal a crippling blow to the struggling American Association. Further weakened when some of the best Players' League personnel were reassigned to the National League, the American Association went under in 1891, no longer able to meet rising operating expenses with the twenty-five cent admission.

In one year, major league baseball went from twenty-four teams to twelve. With just the strongest pitchers remaining, batters suddenly found themselves struggling (only eleven batters hit over .300 in 1892, as compared to twenty-three the previous year). Fearing that interest in the game might dwindle, the baseball owners moved the pitcher's rubber back from 50 feet to 60 feet, 6 inches for the 1893 season. After forty-seven years of constant change, the measurements and configuration of the baseball diamond, as well as most of the rules of the game, had finally stabilized (and remain substantially the same to this day).

In 1901, the National League was again threatened. Ban Johnson, who for seven years had been carefully grooming a successful minor league recently renamed the American League, moved four well-financed franchises into Eastern cities, withdrew from the National Agreement, and proclaimed the new eight-team American League a full-fledged major league. With rosters made up of former National League players, including future Hall of Famers Cy Young, "Iron Man" Joe McGinnity, John McGraw, and Nap Lojoie (who jumped from the National League Philadelphia Phillies to the American League Philadelphia Athletics), the new league was a credible competitor the first season, even managing to outdraw the senior circuit in two long-time National League strongholds, Boston and Chicago. Within two years the National League was forced to recognize the new league as an equal, and the first World Series was played at the end of the 1903 season and won by the American League Boston Pilgrims over the Pittsburgh Pirates. The modern era of baseball had begun.

Thereafter, nothing, including scandal (the shocking discovery that some key Chicago White Sox players had thrown the 1919 World Series with Cincinnati) or war, could come between the American people and the sport embraced as the "National Pastime". Chronicled with skill and care by some of America's keenest observers, from Ring Lardner, Damon Runyon and Grantland Rice to Red Smith, no other sport has made more colorful or numerous contributions to the history and lore of American sport or to everyday language than baseball. Ty Cobb, Christy Mathewson, the legendary Babe Ruth, Lou Gehrig, Dizzy Dean, Joe DiMaggio, Bob Feller, Ted Williams, Jackie Robinson, Stan Musial, Willie Mays, Mickey Mantle, Sandy Koufax, Roberto Clemente, Hank Aaron, Carl Yastrzemski, and Pete Rose are just some of the heroes the game has created. Today, baseball, for so long the most popular sport in America, has spread far beyond the North American continent, and is now played in many countries including Australia, England, Japan, and China.

aboard: On base. (two away with one aboard and the tying run at the plate)

ace: A very good pitcher, usually a team's best. In 1869 the first professional baseball club, the Cincinnati Red Stockings, won fifty-six out of fifty-seven games (one tie), incredibly using only one pitcher, Asa Brainard. The following year, any pitcher who put together a string of victories or pitched a particularly impressive game was likened to Brainard and called an "Asa," which eventually became ace. also *stopper*.

••One who excels in any field. (ace reporter)

air it out: To hit the ball a long distance.

alley: The area of the outfield between the players in center field and left field or center field and right field.

All-Star break: The three-day suspension of regular season games by both the American League and the National League to provide for the annual All-Star Game.

All-Star Game: The annual July exhibition game between the best players of the American League and the National League, as chosen by baseball fans through ballots. At the suggestion of *Chicago Tribune* sports editor Arch Ward, the first All-Star Game was played at Comiskey Park in Chicago on July 6, 1933 and was won by the American League.

aluminum bat: A round, one-piece tubular metal bat used in softball (maximum length: 34 inches; maximum barrel diameter: 2-1/4 inches), welded at the knob end and plugged at the barrel end with a contoured hard rubber insert. A grip-improving wrap or material is mandatory for softball (maximum length: 10 inches, and extending no more than 15 inches

from the end of the handle) and optional for amateur baseball (extending no more than 18 inches from the end of the handle).

American League: One of the two major professional baseball leagues in the United States. Created in 1900 by Byron "Ban" Johnson, the American League played its first game on April 24, 1901. At that time, there were teams in Chicago, Boston, Detroit, Philadelphia, Baltimore, Washington, Cleveland, and Milwaukee. Although even today the American League is sometimes referred to as the "junior circuit" by members of the older National League, the American League has been considered an equal competitor since the first World Series competition between the two leagues in 1903. The American League Boston Pilgrims won that first best-of-nine series five games to three against the National League Pittsburgh Pirates. The American League is now split into two divisions. In the Western Division, the teams are California, Chicago, Kansas City, Minnesota, Oakland, Seattle, and Texas. In the Eastern Division, the teams are Baltimore, Boston, Cleveland, Detroit, Milwaukee, New York, and Toronto. Abbreviated AL.

American Legion Baseball: A league sponsored by the American Legion since 1926 providing a program of summer baseball for fifteen to eighteen-year-olds. Headquartered in Indianapolis, Indiana, American Legion Baseball conducts an annual World Series tournament for the eight regional United States champions in the month of August.

angel: A cloud that shields the sun from the

3

eyes of an outfielder preparing to catch a high fly ball. also *guardian angel.*

Annie Oakley: 1. A free ticket to a baseball game. Named by American League president Ban Johnson, because of the resemblance of complimentary baseball tickets (punched with holes) to the playing cards the legendary Annie Oakley shot holes through at Buffalo Bill's Wild West shows in the late 1800s. 2. A base on balls. A walk is considered a free pass, or free ticket, or free trip to first base.

appeal: The official notification to an umpire of a rules infraction such as batting out of order, or a baserunning infraction, or an official request to consult a base umpire in the case of a half swing that has been called a ball. see *appeal play, batting out of order, half swing.*

appeal play: A play made in conjunction with an appeal when a base runner fails to tag up after a fly ball is caught or fails to touch a base when advancing or when returning to his original base. If a member of the defensive team tags the runner or touches the missed base while holding the ball and makes an appeal to the umpire before the next pitch, the runner is out.

apple: A slang word for ball, popularized in the 1920s by players and sportswriters. also *horsehide.*

arbiter: An umpire.

arm: 1. The ability to make a strong, accurate throw, particularly a long throw from the outfield. 2. A player known for the ability to make strong, accurate throws from the outfield. A list of the great arms in baseball history would have to include Al Kaline of the Detroit Tigers, Bob Kennedy, who played both infield and outfield, Carl "The Reading (Pa.) Rifle" Furillo, and Hall of Famers Chick Hafey, Joe DiMaggio, Mickey Mantle, Roberto Clemente, and Willie Mays. California Angels outfielder Ellis Valentine is among those most frequently mentioned as the best arm in contemporary baseball.

around the horn: 1. The ritual of throwing the ball around the infield after an out (when there are no base runners). 2. A double play in which the third baseman fields the ball and throws to the second baseman, who throws to first base. From the old nautical expression, comparing the flight of the ball to the only route between the Atlantic and Pacific before the Panama Canal was built: all the way around South America, with second base representing Cape Horn, the halfway mark.

artificial turf: A synthetic grass substitute used in some ballparks and sold under a variety of trade names.

aspirin: A fastball. see *fastball.*

assist: A throw or deflection of a batted or thrown ball to a teammate, resulting in a putout, or one that would have resulted in a putout except for a subsequent error by a teammate.

AstroTurf: A brand of artificial turf.

at bat: 1. Now batting or about to bat. Part of the expression "at bat, on deck, in the hole," a corruption of the original "at bat, on deck, in the hold," first uttered in 1872 at a game between a local team and the Boston Red Stockings in the small coastal city of Belfast, Maine. This nautical imagery was chosen to inform the watching crowd of seamen and their families who was batting, who was next, and who was waiting to follow. also *at the plate, up.* 2. A turn as a batter that is charged to a player in statistical records and considered in calculating the player's batting average, slugging average, and home run percentage. An "at bat" is not charged when a player hits a sacrifice bunt or fly, receives a base on balls, is hit by a pitched ball, or is interfered with or obstructed by a defensive player.

atom ball: A ball hit right to a defensive player, or "at 'im."

at the plate: see *at bat.*

automatic take: A situation in which the batter is virtually certain to take the next pitch because of the favorable chances of receiving a base on balls, as with a count of three balls and no strikes.

away: Out. (one man on and two away)

Babe Ruth Baseball: A nonprofit educational organization that sponsors summer baseball leagues for youths aged nine through twelve, thirteen through fifteen, and sixteen through eighteen in cities throughout the United States and Canada, and in Guam. Founded in 1951, Babe Ruth Baseball is headquartered in Trenton, New Jersey.

1. backhand: To catch or field a ball by

reaching across the body with the glove hand turned so that the thumb is down.

2. backhand: A backhand catch.

backstop: 1. A screen or barrier behind home plate for the protection of spectators. 2. A catcher. An old term that dates back to the eighteenth century game of rounders and describes a player positioned to field balls missed by the batsman.

back up: To position oneself behind a teammate to be able to assist if the teammate should misfield a hit ball or a throw.

bad head: Players' slang for an ugly teammate or opponent. (such a bad head, he should always wear a catcher's mask)

bad hop: The sudden and unlikely bounce or carom of a hit ball off a flaw in the turf.

bag: A base. So called because canvas bags are used as bases. see *base*.

bail out: To suddenly move out of the way of a pitch while at bat to avoid being hit by the ball. (had to bail out from a head-high wild pitch) also *hit the dirt*.

balk: An illegal act by the pitcher that allows one-base advance by all runners. A balk is called if, in the judgment of the umpire, a pitcher does not make the pitch after initiating the normal delivery motion; stands in the pitching position near or on the pitcher's rubber without the ball; makes a throw to a base in order to take out a runner but neglects to step directly toward that base; fails to come to a set position and stop before pitching but instead pitches directly from a stretch; pitches when the catcher is not in position in the catcher's box; makes any kind of an illegal pitch, including a quick pitch; feints a throw to first base, homeplate, or any unoccupied base; or winds up for the pitch using more than two pumps. If, in the judgment of the umpire, the pitcher commits one of these actions when the bases are empty, a ball is called. The balk rule was adopted in 1899.

ball: 1. A baseball (hardball or softball). see *baseball, softball*. 2. A pitched ball that misses the strike zone and at which the batter does not swing. If the count reaches four balls in one turn at bat, the batter is awarded first base.

•• To "be on the ball" or to "have something on the ball" means to be clever or intelligent. To "drop the ball" is to make an error or lose an opportunity.

ball boy, ball girl: A young person who fields foul balls throughout the game and keeps the plate umpire supplied with new balls.

ballgame: A baseball game.

•• Just as a pivotal offensive or defensive play or other factors can suddenly make a game in progress "a new ballgame," the introduction of a new factor can be said to figuratively make a new ballgame out of any circumstance. (after the results of the election, it's a whole new ballgame in Congress)

ball hawk: An outfielder skilled at fielding fly balls. (that ball hawk can catch anything that doesn't clear the fence)

ballpark: A stadium or stadium-type area designed for the playing of baseball.

•• Although a ballpark is large, it is enclosed by fences or walls. Therefore, anything said to be within it cannot be too far distant. (still an unacceptable offer, but at least within the ballpark) (a ballpark estimate)

ballplayer: A baseball player.

Baltimore chop: A fair ball that is topped so it will bounce on the ground just in front of home plate and high into the air, often allowing time for the batter to reach first base without a play. Originated as a deliberate tactic by the Baltimore Orioles in 1896.

banana stick: see *morning journal*.

band box: A small ballpark. Players' slang dating from the turn of the century, a comparison to the outdoor bandstands or band boxes then prevalent in the parks of American cities.

bang-bang play: 1. A very close play, such as when the ball barely beats the runner to a base. 2. A defensive play (often a double play) completed with machinelike ease and speed.

banjo hit: An accidental ground ball (such as one hit on a check swing), named in 1924 by Jersey City second baseman, Ray "Snooks" Dowd, for the way the ball "plunks" off the bat. also *bleeder, nubber*.

barber: 1. A pitcher with the reputation of throwing "Gillettes," pitches thrown close to the batter's head that deliver "close shaves." also *headhunter*. 2. A pitcher with enough control to be able to "shave the corners," or throw strikes that pass barely within the strike zone

5

corners. Sal "The Barber" Maglie was known for throwing Gillettes, as well as for his ability to "shave the corners" when he got his nickname pitching for the New York Giants in the early 1950s. 3. A talkative player. From a comparison to constantly talking barbers. First associated with Waite Hoyt, a talky young pitcher who came to the New York Yankees in the 1920s, but popularized later when Red Barber, a master of colorful description, began to broadcast· the Brooklyn Dodgers games.

base: One of four objects set at each corner of a baseball diamond and which the runner must contact in sequence in order to score a run. First, second, and third bases are stuffed, 15-inch-square white canvas bags attached to the ground. First and third bases butt up against the infield sides of their baselines. Second base is positioned at the perpendicular angle formed by the baselines which extend from the outfield sides of first and third bases. Home base (almost always referred to as home plate, home, or the plate) is the last base with which the runner must make contact in order to score. It is a flat piece of white rubber with five sides, set into the ground directly opposite second base. The leading edge, which faces the pitcher, is 17 inches wide. Two perpendicular sides extend 8-1/2 inches back from the leading edge, and then taper to meet in a point 8-1/2 inches farther back. This endpoint is placed on the intersection of the first and third baselines. The distance between bases is 90 feet (50 to 80 feet for youths). The distance between softball bases is 60 feet. Originally the bases were 4-foot-high vertical stakes from the game of rounders. In the late 1830s, in order to prevent injuries from collisions, these were replaced by large flat stones for a time, then by sand-filled sacks similar to modern bases. also *bag, sack.*

●●To "touch base" means to figuratively make contact. (should touch base with her office before leaving) Just as it is a mistake for a base runner to be caught off base by the defending team, the expression "off base" connotes a deviation from what is correct or true. (an off base premise)

baseball: 1. A game played on a fan-shaped field, with a ball and bat, by two teams of nine players each. The field is divided into the infield at the small end, a 90-foot (sometimes less for youths) square called a diamond with a base at each corner; and the outfield, the remaining area beyond the diamond at the larger end. From home plate, which is located at the corner of the diamond at the small end of the field, the other three bases (in the counterclockwise order they must be touched by an offensive player on the way back to home plate to score) are first base, second base, and third base. Teams alternate playing on offense and defense. The defensive team has three players in the outfield who are responsible for catching or fielding balls hit to their respective zones: a right fielder, a center fielder, and a left fielder. The infielders assume the following positions: a first baseman near first base, a second baseman between first and second base, a shortstop between second and third base, and a third baseman near third base. A catcher stands behind home plate, facing a pitcher who stands 60 feet, 6 inches away from· him (sometimes less for youths) on a direct line through the diamond toward second base. A batter from the opposing team tries to hit a ball thrown by the pitcher into the playing area, but between or away from any fielders so that, without being thrown or tagged out, he may run to at least one base. Offensive players may be put out by striking out (any combination totaling three of missed swings, good pitches thrown within the strike zone not swung at, or balls hit foul—although a foul ball is not applicable for the third strike), hitting a fly ball that is caught in the air, having a fielded ball thrown to a defensive player touching first base (or any base one is forced to run to) before the offensive player can get to the base, or by being tagged with the ball while off base. If a batter receives four pitched balls not in the strike zone and does not swing at them, or if the batter is hit by a pitched ball, the batter is allowed to proceed to first base. When the base runner has successfully reached all the bases as well as home plate in succession and has not been put out, a run is earned for the offensive team. The offensive team's players continue to bat in order (according to the batting sequence established before the game) until three players have been declared out. When three players have been put out, the offensive team switches positions with the team in the field, which then takes its turn at bat. Each cycle (both teams bat until three putouts are made) is an inning. Whichever team has scored more runs at the end of nine innings (sometimes less for youths) is the winner of the game. If the home team (which always bats in the second half of each inning) is leading after eight and one-half innings, the game is over. If the home team scores the winning run during the ninth inning, the game is over. At any time during its turn at bat in the ninth inning, the home team can score the winning run and end the game, no matter how many outs have been made. A margin of only one run is needed to win the game. However, if a home run causes a win, the final score will include runs driven in by it. If, at the end of nine innings, the score remains tied, extra innings are played until one team leads after a complete inning. When rain or darkness force a game to end prematurely, it is regarded as a complete game after five innings. The umpire-in-chief, under whose control the game is played, decides whether or not a game can be called off on account of darkness or rain. Positioned behind home plate, the umpire calls balls and strikes, judges whether a hit ball is fair or foul, and rules on plays at home plate. The umpire-in-chief initiates play with the call "play ball" and has the authority to call time out, eject a manager, player, or coach, or forfeit a game. In professional baseball, there are field umpires at each base to call plays there, and, during the World Series, on the foul lines to help rule on balls hit down the lines. 2. A ball with which the game of baseball is played. A sphere wrapped in white leather, the seams of which are in raised relief, it is 9 to 9-1/4 inches in circumference and weighs 5 to 5-1/4 ounces. Its center is cork, which is then wound in twine.

Baseball Annie: A woman or girl, sometimes known as a baseball groupie, who actively pursues the company of members of a professional baseball team. also *green fly.*

baseball mud: A special composition of fine earth used by major league umpires to rub up new baseballs before a game to insure proper and uniform gripping characteristics.

base hit: A batted ball hit within the playing area, enabling the batter to successfully reach a base, unaided by a defensive error, a force play, or an attempt to put out the preceding base runner. also *hit, safe hit, safety.*

baseline: Either of the lines extending at right angles from the rear of home plate through the outer edges of first base and third base respectively to the far boundary of the outfield. Within these lines, also called foul lines, is fair territory. Baselines were first marked with whitewash in 1860.

base on balls: A free passage to first base given to a batter who does not swing at four "balls," pitches thrown outside the strike zone, during one turn at bat. Abbreviated bb. Before 1880, a batter had to receive nine balls in order to be awarded a base on balls. The number of balls required changed to eight in 1880, to seven in 1882, to six in 1884, back to seven in 1886, to five in 1887, and finally, in 1889, to the present four balls. Babe Ruth holds both the single season (170 in 1923) and lifetime (2,056) records for bases on balls. also *Annie Oakley, free pass, free ticket, free trip, pass, walk.*

base path: The lane or path on which base runners travel from base to base. Base runners may deviate from a straight line in order to turn less severe (therefore faster) corners around the bases or to stay out of the way of a defensive player fielding a batted ball, but are restricted from running more than three feet from that line in attempting to evade a tag.

base runner: A member of the offensive team who has taken a turn at bat and subsequently is on base or running toward a base. also *runner.*

bases empty: No member of the team at bat is on base.

bases full: see *bases loaded.*

bases loaded: Base runners on first, second, and third base. also *bases full, ducks on the pond, the table is set.*

basket catch: The fielding of a fly ball

holding the glove at waist height with the palm facing up. A difficult technique first popularized by then-New York Giants player, Willie Mays.

1. **bat:** A tapering, cylindrical hardwood (or, optionally in amateur baseball and softball, metal of the same shape) stick with which the batter tries to hit the ball. The maximum diameter for the larger end is 2-3/4 inches (2-1/4 inches for softball and Little League). The end of the bat that is held is approximately 1 inch in diameter, and is wrapped up in tape or a composition material up to a maximum of 18 inches from the end. This wrapping allows for easier gripping. (The maximum for softball is 15 inches, with an option of a cork-covered grip.) The length of the average baseball bat is 36 to 37 inches, but the maximum is 42 inches (34 inches for softball, 33 inches for Little League). also *hickory, lumber, mace, stick, wand, willow.*

●●The expression "right off the bat" is used to mean initially or immediately. (liked her right off the bat)

2. **bat:** To take a turn as a batter.

BATTER

●●To figuratively "go to bat for" is to speak or argue on behalf of. (promised to go to bat for lower taxes)

bat around: To have, in one inning, a team's entire lineup come to bat in rotation.

bat boy, bat girl: The boy or girl who is responsible for returning bats to the bat rack after use and for assisting with the preparation and maintenance of the team's equipment.

bat rack: The grating or frame in which a team's bats are arranged and placed.

batsman: A batter. Originally from the sport of cricket, later rounders. see *batter.*

batter: The player at bat. During a turn at bat, the player takes his position in the batter's box and tries to hit the ball pitched by the opposing pitcher.

batter's box: One of two rectangles appropriately placed for the batting position, measuring 6 feet by 4 feet, indicated on the ground parallel to and 6 inches away from each side of home plate (5-1/2 feet by 3 feet and 4 inches from home plate for Little League).

batter up: The umpire's notification to the player whose turn it is to bat, to step into the batter's box so that play can commence.

battery: The pitcher and the catcher. From the mid-nineteenth century military description of the components of an artillery unit.

batting average: A statistic expressing the batting efficiency of a player or team. It is calculated by dividing the number of base hits by the number of official at bats and carrying the quotient three decimal places. Abbreviated ba. In 1894, Hugh Duffy of the Boston Beaneaters (later Braves) set the all-time record for the highest batting average in a single season, .438. The last major league player to bat over .400 was Ted Williams, who batted .406 in 1941. The record for the highest lifetime batting average is held by Ty Cobb at .367.

●●A record of success or failure. To "bat a thousand" is to enjoy a perfect record or unqualified success. (the neighborhood grocer is batting a thousand with this week's special)

batting cage: A cagelike apparatus, constructed with wire fencing, and portable in spite of its large size. It provides a space for the batter during batting practice and serves as a collection area for fouled or missed pitches.

batting helmet: A caplike plastic protective helmet, the latest examples of which extend down to cover the ear and temple area. Helmets were first used in 1941 by Brooklyn Dodgers batters and are now mandatory, not only in youth leagues, but in both major leagues.

batting order: The specific sequence in which turns at bat are taken by the players of a team. Established and submitted to the umpire on a lineup card prior to every game, the order is strictly maintained. A substitute player must assume the place held by the replaced player in his team's batting order.

batting out of order: Taking a turn at bat contrary to the fixed batting order on the lineup card submitted to the umpire before the game. If appealed by the defensive team at any time before the first pitch is made to the next batter, the proper batter is declared out, and any advance or score made by or because of the improper batter is nullified.

bat weight: A warm-up device, shaped like a doughnut and heavily weighted, which players slide onto the bat to warm up with just before batting (instead of swinging multiple bats). When the weight is discarded, the player's bat seems particularly light and manageable. also *doughnut.*

bb: Abbreviation for base on balls.

BB: A fastball. see *fastball.*

bean: To pitch a ball so that it strikes the batter on the head. also *skull.* see *beanball.*
●●To hit someone in the head, especially with a thrown object. (beaned by a cushion thrown from the bleachers)

beanball: A pitched ball that is intentionally thrown at or strikes a batter's head. The combination of bean (slang for head) with ball is thought to be the creation of sportswriter Charlie Dryden in 1906. Major league baseball's only fatality occurred in 1920, when a beanball thrown by Yankees pitcher Carl Mays struck and killed Ray Chapman, shortstop for the Cleveland Indians. also *beaner, chin music.* compare *brushback, duster, Gillette, knockdown pitch, purpose pitch.*

beaner: see *beanball.*

beat out: To arrive at first base ahead of an infielder's throw, enabling what would ordinarily be a ground out to be a base hit. (the batter beat out his grounder to third)

behind: To be at a disadvantage because of the count. When a pitcher gets behind, the batter knows the pitcher must now throw strikes or risk a base on balls. also *in the hole.*

belt buckle ball: A ball that is illegally scratched or cut on the pitcher's belt buckle in order to make it curve in an unnatural way when pitched.

1. bench: 1. The long seat in the dugout where reserve players and players waiting to bat sit. 2. Players a team has on reserve, ready to substitute for the current players. (went to his bench for a pinch hitter against the left-hander) 3. The dugout.
●●A figurative place for nonparticipants. (relegated to the bench while his wife attempted to paint over his mistakes)

2. bench: To take a player out of the lineup either before or during a game, for the duration or remainder of the game.

bench jockey: 1. A substitute player who seldom plays. One who "rides" the bench. also *bench warmer.* 2. A player who harasses or "rides" opponents from the bench.

bench warmer: A substitute player who seldom plays. One who "warms" the bench by sitting on it. In use since the 1920s. also *bench jockey.*

between the lines: Players' slang for being engaged in a baseball game. The term refers to being between the foul lines.

big inning: An important inning for a team because of the number of runs scored. (turned the game around with a big inning in the ninth)

big league: 1. Either or both of, or pertaining to either or both of the two existing major professional baseball leagues: the National League and the American League. 2. Any or all of, or pertaining to any or all of, the six major professional leagues in the history of organized baseball: the National League (1876 to the present), the American League (1901 to the present), the American Association (1882 to 1891), the Union Association (1884), the Players' League (1890), and the Federal League (1914 to 1915). also *major league.*
●●The highest level of any enterprise or endeavor. (when the limousine called,

the new vice president knew she'd made the big league)

bigs: The big leagues, or major leagues. also *majors.*

bingle: A hit, usually a single. Probably a combination of "bingo" (an early term for a hit) or "bing" with single, dating from the early 1900s.

bird dog: see *ivory hunter.*

black: The areas just inside and outside the strike zone, above the side sections of the thin black border around the plate. see *paint the black.*

Black Betsy: A large or strong bat. Originally the nickname for a large dark bat used by Cleveland and Chicago slugger, Shoeless Joe Jackson. Jackson's professional career ended when he was banished from baseball for being one of the eight White Sox players responsible for the infamous Black Sox scandal, in which the 1919 World Series was fixed.

blank: To prevent an opposing team from scoring any runs in a game. also *shut out.*

bleachers: Seats which are usually located beyond the outfield walls or fences and in the open with no roof; not reserved and less expensive than regular grandstand seats. Called bleaching boards or bleachers from the late 1800s because of the sun exposure.

●●Outdoor, or simply inexpensive, seating at any kind of spectator event.

bleeder: see *banjo hit.*

block the plate: To try to tag out the base runner by standing between him and home plate. Only legal when the catcher is in possession of the ball.

bloop: To hit a short fly ball that falls between the infielders and outfielders. (blooped a single to right field)

blooper: 1. see *Texas leaguer.* 2. A slow pitch lobbed in a high arc to the batter that, if not hit or caught, bounces just behind the plate. Originated in 1941 by Pittsburgh Pirates pitcher Rip Sewell (the "ephus pitch"), the blooper was revived in the mid to late 1960s by New York Yankees relief pitcher Steve Hamilton (the "Folly Floater"), and in the 1980s by Yankees reliever Dave LaRoche (the "La Lob").

bloop single: see *Texas leaguer.*

blow smoke: To throw a fastball, or fastballs. (no curveballs, he was just blowing smoke)

blue darter: A low line drive. An allusion to the speed of such a hit, the term dates back to the 1890s. also *darter.* see *line drive.*

1. bobble: To drop or lose control of a ball instead of fielding or throwing it effectively. compare *boot.*

2. bobble: The bobbling of a ball while attempting to field or throw it.

boot: To make an error fielding a ground ball, sometimes by actually kicking it. compare *bobble.*

●●To err or figuratively mishandle. (got careless and booted the decision)

bottom of the inning: The last half of an inning, when the home team has the opportunity to bat.

box: To awkwardly field a ground ball.

box score: A condensed report of a baseball game which lists the lineup and batting order of both teams and basic offensive and defensive information on the performances of all the participating players, including the number of times at bat, runs batted in, etc.

Boys Baseball: A summer program of amateur baseball for boys aged thirteen and fourteen, formerly the Pony League.

boys in blue: The umpires in a baseball game. also *men in blue.* see *umpire.*

1. break: The rise, dip, or curving motion of a pitched ball. (a sidearm pitch that breaks over the plate)

2. break, break off: To pitch a ball so that it breaks. (broke off a roundhouse curve)

breaking ball: A pitched ball that breaks or changes direction, such as a curveball. see *curveball.*

break the wrists: To bring the action of the wrists into play when swinging the bat at a pitched ball. If the wrists are not "broken" or moved, then the batter is said to have checked the swing (or to have made a half swing) and is not charged with a strike if the pitched ball is out of the strike zone.

break up the double play: To, while in the course of sliding into a base, physically contact or obstruct a defensive player at the base in such a way as to delay or prevent the player from throwing the ball to another base for a second out. (upended the second baseman and broke up the double play)

bring it: To throw a fastball with great velocity. (lull the batter with a slow curve and then really bring it)

broken bat single: A safe hit in which the bat breaks at the moment of contact with the ball.

Bronx cheer: A sound expressing derision or contempt, made by extending the tongue between the lips and forcibly expelling air. Some claim that the Bronx cheer, long popular among New York baseball fans, originated in the National Theater in the Bronx. also *razz, razzberry.*

brush back: To throw a high, inside pitch that forces the batter to move away from the plate. also *dust, dust off.*

brushback: A high, inside pitch thrown to move the batter away from the plate, or to intimidate the batter. also *duster, Gillette, knockdown pitch, purpose pitch.* compare *beanball, beaner, chin music.*

bullet: A hard hit line drive. see *line drive.*

bullpen: 1. The part of a field used throughout the game by relief pitchers warming up. Often a fenced in area just beyond the outfield boundary of the playing field. Originally a low-cost spectator area in some ballparks which came to be shared by warming-up relievers, the bullpen got its name around the 1880s for the way spectators were "herded" in. The term was further popularized by Bull Durham tobacco advertisements on outfield walls. 2. A team's group of relief pitchers. (only two good starters, but a great bullpen)

1. bunt: A slow-rolling infield ground ball propelled by a bat which the batter has held virtually still. Although introduced ten years earlier by Brooklyn Atlantics shortstop Dickey Pearce, the bunt achieved popularity in 1876 because of Boston's Tim Murnane, who used a special bat with one flat side to "butt" the ball. "Bunt" is a corruption of "butt."

2. bunt: To execute a bunt. (bunt one down the third base line)

bush, bush league: A derogatory term meaning small-time or amateur. Originally an unflattering reference to backwoods minor league towns and their crude playing grounds. also *high school.*
●●Small-time or unworthy. (has no class, strictly bush league)

bushel basket: A larger than usual, scooplike fielder's glove with a deep pocket. compare *pancake.*

busher: 1. A minor league player. 2. A player who, because of a lack of ability or unprofessional behavior, is undeserving of major league status.

cactus league: The unofficial name for the major league teams that conduct spring training and play preseason exhibition games in the Southwest. compare *grapefruit league.*

cage: 1. A spacious, often glass-roofed facility for foul weather and winter baseball (and track and field practice), offering a floor of dirt or artificial turf and a running track. 2. see *batting cage.*

called strike: A pitch that is neither hit nor swung at by the batter, but is judged by the umpire to have passed through the strike zone.

cannon: see *rifle.*

can of corn: An easily played fly ball. Reported to have originated with the grocers' practice in the early 1900s of storing cans of corn on a high shelf. When a grocer needed one, he'd simply tip it forward with a rod or a broom handle so that it would tumble easily into his waiting hands.

carpet: see *artificial turf.*

1. catch: 1. To halt the flight of a thrown or hit ball by grasping and controlling it. (catch a fly ball) 2. To play the catcher's position.

2. catch: 1. The act of catching a thrown or batted ball. (a diving catch to end the inning) 2. An unstructured recreation, practice, or game, in which two or more people throw a ball back and forth. (playing catch)

catcher: The defensive player behind home plate who catches pitched balls that the batter does not hit. Equipped with a face mask, chest protector, and shin guards to protect against foul balls, the catcher also wears a mitt or glove with extra padding. Until the ball is pitched, the catcher must stay inside the catcher's box, after which he may move out to retrieve a passed ball, to attempt to catch a pop foul, to field a ground ball hit toward the pitcher's mound or first or third base, to back up the first or third baseman on a routine putout, to throw to or feint throwing to a teammate to prevent a base runner from stealing a base, or to receive a throw from a teammate and tag a runner attempting to score. The catcher also, by means of hand signals, calls for cer-

11

tain pitches and prearranged defensive shifts and strategies. also *backstop, receiver*.

catcher's box: A rectangular area behind home plate, 4 feet wide and extending 6 feet behind the rear edge of the batter's box. The catcher must remain within this area until the pitcher releases the pitch.

catcher's mask: A padded metal grating that covers and protects the face of the catcher. The catcher's mask was invented in 1875 by Fred Thayer and first worn by Harvard catcher, James Tyng. Professional catchers began using them two years later. also *face mask, mask*.

catcher's mitt: A special glove with two sections, one for the thumb and one for the four fingers. It is round in shape, with heavy padding in front of the thumb, the heel of the hand, and the four fingers, but little or no padding in the central area, or pocket. A heavy leather web connects the thumb and fingers sections. Special padded catcher's mitts were introduced in 1891.

caught leaning: Picked off by a quick throw from the catcher or pitcher, made as the base runner takes a lead off and "leans" toward the next base.

cellar: The lowest standing in a league. (a poor team that finished in the cellar)

CATCHER

center field: 1. The outfield's central area, between right and left field and reaching behind second base. 2. The position of the player in the central outfield. (to play center field)

center fielder: The defensive player responsible for fielding balls hit to center field. also *middle gardener*.

chance: The opportunity to put out a base runner by either fielding a batted ball or making a play on a base runner, which then is computed in determining the fielding average as an error, assist, or putout.

change of pace: see *changeup*.

changeup: A slow pitch, identical in motion to the fastball, thrown to deceive the batter. also *change of pace, letup*.

charley horse: A pain or stiffness in the leg muscles, particularly the thigh. Often in the 1800s, old workhorses kept on the grounds of ballparks were called Charley. The movements of injured, stiff-legged ballplayers were likened to the labored plodding of these old horses, and the injury itself eventually became known as a "charley" or "charley horse."

1. chart: see *pitching chart*.

2. chart: To record pitches for a pitching chart.

chase: 1. To force the removal of a pitcher by rallying with a number of hits. also *knock out of the box*. 2. To officially throw a player, coach, or manager out of a game. (chased by the umpire)

check swing: see *half swing*.

chest pad: see *chest protector*.

chest protector: 1. A protective pad worn by a catcher or plate umpire covering the area from shoulders to waist or crotch. Padded chest protectors for catchers were introduced in 1885. 2. A foam rubber or inflated shield held, rather than worn, by some plate umpires. also *chest pad*.

Chicago slide: The original hook slide. Originated in the 1880s by Hall of Famer Mike "King" Kelly (about whom the song "Slide, Kelly, Slide" was written), then catcher for the Chicago White Stockings; thus, the name Chicago slide. see *hook slide*.

Chinese homer: A short or "cheap" home run, as one hit out of a small ballpark or down a particularly short foul line. Though there are conflicting claims from the East and West coasts as to the exact origin of the term, it is very probably an allusion to the low wages paid in the 1880s to immigrant Chinese laborers.

chin music: A beanball. see *beanball*.

1. choke: To become incapable of good performance because of tension or fear. also *choke up*. (choked under pressure)

2. choke: A poor performance because of tension or fear.

choke up: see *1. choke*.

choke up on the bat: To assume a shortened or raised grip on the handle of a bat resulting in better control, if slightly less power.

chop: To top, or swing the bat downward at a pitched ball, to make the ball hit the ground and bounce.

chopper: A ball batted down to the ground so it will bounce high in the air.

circus catch, circus play: 1. A seemingly impossible catch or play. also *Jawn Titus*. 2. A simple play made to appear exceptional in order to impress onlookers. Believed to be originated by Chicago sportswriter Charlie Seymour in 1885.

clean the bases: To render all bases empty or "clean" by virtue of a home run that enables all base runners to score. also *clear the bases*.

cleanup: The fourth position in the lineup, usually filled by a player with a strong hitting record, who can possibly score any of the first three batters who may be on base.

●●The final and strongest, or most skillful. (cleanup witness for the defense)

clear the bases: see *clean the bases*.

closed stance: A batting stance in which the front foot is positioned closer to the inside of the batter's box than the rear foot. compare *open stance*.

clothesline, clothesliner: A line drive. see *line drive*.

clout: A ball hit with power.

clubhouse lawyer: A player who habitually complains or makes excuses.

clutch hitter: A player known for the ability to get a hit in crucial game situations.

coach's box: One of two rectangular areas located 8 feet behind first and third bases, extending 20 feet toward home plate (6 feet outside the bases, extending 15 feet for softball). While the ball is in play, first and third base coaches are required to remain in their respective boxes.

cockeye: Left-handed. also *corkscrew arm, crooked arm, twirly-thumb*.

comebacker: A ground ball batted straight back to the pitcher.

come in: To pitch so the ball passes directly over the plate. (to come in with his curve)

complete game: A game that is finished by the same pitcher who started. The all-time single season record for complete games (50) was set in 1893 by New York Giants pitcher Amos Rusie. Cy Young holds the lifetime record with 753 complete games in his twenty-two-year career.

connect: 1. To successfully hit a pitched ball. (connected for a double off the left field wall) 2. To hit a home run.

contact hitter: A batter who is known less for power hitting than for the ability to collect base hits by making good contact with the ball.

control: A pitcher's skill at changing the speed, trajectory, and placement of a pitched ball.

corked bat: see *doctored bat*.

corkscrew arm: see *cockeye*.

count: A tally of balls and strikes, expressed in that order, charged to a batter at any point during a turn at bat. (a full count of 3 and 2)

country-fair hitter: A good hitter. Originally an allusion to the big strong farmers who played baseball at country fairs. Later, the expression evolved into a "pretty fair country hitter," or "pretty fair country player."

●●A person, object, or endeavor deserving merit. (served a pretty fair country chili)

country-fair player: 1. see *country-fair hitter*. 2. A show-off player. also *grandstander*.

courtesy runner: A player allowed to run the bases for a teammate without forcing that player out of the game. Used in some informal and nonprofessional games only.

cousin: An easy opponent (whether a particular batter, pitcher, or team). The term was first used in the 1920s by New York Yankees pitcher Waite Hoyt who likened some of his perennial victims at the plate to cooperating family members or "cousins." Later, the meaning was expanded to include any easy-to-defeat pitchers or teams.

cover: To protect a base by positioning oneself at or on it, ready to make a

13

putout. (moved in to cover second base)

cripple: To put the pitcher into a situation where he must throw a strike because he is behind the batter in the count. With a count such as three balls and no strikes, or three balls and one strike, a pitcher is considered crippled without the normal options of deception, placement, and delivery.

crooked arm: see *cockeye*.

crossfire: A sidearm pitch that seems to cross the plate on a diagonal.

cross-handed grip: A reverse hold on the bat, with the hands crossed, as opposed to the usual grip.

crowd the plate: To assume a batting stance at the inner edge of the batter's box.

crush: To hit a pitched ball with great power. (can really crush the ball) also *hammer*.

Cuban forkball: A spitball. also *drooler, spitter*.

cunning thumb, cunning thumber: A player who is a poor thrower.

cup of coffee: A short stint on the roster of a major league club by a minor league player, just long enough to be observed by the parent club before the end of the season, or long enough to "drink a cup of coffee."

1. curve: A curveball. see *curveball*.

●●A surprise or something unexpected. (the last question on the test threw me a curve)

2. curve: To throw a curveball. (threw two fast balls, and then curved him)

curveball: A pitch thrown in such a way as to impart a spin that causes the ball to break or veer downward and to the side. A right-hander's curve breaks to the left, a left-hander's to the right. Although others had thrown the pitch before, the first person to study and understand the mechanics of the curveball and intentionally use it was William A. "Candy" Cummings in the early 1860s. Cummings introduced the pitch to the major leagues in 1872. also *breaking ball, curve, dipsy-do, fish, fish hook, hook, jug handle curve, mackerel, number two, pretzel, rainbow, roundhouse curve, snake*. compare *fastball, knuckleball, screwball, slider*.

cut: A swing with the bat. An attempt to hit the ball. (took a cut at the slow curve)

cut ball: A ball that is surreptitiously slit, scratched, or cut so as to make it break or swerve in an unnatural way when pitched. see *doctored ball*.

cut down: To throw out a base runner. (cut down at the plate) also *gun down*.

1. cut off: The interception of an outfielder's throw toward home plate by an infielder, who then may relay the throw to the plate, or make a play at another base.

2. cut off: To cut off a throw from the outfield.

cutoff man: The player who cuts off a throw from the outfield.

Cy Young Award: An award made annually to the pitcher who demonstrates the most outstanding performance in the major leagues as voted by the Baseball Writers Association of America. Named in honor of the legendary Cy Young, who from 1889 to 1911 won a record 511 games pitching for the Cleveland Spiders, St. Louis Cardinals, and the Boston Pilgrims. The award was first given in 1956 to Brooklyn Dodgers pitcher Don Newcombe. Since 1967, a Cy Young Award has been given to a pitcher from each major league. In 1982, Steve Carlton of the Philadelphia Phillies became the only four-time Cy Young Award winner.

daisy clipper, daisy cutter: A low ground ball hit through to the outfield. also *grass clipper, grass cutter, lawn mower*.

Daniel Webster: A player known for debating or arguing with the umpires. Named after the U.S. statesman and great orator of the 1800s, Daniel Webster.

darter: A line drive. see *line drive*.

delayed steal: A steal in which the base runner does not go on the pitch, but waits for the catcher to return the ball to the pitcher or for the defensive team to make a play on another player.

delivery: 1. The act of throwing a pitch. (impatient slugger waiting for the delivery) 2. The manner in which a pitch is thrown. (changed the delivery for the knuckleball)

designated hitter: A player who bats in the lineup but does not play in the field. Technically, the designated hitter takes the pitcher's batting turn throughout the game. The designated hitter rule was introduced by the American League in 1973 and applies to the All-Star Game (as long as both leagues agree) and every other year to the World Series. Although a designated hitter is still not permitted in the National League, the first to suggest an official batter for the pitcher was National League president John H. Heydler in 1928. The always controversial Charles O. Finley, then owner of the American League Oakland A's, led the movement to adopt the designated hitter rule. also *dh*.

dh: see *designated hitter*.

diamond: 1. That part of the playing field which is comprised of the infield. When seen from home plate, this square area looks like a diamond. 2. The entire playing field.

Dick Smith: A nondescript name for a player who does not fraternize with teammates, a loner.

die: To be stranded on base at the end of an inning or half inning.

dig in: To dig one's spikes into the dirt in order to get a better footing from which to push off with the rear foot for a particularly powerful swing.

dig out a throw: To grasp and control a low, bouncing throw. (first baseman digs out the throw in time for the third out)

dinger: A home run. see *home run*.

dipsy-do: A curveball. see *curveball*.

disabled list: A team list of players who are unable to play several games on account of severe injuries. A player whose name appears on the disabled list is still included on the team's roster, but for a term of either fifteen or twenty-one days, he may not play. A team may add a player to the roster to substitute for a disabled player until such time as he comes off the disabled list.

dish: Home plate. see *home plate*.

doctor: 1. To surreptitiously change or modify the playing field or equipment in order to gain an advantage. (the doctored base paths were so soft, it was impossible to steal) 2. A pitcher who doctors the ball.

doctored ball: A ball that has been illegally modified to make it break or swerve in an unnatural way. This can be accomplished by adding a foreign substance to the surface of the ball (greaseball, jellyball, mud ball, pine tar ball, powder puff ball, and spitball), or by scratching, scuffing, or in any other way marking the surface of a ball (belt buckle ball, cut ball, emery ball, marked ball, sandpaper ball, scuffer, and shine ball).

doctored bat: A bat that has been illegally modified, generally to make it lighter or more lively. The most often used method is to drill a 1/2-inch to 3/4-inch-diameter hole approximately one foot into the large end of the bat. This cavity is either left hollow or filled with a light material such as cork, then capped with a mixture of wood shavings and glue. The cap is then blended in and disguised by careful sanding. The result is a lighter, livelier bat with the mass of a heavy bat. also *corked bat, hollow bat, plugged bat*.

doctored grounds: Areas of the playing field, boundaries, or boundary markers that have been modified (sometimes to an illegal extent) in order to gain an advantage for the home team. In the major leagues, groundskeepers regularly adjust the condition of the playing field according to the relative strengths and weaknesses of the home and visiting teams. Quick teams with speedy base runners prefer the fast surface provided by short, unwatered grass and dry, hard base paths, while slow teams favor the opposite. A particularly wet or soft area near first base can prevent a base-stealer from getting a quick start. (A flagrant and notorious example would be the crucial season-ending series at Candlestick Park in 1962, when the San Francisco Giants successfully employed this trick against baserunning sensation Maury Wills and the Los Angeles Dodgers. The Giants swept the series and eventually went on to the World Series.) Foul lines can be graded to tilt inward or outward in order to influence whether bunts will roll fair or foul. The pitching mound can be raised over the legal 10-inch maximum height in order to give overhand pitchers an advantage over the batter. Even the mound in the visitors' bullpen can be tilted slightly to throw off relief pitchers. To help or hinder a certain hitter, the batter's box can be illegally extended, shortened, or slightly moved in relation to home plate. One of the most spectacular examples of doctored grounds was onetime Cleveland Indians owner Bill Veeck's moveable fence in Cleveland Municipal Stadium. Depending on the hitting strength of the visiting team relative to the weak-hitting Indians, the outfield fence could be moved in or out the night before a game. Six sets of sleeves were installed in the outfield for the fence posts, each set a different distance from home plate.

donkey: A rookie. see *rookie.*

1. **double:** A hit that allows the batter to safely arrive at second base. also *two-bagger, two-base hit.*

2. **double:** 1. To hit a double. (doubled off the left field wall) 2. To advance a base runner by hitting a double. (doubled him to third) 3. To score another runner by hitting a double. (doubled in the tying run)

doubleheader: Two consecutive games on the same day. A ticket holder for that day needs only one admission ticket for both games. Doubleheaders are frequently scheduled to play games postponed earlier in the season. also *twin bill.*

••Two consecutive events. (attended both the wedding and the reception—a doubleheader)

double play: A putout of two runners or the batter and a runner on one pitch. Two runners may be forced out on a quickly fielded grounder and relay to two bases; the batter may hit a fly ball that is caught for the first out and the

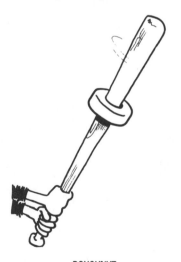

DOUGHNUT

base runner thrown out before tagging up or while running to the next base; or the runner may be caught stealing while the batter strikes out. Hall of Famer George Wright, shortstop for the Cincinnati Red Stockings, is credited with making baseball's first recorded double play, using the "hidden ball" trick. also *twin killing.*

••Two simultaneous accomplishments. (not only won the case, but established an important legal precedent—a double play)

double play ball: A ball hit to or near a defensive player, virtually assuring the completion of an easy double play.

1. **double pump:** The double swinging of the arms back and then forward over the head during a pitcher's windup.

2. **double pump:** To swing the arms back and forward over the head twice during a windup.

double steal: A single play whereby two runners both advance by stealing. Often a delayed steal with men on first and third base. The base runner on first breaks for second base to draw a throw from the catcher. When the catcher makes the long throw to second base, the base runner on third breaks for home.

double up: To put out a base runner as the second out in a double play.

doughnut: see *bat weight.*

down: Out. (hit a homer in the top of the ninth with one down) also *away, gone.* see *out.*

••Finished, dispensed with, or out of the way. (starting my senior year—three down and one to go)

downtown: A home run, particularly one hit especially far. (hit one downtown to win the game) also *gone.*

drag: To execute a drag bunt.

drag bunt: A surprise bunt made to get on base (as opposed to a sacrifice bunt) in which the batter bunts the ball without squaring around to face the pitcher. Left-handers are able to turn the body and start for first base, actually leaving the bat to trail or "drag" behind them just before the bunt is made.

1. **drive:** To hit a pitched ball with great power. (drove a fastball into the hole)

2. **drive:** A pitched ball hit with great power. (a drive to deep centerfield)

drive in a run: To hit a ball that allows a base runner to score.

drooler: see *spitball.*

dropball: A fast pitch softball pitch in which the ball drops as it nears the plate.

ducks on the pond: 1. Bases loaded. also *bases full, the table is set.* 2. Runners on base.

dugout: One of two enclosures housing the players' benches and located on each side of the infield, usually sunken slightly beneath ground level so as not to interfere with the view of the spectators. The dugouts are usually directly linked to the dressing room areas.

dust, dust off: see *brush back.*

duster: see *brushback.*

dying quail: An apparently playable routine fly ball that unexpectedly drops in for a base hit, often due to wind.

early bloomer: A rookie who looks particularly promising in spring training, but fades and eventually fails before the start of the regular season. also *morning glory.*

earned run: A run scored before the third putout in an inning that is not the result of an error, and that is charged to the pitcher in computing the pitcher's earned run average.

earned run average: A statistic that reflects the average number of earned runs allowed by a pitcher for every nine innings. The earned run average, or ERA, of a pitcher is calculated by dividing the total of earned runs by the total number of innings pitched and multiplying by nine. (A pitcher charged with sixty-eight runs in 340 innings has an earned run average of 1.80) The single season record for the lowest ERA (1.01) was set in 1914 by Boston Red Sox pitcher Dutch Leonard. The record for the lowest lifetime earned run average is held by spitballer "Big Ed" Walsh who, in his fourteen-year career, won 194 games with an ERA of 1.82.

easy out: A batter who is easily retired, posing little or no threat to the defensive team or pitcher. (like most pitchers, an easy out) also *out man.* compare *hard out.*

emery ball: An illegally altered baseball. When pitched, the ball will swerve or dip abnormally because it has been scratched on one side with emery cloth or powder. also *sandpaper ball.*

error: A fumble or misplay made by a player in the field on a batted or thrown ball, preventing what would normally have been a putout or allowing a base runner to advance. If a player throws a wild ball, misses or fumbles a playable fly, or cannot field a playable gound ball, the scorer records an error against that player and team.

errorless: No errors charged against a player or team. (eighteen consecutive errorless games)

extra-base hit: A hit that allows a batter to advance further than first base, such as a double, triple, or home run.

extra innings: Innings played beyond the ninth inning in order to break a tie.

face: 1. To bat opposite a pitcher. (goes hitless every time he faces a knuckleballer) 2. To pitch to a batter. (on a good day, could strike out every batter he faced)

face mask: A cagelike protective mask worn by the catcher and plate umpire. also *mask.* see *catcher's mask.*

fadeaway: The original screwball, a reverse curve. Pioneered and named in 1900 by the New York Giants' charismatic pitcher Christy Mathewson (though some claim that New York sportswriter Bozeman Bulger coined the name). The last lines of a Ring Lardner memorial for "Matty" in 1925 read: "may the flowers ne'er wither, Matty/on your grave in Cincinnati/which you've chosen for your final fadeaway." see *screwball.*

fadeaway slide: Old name for a hook slide, perfected in the early 1900s by Ty Cobb of the Detroit Tigers. see *hook slide.*

fair: In fair territory.

fair ball: A batted ball that hits the ground within fair territory (between the foul lines), or lands and remains within the foul lines until it passes first or third base, or, on a home run, remains within the foul lines until it clears the outfield fence or wall.

fair territory: The playing area within the foul lines.

fallaway slide: see *hook slide.*

fall classic: The World Series.

fan: 1. To strike out a batter. (fanned the last three batters to retire the side) also *K, whiff.* 2. To swing and miss. (fanned on a letter-high fastball)

●●To swing at an object and miss. (with the goalie on the ice and an open net, he fanned on the shot)

farm, farm club, farm team: A minor league team that is subsidized by or linked with a parent club in the major leagues. Most young major league prospects break into professional baseball and receive training as well as game experience with a farm club. Minor league teams were known as "farms" even before the farm system existed, because of the rural towns in which they often played. see *farm system*.

farm out: To send a player to an associated minor league club. see *farm system*.

●●To send away. (made so much trouble he was farmed out to a boarding school) To subcontract work or part of a job. (the parts are factory-made, but all the assembling and finishing is farmed out)

farm system: The system pioneered and made popular by St. Louis Cardinals manager-executive, Branch Rickey, in the early 1900s in which individual major league teams (parent clubs) operate or subsidize their own minor league teams (farm clubs) to train and season promising new players.

fastball: A powerfully pitched ball that travels extremely fast (up to 100-plus m.p.h.) and can dip or rise somewhat upon approaching the plate. Colorful synonyms for a fastball refer to the sound or high temperature of its "blazing" speed (hummer, heat, smoke, smoker), or to the difficulty in seeing it (fog), particularly because of its apparent small size when trying to hit it (aspirin, BB, pea). compare *changeup, curveball, knuckleball, palmball, screwball, sinker, slider*.

fast hook: A manager's inclination to remove and replace a pitcher at the first sign of trouble.

fast pitch softball: A variety of softball in which the pitcher is allowed to use a full-power underhand pitch. As in baseball, there are nine players on a side. Bunting is allowed as is stealing, but the runners are not permitted to leave the base before the pitcher lets go of the ball. compare *slow pitch softball*.

fat pitch: A pitch that is easily hit.

fence buster: An strong hitter known for regularly hitting the ball to the outfield boundaries or fences.

field: 1. The playing area for a baseball game. 2. To grasp and control a fly ball or ground ball. (goes to his left to field a high bouncer)

●●To control or handle. (fielded some difficult questions from persistent reporters)

fielder: 1. One who is called upon to field a batted ball. (good fielder, good arm, and can hit) 2. A player in a defensive position other than the pitcher or catcher.

fielder's choice: A scorekeeper's ruling reflecting the opportunity for a fielder to choose between two possible putouts, and in which he decides to throw to a base other than first in order to throw out a preceding base runner instead of the batter. When a fielder's choice ruling is made, the batter is charged with a turn at bat, but does not earn a base hit.

fielding: Catching or stopping and controlling a batted ball with the aim of getting a base runner or batter out.

fielding average: The statistic used to measure the fielding effectiveness of a player or team, determined by dividing the total number of putouts and assists by the total number of chances and rounding off the answer to three decimal places. A player credited with 400 putouts and assists in 425 chances has a fielding average of .941.

field umpire: An umpire positioned on the playing field (as opposed to behind home plate). In the major leagues, there are field umpires positioned at each base. Two umpires are added during the World Series to help with foul rulings from the outfield foul lines. see *umpire, umpire-in-chief*.

find the handle: To keep a solid grip on the ball when both catching and throwing. (plenty of time to throw out the runner, but the fielder couldn't find the handle)

fireballer: An excellent fastball pitcher. One who consistently throws fastballs. also *flamethrower*.

fireman: 1. A relief pitcher who can "put out the fire" when the opponent gets "hot" and appears ready for a big inning. John Murphy, a New York Yankees relief pitcher in the thirties and forties, was the first to be called a fireman. also *ice man*. 2. One who is known for showering, dressing, and leaving the dressing room quickly after a game.

first: First base. (rounding first and headed for second base)

first base: 1. The base located on the baseline on the right side of the diamond when facing the field from home plate. When rounding the bases, this is the first base reached by the runner. also *first, gateway.* 2. The position played by the first baseman. (to play first base) also *first.*

••The preliminary step in a relationship or endeavor. (couldn't get to first base with her)

first base coach: The coach or member of the team at bat who stands in the marked coach's box adjacent to first base to direct base runners and, through prearranged signals, to relay special batting and baserunning instructions from the manager in the dugout.

first baseman: The defensive player stationed just left of first base who is expected to field the balls hit to the surrounding area and to receive throws from other infielders in order to put out the base runner. also *first sacker.*

first baseman's mitt: A special thinly padded glove, generally with two sections, one for the thumb and one for the four fingers, connected by a web that may not exceed 5 inches from its top to the base, 4 inches in width at the top, and 3-1/2 inches at the base. Some mitts are made in three equal sections (one for the thumb and two for the fingers) laced together to form a scooplike glove. Neither kind may exceed 12 inches in length, top to bottom, or 8 inches in width across the palm.

first leg of a double play: The first out in a double play.

first sacker: The first baseman. see *first baseman.*

fish, fish hook: A curveball.

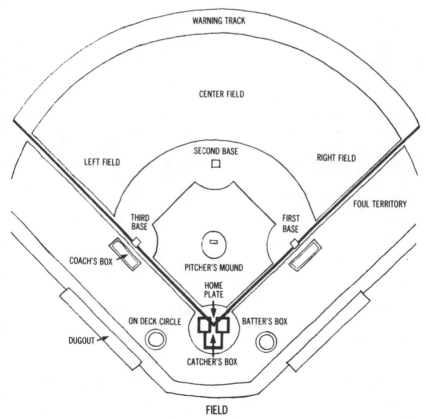

FIELD

fist: To hit a pitched ball with the small end of the bat right next to the hands. (fists an inside pitch right back to the mound)

flag: To catch, or stop and control, a thrown or batted ball.

flake: A peculiar or eccentric player. A noun form created in the 1960s from the adjective "flakey." see *flakey.*

●●An odd or irresponsible person. (can't depend on that flake)

flakey: Off-beat, peculiar, or eccentric. San Francisco Giants outfielder Jackie Brandt is thought to be the first ever to be described as flakey when he was given the nickname in the 1950s.

●●Strange or irresponsible. (so flakey he's probably forgotten where to go)

flamethrower: see *fireballer.*

flutterball: A knuckleball. see *knuckleball.*

1. fly: 1. A fly ball. (hits a high fly to short right field) see *fly ball.* 2. A bothersome fan, an insectlike pest. compare *green fly.*

2. fly: To hit a fly ball that is caught. (flied to centerfield for the third out) also *fly out.*

fly ball: A batted ball which soars high into the air to the outfield. (misjudged a fly ball)

fly out: To hit a fly ball that is caught for an out. (flied out to the left fielder)

fog: A fastball or fastballs. see *fastball.*

foot in the bucket: The movement of the front foot away from the plate (toward the dugout water bucket) during the batter's stride into a swing, usually a detriment to good hitting.

1. force: A force-out. (out at second on a force)

2. force: To put out a base runner on a force play. (forced the runner at second)

force-out: The instance of throwing a base runner out as a result of a force play. also *force.*

force play: An automatic putout arising from the circumstance of a base runner being required to vacate his base and reach the next base because the batter has hit a fair ball and is running to first base. When the batter reaches first base, the base runner previously there is forced to advance. Regardless of the base, any runner on a base that the runner behind him is attempting to reach must also advance. A fielder is not required to tag the runner on a force play in order to make a putout; the runner is out at the moment a fielder in possession of the ball touches the base the runner is trying to reach. If the batter or any runner behind a given base runner is put out, the force play is no longer in effect.

1. forfeit: To lose a game due to an inability or refusal to play or because of a serious rules infraction. The opposing team is awarded a 9-0 victory (7-0 in softball).

2. forfeit: A game that has been forfeited.

forkball: A somewhat unpredictable, but usually downward-breaking pitch, thrown with the index and middle fingers spread wide like the prongs of a pitchfork. Though the exact origin is unknown (pitches with a similar grip were used near the turn of the century), Boston Red Sox pitcher "Bullet" Joe Bush popularized the forkball in 1920.

1. foul: Outside the foul lines. (the ball rolls foul)

2. foul: To hit a ball foul. (fouls one back into the stands)

3. foul: A foul ball. (a long foul down the right field line) see *foul ball.*

foul ball: A ball batted into the area outside the foul lines, or that hits the ground in fair territory but proceeds to roll behind the first or third base foul lines before reaching one of those

FIRST BASEMAN

bases. If a fly ball is caught in foul territory, the batter is called out, but the base runners may try to advance after tagging up. A foul ball not caught on the fly is charged as a strike unless the batter already has two strikes charged against him. also *foul.*

●●An undesirable person. (finally asked the uninvited guest, a real foul ball, to leave)

foul line: One of the two lines that mark the boundaries of fair territory, and which run at right angles from home plate through the outer edges of first and third bases and end at the outfield boundary. Also called baselines.

foul out: To hit a fly ball that is caught in foul territory and results in an out. (fouled out to the third baseman)

foul pole: One of two upright poles marking the foul lines at the outfield boundary. These poles enable the umpire to determine fair and foul balls hit to the outfield. If a long drive hits the foul pole, it is a home run.

foul territory: The entire portion of the field outside the foul lines.

foul tip: A batted ball that travels directly back to be caught by the catcher. The ball is declared in play and the batter is charged with a strike. If the batter hits a foul tip after two strikes, he is called out. If, however, the catcher fails to directly catch the ball, drops it, or traps it, a foul ball is not charged and the batter is not out.

four-bagger: A home run.

frame: An inning. The term dates back to the days when there were no mechanical or electronic scoreboards. Numbers painted on rectangular pieces of wood were set by hand into frames for each inning. also *stanza.*

free agent: Not under contract, free to negotiate with any team.

free pass, free ticket, free trip: A base on balls. see *base on balls.*

frozen rope: A line drive. see *line drive.*

full count: Three balls and two strikes.

fungo: A fielding drill in which a player or coach tosses balls in the air and hits grounders and fly balls to fielders with a special fungo bat. Fungo hitting dates back to the late 1860s, but the exact origin of the term is unknown. Some believe it comes from the rhyme allegedly recited in early versions of the game just as a ball was to be hit.

Others claim that fungo is from "fungus," an allusion to the soft wood used in the strange fungo bats. Yet another theory holds that the term comes from an old Scottish verb, *fung,* meaning "to toss," since the ball is tossed up before hitting fungos.

fungo bat: A bat with a long thin handle and a short thick head specially designed for fungo hitting.

gamer: A "game" ballplayer who plays in spite of injuries. compare *jake.*

●●A courageous and persistent individual as one who continues in an endeavor in spite of great difficulty.

garden: The outfield. also *orchard pasture.*

gardener: An outfielder. also *orchardman pastureworker.*

gateway: First base. So-called because it is the "gateway" to a batter's journey around the bases.

get all of the ball: To connect with a pitched ball, hitting it perfectly and with full power.

get a piece of the ball: To hit or make contact with a pitched ball even if just to foul it off when two strikes are charged against the batter.

get around on a fastball: To be able to execute a complete swing of the bat with full wrist action and power before a fastball is already in the catcher's mitt. Requires great quickness and anticipation, but when a batter connects with a fastball on such a swing, the result is a particularly powerful drive. (gets around on a fastball, and goodbye, that ball is gone)

get hold of the ball: To connect with or hit a pitched ball. (got hold of a fastball for a double)

get the thumb: To be ejected from a game by the umpire.

Gillette: A brushback pitch near the batter's head. A "close shave." see *brushback.*

glass arm: 1. A pitching arm that is susceptible to soreness or injury. 2. A throwing arm susceptible to injury or weakness. Although the exact origin is unknown, the term has been in use since the 1800s.

1. glove: 1. A padded leather covering worn on one hand by all defensive players to aid in catching and controlling a batted, thrown, or pitched ball. 2. A padded leather covering usually having a separate section for each finger (as opposed to a catcher's or first baseman's mitt), worn by fielders to aid in catching and controlling batted or thrown balls. It may not exceed 12 inches in length or 8 inches in width. Padding protects the thumb, heel, and finger sections, which are generally laced together at the top. A leather webbing that may not exceed 4-1/2 inches at the top, and 3-1/2 inches at the base, connects the space between the thumb and forefinger sections. The middle, or palm area, of the glove is unpadded and known as the pocket. compare *mitt.*

2. glove: Skill as a fielder. (can't hit, but he's got a great glove)

3. glove: To catch or grasp and control a batted or thrown ball. (gloved a pop fly for the third out)

glove man: 1. A good fielder. also *leather man.* 2. A poor hitter who plays only because of his skill with a glove; primarily a defensive player. also *leather man.*

goat: A derisive name for a player who makes a critical or game-losing mistake or error. (went from the hero who scored the winning run to the goat when he missed third base)

go down looking: To take a called third strike for an out. compare *go down swinging.*

go down swinging: To swing and miss for the third strike and an out.

go for the fences: To swing with full power and attempt to hit a home run. (jump on the first pitch and go for the fences)

Golden Glove Award: The annual award given by both major leagues to the player voted the best fielder at each position.

gone: 1. Over the outfield boundary, a home run. Popularized by former New York Yankees broadcaster Mel Allen with his famous phrase, "going, going, gone!" also *downtown.* 2. Out. (with two gone in the bottom of the eighth) also *away, down.* 3. Ejected from the game by the umpire. (the ump is motioning, he's gone)

good wood on the ball: To connect and hit the ball well. (got good wood on the

ball and gave it a ride to center field)

go on the pitch: To try to steal a base the moment the pitcher throws the ball toward the plate.

goose egg: An inning with no runs scored, represented on the scoreboard by an egglike zero.

gopher ball: A pitched ball hit for a home run. New York Yankees pitcher, Vernon "Lefty" Gomez coined the term, saying that such pitches "go fer" home runs.

go-sign: 1. A coded signal from the manager or coach telling the base runner to attempt to steal a base. 2. A signal from a coach to a moving base runner to continue to the next base or to home plate. also *green light.*

go the distance, go the route: Pitch an entire game. (went the distance, giving up only one run and five hits)

go with the pitch: To hit an outside pitch toward the outfield on the opposite side of the plate as the batter stands. A right-handed batter goes with the pitch into right field; a left-handed batter into left field. compare *pull.*

grand slam, grand slammer: A home run with the bases full.

grapefruit league: The unofficial name for the major league teams that conduct spring training and play preseason exhibition games in the citrus-growing state of Florida. compare *cactus league.*

grass clipper, grass cutter: see *daisy clipper.*

greaseball: An illegal pitch in which a greasy foreign substance, such as petroleum jelly or hair oil, is surreptitiously rubbed on one part of the ball, so as to make it break or swerve unpredictably when thrown. Tommy Bond, pitcher for the National League Hartford Blues, may have been the first to use a greaseball when he experimented with the application of glycerine in 1876. also *jellyball.* see *doctored ball.*

green fly: A girl or woman who persistently seeks to be in the company of professional baseball players. A baseball groupie. Named after the supposedly most persistent variety of fly, the green fly. also *Baseball Annie.* compare *fly.*

green light: 1. see *go-sign.* 2. A coded signal from the manager or coach freeing the batter to swing if he gets a good pitch instead of taking, as with a 3 and 0 or 3 and 1 count.

1. groove: The central strike zone directly over home plate, where the batter is most likely to get a solid hit.

2. groove: To throw a pitch directly over home plate where it can most easily be hit with power.

ground: To hit a ground ball. (grounded right back to the pitcher for an easy out)

ground ball: A batted ball that rolls or bounces on the ground. also *grounder.* compare *fly ball.*

grounder: A ground ball.

ground out: To hit a ground ball that is fielded and thrown to first base in time for an out. (grounded out to the shortstop)

ground rule: A special regulation applying to a specific ballpark that considers the abnormal conditions of a playing field (field obstructions or unusual outfield fences, for example) and makes appropriate changes in game procedure. Although some ground rules designate certain home runs as automatic, most specify conditions under which a ball is considered dead, in which case base runners are permitted to advance a certain number of bases.

●●A basic rule of procedure. (must establish ground rules for the debate)

ground rule double: A two-base hit automatically given to the batter whose ball lands in fair territory, but bounces over an outfield fence.

groundskeeper: The person in charge of the preparation, maintenance, and marking of the playing field. A job of critical and often strategic importance in professional baseball. also *manicurist.* see *doctored grounds.*

guardian angel: see *angel.*

guarding the lines: A defensive strategy in which the first and third basemen position themselves almost on the foul lines to prevent an extra-base hit down the lines. Often used in the late innings of a close game.

guard the bag: To take a position near a base so as to be ready to receive the throw and make a putout on a base runner.

guess hitter: A batter who attempts to determine what type of pitch he can expect in a given circumstance.

gun: see *rifle.*

gun down: To throw out a base runner. also *cut down.*

half swing: An interrupted swing of the bat in which the wrists are not allowed to "break" or move. Not considered a strike unless the ball passes through the strike zone, or is fouled off accidentally. If the plate umpire calls a "ball" on a half swing, the manager or catcher may request the plate umpire to ask a field umpire on first or third base for help. If the base umpire calls the pitch a "strike," the strike call prevails. also *check swing.*

Hall of Fame: Baseball's most prestigious award, honoring outstanding individuals and their career achievements in the game. In 1936, the first five men were enshrined in the Hall of Fame. They were, in the order of votes received from the Special Committee appointed by Commissioner Kenesaw Mountain Landis: Ty Cobb, Babe Ruth, Honus Wagner, Christy Mathewson, and Walter Johnson. In 1939, the National Baseball Hall of Fame was established in Cooperstown, New York, and several years later, the annual voting was turned over to the Baseball Writers Association of America. In order to qualify for induction into the Hall of Fame, a player must have had ten years of major league experience, must have been retired for a minimum of five years, and must receive votes from 75 percent of those polled.

Hall of Famer: One who has been inducted into the Hall of Fame.

hammer: To hit a pitched ball with great power. (hammers a line drive up the middle) also *crush.*

handcuff: 1. To render the ball unplayable, difficult, or almost impossible to control. (ripped a ball up the line, handcuffing the third baseman) 2. To allow a batter or team few or no hits.

hang a curve: To throw a curveball that fails to break, or "hangs" in the air. The result is an easy-to-hit, high, relatively slow pitch. (lost the shut-out when he hung a curveball that was belted into the right field bleachers)

hardball: 1. The ball used in the game of baseball. Smaller in size (though not much harder) than a softball, and consequently more difficult to hit and field. see *baseball.* compare *softball.* 2. The game of baseball. Considered more difficult (and dangerous) to play than the game of softball, because of the size of the ball used. see *baseball.* compare *softball.*

●●To "play hardball" means to hold nothing back, to mean business, no holds barred. (evident that the prosecutor is playing hardball in that case)

hard out: A batter who is hard to retire. A good hitter who poses a threat to the pitcher and the defensive team every time at bat. compare *easy out.*

hat trick: To hit in one game a single, double, triple, and home run. Originally from the sport of cricket, where in the 1800s teams began to award a new hat to a bowler who took three wickets with three balls consecutively. also *hit for the cycle.*

●●In horseracing, three wins in three consecutive races by a jockey, or the winning of an annual race for three successive years. In hockey and soccer, three goals scored in one game by a single player.

headfirst slide: The attempt by a base runner to reach or return to a base (and sometimes to avoid a tag) by diving headfirst and skidding along the ground with the arms outstretched to touch the base. see *slide.*

heat: A fastball, or fastballs. (not throwing anything fancy, just heat) see *fastball.*

heavy pitch: A pitch that breaks downward near the plate.

hesitation pitch: A pitch in which the pitcher slows or stops momentarily after the windup and before throwing.

hickory: A baseball bat.

high: Above the strike zone.

high and tight: Above the strike zone and inside, or close to the batter.

high-five: A congratulatory hand slap made high in the air, and usually exchanged between one or more players and a teammate who has just made an important play (home run, putout, etc.), or among teammates after an important or gratifying win. The high-five was originated in 1977 by Los Angeles Dodgers outfielder Glenn Burke.

●●The high-five is now used in many sports as well as in nonsports activities.

high school: Amateur, small-time. also *bush, bush league.*

hill: The pitcher's mound. also *mound.*

1. hit: A batted ball hit into fair territory that enables the batter to safely reach a base, unaided by a defensive error, a force play, or an attempt to put out the preceding base runner. In 1920, George Sisler, then of the American League St. Louis Browns, set the all-time record for the most hits in a single season (257). Ty Cobb holds the lifetime record (4,191), although Pete Rose is

HEADFIRST SLIDE

closing in, having overtaken Stan Musial (3,630) in 1981 and Hank Aaron (3,771) in 1982. also *base hit, safe hit, safety.* ●●A success. (new show is sure to be a hit) **2. hit:** 1. To bat or take a turn at bat. (came in to hit for the pitcher) 2. To get a base hit. In 1941, New York Yankee Joe DiMaggio hit safely in fifty-six consecutive games, considered one of the greatest records in sports. 3. To have the ability to bat successfully. (good fielder, but can't hit)

l. hit and run: An offensive strategy for advancing a base runner. On the pitch, a base runner at first runs toward second base while the batter tries to hit the ball, ideally to the space left open by the infielder who must now cover second base (between first and second, if the second baseman covers; between second and third, if the shortstop covers). In a hit and run play, it is important that the batter makes contact with the ball to protect the runner. If the ball is successfully hit through the vacant spot in the infield, the base runner can often take an extra base and sometimes even score. If the ball is hit to an infielder, the base runner is most often able to reach second base safely because of the early start, though the batter may be thrown out at first. If the ball is hit foul, the base runner must return to first but is in no danger. If the batter misses the ball, there is the chance that the catcher can throw the runner out at second base. compare *run and hit.* **2. hit and run:** To execute a hit and run play. compare *run and hit.*

hit away: To use a full swing and attempt to hit the ball with power. (with two out and the tying run on third, look for the batter to hit away) also *swing away.*

hit batsman, hit batter: A batter hit by a pitch and walked.

hit behind the runner: To hit a pitched ball between first and second base, behind a base runner already moving to second (as in the case of a hit and run play).

hitch: A slight dropping or pulling back of the bat immediately prior to swinging. Usually considered a bad habit and detrimental to a good swing.

hit for the cycle: To hit a single, double, triple, and home run in one game. also *hat trick.*

hit into a double play: To hit a ball to or

near a defensive player that can be fielded and relayed from base to base in time to force or tag out two base runners, or can be caught on the fly and thrown to a base before an advancing base runner can return.

hitless: Without a base hit. (held them hitless for the last two innings to hold on for the win)

hitter: 1. A batter. 2. Used with an appropriate number to describe the number of hits given up by a pitcher during a game or part of a game, as in two-hitter, three-hitter, etc. (pitched a two-hitter)

hit the corners: To throw pitches for strikes that pass barely within the strike zone corners. Often taken for a called strike by the batter because they appear to be outside the strike zone. (fooled him with a curveball that hit the corner) also *shave the corners.*

hit the dirt: 1. see *bail out.* 2. To slide into a base to avoid being tagged out. see *slide.*

hold the runner: 1. To prevent a base runner from taking a big lead. Accomplished by frequent looks from the pitcher and occasional throws to the base. 2. To prevent a base runner (one not forced to run) from advancing while a play is being made on another base runner or the batter. Accomplished by a momentary feint toward the unforced base runner by the defensive player fielding the ball before the throw is made to force another base runner or the batter. (stops the ball on one bounce, looks toward second to hold the runner, then throws to first for the out)

hole: 1.The open space between the shortstop and the third baseman. (base hit into the hole) 2. The open space between any two infielders.

holler guy: A team member who loudly encourages fellow players on a regular basis during games. ●●A person noted for enthusiasm and encouragement. (the captain of their bowling team is a real holler guy)

hollow bat: see *doctored bat.*

home: 1. Home plate. 2. Across home plate to score. (drove the runner home) *also in.*

home base: see *home plate.*

home plate: A flat piece of white rubber with five sides placed in the dirt at the opposite corner of the diamond from second base, and the last base a runner must contact when scoring a run. The leading edge, which faces the pitcher, is 17 inches wide. Two perpendicular sides (the lateral boundaries of the strike zone) extend 8-1/2 inches back from the leading edge, and then taper to meet at a point 8-1/2 inches further back. This point rests on the intersection of the first and third base lines. also *dish, home, home base, plate.*

1. homer: 1. A home run. (hit a homer to clean the bases) 2. An umpire who favors the home team.

2. homer: To hit a home run. (homered over the left field wall)

home run: A hit that travels so far or in such a manner that the batter can round the bases and reach home plate before any opposing player can make a putout. Most home runs are hit over the outfield boundaries, but sometimes, with a fast runner, a home run is possible when the ball stays in fair territory. In 1961, Roger Maris of the New York Yankees set the all-time record for the most home runs in a single season, 61. Hank Aaron holds the lifetime record with 755 home runs, followed by Babe Ruth (714), Willie Mays (660), and Frank Robinson (586). also *dinger, four-bagger, homer, round tripper, tater.*

home stand: A number of successive games played at a team's home ballpark.

hook: 1. The removal of a pitcher in trouble from the game. (got the hook after only two innings) 2. A curveball.

hook slide: A method of avoiding the tag when approaching a base, in which the base runner, instead of sliding feetfirst straight into the bag, drops to the side and bends one leg back, which hooks the bag as the player slides by. Though an early version of the technique, the Chicago slide, was practiced in the 1880s by Chicago White Stockings catcher Mike "King" Kelly (of the song, "Slide, Kelly, Slide"), the modern hook slide was first perfected as the fade-away slide after 1905 by Ty Cobb of the Detroit Tigers. also *fallaway slide.*

hopper: A batted ball that bounces. (a high hopper to the hole)

horse-and-buggy league: A minor league. An allusion to the horse and buggy transportation which was common in traveling between many rural minor league towns in baseball's early days. also *minors.*

horsecollar: No hits, likening the resulting zero in the box score to the thick collars worn by workhorses. To "wear the horsecollar" is to go without a hit for a game.

horsehide: A baseball. A reference to the material with which a baseball is covered. also *apple.*

hot corner: Third base. Coined by Cincinnati writer Ren Mulford in 1889 in reference to a particular game in which Redlegs' third baseman Hick Carpenter was peppered with repeated powerful drives.

●●An either busy or difficult location. (complaint department is the hot corner)

hot dog: A show-off player.

●●A show off. Also can be complimentary, meaning an outstanding performer, such as in motor racing. (qualified right up there with the hot dogs in the first row)

hot stove league: Off-season conversations among rabid baseball fans (such as might be carried on around a hot stove in winter) during which past games are rehashed. The term is believed to have been coined by Cincinnati writer Ren Mulford around the turn of the century. also *winter league.*

●●The rehashing of past events.

hummer: A fastball. see *fastball.*

hung up: A situation in which a player is caught in a rundown between bases. (hung up between second and third)

hurl: To pitch in a game. (hurled a strong two innings)

hurler: A pitcher.

ice man: A relief pitcher who can "cool" a suddenly "hot" opponent's rally. also *fireman.*

in: Across home plate to score. (drove in two runs to tie the score) also *home.*

infield: 1. The area of the playing field enclosed within the 90-foot square (60-foot or 75-foot for youths) made by home plate and the three bases. 2. The area of the playing field bounded on the sides by the baselines and extending from home plate to the outside edge of the dirt area in which the bases are set. On playing fields with artificial surfaces, this perimeter is marked with a painted white line that arcs from baseline to baseline. 3. The players who play infield positions. (not much of a hitting team, but they have a great infield)

infielder: A defensive player who plays in the infield.

infield fly rule: A special rule in effect only in the case of a fair infield fly ball judged catchable with less than two out and base runners at first and second, or loaded bases. In this circumstance, the batter is automatically called out whether or not the ball is actually caught, thus removing the force on the base runners should the fly not be caught. This prevents an infielder from choosing not to catch the fly so he can make a double play on the other runners (who must stay near their bases so they won't be trapped off base in the event of a fielded fly).

infield hit: A base hit in which the ball does not pass through the infield.

infield out: A batted ball resulting in a putout by an infielder.

inning: 1. A division of a game in which each team gets a turn at bat. also *frame*. 2. One team's turn at bat, ending when three players have been put out. From the cricket term "innings," which signifies a turn at bat for either a single batsman or a side.
●●A turn or period of play in badminton, billiards, bowling, croquet, curling, handball, horseshoes, and trapshooting.

in play: Able to affect or be acted upon by the batter, base runners, or defensive players. While the ball is in play, the batter and base runners can be put out, and runs can be scored. The ball is in play until it leaves the playing area, the umpire calls time out, or the third out of an inning is made. The expression originated in the sport of cricket in the eighteenth century.

inside: Between home plate and the batter. (the pitch is high and inside for a ball)

inside-out swing: A swing of the bat in which the hands are ahead of the barrel of the bat at the moment of contact with the ball, usually sending the ball to the opposite field.

inside-out the ball: To hit a pitched ball to the opposite field with an inside-out swing. compare *pull*.

inside-the-park home run: A fair hit that remains within the boundaries of the playing field, but provides enough time for the batter to round the bases and score before a play can be made.

instructional league: A winter league sponsored by major league baseball to provide instruction for prospective players and special or recuperative training for injured veterans.

intentional pass: see *intentional walk.*

intentional walk: A base on balls deliberately given to an opposing batter, usually either to avoid a strong batter or to set up a possible force play if first base (or sometimes first and second) is unoccupied. also *intentional pass.*

in the hole: 1. Due to bat after the player who is on deck. Part of the expression, "at bat, on deck, in the hole," a corruption of the original nautical form, "at bat, on deck, in the hold." see *at bat.* 2. At a disadvantage to the batter with a count of more balls than strikes. also *behind.* 3. At a disadvantage to the pitcher with two strikes in the count.

iron man: 1. A durable ballplayer who seldom, if ever, misses a game because of illness or injury, or one who accumulates a record of consecutive games played over a period of time. Baltimore Orioles and New York Giants pitcher Joe "Iron Man" McGinnity (actually a former iron foundry worker) was among the first to popularize the term. In 1903, pitching for the Giants, McGinnity won both games of a doubleheader three times in one month. He also once won five games in six days and continued to play in the minors until he was fifty-four years old. Certainly the most famous Iron Man in modern baseball was New York Yankees immortal Lou Gehrig, who in his fourteen-year career (1925-1939) played in 2,130 consecutive games before removing himself from the lineup, already suffering from amyotrophic lateral sclerosis, the incurable disease that killed him two years later. 2. A baseball announcer, presumably because of the iron microphones used by early announcers. 3. An archaic name for the price of admission to a ballgame. From the days when a general admission ticket could be bought with a single silver dollar, once known as an "iron man."

Iron Mike: An automated pitching machine used by hitters taking batting practice.

ivory: A rookie. Though the exact origin is unknown, the term likens a rookie's potential worth to precious ivory. see *rookie.*

ivory hunter: A baseball scout. One who

tracks down or "hunts" for valuable prospects. also *bird dog.*

jake, jaker: A player who makes excuses (such as illness or injury) to keep from playing. The term is associated with Boston Red Sox player-manager Jake Stahl (early 1900s), although whether its present use stems from a particular incident of not wanting to play or simply to the association of the name Jake (Stahl) with a player who would "stall" rather than play is a matter of question. compare *gamer.*

jam the batter: To pitch inside to a batter in order to prevent a full and powerful swing.

Jawn Titus: A exceptional or spectacular catch; a circus catch. A corruption of the name John Titus, a Philadelphia Phillies and later Boston Braves outfielder, who was known for his heroic fielding in the early 1900s.

jellyball: see *greaseball.*

John Anderson: A rare and embarrassing baserunning mistake in which an over-anxious player attempts to steal a base that is already occupied by a teammate. Named after "Honest" John Anderson, a utility player for the New York Highlanders, who in 1904 attempted to steal second with the bases loaded.

Judy: see *punch hitter.*

jughandle curve: A curveball that travels in a broad arc. also *rainbow curve, roundhouse curve.*

jump all over: To quickly hit and score runs against the opposing pitcher. (jumped all over the starting pitcher for three runs in the first inning)

jump on: To swing at and connect with a pitch. (jumps on a fastball and drives it all the way to the right field wall)

junior circuit: The American League. Although still sometimes referred to in this way, the American League has been considered an equal competitor to the National League since 1903, when the American League Boston Pilgrims won the first World Series against the National League Pittsburgh Pirates.

junk, junk pitch: A slow pitch, such as a forkball, knuckleball, or other pitch, that requires an unorthodox grip and delivery. Though regarded as "junk" by some in comparison to the classic fastball and curveball, these deceptive pitches are nonetheless effective when

well thrown. (just waiting for a fastball, but saw nothing but junk)

junk man: A pitcher who relies heavily on junk pitches rather than the more orthodox fastball and curve. In the late 1940s, New York Yankee pitcher Ed Lopat became the first pitcher to be called a junk man.

1. K: 1. The symbol used by scorers to indicate a strikeout. Originated in the 1860s by *New York Herald* sportswriter M.J. Kelly, who chose the last letter of "struck" (out) to differentiate between a strikeout and a sacrifice, indicated by the symbol "S." 2. A strikeout.

2. K: see *strike out.*

keystone: Second base. So called because second base is of "key" importance and halfway around the bases (like the keystone in an arch).

keystone sacker: Second baseman.

knob: The end of the bat handle, which has slightly raised rounded edges.

knockdown pitch: A pitch deliberately thrown at or near the batter, forcing him to bail out, or drop to the ground, in order to avoid being hit. Although against the rules, a knockdown pitch is sometimes thrown as a warning against or retaliation for other unsportsmanlike behavior. also *brushback, duster, Gillette, purpose pitch.* compare *beanball, beaner, chin music.*

knock out, knock out of the box: To force the opposing pitcher out of the game with a number of consecutive hits. also *chase.*

●●To render ineffective, to defeat. (her rebuttal knocked my argument right out of the box)

Knothole Club: Special blocks of seats reserved in most ballparks for use by youth groups at nominal or no cost. Cardinals manager-executive Branch Rickey originated the practice in St. Louis in the 1920s with the idea of encouraging future paying customers. The name came from the knotholes in the outfield fences of most early ballparks, through which many neighborhood children watched their first baseball games.

knuckleball: A pitch in which the ball is gripped with the thumb and the tips or fingernails of the first two fingers and released in such a way as to impart little or no spin. The result is a relatively slow pitch that dips, hops, or breaks in an unorthodox and unpredictable manner as it nears home plate. Often the catcher must use a larger than normal mitt when working with a knuckleball pitcher. also *flutterball, knuckler.*

knuckleballer: A pitcher known for his knuckleball.

knuckle curve: A curveball that is thrown with the grip used for a knuckleball.

knuckler: see *knuckleball.*

lawn mower: see *daisy clipper.*

lead: The position away from a base in the direction of the next base which a runner takes in order to gain an advantage by shortening the distance to the next base. The runner must, however, remain near to the base so he can run back in the event of a pickoff attempt by the pitcher or the catcher.

lead off: To be the first batter in a team's or inning's lineup.

leadoff: 1. The first to bat in a team's or inning's lineup. (leadoff batter) 2. Of, by, or made by the first to bat in a team's or inning's lineup. (leadoff bunt single)

leather man: see *glove man.*

leave: To have or strand a specified number of base runners on base at the end of the inning. (still can't seem to score a run as they leave two men on in the eighth) also *strand.*

left field: 1. The left (as viewed from home plate) side of the outfield past third base. 2. The player position in left field. (to play left field)

•• Because of the relative vastness of the outfield and its distance from home plate, something said to have come out of left field carries the connotation of something remote or unexpected. (that question came out of left field)

left fielder: The defensive player responsible for fielding balls hit to left field.

leg hit: A bouncer or ground ball that the batter beats out for a base hit.

letter high: The same height (distance from the ground) as the team initials or name generally printed on the chest portion of a uniform. (letter high fastball)

letup: see *changeup.*

line: 1. Baseline or foul line. (hits one down the line toward left field) 2. To hit a line drive. (lines a single through the hole)

line drive: A sharply hit ball that travels close to the ground in a fairly direct path. also *blue darter, clothesliner, darter, frozen rope, liner, rope.*

line out: To hit a line drive straight to a

fielder who catches the ball for an out. (lined out to the shortstop)

liner: A line drive. see *line drive.*

line score: A summary of the results of a game that lists team totals of runs, hits, and errors. A line score may also list each team's lineup and the names of the game's home run hitters. compare *box score.*

lineup: 1. All the players participating in a game. (injured and out of the lineup) 2. A list of the players participating in a game.

•• A list of participants or activities in an event. (a star-studded lineup for tonight's program)

lineup card: A prepared list of participating players and the order in which they bat, presented to the plate umpire by a representative from each team before the start of a game.

Little League: An international organization (twenty-nine countries participated in 1981) of baseball leagues in individual towns and cities for youths between the ages of nine and twelve years old who play on a diamond two-thirds the size of a regulation field. The first Little League was founded by Carl E. Stotz in 1939 in Williamsport, Pennsylvania, the present international headquarters and site of the annual Little League World Series.

live bat: Currently hitting well. (has a live bat in this series, so they will walk him)

live fastball: A fastball that moves around, rising (or occasionally dropping) as it nears homeplate.

load the bases: 1. To allow the opposing team to get base runners on all three bases at one time. (pitcher is in trouble again as he loads the bases with only one out) 2. To get base runners on all three bases at one time. (Yankees load the bases in the bottom of the ninth)

load up the ball: To surreptitiously apply saliva or some foreign substance to a baseball so as to make it break or swerve in an unnatural way when pitched. An illegal practice, which, if proved, results in ejection from the game and disciplinary action from the league.

long ball: A ball batted near or over an outfield wall or fence. (known as a long ball hitter)

long man: see *long reliever.*

long relief, long relief man: see *long reliever.*

THE LANGUAGE OF SPORT

long reliever: A relief pitcher who is able to pitch five or more innings, and can therefore relieve a starting pitcher early in a game. also *long man, long relief, long relief man.* compare *short reliever.*

1. look: The visual check of a base runner taken by a pitcher in the set position, just before delivering a pitch. (gives the look, and the pitch)

2. look: To hold, with a hit or thrown ball in hand, a base runner with a visual check before making a play on the batter or another base runner. (fields the ball on one hop, looks toward third to hold the runner, and throws to first for the out)

look at: To not swing at a pitch. (looks at a fastball inside for ball four) also *take.*

look for: To expect a certain type of pitch. (with a count of three balls and no strikes, looking for a fastball over the plate)

loop: 1. A league. (best pitching staff in the loop) 2. To hit a pitched ball in a high arc. (loops a single into center field)

losing pitcher: The pitcher charged with the loss of a game. A starting pitcher gets the loss if he pitches a complete game or his team is losing when he is taken out of the game and subsequently never gains the lead. A relief pitcher brought in when the team is leading or tied can be charged with the loss if he gives up the winning run (pitches the ball that puts the runner on base who subsequently scores the winning run). compare *winning pitcher.*

Lowdermilk: A pitcher with control problems, prone to wildness. Named after early 1900s pitcher Grover Cleveland Lowdermilk, a journeyman who was notorious for his lack of control.

lumber: A bat, or bats. see *bat.*

mace: A bat. see *bat.*

mackerel: A curveball. From the old saying "dead as a mackerel," which is how a curveball appears when compared to a fastball.

magic number: The total number of games the leading team in a division, conference, or league must win and/or the second place team must lose in order to mathematically guarantee the championship title for the leading team. (With five games left on the schedule, if the leading team has a two-game lead over the second place team, the magic num-ber for the leader is four. Four wins by the leader, four losses by the second place team, or any combination of wins and losses by the first and second place teams respectively that total four, mathematically guarantee that the leading team will finish with a better record than the second place team.)

major league: 1. Either or both of, or pertaining to either or both of, the two existing top level professional baseball leagues, the American League and the National League. 2. Any or all of, or pertaining to any or all of, the six top level professional leagues in the history of organized baseball; the National League (1876 to the present), the American League (1901 to the present), the American Association (1882 to 1891), the Union Association (1884), the Players' League (1890), and the Federal League (1914 to 1915). (a major league baseball player) also *big league.*

●●The top level of a sports endeavor, enterprise, or competition. The highest degree. (a major league personality problem)

Major League Baseball Players Association: The union that represents major league baseball players in collective bargaining. Founded in 1953, the union has national headquarters in New York City. The first labor organization in major league baseball was the National Brotherhood of Professional Baseball Players founded in 1885. In 1890, led by Hall of Fame pitcher and shortstop Monte Ward, Brotherhood members seceded from organized baseball and formed the Players League with teams in most of the National League cities. Although the new league was successful and competitive, after a year the players allowed themselves to be talked back into the fold and ultimately won few concessions from the powerful National League owners.

major leagues: The two top level professional baseball leagues in the United States: the American League and the National League. also *big leagues, bigs, majors.*

●●The top level of any sport, enterprise, or endeavor.

majors: see *major leagues.*

manicurist: see *groundskeeper.*

marked ball: A ball that has been surreptitiously cut, scratched, or scuffed in order to make it break or swerve in an unnatural way when pitched. see *doctored ball*.

mark the ball: To surreptitiously cut, scratch, or scuff the surface of a ball in order to make it break or swerve in an unnatural way when pitched.

mask: see *catcher's mask*.

matador: An infielder who goes through toreadorlike motions to move his body out of the way when fielding a batted ball.

McGrawism: Roughhouse, hard-hitting baseball as epitomized by John "Muggsy" McGraw, third baseman for the Baltimore Orioles in the 1890s (later Orioles and New York Giants manager). McGraw practiced and preached a brutal, anything goes style of play in which opposing infielders were bumped and spiked on the base paths, while their base runners would be tripped, held, or hit as they ran by.

meal ticket: A consistently excellent player, particularly a pitcher. The legendary New York Giants pitcher Carl Hubbell of the 1930s was a classic example. Known as "King Carl, the Meal Ticket," Hubbell was said to be the man who "kept the groceries on his manager's table."

••Any person, object, or quality that guarantees success. (admirable combination of intelligence and integrity will continue to be her meal ticket)

men in blue: The umpires. also *boys in blue*.

middle: 1. The center or middle of the strike zone. (didn't try to hit the corners, just blew a fastball by him right down the middle) 2. Over or near second base, between the normal fielding positions of the second baseman and the shortstop. (a base hit up the middle)

middle gardener: A center fielder.

minor league: Any, or pertaining to any, professional baseball league other than the two major leagues. Often minor league teams are owned and operated by, or affiliated with major league teams. also *minors*.

••Of small importance or little prestige. (just a pushy minor league bureaucrat)

minors: see *minor league*.

mitt: A padded leather covering worn in place of a normal glove by a catcher or first baseman, generally consisting of two sections, one for the thumb and

one for the four fingers (some first baseman's mitts have three sections). compare *glove*.

money player: A player who performs best under pressure or when the stakes are high (as in playoff or championship games).

morning glory: see *early bloomer*.

morning journal: A bat made of poor or soft wood, of no more use than a rolled-up newspaper. also *banana stick*.

motion: The movement of a pitcher's arms and body during the windup for a pitch. Often used to distract or deceive a batter by establishing a false or misleading rhythm.

mound: see *pitcher's mound*.

move: The throw used by a pitcher to pick off a runner caught off base. (picked off the runner with a great move to first)

moxie: A slang expression similar to "guts," meaning a combination of strength and courage or nerve. Moxie was a popular soft drink hawked in East Coast ballparks in the 1880s. The familiar call, "ice-cold moxie" in the stands during a game was eventually associated with the "ice-cold nerves" of courageous players.

••Spirit, courage, or resolution.

mud ball: An illegal pitch in which mud is applied to (or packed in the seams of) a ball in order to make it break or curve unnaturally when thrown.

muff: To fumble or misplay the ball; to bungle a play. In use since the late 1860s and derived from the early baseball term "muffin," an unskilled or casual player.

••To make a mistake or bungle something. (muffed his first line in the second act)

MVP: Most valuable player. An annual award given by the Baseball Writers Association of America (since 1931) to the most outstanding player in each league. The American League's first Most Valuable Player was George Sisler of the St. Louis Browns, selected by a special committee in 1922. In 1924, a special committee selected Dazzy Vance of the Brooklyn Dodgers as the National League's first Most Valuable Player. Frank Robinson is the only player ever to be selected MVP in both major leagues (National League MVP in 1961 with the Cincinnati Reds, American League MVP in 1966 with the

Baltimore Orioles). An MVP award is also given to one player (or occasionally more than one) in each World Series.

●●An actual or figurative award to the best or most valuable player or person in any sport, event, or circumstance. (whoever remembered to fill the canteen gets my vote for MVP)

National Baseball Hall of Fame and Museum: The official museum of baseball, where historic photos and memorabilia are on display, located in Cooperstown, New York, at the site where popular legend says General Abner Doubleday laid out the first baseball diamond in 1839. One section of the museum, the Baseball Hall of Fame, houses a permanent display of plaques honoring outstanding individuals in the sport of baseball, as selected in an annual balloting of the Baseball Writers Association of America. also *Hall of Fame.*

National League: The older of the two major professional baseball leagues in the United States. Created in 1876 by William A. Hulbert, the National League played its first game on April 22, 1876. At the time, there were teams in Boston, Chicago, Cincinnati, St. Louis, Hartford, New York, Philadelphia, and Louisville. The National League is now split into two divisions. In the Western Division, there are teams in Los Angeles, Cincinnati, Atlanta, San Francisco, Houston, and San Diego. In the Eastern Division, there are teams in St. Louis, Montreal, Philadelphia, Pittsburgh, New York, and Chicago. abbreviated NL.

National Pastime: The nickname the game of baseball came to be known by in the early twentieth century, especially after World War I.

nightcap: The second game of a doubleheader, often played in the evening.

nine: A baseball team.

no-hit: Pertaining to a game or part of a game during which a pitcher allows no base hits. (came in to pitch three no-hit innings)

no-hitter: A game in which a pitcher or pitchers give up no base hits to the opposing team. The first professional no-hitter was pitched in 1875 by Joe Borden on the Boston Red Stockings, then in the old National Association. In 1876, Borden pitched the first ever no-hitter in the National League. In 1981,

Nolan Ryan of the Houston Astros became the first pitcher in major league history to have pitched five no-hitters.

nubber: see *banjo hit.*

number two: A curveball, usually called for by the catcher with a hand signal of two fingers.

obstruction: Contact with a runner deliberately made by a defensive player neither in possession nor trying to obtain possession of the ball, illegally interfering with the progress of the runner. If the umpire rules that the base runner would have safely made the base without the obstruction, the base runner is awarded the base.

off-field hit: A base hit to the field on the opposite side of the plate as the batter stands. also *wrong-field hit.*

official scorer: The person officially designated scorekeeper and who makes decisions as to whether a defensive player is to be charged with an error.

off-speed pitch: A slower than normal pitch, particularly deceptive when mixed with fastballs.

on, on base: Occupying a base as a runner. (with one man on, and the winning run at the plate)

on-base percentage: The statistic used to measure the effectiveness of a batter at getting on base, obtained by dividing the number of times the batter reaches a base by the number of plate appearances (at bats, walks, hit batters, catcher's interference) and carrying the quotient three decimal places.

on deck: Next to take a turn at bat. Part of the expression, ''at bat, on deck, in the hole,'' a corruption of the original nautical form, ''at bat, on deck, in the hold.'' see *at bat.*

●●Due, or next on the agenda. (weather bureau reports we have clear skies on deck today)

on-deck circle: Either of two circles marked on each side of the field between the dugout and home plate, in which the batter due to bat next waits.

one-bagger, one-base hit, one-baser: A single.

one-cushion shot: A batted ball that caroms off an outfield wall.

one o'clock hitter: see *two o'clock hitter.*

on the fists: An inside pitch that passes close to the batter's hands, effectively jamming the batter. If contact is made with the ball, it is with the less powerful handle end of the bat. see *jam the batter.*

on the fly: In mid-air. (catches it on the fly for the third out)

open stance: A batting stance in which the front foot is positioned further away from the plate than the rear foot. compare *closed stance.*

opposite field: The field on the opposite side of the plate as the batter stands. (all caught off guard as he lined one to the opposite field)

orchard: 1. A ballpark. 2. The outfield. also *garden, pasture.*

orchardman: An outfielder. also *gardener, pastureworker.*

1. out: The termination of a player's turn as a batter or base runner. Three strikes put a batter out, as do the following: fouling off an attempted bunt with two strikes on the count (an automatic third strike); hitting a fly ball (fair or foul) that is caught in the air; being tagged with the ball after hitting a fair ball and before reaching base; hitting a fair ball and reaching base after a defensive player has touched the base while holding the ball; hitting an infield fly; interfering with the catcher while he attempts to play the ball; batting out of order. A base runner is called out upon being tagged with the ball while off base; reaching a base on a force play after a defensive player in possession of the ball touches that base; being hit by a batted ball before it travels past an infielder; interfering with a fielder's attempt to play the ball; running runs outside the base path to avoid a putout. Originally from the eighteenth century British game rounders. also *away, down, gone.*

2. out: 1. The putting, throwing, or calling out of a player from the opposing team. (got the out that ended the game) also *putout.* 2. The act of being put out or making an out. (made an out his last time at bat) 3. A player who has been put out. (he was caught stealing and became the third out)

outfield: 1. The area of the playing field that is beyond the perimeter of the infield (the grass or turf line behind the bases) and is bounded by the foul lines. The outfield is divided into three general areas, which are, as viewed from home plate, left field, center field, and right field. (to take the relayed throw

from the outfield) 2. The players who play the outfield positions. (a strong throwing outfield)

outfielder: A defensive player who plays in the outfield. also *gardener, orchardman, pastureworker.*

out in front of: Swinging or beginning to swing at a pitch too soon, especially a changeup or slow curve when a fastball is anticipated.

out looking: Out on a pitch that is taken for a called third strike. compare *out swinging.*

out man: see *easy out.*

out of play: Unable to affect or be acted upon by the batter, base runners, or defensive players.

out pitch: One's best or most reliable pitch, the one that most often results in an out. (uses the fastball as his out pitch)

out swinging: Out on a swing and a miss for the third strike. compare *out looking.*

overhand: A type of throw or delivery in which the hand is swung down from over the shoulder in a forward arc. compare *sidearm, underhand.*

overslide: To slide past (instead of safely into) a base. (overslides the base and is tagged out)

1. overthrow: To throw the ball beyond the desired destination. (overthrows the cutoff man and the base runners advance)

2. overthrow: A throw that goes past its desired destination. (takes second base on the overthrow)

paint the black: To throw pitches in the black. Pitchers who are able to paint the black often get these pitches called as strikes or entice batters to swing at them. see *black.*

palm ball: An off-speed pitch in which the ball is gripped between the thumb and the palm (instead of the fingertips) and released in such a way as to impart little or no spin. The result is a pitch that breaks in an unorthodox and unpredictable manner as it nears home plate.

pancake: A thinly padded, rather flat glove preferred by some infielders. The shallow pocket in such a glove allows a fielded ball to be quickly grasped and thrown, particularly important in a double play situation. compare *bushel basket.*

1. pass: A base on balls.

2. pass: To walk, or give a base on balls to a batter.

passed ball: A normally catchable pitch, untouched by the batter, which the catcher misses, enabling base runners to advance. The ruling of passed ball is made by the official scorer. compare *wild pitch.*

pasture: The outfield. also *garden, orchard.*

pastureworker: An outfielder. also *gardener, orchardman.*

pebble picker: An infielder who uses the alibi of a "bad hop" when a ground ball gets by, sometimes picking through the turf for the guilty pebble.

1. **peg:** To throw a ball. (can really peg the ball)

2. **peg:** A throw. (out at the plate on a great peg from left field)

pennant: A league championship. The Brooklyn Bridegrooms (later nicknamed the Dodgers) are the only professional team to have won pennants in two different major leagues in successive years: in the old American Association in 1889, and in the National League in 1890. also *flag.*

pennant race: The competition for a league championship, especially near the end of a season.

pepper: A warm-up drill in which a batter hits a series of ground balls in rapid succession to several players a short distance away, who field them and throw them briskly among themselves before returning them to the batter. The term is probably an allusion to the fast or "peppy" quality of the drill.

perfect game: A no-hitter in which all opposing batters are retired in succession, without reaching first base. Since the first major league perfect game by Worcester pitcher John Richman in 1880, only ten more occured in the next 101 years. The most famous may have been New York Yankees pitcher Don Larsen's perfect game against the Brooklyn Dodgers in the 1956 World Series, the first no-hitter ever pitched in a World Series.

pickle: A rundown. From the colloquialism "in a pickle," meaning caught in an embarrassing or dangerous predicament. see *rundown.*

pick off: To put out a base runner who is off base by quickly throwing the ball to a fielder at the base who tags the runner before he can return. The throw to pick off a runner can be made by the pitcher or catcher.

pickoff: The act or an instance of picking off a base runner.

piece of iron: A particularly good bat. From the early days of baseball, when players would sometimes plug bats with nails or bits of metal in the hopes of making them more powerful.

pinch: Made with a pinch-hit. (a pinch double) also *pinch-hit.*

pinch hit: 1. To replace another player at bat. Legal since the baseball rule permitting substitutions was passed in 1892. (will pinch hit for the pitcher) 2. To make a base hit while pinch hitting for another player. (pinch hit a single to start off the inning)
●●To take another's place. (will pinch hit behind the counter until the salesman returns)

1. **pinch-hit:** A base hit made while pinch hitting for another player. Los Angeles Dodger Manny Mota (retired in 1980) holds the major league lifetime record of 150 pinch-hits.

2. **pinch-hit:** Made by a pinch hitter. (a pinch-hit double) also *pinch.*

pinch hitter: A player who is sent in to take another player's turn at bat, and who is usually himself replaced by another player who continues in the position vacated by the player whose batting turn was taken. A pinch hitter is generally used at a critical juncture, often to bat for the pitcher or a poor hitter, to face a particular pitcher because of previous success, or to bat from the opposite side of the plate as the player being replaced. Cleveland Spiders player John "Dirty Jack" Doyle became the first pinch hitter in baseball history when he hit successfully in his only attempt in 1892. In the same year, sportswriter Charlie Dryden coined the term "pinch hitter" because the player who came into the game to bat was in a "tight spot," or "in a pinch." compare *designated hitter.*

pinch-run: To act as a pinch runner. (putting in a speedster to pinch run for him)

pinch runner: A player who is sent in to run for a teammate on base, and who is usually himself replaced by another player who continues in the fielding position vacated by the player removed for the pinch runner. In 1974, then Oakland A's owner Charles O. Finley hired Herb Washington, a sprinter with no previous professional baseball experience, to use purely as a pinch runner (Finley called him his "designated runner"). compare *courtesy runner*.

pine tar ball: An illegal pitch in which pine tar (normally rubbed on the handle of a bat to make it sticky) is surreptitiously rubbed on one part of the ball so as to make it break or swerve unpredictably when thrown.

pine tar towel: A pine tar-soaked cloth that is rubbed on the handle of a bat to make it sticky, providing a better grip.

1. pitch: 1. To throw the ball to the batter. To be legal, a pitch must be thrown with an overhand or sidearm delivery (underhand for softball), must not be interrupted or stopped in any way (except when the stretch or set position is used), and must be made with the pitcher's foot touching the rubber until the ball is released. (In slow pitch softball, the ball must travel in an arc between three feet and ten feet high on its way to the batter.) (pitched more fastballs than curveballs) 2. To play the position of the pitcher. (pitched three innings before giving up a hit) also *twirl*. 3. To throw in a specific manner. (pitched him high and inside to move him away from the plate) 4. To start a certain pitcher in a given game. (pitched his two left-handers in the first two games of the series)

●●To be "in there pitching" means to be trying or making an effort.

2. pitch: The ball delivered by the pitcher. (first pitch was a hummer)

pitch around: 1. To pitch so carefully as to risk a base on balls in order to prevent the batter from getting a hit. 2. To intentionally walk a batter.

pitcher: 1. The player who delivers the ball to the batter. Originally "bowler" from cricket, and later, rounders. also *hurler, soupbone*. 2. The player position of the pitcher.

pitcher of record: 1. The pitcher credited with the victory or charged with the loss at the end of a game. 2. The pitcher who would be credited with the victory or charged with the loss if the score remains unchanged when the game is ended.

pitchers' duel: A close game in which both pitchers allow the opposite side few, if any, scoring opportunities. A low scoring game. Any low scoring game or contest, usually featuring defense rather than offense. Also often used facetiously to refer to a wide-open high scoring game. (the final score was 14-12—a real pitchers' duel)

pitcher's mound: The slightly elevated portion of the playing field in the middle of a diamond on which the pitcher stands to pitch the ball. Eighteen feet in diameter, the mound rises gradually to a maximum height of 10 inches at the leveled-off central area, which contains a 24-inch-long by 6-inch-wide white rubber slab. The front edge (long side) of this slab, called the pitcher's rubber, lies exactly 60 feet 6 inches from the rear corner of home plate. Before the late 1880s, the pitcher's mound was called the pitcher's box, which was taken from the bowler's box in the game of rounders. also *hill, mound*.

pitcher's plate: see *rubber*.

pitcher's rubber: see *rubber*.

pitch from the stretch: To pitch with the special abbreviated motion used instead of a full windup when runners are on base. see *stretch*.

pitching chart: A written log of every pitch made by a particular pitcher to every opposing batter and the subsequent results. The pitching chart, usually kept by a coach or teammate, can help the

PITCHER

pitcher and his manager assess the effectiveness of certain pitches to certain batters, improving his future performance.

pitching coach: A coach (often an ex-pitcher) whose sole responsibility is to teach, train, and console the pitchers on a team.

pitching machine: see *Iron Mike.*

pitching staff: The pitchers on a team. (strongest pitching staff in the league)

pitchout: A pitch that is intentionally thrown wide of the plate and away from the batter to enable the catcher to throw out a base runner who is stealing a base or to prevent one from stealing a base.

plate: Home plate.

plate umpire: The umpire-in-chief, positioned behind home plate. see *umpire, umpire-in-chief.*

play ball: The traditional signal for play to begin or restart after a time-out, called out by the umpire.
●●To "play the (ball) game" or cooperate. (if the two sides will play ball, the case will be settled in no time)

play-by-play: A running description of the action of a game for a radio or television broadcast. On August 5, 1921, station KDKA of Pittsburgh broadcast the first major league baseball game on the radio, between the Pittsburgh Pirates and the Philadelphia Phillies. Harold Arlin was the play-by-play announcer. On August 26, 1939, Red Barber did the play-by-play on the first major league telecast, a doubleheader between the Brooklyn Dodgers and the Cincinnati Reds.
●●A running commentary on or point-by-point reconstruction of an event. (gave us a play-by-play description of her vacation along with a slide show)

playoff: 1. One of a series of extra games at the end of a season (as between division leaders) to decide the league champion. 2. An extra game or contest or series of games or contests to decide a winner or championship in case of a tie at the end of regular play. 3. Of or pertaining to a playoff or playoffs.

plugged bat: see *doctored bat.*

pocket: The deep central area of a glove or mitt, optimum and most secure for catching or fielding a ball.

1. pop: A pop fly. also *popper, pop-up.*

2. pop: To hit a pop-up. (popped to the shortstop)

pop fly: A short, high fly ball. also *pop, popper, pop-up.*

pop foul: A pop fly that goes foul.

pop out: To hit a pop fly that is caught for an out.

pop-out: A pop fly that is caught for an out.

popper: A pop fly. also *pop, pop-up.*

pop up: To hit a short, high fly ball, usually for an out. (popped up to the second baseman) also *pop.*

pop-up: A short, high fly ball, usually an out. (hits a little pop-up to the pitcher) also *pop, pop fly, popper.*

pop-up slide: A feetfirst slide into a base in which a base runner "pops up" into a standing position on the base, ready to advance to the next base.

powder puff ball: An illegal pitch in which the ball is coated with resin powder (which some claim is mixed with white flour), accumulated in the pitcher's hand from the rosin bag. When the ball is thrown, it arrives at the plate amid a cloud of white dust. Veteran pitcher Gaylord Perry invented the powder puff ball. also *puff ball.* see *doctored ball.*

power alley: Either of two hypothetical lanes in the outfield between the center field and right field and between center field and left field, through which home runs are frequently hit.

pretzel: A curveball. Two derivations: one from the curved shape of a pretzel, and the other from the fact that a curveball can "tie a batter up in a knot" like a pretzel.

protect the plate: To avoid being called out on strikes by attempting to foul off all pitches which might be called strikes if not swung at, while waiting for a hittable pitch.

protect the runner: To give a base runner an opportunity to steal by swinging at any pitch (even a bad one), and thus either hitting the ball or delaying the catcher's attempt to throw out the runner. 2. To attempt to hit the ball during a hit-and-run play.

puff ball: see *powder puff ball.*

pull, pull the ball: To hit the ball to the outfield on the same side of the plate as the batter stands when at bat. A left-handed batter pulls the ball to right field.

pulled off the bag: Made to lose contact with the base in order to catch an errant throw, resulting in the loss of a force play unless contact can be reestablished before the runner reaches the base.

pull hitter: A batter who usually tends to pull the ball.

pull the string: To throw a changeup after a fastball or a series of fastballs, often causing the batter to begin to swing too soon, as though the pitcher had pulled a string attached to the ball before it reached the plate.

1. pump: The part of a pitcher's windup in which he swings his arms back and forward over his head.

2. pump: The raising and swinging of the arms back and then forward over the head in the windup.

Punch and Judy hitter: see *punch hitter*.

punch hitter: A batter who gets hits by punching at the ball (in contrast to using a full swing). also *Judy, Punch and Judy hitter*.

purpose pitch: see *knockdown pitch*.

put out: To cause a player on the opposing team to be out. The expression comes from the game of cricket, and later, rounders.

putout: The putting out of a player, officially credited to the player who completes the putout. To be credited with a putout, a player can tag a base runner, touch a base and force out a runner, or catch a fly ball. If the batter strikes out, hits a foul bunt after two strikes, or is thrown out for obstructing the catcher or batting improperly or in the wrong order, the putout is credited to the catcher. If the runner is put out because of being struck with a batted ball or interfering with a defensive player, the closest player, or the player who would have made the play if unobstructed, is credited with the putout. compare *assist*.

quick hook: 1. The tendency of a manager or coach to immediately remove and replace a pitcher in trouble. 2. The quick or early removal of a pitcher from a game.

quick pitch: 1. An illegal pitch in which the pitcher throws the ball before the batter is ready. If the bases are empty, the quick pitch is called a ball (unless the batter otherwise reaches first base on the pitch, in which case the illegal pitch

is disregarded). If there are runners on base, the quick pitch is ruled a balk and all runners advance one base (unless the batter otherwise reaches first base, causing the runners to advance normally). also *quick return pitch*. 2. A legal pitch made without a windup, but with a simple pivot on the rubber.

quick-pitch: To make a quick pitch.

quick return pitch: see *quick pitch*.

rabbit: The bounce or liveliness of a baseball. (more rabbit in the modern-day baseball)

rabbit ball: The lively ball used in modern baseball, first adopted in 1920 by the American League and one year later by the National League. The rabbit ball (it bounces or jumps like a rabbit) was introduced to take advantage of the box office potential of slugger Babe Ruth (in 1920, Ruth hit fifty-four home runs, his batting average soared fifty-four points to .376, and the American League's collective batting average was twenty-five points higher than the year before).

race to the bag: A footrace between a base runner and a fielder in possession of the ball who will force the runner out if he reaches the base first. (to the pitcher who wins the race to the bag for the third out)

rainbow, rainbow curve: A curveball that travels in a wide sweeping arc. also *jughandle curve, roundhouse curve*.

rain check: The part of the ticket which can be used for admission to another, usually specified, game if a game is rained out. The practice of giving rain checks originated in baseball in the 1880s.

●●When one cannot attend or participate in some activitiy, it is common to ask for a ''rain check,'' another invitation or opportunity at some future time. (already have plans tonight, but I hope you'll give me a rain check)

rain out: To rain hard enough to cause the postponement of a game. (if it continues, the game might be rained out)

●●To rain hard enough to cause the postponement of any event. Also, to be ''rained out'' connotes a lack of success or the opportunity for success at any endeavor due to circumstances beyond one's control. (''you win some, you lose some, and you'll get rained out of a few'')

rainout: A game that is suspended or postponed because of rain.

1. razz: see *razzberry.*

2. razz: To heckle or deride. Derived from *razzberry.*

••To tease or heckle. (got razzed because of his mismatched socks)

razzberry: A sound expressing derision or contempt, made by extending the tongue between the lips and forcibly expelling air. Some believe that the proper and original spelling of the present term, "raspberry," was a play on the word "rasp," meaning to make a coarse or abrasive sound. also *Bronx cheer, razz.*

••An expression of derision or contempt.

RBI: Run(s) batted in. also *ribby.*

receiver: A catcher. see *catcher.*

relief: A relief pitcher's work in a given game. (pitched two innings in relief)

reliefer: see *relief pitcher.*

relief man: see *relief pitcher.*

relief pitcher: A pitcher who does not start, but who is used to relieve another pitcher, particularly one who is used consistently in this capacity. In 1981, Rollie Fingers of the Milwaukee Brewers became the first relief pitcher ever to win both the MVP award and Cy Young Award in the same year. also *reliefer, relief man, reliever.* compare *starting pitcher.*

relieve: To replace or take over for another pitcher during a game.

reliever: see *relief pitcher.*

resin bag: see *rosin bag.*

retire: To put out a batter, batters, or a side. Originally from the sport of cricket, then later, rounders. (retired the last six men in a row) also *set down.*

retire the side: To put out three batters, ending the opposing team's turn at bat until the next inning.

rhubarb: A noisy argument or heated discussion on the field. The expression was first popularized by Brooklyn Dodgers play-by-play man Red Barber. He first broadcast the term at a game in Cincinnati in 1938, after hearing New York writer Garry Schumacher exclaim "What a rhubarb!" during a game-stopping fracas. Though it was common for film, theater, and radio actors to repeat the word "rhubarb" over and over again to simulate an angry and excited mob, Schumacher explained that his use of the expression probably came out of the subconscious memory of boyhood fights with unpopular rhubarb sandwiches (provided as a mild laxative) in the streets of Brooklyn.

••An argument, sometimes with comic results. (small disagreement that turned into a real rhubarb)

ribby: Run batted in. A pronunciation of the abbreviation for runs batted in, RBI. (the ribby king of the team) also *RBI, run batted in.*

1. rifle: A great throwing arm, especially from the outfield. also *cannon, gun.*

2. rifle: To make a long accurate throw. (rifles the ball home in time for the tag)

right field: 1. The right (as viewed from home plate) side of the outfield past first base. 2. The player position in right field. (to play right field)

right fielder: The defensive player responsible for fielding balls hit to right field.

riseball, riser: A softball pitch that rises as it nears the plate.

rook: Short for rookie.

1. rookie: An inexperienced player. Army slang for, and probably an alteration of, the word recruit. also *donkey, ivory, rook, yan, yannigan.*

••An inexperienced or unskilled person. (drives a car like a rookie)

2. rookie: First year. (won eight games in his rookie season)

Rookie of the Year: An annual award given by the Baseball Writers Association of America to the outstanding first year player in each league. The first Rookie of the Year Award was given to Jackie Robinson of the Brooklyn Dodgers in 1947 (the first two years, only one player was selected from both leagues combined).

root: To cheer or encourage a player or team. The term has been popular in baseball since the late 1800s and derives from the notion that a partisan fan is almost "rooted" to his or her team. (root for the home team)

••To encourage, cheer for, wish the success of, or lend support to someone or something.

rooter: A fan who roots for a player or team. The first recorded use of the expression in print appeared in the July 8, 1890 edition of the *New York Press.*

rope: A line drive. Short for frozen rope. see *line drive.*

rosin bag: A cloth bag of powdered rosin that, when handled by a pitcher, leaves enough rosin in the hand to give him a good grip on the ball. also *resin bag*.

rotation: The regular order in which starting pitchers are used. (trying to work his way into the pitching rotation)

roundhouse curve: A curveball that travels in a wide sweeping arc somewhat like the circular revolving floor of a railroad roundhouse. also *jughandle curve, rainbow curve*.

round-tripper: A home run. A round trip around all the bases and back to home plate. see *home run*.

rubber: A 6-inch by 24-inch rectangular slab of white rubber set into the ground atop the pitcher's mound. The front edge (long side) is 60 feet, 6 inches (46 feet for softball) from the rear corner of home plate. Although he must be in contact with the rubber while making a pitch, the pitcher must leave the rubber before attempting to pick off a base runner. The original regulation distance between the rubber and home plate was 45 feet. In 1881, the rubber was moved back to 50 feet. In 1891, the old American Association failed, cutting the number of major league baseball teams from twenty-four to twelve in one year. With just the strongest pitchers remaining, suddenly batters found themselves struggling (only eleven batters hit over .300 in 1892, as compared to twenty-three the previous year). Fearing that interest in the game might dwindle, the baseball owners moved the rubber back to its present distance for the 1893 season. The move had the desired effect, with no less than forty-three batters exceeding the .300 mark that year. also *pitcher's plate, pitcher's rubber*.

rubber arm: A durable pitching arm. Said of a pitcher who is able to pitch often and/or for long periods without soreness or stiffness.

run: 1. A point scored, accomplished each time a member of the offensive team touches all the bases and home plate in succession without being put out. A run is credited to both the player and the team in statistical records. The term comes from the game of cricket. In 1894, Philadelphia Phillies outfielder "Sliding Billy" Hamilton scored 192 runs, the all-time single season record.

Ty Cobb holds the lifetime record for the most runs scored, 2,244. 2. To eject, or throw a player out of a game. (said something he shouldn't have, so the umpire ran him)

run and hit: A prearranged play in which the runner on first starts for second base on the pitch, while the batter, under no obligation to protect the runner, chooses whether or not to swing at the pitch. If the ball is successfully hit through the infield, the base runner can often take an extra base and sometimes even score. If the ball is hit to an infielder, the base runner is most often able to reach second base safely and prevent a double play. If the ball is not swung at or is swung at and missed, the base runner may be thrown out or come up with a stolen base, depending upon the speed and accuracy of the catcher's throw. compare *hit and run*.

run batted in: A run caused by and credited as a run batted in to a particular batter. A batter is credited with a run batted in when he causes a runner to score by getting a base hit or base on balls, by being hit by a pitch, by making a sacrifice or sacrifice fly, or because of an error when there are fewer than two outs and a runner on third who could have scored had the error not occurred. In 1930, Hack Wilson of the Chicago Cubs set the all-time single season record of 190 runs batted in. Hank Aaron holds the lifetime record of 2,297 runs batted in. also *RBI, ribby*.

run down: To put out a base runner in a rundown.

rundown: A situation in which a base runner is trapped off base between two fielders in the base path who toss the ball back and forth and move closer until the runner can be tagged out. Usually the result of an error on the part of the base runner, but occasionally a strategic ploy in a double steal to take the attention of the defensive team while another base runner breaks for home plate. also *pickle*.

runner: A base runner.

runners at the corners: Base runners at first and third bases.

run out a fly ball: To run, after hitting what appears to be a routine fly ball, as hard as possible until the ball is actually caught. This kind of effort can result in a base hit or even extra bases if the fly ball is misjudged or dropped.

rush seats: Unreserved or bleacher seats. The term dates back to the early days of baseball and the custom of opening the gates and allowing the crowd to pour in all at once to fill up the unreserved seats on a first-come-first-served basis.

sack: Base. Named for the stuffed 15-inch-square white canvas bag or "sack" that is attached to the ground for use as a base. also *bag*.

1. sacrifice: A bunt on which a batter is put out, but which allows a base runner to advance. However, if the putout of the batter is the third out, the inning is ended and a sacrifice is not credited. If the batter is not put out because of an error, but would have been without the error, the sacrifice is credited and the base runner advances. In statistical records, a sacrifice does not count as a time at bat and so does not affect the batting average of the batter. If a run scores as a result of a sacrifice, the batter is credited with an RBI. also *sacrifice hit*.

2. sacrifice: To make a sacrifice or sacrifice fly.

sacrifice fly: A fly ball (fair or foul) caught for the first or second out, but hit far enough to enable a base runner to tag up and reach home plate without being put out. In statistical records, a sacrifice fly does not count as a time at bat and so does not affect the batting average of the batter. Since a run is scored on a sacrifice fly, the batter is credited with an RBI.

sacrifice hit: see *sacrifice*.

safe: Successful in reaching a base without being put out. (slides under the tag and is safe)

safety: A base hit.

safety squeeze: see *squeeze play*.

sandlot baseball: 1. Crude, unorganized baseball games played in vacant lots in or near urban areas, historically the place where many youths are first exposed to the game. 2. Crude or unskilled baseball. An uncomplimentary comparison to the rudimentary game played by youths in sandlots.

save: The credit awarded to a relief pitcher who enters a game with his team in the lead and preserves that lead for the remainder of the game. If a relief pitcher does not finish the game, he cannot

be credited with a save unless he is removed for a pinch hitter or a pinch runner. If more than one relief pitcher qualifies for a save, the official scorer will credit the save to the relief pitcher judged to have been the most effective. Only one save can be credited in any game. In 1973, Detroit Tiger reliever John Hiller set the all-time record for the most saves in a single season, thirty-eight. also *vultch*.

scoring position: Either second or third base. So called because a base runner can be expected to score on a base hit when he is on one of these bases. (pitched himself into a jam, with only one out and a man in scoring position)

scratch hit, scratch single: A weak hit that enables a batter to reach first, but would not normally be expected to do so.

screen: The wire protective barrier behind home plate, between the playing field and the spectators. (fouls one back into the screen)

screwball: A breaking ball that breaks the opposite way as a curveball (away from a right-handed batter when thrown by a left-hander), a reverse curve. A difficult pitch to throw, the ball is delivered with an elongated arc with the arm extended almost over the head, and released out of the back of the hand with a snap of the wrist. The earliest version of the screwball (the fadeaway) was pioneered in 1900 by the New York Giants' charismatic pitcher, Christy Mathewson. In 1928, another legendary Giants pitcher, Carl Hubbell, popularized the modern screwball, which he had perfected and renamed three years earlier as a minor league player in Oklahoma City. also *scroogie*.

scroogie: see *screwball*.

scuffer: A ball that is illegally scuffed or scratched in order to make it curve in an unnatural way when pitched.

second: Second base. (will hold up at second with a stand-up double)

second base: 1. The base located on the corner of the diamond diagonally opposite home plate, which must be touched second by a base runner. 2. The name of the position played by the second baseman. (to play second base) also *keystone, second*.

second baseman: The defensive player

positioned usually to the right of second base who makes plays at second base and fields balls hit to the area between second base and first base. also *keystone sacker, second sacker.*

second sacker: Second baseman.

seeing-eye single: A base hit that seems to "find" its way through a narrow gap between infielders, as though led by a seeing-eye dog. also *tweener.*

senior circuit: The National League. So called because the National League is older than the American League, sometimes referred to as the junior circuit.

set down: To cause a batter, batters, or a lineup to be put out. (set down the first three batters in the second inning) also *retire.*

set position: The position a pitcher assumes for the momentary pause that must follow the abbreviated windup or "stretch," during which the pitcher checks a base runner before throwing to a base, delivering the ball to the batter, or stepping off the rubber with the pivot foot. While in the set position, the pitcher stands with one foot (the pivot foot) on the rubber and the other foot in front of the rubber, holding the ball with both hands in front of his body. If the pitcher does not come to a complete stop in the set position, a balk is charged and the runner or runners advance.

seventh-inning stretch: The tradition of standing and stretching for a brief period before one's favorite team comes to bat in the seventh inning. The custom was practiced as far back as 1869 by the fans of the first professional team in baseball, the Cincinnati Red Stockings, and is believed to be related to the age-old superstition about the lucky number seven.

shade: To take up defensive positions slightly to the left or slightly to the right of normal, because of the tendency of a certain batter to hit to one side or the other. (outfield shading to the left) also *shift.*

shag flies: To catch fly balls in practice. ●●To "shag" is to catch, or to run after and retrieve.

shake off a sign: To reject a catcher's sign or signal calling for a certain pitch, usually by shaking the head negatively or flicking the glove.

shave the corners: see *hit the corners.*

shift: see *shade.*

shine ball: An illegal pitch in which one part of the ball is rubbed or polished smooth (in the glove or against some part of the pitcher's uniform) to make it break or swerve unnaturally when pitched. see *doctored ball.*

shin guard: The protective covering worn by the catcher over each shin. Invented and first used in 1907 by New York Giants catcher Roger Bresnahan.

shoestring catch: A catch of a fly or line drive made by a running fielder just before it lands. To make a shoestring catch, the player must lean forward with his glove extended forward almost to the ground.

short: Shortstop.

short fielder: 1. In slow pitch softball, an additional player who is placed just outside the infield. 2. The player position of a short fielder.

short-hop: To catch a ball (especially a batted ball) close to the ground immediately after it bounces. (short-hops the ball and makes the throw to first in time for the out)

short hop: Immediately after the bounce of a ball. (catches it on the short hop)

short man: see *short reliever.*

short relief, short relief man: see *short reliever.*

short reliever: A reliever routinely used for only a few innings, such as during the last couple of innings to protect a close lead. also *short man, short relief, short relief man.* compare *long reliever.*

shortstop: 1. The defensive player positioned usually to the left of second base who is responsible for making plays at second base and for fielding balls hit to the area between second and third base. 2. The position played by the shortstop. (to play shortstop)

shut out: To prevent the opposing team from scoring. Originally from the sport of horse racing in the 1870s and still in use. A bettor who reaches the window too late is shut out and prevented from placing a bet. (the starting pitcher shut them out for the first four innings) also *whitewash.*

shutout: A game (either completed or in progress) in which the opponent is prevented from scoring. Hall of Fame Washington pitcher Walter Johnson pitched a record 110 shutouts in his twenty-one-year career. In 1916,

Grover Cleveland Alexander of the Philadelphia Phillies set the record for the most shutouts pitched in one season, sixteen. also *whitewash.*

●●Any contest or situation where an opponent is prevented from scoring (literally, comparatively, or figuratively), or where a team, group, or individual is particularly successful or dominant. (the prosecutor is pitching a shutout so far)

sidearm: A type of throw or delivery made with the hand and wrist brought forward almost parallel to the ground. compare *overhand, underhand.*

sign: A signal determined prior to the game (a word, gesture, or number of fingers) that managers, coaches, and players use to secretly convey information and instructions. Catchers may ask for particular pitches by giving their pitchers a sign. Coaches in the boxes at first base and third base give signs to the batter and to base runners.

1. single: A base hit enabling the batter to reach first base. (a single up the middle) The term originates from the game of cricket. also *bingle, one-bagger, one-base hit, one baser, singleton.*

2. single: 1. To make a single. (singled up the middle to start the inning) 2. To hit a single that allows a base runner to advance. (singled him to third) 3. To hit a single that causes a run to score. (singled in the tying run in the eighth)

singleton: A single.

sinker: A pitch that drops suddenly (usually without curving) as it nears the plate. also *sinker ball.*

sinker ball: A sinker.

skull: see *bean.*

sleeper rabbit play: A prearranged play with base runners on second and third, wherein the runner on second gets the attention of the catcher by being slow to return to the base after the first pitch. In the hopes of drawing a throw from the catcher, the base runner repeats his "careless" return after the next pitch. When and if the catcher does throw, the runners break for home and third the moment the ball leaves his hand. The sleeper rabbit play was invented by Detroit Tigers third baseman George Moriarty in the early 1900s. In recent years, the play has been revived and used with some success by the Montreal Expos.

1. slide: To leap or dive feetfirst or head-

first when approaching a base, then skid along the ground (away from or under a tag) until the base is safely contacted with an outstretched foot or hand.

2. slide: The action or an instance of sliding feetfirst or headfirst into a base.

slider: 1. A pitch thrown with the speed of a fastball that breaks in the same direction as a curve, just as it crosses the plate. Although the exact origin is unknown, George "The Bull" Uhle of the Detroit Tigers and George Blaeholder of the St. Louis Browns were among the first to throw it in the 1930s. 2. An abrasion from sliding into a base. also *strawberry.*

slip pitch: An off-speed pitch that drops just before it reaches the plate. To deliver the pitch, the ball is held between the thumb and palm, not touched by the fingertips, and released in such a way as to impart little or no forward spin.

slo pitch: Slow pitch softball.

slow pitch: Slow pitch softball.

slow pitch softball: A variety of softball in which pitches are thrown at a moderate speed and must arc higher than the batter's head (a minimum of three feet and a maximum of ten feet above the point of release) on the way to the plate. Each side consists of ten players, with the extra player (short fielder) usually playing in a shallow outfield position. Bunting and base stealing are illegal (base runners must remain on base until the ball reaches the batter). A batter who is hit by a pitch does not walk to first base. also *slo pitch, slow pitch.* compare *fast pitch softball.*

slugfest: A high-scoring game with many hits.

slugger: A batter who is known for hitting extra base hits and home runs. With nine home runs and sixty-two runs batted in, Boston left fielder Charley Jones became baseball's first real slugger in 1879. A list of the greatest sluggers of the game would include Babe Ruth, Lou Gehrig, Stan Musial, Ted Williams, Joe DiMaggio, Willie Mays, Mickey Mantle, and Hank Aaron, who hit more home runs in his career (755) than any man in the history of major league baseball.

slugging average: An official statistic that measures the ability of a batter to hit for extra bases, determined by dividing the total bases reached safely on hits by the total times at bat and carrying the quotient three decimal places. Babe Ruth holds both the all-time single season record slugging average, .847, set in 1920, and the lifetime slugging average, .690.

slurve: A pitch that is faster than a curve, but curves more than a normal slider.

1. smoke: A fastball, or fastballs. (reaching back and throwing smoke) see *fastball*.

2. smoke: To throw hard. (smoked one by him)

snake: A curveball.

sno-cone: A catch in which the ball is barely caught in the top part, or webbing, of the glove and protrudes from the top of the glove like the top of a sno-cone.

softball: 1. A game similar to and derived from baseball, played on a field with the same configurations but smaller dimensions (pitching distance 46 feet, bases 60 feet apart), and using a ball slightly larger than a baseball, which is pitched underhand. Invented in the 1880s, softball was originally intended as an indoor game, known as indoor baseball. There are two varieties of softball: fast pitch softball, in which a great deal of emphasis is put on the speed of the pitching (about equal to hardball, given the shorter pitching distance), and slow pitch softball, which prohibits fast pitching and places more emphasis on the hitting and fielding aspects of the game. see *fast pitch softball, slow pitch softball.* 2. The ball used to play the game of softball. A white horsehide or cowhide-covered sphere sewn together with flat seams, 11-7/8 to 12-1/8 inches in circumference, weighing 6-1/4 to 7 ounces. The center of a softball is kapok, or a mixture of cork and rubber, wound with yarn.

solo home run: A home run with the bases empty, scoring only the batter.

soupbone: 1. A pitcher's arm. 2. A pitcher. The term dates back to the early 1900s, comparing the value of a pitcher or his arm to the team with the value of a soupbone to a soup.

soupboning: Pitching.

southpaw: A left-handed pitcher. From the early practice of orienting baseball parks with home plate towards the west, so that the batter would not have to look into the afternoon sun (nor would the people in the expensive seats behind home plate). When a left-handed pitcher faces west (home plate), his pitching arm is to the south. The exact origin of the term is unknown, but *Chicago Inter-Ocean* sportswriter Charlie Seymour and humorist Finley Peter Dunne both used the term in baseball stories written in the 1880s.

spear: To make a lunging catch with the glove hand extended. (diving to his right to spear a line drive)

speed: 1. The baserunning ability or speed of a team. 2. The ability of a pitcher to throw a fastball. (his speed is a little off but the curveball is really breaking)

speed gun: A radarlike apparatus used to measure the velocity of pitches. A novelty at first, the speed gun is now often used by coaches to aid in evaluating new prospects or in judging any pitcher's speed and effectiveness on a given day.

1. spike: A metal projection on the sole of a baseball shoe to provide traction.

2. spike: To cut or scrape a player with the spikes of a baseball shoe.

spikes: Baseball shoes with spikes on the soles.

spitball: An illegal pitch in which saliva is surreptitiously applied to one part of the ball, so as to make it break and swerve unpredictably when thrown. It is possible that "Smiling Al" Orth, "The Curveless Wonder," threw the first real spitball in 1892, when pitches were delivered underhand from a distance of 50 feet. Pitcher Elmer Stricklett is generally given credit for reintroducing the overhand version of a spitball to the major leagues in 1904 when he came up to play for the Chicago White Sox. He had learned the pitch in the minors two years before from outfielder George Hildebrand (later an umpire) who had been working on a pitch he called a "wet ball." In his one season with Chicago, Stricklett taught the pitch to "Big Ed" Walsh. Walsh went on to become arguably the greatest spitballer in all of baseball, winning 194 games over a fourteen-year period with the lowest lifetime earned run average in the history of the game, 1.82. The term "spitball" has been in use since 1905. In 1920, the spitball was banned—except for seventeen pitchers (each team could select two) who were allowed to continue to use the pitch until they retired, the last of these being Hall of Famer Burleigh Grimes, who retired in 1934. Though the pitch was illegal, many players and managers accused such pitchers as Preacher Roe, Lew Burdette, Whitey Ford, and Don Drysdale of throwing the spitball regularly in the 1950s and 1960s (only Ford admits it). In 1968, regulations were tightened to prohibit any contact whatsoever between a pitcher's throwing hand and his mouth while he is on the mound. Through the seventies and going into the eighties, veterans Tommy John, Don Sutton, and Gaylord Perry have acquired the reputation of throwing the unpredictable pitch. Aware of the psychological advantage of his reputation, Perry (who became a 300-game winner in 1982) has even encouraged it by writing a book called *Me and the Spitter*. also *Cuban forkball, drooler, spitter.*

spitter: A spitball. The term "spitter" has been in use since 1908.

split a doubleheader: To win one game and lose one game of a doubleheader.

spot pitcher: A pitcher who has enough control to be able to pitch the ball to certain spots, areas in and around the strike zone where individual batters are known to have a problem hitting the ball.

spot reliever: A relief pitcher who is occasionally brought into games to pitch for a short period of time, such as to one or two batters, or to finish an inning.

spray hitter: An unpredictable batter who hits to all fields.

spring training: The time during which annual training and conditioning camps are held by major league teams, also used to play exhibition games and try out rookies. Spring training traditionally starts around the beginning of March and ends just before the start of the regular season.

square around: To move the batting stance from the normal position to one facing the pitcher with the feet side by side, as to bunt. (the runners go as the batter squares around to bunt)

1. squeeze: To make a squeeze play that enables a runner on third to come home. (will try to squeeze in the winning run)

2. squeeze: A squeeze play. (the infield is up, expecting the squeeze)

squeeze bunt: A bunt made in a squeeze play.

squeeze play: A prearranged play (with less than two out) in which a runner at third breaks for home on the pitch and the batter attempts to bunt the ball. The play is called a suicide squeeze if the runner does not wait to see if the batter makes contact with the ball but commits himself as the ball leaves the pitcher's hand, and a safety squeeze if the runner waits until the batter makes contact with the ball before running toward the plate at top speed. also *squeeze.*

stand-up double: A two-base hit in which the batter is able to reach second base without having to slide.

stand-up triple: A three-base hit in which the batter is able to reach third base without having to slide.

stanza: An inning. also *frame.*

Statue of Liberty: A derogatory name for a player who takes a called third strike, originally called a "statue stunt." also *wooden Indian.*

1. steal: 1. To suddenly run for the next base in an attempt to reach it safely before the opposing team can get the ball to a defensive player at the base in position to make a tag. (out stealing on a perfect throw from the catcher) 2. To break for and reach safely the next base, taking advantage of the opposing team's momentary inattention to the runner, rather than because of a teammate's hit or a defensive misplay. (stole home to tie the score) also *steal a base.*

2. steal: The action or an instance of stealing. (got to third on a steal)

steal a base: see *steal.*

steal a sign: To intercept and decipher a signal meant for the opposing team, such as the opposing catcher's sign to the pitcher calling for a certain pitch, or a coach's sign to a batter or base runner.

step off the rubber: To disengage the pivot foot from the pitcher's rubber. Before initiating the windup for a pitch, the pitcher must have the pivot foot in contact with the pitcher's rubber.

stick: A bat.

stickball: A crude form of baseball played by youths in confined areas such as city streets with a broomstick and a lightweight ball. Ground rules vary greatly with the condition of the playing area.

stolen base: A successful steal credited to a base runner in official records. Abbreviated sb. Lou Brock of the St. Louis Cardinals holds the lifetime major record for stolen bases with 938 in his nineteen-year career. Brock's single season record (118 in 1974) was broken by Oakland A's baserunning sensation Ricky Henderson, who stole 130 bases in 1982.

stopper: A team's best pitcher, one who can regularly "stop" the opponents. also *ace.*

strand: 1. To have or leave a base runner or base runners on base at the end of an inning. (goes down swinging, stranding the tying run at third) 2. To retire a batter for the third out in an inning, preventing a base runner or base runners from being able to advance or score. (struck him out on a fastball, stranding the tying run at third)

strawberry: An abrasion from sliding into a base. also *slider.*

stretch: An abbreviated windup. In the stretch, the pitcher lifts his hands to head level, then lowers them both in front of the body to a complete stop in the set position prior to throwing to a base, delivering the ball to the batter, or stepping off the rubber. Usually used when there are runners on base.

strike: A pitched ball at which the batter swings at and misses, does not swing at even though it passes through the strike zone, or hits foul for the first or second strike. When there are two strikes in the count, a ball hit foul and not caught is not charged as a strike, except in the case of an attempted bunt. A batter is out when three strikes are charged against him during one time at bat. ●●A perfectly thrown object. (threw a strike into the wastebasket) Also a flawless performance. (author was throwing strikes until the last chapter, which must be rewritten) A strike can figuratively be charged against one, as it is literally to a batter. (his appearance and manners are two strikes against him)

strike out: 1. To be out as a result of being charged with three strikes. (struck out looking) also *K.* 2. To put a batter out by throwing or causing three strikes. (struck him out to retire the side) also *fan, K, whiff.*

●●To fail. (struck out in her attempt to renegotiate the contract)

strikeout: The out made by a batter by getting three strikes. A pitcher's record is credited with the number of strikeouts he has made. In 1972, Nolan Ryan, then with the California Angels, set the all-time record for the most strikeouts in a single season, 383. In 1983, Nolan Ryan (Houston Astros) and Steve Carlton (Philadelphia Phillies) both surpassed Hall of Famer Walter Johnson's lifetime record of 3,508 strikeouts. also *K.*

strike zone: The area through which a ball must pass in order to be ruled a strike; that is, between the batter's armpits and the top of his knees when he is in his usual batting position, and over home plate.

stuff: The movement or liveliness of a pitch or pitches on the way to the batter. (has the best stuff since he pitched the no-hitter last season)

1. submarine: A pitching delivery in which the arm is brought forward in a low arc with the hand at or just below waist level.

2. submarine: To pitch the ball using a submarine delivery.

submariner: A pitcher who uses a submarine delivery.

suicide squeeze: see *squeeze play.*

suspended game: A called game that is to be completed at a later date.

1. swat: A long hit, especially an extra-base hit or home run. One of the nicknames given by the press to New York Yankees slugger Babe Ruth was "The Sultan of Swat."

2. swat: To hit a long ball, especially an extra-base hit or home run.

sweetheart: A great player whose quiet, consistent style of play, game after game, season after season, is the kind most respected by professional ballplayers, as compared to the more visible "heroics" of glory hogs and headline hunters. Lifetime home run king Hank Aaron was a classic example of a sweetheart player.

sweet spot: The optimum part of a bat with which to hit the ball.

1. swing: To move the bat through an arc in order to hit a pitched ball. (swung at the first pitch and hit a line drive to left field)

2. swing: The movement of a bat in an arc in an attempt to hit a pitched ball. (took a swing at a fastball and missed for strike three)

••To "take a swing at" is to make an attempt. (took a swing at playing quarterback in high school)

swing away: see *hit away.*

swing for the fences: To swing as hard as possible in order to hit the ball to or over the outfield wall or fence. also *swing from the heels.*

••To make an all-out effort. (decided to swing for the fences rather than play it safe)

swing from the heels: To swing as hard as possible in an attempt to hit a pitched ball with full power. also *swing for the fences.*

••To go all-out or to hold nothing back. (the debate ended with both candidates swinging from the heels)

swinging bunt: A ball that is swung at normally, but topped so that it dribbles slowly along the ground like a bunt.

switch-hit: To bat or be able to bat both left-handed and right-handed.

switch hitter: A batter who is able to bat left-handed and right-handed.

1. tag: 1. To put out a runner who is off base by touching the runner with the ball or with the hand or glove that is securely holding the ball. (tags the runner going by and throws to first for the double play) also *tag out.* 2. To, while holding the ball securely, touch a base a runner must attain because of a force, before the runner arrives. (tags second for the force) 3. To get a hit or a run, or hits or runs, off a pitcher. (was tagged for three runs in the second inning)

2. tag: 1. The act or an instance of tagging a runner out. (makes the tag on the runner at third and the inning is over) 2. The act or an instance of tagging a base for a force-out.

tag out: see *tag.*

tag up: To return to and touch, or stay in contact with a base until after a fly ball is caught, so as to be able to advance to the next base. (tagged up and beat the long throw home to score)

take: To let a pitch go by without swinging. (takes a strike to even the count at two and two) also *look at.*

take sign: A prearranged (and coded) signal from a coach, instructing the batter to take the next pitch.

take something off a pitch: To throw a changeup after a fastball or fastballs. (took something off the pitch and caused the batter to be way out in front)

tape-measure shot: A particularly long home run. In 1953, New York Yankees slugger Mickey Mantle hit a booming home run off of Chuck Stobbs of the Washington Senators. Red Patterson, then public relations director for the Yankees immediately left the ballpark and found a witness who showed him the spot where the ball hit the ground. Patterson measured the total distance at 565 feet (among the longest in baseball history) and reported his findings to the press, and the expression tape-measure shot was born.

Tartan Turf: A brand of artificial turf used in some baseball stadiums.

tater: A home run. Originally derived from the use of the word "potato," then "tater" as synonyms for "ball" in the 1920s. A home run came to be known as a "long tater," shortened subsequently to "tater."

Texas leaguer: A short fly ball that falls between the infielders and outfielders. In 1890, a Toledo sportswriter described a hit that was the specialty of Toledo ballplayer Art Sunday, a veteran of the old Texas League, as a "Texas League hit." Shortened to "Texas leaguer," the expression soon became popular and is in use throughout baseball today. also *blooper.*

The Sporting News: A national sports weekly founded in 1886. Although now expanded in format to include seasonal coverage of football, basketball, hockey, and other sports, *The Sporting News* has throughout the years served as a chronicle of the sport of baseball with comprehensive statistical information and analysis.

the table is set: Bases loaded.

third: Third base.

third base: 1. The base located on the baseline on the left side of the field, which must be touched third by a base runner. (rounds third base, heading for home) 2. The position played by the third baseman. (to play third base) also *hot corner, third.*

third base coach: The coach or member of the team at bat who stands in the marked coach's box adjacent to third base to direct base runners, and, through prearranged signals, to relay special batting and baserunning instructions from the manager in the dugout.

third baseman: The defensive player who normally stands to the right side of third base who makes plays at third base and fields balls hit to the infield between shortstop and third base. also *third sacker.*

third sacker: Third baseman.

three-bagger: A triple. also *three-base hit.*

three-base hit: see *three-bagger.*

three up, three down: An inning in which three batters come to bat and are retired in succession.

through the wickets: A batted ball that goes through the pitcher's legs, as a croquet ball is knocked through wire wickets.

throw ground balls: To be known for throwing the kind of pitch (a low ball, especially a sinker) that usually results in ground balls when it can be hit.

throw out: To cause a batter or base runner to be put out with a good throw of a fielded or pitched (in the case of a catcher) ball or a ball relayed from another defensive player.

tools of ignorance: The equipment of a catcher: catcher's mask, chest protector, shin guards, and catcher's mitt. Unlike modern-day catchers, who must constantly make strategic decisions and who, in subtle ways, affect many aspects of a game, catchers in the late 1800s and early 1900s were known mostly for their brawn, not their brains. The man who first called the equipment of a catcher "the tools of ignorance" was an obvious exception. Muddy Ruel, who caught 1,422 games in a nineteen-year career, and played in the World Series for Washington in 1924 and 1925, was a practicing attorney between baseball seasons.

top of the inning: The first half of an inning, when the visiting team has the opportunity to bat.

top of the order: The first batter or batters in the batting order. (will come in to face the top of the order)

total bases: The total number of bases (single equals one base, double equals two bases, triple equals three bases, home run equals four bases) reached on hits by and credited in official records to batters and teams. In 1921, Babe Ruth set the all-time single season record for

total bases, 457. Hank Aaron holds the lifetime record for total bases, 6,856.

1. trap: To seemingly catch a fly or line drive, but in reality stopping it or picking it up just as or moments after it first touches the ground. A ball that is trapped is often difficult to distinguish from one caught on the fly.

2. trap: The action or an instance of trapping a ball.

1. triple: A hit that allows the batter to reach third base safely. also *three-bagger, three base hit.*

2. triple: 1. To hit a triple. (tripled off the wall in center field) 2. To advance a base runner by hitting a triple. (tripled in the tying run)

Triple Crown: The distinction of leading a league at the end of a season in the three major batting categories in official records: batting average, home runs, and runs batted in. The first Triple Crown winner in major league history was Providence Gray center fielder Paul Hines, who in 1878 led the National League with a batting average of .358, four home runs, and fifty runs batted in.

triple play: A play in which three players are put out.

turn a double play: To execute a double play. (able to turn a double play and end the inning)

turn around a fastball: To hit a fastball, thereby changing its direction, or "turning it around."

turned away: Out, retired without scoring. (home team was turned away in the ninth, losing 3-0)

turn the ball over: To throw a screwball. Because a screwball comes out from the back of the hand, the pitcher must turn the hand (and the ball) over just before the release.

tweener: A base hit through a narrow gap between infielders. also *seeing-eye.*

twin bill: A doubleheader.

twi-night doubleheader: A doubleheader with the first game scheduled in late afternoon, followed by an evening game. also *twi-nighter.*

twi-nighter: A twi-night doubleheader.

twin killing: A double play.

twirl: To pitch in a baseball game. (twirled the first game of the doubleheader)

twirly-thumb: see *cockeye.*

two-bagger: A double.

two o'clock hitter: A player who hits

impressively in batting practice, but not in a game. When the term was originated, day games began at 3:00 p.m. with batting practice at 2:00 p.m. Now that games (and batting practice) start earlier, the expression "one o'clock hitter" has also come into use.

ump: An umpire.

1. umpire: The official or one of the officials responsible for the conduct of a game and for interpreting and enforcing the rules. Umpires make decisions regarding proper playing conditions, when to begin, end, suspend, or forfeit a game, when the ball is in play, when time is to be called, whether a pitch is a ball or a strike, whether a ball is hit fair or foul, whether a base runner is out or safe at a base, and whether a player or coach has committed an infraction of the rules. If there is only one umpire, he or she will usually take a position behind the plate (or sometimes behind the pitcher with runners on base). If there are two or more umpires, one, the plate umpire, is designated umpire-in-chief and the others field umpires. In major league baseball, four umpires are usually used: the umpire-in-chief behind the plate, who presides, calling balls and strikes and ruling on plays at home plate, and field umpires at each base, who assist the plate umpire, calling plays at their respective bases. During the World Series, two additional field umpires are positioned in the outfield on the foul lines to help rule on foul balls. Originally from the sport of cricket, then later, rounders. also *arbiter, ump.* see *field umpire, umpire-in-chief.*

2. umpire: To be or act as umpire in a game.

umpire-in-chief: The presiding umpire, positioned behind the plate when there are two or more umpires. The umpire-in-chief is in full charge of and responsible for the proper conduct of the game and has authority to call and count balls and strikes, call and declare fair balls and fouls (except those commonly called by field umpires because of better position), to make decisions about the procedures and play of the batter, the pitcher, the catcher, infielders, and base runners (except those commonly made by field umpires because of better position), to make decisions about

plays around home plate or in the infield (except those commonly made by field umpires because of better position), to call field umpires into consultation (when different decisions are made on a play by two umpires) and determine which decision shall prevail, to announce special time limits or ground rules, to inform the official scorer of the batting order and any changes in the lineups and batting order, to (concurrent with the jurisdiction of field umpires) call time out, to enforce the rules of baseball, to eject a player or coach from a game if necessary, and to start, suspend, or forfeit a game. also *plate umpire.*

unearned run: Any run scored because of an error or interference by the catcher, or following an error on an earlier play that would have ended the inning. An unearned run is not charged against a pitcher in computing his ERA. compare *earned run.*

up: At bat, or due to bat. (will pinch hit for the pitcher, who is due up next)

●●**Ready,** or next to take a turn. (the quartet is up after this number)

voodoo ball: A baseball sewn together in Haiti, but with parts made in the United States.

vultch: A save by a relief pitcher. From the word "vulture." In the 1960s, pitchers likened relievers, who came into well pitched games in the late innings and got credit for saves and sometimes wins, to vultures, figuratively picking over the bones of starting pitchers. Los Angeles Dodgers reliever Phil "The Vulture" Regan was so-named in 1966 by Dodgers pitcher Claude Osteen.

1. walk: A base on balls. (gave up a walk, and then struck out the next three men in order) also *Annie Oakley, free pass, free ticket, free trip, pass.*

2. walk: 1. To be awarded first base on four balls. (walked his first time at bat) 2. To pitch four balls to a batter during one turn at bat, allowing him a free passage to first base. (walked the first two men he faced) 3. To allow a run by giving up a base on balls with loaded bases. (walked in the tying run)

Wally Pipp: An instance of taking a day off from one's regular starting position in the lineup. Wally Pipp, who had played first base for the New York Yankees for ten years, elected not to play on June 1, 1925. He had been beaned in a previous game and was still suffering from a headache. Pipp never regained his job, for the twenty-one-year-old player who replaced him on that day was the legendary Lou Gehrig, who would go on to play first base for the Yankees for the next fourteen years and a record 2,130 consecutive games. Because of Pipp's experience, regular players who want a day off (and risk a similar fate) are said to be doing a Wally Pipp.

wand: A bat.

warning path, warning track: The area bordering the outer edge of the outfield, consisting of a dirt or cinder track in many ballparks. So called because it warns a fielder that he is nearing the wall as he backs up to make a catch.

wave on: To signal a base runner to continue on to the next base without stopping.

web, webbing: The leather panel or lacing in the crotch between the thumb and finger sections of a glove or mitt.

wheelhouse: The part of the strike zone (approximately chest high) in which the ball can most easily be hit with full power.

1. whiff: 1. To strike out. (whiffed his first time at bat) also *K.* 2. To strike out a batter. (whiffed the last two batters to end the inning) also *fan, K.*

2. whiff: A strikeout.

whip: A lightweight bat.

1. whitewash: To hold an opposing team scoreless. The term has been used since the mid-1800s. also *shut out.*

2. whitewash: A shutout.

••A contest or situation in which an opponent is held literally or figuratively scoreless.

wide: 1. Outside, or out of the strike zone on the side of the plate opposite the batter. (the pitch is wide for ball three) 2. To either side of a base, or a defensive player waiting for a throw. (throw is wide, and the runners keep going)

wild: 1. Lacking control. (a little wild in the first inning, but throwing nothing but strikes now) 2. Away from, and beyond the grasp of the intended receiver. (the pitch is wild, and the runner at third will score) (the throw is wild, and the runner is safe)

wild pitch: A pitched ball not touched by

the batter that is so high, so wide, or so low that it is unable to be stopped and controlled by the catcher (and could not be expected to be stopped and controlled by ordinary effort in the judgment of the official scorer) and enables a runner or runners to advance. compare *passed ball.*

wild-pitch: 1. To pitch a wild ball. (threw two strikes and then wild-pitched) 2. To throw a wild pitch which results in a run scored. (wild-pitched in the tying run)

willow: A bat.

wind up: To go into a windup before delivering a pitch to a batter.

windup: The motion of a pitcher prior to delivering a pitch in which, with the pivot foot on the rubber, the pitcher swings both arms back over the head, turns the body away and then back as he steps toward the plate and brings the ball forward to release it. Once initiated, the windup must be completed and the ball delivered to the plate or a balk is called. When there are runners on base, an abbreviated windup, the stretch, is used in order to give the runner less time to steal a base.

windmill, windmill pitch: An underhand delivery of a pitch in softball in which the pitching arm makes a 360 degree vertical revolution before the ball is delivered to the plate.

wing: To throw with strength and accuracy. (one of the best arms in the league who can really wing it)

winning pitcher: The pitcher on the winning team who is given credit in official records for a victory. To be credited with a win, a starting pitcher must have pitched five complete innings (four in a five-inning game) and be leading when the game ends or when replaced. If a starting pitcher has completed less than the required innings and is leading when replaced, the relief pitcher who maintains the lead until the game ends (or, if there is more than one, the relief pitcher judged by the official scorer to be the most effective) is credited with the win. If, while a relief pitcher is pitching, his team assumes a lead that he maintains until the game ends, the relief pitcher is credited with the win. compare *losing pitcher.*

winter ball: Organized baseball played by major league and minor league players during the off season, often in instructional leagues or in organized leagues in foreign countries.

winter league: see *hot stove league.*

wolves: Abusive baseball fans who persistently harass and heckle players.

wooden Indian: A derogatory name for a player who takes a called third strike. The term originated in the 1900s when cigar-store Indians were common. also *Statue of Liberty.*

wood man: 1. A good hitter. 2. A poor fielder who plays only because of hitting ability.

World Series: A championship series played at the end of the season between the National League and American League pennant winners. In 1903, in order to prevent further destructive player raids and territorial competition, the National League was forced to recognize and grant equal status to the fledgling American League and agreed to the first "World's Championship Games" or "World's Championship Series," a best-of-nine series to be played in the fall. Much to the embarrassment and anger of the National League, the American League representative, the Boston Pilgrims behind the pitching of Cy Young and "Big Bill" Dinneen, won that first series five games to three over the Pittsburgh Pirates. The following year, the New York Giants refused to play the American League repeat pennant winner, Boston, but from 1905 on, pennant winners from both leagues have met annually. The World Series is now a best-of-seven series. also *fall classic.*

••The championship or highest level, literally or figuratively.

worm burner: A hit ball that skims along the ground.

wrong-field hit: see *off-field hit.*

yan, yannigan: A rookie. It is reported that Jerry Denny, third baseman for the National League Providence Grays in the early 1880s, was the first to reserve the names "yan" and "yannigan" for rookies. Derived from the "yannigan bag," a kind of carpetbag used by prospectors and traveling performers, the term originally applied to all ballplayers, because of their similar lifestyle and low social status. see *rookie.*

BASKETBALL

Basketball is unique among major sports. It did not evolve from other games over a period of years, but rather was invented by one man to fill a particular need.

In the autumn of 1890, faced with the annual drop in membership during the winter, leaders of the International YMCA Training School in Springfield, Massachusetts (now Springfield College), concluded that there should be a game that could be played indoors in the winter months. Dr. James Naismith, a Presbyterian minister at the institution's School of Christian Workers was given the assignment to create such a game.

Naismith observed that all team games used some kind of ball, but concluded that a method would have to be found to take the speed and physical contact out of the new game if it was to be popular and able to be played in a confined area. Noting that much of the roughness of American football came from the physical contact between the ballcarrier and tacklers, Naismith decided that one fundamental principle in his game would be that the offense should not be able to run while holding the ball, thereby eliminating the need for tackling. Next he had to devise a goal for the ball to pass through in a manner so that the player did not benefit from speed or power. A horizontal goal placed above the reach of the players was the answer. It made it necessary to curve or lob the ball rather than drive it, and its height and configuration made it difficult for players to block off the goal or interfere with the ball once it was shot. It was forbidden to play the ball with anything but the hands and all rough physical contact was specifically banned. To start play, the ball was to be thrown up between two players in the middle of the court.

Naismith drew up a set of thirteen rules and in December of 1891, the first game was played between teams of nine players inside the gymnasium at the Springfield YMCA Training School, using a soccer ball (football) as the ball and peach baskets attached to the gymnasium balconies as goals — the source of the name "basket ball", changed to one word after 1921.

The game was an immediate success, and in little time was being played in school gymnasiums all around Springfield, though the exact rules often varied from the first printed rules that appeared in the *Triangle*, a paper at the School for Christian Workers, on January 15, 1892. Within a year, baskets with iron rims and braided cord netting were introduced, eliminating the need to retrieve the ball after each field goal (by a person on a ladder in the first games, and then by pulling on a chain when the peach basket was replaced shortly thereafter by cylindrical baskets of heavy woven wire).

Another major rule change was introduced in 1893. Overenthusiastic fans in the balcony seats in gymnasiums had begun to interfere with shots at baskets, using their hands, umbrellas, and sticks to "help" their team's shots into the goal and block the other team's. To counter this, it was required that 12-foot by 6-foot barriers be erected behind the basket, wire mesh at first, and later, wood. These early backboards suddenly made it possible to bank shots in and rebound. Real basketballs replaced soccer balls the following year, and free throws were introduced (until 1924, any teammate, not just the fouled player, could shoot them).

The first intercollegiate game was played in 1895 between Hamline of St. Paul, Minnesota and the Minnesota State School of Agriculture. In 1896, the University of Chicago defeated the University of Iowa in Iowa City in the first college game with only five players on a side (accepted by most within a year).

In 1898, a professional league was formed, the National Basketball League, comprised of six teams: Trenton, New Jersey; Camden; Millville, Pennsylvania; Bicycle Club; Hancock Athletic Club; and Germantown Club. The professionals played a version of basketball known as the "cage game". In it, a heavy wire mesh fence, 11 feet high, enclosed the entire court, both to keep the ball in play and to prevent spectator interference. The result was a fast, relentless, and sometimes rough style of play. Players of this kind of basketball came to be known as "cagers", a name that remains popular even today, though the wire fences were eliminated from basketball by regulation in 1929. The National Basketball League lasted only two seasons, and other attempts to operate a professional league in the next few years were even less successful.

Basketball first left the United States as early as 1892, when it was introduced in Mexico, but the first international basketball tournament was the Inter-Allied Games in Paris in 1919, won by the United States team comprised of players from the US Armed Forces. The final game (United States 93–France 8) was witnessed by Dr. James Naismith and General John Pershing, who presented the championship trophy to Basketball Hall of Famer Max "Marty" Friedman.

In 1931, a three-night tournament in Peking (then Peiping) drew 70,000 spectators. The following year in Geneva, Switzerland, the Federation of International Basketball Amateur (FIBA) was formed as the governing body of international amateur basketball. The sport became an Olympic event in 1936 at the Berlin Olympics, where the United States defeated Canada 19–8 in the final, which was played outdoors on an earthen "floor" in driving rain. It was estimated that before the outbreak of World War II, between 18 and 20 million people were playing basketball in seventy-five countries.

In 1937, a rule change eliminating the center jump after each field goal revolutionized the game. The center and guards, formerly involved in the tipoff and defensive play only, now became part of the offense. This innovation, together with the introduction of the quick one-handed shot soon after by three-time Stanford University All-American Hank Luisetti forever changed basketball from a low-scoring defensive struggle to the exciting modern game.

In 1939, the NCAA held the first National Collegiate Basketball Championship Tournament, won by Oregon, with Ohio State the runner-up. The following year, basketball made its first appearance on American television, a doubleheader from Madison Square Garden, New York City, in which Pittsburgh defeated Fordham, 57–37, and NYU defeated Georgetown, 50–27. The popularity of college basketball continued to grow until the sport was rocked by a major scandal in 1951, and in the New York Grand Jury's 1953 report, it was revealed that forty-nine games had been fixed in twenty-three cities in seventeen states.

From the mid-fifties on, the US college game was again on the rise with such outstanding players as Frank Selvy, who in 1954, scored a major college record: 100 points in a game for Furman against Newberry; Tom Gola of LaSalle; Bill Russell of the University of San Francisco; and Cincinnati's Oscar Robertson.

Professional basketball, after some lean early years, was also healthy, with the National Basketball Association beginning to stabilize. Formed in 1946 under the name of the Basketball Association of America, the NBA adopted its present name in 1949, after absorbing its older rival, the National Basketball League. Weighted down at first by several weak franchises, the league and individual teams struggled to find an audience, often scheduling exhibition and preliminary games with the Harlem Globetrotters to bring new people into the arenas. The Globetrotters, an all-black touring team founded in 1927 by Abe Saperstein, had become a great box office draw with a unique blend of dazzling skills and comedic showmanship. In 1951, a record crowd of 75,000 people saw the Globetrotters play in Berlin's Olympic Stadium.

In 1954, the NBA adopted a rule requiring the offensive team to shoot at the basket within twenty-four seconds of gaining possession of the ball. The change was an immediate success, speeding up the game and placing more emphasis on scoring than the slow-tempo ball control style of play that had evolved, as well as eliminating dull "slowdown" tactics used to freeze the ball and protect a lead.

Beginning with the 1956–57 season, one team, the Boston Celtics, led by the sharpshooting and playmaking of Bob Cousy and the intimidating defense of Bill Russell, dominated basketball as no professional team has dominated a sport in modern history. In ten years, the Celtics won the NBA championship nine out of ten times, losing only in the 1957–58 season to the St. Louis Hawks.

No less impressive, however, was the University of California, Los Angeles' (UCLA) record in college play from the mid-sixties through to the mid-seventies. From 1964 to 1975, UCLA was NCAA champion nine out of eleven times, losing only to Texas-El Paso in 1966 and to North Carolina State in 1975. Unbeaten for an entire season four times, UCLA also set the NCAA record for the most consecutive victories, eighty-eight, from January 30, 1971, through to January 17, 1974 (both the last loss before the streak and the streak-ending loss came at Notre Dame).

Another long winning streak came to an end at the 1972 Munich Olympics. Undefeated in sixty-three games dating back to 1936 (the first year basketball was an Olympic event), the United States stumbled in a controversial loss to the USSR. A dispute between officials and an improperly set game clock caused the final three seconds to be replayed twice. The Russians scored during the second replay, winning the game 51–50.

Although tested by the rival American Basketball Association from 1967 through to 1976, the NBA has remained the premiere basketball league in the world since the Boston Celtics "dynasty" of the 1950s and 1960s, showcasing the greatest players in the game, such as superstar Wilt Chamberlain, Elgin Baylor, John Havlicek, Oscar Robertson, Jerry West, all-time scoring leader Kareem Abdul-Jabbar, Bill Walton, Moses Malone, Julius Erving, Larry Bird, Earvin "Magic" Johnson, Ralph Sampson, Akeem Olajuwon, and Michael Jordan.

ABAUSA: The Amateur Basketball Association of the United States of America.

air ball: A missed shot that touches neither the rim, backboard, nor the net. The expression was coined by Los Angeles Lakers broadcaster Chick Hearn in the early 1970s. compare *glass ball*.

air dribble: An archaic technique, once allowed in conjunction with a bouncing dribble, in which a player could throw the ball in the air, run, and handle it again before it hit the floor or was touched by any other player. In modern basketball, an air dribble would be considered a traveling violation, resulting in the loss of the ball and a throw-in by the opposing team from the sideline.

alley-oop shot: 1. A shot in which the ball travels in a high arc. The expression was coined in the late 1960s by Los Angeles Lakers broadcaster Chick Hearn to describe a shot used by Lakers guard John Egan when he had to shoot over taller players. 2. A leaping tip-in of a high lobbed pass near the basket.

Amateur Basketball Association of the United States of America: The governing body of amateur basketball in the United States, responsible for the preparation and supervision of national teams to participate in international and Olympic competition. Founded in 1975, the Amateur Basketball Association of the United States is an affiliate member of the Federation of International Basketball Amateur, and is headquartered in Colorado Springs, Colorado. also *ABAUSA*.

around the world: An informal game for two or more players in which contestants take turns shooting, and try to move through seven stations placed outside of and around the free throw area (three on each side, and one at the top of the key), advancing to the next station only when a shot has been successfully made. The first player to move around all seven stations (after all have had the same number of turns) wins the game. Sometimes a variation is played in which a player who misses a shot moves back one station. Around the world is a game that emphasizes pure shooting skill, rather than the trick shots that often characterize the game of H.O.R.S.E. compare *H.O.R.S.E.*

assist: A pass that leads directly to a score, such as one to a teammate who shoots immediately and scores, or drives to the basket and scores. No assist is given if the receiver stops, holds the ball, or dribbles back and forth for position before shooting. The all-time NBA record for the most assists in a single game is held by Kevin Porter, who, while playing for the New Jersey Nets, was credited with twenty-nine assists in a game against the Houston Rockets on February 24, 1978. Porter also holds the NBA single season record of 1,099 assists, set in the 1978-79 season when he played for the Detroit Pistons. Oscar Robertson, credited with 9,887 assists in his career, holds the NBA lifetime record.

back: To guard an opponent by playing behind him (between the guarded player and the basket). compare *front*.

backboard: Either of two opaque or transparent flat 4-foot by 6-foot-wide rectangular (or 35-inch by 54-inch-wide, with a 29-inch radius, fan-shaped) surfaces, suspended above and perpendicular to the floor, 4 feet inside and parallel to the boundary line at each end of the court, to which the basket rings are fastened. NBA regulations call for a transparent rectangular backboard. A small rectangle (18 inches by 24 inches wide) centered behind the ring, is marked on the surface by a 2-inch-wide white line. Players bank shots off the backboards, which also serve to keep the ball in play if a shot is missed. The first backboards were 6 feet by 12 feet wide, and made of wire mesh (then later, wood). They were put behind the baskets in 1893 as a barrier to keep overenthusiastic fans from interfering with shots at the basket from the balcony seats behind each goal. Rectangular backboards were reduced to the present dimensions in 1895, and fan-shaped backboards were approved in 1940. also *board, boards, glass*.

backcourt: 1. The half of a court a team defends, and which contains the basket at which the opposing team shoots. (across the center line from the backcourt) 2. The guards. (their backcourt can really move the ball around)

backcourtman: A guard.

backcourt violation: 1. A violation of the ten-second rule (in continuous control of a ball in the backcourt for more then ten consecutive seconds), which results

in the loss of the ball to the opposing team for a throw-in from out of bounds near where play stopped. see *ten-second rule*. 2. A violation resulting from the return of the ball to the backcourt from the frontcourt by dribbling, passing, or tapping the ball across the division line. This results in the loss of the ball to the opposing team for a throw-in from the sideline at the center of the court. also *over and back*.

backdoor: Next to the end line, under the basket. (came through the backdoor and scored on a reverse lay-up)

backdoor play: A play in which an offensive player momentarily slips in behind the defense along the end line to receive a pass under the basket for a lay-up.

ball control: 1. The ability to dribble, pass, and maintain possession of the ball. (not much of a shooter, but an expert at ball control) 2. A strategy used in amateur, college, and high school basketball, in which a team attempts to maintain possession of the ball. Ball control is used offensively to encourage the opposing team to make defensive mistakes, or vary from a game plan or customary style of play, or as a ploy to maneuver players into certain positions for a set play, or defensively to deny the opposing team a chance to score (as in the case of a stall or freeze), or simply to protect a lead near the end of a game. also *stall ball*.

ball fake: A fake pass or shot by the player with the ball in order to momentarily deceive a defender.

ball handler: 1. The player in possession of the ball. 2. A player with good ball control, adept at dribbling and passing.

BACKBOARD AND BASKET

bang the boards, bang the glass: To rebound aggressively under the backboards. (got the opportunity for the second shot because he bangs the boards) also *crash the boards, hammer the boards, pound the boards, pound the glass.*

bank: To bounce the ball off the backboard toward the basket. To make a bank shot. (banks one in from the side of the key)

bank shot: A shot in which the ball is made to bounce off the backboard towards the basket.

baseball pass: A one-arm overhand pass (often long) in which the ball is thrown like a baseball.

baseline: 1. The boundary line at each end of the court, 50 feet long and marked with a 2-inch-wide line. also *end line.* 2. The area of the court just inside the end line. (a 15-foot jump shot from the baseline)

basket: 1. Either of the goals at the ends of a court, consisting of a metal ring, 18 inches in inside diameter, with a 15 to 18-inch-long sleeve, made of white cord net, suspended below. The basket ring is attached to the backboard with its upper edge 10 feet above and parallel to the floor, and equidistant from the vertical edges of the board. For regulation play, the basket ring is painted orange, and mounted so that the nearest point of the inside edge of the ring is 6 inches from the front surface of the backboard. The term "basket" originated from the use of a peach basket as a goal when the game was invented in 1891 (the ball had to be retrieved with the aid of a ladder after each goal). Within a year, the peach basket was replaced by a cylindrical basket made of heavy woven wire, with a pull chain attached to drop the ball. Baskets with iron rims and braided cord netting were introduced in 1893. also *bucket, hoop.* 2. A field goal. also *bucket, deuce.*

basketball: 1. A game played between two teams of five players on a 94-foot-long by 50-foot-wide court (84 feet by 50 feet for high school play), with a horizontal 18-inch metal ring mounted 10 feet above the floor on a vertical backboard suspended over each end of the court. Points are scored by tossing an inflated ball (leather or rubber, 9-1/2 inches in diameter) through the metal ring, or basket, defended by the opposing team. A player with the ball may shoot or pass to a teammate at any time, but may not walk or run without dribbling the ball (bouncing the ball off the floor with successive taps of the hand). A player who stops dribbling may not start again, but must pass or shoot. If a player takes steps without dribbling the ball, or resumes a dribble after stopping, possession of the ball is awarded to the opposing team, to be thrown in from the sideline. In an attempt to prevent an opponent from advancing the ball or scoring, a player may bat away, intercept, or block a ball being dribbled, passed, or shot by the opposing team, but may not hit, push, hold, or trip an opponent. These actions are considered fouls, and result in the loss of possession of the ball to the opponent (to be thrown in from the sideline), or in the fouled player being awarded one or more free throws (an undefended shot at the basket from a line drawn 15 feet away). If, during the course of a game, a player is charged with a specified number of fouls (five fouls in high school, collegiate, women's, and international amateur basketball, six fouls in the NBA), the player is put out of the game. A player charged with a dangerous or violent foul is immediately ejected from the game. A team is made up of a center (usually the tallest on the team), who often takes a position in the middle of the frontcourt near the basket to receive and relay passes, shoot, and rebound; two guards, good ball handlers who usually bring the ball out of the backcourt, start plays, and distribute the ball to teammates closer to the basket; and two forwards, usually positioned to the side of the basket near the baseline, from where they may shoot or break in toward the basket to shoot or rebound. A referee is in charge of the game, assisted by another (or by two others in some college conferences). Both have the authority to call fouls and violations. In the NBA, a game consists of four twelve-minute quarters. College and international amateur games are divided into two twenty-minute halves. High school games consist of four eight-minute quarters. A game (and each period in international amateur and high school games) is started by a jump ball (the ball is thrown up between two opponents to be tapped to a teammate) in the center of the court, and play continues to the end of the period, except for fouls, violations, or time outs. When a team scores, the ball is given to the opposing team for a throw-in from outside the end lines under the basket. If a ball goes out of bounds, the ball is given to the team opposing the player who last touched it, for a throw-in from the sideline. Each field goal is two points. In the NBA, a field goal made from outside an area marked by parallel lines 3 feet inside the sidelines, extending from the baseline to intersect with a line drawn in an arc of 23 feet, 9 inches from the middle of the basket, is three points (a provision that was adopted experimentally by some college conferences in the early 1980s and may ultimately be universally adopted). A free throw is one point. If, at the end of regulation play, the score is tied, overtime periods (five minutes in NBA, international amateur, and college games; three minutes in high school games) are played until one team is leading at the end of a period. Basketball (written "basket ball" before 1921) was also known as "roundball." 2. The ball used in a basketball game: an inflated bladder with a leather, rubber, or synthetic covering, 9-1/2 inches in diameter, weighing 20 to 22 ounces. The first specially designed basketball was introduced in 1894 to replace the soccer balls originally used.

Basketball Hall of Fame: The Naismith Memorial Basketball Hall of Fame. The institute that honors the achievements of the outstanding figures of basketball, located on the campus of Springfield College in Springfield, Massachusetts, where Dr. Naismith invented the game of basketball. The first members of the Hall of Fame were elected in 1959, fifteen individuals and two teams: Dr. Naismith's original team and the original Celtics, a pioneer barnstorming professional team of the 1920s. The permanent headquarters and museum opened in 1968. Nominations for the Hall of Fame are voted on annually by an anonymous Honors Committee. also *Hall of Fame.*

basket-hanger: A player who leaves the backcourt early or remains in the frontcourt near the basket when play is at the other end of the court, waiting for a long pass in order to take an undefended shot at the basket. also *cherry picker, hanger.*
basket interference: see *goaltending.*
big man: The center on a basketball team, usually the tallest player.
blind screen: A screen that is established out of the line of sight of an opponent (as to the side of or behind).
1. block: 1. To legally obstruct or deflect an opponent's shot with the hands. Elmore "The Rejector" Smith of the Los Angeles Lakers holds the NBA record for the most blocked shots in one season (393, 1973-74). Smith also holds the single game record (17, vs. Portland, October 28, 1973). also *reject.* 2. To legally obstruct or deflect an opponent's pass with the hands. 3. To cause physical contact by stepping into the path of an opponent. A personal foul. see *blocking.* compare *charge.*
2. block: 1. The act or an instance of blocking an opponent's shot or pass with the hands. 2. The act or an instance of physical contact as a result of stepping into the path of an opponent. A personal foul. see *blocking.* compare *charge.*
blocking: A personal foul in which physical contact occurs as a result of illegally impeding the progress of an opponent, such as by stepping or extending an arm, shoulder, hip, or leg into the path of a moving opponent. see *personal foul.* compare *charging.*
block out: see *box out.*
board: 1. Backboard. (banks a shot off the board) 2. A rebound. (he's got eleven boards in the game so far)
boards: Backboard.
bomb: A long distance low percentage shot.
bonus, bonus free throw: An additional free throw awarded to a fouled player when the opposing team has reached a specified number of team fouls during a period of play (five fouls in one quarter in NBA games, seven fouls in one half in college and women's games, nine fouls, including technical fouls, during a half in international amateur games, and five fouls during a half in high school games). In college and high school

games, the bonus applies only to one-shot fouls and is not given if the first free throw is missed (called a one-and-one situation). In the NBA, a bonus free throw is called a penalty free throw.

bonus situation: A situation in which a team has reached a specified number of team fouls for a period of play (five fouls in one quarter in NBA games, seven fouls in one half in college and women's games, nine fouls, including technical fouls, in international amateur games, and five fouls during a half in high school games), and each foul thereafter yields a bonus free throw to the opposing team. In the NBA, a bonus situation is called a penalty situation or penalty stage.

bounce pass: A pass in which the ball is bounced off the floor between the passer and the receiver. A bounce pass is easy to handle at full speed and difficult to intercept.

box, box-and-one: A defensive strategy which employs a four-man zone, with players deployed in a "box" around the free throw lane (two on each side) leaving one defender to play man-to-man against the most dangerous scorer on the opposing team. compare *diamond-and-one*.

box out: To take a position between an opponent and the basket, to prevent the opponent from having access to a rebound or tip-in. also *block out, screen out*.

brush-off: To maneuver so that a defending opponent is blocked by the screen or pick of a teammate and left behind.

bucket: 1. A field goal. also *basket, deuce*. 2. The basket ring and net. also *basket, hoop*.

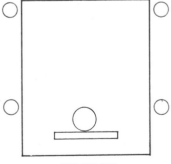

BOX-AND-ONE

buzzer shot: A shot made just as a period is ending, with the ball in the air at the buzzer.

cager: A basketball player. In the 1890s, one version of basketball, the "cage game," used a heavy wire-mesh fence, 11 feet high, to enclose the entire court, both to keep the ball in play and to prevent spectator interference. Players of this fast and sometimes rough kind of basketball came to be known as cagers, a name that remains popular today, though wire fences were eliminated by regulation in 1929.

carry: see *palm the ball*.

center: 1. The player on a team (usually the tallest) responsible for the tipoff or center jump, for defending against the opposing center, and for playing the "pivot" in the middle of the frontcourt near the basket, from where he can set screens, receive and relay passes, shoot, and position himself for rebounds. Called "center" because, prior to the 1937 rule change, the jump ball after each field goal in the center circle was the main responsibility of the center. also *frontcourtman*. 2. The position played by a center.

center circle: 1. The 12-foot restraining circle for jump balls in the center of the court, divided by the center or division line, with (except in international amateur play) a 4-foot jumping circle marked in the middle. also *circle, restraining circle*. see *jump ball*.

center line: see *division line*.

1. charge: To run into a defensive player who has established position. A personal foul. see *charging*. compare *block*.

2. charge: The act or an instance of running into a defensive player who has established position. A personal foul. see *charging*. compare *block*.

charging: A personal foul in which an offensive player runs into a defensive player who has established position. also *charge*. see *personal foul*. compare *blocking*.

charity line: The free throw line. also *charity stripe, foul line, line*.

charity shot: A free throw.

charity stripe: The free throw line. also *charity line, foul line, line*.

check: 1. see *hand check*. 2. To guard an opponent.

cherry-pick: To leave the backcourt early, or to remain in the frontcourt near the basket when play is at the other end of the court, waiting for a long pass in order to take an undefended shot at the basket.

cherry picker: One who cherry-picks. also *basket-hanger, hanger.*

chest pass: A two-handed pass in which the ball is pushed away from the body by a quick extension of the arms and released with a snap of the wrists.

chippie: see *cripple.*

chucker: see *gunner.*

circle: see *center circle.*

clutch shooter: A player who can be counted upon to make a basket or baskets in crucial, game-deciding situations. Los Angeles Lakers guard Jerry West, "Mr. Clutch," who played from 1960 to 1974, is thought to have been one of the all-time great clutch shooters in the NBA.

coast to coast: From one end of the court to the other, as in a court-length pass.

cold: Temporarily unable to score. (gone cold in the second quarter)

collapse: To, with two or more defenders, converge on the opposing center the moment the ball comes into him at the pivot, in order to pressure him and deny the easy pass or shot.

common foul: A personal foul that is neither flagrant nor intentional, nor a part of a double or multiple foul (and, in the NBA only, that is not committed against a player in the act of shooting). When a player commits a common foul, the result is a loss of the ball to the opposing team for a throw-in from out of bounds, except in the case of a bonus situation, when the fouled player is awarded a bonus free throw.

continuation: A shot, or the follow through or consequences of a shot attempt committed to by the fouled player at the moment of, or just prior to, the foul. Though the actual shot may not be made until after the foul, in the NBA, if the shot goes in, the field goal counts in addition to the free throw awarded for the foul.

conversion: A successful free throw. (if he makes the conversion, it's a three-point play)

convert: To make a successful free throw.

cord: The net. (his shot hit nothing but the cord)

corner: Any of the four areas of the court where the sidelines and baselines intersect.

cornerman: A forward.

court: The rectangular playing area for a basketball game (94 feet long by 50 feet wide for NBA and college play, 84 feet long by 50 feet wide for high school play), divided by a line across the middle between the sidelines, the center or division line. At each end of the court, a 10-foot-high, horizontal 18-inch metal ring is attached to a flat rectangular (6 feet wide by 4 feet high) or fan-shaped (54 inches wide by 35 inches high, with a 29-inch radius) white or transparent surface, which is suspended above and perpendicular to the floor 4 feet inside the end line. A 12-foot circle, the restraining circle, is marked in the middle of the court, and divided into equal parts by the center or division line (an additional 4-foot concentric circle is marked for NBA, college, and high school play). Nineteen feet in from and parallel to each end line, and centered on the middle of the basket, the 2-inch-wide, 12-foot (16-foot in the NBA) free throw line is marked. The free throw line bisects a marked 12-foot circle. Two lines extend from the end line to the ends of the free throw line to enclose the free throw lane in the rectangle formed (in international amateur play, the lines form a trapezoid, with a 19-foot, 8-1/4-inch base on the end line). In the NBA, the three-point field goal area is marked by lines extending from the end line 3 feet from and parallel to the sidelines, intersecting an arc of 23 feet, 9 inches from the middle of the basket. (The three-point field goal and similar markings were adopted experimentally by some college conferences in the early 1980s and may ultimately be universally adopted.) In addition, two 2-inch-wide, 3-foot-long "hashmarks" extend inward from and perpendicular to each sideline, 28 feet from the end lines. Although informal games can be played outdoors on asphalt or dirt courts, regulation basketball is played indoors on a hardwood court.

crash the boards: see *bang the boards.*

cripple: An easy, unhindered shot, made from close to the basket. also *chippie.*

1. cut: To suddenly move at an angle, or change directions to leave a defender behind, receive a pass, or move toward the basket. (faked a shot, then cut in to the basket)

2. cut: The act or an instance of cutting.

defensive boards: The backboard of the basket a team is defending. (took charge of the game by controlling the defensive boards)

defensive rebound: A rebound from an opponent's shot at the basket a team is defending.

deuce: A field goal. (hit the jumper for a deuce) also *basket, bucket.*

diamond-and-one: A defensive strategy which employs a four-man zone, with players deployed in a "diamond" around the free throw lane (one at each end of the free throw line and one at high and low post positions), leaving one defender to play man-to-man against the most dangerous scorer on the opposing team. compare *box.*

disqualification: The suspension of a player for the remainder of a game for "fouling out" or committing a specified number of fouls during a game (five fouls in high school, college, women's, and international amateur basketball; six fouls in the NBA). Don Meineke of the Ft. Wayne Pistons holds the NBA record of twenty-six disqualifications in one season (1952-53). Vern Mikkelsen of the Minneapolis Lakers holds the all-time career mark of 127 disqualifications in his ten-year NBA career (1949-59).

division line: A line parallel to the end lines that divides a basketball court in half. The division line, which separates a team's backcourt from the frontcourt, is

used to enforce the ten-second rule and determine backcourt violations. also *center line, midcourt line, ten-second line, time line.*

double-cover: see *double-team.*

1. double dribble: To resume dribbling after a dribble has been stopped, or to dribble with both hands simultaneously. A violation that results in the loss of the ball to the opposing team for a throw-in from a spot out of bounds near the violation.

2. double dribble: A violation that occurs when a player resumes dribbling after a dribble has been stopped, or dribbles the ball with both hands simultaneously. This results in a loss of the ball to the opposing team for a throw-in from a spot out of bounds near the violation.

double figures: Ten or more points, rebounds, or assists in a game. also *doubles.*

double foul: Approximately simultaneous fouls committed by opponents against each other. Penalties are cancelled out, and play resumes with a jump ball between the two players involved at the center circle (except in college, where the ball is awarded to the teams on an alternate basis), unless the foul was committed away from the ball, in which case play resumes where it was interrupted (and in the NBA the twenty-four-second clock is reset to twenty-four). compare *multiple foul.*

1. double pump: To fake a shot at the basket twice in rapid succession in order to momentarily deceive a defender (especially to make him leave his feet) before a real shot, a pass, or a dribble. (double pumps, then scores with a thirteen-foot jumper)

2. double pump: The act or an instance of double pumping.

doubles: Double figures in points, rebounds, or assists in a game.

double-team: To guard or defend against an opponent with two players at the same time. (double-team the center, and force him to pass) also *double-cover, two-time.*

downcourt: To or toward the end of the court containing the basket at which a team is shooting. also *upcourt.*

draw a foul: 1. To deliberately maneuver in such a way as to be fouled. 2. To be fouled.

draw iron: To hit the rim of the basket on a shot. Chick Hearn, broadcaster for

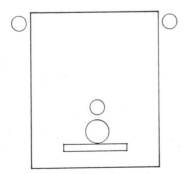

DIAMOND-AND-ONE

the Los Angeles Lakers, popularized the expression in the late 1960s. (a poor shot that didn't even draw iron)

1. dribble: 1. To bounce the ball off the floor, giving impetus with successive taps of the hand. A player with the ball may not walk or run without dribbling. Once a dribble has ended (when the ball is allowed to come to rest in one or both hands), the player may not resume dribbling until after control of the ball has been lost and regained (the ball is shot and recovered, passed and returned, batted away by an opponent and recovered). 2. To move or maneuver while bouncing the ball. (dribbles into the frontcourt)

2. dribble: The act or an instance of dribbling the ball.

dribble drive: A determined advance with the ball, especially toward the basket or baseline. Los Angeles Lakers broadcaster Chick Hearn originated the expression in the mid-1960s to describe the penetrating drives of Hall of Famer Laker Elgin Baylor. also *drive.*

dribbler: 1. The player who is dribbling the ball at a given time during a game. 2. A player who is skilled at, or known for dribbling. (not much of a shooter, but a great playmaker and dribbler)

1. drive: To make a determined advance with the ball, especially toward the basket or baseline. (drives into the lane and shoots)

2. drive: A determined advance with the ball, especially toward the basket or baseline. also *dribble drive.*

drive the lane: To make a determined advance with the ball through the key or lane toward the basket.

drop pass: A pass in which the dribbler leaves the ball for, or pushes it back to a trailing teammate. The passer often continues forward to momentarily draw away a defender.

drop step: A technique in which a player with the ball, positioned at the post with his back to the basket, takes a step back, just to the side of a defender behind him, before turning and driving around him in that direction.

1. dunk: To leap up and push the ball down into the basket from above. Though the exact origin is unclear, the expression stems from "dunking a doughnut." also *jam, stuff.* compare *slam dunk.*

2. dunk: A field goal made by leaping up and pushing the ball down through the basket from above. also *jam, stuff, stuff shot.* compare *slam dunk.*

elbowing: The illegal use of an elbow to hit an opponent, a personal foul. see *personal foul.*

end line: see *baseline.*

fadeaway, fadeaway jumper: see *fallaway.*

fallaway, fallaway jumper: A shot taken while moving back, or "falling away" from the basket. The expression "fallaway jumper" was coined by Los Angeles Lakers broadcaster Chick Hearn in the early 1960s to describe a particular shot favored by Laker guard Dick Barnett. Hearn also applied the expression to NBA superstar Wilt Chamberlain's "fallaway bank shot". also *fadeaway, fadeaway jumper.*

false multiple foul: A situation in which two fouls are committed in succession (rather than simultaneously) by teammates against a single opponent, the second foul occurring before the clock is started following the first foul. A free throw is awarded for each foul if the fouled player was in the act of shooting, if the foul was flagrant, or if the bonus situation applies.

fast break: An offensive strategy and concept of play in which a team breaks toward the frontcourt immediately after gaining possession of the ball or putting it in play, in order to constantly pressure the opponents and deny them the

DRIBBLER

time to organize defensively. Ward "Piggy" Lambert, coach of Purdue University (1917, 1919-45) was an early exponent of the fast break or "firewagon basketball," popularized further after the center jump was eliminated in 1937. One of Lambert's star players, three-time All-American John Wooden, later coached UCLA to ten NCAA championships in the 1960s and 1970s using the fast break.

Federation International Basketball Amateur: The international governing body of amateur basketball. Founded in Geneva, Switzerland, in 1932, it is headquartered in Munich, Germany. also *FIBA*.

1. feed: To pass to a teammate near the basket. (feeds to the big man, who turns and dunks for two points)

2. feed: A pass to a teammate near the basket.

FIBA: The Federation International Basketball Amateur.

field goal: A two-point score made by throwing the ball through the basket (three points in the NBA and some college conferences, if shot from outside the three-point field goal area, approximately 23 feet from the basket). Before the mid-1890s, all field goals were three points. NBA superstar Wilt Chamberlain holds the all-time record for the most field goals scored in a single game (36 for the Philadelphia Warriors on March 2, 1962) and one season (1,597 for the Philadelphia Warriors, 1961–62). In 1984, Kareem Abdul-Jabbar of the Los Angeles Lakers surpassed Chamberlain's career record of 12,681 field goals to become the all-time NBA field goal scorer. also *basket, bucket, deuce.*

fill the lane: To run toward the opponent's basket in one of the imaginary alleys or lanes near the sidelines on a fast break, thereby spreading the attack and increasing the difficulty for the defense.

finger roll: A shot from close range in which the ball rolls gently off the fingertips into the basket. The expression was coined by broadcaster Chick Hearn to describe a shot often made by Wilt Chamberlain.

five: A basketball team. also *quintet.*

five-second rule: 1. A rule in college and high school play that requires a closely guarded player holding or dribbling the ball in the frontcourt, or holding and/or dribbling in the midcourt, to shoot or pass within five seconds. A violation (held ball) results in the ball being awarded to the opposing team for a throw-in. 2. A rule in women's and international amateur play that requires a closely guarded player holding the ball to shoot, pass, or dribble within five seconds. A violation (held ball) results in a jump ball.

flagrant foul: A foul in which a player deliberately attempts to hurt an opponent by violent contact, such as kicking, kneeing, or running under a player who is in the air. A flagrant foul is charged as a personal foul and a team foul, and carries a penalty of two free throws. The offending player is ejected (and, in the NBA, may be subject to suspension and/or a fine).

floor: 1. The playing surface of a basketball court. 2. The playing area of a basketball court. (will put the five best men on the floor to finish the game)

forecourt: The area of a team's frontcourt between the hashmarks (midcourt area markers) and the end line. see *five-second rule.*

forward: 1. Either of two players who operate from a position near the base-

DUNK

line, on either side of and close to the basket. The two general types of forwards are the "power forward," usually large and strong and an aggressive rebounder, and the "small forward," usually noted for quickness and mobility, and often a particularly good shooter. Before the center jump after each field goal was abandoned in 1937, the offensive players often remained in the frontcourt, in a "forward" position. also *frontcourtman.* 2. The position played by a forward. (can play forward or center)

1. **foul:** An infraction of the rules that prohibit illegal physical contact (personal fouls such as pushing, charging, etc.), actions that violate game regulations (technical fouls such as too many players on the court, delay of game, etc.), or those which call for sportsmanlike conduct (technical fouls such as disrepect of officials, profanity, etc.). A foul is charged to the player who commits it (and sometimes toward the number of team fouls allowed before the bonus situation applies), and (depending upon the nature and gravity of the foul, whether it is committed by an offensive or defensive player, and whether the bonus situation applies) is penalized by awarding the opposing team possession of the ball, or by awarding one or more free throws. see *bonus situation, personal foul, technical foul.* compare *violation.*

2. **foul:** 1. To commit a foul. 2. To commit a foul against a specific player. (fouled him in the act of shooting)

foul lane: see *free throw lane.*

foul line: see *free throw line.*

foul out: To be put out of a game for committing a specified number of fouls during a game (five fouls in high school, college, women's, and international amateur basketball; six fouls in the NBA). see *disqualification.*

foul shot: A free throw.

four-corner offense: A ball control strategy in high school and college basketball in which offensive players form a large box, with one player near each of the four corners in the frontcourt and the fifth player near the center circle. Used as a control type offense to spread the defense, or as a stalling tactic employed to prevent the opposing team from gaining possession of the ball, such

as at the end of a game to protect a lead. Extensive use of the four-corner offense usually results in a low-scoring game. The four-corner offense was developed by University of North Carolina coach Dean Smith in the mid-1960s.

four-point play: 1. A situation in an NBA game (or a college game in a conference where the three-point field goal is used) in which a player as he shoots and makes a field goal from outside the three-point area (approximately 23 feet away from the basket). The basket counts, and if the free throw is made, the total is a four-point play. 2. A situation in a college, women's, or high school game in which a player is fouled flagrantly or intentionally as he or she shoots and makes a field goal. The basket counts, and two free throws are awarded. If both are made, the total is a four-point play. 3. A situation in a college, women's, or high school game in which a player is fouled after shooting a field goal (or his or her teammate is fouled). The basket counts and a one-and-one free throw is awarded. If both are made, the total is a four-point play. 4. A situation in a women's game in which a player is fouled flagrantly as she shoots and misses. Four free throws are awarded to the fouled player. If all are made, the result is a four-point play.

free ball: see *loose ball.*

free throw: An uncontested shot at the basket from behind the free throw line (15 feet from the basket) awarded to the fouled player when an opponent has committed a personal foul, or to any player chosen by the coach when an opponent has committed a technical foul. After a personal foul, players from the two teams line up in alternate positions along both sides of the free throw lane, with two players from the fouling team closest to the basket. If a free throw attempt is unsuccessful, the ball is in play as soon as it makes contact with the backboard, rim, or net, and players may then enter the lane to contend for it (if more than one free throw is awarded, the ball is not in play until the second attempt). If the free throw is successful, the ball is dead until put into play by the opposing team with a throw-in from outside the baseline under the basket. After a technical foul, the ball is dead and is put into play (usually by the team shooting the foul) with a throw-in from the sideline. Each successful free throw scores one point. Free throws were introduced in 1894 and were valued at three points each until 1895. NBA superstar Wilt Chamberlain set the all-time record for the most free throws in a single game on March 2, 1962, when he made 28 free throws for the Philadelphia Warriors. Jerry West of the Los Angeles Lakers set the record for the most free throws in one season, 840, in 1965–66. Houston Rockets guard Calvin Murphy holds the record for the highest free throw percentage in one season (95.8 percent in 1980–81, including a record 78 consecutive free throws made). Rick Barry owns the highest career percentage, making 90 percent of his attempted free throws during his ten year NBA career (1965–1967 and 1972–1980). Oscar Robertson holds the NBA lifetime record of 7,694 free throws in his fourteen-year career (1960–1974). also *charity shot, foul shot.*

free throw area: 1. The free throw lane. 2. The free throw lane and the free throw circle. also *key, keyhole.*

free throw circle: Either of the two 12-foot restraining circles that form the top of the key at both ends of the court and are bisected by the free throw lines. The free throw circle is sometimes used for jump ball situations.

free throw lane: The rectangular (19 feet long by 12 feet for college and high school play, 19 feet long by 16 feet in the NBA) or trapezoidal area (19 feet

long by 12 feet wide at the free throw line and 19 feet, 8-1/4 inches wide at the end line for international amateur play) marked at each end of the court between the free throw line and the end line. No player may remain within his offensive free throw lane for more than three consecutive seconds while his team has possession of the ball in the frontcourt. No player may enter the lane on a free throw until the ball has made contact with the backboard, the rim, or the net. also *foul lane, free throw area, key, keyhole, lane, paint, three-second area, three-second lane.*

free throw line: Either of two 2-inch-wide, 12-foot-long lines (16 feet in the NBA) marked 19 feet from and parallel to the end line (15 feet from the basket) at both ends of the court. A player attempting a free throw must stand behind the free throw line and within the 12-foot free throw circle it bisects. The free throw lines were moved from 20 feet to 15 feet from the basket shortly after free throws were introduced in 1894. also *charity line, charity stripe, foul line, line.*

1. freeze: To stall. see *stall.*

2. freeze: The act or an instance of stalling.

front: To guard an opponent (especially a taller opposing center or pivot) by playing in front of him in the passing lane (between him and the ball), instead of between him and the basket. compare *back.*

frontcourt: 1. The offensive half of a court, which contains the basket at which a team shoots. (bring the ball into the frontcourt) 2. The center and forwards. (overmatched if you try to go man-to-man on their frontcourt) also *front line.* 3. The positions played by the center and forward.

frontcourtman: A center or forward; one who plays in the frontcourt.

front lay-in: see *front lay-up.*

front lay-up: A lay-up made while in front of and facing the basket. also *front lay-in.* see *lay-up.* compare *reverse lay-up.*

front line: see *frontcourt.*

full-court press: A defensive tactic in which opponents are closely guarded man-to-man the full length of the court, from the moment the ball is put in play after a basket. Used to disrupt an

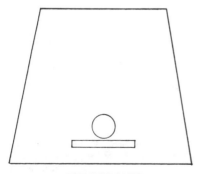

FREE THROW LANE

opposing team's normal offensive flow, to apply intense pressure and force mistakes, or as a part of a concerted effort to steal the ball for a quick score. compare *half-court press, zone press.*

game clock: The clock that indicates the remaining time to be played in a period. compare *shooting clock.*

garbage: 1. An easy or uncontested basket, or of or pertaining to an easy or uncontested basket, made from close range. (grabbed the rebound for a garbage two points) 2. The closing minutes of a game in which one team has such a commanding lead that the outcome has been decided, and substitutes are sent in to finish up. also *garbage time.*

garbage time: see *garbage.*

give and go: To execute a give-and-go.

give-and-go: A play in which the ball handler passes to a teammate, then breaks past a defender or defenders to receive a return pass in the clear. In the early 1930s, Nat Holman, coach of City College of New York, helped to refine the give-and-go into a system of play that eventually was adopted and practiced by many East Coast colleges. (worked the give-and-go into the lane)

glass ball: A missed shot that touches only the glass backboard and rebounds. compare *air ball.*

Globetrotters: see *Harlem Globetrotters.*

goaltending: Interference with a shot by touching the ball or the basket while the ball is on, over, or within the rim, touching the ball on its downward flight to the basket before it hits the rim, touching the ball on its upward flight to the basket after it has touched the backboard (as on a lay-up), or trapping the ball against the backboard. A violation, resulting in the loss of the ball to the opposing team for a throw-in from the sideline even with the free throw line if committed by an offensive player, or by the awarding of two points (three points in the NBA and some college conferences if the shot was taken from outside the three-point line) to the shooter. The ball is then inbounded in the normal manner after a field goal. The first goaltending rule was introduced in 1944. also *basket interference.*

guard: 1. Either of two players (often smaller and better ball handlers than the forward) who usually bring the ball out of the backcourt, start plays, and dis-

tribute the ball to teammates closer to the basket. Before the center jump was abandoned in 1937, the main responsibility of the two guards was to play defense and to "guard" the opposing forwards. (best outside-shooting guard in the league) also *backcourtman.* 2. The position played by the guards. 3. To prevent an opponent from being able to maneuver, pass, or receive a pass, or shoot effectively.

gunner: A player who shoots at every opportunity, even when teammates are more open or in a better position to score. also *chucker, pump.*

1. hack: To hit an opponent on the arm with the hand or forearm, in an attempt to knock the ball away; a personal foul. see *hacking.*

2. hack: The act or an instance of hacking.

hacking: A personal foul in which a player hits an opponent's arm with his hand or forearm. see *personal foul.*

half-court press: A defensive strategy in which the opponents are closely guarded man-to-man as soon as they enter a team's backcourt. compare *full-court press, zone press.*

Hall of Fame: see *Basketball Hall of Fame.*

hammer the boards: see *bang the boards.*

hand check: To maintain intermittent or continuous physical contact with the hand while guarding an offensive player, especially the ball handler. A personal foul. also *check.* see *personal foul.*

hanger: see *basket hanger.*

hardship case: A situation in which a college basketball player, not yet in his senior year, claims eligibility for a special NBA draft before graduating, under the "hardship" rule. NBA regulations originally forbade the playing or drafting of any college player before his class graduated. A court decision in the early 1970s ruled in favor of Seattle SuperSonics owner Sam Sullivan's attempt to hire Spencer Haywood, who had left the University of Detroit to play in the rival ABA. Ruling that the NBA regulation denying his right to play would work a hardship on Haywood, the court opened the way for other underclassmen to be drafted if they claim a hardship.

Harlem Globetrotters: A touring all-black

65

team that travels all over the world to play exhibition games that feature a unique blend of dazzling basketball skills and comedic showmanship. Founded in 1927 by Abe Saperstein, the Globetrotters have introduced the game of basketball to millions of fans and have become one of the all-time great attractions in sports. Some credit the Trotters with saving professional basketball when they played prior to some NBA games in the 1950s and drew many new fans to the arenas. Superstar Wilt Chamberlain played with the Harlem Globetrotters before his NBA days. also *Globetrotters, Trotters.*

hashmark: see *midcourt area marker.*

held ball: 1. A situation in which two or more opponents have their hands so firmly on the ball that neither can gain sole possession without undue roughness. This results in a jump ball at the circle nearest the spot where the held ball occurs (except in college games, where the ball is given alternately to the teams). also *tie ball.* 2. A violation of the five-second rule in college and high school play in which a closely guarded player holds or dribbles the ball in the frontcourt, or holds and/or

HOOK SHOT

dribbles the ball in the midcourt for five seconds without shooting or passing, resulting in the opposing team being awarded the ball for a throw-in. 3. A violation of the five-second rule in women's and international amateur play in which a closely guarded player holds the ball for five seconds without shooting, passing, or dribbling, resulting in a jump ball.

high post: A position just outside the lane near the free throw line in the frontcourt where a team's center often plays, and around which the offense maneuvers as he sets screens, receives and relays passes, and shoots. compare *low post.*

holding: A personal foul in which a player uses the hands to interfere with the movement or impede the progress of an opposing player. see *personal foul.*

1. hook: 1. A one-handed overhead shot made with the back arm when the body is turned sideways to the basket. With the shooting arm extended, the ball is lifted in an arc, then released with a flick of the wrist. Because the ball is released high, out of reach, and because it is further protected from defenders by the width of the shooter's body, an accurate hook is almost unstoppable. also *hook shot.* 2. An illegal, but common tactic in which a player with the ball, positioned with his back to a defender close behind, subtly moves a hand or elbow back to hold or "hook" the defender just before wheeling around him in that direction on a drive. If the infraction is detected, a personal foul results. see *personal foul.*

2. hook: 1. To execute a hook shot. (hooked right over the big man for two points) 2. To use an illegal hook to turn and dribble around an opponent.

hook pass: A pass made with the overhead motion of a hook shot.

hook shot: see *hook.*

hoop: The basket. also *bucket.*

H.O.R.S.E.: An informal game for two or more players in which contestants take turns making various kinds of shots from different locations around the court. When a shot is made, all players must then duplicate that shot. Each time a player fails to duplicate another player's shot, the unsuccessful player is assigned one letter of the word "horse" (other longer or shorter words are sometimes substituted). When a player misses enough times to spell out the word "horse" (or the substitute word), that player is eliminated from the game. The last player left in a game is the winner. Because of the requirement to duplicate the style of a shot, as well as the distance and type, and because there is usually no penalty to a player who misses an original shot (the next player makes his original shot attempt), low-percentage trick-shots are often employed in the game of H.O.R.S.E. compare *around the world.*

hot hand: A temporary heightened ability to make baskets, lasting for an indeterminate period of time. (had a hot hand for the three games he's played since coming off the bench)

●●A temporary heightened ability to accomplish or perform a task or activity. (got the hot hand at picking winners today)

inbound: To put the ball in play by a throw-in from out of bounds. If the ball is not inbounded within the five-second time limit, the opposing team is awarded the ball for a throw-in. (will inbound the ball from the sideline)

inbound pass: A throw-in from out of bounds. (takes the inbound pass and immediately moves the ball upcourt)

in bounds: Within the boundary lines of the playing court. (the ball is still in bounds)

inbounds: Of or pertaining to putting the ball in play with a throw-in from out of bounds. (broke up the inbounds play with a steal)

incidental contact: Legal physical contact with an opponent that is incidental to an effort by a player to perform normal defensive or offensive movement or to reach a loose ball.

in one's face: Disrespectfully, disdainfully, in spite of one's best efforts to oppose, as of a direct and deliberate challenge. (drove the lane right at their big man and scored two points in his face)

1. inside: The area in and around the free throw lane, close to the basket. (dominate the boards with the big man on the inside)

2. inside: To or toward the area in and around the free throw lane, close to the basket.

inside game: The ability of an individual or team to maneuver, shoot, and rebound close to the basket. (can't shoot from the outside, but his inside game is great)

intentional foul: A deliberate foul to stop the clock by a defensive player whose team is behind late in a game, conceding one or two free throws (which might be missed) for possession of the ball and the opportunity to score. Two free throws are awarded to the opposing team, except in the NBA in the final two minutes of play or an overtime period if the foul is committed against someone other than the ball handler. In such a case, one free throw is awarded to the opposing team.

in-your-face: Aggressively challenging, disrespectful, or disdainful. (scored with an in-your-face slam dunk)

isolate a defender: To maneuver a defender into a situation in which an offensive player is able to go one-on-one against him.

jab step: A technique in which the player with the ball takes a sudden step (without lifting the pivot foot) to fake a drive and momentarily deceive a defender, as before a shot, pass, or a drive in another direction. (backed the defender off with a jab step just long enough to shoot)

1. jam: To dunk the ball. also *stuff.*

2. jam: A dunk. also *stuff, stuff shot.*

jump ball: 1. A method of putting the ball in play in which two opponents within one of the three restraining circles jump up to try to tap a ball thrown in the air between them by the referee to a teammate outside the circle. A jump ball occurs in the center circle at the beginning of a game or overtime period (and at the beginning of every period in international amateur, women's, and high school play), and (except in college play) when a double foul on the ball is called. Except in college play, a jump ball occurs in the nearest circle in the case of a held ball, an out of bounds ball caused by both teams, a double-free throw violation, a ball lodged in a basket support, or a dead ball that neither team controls when no goal or infraction is involved. Jumpers must remain within, and teammates may not enter, the restraining circle before the ball is tapped. When a jump ball occurs in the center circle, jumpers must have at least one foot within a 4-foot jumping circle marked in a middle of the 12-

foot restraining circle (except in international amateur play). also *toss-up*. 2. A held ball.

●●A conflict in which there is no winner, or an even choice between options; a toss-up. (by train or by car, it's a jump ball)

jumper: A jump shot. (sinks a 15-foot jumper)

jumping circle: A 4-foot circle marked in the middle of the center circle in high school, college, and NBA play, inside which each jumper must have at least one foot before a jump ball.

jump pass: A pass made while jumping, often disguised as a jump shot.

jump shot: A shot in which the ball is released over the head at the peak of a jump. Difficult for a defender to block because of the height of the release. Though a two-handed jump shot was used as early as 1939 and 1940 by University of Arkansas forward Johnny Adams, and Minneapolis Laker Jim Pollard showed an unorthodox jump shot in the NBA in 1948, one of the earliest to use the modern jump shot was Universi-

JUMP SHOT

ty of San Francisco All-America forward Don Lofgran. After seeing him in a 1949 tournament, New York sportswriters dubbed his shot the "kangaroo shot." also *jumper*.

key, keyhole: The free throw area (including the restraining circle) or the free throw lane. The terms date from the early days of basketball and refer to the keyholelike appearance of the pre-1950s free throw area, with a 6-foot-wide lane extending from one end of the 12-foot restraining circle. (misses a jump shot from the top of the key)

lane: 1. The free throw lane. 2. Either of two imaginary alleys near the sidelines that offensive players attempt to fill during a fast break in order to spread the attack and increase the difficulty for the defense.

lay-in: A lay-up.

lay-up: A relatively easy shot made usually off the backboard from close to the basket at the peak of a jump. (steals the ball in the backcourt and scores with an easy lay-up) also *lay-in*.

lead official, leading official: The official who precedes play down the court and takes a position off the court near the basket. On a fast break, the lead and trail officials usually switch roles. compare *trail official*.

line: The free throw line.

loose ball: A ball that is in play but not in the possession of any player (such as a ball in the air on a pass or rebound, or rolling on the floor uncontrolled), and recoverable by either team. also *free ball*.

loose ball foul: In the NBA, a personal foul committed while the ball is in the air for a shot or a rebound, or otherwise in possession of neither team. The offending player and the team are charged with a foul, and the ball is awarded to the opposing team for a throw-in from out of bounds near where the foul occurred. If a loose ball foul occurs during a penalty situation, the number of free throws that normally applies on the personal foul are awarded.

lowbridge: To knock the legs out from under an opponent who is in the air to make a play (such as a shot, rebound, or pass). A personal foul that results in the awarding of two free throws to the fouled player. also *submarine, undercut*.

low post: A position close to the basket just outside the free throw lane in the frontcourt where a team's center often plays, and around which the offense maneuvers as he sets screens, receives and relays passes, shoots, and rebounds. compare *high post.*

makeup foul: A dubious or questionable foul that is called to "make up" for an earlier dubious or questionable foul called against the other team.

man defense: Man-to-man. also *man-for-man, man-on-man.*

man-for-man, man-on-man: Man-to-man. also *man defense.*

man-to-man: A defense in which each player guards a specific opponent. also *man defense, man-for-man, man-on-man.*

midcourt: The area of a team's frontcourt between the center line and the hashmarks (midcourt area markers). see *five-second rule.*

midcourt area marker: Either of two 2-inch-wide lines extending 3 feet in from each side boundary line 28 feet from and parallel to the end line. also *hashmark.*

midcourt line: see *division line.*

moving pick: An illegal maneuver in which an offensive player fails to come to a stop or remain stationary in an attempt to screen an opponent. If physical contact results, a personal foul is charged against the guilty player. see *personal foul.*

multiple foul: A situation in which two or more players on a team foul the same player at approximately the same time. A multiple foul results in the fouled player being awarded one free throw for each foul. compare *double foul.*

muscle player: A player who uses physical strength to maneuver for or maintain position, and rebound.

National Basketball Association: The major professional basketball league in the United States, founded in 1946 under the name of the Basketball Association of America. When the first games were played on November 1, 1946, there were eleven charter member teams. The league adopted its present name in 1949, after absorbing the rival National Basketball League. Today there are twenty-four franchises in the National Basketball Association in two conferences, each with two divisions. In the Eastern Conference, the Atlantic Division is made up of the Boston Celtics, the New Jersey Nets, the New York Knicks, the Philadelphia 76ers, and the Washington Bullets, and the Central Division is made up of the Atlanta Hawks, the Chicago Bulls, the Cleveland Cavaliers, the Detroit Pistons, the Indiana Pacers, and the Milwaukee Bucks. In the Western Conference, the Midwest Division is made up of the Dallas Mavericks, the Denver Nuggets, the Houston Rockets, the Kansas City Kings, the San Antonio Spurs, and the Utah Jazz, and the Pacific Division is made up of the Golden State Warriors, the Los Angeles Lakers, the Phoenix Suns, the Portland Trail Blazers, the San Diego Clippers, and the Seattle Super-Sonics. Abbreviated NBA.

NBA: The National Basketball Association.

net: The white mesh cord sleeve (15 to 18 inches in length) attached beneath the 18-inch metal rim to slow the ball momentarily as it passes through the basket. also *cord.*

no harm, no foul: The guiding philosophy of professional basketball officiating. If a foul is inconsequential, and no harm is done nor advantage gained, play is usually allowed to continue. "No harm, no foul" was coined by Los Angeles Lakers broadcaster Chick Hearn.

●●The expression is now used in sports other than basketball, as well as figuratively in nonsports circumstances where the same sentiment applies. (though his car did tap my bumper, no harm, no foul)

offensive boards: The backboard of the basket at which a team is shooting. (always got a second shot because they controlled the offensive boards)

offensive foul: A personal foul committed by a player of the team in control of the ball in NBA, international amateur, and women's play. When an offensive foul is committed, the guilty player and (except in the NBA) the team are charged with the foul, and the ball is awarded to the opposing team for a throw-in from out of bounds near where the foul occurred. In college and high school play, an offensive foul committed by a player other than the ball handler is a common foul and results in the ball being awarded to the opposing team for a throw-in (except in a bonus situation, when a one-and-one free throw is awarded to the fouled team). compare *player control foul.*

offensive rebound: A rebound taken off the backboard of the basket at which a team is shooting. (got the offensive rebound for his own shot)

official: Either of the two referees (or any of the three in some college conferences) who administer the rules of the game, or any of the individuals responsible for the timing and scoring of a game (in the NBA there is a lead official, a referee, a timer to operate the game clock, a timer to operate the twenty-four-second clock, and a scorer to compile game statistics). see *lead official, trail official.*

one-and-one: A situation in college, women's, and high school play in which a bonus free throw is awarded to a fouled player if the first free throw is successful during a bonus situation. A bonus situation applies when the opposing team has committed a specified number of team fouls during a period of play (seven fouls in one half in college and women's games, five fouls during one half in high school games). also *one-plus-one.*

one-handed push: see *one-hand set.*

one-hand set: A shot in which the ball is held shoulder high in the palm of one hand (knuckles toward the basket), and pushed toward the basket by the fingertips of the other hand with a snap of the wrist. Three-time Stanford All-American Hank Luisetti is credited with popularizing the one-handed set shot in the late 1930s, a major contribution to the modern high-scoring game. With his quick, hard to defend against one-hand shot, Luisetti once managed to score fifty points against Duquesne University, at a time when it was not uncommon for the winning team to score less than twenty points. The introduction of the one-hand set shot (out of which later came the jump shot) and the abolishing of the center jump after each field goal in 1937 (which integrated the center and guards into the offense and allowed the fast break to be developed) were the two most revolutionary changes in the game of basketball. also *one-handed push.*

one-on-one: 1. A situation in which a player offensively or defensively confronts

or is confronted by a single opponent. Often a team with the ball will maneuver to create a situation where a good ball handler and shooter can go "one-on-one" against a defender. 2. An informal basketball game between two players.

••Any contest or situation (athletic or nonathletic) that pits one individual against another. (broke through the secondary to be one-on-one with the free safety on the 10-yard line) Also a situation that allows one individual to talk or interact with another individual, unbothered by other people. (a productive one-on-one discussion after everybody left)

one-plus-one: see *one-and-one.*

open: Unguarded by or away from any opponent. (fed the open man under the basket for an easy two points)

OT: see *overtime.*

outlet: To start a fast break after a defensive rebound with a pass to a teammate. (outlets the ball right up the middle, and the fast break is on)

outlet pass: A pass to a teammate to start a fast break, made by a player who pulls down a rebound from the defensive boards.

out of bounds: Beyond the boundaries of the playing area and out of play. A player is out of bounds when he touches the floor, a person, or any object on or outside a boundary. A player in the air who takes off from in bounds is not out of bounds until he touches the floor, a person, or any object on or outside a boundary. The ball is out of bounds when it touches the floor, a person, or any object on, above, or outside of a boundary, or the supports or back of the backboard. When a ball goes out of bounds, the ball is awarded to the team opposing the player who last touched it for a throw-in.

out of bounds play: A special play used by a team awarded a throw-in in the frontcourt, in which players maneuver so that one, or more than one, designated teammate will be open to receive the throw-in. Often players crowd into a line perpendicular to the boundary line in front of the thrower-in, then break suddenly in different prearranged directions for the inbound pass.

1. **outside:** The area near the sides and back of the frontcourt, away from the

basket and free throw lane. (good shooters from the outside)

2. outside: To or toward the area near the sides and back of the frontcourt, away from the basket and free throw lane, near the division line or sidelines.

outside shooter: A player who can make shots from far away from the basket.

over and back: see *backcourt violation.*

overhead pass: A two-hand pass in which the ball is released over the head by snapping the hands forward. Often used to feed the post, over the defense.

overload the zone: To send more offensive players into an area than there are defenders.

overplay: To bias one's defense toward the strongest or favorite side of an opponent to make him go the other way.

over the top: 1. A situation in which a player leaps, or extends arms or part of the body over a player who has established position. A personal foul if physical contact results. see *personal foul.* 2. A shot from the outside, over the defense.

overtime: An extra five-minute period of play (three minutes in high school games) to decide a game tied at the end of regulation play. Overtime periods continue to be played until one team wins. also *OT.*

paint: The free throw lane. The expression was coined by Al McGuire, coach of Marquette University from 1965 to 1977. (into the big man on the paint) see *free throw lane.*

palm the ball: 1. To hold the ball in the palm of the hand momentarily while dribbling, or "catch" the ball between bounces. A violation, resulting in the loss of the ball to the opposing team for a throw-in from the sideline. also *carry.* 2. To hold a ball in one hand, with the palm facing down. (could palm a regulation ball by the time he was sixteen)

passing lane: A safe path or channel for a pass to a teammate.

penalty situation: A situation in NBA games in which a team has reached five team fouls, and each foul thereafter yields an additional free throw to the opposing team. also *bonus situation, penalty stage.*

penalty stage: see *penalty situation.*

personal foul: A foul in which there is physical contact with an opponent

(holding, pushing, charging, hacking, elbowing, blocking, etc.). If a personal foul is committed by an offensive player, the player and (except in the NBA) the team are charged with a foul, and the ball is awarded to the opposing team for a throw-in. Free throws are awarded instead in international amateur play (two free throws) and college, women's, and high school play (one-and-one) if the foul occurs during or causes a bonus situation. If a personal foul is committed by a defensive player, the player and the team are charged with a foul, and the fouled team is awarded a throw-in. Free throws are awarded (two in NBA, international amateur, and high school play, one-and-one in college and women's play) if the foul occurs during or causes a bonus situation (penalty situation in the NBA). If the foul is flagrant (an automatic disqualification for the guilty player) or intentional (or, in the NBA, if it is committed before the ball is inbounded), two free throws are awarded. If the foul is committed against a shooter who misses or is prevented from shooting, two free throws are awarded (three-to-make-two in international amateur play). One free throw is awarded if the foul is committed against a shooter who scores. see *flagrant foul, intentional foul.* compare *technical foul, violation.*

pick: see *screen.*

pick and roll: A play in which an offensive player sets a screen, then wheels towards the basket in order to receive a pass.

1. pivot: 1. The post position. see *post.* 2. The player who plays the pivot or post position. (their pivot can play in a high post or low post position) also *pivotman, post, post man.* 3. The act of, while holding the ball, stepping forward, backward, or to the side with one foot while the other foot (pivot foot) remains in contact with the floor in one place. see *pivot foot.*

2. pivot: To execute a pivot. see *pivot foot.*

pivot foot: The foot on which a player pivots, and which must remain in contact with the floor in one place while the player holds the ball. As long as the pivot foot remains in one place, any number of steps taken with the other foot count as the one step a player is permitted to take while holding the ball. If the pivot foot is moved from its original point of contact (except in the case of a jump pass or jump shot), or if a player, in attempting to make a jump pass or jump shot, touches the floor with either foot before the ball leaves his hands, the player is guilty of traveling. A traveling violation results in the loss of the ball to the opposing team for a throw-in from out of bounds near where the violation occurred. Either foot may be used as the pivot foot if a player receives the ball while standing still, or receives the ball while in the air and lands on both feet. If a moving player stops a dribble or receives a pass, the pivot foot is the first foot to touch the floor after the dribble stops or the ball is caught. If a moving player receives a pass while both feet are in the air, the pivot foot is the first foot to touch the floor after the ball is caught.

pivotman: The player (usually the center) who plays in the pivot or post position. also *pivot, post, post man.*

player control foul: A personal foul committed by the player in control of the ball in college and high school basketball. When a player control foul is committed, the guilty player and the team are charged with a foul, and the ball is awarded to the opposing team for a throw-in from out of bounds near where the foul occurred. compare *offensive foul.*

play for one: To play for one shot only, to maintain control of the ball near the end of the period or game so that when a shot is taken, there will not be enough time remaining for the opposing team to score.

point: 1. The basic scoring unit in basketball. A field goal counts for two points (in the NBA and some college conferences, a field goal made from outside the three-point line, approximately 23 feet from the basket, counts for three points). A successful free throw counts for one point. 2. The area toward the back of the frontcourt from where the point guard runs the offense.

point guard: The guard who runs the offense from a position near the back of the frontcourt.

point shaving: The deliberate (and illegal) limiting of the amount of points scored in a game by a team by one or more players to conform to the interests of gamblers.

post: 1. A position in the frontcourt, just outside the free throw lane, either close to the basket (low post), or near the free throw line (high post), occupied by the player (usually the center) around which the offense maneuvers as he sets screens, receives and relays passes, and shoots. Some teams use a two-post offense, with one player at the high post, and another at the low post. also *pivot.* 2. The player who plays the post position. also *pivot, pivotman, post man.*

post man: The player who plays the post position. also *pivot, pivotman, post.*

post-up: To establish a post position close to the basket.

pound the boards, pound the glass: see *bang the boards.*

power forward: A strong forward, usually large, primarily responsible for establishing and maintaining good position in front of the basket in order to be able to rebound aggressively, and to inhibit drives toward the basket by players on the opposing team. Minneapolis Lakers forward Vern Mikkelson, a six-time NBA All-Star in the 1950s, was the prototype for the modern power forward.

1. press: A defensive tactic in which opponents are closely guarded man-to-man either from the moment the ball is put into play after a basket (full-court press), or as soon as they enter a team's backcourt (half-court press), or when they enter specific zones defended by individual players (zone press). Used to disrupt an opposing team's normal offensive flow, to apply intense pressure and force mistakes, or as a part of a concerted effort to steal the ball for a quick score.

2. press: To execute a press against the opposing team. (press them and try to come up with a steal)

1. pump: To fake a shot at the basket in order to momentarily deceive a defender before a real shot, a pass, or a dribble. (pumps, then drives into the lane)

2. pump: 1. The act or an instance of pumping. (fakes with a pump, then sinks a 15-foot jump shot) 2. A gunner. see *gunner.*

pure shooter: A player with the ability to consistently make baskets, a very good shooter.

quintet: A basketball team. also *five*.

racehorse: see *run-and-gun*.

1. rebound: 1. The carom off the rim or backboard of a missed shot at the basket. (goes up for the rebound) 2. The act or an instance of gaining control of a ball that caroms off the rim or backboard from a missed shot at the basket. Wilt Chamberlain set the all-time NBA records for the most rebounds in a single game (55 on November 24, 1960) and in one season (2,149 in 1960-61) when he played for the Philadelphia Warriors. Chamberlain also holds the lifetime record, with 23,924 rebounds in his fourteen-year NBA career. also *board*.

2. rebound: To gain possession of a rebound. (rebounds and immediately outlets the ball)

ref: A referee.

referee: One of two officials (called the "umpire" and "referee" in high school and college play, and "lead official" and "referee" in the NBA, though all are commonly referred to as "referees") responsible for administering the rules of the game. Some college conferences require three officials, one "referee" and two "umpires." All call violations and fouls, and indicate successful goals. also *ref*.

reject: To block a shot at the basket. (rejected by the big man) see *block*.

release: To leave one assignment, such as guarding an opponent, for another (such as to double-team the player with the ball).

release early: To leave the backcourt early, as to start a fast break or to cherry-pick.

restraining circle: Any of three 12-foot circles (one in the middle of the court, bisected by the division line, and one at each end of the court, bisected by the free throw lines) within which a jump ball may be held, and inside which no other player may step until a jump ball has been tapped.

reverse dunk: A dunk shot made back over the head from underneath the basket, with the player facing out.

reverse lay-in: A reverse lay-up.

reverse lay-up: A lay-up made back over the head from underneath the basket. also *reverse lay-in*. see *lay-up*. compare *front lay-up*.

rim: Either of the 18-inch metal rings attached to the backboards at both ends of the court, from which a white cord net is suspended, and through which the ball must pass to make a basket. The most advanced model rims are designed with a hinge that allows the rim to give way under a certain amount of weight, and snap back when the pressure is released. This is to prevent injuries from shattered glass backboards that can result from hanging on the rim or from a particularly powerful slam dunk. These spring-loaded rims were adopted by the NBA (and approved for college use) in 1981-82.

rim shot: A shot that is banked in off the rim.

rocker step: A technique in which a player with the ball fakes a drive by taking a step (without lifting the pivot foot), then pulls back to shoot (or sometimes, to fake a shot before actually driving, appearing to "rock" back and forth).

roll: To suddenly wheel around from a stationary position (such as from a pick) and break toward the basket.

run-and-gun: A wide-open offensive style of play, characterized by a fast break and relentless attacks on the offensive basket rather than deliberate or complicated offensive and defensive strategies. also *racehorse, run-and-shoot*.

run and gun: To employ a run-and-gun offense. (will be forced to run and gun now to cut down the lead) also *run and shoot*.

run-and-shoot: see *run-and-gun*.

run and shoot: see *run and gun*.

run the break: To play the key part in and direct a team's fast break offense. (a great ball handling guard who runs the break)

sag: see *slough off*.

scoop, scoop lay-up: A lay-up in which the ball is brought up to the basket with an underhand motion.

scorer: The official responsible for keeping a record of field goals made, free throws made and missed, and a running summary of points scored. Scorers also record the personal and technical fouls called on each player and the time-outs charged to each team, and notify the nearest official when the maximum number of fouls permitted a player, or time-outs permitted a team is reached. Scorers record the names, numbers, and positions of all starting players and substitutes, as well as the time of any substitutions. When a player is disqualified from the game, or when a penalty shot is being awarded, a buzzer, siren, or some other audible sound is used by the scorer (or sometimes the timer) to notify the game officials.

1. **screen:** A maneuver in which an offensive player without the ball takes a stationary position in back of, to the side of, or in front of a defensive player in order to momentarily obstruct his path and free the ball handler. Legal only if the offensive player remains stationary, and leaves enough room for the defensive player to avoid a collision. also *pick.*

2. **screen:** To take a stationary position in back of, to the side of, or in front of a defensive player in order to momentarily obstruct his path and free the ball handler. (screened the defender off the ball handler) also *set a pick.*

screen out: see *box out.*

set a pick: To screen a defensive player or to execute a screen.

set offense: An offense that utilizes practiced patterns of movement in order to maneuver for a good shot at the basket.

set play: An offensive play in which specific patterns of movement are used to maneuver for a good shot at the basket.

set shot: A shot that is taken with both feet on the floor, as opposed to a jump shot. see *one-hand set shot, two-hand set shot.*

shave points: To deliberately (and illegally) limit the amount of points scored in a game by one's team to conform to the interest of gamblers.

shoot: To make an attempt to throw the ball through the basket. (shoots from the top of the key)

shootaround: A short, midday practice session consisting of stretching and skill and shooting drills designed to promote "muscle memory" and reinforce specific tactics between closely scheduled games. Basketball Hall of Fame coach Bill Sharman introduced the now widely used shootaround in 1961 with the ABL Los Angeles Jets, bringing it to the NBA San Francisco Warriors in 1966, and then to his 1971-72 NBA champion Los Angeles Lakers.

shooting clock: A clock that tells the amount of time a team has left to make a shot at the basket under the thirty-second rule (women's and international amateur play) or twenty-four-second rule (in the NBA). A shooting clock was adopted experimentally in the early 1980s by some college conferences and may ultimately be universally adopted. also *shot clock, thirty-second clock, twenty-four-second clock.*

shoot over the zone: To make shots from the outside in order to force a team to abandon a zone defense and play man-to-man instead.

shot: An attempt to throw the ball through the basket for a score.

shot clock: see *shooting clock.*

shovel pass: An underhand pass used occasionally for short distances.

1. **simulcast:** To simultaneously broadcast a game on radio and television. Chick Hearn, play-by-play announcer for the Los Angeles Lakers began to regularly simulcast Lakers games in 1966, an idea credited to then Laker owner Jack Kent Cooke and subsequently adopted by others.

2. **simulcast:** The simultaneous broadcast of a game on radio and television.

sink: To make a successful shot.

sixth man: The player who normally substitutes first when a starting player must be rested or is in foul trouble, or when a team needs a change of pace.

sky: To jump high and almost sail through the air. (can really sky) also *talk to God.*

skyhook: A high hook shot, released above the level of the basket. The expression was coined by Milwaukee Bucks broadcaster Eddie Doucette in 1969 to describe a shot perfected by future all-time NBA scoring champion, Kareem Abdul-Jabbar (then Lew Alcindor) in his first year with the Bucks.

1. **slam dunk:** A particularly forceful dunk shot. The expression was coined by Los Angeles Lakers broadcaster Chick Hearn to describe the technique first popularized by NBA superstar Wilt Chamberlain. Because of the increasing incidence of shattered glass backboards, usually the result of a violent slam dunk, in the 1981–82 season the NBA (and some colleges) began to use a hinged, spring-loaded rim, which is designed to give way under a certain amount of pressure, and return when the pressure is released. compare *dunk.*

2. **slam dunk:** To execute a slam dunk.

(gets the rebound and slam dunks for two points) compare *dunk.*

slough off: To leave the opponent one is guarding in order to play a passing lane, double-team, double-team another opponent, or get a good position under the basket for a rebound. also *sag.*

small forward: A forward who is known more for quickness, mobility, and shooting rather than rebounding, unlike the usually larger "power forward."

spread-court offense, spread offense: A control-type offense in which the team with the ball attempts to spread the defense (leaving the middle open for scoring opportunities) by keeping the ball outside or near the perimeters of the frontcourt until the defensive team abandons zone coverage and moves out to cover man-to-man.

stack: An offensive alignment in which the two forwards (or the center and one forward) begin play in the frontcourt from a low post position on one side of the lane with the center (or other forward) at a low post position on the other side of the lane. Occasionally a variation is used with all three players beginning from a low post position on one side of the lane.

1. stall: To attempt to maintain possession of the ball, not for the purpose of scoring, but to prevent the opposing team from gaining possession and having the opportunity to score. Most often a team will stall the ball to protect a lead near the end of a game, but occasionally, when faced with a particularly strong, high-scoring opponent, a team will stall the ball for an entire game in order to keep the score low, and an upset victory within reach. also *freeze.*

2. stall: The act or an instance of stalling the ball. also *freeze.*

stall ball: see *ball control*

1. steal: To take possession of the ball from an opponent by batting it away, or intercepting a pass.

2. steal: The act or an instance of stealing the ball. (makes a steal, and the fast break is on)

steps: see *traveling.*

1. stuff: see *dunk.*

2. stuff: A field goal made by dunking the ball. see *dunk.*

stuff shot: see *stuff.*

stutter step: A momentary change in rhythm or pace (and sometimes direc-

tion) while moving, or a feint in one direction with a quick step and return, in order to "freeze" or confuse an opponent for an instant.

stutter-step: To execute a stutter step. (stutter-stepped, then drove to the baseline)

submarine: see *lowbridge.*

swing: To play or be able to play in two different positions, usually guard and forward. To be a swingman.

swingman: A player who is able to play two different positions on a team. (a swingman who can play at guard or forward)

1. swish: A shot that travels through the basket without hitting the backboard or rim. also *swisher.*

2. swish: To shoot a swish, or swisher. (swished a 10-footer).

swisher: see *swish.*

1. switch: To momentarily change defensive assignments with a teammate or to pick up an open or free man.

2. switch: The act or an instance of switching, or switching off.

T: A technical foul. (picked up a T for unsportsmanlike conduct)

talk to God: To jump high and almost sail through the air. also *sky.*

tap: A tipoff. also *tapoff, tip.*

tapoff: A tipoff. also *tap, tip.*

team foul: Any personal foul (except an offensive foul in the NBA) charged toward the specified number of fouls a team is allowed within a certain period of play before a bonus or penalty situation exists (four in one quarter or three in an overtime period in NBA games, eight, including technical fouls, in one half in international amateur games, six in one half in college and women's games, and four in one half in high school games.

technical foul: A foul committed by a player, coach, or bench personnel that does not involve contact with an opponent, or that involves intentional or flagrant contact with an opponent (such as punching or fighting) when the ball is dead and the clock has stopped, unsportsmanlike conduct (such as profanity, disrespect for an official, illegal substitutions), or (in the NBA only) the use of a zone defense. When a player commits a technical foul in high school, women's, or college play, the opposing team is awarded one free throw, or two free throws if the foul is flagrant or intentional, or if committed by a coach or bench personnel (one free throw for coach or bench personnel in women's basketball). The player or coach is automatically ejected from the game if the foul is flagrant, or if it is his third technical foul. When a player or coach commits a technical foul in the NBA, the opposing team is awarded one free throw, and the ball is returned to the team having possession at the time the foul was called for a throw-in from out of bounds near where play ended. The player or coach is automatically ejcted from the game if the infraction is his second technical foul. When a player commits a technical foul in international amateur play, the foul is charged against the player and the team, and the opposing team is awarded two free throws (one free throw if the foul was committed by a coach). Play resumes with a jump ball. In college basketball, the ball is awarded alternately to the teams after a technical foul. also *T.* compare *personal foul, violation.*

ten-second line: The division line when used in conjunction with the ten-second rule. also *time line.*

ten-second rule: A rule that states that a team may not be in continuous control of a ball in its backcourt for more than ten consecutive seconds. If, within ten seconds of inbounding or gaining possession of the ball in the backcourt, a team fails to bring the ball across the division line, a violation occurs, resulting in the loss of the ball to the opposing team for a throw-in from out of bounds near where play stopped. The ten-second rule was introduced in 1937.

thirty-second clock: A clock that tells the amount of time a team has left to make a shot at the basket under the thirty-second rule used in international amateur and women's basketball. When a shot is attempted, or when the opposing team gains possession of the ball, the clock is reset for another thirty seconds. also *shooting clock, shot clock.*

thirty-second rule: A rule in international amateur and women's basketball that requires a team to attempt a shot at the basket within thirty seconds of gaining possession of the ball or putting it in play. see *thirty-second violation.*

thirty-second violation: A violation of the thirty-second rule, resulting in the loss of the ball to the opposing team for a throw-in.

three-point field goal: A field goal made from outside the three-point line, an arc drawn from each baseline, approximately 23 feet from the basket. The three-point field goal was first used by Abe Saperstein (founder of the Harlem Globetrotters) in 1961 in his short-lived professional league, the American Basketball League. The three-point field goal was reintroduced in 1967 by the American Basketball Association, adopted by the NBA in 1978, and tried on an experimental basis by some college conferences in the early 1980s. In time, it may be universally adopted.

three-point line: A 2-inch-wide semi-circular line marked at each end of the court, in games where the three-point field goal is used, by lines extending from the end line 3 feet from and parallel to the sidelines, intersecting an arc of 23 feet, 9 inches from the middle of the basket (23 feet from the basket). Any field goal made from outside the three-point line counts three points. see *three-point field goal.*

three-point play: A situation in which a foul is committed against a player as he shoots and scores. The basket counts, and if the awarded free throw is made, the total is a three-point play.

three-second area, three-second lane: The free throw lane when used in conjunction with the three-second rule.

three-second rule: A rule that states that no offensive player may remain within the free throw lane (between the end line and the outer edge of the free throw line) in the frontcourt for more than three consecutive seconds while his team is in possession of the ball.

three-second violation: A violation of the three-second rule, resulting in the loss of the ball to the opposing team for a throw-in from out of bounds.

thrower-in: The player who inbounds the ball on a throw-in.

throw-in: A method of putting the ball in play from out of bounds (as after a score, a violation, a foul for which no free throws are awarded, or when the ball goes out of bounds) in which a player is given five seconds to pass, roll, or bounce the ball to a teammate from out of bounds. A throw-in begins when the ball is at the disposal of the team or player entitled to it, and ends when the passed ball touches or is touched by an inbounds player other than the thrower-in. If a player is unable to inbound the ball within five seconds, a violation occurs, resulting in the loss of the ball to the opposing team for a throw-in from out of bounds at the point of the infraction.

ticky-tack foul: A questionable or inconsequential foul which could (or should) go uncalled by an official. Los Angeles Lakers broadcaster Chick Hearn coined the expression.

tie ball: A held ball.

time line: see *ten-second line*.

timer: Either of two officials responsible for the operation of game clocks (and shot clocks in international amateur and NBA play), recording and timing time outs, and signaling the beginning and end of a period.

tip: A tipoff. also *tap, tapoff*.

tip in, tip-in: A field goal made from close to the basket by tapping in a rebound or a high-arcing pass or shot.

tipoff: The jump ball at the beginning of a game or a period of play. (wins the tipoff) also *tap, tapoff, tip*.

top of the key: The area behind the free throw line just inside or outside the restraining circle. (the ball goes into the high post at the top of the key)

toss-up: A jump ball.

●●A conflict in which there is no winner, or an even choice between options. (either the apple pie or the chocolate cake, it's a toss-up)

trail official: The official or referee who follows play down the court and takes a position near the division line, with the primary responsibility of signaling if a field goal counts. The trail official shares the responsibility of calling fouls and violations with the lead official. On a fast break, the lead and trail officials usually switch roles. compare *lead official*.

transition: The change from defense to offense after a team gains possession of the ball in its backcourt.

transition game: The ability of a team to change from defense to offense after gaining possession of the ball in the backcourt.

1. trap: 1. To suddenly double-team and pressure the ball handler in the hopes of forcing a mistake. 2. To pin the ball against the backboard, a violation. see *goaltending*.

2. trap: 1. The act or an instance of trapping the ball handler. 2. The act or an instance of pinning the ball against the backboard, a violation. see *goaltending*.

travel: To take more than the allowed number of steps while holding the ball or at the end of a dribble, or to lift or drag the pivot foot. A traveling violation. see *traveling*.

traveling: A violation in which a player with the ball takes more steps than allowed without dribbling, or at the end of a dribble, or lifts or drags the pivot foot. A traveling violation results in the loss of the ball to the opposing team for a throw-in from out of bounds near where the violation occurred. also *steps, walking*.

triple doubles: Double figures in points, rebounds, and assists in a game by a player. Incredibly, Hall of Famer Oscar "The Big O" Robertson averaged triple doubles for five consecutive seasons for the Cincinnati Royals (30.3 points, 10.4 rebounds, and 10.6 assists per game from 1960-61 through 1964-65).

triple-team: To guard an opponent with three players at the same time.

Trotters: The Harlem Globetrotters.

turnaround jumper: A turnaround jump shot.

turnaround jump shot: A jump shot that a player facing away from the goal pivots toward the basket, jumps, and shoots. also *turnaround jumper*.

turnover: The loss of possession of the ball, whether because of a mistake, a steal, or as a result of a violation.

twenty-four-second clock: A clock that tells the amount of time a team has left to make a shot under the twenty-four-second rule in NBA play. When a shot is attempted, or when the opposing team gains possession of the ball, the clock is set for another twenty-four seconds. also *shooting clock, shot clock*.

twenty-four-second rule: A rule in the NBA that requires a team to attempt a shot at the basket within twenty-four seconds of gaining possession of the ball or putting it in play. The twenty-four-second rule was first adopted by the NBA for the 1954-55 season to combat the slowdown tactics used to freeze the ball and protect a lead. Bitterly opposed at first by some owners, the change proved to be a great success, providing an immediate speed-up in play and placing more emphasis on scoring. see *twenty-four-second violation.*

twenty-four-second violation: A violation of the twenty-four-second rule, resulting in the loss of the ball to the opposing team for a throw-in.

two-handed push: A two-handed shot in which the ball is held above the head and pushed toward the basket with a flick of the wrists. Occasionally used for a short to mid-range jump shot. Nicknamed the "Illinois kiss" around the 1930s (because of the proximity of the ball to the shooter's face), the two-handed push was a specialty of New York Knicks guard (late 1940s to early 1960s) Carl Braun.

two-hand set shot: A shot in which the ball is held with the fingertips of both hands about neck-high with the body slightly crouched, then pushed up and out and released over the head as the legs and body spring straight. Seldom used in modern basketball, except from the outside against a zone defense, when there is sufficient time to get set.

two-shot foul: A personal or technical foul that carries a penalty of two free throws. see *personal foul, technical foul.*

two-time: see *double-team.*

umpire: One of the two officials in international amateur play (one called the "referee" and one called the "umpire" but both commonly referred to as referees) equally responsible for the conduct of a game, and calling fouls and violations.

undercut: see *lowbridge.*

unsportsmanlike conduct: Unfair, unethical, dishonorable, or violent behavior, such as using profanity or abusive language, unfairly distracting or blocking the vision of an opponent, fighting, striking, or physically contacting an official (by a coach or player), etc. Unsportsmanlike conduct is penalized by a technical foul, and, depending upon the nature and severity of the infraction, ejection from the game and possible further disciplinary action by the league or conference under whose auspices the game is played.

upcourt: To or toward the end of the court containing the basket at which a team is shooting. also *downcourt.*

violation: An infraction of the rules by the team in control of the ball (traveling, stepping out of bounds with the ball, etc.) that results in the opposing team being awarded the ball for a throw-in. compare *personal foul.*

walking: see *traveling.*

1. weave: An offensive strategy in which players move laterally in the frontcourt between the division line and the top of the key in a figure-eight pattern, passing and handing the ball off as they move past each other and edge closer to the basket until a player who is momentarily left unguarded can shoot or drive in toward the basket. A popular strategy in college play in the 1950s, but less effective against modern zone or switching man-to-man defenses.

2. weave: To execute a weave.

white legs: see *white man's disease.*

white man's disease: Locker room humor for a player's lack of speed or jumping ability, originating from vulgar racial stereotyping of athletic or intellectual superiority or inferiority. (a great ball handler, but he has white man's disease) also *white legs.*

wing: 1. A position played by a forward in the frontcourt near the baseline on either side of the lane. 2. A player who plays in the wing position.

yo-yoing: Dribbling the ball continuously in one spot, as one might play with a yo-yo. Coined by broadcaster Chick Hearn.

zone: 1. A specific area of the court a defender is responsible for in a zone defense. 2. A zone defense.

zone defense: A defensive strategy in which each player defends a specific area of the court, rather than an opponent. A defender guards an opponent only when the opponent moves into the area of the zone the defender is assigned to cover. A zone defense is not permitted in NBA games, and its use results in a technical foul. also *zone.*

zone press: A defensive strategy in which close, man-to-man coverage is applied only when the ball or ball handler enters a specific area or zone that a defensive player is assigned to cover. compare *full-court press, half-court press.*

BOXING

The earliest record of boxing as a sport was found in a temple in Khafaja near Baghdad, Iraq. There, a stone slab dating back to the fifth millennium B.C. clearly shows two fighters boxing, their hands wrapped with pieces of leather: the first crude boxing gloves.

Ancient Mycenaean and Minoan civilizations enjoyed the sport, the latter evidenced beautifully by a vase discovered at Hagia Triada on the island of Crete. Minoan boxers are portrayed on the vase, which dates back to 1600 B.C.

It was the Greeks of later years, however, who took the greatest interest in boxing. Homer's *Iliad* tells of a famous boxing contest between Epeus and Euryalas at the funeral games of Patroclus, killed in the final days of the siege of Troy, now thought to have occurred in the fourteenth century B.C. Greek boxers, from this period until the end of the fifth century B.C., had their hands and forearms wrapped with "soft gloves", 10 to 12-foot-long thongs of ox-hide, sometimes dressed with fat to make them supple. Greek boxers resembled their modern counterparts to a surprising degree. They fought two-handed, cocking the right hand high with the left slightly extended, and trained with meal or sandfilled leather punching bags. References to knockouts and cauliflower ears by both Homer and Plato attest to the punching power of the Greeks, presumed to be mostly heavyweights in the absence of actual weight divisions. Some historians believe the word "boxing" comes from the Greeks' comparison of the clenched fist with a box (*pyxis*).

The rules for Olympian boxing were drawn up in 688 B.C. by Onomastus of Smyrna, the first boxing champion at Olympia. According to Diogenes Laertius, the first scientific boxer was Pythagoras of Samos, who was champion at the Olympia games in 588 B.C. and possibly an uncle of the mathematician-philosopher Pythagoras.

The greatest Greek boxer of them all was Theogenes of Thasos. After winning at Olympia in 480 B.C., it is claimed that Theogenes remained undefeated for twenty-two years, winning over 1,400 matches. With his awesome record and reputation, undoubtedly some of Theogenes' victories were barely contested. Greek jargon for such a walkover was *akoniti*, a "victory without dust".

Early in the fourth century B.C., boxers began to use "sharp gloves" (*sphairi*), still made of leather thongs, but with a hard leather ring with sharp edges over the knuckles. The sport took a turn toward violence, a trend that would continue when the conquering Romans introduced the *caestus* (cestus), a thong handwrapping that included bits of lead and sharp pieces of metal projecting from the knuckles.

79

Soon the sporting aspect of boxing gave way to the bloody gladiatorial spectacles favored by the Romans. By the first century B.C., first the cestus, then boxing itself were prohibited, and the sport would not surface again in history or literature for some seventeen hundred years, except, ironically, in one report which raises the possibility of a link between boxing and a canonized saint of the Catholic church.

In Siena, Italy, in the early thirteenth century, a priest (later St. Bernardine) is alleged to have taught his male parishioners the art of fisticuffs as an alternative to dueling and served as the referee for these contests of honor. Some believe that Bernardine's special instructions for "boxing up" (blocking with the hands and arms) an opponent's punches were the origin of the word "boxing".

In the seventeenth century, English men began to settle differences with their fists as well as knives and cudgels, some even betting on the outcome. Eventually, as many of these crude anything-goes contests were fought for "purses" as were fought for anger, honor, or ego. Thus, England, and particularly London, soon became the center of "prize fighting".

By 1719, one young man had begun to emerge as England's best fighter. At the age of twenty-four, James Figg had won fifteen consecutive fights. Though handy with weapons and a good wrestler, it was Figg's devastating punches that won fights and a reputation for him. All of London began to hear of the pugilist, James Figg and his "Figg Fighting".

Because of his following, Figg was able to open a boxing academy, called Figg's Amphitheater, where he staged fights and taught wrestling and boxing, and was always prepared to accommodate any challenger. James Figg, the first heavyweight champion, retired undefeated at the age of thirty-five and died ten years later, in 1740 of pneumonia.

Three years later, another famous English fighter and teacher, Jack Broughton, framed the first set of rules to civilize the sport. Broughton's rules forbade hitting below the waist, hair pulling, and hitting a downed man, and they allowed a fighter thirty seconds of rest before having to return to the square drawn in the center of the fighting area to "toe the line". Regarded as the father of boxing, Broughton also invented padded leather boxing gloves, which he allowed his young noblemen students to wear while sparring.

In 1838, Broughton's code formed the basis of the London Prize Ring Rules, which, with revisions, were to regulate prize fighting until its final evolution from bareknuckles to boxing fifty years later. London Prize Ring Rules called for a 24-foot-square ring, specified the end of a "round" to be whenever a fighter hit the floor, and replaced Broughton's chalked square with a line drawn at the center of the ring (the scratch line). To avoid defeat by being "knocked out of time", a downed fighter had eight seconds after the thirty-second rest allowed, to come "up to scratch" unassisted.

The first big international fight took place in 1860 at Farnborough, Hampshire in England. American "champion" John Carmel Heenan and English champion Tom Sayers fought forty-two grueling rounds before the match ended controversially as a draw because of crowd interference.

In 1865, John Sholto Douglas, the ninth Marquis of Queensberry, sponsored a set of rules framed by John Graham Chambers, which were to become the basic rules for modern boxing. They called for a 20-foot-square ring, three-minute rounds with a one-minute rest in between, padded gloves, a ten-second count for a downed boxer, and outlawed wrestling, gouging and clinching.

In England, bareknuckle fights, though often illegal, had gained a wide following, particularly among the gentry, who were called the "fancy" (later shortened to form the word "fan").

When John L. Sullivan became the bareknuckle world heavyweight champion in 1882 by knocking out Paddy Ryan in nine rounds, his victory went almost unnoticed. But Sullivan had the answer. In a bold and clever move with far-reaching consequences for the sport of boxing, he began to tour the United States with a theatrical troupe, performing boxing exhibitions on stage with gloves and under Queensberry Rules (thereby, neatly sidestepping the police, who were more tolerant of gloved matches and the new rules).

The public responded, and Sullivan's reputation grew, especially after he abandoned his regular sparring partners and began challenging all comers in each American city. Across the country, people flocked to theaters to see Sullivan flatten the local bruisers, who were offered $500 if they could last four rounds with him. Though still officially banned in most states, boxing was becoming popular, and "The Great" John L. Sullivan was its biggest attraction.

By 1885, Sullivan not only held the bareknuckle title, but claimed the first Queensberry heavyweight championship, after defeating Dominick McCaffrey in six rounds. In 1889, in the last bareknuckle championship fight, John L. Sullivan defeated Jake Kilrain by a knockout when Kilrain was unable to answer the bell for the seventy-sixth round.

In 1892, Sullivan lost the heavyweight title (Queensberry) to James J. Corbett in New Orleans, Louisiana, by a knockout in the twenty-first round.

In 1896, New York became the first state to sanction boxing matches, followed shortly thereafter by Nevada. But the New York law was changed and revoked. For years, bouts could be held, but for ten rounds only, and no decision could be rendered. Until the Walker Law (sponsored by the Speaker of the New York Senate, James J. Walker) legalized boxing in 1920, all decisions in fights not ending by a knockout were made by boxing writers.

In 1904, boxing was included in the Olympics of St. Louis, though there were few non-American entries, and the United States boxers won all eight gold medals. The year before, Englishman Bob Fitzsimmons, who had won the heavyweight title from Corbett in 1897 (the first title fight ever filmed), and lost it in 1899 to James J. Jeffries, won the world light heavyweight championship to become the first boxer ever to win titles in three divisions (he had won the middleweight championship in 1891).

Boxing was first included in the Olympic Games in 1904. The United States and Great Britain dominated the sport for many years. In 1904 the United States won all titles available. Great Britain did the same in 1908. Harry Mallin of Great Britain became the first boxer to successfully defend an Olympic title when he won the middleweight title in 1920 and 1924.

George "Little Chocolate" Dixon had become the first black world champion when he claimed the bantamweight title in 1890. In 1908, Jack Johnson became the first black heavyweight champion, knocking out Tommy Burns in fourteen rounds. A superb defensive fighter, Johnson was the subject of controversy during his seven-year reign. His arrogance, womanizing, and well-publicized trouble with the law only served to infuriate those who raised the racial cry for a "white hope" to topple him. Finally, in 1915 in Havana, Cuba, 6-foot, 6¼-inch, 240-pound Jess Willard knocked out Johnson in the twenty-sixth round to win the heavyweight championship and a reputation as the "great white hope".

In 1921, heavyweight champion Jack Dempsey (he had taken the title from Willard in 1919) knocked out Georges Carpentier in four rounds. It was the first title fight ever broadcast on the radio and the first fight ever to gross over one million dollars.

In spite of political maneuvering and occasional scandals, boxing's popularity grew, and by 1937, Joe Louis had become heavyweight champion. He would hold the title until 1949, longer than any other man. Late in 1937, Henry Armstrong won the featherweight championship. It was the first of three titles he would win within a year (welterweight, May, 1938, and lightweight, August, 1938), becoming the only man in the history of boxing to hold three world championships simultaneously.

After retiring undefeated in 1949, Joe Louis tried unsuccessfully to take back the heavyweight crown from Ezzard Charles in 1950. It was the first fight shown on closed-circuit television, a medium that, in the 1970s and 1980s, would make millionaires out of boxers and promoters.

In the late 1940s and early 1950s, great champions like welterweight and middleweight king Sugar Ray Robinson (some say the all-time greatest "pound-for-pound", an expression coined to describe him) and undefeated heavyweight champion Rocky Marciano dominated the sport. Jimmy Carruthers of Australia was at this time reigning bantamweight champion.

In 1964, boxing fans greeted a new champion who would single-handedly raise boxing to new heights and would ultimately become one of the two most popular athletes in the world, challenged only by soccer's legendary Pele. The 1960 Olympic light heavyweight champion, Cassius Clay, knocked out the seemingly invincible Sonny Liston to become world heavyweight champion at the age of twenty-two.

Brash and controversial, Clay adopted the Muslim name Muhammed Ali and refused to fight in the Vietnam War on religious and moral grounds, braving a possible jail sentence. Though ultimately he would emerge a hero, Ali's position was a courageous and unpopular stand at the time. At the physical prime of his life, Ali was prevented from fighting in 1968 and 1969. In 1971, Ali lost a fifteen-round decision to the new heavyweight champion, Joe Frazier. In 1973, he became only the second man in boxing history to regain the heavyweight title when he knocked out George Foreman in eight rounds. (In 1960, Floyd Patterson had regained the title he lost the previous year to Ingemar Johansson.) Then, incredibly, in 1978 at the age of thirty-six, Ali became the only man ever to regain the heavyweight championship twice when he lost and regained the title from 1976 Olympic light heavyweight champion, Leon Spinks.

In the early 1980s, another Olympic gold medalist (1976), with the help of closed-circuit television, emerged as the greatest money-winner of all time, out-earning even Ali who set all previous records. Bright, charismatic, and able Sugar Ray Leonard took the world welterweight championship from Wilfred Benitez in 1979 and lost and regained it in 1980 from seven-year lightweight title holder Roberto Duran. Leonard won the junior middleweight championship from Ayub Kalule in 1981, and then unified the welterweight title by defeating WBA welterweight champion Thomas Hearns, before retiring in 1982.

As one of the oldest sports in the history of mankind, it is fitting that boxing has made one of the largest and most colorful contributions to our spoken language.

AIBA: The Association Internationale de Boxe Ameteur.

Ali shuffle: A rapid series of changes in the lead foot of the boxing stance. The invention of three-time heavyweight champion Muhammad Ali in the mid-seventies. Ali used the showy technique more to gain a psychological advantage than a physical or tactical advantage.

answer the bell: To resume fighting when the bell rings for the next round. If a boxer is unable to answer the bell, he is declared the loser by a knockout in that round. (took so many punches in the eighth round, he couldn't answer the bell for the ninth)

●●To resume or continue an activity. (won't be able to answer the bell tomorrow if he stays out too late)

apron: The section of the ring floor that extends approximately 2 feet outside the ropes.

arm puncher: A boxer who uses only the

strength of the arms rather than the whole body in his punches.

arm weary: Fatigued in the arms from throwing punches, no longer able to punch or defend properly. also *punched out*.

Association Internationale de Boxe Ameteur: The sanctioning body formed in 1946 to control and oversee international amateur boxing.

babyweight: 1. Any weight division below lightweight. (a card of babyweight fights) 2. A boxer whose weight classes him below the lightweight division.

backpedal: To retreat or back up in the ring. (backpedalled after taking a straight right to the chin)

●●To literally or figuratively retreat or back up from someone or something. (backpedalled until he could think of an answer)

bag: A punching bag. Either a heavy bag, speed bag, or double-end bag.

bagged fight: A fight that is fixed, the outcome illegally decided before the match takes place. also *tank job*.

bandage: To apply the protective gauze bandages to a boxer's hands. also *wrap*.

bandages: The 1-1/2 to 2-inch protective gauze wrappings that are placed over a boxer's hands and taped at the wrist. also *wrapping*.

bang: To punch hard. (not much of a boxer, but he can really bang) also *belt, bomb, slug*.

banger: see *slugger*.

bantam: Bantamweight. also *banty*.

bantamweight: 1. The 118 pound weight division (119 pounds in amateur boxing. also *bantam, banty*. 2. A boxer who fights in the bantamweight division. Originally the smallest weight division (105 pounds, then 112, 115, and finally 118 pounds), bantamweight boxers were called "bantams" or "little chickens." Early records are incomplete, but in 1856, American Charlie Lynch claimed the world bantamweight title after defeating British boxer Simon Finighty in forty-three rounds. Lynch retired undefeated in 1861 and the division was inactive until 1887. Though several fighters claimed supremacy, no clear champion emerged until 1890 when George "Little Chocolate" Dixon claimed the title. Dixon, the first black world champion, held onto the title until

1892 when he outgrew the division. He was elected to the Boxing Hall of Fame in 1956. also *bantam, banty*.

banty: Bantamweight. also *bantam*.

beat a tattoo: To pummel an opponent or score repeated hits. also *pepper, tattoo*.

●●To hit repeatedly. (beat a tattoo on the conga drum)

beat the count: To get up before being counted out.

●●To recover from a serious problem or illness. (broke his back, but he beat the count and is walking today)

beat to the punch: To score with a punch faster than or before an opponent can land one of his own. (making use of his great hand speed and consistently beating the challenger to the punch)

●●To act faster than another. (was well qualified for the work, but someone beat him to the punch and got the job)

bell: A bell that is rung to mark the beginning and end of each round.

●●The beginning or end of an activity or period of time. (may seem confused now, but when the bell rings, she'll be ready to present her case)

belly jab: A straight jab to the abdomen.

below the belt: Below an imaginary line drawn across the body at the top of the hipbones. A punch delivered below this line is a foul, resulting in the loss of points, the round, or disqualification if repeated, depending upon the sanctioning body of the match. also *south of the border*. see *low blow*.

●●Unfair or cowardly. (tried to influence the vote with below the belt smear tactics)

belt: 1. To deliver a powerful punch. also *bang, bomb, connect, nail, slug, tag*. 2. see *championship belt*.

big: Particularly powerful. (ended the fight with a big right hand in the ninth round)

big bag: see *heavy bag*.

bleeder: A boxer who cuts easily.

bob and weave: To move the head and upper part of the body back and forth and up and down, becoming a moving target that is difficult to hit.

body punch: A punch delivered to the abdomen or ribs. Effective body punches tend to weaken an opponent and/or cause an opponent to lower his guard, leaving the chin unprotected.

body puncher: A boxer who specializes in body punches.

bolo, bolo punch: An uppercut that is delivered from a point below the hip with an exaggerated pendulum swing and the arm extended. The bolo punch was popularized by Boxing Hall of Fame member and World Middleweight Champion (1939, 1940) Ceferino Garcia, who compared its sweeping underhand delivery with the path of a bolo knife used to cut through the jungles of his native country, the Philippines. Cuban sensation Kid Gavilan, World Welterweight Champion in 1952, 1953, and 1954, also frequently made use of the bolo punch.

1. bomb: A powerful punch. also *haymaker, Sunday punch*.

2. bomb: To throw a bomb. see *belt*.

bomber: see *slugger*.

bout: A boxing match that consists of a specified number of three-minute rounds (usually three to fifteen) and ends in a decision by the referee and/or the judges, or by a knockout or technical knockout. also *fight, prizefight*.

box: 1. To engage in the sport of boxing. also *fight*. 2. To practice the skills of boxing, defensive as well as offensive, instead of just slugging.

boxer: 1. One who engages in the sport of boxing. also *fighter, gladiator, prizefighter, pug, pugilist*. 2. One who possesses the offensive and defensive skills of boxing as opposed to just being a slugger. (just a fair puncher, but a skillful boxer)

boxing: A sport in which two opponents fight each other with fists (covered with protective gloves) for a specified number of three-minute rounds (three to fifteen, with one-minute rest periods in between) inside a usually elevated "ring" (a square canvas-covered mat enclosed by ropes strung from posts in each corner). Boxers attempt to score points by hitting the opponent above the waist on the front or the sides of the body and the head with the knuckle part of the gloved hands. One referee in the ring presides over a boxing match making sure that all blows are fair, separating the boxers when they clinch, giving the count in case of a knockdown, and sometimes (depending on the sanctioning body and location of the match) assisting the judges in scoring the match. A boxing match can be won by a decision (the winner of a round being awarded a specified maximum number of points depending upon the sanctioning body and location of the match, and the loser a fewer number of points), by a technical knockout (when the referee stops a match because the opponent is injured or unable to continue), or by a knockout (when an opponent is unable to get up after being knocked down before a count of ten, measured by a timekeeper and given out loud by the referee). To insure fair competition, boxing matches are conducted in weight divisions, the parameters of which vary according to the sanctioning body. Some historians believe the term "boxing" came from the Greeks (some of the earliest practitioners of the sport) and their comparison of the clenched fist with a box (*pyxis*). Others attribute the origin to a priest in Siena, Italy, who was later canonized as St. Bernardine. Early in the thirteenth century, Bernardine is alleged to have taught his male parishoners to fight with their fists rather than deadly weapons, emphasizing special techniques to "box up" (block) an

BOLO PUNCH

opponent's punches with the hands and arms.

boxing gloves: Padded leather-covered mitts (having one section for the thumb and another for the four fingers) with laces on the inside of the wrist, worn to somewhat cushion the blows to an opponent, as well as to protect a boxer's hands. "Thumbless" gloves, which considerably lessen the chances for eye injuries, were introduced in 1981. British boxing pioneer Jack Broughton invented modern boxing gloves in the mid-1700s. For training and sparring, Broughton fitted padded leather gloves ("mufflers") on the hands of the young noblemen to whom he taught the science of pugilism. Eight-ounce gloves are now used in amateur bouts. In professional boxing, six, eight, and ten-ounce gloves are used, depending upon the sanctioning body, the weight division, and the location of the boxing match. also *gloves.*

breadbasket: The belly or abdomen.

1. break: To withdraw from a clinch when so ordered by a referee.

2. break: The withdrawal from a clinch when so ordered by a referee.

break clean: To separate from a clinch without throwing a punch. It is a foul to throw a punch after being ordered to break from a clinch, resulting in a loss of points or disqualification.

brittle chin: see *glass chin.*

bum: An unskilled or no longer skilled boxer. also *chump, ham, ham-and-egger, palooka, stiff, tomato can.*

bust up: A slang expression meaning to inflict or suffer cuts on the face during a boxing match. (got the decision, although he was all busted up)

busy fighter: A boxer who moves constantly and throws a lot of punches.

1. butt: To use the top of the head for striking an opponent. To butt an opponent intentionally is a foul that can result in a loss of points or disqualification.

2. butt: The act or an instance of butting an opponent. also *head butt.*

button: The point of the chin. In use since the 1920s. (took a straight right to the button)

●●The expression "on the button" means in the exact spot or at the exact moment in time. (called at seven o'clock on the button)

can't break an egg: Has no power in his punches; can't punch.

●●Has no power or strength. (looks big, but he can't break an egg)

can't lay a glove on: Unable to connect due to an opponent's boxing skill.

●●Unable to harm. (tried to discredit the witness, but couldn't lay a glove on him because his record was clean)

canvas: The floor of a boxing ring, a canvas covering stretched over a mat. (a left hook sent him to the canvas for the third time)

●●To "get up off the canvas" is to recover from a defeat or setback. (after his misfortune, he got up off the canvas to become a success)

canvasback: A fighter who gets knocked down or knocked out often.

card: see *fight card.*

carry: To hold back in order to make a weaker opponent look good. (carried him for a couple of rounds before taking him out in the third)

carry the fight: To dominate in a boxing match.

catcher: A boxer who takes a lot of punches during the course of a fight. also *punching bag.*

cauliflower ear: A deformity of the ear caused by repeated blows, and the resulting growth of excess scar tissue.

cement chin: The ability to take a punch on the chin without fear of a knockout. also *granite chin.* compare *brittle chin, china chin, glass chin, glass jaw, round heels.*

challenger: A boxer who fights a champion for the title.

champ: A champion. also *titleholder, titlist.*

●●The best, of superior quality. (when the chips were down, she came through like a champ)

championship: The title held by a champion; the highest accomplishment in boxing. also *crown, title.*

●●The highest level of any competition or endeavor. (will compete tomorrow in the pie-baking championship)

championship belt: The ornamental belt awarded to the champion of a weight division. also *belt.*

championship fight: A boxing match to decide a championship, as in a title defense. also *title fight.*

china chin: see *glass chin.*

chump: see *bum.*

class: see *weight division.*

clean break: The separation from a clinch

on the orders of the referee, with no illegal punches thrown by either fighter while disengaging.

clean up: To score with repeated unanswered blows against an opponent.

1. **clinch:** To hold an opponent with one or both arms so that no effective punches can be thrown, usually for the purpose of resting or for recovering after being hurt. When boxers clinch, the referee may order them to break or step back in order to keep the action going. also *tie up.*

2. **clinch:** The act or an instance of clinching.

close the distance: To maneuver closer to an opponent. also *cut the distance.*

clubber: Clubfighter.

clubfighter: 1. The product of a neighborhood boxing club, often noted for the ability to absorb punishment and keep punching. 2. A small-time boxer with modest skills. also *clubber.*

coldcock: To knock an opponent unconscious with a single blow. also *lower the boom.*

combination: Two or more different punches delivered quickly and in sequence, most often in a pattern planned and practiced before the fight. (floored by a left-right combination)

combination puncher: A boxer who throws punches in combinations.

connect: 1. To successfully hit an opponent; to land a punch. (has found the range and is beginning to connect with the jab) also *land.* 2. To land a particularly strong punch. (when the champ really connected, the challenger went down for the count) also *bang, belt, bomb, land, nail, slug, tag.*

●●To be particularly successful. (really connected with her last two songs)

contender: A boxer good enough to fight for the championship.

●●A prospect with sufficient qualities for success or the attainment of a particular goal or level of achievement. (definitely a contender for MVP)

cool: To knock out an opponent. see *knock out.*

cop a Sunday: To land a Sunday punch. (trying to cop a Sunday and knock him out)

corner: 1. Any of the four corners of a boxing ring. (had to fight his way out of the corner) 2. One of the two assigned corners (opposite each other) where the

boxers rest between rounds and are attended by seconds. (held on and looked to his corner for help)

●●To be "in one's corner" is to be for that person or on that person's side. (with most of the legislators in his corner, the Governor felt confident that his bill would pass)

cornerman: One of the seconds allowed inside the ring between rounds to attend to and advise the boxer.

count: 1. The calling off of the ten seconds allowed a boxer who has been knocked down. The ten seconds (timed by the timekeeper and called out by the referee) begin as soon as the boxer goes down and the opponent retires to a neutral corner. If the downed boxer is unable to get up before the count of ten, he is "counted out," and the opponent is declared the winner by a knockout. 2. The number of seconds counted against a downed boxer. (got up at the count of nine)

1. **counter:** To counterpunch. (countered with a left hook)

●●To respond to an action, argument, or proposal with an opposing action, argument, or proposal. (countered with her own list of complaints)

2. **counter:** A counterpunch. (knocked out by a right-hand counter)

●●An opposing response to an action, argument, or proposal. (silenced the critic with a witty counter)

1. **counterpunch:** To parry or block an opponent's lead and answer with a punch. (likes to counterpunch over a jab) also *counter.*

2. **counterpunch:** A punch that is a response to an opponent's lead. (never saw the counterpunch) also *counter.*

counterpuncher: A boxer with the ability to counterpunch, or one who prefers to counterpunch. (an effective counterpuncher)

count out: To complete an audible count of ten seconds before a downed boxer can get up, the result being a knockout. (went down three times before being counted out)

●●To be "counted out" is to be finished or defeated. (don't count her out yet, she's full of surprises) .

cover up: To abandon all offense and protect one's head and body as much as possible with the arms. (ran into a right hand near the end of the round and had to cover up until the bell sounded)

crazy bag: A double-end bag.

1. cross: A punch thrown over and across an opponent's lead. (dropped him with a right cross)

2. cross: To throw a cross. (crossed him to counter the jab)

crown: A championship. also *title*.

cruiserweight: 1. The 190 pound (maximum) weight division. Of the two major professional sanctioning bodies, only the WBC recognizes the cruiserweight division. 2. A boxer who fights in the cruiserweight division.

cutie: A clever boxer with deceptive moves.

cut man: The second who is responsible for stopping the bleeding of cuts a boxer may receive during a fight. Television boxing commentator Angelo Dundee, trainer and cornerman for nine world champions (among them three-time heavyweight champion Muhammad Ali and welterweight champion Sugar Ray Leonard) is regarded as one of the premier cut men in boxing.

cut off the ring: To move laterally in such a way as to limit the part of the ring an opponent can maneuver in. (the strategy will be to cut off the ring and keep the challenger in front of him)

cutter: A boxer whose punches spin and tend to open cuts on opponents.

cut the distance: see *close the distance*.

cut the tree: To throw body punches, or direct punches at the "trunk" of an opponent. also *go to the body*.

dance: To use footwork to maneuver and present a moving target to an opponent. (a cutie who will just dance and counterpunch until he sees an opening)

●●To stall, evade, or avoid. (just danced around the issue and never gave a straight answer)

dancer: 1. A fighter who uses footwork and movement as a strategic tactic. also *mover*. 2. A fighter who is not aggressive but fights defensively, always moving away.

●●An individual who is skilled at stalling, avoiding, or evading. (hard to pin down, a real dancer)

1. decision: The awarding of a win to a boxer on the basis of the number of points scored or rounds won in a match in which there is no knockout or technical knockout. A decision can be a unanimous decision (all three officials cast their votes for one boxer), a major-ity decision (two officials vote for one boxer and the third votes for a draw), or a split decision (two officials vote for one boxer and the third votes for his opponent).

●●A less than conclusive victory. (won the argument by a decision)

2. decision: To win a fight by a decision. (won the first fight by a knockout and decisioned him in the rematch)

deck: To knock an opponent down. (decked the challenger in the third round) also *drop, flatten, floor*.

distance: The total number of rounds scheduled for a boxing match if there is no knockout or technical knockout. see *go the distance*.

division: see *weight division*.

double-end bag: A small inflated leather punching bag suspended about head-height between ceiling and floor mounts with elastic cords. Used to improve a boxer's timing and accuracy. also *crazy bag*. compare *heavy bag, speed bag*.

double up: To throw two consecutive punches with the same hand or with alternate hands. (found he could double up on the jab after the first round)

down: 1. Touching the canvas with any part of the body except the feet (or outside the ropes) and subject to the ten second count. 2. Knocked down. (down twice in the eighth round but came back to score a knockout in the ninth)

down and out: Knocked out, unable to rise before the count of ten. also *down for the count*.

●●Poor, desolate, in a hopeless or miserable state. (down and out, and living on charity) To be "down but not out" means to be in a bad state, but not defeated. (we were down but not out, and eventually came back to win the game)

down for the count: Knocked out, unable to rise before the count of ten. (finally went down for the count in the seventh round)

●●Defeated, finished, dying, or dead. (finally went down for the count after a long illness)

downstairs: The abdomen and/or ribs or to the abdomen and/or ribs. (can't take a good punch downstairs) compare *upstairs*.

1. draw: A boxing match that ends in a tie.

2. draw: To gain a tie in a boxing match.

dreadnought: A boxer in the heavyweight division. also *heavy, heavyweight.*

drop: To knock an opponent down. (dropped him in the fourth round) also *deck, flatten, floor.*

drop one's guard: To lower the hand that guards one's chin (right hand for a right-handed boxer, left hand for a left-handed boxer), leaving it unprotected. (got nailed with a left hook when he dropped his guard)

••To relax, leaving oneself unprotected. (presiding judge dropped her guard long enough to reveal a wry sense of humor)

dukes: The fists. Short for "Duke of Yorks," the original Cockney rhyming slang for "forks," which stood for fingers or hands, and later, fists.

••To "put up one's dukes" means to raise the hands or fists to prepare for a fight. To "duke it out" means to fight.

elimination bout, elimination match: One of a series of matches in which winners advance and are matched against each other until a champion emerges.

Enswell: A smooth, slightly convex stainless steel rectangular device (approximately 2 inches by 1 inch, by 1/4 inch thick) with a small flat-ironlike handle, designed specifically to remove swelling from the area under a fighter's eyes. Developed by sports physician and New Jersey State Boxing Commission member Dr. Michael Sabin, the Enswell is kept on ice, then applied with pressure directly against the swollen area between rounds and drawn sideways toward the ear. First tried on middleweight Bobby Czyz by veteran handler Ace Marotta, the device proved to be a convenient and effective replacement for the ice bags and cold fifty-cent pieces previously used. The Enswell received national attention in welterweight champion Sugar Ray Leonard's celebrated 1981 victory over Thomas Hearns, when handlers Angelo Dundee (Leonard) and Emanuel Stewart (Hearns) used the device on their fighters.

even: Tied, no winner. (finally took charge in the third after two even rounds)

1. **exchange:** To trade punches with an opponent. (got the worst of it when they exchanged right hands)

2. **exchange:** Two or more punches traded between opponents. (both fighters scored in the exchange)

face fighter: A boxer who is willing to take punches to the head in order to score his own punches; one who "leads with his face."

fan: An enthusiast or devotee. Though the word "fanatic" was abbreviated and used similarly as early as the 1600s, "fan" was applied to sports independantly, early in the nineteenth century. At that time in London, bareknuckle prize fighting was popular among the gentry, who could be seen dressed up and parading through the streets in their carriages on the way to matches. They were called the "fancy," corrupted to the "fance," then shortened to "fans," from whence came the singular "fan."

featherweight: The 126 pound weight division (125 pounds in amateur boxing). 2. A boxer who fights in the featherweight division. In the late 1800s, a number of boxers laid claim to the championship of the featherweight division (originally 118 pounds, then 122, and finally 126 pounds). New Zealander "Torpedo" Billy Murphy (1890) and Australian Young Griffo (1890, 1891) are both now recognized as worthy early claimants, but when American featherweight titleholder George "Little Chocolate" Dixon knocked out English featherweight champion Abe Willis on July 28, 1891, he became the accepted World Featherweight Champion. Elected to the Boxing Hall of Fame in 1956, Dixon had already become the first black world champion when he claimed the bantamweight title in 1890.

1. **feint:** To quickly move the head, hand, or body in such a way as to momentarily deceive an opponent. A boxer often feints with one hand, then throws a punch with the other.

2. **feint:** A quick movement of the head, hand, or body in order to momentarily deceive an opponent.

1. **fight:** To take part in a boxing match. also *box.*

2. **fight:** A boxing match. also *bout, prizefight.*

fight card: A program of boxing matches. also *card.*

fighter: A boxer. see *boxer.*

finish: To follow up when an advantage is gained and the opponent is stunned or hurt in order to end a match by a knockout.

fistic: Having to do with boxing. (a fistic attraction)

five point must system: A method of scoring a bout in which the winner of a round is awarded five points, and the loser a fewer number (usually the difference is less than one point). In the case of an even round, both boxers are awarded five points. compare *five point system*.

five point system: A method of scoring a bout in which the winner of a round is awarded from one to five points, and the loser a number fewer than those awarded to the winner (usually the difference is less than one point). In the case of an even round, neither boxer is awarded points. compare *five point must system*.

flatten: 1. To knock an opponent down. also *deck, drop, floor.* 2. To knock out an opponent. see *knock out.*

float: To evade an opponent's punches by a combination of footwork and movement of the head and body. Popularized by three-time Heavyweight Champion Muhammad Ali, who fulfilled his friend and cornerman Drew Bundini Brown's prediction that Ali (then Cassius Clay) would "float like a butterfly and sting like a bee" in his 1964 title fight with Sonny Liston. Ali won by a knockout when Liston failed to answer the bell for the seventh round.

floor: To knock down an opponent. also *deck, drop, flatten.*
●●Overwhelm, or surprise. (floored by the warm welcome she got)

flyweight: 1. The 112 pound (maximum) weight division. 2. A boxer who fights in the flyweight division. The flyweight class was created in England in 1910 at 108 pounds, with America following suit in the same year. At that weight (later raised to 112 pounds), Welshman Jimmy Wilde became the first generally accepted World Flyweight Champion in December of 1916 when he knocked out American flyweight Young Zulu Kid in eleven rounds. Wilde was elected to the Boxing Hall of Fame in 1959.

footwork: The movement of the feet in the boxing stance, not only to maneuver in relation to an opponent but to insure maximum balance and leverage for the punches thrown.
●●The term "fancy footwork" can be applied to dancing, or to a quick movement of the feet to recover balance or avoid a collision (some fancy footwork saved him from a terrible fall), or to take "steps" to stall, avoid, or evade. (had to do some fancy footwork to avoid giving away the surprise)

1. foul: An illegal blow or action that generally results in a warning first, followed by a loss of points or disqualification if repeated. This can be a blow below the belt, in back of the head or neck, during a break from a clinch, while an opponent is down or outside the ring, or one delivered with any part of the glove other than that which covers the knuckles, wrestling or butting with the head.

2. foul: To commit a foul. (ahead on points until he fouled twice in the tenth round)

get off: To properly execute one's punches. (tight for the first few rounds and couldn't get off)

gladiator: A boxer. see *boxer.*

glass chin, glass jaw: Easily knocked out. also *brittle chin, china chin, round heels.* compare *cement chin, granite chin.*

gloves: see *boxing gloves.*
●●To "put on the gloves" is to literally or figuratively fight. (seemed ready to put on the gloves if the bill was vetoed) To "hang up the gloves" is to retire. (after forty years with the company, he decided it was time to hang up the gloves)

go into the tank: To intentionally lose a fight. also *swoon, take a dive, throw a fight.*

Golden Gloves: A program of amateur elimination tournaments that take place in many larger United States cities, culminating in an annual Golden Gloves National Championship Tournament in which national titles are awarded in the various weight divisions. In 1926, Arch Ward, sports editor for the Chicago Tribune, got his newspaper to sponsor the first Golden Gloves tournament. A year later, at the urging of sports editor Paul Gallico, the New York Daily News sponsored its own Golden Gloves tournament in New York. In response to a challenge from Gallico, winners from the two cities' tournaments met on March 4, 1928, in Chicago Stadium for the first Golden Gloves Inter-City Championship Tournament. Two youngsters who fought in that first tournament went on to become professional titleholders, Bob Olin, World Light Heavyweight Champion in 1934 and 1935, and National Boxing Association Middleweight Champion (in 1938 and 1939) Solly Krieger. Among other world champions who fought in Golden Gloves tournaments were Barney Ross, Joe Louis, Tony Zale, Sugar Ray Robinson, Rocky Marciano, and Muhammad Ali.

go the distance: 1. To last or be able to last or complete all of the rounds scheduled for a particular bout before tiring or before losing on a knockout or technical knockout. (in good enough shape to go the distance) 2. To last the scheduled amount of rounds without a knockout or technical knockout. (don't expect the fight to go the distance)
●●To last, or go all the way. (finished medical school, surprising all those who thought he'd never go the distance)

go to the body: To punch to the abdomen and ribs of an opponent, or throw body punches. also *cut the tree.*

1. gouge: see *thumb.*

2. gouge: The act or an instance of thumbing an opponent. see *thumb.*

granite chin: see *cement chin.*

guard: The hand held high and close to the head to protect the chin (right hand for right-handed boxers, left hand for left-handed boxers). see *drop one's guard.*

gumshield: see *mouthpiece.*

gym fighter: A boxer who looks good in training but fails in a real bout.

ham: see *bum.*

ham-and-egger: see *bum.*

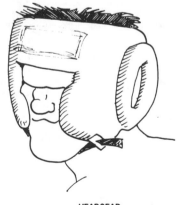

HEADGEAR

handle: To train and act as a second for a boxer.

handler: Someone who trains and acts as a second for a boxer. (his handlers have taught him to pace himself in the early rounds)

hand speed: The speed with which a boxer can throw punches, parry, and block.

hang on: To clinch or tie up an opponent, especially when tired or hurt, or to last until the end of a round.
●●To keep trying; to refuse to give up or give in. (hung on somehow until help arrived)

hard to find: Difficult to hit. Adept at slipping punches and movement. (has good footwork and he's hard to find)

haymaker: A powerful punch, or crushing blow. (landed a haymaker that ended the fight) also *bomb, Sunday punch.*
●●A devastating "blow." (the news of his wrecked car came as a haymaker)
●●An individual's or entertainment event's best song, joke, piece, or performance. (closed the show with a haymaker that brought the crowd to its feet)

head butt: see *butt.*

head feint: A quick movement of the head in order to momentarily confuse or deceive an opponent. (gives a little head feint before he throws the right)

headgear, headguard: A padded protective covering for a boxer's head, worn while sparring and in some amateur bouts. Headgear padding protects the forehead, temples, ears, and cheeks.

headhunter: A boxer who punches mainly to the head and rarely throws a body punch.

heavy: A heavyweight. also *dreadnought.*
●●Important (a Congressional heavy) or meaningful. (made a heavy point)

heavy artillery: Powerful punches. (an even fight until the eighth round when the champ started throwing his heavy artillery)

heavy bag: A large stuffed canvas or leather bag (approximately 3 feet high and 1 to 1-1/2 feet in diameter), suspended about 3 feet off the ground for the purpose of hitting. A boxer uses a heavy bag to develop power and strength. also *big bag.* compare *double-end bag, speed bag.*

heavy hitter: see *slugger.*

heavyweight: 1. The weight division for boxers over 175 pounds (between 179 and 200 pounds for amateur bouts). also *dreadnought*. 2. A boxer who fights in the heavyweight division. The first ever heavyweight champion (under London Prize Ring Rules) was English bareknuckler James Figg, who held the crown from 1719 to 1734. Figg was elected to the Boxing Hall of Fame in 1954. The first modern heavyweight champion (under Marquis of Queensberry Rules) was John L. Sullivan, who won the title in 1885 and held it until he was knocked out in the twenty-first round by James J. Corbett in 1892. Sullivan was elected to the Boxing Hall of Fame in 1954. also *dreadnought, heavy*.

●●Particularly important (a heavyweight in the corporation) or meaningful. (we were all affected by the heavyweight message in the lyric)

1. heel: To shove an opponent or deliver a blow with the part of a glove that covers the heel of the hand. A foul that can result in the loss of points or disqualification. (heeled him as they clinched)

2. heel: The act or an instance of heeling an opponent.

hit on the break: To illegally punch an opponent while in the process of breaking from a clinch as ordered by the referee. A foul that can result in the loss of points or disqualification.

1. hook: A usually short circular blow by the lead hand (left hand for a right-handed boxer, right hand for a left-handed boxer), delivered with the elbow bent and rigid. The hook can be a powerful punch and is used to attack both the body and the head. (hurts him with a hook to the body)

2. hook: To throw or deliver a hook. (hooks twice to the body, then throws an overhand right)

hook off a jab: To immediately follow a jab with a hook, circling the hand into the hook instead of pulling it back after the jab.

hungry: Desperately in need of or desirous of a win. The expression originally applied only to monetarily poor boxers who needed to win in order to eat, but now includes any boxer who has yet to attain success, recognition, or a desperately wanted goal, such as a championship. (no longer trains like a hungry fighter since he won the championship)

●●Desirous, desperately wanting or needing. (artists and athletes alike are told to "stay hungry")

ice: To knock out an opponent. (iced him in the seventh) see *knock out*.

in and out: A maneuver in which a boxer moves close to an opponent in order to deliver one or more blows, then quickly away to avoid being hit. (moved in and out with a beautiful combination to the head)

infighter: A boxer who moves inside and fights at close quarters. (a punishing infighter)

●●A figuratively tough individual, willing and able to take care of oneself in personal/political conflicts. (an adept infighter who quickly rose to a leadership position)

infighting: Fighting inside, close to the opponent.

●●The personal/political struggles between members of a group. (finally left the company, a victim of vicious infighting)

inside: At close quarters with an opponent. (not a pretty boxer, but dangerous inside)

in the bag: Fixed, the outcome decided before the match takes place.

●●A virtual certainty, a sure thing (though not necessarily because of a fix). (with three minutes to go in the final quarter and a three-touchdown lead, he knew the game was in the bag)

in the tank: Throwing a fight, taking a dive. (lost his boxing license when it

HEAVY BAG

was discovered he'd gone in the tank)

in trouble: Stunned and hurt by blows, ready to be knocked down or out. see *on queer street.*

1. **jab:** A rapid and direct punch (often aimed at the opponent's head) made by suddenly extending the arm of the lead hand (left hand for right-handed boxers, right hand for left-handed boxers). Though not always the most powerful punch, a jab can be used to bother or keep an opponent off balance and as a lead punch for another blow or a combination. (likes to hook off the jab)

2. **jab:** To throw a jab. (jabs twice, then crosses with the right) also *shoot the jab, stick.*

jab bag: A stuffed teardrop-shaped leather punching bag, suspended at head height similar to a speed bag, for the purpose of practicing a jab. Used less frequently than the speed bag, double-end bag, and heavy bag.

junior bantamweight: 1. The 115 pound (maximum) weight division. also *super flyweight.* 2. A boxer who fights in the junior bantamweight division. also *super flyweight.*

junior featherweight: 1. The 122 pound (maximum) weight division. also *super bantamweight.* 2. A boxer who fights in the junior featherweight division. also *super bantamweight.*

junior flyweight: 1. The WBA 108 pound (maximum) weight division. also *light flyweight* (WBC). 2. A boxer who fights in the junior flyweight division. also *light flyweight* (WBC).

junior lightweight: 1. The WBA 130 pound weight division (132 pounds in amateur boxing). also *super featherweight* (WBC). 2. A boxer who fights in the junior lightweight division. Artie O'Leary (real name Arthur Lieberman) was the first to claim the title in the junior lightweight division, from 1917 through 1919, but the first generally accepted junior lightweight champion was Italian born Johnny Dundee (real name Joseph Corrara), who won the title in 1921 and held it until 1923. Dundee was elected to the Boxing Hall of Fame in 1957. also *super featherweight* (WBC).

junior middleweight: 1. The WBA 154 pound weight division (156 pounds in amateur boxing). also *super welterweight* (WBC). 2. A boxer who fights in the junior middleweight divi-

sion. The first champion in the junior middleweight class was Dennis Moyer, who held the title in 1962 and 1963. also *super welterweight* (WBC).

junior welterweight: 1. The WBA 140 pound (maximum) weight division. also *super lightweight* (WBC). 2. A boxer who fights in the junior welterweight division. Myron "Pinkey" Mitchell became the first junior welterweight champion in 1922, holding the title until 1926. also *super lightweight* (WBC).

1. **kayo:** To knock out an opponent. see *knock out.*

●●To literally or figuratively knock out, or defeat decisively. (kayoed the opposition with a brilliant proposal)

2. **kayo:** A knockout. see *knockout.*

kidney punch: An illegal blow to the kidneys. A foul that can result in the loss of points or disqualification.

killer instinct: The ability to follow up an advantage, to finish or knock out a stunned or weakened opponent.

kill the body, the head will die: A favorite boxing axiom attesting to the sure result (a knockout) of an effective body attack. First associated with black heavyweight Sam Langford who, in 1906, lost in fifteen rounds to then Negro Heavyweight Champion Jack Johnson, two years before he became World Heavyweight Champion.

kiss the canvas: To be knocked down. (kissed the canvas twice in the sixth round before being knocked out)

knock down: To punch an opponent and cause him to fall to the floor. also *deck, drop, flatten, floor.*

knockdown: The act or an instance of one of the contestants in a bout being knocked down. When a knockdown occurs, a ten second count (timed by the timekeeper and called out by the referee) begins as soon as the standing opponent retires to a neutral corner. If the downed boxer is unable to get up before the count of ten, he is "counted out," and the opponent is declared the winner by a knockout.

knock out: 1. To knock an opponent unconscious. 2. To win a boxing match by a knockout. also *cool, flatten, ice, kayo, KO, put away, put out the lights, starch, stop, stretch, take out.*

●●To be figuratively "knocked out" is to be overwhelmed. (knocked out by the view from the edge of the canyon)

knockout: 1. The act of knocking out an opponent. 2. The termination of a bout when one boxer is knocked unconscious or is knocked down or out of the ring and is unable to resume fighting before the ten-second count has elapsed. also *kayo, KO.* compare *technical knockout.*

●●"Stunningly" attractive (she's an absolute knockout) or good (a knockout finish for the third act).

●●A "knockout blow" describes a decisive or defeating action. (another touchdown in the fourth quarter, which proved to be the knockout blow)

1. KO: To knock out an opponent. see *knock out.*

●●To literally or figuratively knock out, or decisively defeat. (enough votes to KO the motion)

2. KO: A knockout. see *knockout.* compare *TKO.*

lace: To illegally rub the laces of a boxing glove against the opponent's face or head. A foul that can result in the loss of points or disqualification. (laced him and opened up a cut above the eye)

laces: The string or cord used to fasten boxing gloves, located on the inside of the wrist.

land: 1. To successfully hit an opponent; to connect with a punch. (beginning to land the hook) also *connect.* 2. To connect with a particularly strong punch. (really landed that time, and the challenger is hurt) also *bang, belt, bomb, connect, nail, slug, tag.*

lay a glove on: To land or be able to land a punch. (couldn't lay a glove on him for the first three rounds)

●●To literally or figuratively touch, or effect. (in spite of all the money spent and the smear tactics employed, the special interest group couldn't lay a glove on the veteran senator)

1. lead: To start a combination or series of punches, usually used in reference to starting with a particular punch or hand. Most often, a right-handed boxer will lead with a left jab.

●●To "lead with one's chin" is to leave oneself completely unprotected or vulnerable, to invite disaster. (the thief was leading with his chin when he challenged the priest's honesty)

2. lead: 1. The first in a series of punches. 2. The jab or jabbing hand. (occasionally changes to a right-hand lead to confuse his opponent)

left: A punch with the left hand. (lands with two lefts, then throws a right cross)

light flyweight: 1. The WBC 108 pound (maximum) weight division. also *junior flyweight* (WBA). 2. A boxer who fights in the light flyweight division. also *junior flyweight* (WBA).

light heavyweight: 1. The 175 pound weight division (178 pounds in amateur boxing). 2. A boxer who fights in the light heavyweight division. Chicago newsman and boxing promoter Lou Houseman urged the formation of the light heavyweight class just after the turn of the century. A boxer he managed, Jack Root, who could no longer make the weight for the middleweight division but was too light to be a heavyweight, became the first light heavyweight champion in 1903. Root was elected to the Boxing Hall of Fame in 1961.

lightweight: 1. The 135 pound weight division (139 pounds in amateur boxing). 2. A boxer who fights in the lightweight division. Though John Moneghan, an Irishman from Liverpool, England claimed the lightweight title (bare-knuckle rules) as early as 1855, the first recognized World Lightweight Champion (Marquis of Queensberry Rules) was George "Kid" Lavigne, who won the title by knocking out Dick Burge in London, England in seventeen rounds. Lavigne was elected to the Boxing Hall of Fame in 1959.

●●Small-time, not important. (paid no attention to what he said, because he was a real lightweight)

load up: To make sure all one's power is behind a punch. (loading up and throwing bombs)

long count: A count that takes more than the prescribed ten seconds. The most famous long count incident took place

LEFT JAB

93

in the second Jack Dempsey-Tunney World Heavyweight Championship fight in Chicago in 1927. Tunney survived what many have alleged to be a long count in the seventh round to come back and win a unanimous decision in ten rounds and retain the heavyweight title. Jack Dempsey was elected to the Boxing Hall of Fame in 1954 and Gene Tunney, in 1955.

low blow: A blow delivered below the belt of the opponent, or below an imaginary line drawn across the body at the hipbones. A low blow is a foul for which the boxer may be warned, lose points, lose the round, or be disqualified.

●●An unfair or cowardly act. (spreading the lie about his opponent was a low blow)

lower the boom: To knock an opponent unconscious, especially with a single blow. (the challenger dropped when the champ lowered the boom in the fourth round) also *coldcock.*

main event: The most important bout on a fight card, the principal attraction.

●●The principal or most important. (a seven-course gourmet dinner on the last night of the holiday weekend was definitely the main event)

majority decision: A decision in which two of the three officials vote for one boxer and the third votes for a draw. compare *split decision, unanimous decision.*

make him pay: A popular boxing exhortation that urges a fighter to take advantage of a mistake or mistakes made by an opponent.

make the weight: To be able to be within the weight parameters of a particular division at the time of the official weigh-in for a fight (usually by reducing from a higher weight). (called off the bout when the challenger couldn't make the weight)

mandatory eight count: A rule that states that in the case of a knockdown, the count must reach eight before the fight can begin again, whether or not the downed boxer has already reached his feet. The mandatory eight count is a safety measure to protect boxers and is in force in most bouts.

Marquis of Queensberry Rules: The basic rules under which boxing has been conducted since they began to be gener-

ally accepted in 1885, when John L. Sullivan, the Bareknuckle World Heavyweight Champion, defeated Dominick McCaffrey in six rounds to become the first World Heavyweight Champion under Queensberry Rules. There were few rules for the earliest pugilistic contests in seventeenth and eighteenth century England. These were free-for-alls in which contestants kicked, butted, wrestled, gouged, and bit each other with no rest periods until one contestant could not go on. Fists became predominant only when the legendary fighter and boxing pioneer, Boxing Hall of Famer James Figg, demonstrated what a formidable weapon they could be in the early 1700s in London. In 1743, another Boxing Hall of Fame member, Jack Broughton (called the "Father of Boxing") framed the first set of rules to civilize prize fighting. These formed the basis for the London Prize Ring Rules, which were formally adopted in 1838 to govern bareknuckle fighting. The London Prize Ring Rules called for a 24-foot square ring, the end of a round when either fighter was downed, and a 30-second rest period at the end of each round (if a fighter was not ready to resume the contest in thirty seconds, he was declared the loser). The rules forbade grappling, low blows, butting, kicking, and biting. In the mid-1860s, John Sholto Douglas, the ninth Marquis of Queensberry, sponsored a set of boxing rules framed by John Graham Chambers, which eventually came to be accepted as the basic rules of modern boxing. The Queensberry Rules outlawed wrestling or clinching and called for a 20-foot square ring, three-minute rounds with a one-minute rest interval, padded gloves for the fists of the boxers, a ten-second count for a downed boxer, and the withdrawal of the standing boxer to a neutral corner during the count.

measure: To leave the lead hand propped against a stunned opponent to use as a "guide" for a big punch. (got the challenger in trouble and is just measuring and bombing at will)

mechanic: A boxer with good technical skills.

middleweight: 1. The 160 pound weight division (165 pounds in amateur boxing).

2. A boxer who fights in the middleweight division. Irishman Jack "The Nonpareil" Dempsey (not to be confused with heavyweight Jack Dempsey) became the first World Middleweight Champion in 1884 when he knocked out George Fulljames in twenty-two rounds. Dempsey was elected to the Boxing Hall of Fame in 1954.

mini flyweight: The 106 pound (maximum) weight division in amateur boxing. **2.** A boxer who fights in the mini flyweight division.

mix it up: 1. To fight, or exchange blows. (felt each other out in the first two rounds but began to mix it up in the third) also *trade, trade punches*. **2.** An exhortation advising a boxer to throw a combination, or a series of different kinds of punches.
●●To fight. (shoved each other after the whistle, but the linesman skated between them before they could drop their gloves and mix it up)

mouse: A swelling and discoloration around the eye, the result of a blow. (a left hook, which raised a pretty good mouse under the challenger's eye)
●●A black eye, or swelling around the eye from a collision or blow. (suffered only a mouse under one eye from the fall)

mouthpiece: A rubberized protector worn inside the mouth to protect the teeth and lips of a boxer. Invented in the early 1900s by London dentist Jack Marks. Popularized (after considerable resistance) in 1913 by British fighter, two-time Welterweight Champion Ted "Kid" Lewis, who introduced the device in the United States on November 19, 1914, at Madison Square Garden, when he fought a ten round no-decision bout against Phil Bloom. Lewis was elected to the Boxing Hall of Fame in 1964. also *gumshield*.

mover: see *dancer*.

nail: To deliver a powerful punch. (got nailed with a haymaker and went down for the count) also *bang, belt, bomb, slug, tag*.

neutral corner: Either of the two corners not assigned to a boxer that face each other diagonally across the ring. After a knockdown, the standing boxer must retire to a neutral corner for the duration of the ten-second count.

no contest: The termination of an inconclusive boxing match by the referee before the scheduled number of rounds is completed, due to a lack of action, disqualifications, or uncontrollable circumstances (such as a sudden downpour, a structural failure of the ring or other equipment, etc.).

no decision: A boxing match in which the scheduled number of rounds is completed, but no official decision is reached. A rare occurence in modern boxing, a no decision ruling can result from the invalidation of a bout's scoring by the sanctioning body under whose authority the match is made. In the early 1900s, many bouts that were not ended by a knockout were called "no decision" because of rules in various states and countries that forbade the rendering of a decision in a prize fight. In such cases, boxing writers would often later declare a winner, but officially the fight was ruled "no decision."

no foul rule: A rule that prohibits the automatic awarding of a bout to the victim of a low blow. Before the no foul rule, many fights were won and lost on fouls. It was not uncommon for a fighter who knew he was overmatched to intentionally hit his opponent with a low blow and lose on a foul. Since all bets were off in such a situation, a fighter could not only save himself discomfort and a more serious blemish on his record, but could save some money for himself and his backers as well. A fed-up ringside telegraph operator for the newspapers, Stan Taylor, finally did something about the problem. Taylor invented a device that would come to be known as a "protective cup," now mandatory equipment for all boxers. So effective was his invention (he actually wore it to the fights and had people kick him and hit him below the belt to demonstrate its worth), that Commissioner James J. Farley of the New York State Athletic Commission amended the boxing regulations in 1930 with the no foul rule.

no knockdown: A judgment and declaration by the referee that an instance of a boxer dropping to the canvas was due to a slip or a push and is not to be scored a knockdown.

on a bicycle, on one's bicycle: Using footwork to stay away from an opponent. (been on his bicycle since he got tagged in the second round)

one-hand fighter: A boxer who can or does punch with one hand only, rarely using the other.

one-two: A two-punch combination, consisting of a short left jab followed immediately by a hard right cross, usually to the jaw of an opponent. Left-handed boxers use a right jab followed by a left cross. (connects with a good one-two)

••A two-step or two-phase action or program. (a good one-two combination of sales and service)

on one's toes: Dancing, moving. In order to move quickly and maneuver properly, a fighter must be up on his toes, rather than flat-footed. (fresh, up on his toes, and moving as though it were the first round)

••To "stay on one's toes" means to stay alert, ready to act or react quickly. (had to stay on her toes backstage, or she would have missed her cue)

on queer street: Stunned and hurt by blows, ready to be knocked down or out. (caught with a big right hand, and all of a sudden, the champion was on queer street) also *in trouble, on the ropes, out on one's feet, ready to go, walking on one's heels.*

••Dazed, confused, not in possession of one's senses. (was on queer street for about an hour after the accident)

on the button: Directly on the chin. (took a left hook on the button)

••Exact, precisely correct. (her directions were right on the button)

on the ropes: Leaning helplessly against the ropes, stunned and hurt by blows, ready to be knocked down or out. see *on queer street.*

••Close to ruin or failure. (the company is on the ropes because of years of mismanagement)

open hook: A hook that is thrown alone, rather than following a jab or in a series. (went down when he walked into an open hook)

open up: To throw a number of punches with little or no thought of defense. (began to open up in the second round)

out: Knocked out, unconscious. (out before he hit the floor)

••Unconscious, asleep. (so tired he was out just after dinner)

out on one's feet: Stunned, almost unconscious, ready to be knocked down or out. see *on queer street.*

••Dazed, sleepy, barely conscious. (hadn't slept for two days and was out on his feet)

outpoint: To win a boxing match by a decision. (got outpointed in the rematch)

over and under: A punch to the head followed by a body punch, often both hooks.

overhand punch: A punch made with the fist brought forward and down from above shoulder level, such as a straight right or cross (or left for a left-handed boxer).

paint job: An instance of scoring repeated blows against an opponent, "covering" an opponent with blows. (did a paint job on the challenger after stunning him with a big right hand)

palooka: An unskilled, or sometimes no longer skilled boxer. Coined in the 1920s by journalist Jack Conway. see *bum.*

••A lout or lummox. (two big palookas blocking the doorway)

peanut bag: A small speed bag, 4 to 5 inches in diameter. Because of its size and quick bounce, the peanut bag is difficult to hit, and is used to develop hand speed and timing.

peek-a-boo: A relatively unorthodox boxing stance, in which both hands are held high to protect the front and sides of the face. The name comes from the appearance of "peeking" over the boxing gloves. Boxing Hall of Famer Floyd Patterson, World Heavyweight Champion in 1956, 1957, 1958, 1959, 1960 (after losing in 1959, then becoming the first man ever to regain the Heavyweight Title), 1961, and 1962, popularized the peek-a-boo defense.

pepper: see *beat a tattoo.*

pick off: To block an opponent's punch. (seems to be able to pick off the left jab)

preliminary bout: An opening bout before the main event that most often involves boxers of less skill and experience.

prizefight: 1. A professional boxing match. 2. A boxing match. also *bout, fight.*

prizefighter: 1. A professional boxer. 2. A boxer. also *fighter, gladiator, pug, pugilist.*

prize ring: A boxing ring. also *square circle.*

pug: A boxer. Short for pugilist.

pugilism: The art of boxing. From the Latin words *pugunus* (fist) and *pugil* (boxer).

pugilist: A boxer. also *fighter, gladiator, prizefighter, pug.*

pull a punch: To punch with less than full strength; to hold back.

●●To hold back. (up before a tough judge who pulls no punches)

pumper: A bad cut that bleeds profusely.

1. punch: To strike a blow or blows with the fist or fists. also *stick, throw a punch, throw leather.*

2. punch: A blow with the fist. also *shot.*

●●Vitality, force. (a thought-provoking editorial with a lot of punch)

punch-drunk: Suffering the long term effects of repeated blows to the head, slow in movement and speech. also *punchy.*

●●Dazed, or confused. (still punch-drunk from sitting next to the speaker at the rock concert)

punched out: Arm weary, exhausted from throwing punches.

punching bag: 1. One of several kinds of suspended stuffed or inflated bags used for training in boxing. see *heavy bag, double-end bag, speed bag.* 2. see *catcher.*

punchy: Punch-drunk.

●●Dazed, groggy. (punchy from lack of sleep)

put away: To knock out an opponent. (finally put him away in the eleventh round) see *knock out.*

●●To destroy or defeat (put him away with three straight service aces) or to captivate, delight, or spellbind. (her closing number put me away)

put out the lights: To knock out an opponent. see *knock out.*

quick count: An unfair count that takes less than the allotted ten seconds.

rabbit punch: An illegal clubbing blow to the back of the neck. A foul that results in the loss of points or disqualification.

reach: A measurement of the arm fully extended. A boxer must sometimes alter his strategy due to a reach advantage held by himself or his opponent.

ready to go: Stunned and hurt by blows, ready to be knocked down or out. see *on queer street.*

ref: Short for referee.

referee: The official in the ring who presides over a boxing match. A referee makes judgments about rules infractions and fouls, issues warnings and removes points when he or she deems it necessary, separates the boxers when they clinch, gives the count when a boxer is knocked down, and has the authority to stop the bout if a boxer is injured or unable to continue. Referees also sometimes assist the judges in scoring the bout, depending on the sanctioning body and location of the match. also *ref, third man in the ring.*

rematch: A bout in which two boxers who have fought each other previously meet again. In most cases, a clause in the contract for a championship fight guarantees the champion a rematch should he lose the title.

right: A punch with the right hand. (decked by a straight right)

right lead: 1. A straight right or right cross that is not preceded by a jab or combination. A surprise, and somewhat risky, maneuver. 2. A right jab for a left-handed boxer.

ring: A usually elevated 18 to 20-foot-square area surrounded by three (and sometimes four) 1 to 2-inch cloth-wrapped ropes attached to padded turnbuckles on the posts in each corner, and in which a boxing match is conducted. The ring floor, a canvas-covered rubber or felt mat, usually extends an additional 2 feet outside the ropes on all four sides of the ring. also *prize ring, square circle.*

●●To "toss one's hat into the ring" is to enter into a competition.

Ring Magazine: see *The Ring.*

ring post: One of the four posts at the corners of a boxing ring, to which the ropes are attached that surround the ring.

ring rust: The inability to time punches or maneuver properly due to an absence from the ring. (showed some ring rust in his first comeback fight)

ring savvy: Knowledge and understanding of the techniques and tricks used in a boxing ring. (up against a veteran with a lot of ring savvy)

ringside: Next to or close to the ring. (saw it all from ringside seats)

●●A good or close vantage point. (ringside seats for the whole performance)

roadwork: The part of a boxer's training program that involves long-distance running, often on public roads.

●●Long-distance running as part of an athlete's training.

roll with a punch: To move the head or body in the same direction of an opponent's blow in order to diminish its effect. (would have been a sure knock-out if he hadn't rolled with the punch)

●●To take a setback in stride; to be resilient. (can survive corporation politics because he knows how to roll with a punch)

rope: One of the three (or four) parallel ropes surrounding a boxing ring, attached by means of padded turnbuckles to the four posts at the corners of the ring. The ropes are strung at 2, 3, and 4-foot heights measured from the floor of the ring (international amateur boxing requires 40, 80, and 130 centimeters). Four ropes, when used, are strung 18, 30, 42, and 54 inches high.

rope-a-dope: An unorthodox strategy devised by three-time World Heavyweight Champion Muhammad Ali in which a boxer leans back against the ropes in a defensive shell, in the hopes that an opponent will tire himself out by throwing punches that can be blocked with the arms. Ali named the technique after using it in his successful bid to regain the heavyweight title from then champion George Foreman in 1974,

knocking out Foreman in the eighth round.

round: The three-minute periods into which a bout is divided (two minutes in some amateur competitions), with a one-minute rest period after each round. The idea of a time-limited round was first introduced in the Marquis of Queensberry Rules in 1865. In bareknuckle contests prior to that time, a round had ended only when one of the combatants slipped to or was knocked or pushed to the ground. One fight under such rules, between Mike Madden and Bill Hays in England in 1849, was contested for 185 rounds over a period of six hours and three minutes. The longest fight under Marquis of Queensberry Rules was in 1893 between Andy Bowen and Jack Burke, who both were unable to continue after fighting 110 three-minute rounds, taking a total of seven hours and nineteen minutes. The match was called "no contest." also *stanza.*

rounder: A bout lasting a specific number of rounds. (decisioned him in a grueling fourteen-rounder)

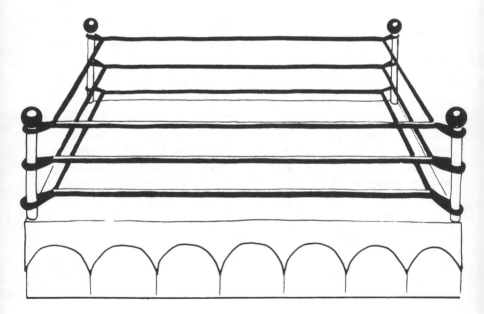

RING

round heels: see *glass chin.*

1. **roundhouse:** A punch delivered with a wide-sweeping arc. Named after the circular revolving floor of a railroad roundhouse. (got tagged with a roundhouse)

2. **roundhouse:** Of or pertaining to a punch delivered with a wide-sweeping arc.

saved by the bell: About to be counted out when the bell rings, ending the round. Sanctioning bodies in some locations do not allow a fighter to be saved by the bell but require that the count be continued. In this case, a fighter who is not able to rise unassisted by the count of ten is counted out, and the match is ended. Regardless of the sanctioning body, no fighter may be saved by the bell in the final round of a match.

●●To be saved just in time from something bad or unpleasant. (saved by the bell when his wallet was found just before the plane left)

scar tissue: Layers of new skin that remain after healing in and over wounds or cuts, especially over an area that has been wounded or bruised repeatedly.

scorecard: A card on which an official keeps a tally of rounds or points awarded to the boxers in a bout.

second: One of the cornermen allowed inside the ring between rounds to attend to and advise a boxer.

shadow box: To spar with an imaginary opponent as a training exercise.

shadow boxing: A training exercise in which a boxer spars with an imaginary opponent.

shake the cobwebs: To attempt to clear one's head after being dazed by a blow or blows. (backing up now and just trying to stay out of range of the champion until he can shake the cobwebs)

●●To clear one's head; to wake up. (takes her about fifteen minutes to shake the cobwebs after the alarm goes off in the morning)

shoot the jab: To quickly throw a jab. (shoots the jab, then crosses with the right) also *jab, stick.*

shop fighter: A journeyman, experienced but less than first class.

shot: A punch. (scored with some good shots in the first two rounds)

slide rule decision: A close decision.

slip: 1. To dodge a punch by moving the head sideways. 2. An instance in which a boxer falls to the canvas as a result of a loss of footing rather than a punch. In such a case, there is no knockdown and no count.

slug: To punch hard. (a banger who can slug with anybody) also *bang, belt, bomb.*

slugfest: A boxing match between two sluggers, with each swinging from the heels to score a knockout. also *war.*

●●A literal or figurative brawl. (a disagreement that quickly turned into a verbal slugfest)

slugger: 1. A fighter who prefers to slug, rather than rely on boxing skill or style. 2. A powerful puncher. also *banger, bomber, stiff puncher.*

smoking: Relentless punching. "Smoking" Joe Frazier, Heavyweight Champion in 1968, 1969, 1970, 1971, 1972, and 1973, got his nickname for just such a style. Frazier was elected to the Boxing Hall of Fame in 1980.

south of the border: Below the belt. see *below the belt, low blow.*

spar: To box in a practice or exhibition bout.

●●To argue, or bandy words. (the judge looked on as the two attorneys sparred with each other)

sparmate: A sparring partner.

●●A humorous name for one's mate or spouse.

sparring partner: An individual who spars with a boxer in training. Sparring partners are often young up-and-coming boxers. also *sparmate.*

SLIP

••A humorous name for one's mate or spouse.

speed bag: A leather punching bag that hangs at head level from the middle of a round, horizontal board or frame so that when the bag is hit, it bounces back rapidly. The inflated, pear-shaped speed bag is used in training to develop speed and timing. compare *double-end bag, heavy bag.*

split decision: A decision in which two officials vote for one boxer, and the third votes for his opponent. compare *majority decision, unanimous decision.*

square circle: A boxing ring. also *prize ring.*

standing eight count: A count of eight given, at the discretion of the referee, when a boxer has been stunned or hurt. In professional boxing, a standing eight count is scored as a knockdown.

stanza: A round.

starch: To knock out an opponent. (starched him in the third round) see *knock out.*

stay there: To stay in front of and close to an opponent; to remain inside. (has to stop dancing and stay there)

steal a round: To flurry and step up one's performance in the closing minute of a round, impressing and influencing the judges' scoring. An acknowledged master at this technique was three-time heavyweight champion Muhammad Ali.

SPEED BAG

step back: To break from a clinch. When fighters clinch, a referee will order them to "break" or "step back."

stick: 1. To throw a jab. (he would stick, stick, then hook) also *jab, shoot the jab.* 2. To punch.

stick and move: 1. To jab and immediately move, in order to present a more elusive target for an opponent. 2. To throw a punch and immediately move, in order to present a more elusive target to an opponent.

stiff: see *bum.*

stiff jab: A strong, stinging jab.

stiff puncher: see *slugger.*

stop: To knock an opponent unconscious. see *knock out.*

stop a fight: To officially end a boxing match before the completion of all the rounds scheduled. A referee has the authority to stop a fight by declaring a technical knockout if one of the contestants is injured or unable to continue, to disqualify one of the contestants, or to declare a bout "no contest."

straight punch: A right-hand or left-hand punch that travels in a direct line to the opponent, as opposed to hooking, crossing, or traveling upward or downward. (dropped him with a straight right)

straight-up fighter: A boxer who does not crouch, bob, or weave, but stands erect.

stretch: To knock out an opponent. (took him only two rounds to stretch his last opponent) see *knock out.*

1. sucker punch: An unexpected or deceptive punch, as one thrown before an opponent is ready.

2. sucker punch: To throw a sucker punch. (tried to sucker punch him as he reached to touch gloves)

Sunday punch: One's best or most powerful punch. also *bomb, haymaker.*

••A powerful "blow." (opened the negotiations with his Sunday punch)

super heavyweight: 1. The amateur weight division for boxers over 200 pounds. 2. An amateur boxer who fights in the super heavyweight division.

super lightweight: 1. The WBC 140 pound (maximum) weight division. also *junior welterweight* (WBA). 2. A boxer who fights in the super lightweight division. also *junior welterweight* (WBA).

swing from the heels: To put all one's power behind a punch or punches.

(both fighters stood toe-to-toe, swinging from the heels) also *tee off, unload.*
●●To make one's best effort, holding nothing back. (it was obvious from the opening statement that the committee intended to swing from the heels)

1. swoon: 1. To intentionally lose a fight, especially by a faked knockout. also *go into the tank, take a dive, throw a fight.* 2. To be knocked out. (after being hurt in the second and third, he finally swooned at two minutes and twelve seconds into the fourth round)

2. swoon: The act or an instance of intentionally losing a fight, especially by a faked knockout.

take a dive: To intentionally lose a fight, especially by faking a knockout. (lost his boxing license for taking a dive) also *go into the tank, swoon, throw a fight.*
●●To intentionally lose a contest.

take a punch: To withstand or be able to withstand a blow or blows from an opponent. (proved he could take a punch in his first two fights)

take out: To knock out an opponent. (took him out with a vicious left hook) also *cool, flatten, ice, kayo, KO, put away, put out the lights, starch, stop, stretch.*

take the count: 1. To allow oneself to be counted out after being knocked down. A fighter who has been badly beaten and is exhausted is sometimes told to take the count by his corner in order to prevent an injury.

tale of the tape: The weight and measurements of a boxer, or of two boxers who are about to meet in a boxing match. The exact origin of the expression is unclear, but television sports commentator Howard Cosell did much to popularize it in the 1970s.

tank job: see *bagged fight.*

tattoo: see *beat a tattoo.*

technical draw: The termination of a boxing match due to an injury incurred accidentally (most often a cut from an accidental butt) by one or both boxers. If neither boxer is ahead on points at the time of the injury, or if the injured boxer is behind on points at the time the match is stopped, a technical draw is declared under the rules of some sanctioning bodies.

technical knockout: The termination of a

boxing match by the referee when one of the contestants is injured, unwilling to continue, or, in the referee's judgment, unable to defend himself. also *TKO.* compare *knockout.*

tee off: To put all one's power behind a punch or punches. Originally from golf, meaning to strike the ball off of a golf tee, starting play. (just standing in the middle of the ring, teeing off on each other)
●●To hit something with all one's power (tees off on the first pitch and sends it to deep center field) To severely reprimand or openly express anger. (teed off on her son for disrupting the picnic)

telegraph a punch: To unintentionally communicate to an opponent (as by a glance or some movement) the blow that one intends to deliver next. (he drops his shoulder and telegraphs the punch)
●●To "telegraph" a word or an action is to involuntarily signal one's intention. (clumsily telegraphed his next move and quickly found his king in check)

ten point must system: A method of scoring a bout by awarding ten points to the winner of a round and a lesser number to the loser (usually the difference is less than two points). Both boxers are awarded ten points in the case of an even round.

The Ring: A national sports magazine, published monthly since 1922. Founded by boxing authority Nat Fleisher, *The Ring* is the oldest sports magazine in the United States and has, since 1924, issued ratings that have served as a practical, if not official, measure of the ascension of challengers to championships in the various weight divisions. Writers such as Paul Gallico, Dan Daniel, Ed Sullivan, Bud Schulberg, Red Smith, Damon Runyon, and others have contributed to *The Ring,* known as "The Bible of Boxing." also *Ring Magazine.*

third man in the ring: The referee. also *ref.*

three knockdown rule: A rule in effect in some locations that requires a bout to be stopped automatically if one boxer is knocked down three times in any round. In such a case, the opponent of the downed boxer is awarded a victory by a knockout in the round the bout is stopped.

throw a fight: To intentionally lose a fight. also *go into the tank, swoon, take a dive.*

throw a punch: To punch, or attempt to hit an opponent. also *stick.*

throw in the towel: To concede defeat for a boxer by throwing a towel into the ring from the boxer's corner. To prevent a serious injury, a boxer's seconds may throw in the towel even if the boxer himself wants to continue. The act of throwing in the towel is not recognized by some sanctioning bodies, but in practice, if the cause is obvious, the referee will usually stop the match and award a victory by a technical knock-out to the opponent.

•• To give up, to concede defeat. (finally threw in the towel and went along with the majority opinion)

throw leather: To deliver punches, especially flurries of hard punches. (backs up the champion as he begins to throw leather)

1. thumb: To illegally stick the thumb of a boxing glove in an opponent's eye. A foul that can result in the loss of points or disqualification. (a dirty fighter who would thumb and lace his opponents) also *gouge.*

2. thumb: The act or an instance of thumbing an opponent. also *gouge.*

tie up: see *clinch.*

TIMEKEEPER

timekeeper: The official at ringside responsible for timing rounds, the interval between rounds, and the ten-second count in case of a knockdown.

title: A championship. (held the middleweight title for two years) also *crown.*

•• The highest level of any competition or endeavor. (will compete in the final race to decide the national title)

title defense: see *championship fight.*

title fight: see *championship fight.*

TKO: A technical knockout. (won in the eighth round on a TKO)

toe-to-toe: A furious exchange of punches in which opponents face each other and slug with no effort made to move or defend. (went toe-to-toe in the last round of the fight)

•• An open and heated argument or confrontation. (an unproductive session, with union and management negotiators going toe-to-toe)

tomato can: see *bum.*

trade, trade punches: To exchange punches with an opponent. (stick and move, don't trade with him) also *mix it up, punch.*

twenty point must system: A method of scoring a bout in which the winner of a round is awarded twenty points, and the loser a lesser number. In the case of an even round, both boxers are awarded twenty points.

unanimous decision: A decision in which all officials cast their votes for one boxer. compare *majority decision, split decision.*

under and over: A punch to the body followed by a punch to the head, often both hooks.

undercard: Preliminary bouts before the main event.

unload: To deliver a hard punch or hard punches. (unloaded and knocked the champion off his feet)

1. uppercut: A punch of fairly short extension delivered up toward the head or upper body with either hand from the waist and with a bent elbow.

2. uppercut: The act or an instance of delivering an uppercut. (step in and uppercut him)

upstairs: The head or to the head. (hit him in the gut, then go upstairs) compare *downstairs.*

walk away: To take several steps to the right of an opponent (away from a right-handed boxer's right hand). A boxer usually walks away to take a safe breather, but Boxing Hall of Famer Jersey Joe Walcott, World Heavyweight Champion in 1951 and 1952, used the technique to momentarily lull an opponent before an attack.

walking on one's heels: Stunned, off balance, ready to be knocked down or out. (he's up, but still walking on his heels) see *on queer street*.

waltz: A boxing match characterized by dancing and fancy movement, but little punching.

war: An action-packed and/or brutal boxing match, in which the combatants pummel each other from the opening bell. also *slugfest*.

warning: An official notification to a boxer from the referee that points will be subtracted from the boxer's score if an observed foul is repeated.

WBA: The World Boxing Association.

WBC: The World Boxing Council.

weigh-in: The official weighing of boxers before a match to insure that the weights of both contestants are within the specified limits of their weight division. see *weight division*.

weigh in: To have one's weight measured and recorded at the official weigh-in before a boxing match. (weighed in at 209 pounds)

weight division: The class or category into which boxers are grouped according to weight. also *class, division*.

welter: A boxer in the welterweight division.

welterweight: 1. The 147 pound (maximum) weight division. also *welter*. 2. A boxer who fights in the welterweight division. "Welter" was a weight term used in English horse racing (a weight of 28 pounds sometimes added to a horse's weight for age). In 1792, 145-pound Tom Jones became the first champion of the "welters," a name which had been adopted by a number of small English fighters of the same weight. There was little interest in the division until 1888, when American-born Paddy Duffy claimed the first World Welterweight Championship holding the title through 1889 and 1890. also *welter*.

white hope: A white boxer who is a contender for a title held by a black boxer. A racial expression that originated in the early 1900s, when Boxing Hall of Famer Jack Johnson, the first black World Heavyweight Champion, dominated the heavyweight ranks for seven years (1908-1915). Johnson's arrogance, womanizing, and public scrapes with the law only served to fuel those who clamored for a "white hope." Finally, on April 15, 1915, in Havana, Cuba, 6 foot 6-1/4-inch, 240-pound Boxing Hall of Famer Jess Willard knocked out the controversial Johnson in the twenty-sixth round of their championship fight to win the heavyweight crown and the title of the "Great White Hope."

UPPER CUT

wing: To deliver big, looping punches. (winging punches in the hopes of connecting)

win on points: To win a boxing match by a decision.

••To just barely win. (she won the argument on points this time, but next time, it won't even be close)

work the corner: To act as a second or cornerman for a boxer.

World Boxing Association: One of the two major sanctioning bodies of professional boxing. An outgrowth of the old National Boxing Association in the United States, the World Boxing Association is headquartered in the Republic of Panama. also *WBA*.

World Boxing Council: One of the two major sanctioning bodies of professional boxing. Formed in 1963, the World Boxing Council is headquartered in Mexico. also *WBC*.

wrap: see *bandage*.

wrapping: see *bandages*.

CRICKET

Cricket is a descendant of the traditional folk games that were popular in England as early as the thirteenth century. Country village games, some of which were later known as club ball, tip-cat, cat and dog, trap-ball, and stoolball (still played in a revised form) all contained one or more of the essential elements of cricket; a bat and "ball" (or object to be hit with the bat), a wicket-like object to be defended (with the bat or a hand) from an opponent's deliveries, and the concept of scoring by hitting the ball (and sometimes, by running between objects).

Lacking written rules, local variations of these games were passed on to succeeding generations by word of mouth. Around 1550, a version called cricket was played at the Royal Grammar School in the Borough of Guilford. While less violent than the mob football games of the time, cricket (the increasingly popular name for many similar folk games) was nevertheless under pressure from the law, the church, and from business interests for the remainder of the sixteenth century, and halfway through the seventeenth century. Oliver Cromwell was criticised in 1621 for having taken part in cricket and other sports in his youth. But regardless, the games thrived, particularly in country villages, and eventually, "respectable" people came to view them with more curiosity than suspicion.

In 1677, the Earl of Sussex attended a cricket game at Dicker, becoming the first member of the aristocracy to be officially associated with the growing pastime. By the eighteenth century, "gentlemen" began to take part in eleven-a-side matches in London, with the extra incentive of wagering on the outcome. In 1727, the exact terms of one such bet, as well as the conditions under which a player could be "caught out" or "run out" (wicket downed with the ball in hand), and the powers and responsibilities of the "umpires" were committed to writing as "Articles of Agreement" for two matches between the Duke of Richmond and a Mr. Alan Broderick.

In 1733, the Prince of Wales donated a silver cup for a cricket match. An occasional participant himself, the Prince of Wales was president of the London Cricket Club. In 1744, the London Club formulated the first uniform code of cricket Laws. Many of these rules apply today, though wickets of the time were comprised of two stumps (a third was adopted the following year), cricket bats resembled crooked hockey sticks, bowling was underarm, and the batsman could interfere with a fielder to prevent a catch.

Around 1750, the Hambledon Cricket Club was founded. Often referred to as the "Cradle of Cricket", the Hambledon CC developed the skill and art of cricket, remaining unbeaten until 1769, and often defeating the Rest of England sides in the following decade. In 1787, the Marylebone Cricket Club was founded in London. Soon eclipsing the Hambledon CC in prominence, the MCC would go on to become the central cricket body in the world. Under the increasing influence of the MCC, cricket Laws were refined extensively during the nineteenth century. Round-arm bowling, made legal in 1838, finally gave way to the overarm delivery in 1868.

Having been introduced into Australia in the late 1700s by British soldiers, cricket flourished there as well ás at home. By 1832, Australia's first cricket club had been founded, the Hobart Town Club (changed to the Derwent Club in 1837). In 1877, Melbourne was the site of the first Test match between England and Australia, with the home side prevailing by 45 runs. Five years later Australia stunned England with a Test victory at the Oval, precipitating cricket's most famous tradition; that of "The Ashes", thereafter figuratively awarded to the winner in any England/Australia Test series.

The nineteenth century also produced cricket's first heroes. While batsmen like Fuller Pilch (single wicket Champion of England in 1833) and the "Lion of Kent", Alfred Mynn (single wicket Champion in 1838 and 1846), and the legendary "Grand Old Man of Cricket", all-rounder Dr. William Gilbert Grace drew new admirers to the sport in England, Frederick Robert Spofforth, the world-class "Demon Bowler", and all-rounder George Giffen did the same in Australia.

In the early twentieth century, Australia's Victor Trumper emerged as one of the great batsmen in the history of the sport. Among the bright lights of English cricket at that time were the charismatic Indian batsman, Kumar Shri Ranjitsinhji (whose English first-class career as "Ranji" began in 1893), all-rounders Wilfred Rhodes and George Hirst, and the brilliant batsman, Sir John Hobbs. Called "The Master", Hobbs picked up where he left off after World War I, at a time when another great English batsman, Walter Hammond, was beginning his career.

In 1927, the first play-by-play radio broadcast was made of a cricket match between Essex and the New Zealanders (commentary by Rev. F. H. Gillingham). The first Test match was broadcast in 1930, when England met Australia at Nottingham. On England's 1932–33 tour of Australia, two Australian batsmen were injured by the English fast leg-theory bowlers (among them, Harold Larwood, "The Nottingham Express"), giving birth to the great "bodyline" controversy. In 1938, the first Test cricket match, England vs. Australia, was televised at Lords. The 1930s also produced the West Indies' first outstanding cricketer, George Headley, who would continue to play long after World War II and be called the "Bradman of the Caribbeans", after Australia's brilliant batsman of the 1930s and 1940s, all-time great, Sir Donald Bradman.

Such was Bradman's worldwide reputation that skilled batsmen from other countries were often compared to him; C. K. Nayudu, for example, was known as the "Indian Bradman". But though there have many outstanding world-class players since World War II like Australia's record-setting bowlers, Ray Lindwall (1940s and 1950s) and Richie Benaud (1950s and 1960s), West Indian batsman Everton Weekes (1940s and 1950s), South African bowler Hugh Joseph Tayfield (1940s and 1950s), England's pace bowler F. S. Trueman (1950s and 1960s), and West Indies bowlers, Wesley Hall (1950s and 1960s) and off spinner Lance Gibbs (late 1950s to the 1970s), arguably the greatest modern cricket player of them all has been Sir Garfield Sobers, many of whose first-class and Test records (representing the West Indies) set in the 1950s, 1960s, and 1970s remain unbroken.

agricultural shot: see *cow shot.*

all out: Having had all ten wickets downed, said of a side whose innings has ended. compare *not out.*

all-rounder: A player skilled at batting, bowling, and fielding. The legendary W. G. Grace (1848–1915) of Great Britain served as a prototype all-rounder, but G. S. Sobers of the West Indies (1950s, 1960s, and 1970s) is arguably the most famous example of an all-rounder in the history of cricket.

•• One who excels in many fields or possesses multiple skills, an all-rounder who can do carpentry, plumbing, and electrical work)

analysis: A bowler's statistics, usually consisting of the number of overs bowled, maiden overs bowled, runs allowed, wickets taken, and the bowling average.

1. appeal: The required calling out of "How's That?" to an umpire by one or more fieldsmen before a batsman can be officially declared out, or a plea to an umpire for an out in a close play. In either case, the appeal must be made before the bowler begins his run-up or bowling action to deliver the next ball, or before the umpire calls "time" to suspend play for an arranged interval, at the end of a day's play, or to conclude a match.

2. appeal: The act or an instance of making an appeal.

arm ball: A bowled ball that follows the direction of movement of the bowler's arm, either in the air or upon pitching (a right-handed bowler's arm ball moves away from a right-handed batsman).

Ashes, the: The famous memento of Australia's humiliating 1882 Test match victory over England, after which a mock obituary notice appeared in the *Sporting Times* mourning the death of English cricket. When an England team toured Australia later the same year, the actual burnt ashes of one of the stumps used in the Test match were solemnly presented to the English captain. The velvet-covered urn containing the Ashes is on permanent display at the MCC's Imperial Cricket Memorial Museum in London. Traditionally, however, whoever wins an England vs. Australia Test match series is said to hold the Ashes.

attacking field: A deployment of fieldsmen in positions that are relatively close to the batsman. An attacking field is employed primarily to take wickets (make outs) rather than to prevent runs. compare *defensive field.*

attacking shot: A stroke meant to score runs rather than to defend the wicket. also *forcing shot.* compare *defensive shot.*

at the stumps: Keeping wicket, or wicketkeeping. also *keeping.*

Aunt Sally: Players' jocular term for wicketkeeper, popularized in the late 1890s. also *keeper, stump, stumper.*

away swinger: An outswinger.

back cut: see *late cut.*

back-foot: Of or pertaining to back play or a backstroke. (opened with a back-foot hit) compare *front-foot.*

backlift: The taking back of the bat by the striker just before the forward swing of the stroke is begun.

back play: Batting in which the striker steps back in order to make contact with the ball behind the popping crease.

backstroke: A stroke in which the batsman steps back with the rear foot just before making contact with the ball. compare *forward stroke.*

back up: 1. To position oneself behind a teammate to be able to assist if the teammate should misfield a hit ball or a throw. 2. To, as striker, move forward of the popping crease after the ball has been played in order to be ready to run. 3. To, as nonstriker, move forward of the crease as the ball is delivered by the bowler in order to be ready to run.

backward point: see *gully.*

backward short leg: 1. A fielding position just behind and wide of the wicketkeeper on the leg side, between leg slip and short leg. 2. The fieldsman in the backward short leg position.

bail: Either of two identical 4⅜-inch long pieces of wood that rest end to end in grooves across the top of the stumps of a wicket. When in this position, the bails should not project more than ½ inch. Early wickets had two stumps topped by a single bail. By 1705, wickets of this configuration measured approximately 1 foot high by 2 feet wide. From their resemblance to the small hurdle or wicket gate leading to a sheep pen, the moveable top rail of which was called a bail, came the cricket terms "wicket" and "bail". The 1744 London Cricket Club rules called for two 22-inch high stumps with a single 6-inch bail. Though a third stump was added in 1775, the single bail remained in general use until 1786, when a second was added. The present bail specifications were adopted by the MCC in 1931. In high winds, the umpire may decide to dispense with bails.

ball: A sphere comprised of two red (or for night matches, white) leather hemispheres joined and stitched together with raised seams, 8¹³⁄₁₆ to 9 inches in circumference and weighing 5½ to 5¾ ounces. Its center is cork, which is then wound in twine. Present day specifications for the ball were finalized in 1927, when the circumference was reduced slightly. Early cricket balls were white, changing to red at some time before the 1840s, when reference was made to a red cricket ball in Dickens' *Martin Chuzzlewit*. White balls were introduced again when night cricket was popularized in the late 1970s.

balloon: A batted ball hit high in the air, easy to catch. also *dolly, sitter, skier*.

banana floater: A slow, looping delivery that curves, with a trajectory like a banana. also *dolly, donkey drop, lob*.

barn-door game: The practice of batting defensively or stonewalling.

1. bat: To take one's turn at bat. also *face*.

2. bat: The somewhat paddle-like wooden stick used by a batsman to hit a bowled ball in cricket. The handle end of a cricket bat (approximately one-third of the length) is narrow to facilitate gripping with a batsman's thick gloves. The blade or remainder of the maximum 38-inch total length (35 inches is average) is wider (maximum 4¼ inches) and, near its end, thicker, with a flat striking surface on one side. A shock-cushioning rubber insert inside the handle extends to the point in the blade where the two sections are spliced together. Early cricket bats were curved and weighted at the bottom like a hockey stick to accommodate the underarm style of bowling, in which the ball was delivered on or close to the ground. The first rule to apply to bats (setting the maximum width at 4¼ inches) was framed in 1771 by the Hambledon Cricket Club, two days after Thomas "Shock" White of Reigate used

a bat that was wider than the wicket in a game against Chertsey. John Small of Petersfield, Hampshire is most often credited with making the prototype of the modern straight bat in 1773. By the end of the decade, bats of this configuration were used almost exclusively. There is no regulation governing the weight of a cricket bat, but the average is approximately 2lb 5oz. The present length limit was set in 1835.

bat and pad: An expression descriptive of a situation in which a bowled ball first hits the bat, then the pads of a batsman in front of the wicket, thereby precluding an out under the leg before wicket rule. also *bat-pad*. see *leg before wicket*.

bat-pad: Short for bat and pad.

batting average: A statistic expressing the batting efficiency of a player, calculated by dividing the total number of runs scored by the player by the number of innings in which the player was put out (total innings minus innings not out or retired hurt or ill). The career record for the highest batting average in Test matches belongs to Australia's all-time great, Sir Donald G. Bradman, who in 52 Tests, scored an amazing total of 6,996 runs in 80 innings with 10 not out innings, for an average of 99.94. Ironically, he needed to score just 4 runs in his last Test appearance in 1948 for a batting average of an even 100, but was instead, bowled for a duck by England's W. E. Hollies.

batting pads: The padded fabric-covered shields wrapped around the front and sides of a batsman's legs to protect the area from the ankles to just above the knees. Wicketkeepers also wear batting pads or similar protective equipment. While the first batsman's protective pad is believed to have been worn (on one leg only) by "Long Bob" Robinson of Farnham, Surrey in the late 1700s or early 1800s, and shin pads were used in the mid-1830s, Thomas Nixon of Nottingham is most often thought of as the inventor of the prototype of modern batting pads. In 1841 he introduced innovative cork pads, though even these and their successors were not widely adopted for another twenty-five years. also *leg pads, pads*.

batting pitch: see *easy wicket*.

batsman: 1. The striker. also *batter*. see

striker. 2. The nonstriker. see *nonstriker.*

batter: The striker. also *batsman.* see *striker.*

bat through an innings: To maintain one's turn at bat without being put out through an entire innings. Two Englishmen, the legendary Dr. William G. Grace of the late 1800s and early 1900s and C. J. B. Wood of the early 1900s set the record for batting through an innings in first-class cricket, each accomplishing the feat seventeen times. also *carry a bat through a complete innings, carry one's bat, carry one's bat out.*

beamer: A full-length bowled ball aimed at or near a batsman's head.

big hitter: A powerful hitter.

big hitting: Powerful hitting.

bite: To momentarily grip the ground on pitching so as to turn or break in a manner or direction because of spin imparted, said of a bowled ball. (a sticky wicket that allowed his off-spin deliveries to bite and turn sharply)

blade: The wide paddle-like part that comprises approximately two-thirds of the length of a cricket bat, with the flat front side serving as the hitting surface.

blob: A "duck" or scoreless innings for a batsman. From the late 1890s, the zero marked on a scorecard for the batsman. see *get a blob, make a blob.*

1. block: 1. A defensive stroke made merely to block or protect the wicket. 2. see *block hole.*

2. block: To make a defensive stroke merely to protect the wicket.

block hole: A small hole made by a batsman to mark the spot over which the bat is positioned vertically before each delivery. also *block.* see *take guard.*

bodyline bowling: Bowling that is considered a dangerous and unfair attack by the bowler upon the batsman, such as the repeated use of fast, short-pitched deliveries that bounce up toward a batsman who is not blocking the wicket. The expression was first used in 1933 in an angry cable from the Australian Board of Control to the MCC after a controversial incident during a Test match in Australia in which two Australian batsmen were hurt by balls bowled by England's fast leg-theory bowlers, among them, Harold Larwood. see *direct-attack bowling.*

boots: The white shoes traditionally worn by cricketers, usually with studs attached to the soles. also *spikes.*

bosey, bosie: A googly. From the name of the English bowler B. J. T. Bosanquet, who is credited with introducing the googly in 1900, and popularizing the technique on a tour in Australia in 1903. also *wrong 'un.*

bouncer: A fast-bowled ball that is pitched short so as to bounce high, and often dangerously close to the batsman's head or upper body. also *bumper.*

boundary: 1. The structure, object, or line that marks the outer limit of the playing area around a cricket ground. It is believed that boundaries were introduced at Lords (London) in 1866 for a match between Eton and Harrow, but they were first mentioned in the Laws of Cricket in 1884. see *boundary hit.* 2. A boundary hit. (hit four consecutive boundaries) 3. The award of usually four runs when a thrown or batted ball hits inside, then touches or crosses a boundary. also *four.* 4. The award of six runs when a batted ball carries over a boundary on the fly. also *boundary six, six, sixer.*

boundary catch: A catch for an out by a fieldsman of a batted ball that would otherwise hit or carry over a boundary on the fly.

boundary hit: A batted ball that touches or crosses over a boundary. If the ball touches inside the boundary first, usually four runs are awarded. If the ball carries over the boundary on the fly, six runs are awarded. also *boundary.*

boundary six: The award of six runs when a batted ball carries over a boundary on the fly. also *boundary, six, sixer.*

1. bowl: To deliver the ball to or toward the opposite wicket with an underhand or overhand motion ensuring that the arm is straight just before the ball is released. The Laws of Cricket specify that the bowler must deliver the ball with his front foot behind the popping crease and within the return crease or its extensions, and that the batsman is entitled to be notified whether the delivery is to be made left- or right-handed, underhand or overhand, and over or round the wicket. Originally, all deliveries were made underhanded, with the ball usually rolling or skipping

109

along the ground. Thus, the term "bowl". Gradually, bowlers raised their bowling arms until round-arm bowling (called "throwing" by its critics), with the ball released as high as the armpit, made inroads in the late 1600s. The round-arm technique is believed to have been created by Christina Willes, to clear her full skirts when she practiced bowling to her brother John, of Kent. He was among the first to employ round-arm bowling, which continued to be controversial even after specific regulations permitted an elbow-high release in 1828, and a shoulder-high release in 1835. Finally, in 1864, the Laws of Cricket were changed to allow overhand bowling. Though underhand deliveries remained popular long afterwards, they are rarely ever seen in modern cricket. But in a particularly controversial incident in 1981, during a one-day match in Australia against New Zealand, with the home side ahead, only one ball remaining, and New Zealand's only chance being to score a six, the Australian bowler Trevor Chappell on the instruction of his captain, Greg Chappell, used an underhand delivery on the last ball, bowling a grubber along the ground to make it impossible for the New Zealand batsman to loft a long drive. also *delivery*, *send down*. see *bowled*, *no ball*, *over*, *wide*.

2. bowl: A delivery of the ball by the bowler.

bowled: Having been, on appeal, given out due to the bails being dislodged by a delivery from the bowler, said of a batsman whose turn at bat has been ended in this manner. compare *bowled for a duck*.

●● Since the early 1800s, to "bowl out" or to be "bowled out" have been used as slang expressions meaning to defeat or be defeated.

bowled all over the wicket: Clean bowled.

bowled for a duck: Bowled out without having scored a run. see *duck*.

bowler: The player who bowls the ball toward the wicket defended by the striker. In an over, a bowler is given six or eight chances (depending on prevailing rules) to bowl the ball, not counting wide balls and no balls. A bowler may bowl as many overs as desired by the

team captain, or the number stipulated in limited-over cricket, but may not bowl two consecutive overs in an innings. At the end of each over, the bowler is changed and the new bowler bowls toward the opposite wicket. see *bowl*, *no ball*, *over*, *wide*.

bowler's double: The taking of 100 wickets while scoring just 100 runs in a season by a player obviously more skilled at bowling than batting. From the 1930s, a humorous allusion to the achievement of a true double (100 wickets and 1000 runs in a season). see *double*.

bowler's run-up: see *run-up*.

bowl for timber: To bowl at the batsman's legs. Players' slang from around the turn of the century.

bowling average: A statistic that reflects the bowling efficiency of a player, calculated by dividing the total number of runs allowed during a period of time by the number of wickets taken. In first-class cricket, the amazing English slow bowler Wilfred R. Rhodes set the record for the best bowling average over a career. In his playing years (1898–1930), Rhodes allowed 69,965 runs and took 4,187 wickets, for an average of 16.71.

bowling crease: Either of two 8-foot, 8-inch long parallel lines on which the wickets are centered at opposite ends of a cricket pitch. Originally, with each delivery, the bowler's rear foot had to be behind the bowling crease (and within the return crease) until the ball was released. In 1969 the Laws were changed to require the bowler's front foot to be behind the popping crease (and the rear foot within the return crease or its extensions) until the ball is released. also *crease*.

bowling machine: A mechanical device that automatically bowls various kinds of deliveries to batsmen taking batting practice. The first bowling machine (the "Catapulta") was invented in 1837 by Blackheath schoolmaster and Kent, Surrey, and All-England XI cricketer, Nicholas Felix (or Wanostrocht).

box: 1. An archaic term for gully. 2. A protective cup for the groin.

bread and butter wicket: An easy wicket for batsmen. From the late 1880s. also *batting pitch*, *plumb*, *plumb wicket*. see *easy wicket*.

1. break: The change in direction of a bowled ball when it pitches or bounces, the result of spin imparted by the bowler. also *turn.*

2. break: 1. To change direction after pitching or bouncing due to spin, said of a bowled ball. (will break to the leg side) also *turn.* 2. To bowl a ball with spin so that it will change direction when it pitches or bounces. (broke one too far out for a wide) also *turn.*

break back: A bowled ball that pitches on the off side, then veers back toward the batsman.

break one's duck: To score at least one run in an innings, said of a batsman. Popularized around 1900 from the 1870s expression "save one's duck" or "save one's duck egg". see *duck.*

break the wicket: To dislodge one or both bails or pull out or knock down one or more of the stumps of a wicket. In order to put out a batsman, the bowler attempts to break the wicket with a bowled ball. A batsman is also out if the wicket is broken by his bat or any part of his person, or when he is running and has not made his ground, by a ball thrown by a fieldsman, or by a fieldsman holding the ball. The wicket is then said to be down.

broad bat: The ability to defend the wicket with one's bat. (had reached a point in the match where Edwards' broad bat was necessary)

bump ball: A batted ball bounced high in the air off the ground in front of the batsman. When a bump ball is "caught" by a fieldsman, distant spectators sometimes mistakenly believe the batsman to be caught out.

bumper: see *bouncer.*

butter: To miss a catch by letting the ball slip through one's fingers. Popularized in the 1890s from the earlier expression "butterfingers".

butterfingers: One who is apt to miss catches by dropping the ball. From the early 1800s.

•• One who is clumsy or apt to drop things. Such a person is often described as "butterfingered".

bye: Any run scored on a ball bowled past the batsman without touching his bat or body when the ball is not called "wide" or "no ball" by the umpire. Byes are credited to the batsman's team, but not the batsman. compare *leg bye, wide.*

call: 1. A verbal signal by the striker to his partner to run. 2. The pronouncement of an umpire after making a judgement on a play.

1. cap: A figurative award of merit (and in some countries, an actual tasseled cap) given to a player each time he participates as a member of a national team in international competition. From the nineteenth century custom of English public schools and universities awarding ornate tasseled caps for athletic accomplishments when sports were first organized and popularized. In England, a cap, or "county cap", is awarded to players who distinguish themselves in first-class cricket representing their country. 2. A player who has been awarded an international cap. (a particularly strong team that includes three Australian caps)

2. cap: To award a cap. (played in four games before being capped by his county)

capture a wicket: see *take a wicket.*

carry a bat through a complete innings, carry one's bat, carry one's bat out: To bat through an innings without being put out. From the early days of cricket, when it was customary to leave the bat (sometimes the only one) for the next batsman after being put out. see *bat through an innings.*

•• To prevail after some time, to outlast others.

castle: The wicket at which the ball is bowled.

1. catch: To put out a batsman by grasping and controlling a ball hit into the air before it touches the ground. (was caught at slips to end the innings)

2. catch: The act or an instance of a fieldsman catching a ball hit into the air for an out. The record for catches in a Test match was set in the fifth Test of the 1901–1902 Australian tour, when sixteen English players were caught out.

catches win matches: A popular slogan attesting to the importance of good fielding in cricket.

caught and bowled: Put out by a catch made by the bowler.

caught out: Having been, on appeal, given out after hitting a fly ball that is caught by a fieldsman.

center: see *middle and leg.*

centurion: A player who scores over 100

runs during a turn at bat in an innings. Though John Small of Hambledon (London) probably scored more than 100 runs in an innings on several occasions in previous years, the first recorded centurion was Minshull of the Duke of Dorset's XI who scored 107 in an innings against Sevenoaks in 1769.

century: The scoring of 100 runs during one's turn at bat in an innings. C. Bannerman of Australia scored the first Test match century (165 before retiring hurt) in 1877 at Melbourne against England. also *ton.*

chance: The opportunity for a fieldsman to put out a batsman.

change bowler: A bowler who is brought on after the two opening bowlers.

change of pace: A slow delivery, bowled with the same run-up and motion as a fast ball to deceive the batsman.

change of bowling: The substitution by a team captain, of another player on the field to act as bowler for the next over.

Chinaman: A left-handed bowler's googly or off-break ball. see *googly.*

Chinese cut: A misplayed cut stroke in which the ball deflects off the edge of the bat toward the leg side.

1. chop: A form of late cut in which a bowled ball is deflected down toward the area between point and the slips on the off side. see *late cut.*

2. chop: 1. To hit down at a bowled ball with a short, chopping swing as it passes, sending it down toward the area between point and the slips on the off side. 2. To execute a chop stroke against a particular bowler. (chopped Higson for a quick single)

1. chuck: To illegally throw rather than bowl the ball to the striker. see *bowl.*

2. chuck: An illegal delivery in which the ball is thrown instead of bowled, resulting in a no ball.

chucker: A bowler suspected of or known for illegally throwing rather than bowling the ball. From the 1880s.

clean bowled: Bowled out by a ball untouched by the batsman or his bat. also *bowled all over the wicket.*

clean catch: A precisely executed catch for an out.

1. clip: To hit a full-length bowled ball (such as a yorker) just as it pitches at one's feet.

2. clip: The act or an instance of clipping a bowled ball.

close field: 1. A deployment of fieldsmen in which players are positioned close to the striker in the infield. 2. The area of the infield close to the striker. compare *deep field.*

close-field: Of or pertaining to the area of the infield close to the striker. (moved into a close-field position) compare *deep-field.*

close fielding: Fielding from infield positions close to the striker, or very close such as short leg or silly point. compare *deep fielding.*

close-fielding: Close or very close to the striker, said of a fieldsman or fielding position. (will need a good close-fielding player at silly point) compare *deep-fielding.*

collar: To easily score runs facing a certain bowler, or against a specific type of bowling. (collars all off spin bowlers)

country, the: Slang for the deep field, the area of the outfield near the boundary. From the 1880s.

cover: Short for cover point.

cover drive: A drive hit to the off side toward the area between cover point and extra cover. compare *off drive, on drive, square drive, straight drive.*

cover-drive: 1. To drive a bowled ball to the off side toward the area between cover point and extra cover. 2. To execute a cover drive against a particular bowler. (cover-drove Dean-Smith for a four)

cover point: 1. A fielding position on the off side relatively square to the striker, between point and mid off. also *cover.* 2. The fieldsman in the cover point position. also *cover.*

CLEAN-BOWLED

covers: The general area of cover point and extra cover. (a leg side field with no one in the covers)

cow shot: An unorthodox and awkward stroke (sometimes made on one knee) played across the line of the ball with a nearly horizontal bat, sending the ball toward the leg side. From the early 1900s. Since the 1930s, the stroke has also been called an "agricultural shot", probably because of the mowing action of the swing.

cradle: A concave cradle-like device made of wooden slats into which the ball is propelled at a low angle so that players can practice making slip catches.

crease: 1. The popping crease. 2. The bowling crease. 3. The return crease.

creeper: A bowled ball that rolls along or stays very close to the ground after pitching. also *daisy cutter*, *grub*, *shooter*, *sneak*.

cricket: A game played with a ball and bat on a large field in the shape of an oval or a rectangle with rounded corners, by two teams of eleven players each. At the center of the field, two small structures (wickets) are erected 22 yards apart, centered on 8-foot, 8-inch parallel lines (bowling creases). Four feet in front of and parallel to each bowling crease is a line called the popping crease (minimum length of 12 feet). A batsman from the offensive team is positioned in the area between each popping crease and bowling crease (batsman's ground). Members of the defensive team (fieldsmen) are deployed at various positions around the field. One defender (the bowler) delivers the ball (usually overhand, but with the arm straight) from behind one wicket toward the other. The batsman defending that wicket (the striker) attempts to hit the bowled ball away from the fieldsmen, and to score runs by exchanging places with the batsman at the other wicket (the nonstriker) before either wicket can be knocked down or a part of it dislodged by the ball or a fieldsman holding the ball. Though the batsmen are under no obligation to run after the ball is hit, each safe exchange of places by them counts as one run scored. If a batted ball touches or crosses over the boundary of the playing field (a boundary hit), four runs are automatically awarded. Six runs are awarded if the ball carries over the boundary on the fly. If a batsman's wicket is broken while he is not within his crease (or not touching it with his bat or any part of his body), the batsman is out (run out). The batsman can also be put out if his bat or any part of his body knocks the wicket down (hit wicket), if a bowled ball knocks the wicket down (bowled out), if, after a delivery, the gloved fieldsman positioned behind his wicket (the wicketkeeper) knocks it down unassisted by any other fieldsman while the batsman is out of his ground (out stumped), if any fieldsman catches a batted ball on the fly (out caught), if a bowled ball that would have hit the wicket is obstructed by the body of the batsman (out leg before wicket), or if a ball in play is hit again or a fieldsman is obstructed by the batsman. When a batsman is put out, another follows according to a prearranged batting order until ten outs have been made, ending that team's offensive period of play (an innings). A bowler is allowed to deliver six or (depending on prevailing rules) eight fair balls at one wicket (an over). When an over is completed, another bowler bowls the next over at the opposite wicket. At the option of the team captain, a bowler may bowl any number of overs, as long as two overs are not bowled consecutively in one innings. Though cricket is sometimes played at night, matches traditionally begin in the late morning, with arranged breaks for lunch (lunch interval) and tea (tea interval). A typical match is played over a period of several days, with two innings for each side, played alternatively. Captains toss to determine which side bats first. When the team that bats first leads by a certain margin of runs (dependent upon the length of the match) after both teams have played their first innings, that side's captain has the option to require the other team to take both their innings consecutively (follow on). Unless the opposing team equals or surpasses the margin of runs in their second innings, the team that batted first is proclaimed the winner of the match and need not play its second innings. The captain may also declare an innings closed (a declaration) at any time, or even forfeit his team's second innings if he is confident of an insurmountable lead. These two decisions are irreversible, however, and his team can lose the match if the opponents exceed his side's run total. In the 1960s England developed one-day cricket in which each side plays a limited number of overs, and the one with the most runs at the end of this number of overs is the winner. Cricket matches are played under the authority and control of two umpires. Although attempts have been made to relate the word "cricket" to the fourteenth century game "creag", or to the Old English word *cryce*, meaning "a crooked stick", or to the similar French words *croche* and *croquet*, its exact origin is unknown.

●● From the early 1900s, fair, proper, or honorable. (sensed that something was definitely not cricket about the offer)

cricketana: Collectible items, information, or anecdotes pertaining to the sport of cricket.

Cricket Council: The governing body for English cricket, founded in 1968 and chaired by the president of the MCC.

cricketer: One who plays cricket.

cricketess: Slang for cricketress. From the mid-1860s.

cricket ground: A large field, usually in the shape of an oval or a rectangle with rounded corners, at the center of which are pitched two wickets, 22 yards apart, with a closely shorn 10-foot wide grass area, called the pitch, between. see *field.* also *ground, grounds, pitch.*

cricketress: A female cricket player. From the 1830s. also *cricketess.*

cross-batted: Not made with a straight bat. Swung in an arc that is not vertical, said of a stroke that is made with the bat held at an angle or nearly horizontal.

1. cut: A stroke in which the bat is brought down sharply on a bowled ball, deflecting it toward the off side, either just in front of, behind, or directly beside the batsman. see *forward cut, late cut, square cut.*

2. cut: 1. To bring the bat down sharply on a bowled ball and deflect it toward the off side. 2. To execute a cut stroke against a particular bowler. (opened by cutting Newman for a single)

cutter: 1. Short for leg cutter. 2. A batsman who is known for or proficient at executing the cut stroke.

1. dab: To hit a bowled ball with a sudden, light thrust of the bat.

2. dab: A stroke played with a sudden, light thrust of the bat.

daisy cutter: A bowled ball that rolls along or stays very close to the ground after pitching. From the early 1860s. also *creeper, shooter, sneak.*

dead: Out of play, said of a ball. When a ball is dead, no runs can be scored (except those awarded by an umpire in the case of a boundary six or a penalty). The ball is dead when it is finally settled in the hands of the wicketkeeper or the bowler, when it reaches or pitches over the boundary, when, whether played or not, it lodges in the clothes or equipment of a batsman, the helmet of any of the fielders, or the clothing of an umpire, when a batsman is declared out, and when play is suspended by an umpire at the end of an over or period of play, when a penalty is being

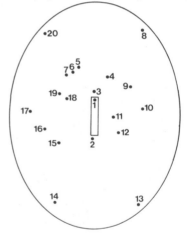

1	BATSMAN	11	SILLY MID-ON
2	BOWLER	12	MID-ON
3	WICKETKEEPER	13	LONG-ON
4	LEG SLIP	14	LONG-OFF
5	FIRST SLIP	15	MID-OFF
6	SECOND SLIP	16	EXTRA COVER
7	THIRD SLIP	17	COVER POINT
8	DEEP FINE LEG	18	POINT
9	BACKWARD SQUARE LEG	19	GULLY
10	SQUARE LEG	20	THIRD MAN

FIELD POSITIONS

assessed, or in the case of an injury. The ball ceases to be dead at the moment the bowler starts his run-up or bowling motion.

declaration: The official notification by a team captain that an innings being played by his side is closed, though less than ten outs have been made. This can be because of a seemingly insurmountable lead or for tactical reasons when time or weather considerations appear unfavorable to the opponents. The Laws of Cricket also provide a captain the option to declare at any time during his team's second innings if he feels his team is in a favorable position to win. However, once exercised, these options are irreversible, and his team loses the match if the opponents are able to exceed his side's run total.

declare: To, as team captain of the batting side, close an innings being played when less than ten outs have been made. see *declaration*.

deep: Relatively far away from the striker or near the boundary, said of a fieldsman or fielding position. compare *fine, short, silly, square*.

deep extra cover: 1. An outfield position on the off side in the area wide of and beyond mid off, near the boundary. 2. The fieldsman in the deep extra cover position.

deep field: The area of the outfield far away from the striker and relatively close to the boundary. also *country, the*. compare *close field*.

deep-field: Of or pertaining to the area of the outfield far from the striker and relatively close to the boundary. compare *close-field*.

deep fielding: Fielding from outfield positions that are far from the striker and relatively close to the boundary. compare *close fielding*.

deep-fielding: Far from the striker in the outfield and relatively close to the boundary, said of a fieldsman or fielding position. compare *close-fielding*.

deep fine leg: 1. An outfield position on the leg side behind the striker, played a short distance wide of the line of flight of a bowled ball and near the back boundary. compare *leg slip*. 2. The fieldsman in the deep fine leg position.

deep midwicket: 1. The midwicket fielding position on the leg side played "deep", or farther away from the striker. see *midwicket*. 2. The fieldsman in the deep midwicket position.

deep square leg: 1. A fielding position almost square to the striker on the leg side near the boundary. compare *square leg*. 2. The fieldsman in the deep square leg position.

defensive field: A deployment of fieldsmen in positions that are generally some distance from the batsman. A defensive field is employed to prevent runs rather than to take wickets (make outs). compare *attacking field*.

defensive shot: A stroke meant to defend the wicket rather than to score runs. compare *attacking shot*.

deliver: To bowl the ball. also *send down, send the ball down*.

delivery: A bowled ball, or the act or an instance of bowling the ball. also *bowl*.

direct-attack bowling: Bowling that is considered a direct attack by the bowler upon the batsman, the unfair practice of systematically bowling fast, short-pitched (so as to bounce high) balls at a batsman standing clear of his wicket. A bowler who persists in making this kind of delivery after being cautioned can be ordered replaced by the umpire and prevented from bowling for the remainder of the innings. also *bodyline bowling*.

dismiss: To put out a batsman.

dismissal: An out.

dolly: 1. A batted ball hit high into the air, easy to catch. From the original "dolly-catch" in the mid 1920s. also *balloon, sitter, skier*. 2. A slow, high-arcing delivery by a bowler. From the early 1900s. also *banana floater, donkey drop, lob*.

donkey drop: A slow, high-arcing delivery by a bowler. From the late 1880s. also *dolly*.

double: The scoring of 1000 runs and taking of 100 wickets in a single season by a player skilled as both batsman and bowler. Wilfred R. Rhodes of Yorkshire holds the career record, achieving 16 doubles between 1903 and his retirement in 1930. compare *bowler's double*.

double century: The scoring of 200 runs during one's turn at bat during an innings. The first recorded double century was by W. Ward of the MCC who scored 278 runs against Norfolk in 1820. Sir Donald Bradman of Australia holds the career record for double centuries, accomplishing this feat thirty-seven times between 1927 and 1949. also *twin century.*

double double: The almost impossible feat of scoring 2000 runs and taking 200 wickets in a single season, accomplished only once in first-class cricket. In 1906, Yorkshire and England all-rounder George Hirst (1871–1954) scored 2,385 runs while taking 208 wickets.

down: One or both bails dislodged or one or more stumps pulled out or knocked over by the ball, the striker, or his bat, or by a fieldsman holding the ball, said of a broken wicket. see *break the wicket.*

drag: 1. To play on to the wicket. also *play on.* 2. To impart reverse spin (backspin) to a bowled ball. 3. To drag one's rear foot at the release of the ball when bowling, a once popular method of "bending" the original rule governing the restriction of the bowler's rear foot before the ball was released. see *no ball.*

1. drive: An attacking shot in which a bowled ball is struck hard and propelled forward from the batsman in a relatively straight trajectory. see *cover drive, low drive, off drive, on drive, straight drive.*

2. drive: 1. To strike a bowled ball hard, causing it to be propelled forward in a relatively straight trajectory. 2. To execute a drive stroke against a particular bowler. (drove Alcott for a boundary)

drop: To drop a ball hit into the air by a batsman. (dropped Tanner prolonging the innings)

dropped catch: A batted ball in the air that is dropped after a fieldsman has attempted to catch it.

duck: An innings in which a batsman is held scoreless. Short for duck egg. Both popularized around 1868 from the earlier (1863) "duck's egg" for the zero marked on a scorecard for the batsman. see *blob, bowled for a duck, break one's duck, king pair, make a duck, on one's duck, pair of ducks.*

easy wicket: A smooth, even pitch, preferably slow, as is sometimes the case when the wicket becomes saturated with water. On such a surface, the ball bounces predictably and can be judged

and timed more easily by batsmen. also *batting pitch, bread and butter wicket, plumb, plumb wicket.*

1. edge: 1. The edge of the bat. Bowlers hope to "find the edge" of a striker's bat, with the result often being an easy catch. 2. A ball hit off the edge of the bat, often for an easy catch.

2. edge: To hit the ball off the edge of the bat rather than the flat front surface of the blade, often resulting in an easy catch.

end: Either of the two wickets or the area around them. (will bowl from the other end for the next over)

extra: Any run that results from a bye, leg bye, no ball, or a wide rather than a hit. Extras are not credited to the batsman but to the team. also *sundry.*

extra cover, extra cover point: 1. A fielding position on the off side that can be played either in the area between cover point and mid off (short extra cover) or beyond mid off, closer to the boundary (deep extra cover). 2. The fieldsman in the extra cover position.

face: To take one's turn as the striker against a bowler.

fall: 1. To be dismissed. (Daly and Cook fell to close the innings) 2. To have one or both bails dislodged or one or more stumps pulled out or knocked over, said of a wicket broken for a dismissal.

fast ball: A bowled ball delivered with great pace. The fastest bowled balls are delivered at close to 100 m.p.h.

●● The expressions "fast one", meaning something tricky or deceptive, and to "pull a fast one", meaning to do something tricky or deceptive, were first

TO FACE

116

popularized around 1938 and referred to the deceptive and difficult to hit fast balls sent down by England's noted fast bowler of the 1920s and 1930s, Harold Larwood.

fast bowler: A bowler who is known for or proficient at delivering fast balls. Modern day fast bowlers are inevitably compared to legendary earlier speed merchants such as C. J. Kortright of Essex (late 1890s), then regarded as faster than any before him, H. Larwood, the "Nottingham Express", England's top bowler in 1927, 1928, 1931, 1932, and 1936, Ray Lindwall (1940s and 1950s), Australia's brilliant fast bowler, and F. S. Trueman (England, 1950s and 1960s), who was the first bowler in history to take over 300 Test wickets, 307 with a bowling average of 21.75. For sheer speed, however, many contend that England's F. H. Tyson (mid-1950s) was the fastest of all time. also *pace bowler, paceman, quick, quickie.* compare *medium-pace bowler, slow bowler, spin bowler.*

fast wicket: A hard, smooth playing surface, one that favors fast bowlers. also *quick wicket.* compare *slow wicket.*

1. field: 1. An oval or rounded rectangle-shaped grass playing area (ideally about 200 yards long by 150 yards wide) at the center of which is a carefully groomed area known as the square or middle, wherein the pitch is made. The pitch is a 22-yard long by 10-foot wide rectangle of close-cut grass (or a smooth artificial surface) with an 8-foot, 8-inch line, the bowling crease, marked across each end on which the wickets are centered. Four feet in front of and parallel to each bowling crease a line called the popping crease (minimum length of 12 feet), is marked. Parallel lines 8 feet, 8 inches apart called the return crease are marked at the ends of and perpendicular to each bowling crease, extending forward to the popping crease and back to a point at least 4 feet behind the wicket. also *cricket ground, ground, grounds, pitch.* 2. The fieldsmen and their alignment or positioning. (changed to an off-side field) 3. A fieldsman. (known as a good field at cover point) also *fielder.*

2. field: To grasp and control a thrown or batted ball.

fielder: A fieldsman. also *field.*

fieldsman: Any of the players on the field while the other team is batting during an innings. Fieldsmen are deployed in various positions on the field (according to specific game conditions) and are responsible for making catches for outs and for participating in runouts by fielding batted balls or those overthrown or bowled past the wicketkeeper (bowlers and wicketkeepers have additional means of dismissing batsmen). also *field, fielder.*

fifty: see *half-century.*

find the gap: To hit a bowled ball into a space between fieldsmen, enabling runs to be scored.

fine: Not far wide of the line of flight of a bowled ball, said of a fieldsman or fielding position. compare *deep, short, silly, square.*

fine leg: 1. A fielding position on the leg side behind the striker, played a short distance wide of the line of flight of a bowled ball. Fine leg can be played relatively close behind the striker (short fine leg) or back near the boundary (deep fine leg). 2. The fieldsman in the fine leg position.

fingerspin: Spin imparted to a bowled ball solely by the motion of the fingertips, as opposed to that imparted by turning the wrist.

first-class cricket: The highest level of cricket competition in a nation. Within each country, certain league matches (often those between county or state teams) and specific traditional or annual competitions are considered first-class cricket.

first slip: 1. One of the slip fielding positions on the off side in back of the wicketkeeper, this one being the closest laterally and the farthest back, just behind and inside second slip. 2. The fieldsman in the first slip position.

1. flight: To bowl a ball in such a way that the vertical trajectory makes it difficult for the batsman to judge where the ball will pitch.

2. flight: 1. A bowled ball with a vertical trajectory that makes it difficult for the batsman to judge where it will pitch. 2. The vertical trajectory of a bowled ball, among the variables controlled by the bowler. compare *length, lift, line, pace, swerve, swing, turn.*

flipper: A delivery (often a leg-break) with top spin imparted by "flipping" the ball

117

off the fingertips on release, causing it to jump forward upon pitching. From the 1920s.

fly slip: 1. An unorthodox fielding position on the off side about halfway between the slips and the boundary. 2. The fieldsman in the fly slip position.

follow on: To, at the option of the opposing team's captain, commence with a second innings (same side batting) directly after the first innings has been completed when behind by a certain number of runs (75 runs in a one-day match, 100 runs in a two-day match, 150 runs in three-day and four-day matches, 200 runs in matches of five or more days). This option can be exercised by the captain of the team that batted first in the first innings if he feels his team has accumulated enough runs to win without batting a second time. A second opportunity to bat is available, however, should the opponents (the team following on) exceed his team's score. The first follow-on rule (1835) made it mandatory for a team to bat again if behind by 100 runs at the end of the first innings. The present rules were adopted in 1971.

follow-on: The act or an instance of a team following on.

forcing shot: see *attacking shot.*

1. forward cut: A seldom seen cut shot in which the bat is brought down sharply on a rising ball, sending it toward the off side between cover point and extra cover.

2. forward cut: 1. To execute a forward cut stroke. 2. To execute a forward cut stroke against a particular bowler.

forward short leg: see *silly mid-on.*

forward stroke: A stroke in which the batsman steps forward with his front leg just before making contact with the ball. compare *backstroke.*

four: 1. Four runs scored as a result of a hit or an overthrow. 2. The award of four runs when a thrown or batted ball hits inside, then touches or crosses a boundary. also *boundary.*

front-foot: Of or pertaining to forward play or a forward stroke. (a well-known front-foot batsman) compare *back-foot.*

full-length: In the air, the full distance between the bowler and the batsman, said of a bowled ball that does not pitch in between. also *full pitch.*

full pitch: see *full-length.*

full toss: A ball bowled so as to travel the full distance between the bowler and batsman without pitching.

gardening: Player's slang for the act or an instance of patting down a damaged portion of the pitch with a bat or picking up loose bits of turf. From the late 1870s.

get a blob: To, as a batsman, be held scoreless in an innings. The expression was popularized in 1905. also *make a blob, make a duck.* see *blob.*
•• Used figuratively since around 1905 to mean to accomplish nothing.

get one's eye in: see *play one's self in.*

give a catch: To hit a bowled ball that is caught for an out, said of a batsman.

given out: Called or judged out by an umpire, said of a batsman who is dismissed.

give the ball air: To, as a bowler, flight a delivery so that the ball travels in a looping arc. Cambridge University and Yorkshire slow bowler E. R. Wilson is credited with being among the first to popularize the expression around 1920.

glide: see *leg glance.*

glance: see *leg glance.*

glass arm: A derogatory term describing a fieldsman's weak throwing arm.

gloves: 1. The short padded gloves worn by a batsman, with individual tubular sections protecting the back of the fingers and hands. Gloves for batting (kid gloves with rubber strips glued on) were introduced by Blackheath schoolmaster and Kent, Surrey, and All-England XI cricketer, Nicolas Felix (or Wanostrocht) around 1835. 2. The protective leather gloves worn by wicketkeepers to protect the hands and wrists. Special gloves for wicketkeepers were introduced by British cricket equipment manufacturer, Duke and Son in the late 1840s.

gluepot: Slang for a sticky wicket. also *sticky dog.*

go away: To veer away from the batsman in the air or upon pitching, said of a bowled ball.

go in: To take one's turn as a batsman.

googler: A bowler who is proficient at or known for bowling googlies. also *googlie merchant, googly merchant.*

googlie: see *googly.*

googlie-merchant: see *googly-merchant.*

googly: An off-break (turns into the batsman after pitching on the off side)

bowled with a leg-break motion to deceive the batsman, but released from the back of the hand as the wrist is turned over to reverse the direction of spin imparted. The introduction of the googly is credited to English bowler B. J. T. Bosanquet in 1900. Bosanquet popularized the technique on an Australian tour in 1903–04, during which his Test average was 25.18 for 16 wickets. also *bosey, bosie, googlie, wrong 'un.*
•• Australian slang from the mid-1920s for a tricky or awkward question.

googly merchant: A googler. From the 1920s. also *googlie merchant.*

go with the arm: To move or veer in the direction of movement of the bowler's arm, either in the air or upon pitching, said of a bowled ball. see *arm ball.*

greasy: Wet from rain or over-watering, said of a saturated pitch or field.

green-top: A smooth, grassy pitch likely to favor fast bowlers, especially if slightly wet.

ground: 1. A stadium or playing field and environs. 2. The playing field. also *cricket ground, grounds, pitch.* see *field.*

grounds: see *ground.*

grub, grubber: An underhand delivery that stays low and skims along the ground, seldom seen in modern cricket. Popularized in the late 1800s or early 1900s from the worm-like larva of certain insects found in the ground. also *sneak.* see *bowl.*

guard: see *take guard.*

gully: 1. The fielding position on the off side between point and the slips. also *backward point.* 2. The fieldsman who plays in the gully position. also *backward point.*

half-century: The scoring of fifty runs during one's turn at bat in an innings. also *fifty.*

half-cock: An awkward stroke made when the batsman misjudges the length of a bowled ball and hasn't time to properly move his feet.

1. half-volley: To hit a bowled ball immediately after it pitches.

2. half-volley: A stroke in which a bowled ball is hit immediately after it pitches.

handle the ball: To, as a batsman, touch the ball with the hands while it is in play. Unless requested by the opposing team, this is illegal and results in the batsman being given out "handled the

ball". Since 1899, a ball lodged in a batsman's clothing has been considered dead and can be removed without fear of a dismissal.

Harrow bat: An undersized bat, as for schoolboys.

hat trick: The taking of three wickets by a bowler with three consecutive balls. From the mid-1800s when certain English clubs began awarding hats to bowlers who accomplished this feat.
•• Three successive, identical accomplishments by the same individual, such as scoring three goals in a single soccer or hockey game, or three related accomplishments, such as hitting for the cycle (a single, double, and triple) in baseball, three consecutive wins in different horse races, or winning a particular race for three consecutive years.

have a boff: To hit out. First used in England in the mid-1950s. From the earlier (1894) "have a go".

have a go: To hit out. Popularized in 1894.
•• To try or make an attempt. (decided to have a go at the crossword puzzle)

haymaker: Players' slang for a stroke in which the bat is swung like a scythe cutting hay.

helmet: A cap-like plastic protective covering for the head, the latest examples of which extend down to cover the ear and temple area. Clear, wrap-around plastic or wire cage visors are often attached to protect the face. Helmets are worn regularly by batsmen and, increasingly in recent years, by players in the close-fielding positions.

hip-pocket shot: An awkward defensive shot in which the ball is hit downward with the bat held high and close to the batsman's body, often the result of leg-theory bowling.

hit a six: To hit a boundary six, a fly ball that clears a boundary without being caught, resulting in six runs being awarded.

hit off the back foot: 1. To execute a backstroke. compare *hit off the front foot.* 2. To practice or specialize in back play. compare *hit off the front foot.*

hit off the front foot: 1. To execute a forward stroke. compare *hit off the back foot.* 2. To practice or specialize in forward play. compare *hit off the back foot.*

hit out: To bat aggressively on one or more deliveries with the intent of scoring runs rather than just protecting the wicket. also *have a boff, have a go.*

hit the ball twice: To strike or be hit by a bowled ball, then wilfully strike it again, except for the purpose of protecting the wicket (which is allowed with the bat or any part of one's person but the hands). A batsman who does this is given out "hit the ball twice".

hit wicket: Having dislodged one or both bails or knocked over one or more of the stumps with the bat or any part of one's person while attempting to play the ball or setting out to run. A batsman who does this is given out "hit wicket".

home: 1. One's crease. 2. Having made one's ground, safely in one's crease.

1. hook: A stroke in which a fast ball pitched short is stepped inside of (so that it passes on the leg side of the striker) and swept back on the leg side between square leg and the wicketkeeper. also *hookshot.*

2. hook: 1. To step inside of a fast ball pitched short (so that it passes on one's leg side) and sweep it back on the leg side between square leg and the wicketkeeper. 2. To execute a hook against a particular bowler.

hookshot: see *hook.*

How's that?: The audible plea made to an umpire by one or more fieldsmen before any batsman can be given out, or after a close play when an out is being called for. The phrase is often abbreviated and almost unintelligible. One variation sounds like "Owzat?".

ICC: The International Cricket Conference.

in: Taking one's turn as a batsman.

infield: The area of the field relatively close to the wicket.

innings: 1. A player's turn at bat. A player's innings continues until he is dismissed. The longest individual Test innings occurred in 1958, when Hanif Mohammad of Pakistan stayed at bat for sixteen hours and thirty-nine minutes for 337 runs against the West Indies. 2. A team's turn at bat. A team's innings continues until ten batsmen have been dismissed or until the captain declares the innings closed. see *declaration.*

in strike: At bat, taking one's turn batting. also *in.*

inswing: The swerving motion of a bowled ball in the air from the off side toward the leg side.

inswinger: A bowled ball that swerves in the air from the off side toward the leg side (into the batsman). compare *outswinger.*

International Cricket Conference: The governing body responsible for international cricket. When it was founded in London in 1909 as the Imperial Cricket Conference, membership was limited to cricket governing bodies within the British Commonwealth where Test matches were played. Original members were England, Australia, and South Africa (dropped after leaving the Commonwealth in 1961). India, New Zealand, and the West Indies were admitted in 1926, Pakistan in 1952. In 1965, the present name was adopted along with new rules permitting other nations to be admitted. To date, cricket governing bodies from fourteen additional nations (including the United States) have been admitted as associate members. also *ICC.*

keeper: The wicketkeeper. also *Aunt Sally, stump, stumper.*

keeping: Acting as the wicketkeeper. also *at the stumps.*

keep wicket: To act as the wicketkeeper.

kick: 1. To cause a bowled ball to rebound erratically, said of the surface of a pitch. (an uneven pitch that kicked the ball all over) 2. To rebound erratically, said of a bowled ball. (kicked back toward his head) also *kick up.*

kick up: see *kick.*

king pair: Two consecutive innings in which a particular player is dismissed without scoring (a "pair of ducks"), each time on the first ball. see *duck.*

last wicket stand: 1. The performance of

KEEPER

or number of runs scored by the last two batsmen in an innings (with 9 wickets already down). 2. The last two batsmen in an innings (with 9 wickets already down).

1. **late cut:** A stroke in which a bowled ball on the rise is hit down at with a short, snappy swing as it passes, sending it back on the off side toward slips. also *back cut.*

2. **late cut:** 1. To hit down at a bowled ball on the rise with a short, snappy swing as it passes, sending it back on the off side toward slips. also *back cut.* 2. To execute a late cut stroke against a particular bowler. (late cut Austin for a quick single) also *back cut.*

Laws: The international rules of cricket. The earliest complete set of cricket rules appear to be those drawn up in 1744 by the London club. The MCC, author of the present Laws of Cricket, made its first revisions in 1788.

LBW: Short for leg before wicket.

leg: Short for the leg side.

leg-before: Short for leg before wicket.

leg before wicket: Having blocked the wicket with part of one's person rather than with the bat, thereby intercepting a bowled ball that, in the judgement of an umpire, would have hit the wicket. A batsman who does this is, on appeal, given out "leg before wicket". First mentioned in the Laws of Cricket in 1774, the leg before wicket rule has been a source of controversy through revisions in 1788, 1823, 1839, the most consequential of all, in 1937. In that year, a ball pitching on the off side of the wicket (as opposed to just between the wickets) was included under the Law, as long as the umpire judged that it would have hit the wicket if not intercepted by the batsman. In 1972, it was ruled that the batsman could be given out on such a ball even if the actual interception was outside the off stump, rather than just between the wickets. also *LBW. leg-before.*

leg-break: A bowled ball that, because of spin imparted to it, breaks or turns from the leg side toward the off side (away from the batsman) after pitching. compare *off-break.*

leg bye: A run scored after a bowled ball is deflected off a batsman attempting to hit or get out of the way of the ball.

leg cutter: A medium to fast delivery in which the fingers of the bowler "cut" across the seam at the point of release, causing the ball to break from the leg side toward the off stump. also *cutter.*

leg glance: A stroke in which a bowled ball is deflected almost straight back on the leg side toward fine leg or long leg. also *glance, glide, leg glide.*

leg glide: see *leg glance.*

leg hit: A bowled ball hit to the leg side.

leg pads: see *batting pads.*

leg side: That side of the field on the side of the wicket on which the striker stands. also *leg, on side.* compare *off side.*

leg-side: Of or pertaining to the leg side. (a leg-side fielder) also *on-side.* compare *off-side.*

leg-side field: A deployment of fielding players in which more fieldsmen are positioned on the leg side, as is often the case in anticipation of the leg-side hits that result from the use of leg-theory bowling. In 1969, a law was passed which limited the number of leg-side fielders behind the popping crease at the moment of delivery to two in order to preclude packing the leg side. also *on-side field.* compare *off-side field.* see *leg-theory bowling.*

leg slip: 1. A fielding position a short distance behind and just wide of the wicketkeeper on the leg side. also *short fine leg.* 2. The fieldsman who plays in the leg slip position. also *short fine leg.*

leg spin: Spin imparted by the bowler to the ball that causes it to swerve from off to leg (toward the batsman) in the air, but to break or turn from leg to off (away from the batsman) upon pitching. compare *off spin.*

leg spinner: 1. A bowled ball with leg spin. compare *off spinner.* 2. A bowler known for or proficient at bowling balls with leg spin. compare *off spinner.*

leg stump: 1. The outside stump on the leg side, closest to the batsman. compare *middle stump, off stump.* 2. A verbal request from the striker to the umpire at the opposite wicket when taking guard to help him position his bat directly in front of the leg stump. also *one leg.* compare *middle, middle and leg.*

leg-theory bowling: The practice of employing a leg-side field in conjunction with medium-fast to fast bowling (often with inswing) aimed at pitching on or outside the leg stump, thereby virtually forcing the batsman to make leg hits. England bowler Fred Root was the first to popularize leg-theory bowling in the 1926 Test matches against Australia. In the years following World War II, the use of the technique increased dramatically. Finally, to stem the negative, defensive aspects of leg-theory bowling, a law was passed in 1969, limiting the leg-side field to two fieldsmen behind the popping crease at the moment of the bowler's delivery. see *leg-side field*.

leg trap: A deployment of fieldsmen around the batsman on the leg side in order to be in position to make a catch. Such a field can consist of a leg slip, a short leg, and a forward short leg.

length: The distance traveled by a bowled ball before it pitches, among the variables controlled by the bowler. compare *flight, lift, line, pace, swerve, swing, turn*.

1. lift: To rise from the ground after pitching, said of a bowled ball.

2. lift: The height, angle, and speed of the rise of a bowled ball after it pitches, among the variables controlled by the bowler. compare *flight, length, line, pace, swerve, swing, turn*.

lifter: A bowled ball that lifts sharply after pitching.

limited-over cricket: Cricket matches in which the innings end after a specified number of overs are completed, regardless of whether or not ten wickets have fallen. In England, limited-over cricket is played in John Player League matches (one 40-over innings for each side) and Gillette Cup matches (one 60-over innings for each side).

line: The direction of a bowled ball, one of the variables controlled by the bowler. compare *flight, length, lift, pace, swerve, swing, turn*.

1. lob: A slow, high-arcing delivery. also *banana floater, dolly, donkey drop*.

2. lob: 1. To deliver a slow, high-arcing ball. 2. To deliver a slow, high-arcing ball to a particular batsman. (tried to lob Maxwell)

long field: The general area of the outfield behind the bowler and near the boundary, where the fieldsmen at long leg and long off play.

long handle: A grip in which the batsman's hands are positioned at the very end of the handle, providing maximum power when hitting out.

long hop: A bowled ball that pitches short (a long way from the batsman), often an easy delivery to hit.

long leg: 1. A fielding position deep in the outfield behind the striker's wicket on the leg side. 2. The fieldsman in the long leg position.

long-off: 1. A fielding position deep in the outfield on the off side, behind the bowler's end of the pitch near the boundary. compare *long-on*. 2. The fieldsman in the long-off position.

long-on: 1. A fielding position deep in the outfield on the leg side, behind the bowler's end of the pitch near the boundary. compare *long-off*. 2. The fieldsman in the long-on position.

long-stop: 1. A fielding position directly behind the wicketkeeper, obsolete in high-level cricket. 2. The fieldsman in the long-stop position. also *long-stopper*.

long-stopper: Slang for the long-stop fieldsman. also *long-stop*.
●● From the early 1900s, Australian slang for a lookout man.

low drive: A powerful drive that stays close to the ground and is, therefore, difficult to catch.

lunch interval: An arranged break for lunch in some cricket matches during which play is suspended. compare *tea interval*.

maiden, maiden over: An over (of 6 or 8 balls, depending on prevailing national rules) during which no runs are scored. The record for the highest number of maiden overs in a Test match was set by South Africa's off-break bowler H. J. Tayfield, who bowled 16 consecutive (8-ball) maiden overs against England at Durban in 1957.

make a blob: To, as a batsman, be held scoreless in an innings. Popularized in 1903. also *get a blob, make a duck*. see *blob*.
●● Used figuratively since around 1905 to mean to make or accomplish nothing.

make a duck: To, as a batsman, be held scoreless in an innings. Popularized in the late 1860s. also *get a blob, make a blob*. see *duck*.

make one's ground: To safely reach or touch (with the bat in hand or any part of one's person) the ground inside the crease one is running toward or returning to before the wicket is downed.

Man of the Match: An award given to the outstanding player in a match.

•• An award given figuratively or facetiously for an outstanding act or performance. (got Man of the Match for his witty parting remark).

Marylebone Cricket Club: The most famous cricket club in the world, founded in 1787 by members of the White Conduit Cricket Club of Islington, London, among them the Earl of Winchelsea, then president of the venerable Hambledon Cricket Club. The Marylebone Cricket Club (MCC) was soon recognized as the leading authority on cricket, not only in England, but wherever the game was played. Until 1968, when the MCC Council was formed, a central authority with representatives from other associations, the Marylebone Cricket Club was solely responsible for the sport and its Laws. Headquarters for the MCC and the Imperial Cricket Museum is at Lord's Cricket Ground, London.

matting: Synthetic turf for the pitch.

MCC: The Marylebone Cricket Club.

meat: The middle of the blade of a bat at its thickest point, the optimum point of contact for power.

medium-pace bowler: A bowler who is proficient at or known for bowling medium fast deliveries. also *medium pacer*. compare *fast bowler, slow bowler, spin bowler*.

medium pacer: A medium-pace bowler.

middle: 1. see *square*. 2. A verbal request from the striker to the umpire when taking guard to help him position his bat directly in front of the middle stump. compare *leg stump, middle and leg*. also *center*.

middle and leg: A verbal request from the striker to the umpire at the opposite wicket when taking guard to help him position his bat directly in front of the space between the middle and leg stumps. also *center, two legs*. compare *leg stump, middle*.

middle it: see *middle the ball*.

middle stump: The center stump in the wicket, in between the leg-side and off-side stumps. compare *leg stump, off stump*.

middle the ball: To hit the ball squarely, making contact with the optimum part of the striking surface of the bat. also *middle it*.

mid-off: 1. A fielding position not far behind the bowler on the off side. compare *mid-on*. 2. The fieldsman in the mid-off position.

mid-on: 1. A fielding position not far behind the bowler on the leg side. compare *mid-off*. 2. The fieldsman in the mid-on position.

midwicket: 1. A fielding position on the leg side approximately in line with or not far in front of the bowling crease. compare *deep midwicket*. 2. The fieldsman in the midwicket position.

military medium: Slang for just under medium or on the slow side of medium fast, said of a bowler or his deliveries.

misfield: To misjudge, drop, or bobble a batted ball.

mow: A stroke in which the ball is hit cross-batted to the leg side. Derived from the "mowing" action of the swing.

nets: see *practice nets*.

night watchman: A batsman from low in the batting order sent in to defend the wicket for the last few overs near the close of play at day's end, thereby saving a more skilled batsman for the resumption of play the next day. Popularized in the mid 1940s.

no ball: 1. A bowled ball declared unfair by an umpire, not counted as one of the six or eight (depending on prevailing rules) balls of an over. If a delivery is thrown (with the elbow bent) rather than bowled, if, in the delivery stride, no part of the bowler's front foot is behind the popping crease (grounded or raised) or his back foot does not land within the return crease (without touching it or its extension), if the bowler fails to notify the striker of a change in the mode of delivery (whether over the wicket or round the wicket, overhand or underhand, left- or right-handed), or if the bowler throws the ball at the striker's wicket in an attempt to run him out before delivering it, a no ball may be declared by an umpire. A no ball may be hit by the striker and any runs that result are credited to him. Any runs made otherwise are scored as "no balls". If no runs are made, one run is awarded. No balls were first recorded in a match between the MCC and Middlesex at Lord's in 1830. 2. Any run resulting from a no ball that is not because of a hit by the batsman.

no-ball: To declare an unfair delivery by

a bowler a no ball.

nonstriker: The batsman that is not "in strike" (at bat attempting to hit the ball), but positioned at the wicket from which the ball is bowled. When one or any other odd number of runs is made, the batsmen exchange wickets, with the nonstriker becoming the striker and the striker becoming the nonstriker. compare *striker.*

not out: 1. Having not been given out and still batting (as striker or nonstriker) at the end of a team's innings, said of a batsman. 2. Having not had ten batsmen dismissed and still batting at the end of a day's play, said of a team. compare *all out.*

off: Short for the off side.

off-break: A bowled ball that, because of off spin imparted to it, breaks or turns from the off side toward the leg side (toward the batsman) after pitching. compare *leg-break.*

off drive: A drive hit to the off side toward the area between the opposite wicket and extra cover. compare *cover drive, on drive, square drive, straight drive.*

off-drive: 1. To drive a bowled ball to the off side toward the area between the opposite wicket and extra cover. compare *on-drive.* 2. To execute an off drive against a particular bowler. (off-drove Wilson on the first delivery) compare *on-drive.*

off side: That part of the field on the side of the wicket opposite the one on which the striker stands. also *off.* compare *leg side.*

off-side: Of or pertaining to the off side. (an off-side fielder) compare *leg-side.*

off-side field: A deployment of fielding players in which more fieldsmen are positioned on the off side in anticipation of hits toward that side. compare *leg-side field.*

off spin: Spin imparted by the bowler to the ball that causes it to swerve from leg to off in the air (away from the batsman), but to break or turn from off to leg (toward the batsman) upon pitching. compare *leg spin.*

off spinner: 1. A bowled ball with off spin imparted to it. compare *leg spinner.* 2. A bowler who is proficient at or known for bowling off spinners. One of the great off spinners of all time, Lance R. Gibbs of the West Indies (1960s and 1970s) was only the second bowler in

history to capture over 300 Test wickets. compare *leg spinner.*

off stump: The outside stump on the off side, the one opposite the side on which the striker stands. compare *leg stump, middle stump.*

off the gloves: Deflected off the striker's gloves, as of a ball mishit then caught for an easy dismissal.

on drive: A drive hit to the leg (on) side toward the area between the opposite wicket and midwicket. compare *cover drive, off drive, square drive, straight drive.*

on-drive: 1. To drive a bowled ball to the leg (on) side toward the area between the opposite wicket and midwicket. compare *off-drive.* 2. To execute an on drive against a particular bowler. (on-drove Hunt for a four off the boundary) compare *off-drive.*

one: A single run. (often good for a one or a two) also *single.*

one leg: see *leg stump.*

on one's duck: To be scoreless while batting in one's innings, said of a batsman. see *duck.*

on side: The leg side.

on-side: Leg-side.

on-side field: A leg-side field.

on the boundary: Close to the boundary, as of a fieldsman or a catch.

open: To go in as first batsman in an innings.

opener: The opening batsman in an innings, usually one of the best batsmen on a side. also *opening bat, opening batsman.*

openers: The two opening batsmen in an innings.

opening bat, opening batsman: The first player to bat in an innings, usually one of the most skilled batsmen on a side. also *opener.*

opening stand: 1. The performance of or number of runs scored by the first two batsmen in an innings. The most successful opening stand in the history of Test cricket was 413 runs, scored in 1955 by India's first-wicket partnership of V. Mankad and P. Roy against Pakistan. 2. The first two batsmen in an innings. also *openers.*

1. out: No longer a batsman, dismissed. On appeal, a batsman is given out if he is bowled, caught, run out, or stumped, or if he handles the ball, hits the ball twice, obstructs the field, or if he knocks the wicket down (out hit wicket), or obstructs the wicket (out leg before wicket).

2. out: The act or an instance of a batsman being dismissed.

outfield: The area of the field relatively far from the wicket, closer to the boundaries.

out of one's ground: Not touching (with the bat in hand or any part of one's body) the ground inside the crease where one is stationed or toward which one is running or returning as a batsman and, therefore, subject to being put out if the wicket is broken.

outswinger: A bowled ball that swerves in the air from the leg side toward the off side (away from the batsman). also *away swinger.* compare *inswinger.*

over: A series of six or (depending on prevailing rules) eight consecutive balls delivered by a bowler from one end of the wicket, not including deliveries judged wide balls or no balls by an umpire. Though a bowler may bowl as many overs as desired, he is not permitted to bowl two consecutive overs in an innings. So, when an over is completed (signaled by the umpire calling out "over"), the following over is bowled by another bowler from the opposite end. The six-ball over was made standard in 1900, though in 1921, the eight-ball over (popular in Australia since 1918) was recognized as legal where preferred.

over rate: The number of overs bowled in an hour.

OUT OF ONE'S GROUND

overspin: Top spin.

over the wicket: Delivered from over or very close to the wicket, said of a bowled ball. According to the Laws of cricket, a bowler must notify the striker whether he intends to deliver the ball overhanded or underhanded, left-handed or right-handed, or over the wicket or round the wicket. A failure to comply results in a no ball. compare *round the wicket.*

1. overthrow: To, as a fieldsman, throw the ball past the wicket and/or past teammates on a return, often allowing one or more runs to be scored.

2. overthrow: 1. A return thrown past the wicket and/or past teammates, often resulting in runs being scored. 2. Any run scored as a result of a return overthrown. Four runs (overthrows) are awarded if a return hits or crosses a boundary.

Owzat?: see *How's that?*

pace: The velocity of a bowled ball.

pace bowler: A fast bowler. also *paceman, quick, quickie, speed merchant.*

paceman: A fast bowler. also *pace bowler, quick, quickie, speed merchant.*

pacey: Fast, said of a bowler or of a delivery.

pad-play: The intentional blocking of the wicket with the pads to intercept bowled balls. see *leg before wicket.*

pads: see *batting pads.*

pad up: 1. To put on batting pads preparatory to taking one's turn as a batsman. 2. To intentionally block the wicket with one's pads in order to intercept a bowled ball. see *leg before wicket.*

pair: Short for a pair of ducks or a pair of spectacles.

pair of ducks: Two consecutive innings in which a batsman is given out without scoring runs. also *pair, pair of spectacles, spectacles.* see *duck.*

pair of spectacles: Two consecutive scoreless innings for a batsman. Popularized in the 1860s from the appearance of two zeros in statistics. also *pair, pair of ducks, spectacles.*

partnership: The two batsmen (striker and nonstriker) at any point in a match. The record for the highest score ever made by a partnership in a Test cricket innings was set in 1934, when Sir Donald G. Bradman and William H. Ponsford of

Australia combined for 451 runs against England.

pavilion: The structure at cricket grounds in which players store equipment, change clothes, and take meals.

1. pitch: 1. To bounce on the ground before reaching the striker's wicket, said of a bowled ball. 2. To cause a bowled ball to bounce on the ground before reaching the striker's wicket, said of a bowler.

2. pitch: 1. The 22-yard long and 10-foot wide rectangle of close-cut grass (or artificial surface) between wickets. also *track, wicket.* see *wicket.* 2. A cricket ground. also *ground, grounds.* see *field.*

play: To hit or attempt to hit a bowled ball.

play and miss: To attempt and fail to hit a bowled ball.

play on: Short for play on to the wicket. also *drag.*

play one's self in: To bat cautiously and defensively until acclimated to the deliveries of the bowler. also *get one's eye in.*

play on to the wicket: To deflect the ball back into the wicket, removing the bails. When a wicket falls in this manner, the striker is, on appeal, out bowled. also *drag, play on.*

play safe: To bat cautiously and defensively.

plumb: 1. Short for plumb wicket. 2. A blatant instance of leg before wicket.

plumb wicket: A wicket that is true and predictable, an easy wicket for batsmen. also *batting pitch, bread and butter wicket, plumb.*

point: 1. A fielding position almost square to the striker on the off side. compare *silly point.* 2. The fieldsman in the point position.

pop: To rebound sharply off the ground, as of a bowled ball upon pitching.

popping crease: Either of two lines (minimum length of 12 feet) marked four feet in front of and parallel to the bowling crease at both ends of the cricket pitch. As long as a batsman has some part of his person or the bat he is holding grounded behind the popping crease, he is not "out of his ground", and cannot be run out or out stumped. While the ball is in play, each time the batsmen cross and ground some part of their person or bat behind the popping crease at the opposite end of the wicket, one run

is scored. On each delivery, the bowler's front foot must be behind the popping crease at the opposite wicket (and the rear foot within the return crease or its extension) at the moment the ball is released. The name popping crease comes from the very early days of cricket when a small hole was dug between the then two bails. To score a run, the batsman had to jam the tip of his bat into the hole before the ball could be "popped" into it. Injuries resulting from the inevitable collisions between the bat and wicketkeeper's hands eventually led to the safer present methods of scoring runs with the adoption of the popping crease. The distance between the bowling crease and popping crease (3 feet, 10 inches in the 1744 London Club Laws) was increased to four feet in 1819. also *crease.*

pop up: To hit a short, high fly ball, often for an easy catch.

pop-up: A short, high fly ball, one that often results in an easy catch.

practice nets: A rectangular enclosure of string netting within which players can practice batting and bowling. Kent, Surrey and All-England XI cricketer Nicolas Felix (or Wanostrocht) introduced practice nets around 1845. also *nets.*

pudding: Players' slang for a soggy, soft wicket that favors batsmen.

1. pull: An attacking shot in which the bat is swung horizontally with the wrists rolled over, sending the ball toward the leg side, usually between square leg and mid on. also *pull shot.*

2. pull: 1. To, with the wrists rolled over, swing the bat horizontally and hit the ball toward the leg side, usually between square leg and mid on. 2. To execute a pull shot against a particular bowler. (pulled Malone to the boundary for four)

pull shot: see *pull.*

put down: To drop a fly ball that should be caught. (prolonged the innings when he put down a sitter on the tenth wicket)

put in: To, upon winning the toss, elect to have the opposing side bat first.

quick, quickie: A fast bowler. also *pace bowler, paceman, speed merchant.*

quick single: A run scored primarily by virtue of daring and precisely timed running by the batsmen.

quick wicket: see *fast wicket.*

rabbit: A weak batter, usually placed well down in the batting order.

remove the bails: 1. To suspend play before an arranged interval or at the end of a day's play. 2. To conclude a match. In all cases, the umpires call "time" and actually remove the bails from both wickets.

retire hurt, retire ill: To voluntarily end one's turn at bat during an innings due to injury or illness. In such a case, the batsman is regarded "not out" and, when able, may resume his innings when a wicket falls or another batsman retires.

return: 1. The throwing back of the ball to the wicketkeeper by a fieldsman in a run-out attempt. 2. The throwing back of the ball to the bowler by a fieldsman or the wicketkeeper.

return crease: Either of two parallel lines drawn at right angles at the ends of the bowling crease and extending forward to the popping crease and back at least four feet behind the bowling crease. The return crease marks the area within which the bowler's rear foot must rest until the ball is delivered. compare *bowling crease, popping crease.*

round the wicket: Delivered from the side of the wicket (often near the return crease), said of a bowled ball. According to the Laws of cricket, a bowler must notify the striker whether he intends to deliver the ball overhanded or underhanded, left-handed or right-handed, or over the wicket or round the wicket. A failure to comply results in a no ball. compare *over the wicket.*

rubber: 1. An odd-numbered set of games. 2. A final, deciding game when teams are tied after playing an even number of games.

run: A point scored, accomplished after a hit or whenever the ball is in play each time both batsmen, having crossed, are able to reach the popping crease of the opposite wicket before that wicket is broken, or when assigned (as in the case of boundary hit allowances and certain penalties) by the umpire. As late as 1863, a run was called a "notch".

run-in: The bounding, accelerating steps taken by a bowler to gain momentum and rhythm before a delivery. also *run-up.*

runner: A substitute player brought in to run for a batsman with an injury that permits him to bat but not to run. A runner may score runs or be put out in the same manner as the batsman.

running between the wicket, running between the wickets: The science or practice of accumulating runs by running the distance between the wickets after a hit or any time the ball is in play. (produced many quick singles with good running between the wicket)

1. run out: To, while the ball is in play, put out a batsman who is not within the popping crease by breaking the wicket toward which he is running with the ball, or if the batsmen have not crossed, by breaking the wicket he has left.

2. run out: Put out due to one's wicket being broken by the ball or a fieldsman holding the ball while one is out of one's ground.

runout: The act or an instance of a batsman being run out.

run the ball away: To cause a bowled ball to move away from the batsman (toward the slips for a right-handed batsman).

run-up: 1. The ground behind the bowling crease on which a bowler takes his momentum-gaining steps before a delivery. also *bowler's run-up.* 2. see *run-in.*

safe pair of hands: Skill at catching or fielding, the mandatory attribute of a good fieldsman.

sanctum: see *square.*

scamper a run, scramble a run: To score a run by virtue of daring and precisely timed running and/or surprise. also *steal a run.*

seam bowler: A swing bowler, because of the importance of the direction in which the seam of the ball is pointed at the time the ball is released in swing bowling. also *seamer.* see *swing bowler.*

seam bowling: Swing bowling, because of the importance of the direction in which the seam is pointed at the time the ball is released. see *swing bowling.*

seamer: A seam bowler.

second slip: 1. One of the slip fielding positions on the off side in back of the wicketkeeper, this one being just inside and behind third slip (the closest behind the wicketkeeper, but farthest out to the side), and just outside and in front of first slip (the closest laterally, but farthest behind the wicketkeeper). 2. The fieldsman who plays in the second slip position.

send down, send the ball down: To bowl the ball. (sent down a beamer) also *deliver*.

session: Players' slang for any of the three periods of play in a match with a lunch interval and tea interval.

shine the ball: To polish one side of the ball on one's pants (often with the aid of saliva or perspiration) in order to alter the flow of air around it in flight and thus maximize its movement or deviation from a straight line when bowled.

shooter: 1. A fast bowled ball that skims along the ground. also *creeper, sneak*. 2. A bowled ball that doesn't rise upon pitching, but "shoots" forward close to the ground.

short: 1. Not having reached one's ground before turning for the opposite wicket and attempting to score another run, said of a batsman. see *short run*. 2. Relatively close to the wicket, said of a fielding position or fieldsman. compare *deep, fine, long, silly*. 3. Closer to the bowler than normal, said of the pitching of a bowled ball. (pitched short to be a bumper)

short fine leg: see *leg slip*.

short leg: 1. The fielding position just behind or in front of the striker, a short distance out on the leg side. 2. The fieldsman who plays at short leg.

short run: An attempt to score in which one or both batsmen fail to make their ground before turning to make an additional scoring attempt. One run is subtracted for each such infraction.

short slip: 1. The fielding position just behind the striker, a short distance out on the off side. 2. The fieldsman who plays in the short slip position.

shoulder arms: Players' slang for the action of a batsman who lifts his bat then lets an off-side ball pass without playing a stroke.

sight screen: A flat, often rectangular structure erected next to or as a part of the boundary behind both wickets in the line of sight of a batsman facing a bowler. Sight screens are employed to provide a uniform background for the batsman to look into when the ball is being bowled, free from spectator distractions.

silly: Close or very close to the batsman (close enough to be considered almost foolhardy or "silly"), said of a fielding position or fieldsman.

silly mid-off: 1. The mid-off position played at a closer-than-normal or "silly" distance from the batsman. see *mid-off*. compare *silly mid-on*. 2. The fieldsman in the silly mid-off position.

silly mid-on: 1. The mid-on position played at a closer-than-normal or "silly" distance from the batsman. also *forward short leg*. see *mid on*. compare *silly mid-off*. 2. The fieldsman in the silly mid-on position.

silly point: 1. The point position played at a closer-than-normal or "silly" distance from the batsman. see *point*. 2. The fieldsman in the silly point position.

1. single: One run scored.

2. single: To score one run.

sitter: A batted ball popped up or hit high into the air, an easy catch. Said to be so easy to catch, one could do it while sitting. From the late 1890s. also *balloon, dolly, skier*.

six: An award of six runs when a batted ball clears a boundary on the fly. The greatest six-hitter of all time was England's A. W. Wellard, who in his career (1927–50) is believed to have hit over 500 sixes. Remarkably, 129 of his sixes were hit in just two seasons (1935 and 1936). also *boundary six, sixer*.

sixer: Slang for a six or boundary six. Popularized in the 1870s.

skier: A batted ball hit high into the air or sky, an easy catch. also *balloon, dolly, sitter, skyer*.

skittle, skittle out: To routinely dismiss the batsmen of the opposing team without giving up many runs. (were skittled out by two incredibly fast bowlers)

sky: To mishit a bowled ball high into the air or sky.

skyer: A skier.

slips: The fielding area behind and just wide of the wicketkeeper on the off side, played at one or more of three possible depths or widths. see *first slip, second slip, third slip*. compare *short slip*.

slow ball: A ball bowled slowly. In modern cricket the term is most often applied to relatively slow change-of-pace deliveries or to those imparted with pronounced spin.

slow bowler: A bowler who is adept at or

primarily known for bowling slow balls. The remarkable left-handed all-rounder Wilfred R. Rhodes of Yorkshire was undoubtedly the greatest slow bowler in the history of cricket. Among his many accomplishments, Rhodes took over 100 wickets in a season a record twenty-three times. He also holds the career record for wickets taken; 4,187 from 1898 through to 1930, with a 16.71 bowling average. True slow bowlers are increasingly rare in modern cricket, though the term is sometimes applied to spin bowlers whose deliveries are relatively slow. compare *fast bowler, medium-pace bowler, spin bowler*.

slow wicket: A wet or soaked pitch, usually favoring, if anybody, batsmen rather than bowlers.

smother the ball: To, with the bat held relatively still and tipped down, make contact with a bowled ball close to the ground (as one that has just pitched) and hit it downward.

sneak: see *shooter*.

1. snick: A batted ball that is mishit and tipped back to one side, often for a catch.

2. snick: To mishit a bowled ball and tip it back to one side, often for a catch.

spectacles: Two consecutive scoreless innings for a batsman. From the appearance of two zeros in statistics. Popularized around 1910. also *pair, pair of ducks*.

speed merchant: A fast bowler. also *pace bowler, paceman, quick, quickie*.

spikes: 1. The most often screw-in (thus,

TO SKY

replaceable) metal studs attached to the bottom of cricket boots. 2. See *boots*.

spin bowler: A bowler who is adept at or primarily known for imparting spin to his deliveries. Though spin bowlers appeared as early as the 1780s, they became a real factor in cricket only after overarm bowling was made legal in 1864. also *spinner*. compare *fast bowler, medium-pace bowler, slow bowler*.

spinner: A spin bowler.

spoon: To loft a bowled ball in the air with a weak stroke of the bat.

1. square: Directly to the side of the striker or of or pertaining to that area, said of a fielding position or fieldsman. compare *fine, deep, short, silly*.

2. square: The closely groomed area in the middle of a cricket ground inside which the pitch is made. also *middle sanctum, table*.

square cut: A batted ball hit with a chopping stroke and deflected to the off side, almost square, ideally between the point and cover point positions. compare *late cut*.

square drive: A drive that is hit sharply to the side, or almost square. see *drive*. compare *cover drive, low drive, off drive, on drive, straight drive*.

square leg: 1. The fielding position almost square to the striker on the leg side. compare *deep square leg*. 2. The fieldsman who plays at the square leg position.

squat: To roll along or stay close to the ground after pitching, said of a bowled ball such as a creeper.

stand: 1. The performance of or number of runs scored by a partnership. (a 116-run opening stand) 2. A partnership.

steal a run: see *scamper a run*.

step down the wicket: To move forward of the popping crease in order to hit a bowled ball.

stick: Slang for a stump.

sticky dog: A sticky wicket. also *gluepot*.

sticky wicket: A tacky, previously soaked but now drying pitch, usually greatly favoring spin bowlers. also *gluepot, sticky dog*. compare *slow wicket*.

●● An awkward or difficult set of circumstances. To "bat on a sticky wicket" is to deal with awkward or difficult circumstances.

1. stonewall: To bat defensively, primarily to defend or block the wicket like a stone wall rather than score runs.

●● To rigidly block or obstruct some course of action, particularly by stalling or lengthy debate in politics. Popularized in the late 1800s.

2. stonewall: see *stonewaller*.

●● One who is known for or adept at stonewalling. From the late 1800s.

stonewaller: A player who bats defensively, primarily to defend or block the wicket like a stone wall rather than score runs. Though the first stonewaller may have been Tom Walker of Hambledon (London), whose relentless defensive batting style earned him the nickname "Old Everlasting" in the late 1700s, it was not until the mid to late 1800s that the Surrey player H. Jupp was actually called "Young Stonewall", introducing the term and its implied concept. William Barnes of Nottinghamshire, known himself as a defensive batsman, further popularized the expression in 1882 when, after bowling to Lancashire's R. G. Barlow for over two and a half hours, he exclaimed, "bowling to thee were like bowling at a stone wall!". also *stonewall*.

●● One who is known for or adept at stonewalling. From the late 1800s.

straight bat: A bat held absolutely vertical so as to hit a bowled ball squarely with the flat contact surface, rather than being angled or tipped in any direction.

straight drive: A drive hit straight over or nearly straight over the opposite wicket. see *drive*. compare *cover drive*, *off drive*, *on drive*, *square drive*.

strike: The activity of acting as striker. A striker is said to be in strike or to have the strike.

striker: The batsman who is currently facing the bowler. compare *nonstriker*.

1. stroke: 1. A hit. 2. A particular type of hit. (connected with a cut stroke)

2. stroke: 1. To hit the ball. 2. To hit the ball gently, as for a defensive shot.

1. stump: 1. Any of three identical 28-inch long vertical poles that, when stuck in the ground in a straight line and topped with two 4⅜-inch bails resting end to end in grooves, serve as wickets at each end of a cricket pitch. Placed in the ground to be 9 inches wide in total, the stumps are of sufficient size to prevent the ball from passing through. Stumps got their name from the original wicket,

a convenient tree stump in a field. By 1705, a wicket comprised two 1-foot long sticks or "stumps" placed in the ground about 2 feet apart with a single horizontal rail across the top. The 1744 London Cricket Club rules called for two 22-inch stumps set 6 inches apart. A third stump was added in 1775, though the single bail was used until 1786. Present specifications were adopted in the 1931 MCC Laws. also *stick*. 2. Short for stumper.

2. stump: To, as wicketkeeper, put out the striker unassisted by any other player by breaking the wicket with the ball while he is not within the popping crease and not attempting a run.

stumped: Out by virtue of a stumping by the wicketkeeper. see *stump*.

stumper: A wicketkeeper. also *keeper*, *stump*, *wicketkeep*.

1. substitute: A player who, with the permission of the opposing captain, enters a game to replace an ill or injured player. A substitute may field but may not bat or bowl.

2. substitute: To, with the permission of the opposing captain, enter a game to replace an ill or injured player.

sundry: Australian slang for an extra. see *extra*.

1. sweep: A batted ball "swept" (with the bat horizontal) to the leg side behind the striker, between fine leg and square leg.

2. sweep: To step into and (with the bat held horizontally) pull or "sweep" a bowled ball back on the leg side between square leg and fine leg.

swerve: The change in the direction of flight of a bowled ball due to spin being imparted at the moment of release, among the variables controlled by the bowler. compare *flight*, *length*, *lift*, *line*, *pace*, *swing*, *turn*.

swerver: A ball that curves in flight due to the spin imparted by the bowler.

swing: The change in the direction of flight of a bowled ball due to the particular direction in which the seam of the ball is pointed at the moment it is released, among the variables controlled by the bowler. Humidity and the condition of the surface of the ball also affect swing. compare *flight*, *length*, *lift*, *line*, *pace*, *swerve*, *turn*.

swing bowler: A bowler who is known for or adept at making a bowled ball curve in flight by manipulating the precise direction in which the seam of the ball is pointed at the moment it is released. also *seam bowler, seamer.*

swing bowling: Bowling in which the ball is made to curve in flight by manipulating the precise direction in which the seam of the ball is pointed at the moment of release. also *seam bowling.*

table: 1. see *square.* 2. A schedule of league standings. (third in the table)

tail: The last or one of the last batsmen in the batting order, usually among the least skillful batters on a side.

take a wicket: To cause an opposing batsman to be made out. The only bowler ever to take all ten wickets in an innings of a Test match was England's J. C. Laker against Australia in 1956. Remarkably, Laker took a record 19 wickets in the Test. also *capture a wicket.*

take block: see *take guard.*

take guard: To determine one's exact position and bat placement in front of the defended wicket before batting in order to be able to judge the direction of a bowled ball relative to that wicket. Usually, the batsman requests assistance from the umpire at the opposite wicket by calling out one of three common locations for his bat to be positioned, "center" or "middle" (in front of the middle stump), "middle and leg" or "two legs" (centered in front of the middle and leg stumps), or "leg stump" or "one leg" (in front of the leg stump). Once the block or guard position is determined, the batsman makes a mark on the ground (the "block hole") for reference. also *take block.*

taking the new ball: Requesting the use of a new ball, an option available to the captain of the fielding side as a tactic once the prescribed number of overs has been bowled (according to prevailing national rules; usually between 75 and 85 six-ball overs or 55 and 65 eight-ball overs). A new ball generally favors a fast bowler over the striker.

tea interval: An arranged break for tea in the afternoon in traditional cricket matches during which play is suspended. compare *lunch interval.*

1. Test: Short for a Test match. (pulled even in the second Test)

2. Test: Having to do with a Test match. (the best ever record in Test cricket)

Test match: A match between national teams, an international match. Test matches represent the highest level of cricket competition. The first Test match, played in Melbourne on March 15, 1877 between Australia and England, was won by the home side by 45 runs. England won the second Test match, played two weeks later. also *Test.*

thigh pad: A protective sponge rubber or composition pad worn by a striker to cover the outside part of the thigh (that which faces the bowler).

third man: 1. The outfield fielding position on the off side behind and outside third slip, in the vicinity of the boundary. 2. The fieldsman who plays in the third man position.

third slip: 1. One of the slip fielding positions on the off side in back of the wicketkeeper, this one being the widest laterally and the closest behind the wicketkeeper, just in front of and outside second slip. 2. The fieldsman who plays in the third slip position.

ton: Slang for a century. see *century.*

top spin: Forward spin imparted by the bowler to the ball to make it dip or drop in flight and jump forward upon pitching.

top-spinner: A bowler who is proficient at or known for sending down deliveries with top spin.

toss: The traditional flipping of a coin between captains before a match to decide who bats first.

track: The pitch. also *wicket.*

trimmer: A fast bowled ball that dislodges the bails without touching the stumps.

triple century: The scoring of 300 runs in a single innings by a batsman.

1. turn: The change in direction of a bowled ball when it pitches or bounces, the result of spin imparted by the bowler. also *break.*

2. turn: 1. To change direction after pitching or bouncing due to spin, said of a bowled ball. (turned toward the off side) also *break.* 2. To bowl a ball with spin so that it will change direction when it pitches or bounces. (turned one to the leg side) also *break, turn the ball.*

turning wicket: A wicket with a surface that promotes turn. One that favors spin bowlers.

turn the ball: see *turn.*

twelfth man: The first substitute for a team or the player who is usually a team's first substitute.

twin century: see *double century.*

two-eyed stance: Players' slang for an open batting stance in which a batsman turns his chest to face the bowler.

two legs: see *middle and leg.*

1. umpire: One of two officials in charge of a cricket match. The umpires are responsible for designating the clock or watch to be used to time a match, determining and making rulings on the condition of the pitch and any special regulations agreed upon by the captains before a match, as well as presiding at the toss. During a match, one umpire is stationed at each end of the wicket (most often on the leg side at the striker's end and behind the wicket, out of the bowler's way at the other end), switching ends after each side has had one innings. Umpires are responsible for the conduct, timing, suspension, or termination of a match, and are solely in charge of interpreting the Laws. No player can be given out except after an appeal to and agreement by an umpire.

2. umpire: To act as an umpire in a match.

visor: A wire cage or piece of transparent plastic wrapped around the face and attached to the front and sides of a helmet, worn by a batsman or fieldsman to protect the eyes and face.

walk: To voluntarily turn away and leave the wicket as a striker, admitting a dismissal after a close play, as when a bowled ball is caught by the wicketkeeper after barely or imperceptibly touching one's bat. A truly sporting gesture by a batsman.

whites: The traditional white or cream colored shirts, sweaters, and pants worn by cricketers. Now sometimes replaced by colorful uniforms for televised matches played at night.

wicket: 1. Either of two 9-inch wide wooden frames set 22 yards apart, at which the ball is bowled. Each wicket is comprised of three identical 28-inch vertical stumps of sufficient size to prevent the ball from passing through, placed in the ground and topped with two bails set end to end in grooves at the tip of the stumps. If a bowled ball dislodges any part of the wicket or if, while the batsman is out of the crease, a fieldsman dislodges any part of the wicket with the ball, the batsman is out. The first wicket was probably a con-

venient tree stump. Next, two sticks or branches, still called "stumps", were stuck into the ground about two feet apart with a third piece balanced between them at the top, about 12 inches off the ground. From this version's resemblance to the small hurdle or wicket gate leading to a sheep pen, the movable top rail of which was called a bail, came the terms "wicket" and "bail". Between the two stumps was a hole large enough to accommodate the ball. If a fieldsman could "pop" the ball into this hole before the batsman reached it with the tip of his bat, the batsman was out. From the so-called "popping hole" came the later term "popping crease". By the time the London Cricket Club framed the first Laws in 1744, two wickets were called for, each comprising two 22-inch high stumps with a single 6-inch bail. A third stump was added in 1775, though the single bail remained in general use until 1786, when the second was added. The present measurements for a wicket were adopted by the MCC in 1931. 2. The rectangular grass area between wickets where the ball is bowled and the batsman and nonstriker run, 22 yards in length and 10 feet wide. (played on a slow wicket) also *pitch, track.* 3. A batsman's turn at bat in an innings until he is put out. (third wicket scored 87 runs) 4. A batsman who has been put out. (a clever spin bowler who took the last two wickets with two consecutive balls) 5. A batsman's turn at bat that is not finished or not taken because the opposing team's full score has already been exceeded. (won by four

VISOR

wickets) 6. The period of play in an innings during a partnership. (a memorable last wicket stand)

•• To be figuratively "on a good wicket" or "on a bad wicket" means to be on "safe" or "unsafe" ground, or to be faced with particularly agreeable or disagreeable circumstances. (would seem to be on a good wicket politically)

wicketkeep: Short for wicketkeeper.

wicketkeeper: 1. The fieldsman positioned behind the wicket at which the ball is being bowled. Equipped with protective gloves and shin pads, the wicketkeeper is primarily responsible for making catches, stumping, participating in runouts, and preventing byes. The wicketkeeper must remain behind the wicket until after a bowled ball touches the batsman or the bat, or passes the wicket, or until the batsman attempts a run. also *keeper, stump, stumper, wicketkeep.* 2. The position played by a wicketkeeper.

wicketkeeping: The act or action of playing wicketkeeper. also *at the stumps, keeping.*

wicket maiden: A scoreless over in which at least one wicket falls that is credited to the bowler.

wide, wide ball: A ball bowled so high over or so wide of the wicket that in the opinion of the umpire, it is out of reach of the batsman in his normal position. A wide ball does not count as one of the alloted six or eight deliveries of an over, and results in the awarding of one run to the batting side. Additional runs can be scored on a wide ball (as when the ball gets by the wicketkeeper and/or is misplayed by other fieldsmen), but the batsmen are then subject to being run out, or can be made out for obstruction or handling the ball. The striker can be made out if he is stumped on a wide ball, or if he breaks the wicket with his bat or any part of his body. Runs scored on a wide ball are considered extras and are not credited to the striker.

winkle out: To, by means of persistence and/or tactics, put out one or more particularly crafty or conservative batsmen.

wrong 'un: Australian slang for a googly. also *bosey, googlie.*

york: To bowl a yorker. (yorked him to end the innings)

yorker: A bowled ball of usually fast to medium pace that ideally pitches just under the tip of the batsman's bat and is, therefore, hard to hit.

FOOTBALL (AMERICAN)

The ancestor of all football games is soccer, but rugby, an offshoot of soccer, served as both the inspiration and departure point for American football.

Rugby was invented in 1823 at Rugby School in England when William Webb Ellis suddenly picked up the ball in frustration during a soccer game and ran with it to the goal line. Though Ellis was soundly criticized, the idea of carrying the ball as well as kicking it was soon accepted and identified with the school.

When Princeton and Rutgers Universities pioneered intercollegiate "football" in the United States in 1869, the game played was international style soccer, albeit with twenty-five players on a side. Soon Yale, Cornell, Columbia, and Michigan Universities organized football teams. In 1873, Yale convened a meeting to form the Intercollegiate Football Association. However, Harvard did not join the Association, having over a period of years developed its own conflicting "Boston game" in which it was permitted to catch, handle, and run with the inflated rubber ball.

Unable to compete with other American schools, Harvard scheduled a series of games with McGill University of Montreal. The initial contest was played by Harvard's rules, but the following day, May 15, 1874, McGill introduced the game of rugby in the United States. Thus began America's fascination for the odd egg-shaped ball and for a game which would soon begin to undergo great changes, although always retaining the running and tackling of rugby. Within two years, a slightly modified form of rugby had been adopted officially by Harvard, Yale, Princeton, Columbia, and Rutgers under a new Intercollegiate Football Association.

The first changes which would separate the American game from rugby occurred in 1880. Led by a twenty-year-old Yale halfback, Walter Camp, the rules committee agreed to a reduction of players from fifteen to eleven players per side, the naming of team positions, and the substitution of scrimmage for the rugby scrum. The scrimmage line, giving unhindered possession of the ball to one team until the ball was "snapped" back by the center to the quarterback, is considered the most important rule of football, allowing variable strategies to be implemented with prearranged plays. Camp also persuaded the committee to change the standard field size from the original 140 by 70 yards to 110 by 53⅓ yards (the maximum width which could be accommodated in Harvard's stadium). In

134

1882, the rules committee introduced "downs", compelling the offensive team to advance the ball 5 yards within three consecutive downs or lose possession to the opponent. In the same year, new scoring values were assigned. For the first time, a total of four touchdowns was given precedence over a goal from the field (field goal) and two safeties were made equal to one touchdown. Changes would continue to be made until 1912, when the present field dimensions and scoring values were codified.

In 1887, Pennsylvania and Rutgers played the first indoor football game in Madison Square Garden. In 1889, Walter Camp chose the first All-American team for Caspar Whitney's magazine, *Week's Sport*. Among his selections was Yale end Amos Alonzo Stagg, a future legendary coach, whose all-time record of 314 victories wasn't surpassed until 1981 by Alabama coach Paul "Bear" Bryant. Also selected from Yale was guard William "Pudge" Heffelfinger, who in 1892 was paid $500 to play for the Allegheny Athletic Association in a game against the Pittsburgh Athletic Club, becoming the first known professional football player.

The same year, Harvard coach L. H. Deland opened the second half of the Yale-Harvard game with the devastating flying wedge. With the quarterback at his own 40-yard line with the ball, his teammates were arranged in two groups, about 20 yards back and wide to either side. On a signal, both groups of players ran toward the quarterback, who put the ball in play (touched it to his foot) just as they passed and overlapped in front of him. The ball was handed off to a halfback who fell in behind the steam-rolling wedge. On that first occasion, the play went 50 yards before Yale could down the ballcarrier, and the era of the flying wedge had begun. Already criticized for being too rough (Harvard had once banned the sport for a year in 1885), football was becoming even more violent, and injuries abounded. At the line of scrimmage, opposing linemen stood toe-to-toe, grappling, punching, and kicking at each other throughout a game. The introduction in 1903 of the neutral zone separating the two lines helped this somewhat, but rules to protect the ballcarrier were largely ignored. The player with the ball was often the object of a violent tug-of-war between the offense and defense, and, to preserve flesh and hair, would have leather handles attached to his uniform.

In 1905, eighteen fatalities and 159 serious injuries were reported. "Dead and wounded of the football battlefields", read the headline of a December feature in the *World*, a New York newspaper. The story called football "the most brutal, perilous, and unnecessary sport sanctioned by any country in the world". All across America, educators, clergymen, and parents clamored for an end to football. Finally, horrified by a newspaper photograph of 250-pound Swarthmore lineman Bob Maxwell (for whom the Maxwell Trophy was later named), bloodied and beaten after a game, President Theodore Roosevelt summoned college athletic leaders to the White House and threatened to ban the sport by executive order if the violence wasn't curbed.

In December of 1905, New York University Chancellor Henry M. MacCracken called a special meeting of the football-playing colleges of the nation, at which it was decided to completely reform the sport. In a second meeting the same month, with representatives of sixty-two institutions in attendance, a new Football Rules Committee was appointed and the Intercollegiate Athletic Association of the United States was formed (in 1910, renamed the National Collegiate Athletic Association).

Sweeping rules changes followed for the 1906 season, the most important of which prohibited almost all mass formations and plays, upped the yards to gain in a series of downs to ten, and legalized the forward pass. Both Wesleyan (vs. Yale) and Yale (vs. Harvard) are said to have been among the first to have used a pass in 1906, but it would be many years before the potential of the forward pass was fully realized.

In 1913, a team from a Catholic university in Indiana traveled to West Point to play what was considered little more than a tune-up game for powerhouse Army. Instead, Notre Dame stunned their hosts 39–13. Quarterback Gus Dorns repeatedly dumbfounded the hulking Army players with pinpoint passes to end Knute Rockne. It was, of course, just the beginning of the legendary exploits of Rockne and Notre Dame, but it was also a turning point in the history of college football. Notre Dame's astonishing feat proved that smaller colleges with relatively modest football programs and normal-sized players could compete with the football juggernauts, by the use of clever strategy and the forward pass.

The first "professional" football game was the one in which Pudge Heffelfinger played in 1892. Subsequent attempts to form a professional league were unsuccessful. Because of competition from the college game, real and imagined scandals, and a lack of finances, only a few individual clubs, such as the team founded in 1898 in Chicago by the Morgan Athletic Club (ultimately becoming the St. Louis Cardinals, the oldest continuing operation in professional football), were able to survive.

In 1902, the Philadelphia Athletics, organized by Connie Mack as a football counterpart to his champion baseball team, played in the first night football game with baseball pitcher Rube Waddell in the lineup, but the Athletics only lasted two seasons. After a betting scandal in 1906 ended an earlier effort in Ohio, the Canton Bulldogs were revived in 1915, with the signing of college star and 1912 Olympic hero Jim Thorpe. Making use of Thorpe's extraordinary ability, Canton won ten straight games in 1916.

Finally, in 1920, twelve teams from five states formed the American Professional Football Association, with Jim Thorpe as league president. Among the teams represented were Thorpe's Canton Bulldogs, the Racine Cardinals of Chicago (later St. Louis), the Decatur Staleys (later the Chicago Bears) with player-coach George Halas, and a year later, the Green Bay Packers. In 1922, the APFA changed its name to the National Football League but had little success until 1925, when University of Illinois three-time All-American Harold E. "Red" Grange left school at the end of the season to play for the Chicago Bears.

Grange, "The Galloping Ghost", was at the time the most spectacular player ever. In his three years at Illinois, he rushed for 3,637 yards, once scoring four touchdowns in the first ten minutes of a game against Michigan in 1924. His enormous popularity made his signing the turning point for professional football and the NFL. Thirty-eight thousand fans watched his first game against the Cardinals, and the Bears immediately launched a barnstorming tour, playing seven games in eleven days. A record crowd of 70,000 saw Grange and the Bears at the Polo Grounds against the New York Giants, 5,000 more than were at the Army-Navy game the week before.

A parade of college stars followed Grange's example and turned pro. Though many weak franchises were forced to drop out, professional football was beginning to attract crowds with well-known college players like Stanford's Ernie Nevers, Michigan's Benny Friedman, the famed Four Horsemen of Notre Dame, and Minnesota's Bronko Nagurski.

Rule changes which slimmed the football in 1929 and 1933 virtually eliminated the drop kick because of the untrue bounce of the more pointed ends, but they also made the ball easier to throw and control. Ten-yard inbounds lines were adopted in 1933 and increased to 15 yards in 1935 (1938 in college play).

In 1934, the NFL legalized the forward pass from anywhere behind the line of scrimmage. The same year, the first College All-Star game was played in Chicago before 79,432 fans, with the collegians holding the Chicago Bears to a scoreless tie. In 1936, the first college draft was held, with the team finishing last in the standings having first choice on each round of the draft. A far-reaching idea, the draft was designed to equalize the strengths of teams throughout the league, and to prevent any one team from dominating the game. This same principle was eventually adopted by other professional sports.

In 1939, a game at Ebbets Field in Brooklyn, New York between the Philadelphia Eagles and Brooklyn Dodgers was broadcast live by the National Broadcasting Co. (NBC) becoming the first NFL game ever to be televised. Only two cameras were used for that game (one at ground level and one in the stands), which was announced by Allan "Skip" Walz.

The following year, the modern T formation, as developed by Stanford coach Clark Shaughnessy and George Halas and coach Ralph Jones of the Chicago Bears (with Shaughnessy as a special advisor), revolutionized football offense with its counterplays, players in motion, and forward pass options. In the first championship carried on network radio, the Bears used the T formation to defeat Washington 73–0 to become the 1940 NFL champions, with sportscaster Red Barber doing the play-by-play for 120 stations of the Mutual Broadcasting System.

In 1946, the Cleveland franchise was transferred to Los Angeles to become the Los Angeles Rams, making the NFL a coast-to-coast league for the first time. An eight-team rival league, the All-American Football Conference, was formed the same year. The two leagues agreed to merge in 1950, with three AAFC teams being added to the NFL: the Cleveland Browns, the San Francisco 49ers, and the Baltimore Colts.

In the 1950s, professional football was to emerge as the most popular spectator sport in America. The 1951 NFL championship game, in which Los Angeles defeated Cleveland 24–17, was televised coast-to-coast for the first time. Wisely, NFL Commissioner Bert Bell formulated a league policy of televising away games, blacking out only the city where the game was being played. Millions who had never seen a game in person now watched on television just at the time football was being made even more exciting by explosive passing attacks by quarterbacks such as Otto Graham of Paul Brown's Cleveland Browns, Bobby Layne of the Detroit Lions, and Johnny Unitas of the Baltimore Colts.

In 1960, an eight-team professional league began to operate as the American Football League. Fueled by generous contracts from television networks, the two leagues battled fiercely for college talent, while on the field, professional football came under the domination of one team, the Green Bay Packers, led by the legendary Vince Lombardi. In last place when he came to coach them in 1959, the Packers were Western Conference Champions by 1960, and NFL Champions by 1961. Though individual stars like Cleveland Brown running back Jim Brown continued to set records (many of which stand even today), and new lights emerged like Chicago Bears middle linebacker Dick Butkus and running back Gale Sayers, defensive linemen Merlin Olsen of the Los Angeles Rams, Bob Lilly of the Dallas Cowboys, and New York Jets quarterback Joe Namath, the 1960s will always be remembered for the dynasty of Vince Lombardi's Green Bay Packers (a total of five NFL championships).

The AFL-NFL war reached its peak in 1966, with the leagues spending a combined total of $7 million to sign their draft choices that year. Later in 1966, a merger was announced, with the leagues agreeing to play separate schedules until 1970, but meeting in a world championship game (the Super Bowl) beginning in 1967.

Lombardi's Green Bay Packers defeated the AFL Kansas City Chiefs in Super Bowl I in 1967 and the AFL Oakland Raiders in Super Bowl II in 1968. In 1969, Joe Namath led the AFL New York Jets to victory over the NFL's Baltimore Colts in Super Bowl III.

Though briefly challenged by the would-be rival World Football League in 1974 and 1975, the NFL became even stronger in the 1970s, with record network television contracts, new expansion franchises in Tampa and Seattle, rule changes adopted in 1978 to stimulate offense by opening up the passing game, and exciting players such as Fran Tarkenton, Bob Griese, Ken Stabler, Roger Staubach, O. J. Simpson, Walter Payton, and Franco Harris.

Though a combination of escalating operating budgets, injuries, and resulting insurance problems began to cause a dropoff in youth and high school-level football programs in the late 1970s, football's place as America's most popular spectator sport seems secure for the

1980s. In 1982, the United States Football League (USFL) was formed to operate from March through to June, normally football's off season. In 1986 the new league will change its schedule to compete directly with the NFL. Undoubtedly, football fans young and old will continue to be thrilled by the gridiron exploits of college and professional players like Tony Dorsett, Earl Campbell, Billy Sims, George Rogers, Marcus Allen, Herschell Walker, Joe Montana, Eric Dickerson, Dan Marino, John Elway, and others following in the footsteps of Jim Thorpe, Red Grange, and Ernie Nevers.

ace formation: see *one-back formation.*

aerial: A pass or pertaining to a pass. (won with an inspired aerial attack)

AFC: The American Football Conference.

A formation: see *one-back formation.*

against the grain: Toward the sideline opposite the direction most players are moving.

air: Pass plays or pertaining to pass plays. (went to the air in the second half)

air it out: To pass or attempt to pass, especially a long pass. (will air it out on third-and-long) also *put it up.*

All-America: A national honor given annually to outstanding college football players at each of the positions on a team. Yale player, coach, and football innovator Walter Camp chose the first All-America team in 1889 for Casper Whitney's magazine, *Week's Sports.* The honor and title of All-America is now also given to athletes who participate in other sports at both the college and high school level.

All-American: A player named to an All-America team.

●●Excellent, or exemplary. (a clean-cut All-American boy)

alley: A gap between players in the offensive line through which a defensive player attempts to rush into the offensive backfield.

All-Pro: 1. An honor and title given annually to outstanding professional football players at each of the positions of an all-star team, as selected by a national news service, or by the Professional Football Writers Association. Among the players selected for the first All-Pro team in 1920 (then called All-League) were Jim Thorpe of the Canton Bull-

dogs, and George Halas of the Decatur Staleys, later to become the Chicago Bears. 2. A player named to an All-Pro team.

all the way: The remaining yards for a touchdown. (to the forty, to the thirty, he's going all the way)

American Football Conference: One of the two conferences of the National Football League, the championship teams of which compete annually for the national championship in the Super Bowl, and from which individual players are selected to compete in the annual AFC-NFC Pro Bowl. The AFC is made up of three divisions: the Eastern Division, which comprises the Indianapolis Colts, the Buffalo Bills, the Miami Dolphins, the New England Patriots, and the New York Jets; the Central Division, which comprises the Cincinnati Bengals, the Cleveland Browns, the Houston Oilers, and the Pittsburgh Steelers; and the Western Division, which comprises the Denver Broncos, the Kansas City Chiefs, the Los Angeles Raiders, the San Diego Chargers, and the Seattle Seahawks. also *AFC.*

angle block: A block in which contact is made diagonally, as when an opponent is lined up just to the left or right of the blocker.

approved ruling: An official ruling for a given set of circumstances.

area blocking: A blocking strategy in which specific areas or zones are assigned to offensive players to protect, and any opponent entering the zone is blocked (as opposed to individual blocking of designated players). also *zone blocking.*

armchair quarterback: One who criticizes or second-guesses a team's play, though neither personally concerned nor necessarily well informed. compare *curbstone coach, grandstand quarterback, Monday morning quarterback.*

●●A kibbitzer, one who second-guesses or offers advice about matters with which he is not concerned.

1. arm tackle: To tackle a ballcarrier using just one or both arms, without the shoulder or body. (a powerful runner who is almost impossible to arm tackle)

2. arm tackle: The act or an instance of arm tackling a ballcarrier.

artificial turf: A synthetic surface used as a substitute for grass in some stadiums.

AstroTurf: A brand of artifical turf developed by Monsanto for use inside the Houston Astrodome in 1965.

audibilize: To call an audible at the line of scrimmage. also *check off.*

audible: A verbal change of the intended offensive play or defensive alignment made in code at the line of scrimmage, as to adjust to a particular deployment of players or anticipated action by the opposing team. An audible is usually called by the quarterback on offense, or the middle linebacker on defense. also *automatic.*

automatic: see *audible.*

back: One who plays in the offensive or

ANGLE BLOCK

defensive backfield. see *defensive back, offensive back.*

backer-up: see *linebacker.*

backfield: 1. The offensive and defensive backs. see *offensive back, defensive back.* 2. The positions played by the offensive and defensive backs. 3. The area behind the line of scrimmage.

backfield in motion: see *illegal motion.*

backfield line: The imaginary vertical plane 1 yard behind and parallel to the line of scrimmage in the offensive backfield (or in high school play, even with the waistline of an offensive lineman). No offensive back except the player "under the center" (usually the quarterback) is permitted to line up in front of the backfield line.

back judge: A football official who, at the snap, is positioned approximately 17 yards downfield on the same side of the field as the line judge, and who is responsible for judging when and where the ball or the ballcarrier go out of bounds downfield on his side, watching for clips and pass interference on his side behind the area covered by the umpire, counting the number of defensive players on each play, ruling with the field judge on conversions and field goals, and recording all time-outs.

backpedal: To run backwards while facing an opponent or a play in progress. Often defensive backs must backpedal while guarding the receivers of the opposing team.

backward pass: see *lateral.*

bait the hole: To fake a pass, pitchout, or handoff in order to lure a rusher through a gap in the offensive line so that he can be trap blocked away from the intended path of the ballcarrier.

balanced line: An offensive alignment with an equal number of players on either side of the center.

ball: see *football.*

ballcarrier: The player (usually a halfback or fullback) who carries the ball on a running play, whether directly from the snap or on a handoff or pitchout. also *runner.* compare *receiver.*

ball control: An offensive strategy in which a team attempts to maintain possession of the ball for as long as possible while advancing methodically toward the opposing team's goal line. A ball control offense usually features a strong running game and conservative short passes to maximize the chances of consecutive first downs. also *possession football.*

ball hawk: A defensive player who often gains possession of the ball; one who is particularly adept at intercepting passes and recovering fumbles and loose balls.

1. bat: The intentional striking of a loose ball or a ball in player possession with the hand, fist, elbow, or forearm. A bat is illegal if used to punch a loose ball in the field of play toward the opponent's goal line, a loose ball in any direction if it is in either end zone, a ball in the possession of a player, or a pass in flight forward toward the opponent's goal line. An illegal bat results in a 10-yard penalty.

2. bat: To punch or strike the ball with the hand, fist, elbow, or forearm.

beat the line: see *beat the spread.*

beat the price: see *beat the spread.*

beat the spread: 1. Betting parlance meaning to win a wager, either by betting on a favored team which wins by more than the point spread or by betting on an underdog which wins, or loses by less than the point spread. If the favored team wins by the same number of points indicated in the point spread, the bet is considered a "push" and is usually cancelled. also *beat the line, beat the price.* see *point spread.* 2. To win a game one's team is favored to win by more than the point spread, or to defeat a favored opponent or lose by less than the point spread. (managed to beat the spread only once in their last three games) also *beat the line, beat the price.* see *point spread.*

belly back: To momentarily carry the ball away from the line of scrimmage on a sweep in order to get around blockers and rushing linemen.

belly series: A series of offensive running and passing plays which begin in the same manner, with a handoff or fake handoff to the midsection of a running back.

1. bench: 1. The long seat adjacent to the sideline, where players sit during a game. Usually, team benches are centered on the 50-yard line on opposite sides of the field. 2. Players not on the first string, but held in reserve as substitutes. 3. The area in front of and immediately around the bench, from where the coach and coaching staff observe

and send plays into a game. (scored with a trick play from the bench) also *sideline.*

2. bench: 1. To take a player out of a game, or to prevent a player from taking part in one or more games. 2. To cause a player to be unable to play. (benched by a pulled hamstring) also *hamstring.*

bench warmer: A reserve player. One who "warms" the bench by sitting on it for long periods of time.

Big Ben: A Hail Mary pass play used in desperation (such as when trailing in the closing moments of a game) in which the ball is passed into a group of receivers in or near the end zone in the hopes that one receiver will be able to leap up over covering defenders and tip the ball to an eligible teammate. Most professional teams now use a version of the Big Ben play, popularized by the Minnesota Vikings in 1980, when a pass from Viking quarterback Tommy Kramer was successfully tipped to receiver Ahmad Rashad to defeat the Cleveland Browns 28-23 in a critical, late-season game.

betting line: The point spread set by oddsmakers for a particular game. also *line, point line, price.*

big play: An important or consequential play, especially one that changes the momentum of a game or insures a victory. A big play can be a spectacular kickoff return or run, the completion of a "bomb," a pivotal goal line stand, or a timely interception or fumble recovery.

birdcage: A cagelike metal face mask attached to the front of a helmet, consisting of several horizontal bars bisected by a central vertical bar. see *face mask.*

black out: To ban or withhold the local telecast of a home game.

blackout: The banning of a local telecast for a home game. First adopted as NFL policy in the early 1950s and modified in 1973 to permit a local telecast if a sellout is declared seventy-two hours before game time.

1. blind side: The side a quarterback cannot see once in position to throw (the left side for a right-handed quarterback). When a quarterback is sacked or injured, it is often the result of a blind side hit.

2. blind side: To hit or tackle a quarterback on his blind side. (blind sided and thrown for a 5-yard loss)

1. blitz: A defensive play used in passing situations in which one or more defensive backs rush the quarterback at the snap in an attempt to sack him, or to block or hurry his throw. In common usage, the meaning of the term is often broadened to include rushing linebackers. The blitz can be an effective tactic against the pass, but if the blitzers are unable to reach the quarterback before he passes, the deep backs are then left to cover receivers man-for-man, and are, therefore, vulnerable. In addition, if detected or anticipated by the quarterback, a blitz can be taken advantage of by a run or a short pass, particularly to the area vacated by the blitzers. compare *red dog.*

2. blitz: 1. To execute a blitz. 2. To have one or more defensive backs or linebackers execute a blitz.

blitzer: A linebacker or defensive back who takes part in a blitz.

1. block: To legally use the shoulders or body (but not the hands) to delay or obstruct a defensive player from the front or side, or to knock him down or move him out of the way in order to protect or clear a path for the ballcarrier or passer.

2. block: The act or an instance of blocking.

blocking back: An offensive back (often the fullback) whose primary responsibility is to block in front of a running back, or block for the quarterback during a pass attempt.

blow a coverage: 1. To miss or poorly execute a defensive assignment to cover a receiver or zone, often resulting in the completion of a pass. 2. To misread a defensive coverage and throw a pass to a well-defended receiver, often resulting in an interception.

blow dead: To signal by blowing a whistle that the ball is no longer in play. The ball is blown dead by an official if it is downed or travels out of bounds, if a time out is called, or because of a rules infraction.

blow in: To break through the offensive line into the backfield. (blew in on a blitz and sacked the quarterback)

body block: A block in which the side of the body is used to hit the opponent instead of the shoulders. Football coach Glenn S. "Pop" Warner is credited with inventing the body block. also *crab block, cross-body block.* compare *shoulder block.*

1. bomb: A long pass, especially a touchdown pass. First used to describe the "aerial bombardment" of the 1951 Los

BOX AND CHAIN CREW

Angeles Rams, with quarterbacks Bob Waterfield and Norm Van Brocklin and receivers Tom Fears and Elroy "Crazylegs" Hirsch, all Pro Football Hall of Famers.

2. bomb: To throw a long pass, or long passes.

bomb squad: see *suicide squad.*

1. bootleg: An offensive play in which the quarterback attempts to deceive the defense by faking a handoff in one direction, then moving toward the opposite sideline (as though finished with the play) with the ball hidden behind his hip, before running or passing. The term "bootleg" derives from the quarterback's "smuggling" action with the ball.

2. bootleg: 1. To execute a bootleg. 2. To gain yardage with a bootleg play. (bootlegged 3 yards for the score)

bowl game: An annual post-season exhibition game between teams invited on the basis of performance during the regular season or all-star teams. The first such annual game was the Tournament of Roses, played in Pasadena, California in 1902. Michigan defeated Stanford that year 49-0. In 1923, the game was moved to the newly completed Rose Bowl stadium, taking its name thereafter to become the first bowl game.

box and chain crew: A group of workers who, under the supervision of the linesman, operate the 10-yard measuring chain and the down box on one sideline of the field. also *chain crew, chain gang.*

boxman: The member of the box and chain crew responsible for operating the down box.

break a tackle: To break out of the grasp of a tackler and continue running with the ball. (not only has good speed, but enough power to break tackles)

breakaway runner, breakaway threat: A runner with the agility and speed to be able to get through or around tacklers for a long gain.

break off a run: To successfully execute a running play, especially for a long gain. (finally managed to break off a long run and score)

bring down: To tackle the ballcarrier.

broken field: The sparsely defended area of the field beyond the line of scrimmage, or away from the point of origin of a play. also *open field.*

broken-field runner: A player who is adept at broken-field running.

broken-field running: Eluding tacklers in an open field, often without the aid of blockers running interference.

broken play: A play that does not go according to plan, usually due to a mix-up between the quarterback and the running backs or receivers. In such a case, the quarterback is forced to improvise to avoid being thrown for a loss. also *busted play.*

brush block: A block that is intended only to momentarily obstruct or delay an opponent rather than knock him down, often used by a receiver.

bubble: The potentially weak and vulnerable spot in an "over" or "under" defense covered only by the middle linebacker who has changed places with the shifted defensive tackle. Because the linebacker is usually physically smaller than the shifted defensive tackle, and because he must play off the line in case of a pass, a quarterback will often call a running play directly at the bubble. see *over, under.*

bullet: A hard straight pass.

bump and go: see *bump and run.*

bump and run: A defensive technique first popularized in the 1960s in the AFL, in which a cornerback covering a wide receiver chucks or makes contact with the receiver as he comes off the line to momentarily delay him and disturb his concentration, then runs with him to defend man-for-man against a pass. Contact on a bump and run is limited to one chuck and may be made only within 5 yards of the line of scrimmage. also *bump and go.*

burner: A particularly fast runner, usually a receiver or running back.

busted play: see *broken play.*

butt-blocking: An illegal technique in which the face mask, front, or top of the helmet is driven directly into an opponent as the primary point of contact either in close line play or in the open field. Dangerous to both the blocker and opponent, butt-blocking results in a 15-yard penalty.

buttonhook: see *comeback.*

cab squad: see *taxi squad.*

cadence: see *signals.*

cage: see *birdcage.*

1. call: 1. A ruling by an official (such as on an infraction, a question of whether

or not the ball or a player was out of bounds, etc.). 2. The choice or selection of a play.
2. call: 1. To make an official ruling. 2. To select a team's plays. (too inexperienced to call his own plays)

Canadian football: A game similar to American football with the following rule differences. In Canadian football there are twelve players on a team instead of eleven (the extra man is a backfield player). The playing field is 110 yards long between goal lines and 65 yards wide, with 25-yard end zones (goal posts on the goal lines). A team is allowed three downs, instead of four, to make 10 yards, and any number of backfield players may be in motion in any direction at the snap, instead of just one back moving backwards or laterally. The offensive line of scrimmage is at the forward point of the football, and the defensive linemen may line up no closer than 1 yard beyond. One point is awarded for a PAT (called a "convert") if it is kicked through the uprights, two points if it is run or passed into the end zone. If a player is unable to run a punted ball out of his end zone, or if a punted ball travels through the end zone and across the end boundary (called the "deadline") or sideline, a "rouge" or "single" is scored, for which one point is awarded. All other scoring is the same as in American football. There is no fair catch on a punt, but tacklers must remain outside a 5-yard area around the receiver until he has touched the ball. Blocking above the waist is permitted on punt returns. The ball is kicked off from the 45-yard line at the start of each half and after a touchdown. After a field goal, the team scored against may take a first down or kick off from its own 35-yard line, or elect to receive a kickoff. After a "rouge," the team scored against gets a first down on its own 35-yard line. Only one time-out per team is permitted, and then, only in the last three minutes of each half. There are 5, 10, 15, and 25-yard penalties (disqualification accompanies the 25-yard foul for rough play or fighting), and no yardage difference between offensive and defensive penalties. A game is played in four quarters of fifteen minutes each. The attacking team is given twenty seconds to put the ball into play, but the referee allows "reasonable" time for teams to line up and make substitutions, before starting the time count. If even one second of a period remains after the previous play ends, one complete play must be permitted.

Canadian Football League: The major professional football league in Canada. Established in 1958, the Canadian Football League is split into two geographic divisions. The Western Division is comprised of the British Columbia Lions, the Calgary Stampeders, the Edmonton Eskimos, the Saskatchewan Roughriders, and the Winnipeg Blue Bombers, and the Eastern Division is comprised of the Hamilton Tiger-Cats, the Montreal Concordes, the Ottawa Rough Riders, and the Toronto Argonauts. Division winners meet annually in late November to play for the national championship and the Grey Cup, put up in 1909 by Earl Grey, then governor general, for "the rugby-football championship of Canada." also *CFL.*

1. carry: To run with the ball. also *run, rush.*

2. carry: The act of running with the ball. (gained 75 yards in fifteen carries) also *run, rush.*

1. center: 1. The player positioned in the middle of the offensive line who snaps the ball between his legs to a back (usually the quarterback) to begin play on each down. The center and quarterback positions were created in 1880 when the intercollegiate rules committee adopted the scrimmage concept with a center snap urged by Walter Camp, a twenty-year-old Yale halfback who is now called the primary architect of American football. also *snapper.* 2. The position played by the center. (at center, a two-time All-Pro)

2. center: To snap the ball to a back to begin play on a down. also *hike, snap.*

center snap: see *snap.*

CFA: The Canadian Football Association.

CFL: The Canadian Football League.

chain: The 10-yard long chain (with a rod attached at each end) used to measure the distance the ball must be advanced by the offensive team in a series of four downs in order to maintain possession of the ball for a new series of downs (first-and-ten). If the ball has been advanced close to the 10 yards necessary for a first down, the referee may request, or be asked by a team captain to request, that the chain be brought out onto the field for an exact measurement. also *measuring sticks, sticks, yardage chain.*

chain crew, chain gang: see *box and chain crew.*

chalk talk: A team meeting in which tactics and specific plays are diagrammed (such as on a chalkboard) and discussed. also *skull session, skull practice.*

●●A meeting or session in which a blackboard is used for diagrams or illustrations.

cheat: To bias one's defensive position toward one side in anticipation of a play in that direction.

check: To execute a brush block, momentarily obstructing or delaying an opponent (as opposed to knocking him down).

check off: see *audibilize.*

chicken-fight: To stand an opponent up and block him from an upright position (sometimes several times in succession while slowly backing up) in order to protect the passer.

chop block: An illegal delayed block at or below the knees against an opponent who is in contact with a teammate of the blocker in the free-blocking zone (a rectangular area extending 4 yards on either side of the point from which the ball is centered, and 3 yards behind

each scrimmage line). In high school play, a chop block results in a 15-yard penalty.

1. chuck: To bump a receiver with the hands, arms, or body as he comes off the line in order to momentarily delay his pass route. Legal one time within 5 yards of the line of scrimmage. also *jam.*

2. chuck: The act of chucking.

1. circle: see *circle pattern.*

2. circle: 1. To run a circle pattern or route. 2. To call a circle pattern for a receiver. (circles the left end and hits him over the middle)

circle pass: A pass thrown to a receiver in a circle pattern or route.

circle pattern, circle route: A pass route in which a receiver circles in toward the middle. also *circle.*

circus catch: An extraordinary or spectacular catch. Originally a baseball expression, first used in the late 1800s.

1. cleat: One of a number of cone-shaped 1/2-inch long projections that extend from the bottom of a football shoe. A cleat may be no less than 3/4-inches in diameter at the free end and must be constructed of a material that does not chip or develop a cutting edge (usually hard rubber or nylon). also *stud.*

2. cleat: To kick or scrape a player with the cleats of a football shoe.

cleats: Football shoes with cleats on the soles.

1. clip: To illegally block or charge into an

CIRCUS CATCH

opponent who is not the ballcarrier below the waist from behind. It is not considered clipping if the opponent is hit within a specified clipping zone or free-blocking zone around the point from which the ball is snapped, as long as the blocker was in the zone at the snap. To clip is a foul that results in a 15-yard penalty.

2. clip: The act of clipping. also *clipping*.

clipping: The act of clipping an opponent, a foul that results in a 15-yard penalty. also *clip*.

clipping zone: A specified rectangular area around the line of scrimmage (extending laterally 4 yards on either side of the spot from which the ball is snapped and 3 yards behind each scrimmage line, or in the NFL, extending laterally to the position occupied by the offensive tackles at the snap and 3 yards back from each line of scrimmage). A player positioned inside the clipping zone at the snap may legally block an opponent below the waist from behind within the zone. also *free-blocking zone*.

clock play: An offensive play used to stop the clock near the end of a period of play, usually a pass thrown to a receiver near the sideline. If the pass is incomplete, or if the pass is complete and the receiver steps out of bounds, the clock automatically stops.

1. clothesline: A dangerous and illegal tackle in which an arm is swung or extended to deliberately catch a ballcarrier by the head, much like an unseen clothesline might. A foul that results in a 15-yard penalty.

2. clothesline: To execute a clothesline tackle.

coffin corner: Any of the four corners of a field where the sidelines and goal lines intersect. Punters aim for a coffin corner in the hopes that the ball will go out of bounds just short of the opponent's goal line, thereby preventing a return and insuring that the opponents will have to put the ball in play dangerously close to their own goal line.

College Football Association: An association within the NCAA of large schools with extensive football programs. Formed in 1976 to lobby for a stronger voice in the determination of NCAA bylaws and policies governing football, the College Football Association came into open conflict with the NCAA in 1981 by offering to negotiate independently with the major networks for the right to televise football games of its members. also *CFA*.

College Football Hall of Fame: The national institution that honors outstanding college football players. The Hall of Fame was opened in 1978 at Kings Island, Ohio (near Cincinnati).

color: Commentary and incidental information that makes the radio or television broadcast of a game more interesting and/or informative, usually provided by someone other than the play-by-play announcer.

color commentator: The member of a radio or television broadcast team who provides commentary or incidental information to augment the play-by-play account of a game. also *color man*.

color man: see *color commentator*.

combination coverage: A defensive strategy that employs double coverage for a receiver on one side of the field, and man-for-man coverage for the receiver on the other side of the field.

comeback, comebacker: A pass pattern in which the receiver runs straight ahead, then abruptly turns back toward the passer. also *buttonhook, hook*.

come off the ball: To react quickly and

CLIPPING

spring forward from a set position the moment the ball is snapped. Play at the line of scrimmage is often dictated by the team that has the ability to come off the ball quickly, or "fire out." also *move off the ball.*

compensation: Money and/or future draft choices given to a team to compensate for the loss of the services of a high-quality veteran player who has played out his option, by the team signing the player at the end of the option year. see *option.*

1. complete: To throw a pass that is caught by the intended receiver. (completes a short pass over the middle to the tight end)

2. complete: Caught by the intended receiver. (a long pass, complete at the 2-yard line)

completion: A completed forward pass. A completion is credited to the passer in statistical records. Fran Tarkenton of the Minnesota Vikings and New York Giants holds the NFL career record for completions, 3,686. San Diego Chargers quarterback Dan Fouts holds the NFL record for the most completions in a season, 348 in 1980. Richard Todd of the New York Jets set the NFL one-game record for completions on September 21, 1980, against the San Francisco 49ers, 42.

conversion: The scoring of one or two extra points on a try for point after a touchdown. see *convert.*

convert: To score on a try for point after a touchdown, either by kicking the ball over the crossbar between the goal posts, or running or passing the ball over the goal line. In college and high school play, two points are awarded for running or passing the ball over the goal line.

corner: see *cornerback.*

cornerback: 1. One of two defensive backs who line up behind and outside the linebackers (usually opposite the wide receivers), and whose primary responsibilities are to prevent the opponents from turning the corner on sweeps and to cover the wide receivers on pass plays. also *corner, cornerman.* 2. The position played by a cornerback. also *corner, cornerman.*

corner blitz: A blitz by one or both cornerbacks. see *blitz.*

cornerman: A cornerback. also *corner.*

corner route: see *flag.*

cough up the ball: To fumble and lose possession of the ball. (coughed up the ball on their own 3-yard line)

count: see *signals.*

counter, counter play: An offensive play in which the ballcarrier runs "against the grain," toward the sideline opposite the direction most players are moving.

cover: 1. To guard a receiver in order to prevent him from catching a forward pass. 2. To defend in a particular area or zone. (the safety covered deep)

coverage: The covering of a receiver or receivers, or the manner in which a receiver or receivers are covered (man-for-man, zone, etc.).

crab block: see *body block.*

crackback block: An illegal block in which a flanking player (2 yards or more outside the tackle) turns in and blocks a defensive player from the side or back within an area 5 yards on either side of the line of scrimmage. A foul that results in a 15-yard penalty.

crawling: An attempt by a runner to advance the ball on the ground after he has been downed, or after the ball has been blown dead. A foul that results in a 5-yard penalty.

cross: A pass pattern in which receivers on opposite sides of the field run downfield and turn inward so that their routes cross. also *crossing pattern.*

1. cross block: A side block made on a defensive lineman positioned to one side of (as opposed to directly across the line from) the blocker, either to move the defensive player laterally to clear a path for a particular play, or to vary from normal blocking patterns by switching assignments with another blocker. Invented by pioneer football coach Amos Alonzo Stagg.

2. cross block: To execute a cross block.

cross-body block: see *body block.*

cross buck: An offensive play in which the quarterback hands the ball off to one of two running backs (faking to the other) who run past him toward the line on diagonally crossing paths. Invention of the cross buck credited to Amos Alonzo Stagg.

crossing pattern: see *cross.*

curbstone coach: see *grandstand quarterback.*

1. curl: A pass pattern in which the receiver runs straight ahead, then turns inside

or outside and curls back toward the line of scrimmage. also *curl-in, curl-out.*
2. curl: To run a curl pattern.
curl-in: see *curl.*
curl-out: see *curl.*
1. cut: 1. To suddenly change direction, often with a burst of acceleration or after a fake in the opposite direction. 2. To eliminate from a team. (cut five men in the final week of practice)
2. cut: 1. A sudden change of direction. (eludes the tackle with a quick cut inside) 2. The elimination of a player from a team. (survived the last cut) see *make the cut.*
cut back: To suddenly almost reverse direction with a cut, such as back into the middle after running wide.
cutback: The act of cutting back.
cut block: A low block (below the knees) made by interior linemen to trip defensive linemen. also *cutoff block.*
cutoff block: see *cut block.*
D: Defense. (the D has held again)
daylight: A gap or open space between defensive players. (moves laterally, looking for some daylight) also *hole.*
D back: A defensive back.
dead ball: A ball that is out of play. A ball is dead if it is downed or travels out of bounds, if a fair catch is made, if a time out is called, or if an official blows a whistle to indicate a rules infraction.
dead man play: see *hideout play.*
decline a penalty: To exercise the option given to the captain of the offended team on most fouls and refuse a penalty, in which case play proceeds with the next down as though no foul had been committed. The captain of the offended team will decline a penalty if the existing field position and down favor his team.
deep: 1. Far away from either side of the line of scrimmage. (sends his receivers deep, looking for the bomb) 2. Close to either team's goal line. (will be forced to put the ball in play deep in their own territory) 3. Having an ample number of players available for or capable of playing a position or positions. (deep in receivers) see *depth.*
deep drop: The movement of the quarterback to a position far back from the line of scrimmage in order to throw a pass. A deep drop is taken to avoid a pass rush and to provide a quarterback with an extra measure of time to find an open receiver.

1. defense: 1. The endeavor to stop the opposing team from advancing the ball or scoring, and whenever possible, to get possession of the ball for one's own team. (a conservative, defense-oriented team) also *D.* 2. The specific plan or alignment used to defend. (use the nickel defense against the pass) 3. The defensive team or its members. also *D, defensive team, defensive unit.*
2. defense: To defend against an opposing player, team, or play. (made some adjustments to defense the pass effectively)
defensive: Pertaining to defense, or the playing of defense. (defensive play) (defensive game plan)
defensive back: 1. One of the players (usually two cornerbacks and two safeties) positioned behind (and outside in the case of cornerbacks) the linebackers in the defensive backfield, and who are primarily responsible for defending against passes, and for preventing long gains on running plays which get through or around the defensive line. For special defensive coverages, extra defensive backs replace one or more linebackers. also *back, D back.* 2. The position played by a defensive back. also *back, D back.*
defensive end: 1. One of the usually two defensive players positioned outside the defensive tackles on the line of scrimmage, and who are primarily responsible for defending against sweeps and other wide running plays, and for rushing the passer. also *end.* 2. The position played by a defensive end. also *end.*
defensive tackle: 1. One of the two defensive players who are positioned on the line of scrimmage between the defensive ends, and who are primarily responsible for defending against inside running plays, and for rushing the passer. 2. The position played by a defensive tackle.
defensive team, defensive unit: The players on a team who regularly play as a unit on defense. also *D, defense.*
1. delay: A deception play on offense or a deceptive part of an offensive play in which a player disguises his actual assignment (to run a pass route, take a handoff, or make a key block) by hesitating long enough to appear to be doing something else.
2. delay: To disguise one's actual assignment on a play with a delay.

delay of game: An infraction of the rules that involves any action or inaction by either team that delays play or the progress of a game, such as, the failure to put the ball in play within the allotted time (twenty-five seconds in high school and college play, thirty seconds in the NFL), remaining on a dead ball or on a downed runner, taking and/or advancing a dead ball, or advancing the ball of a fair catch. Delay of game results in a 5-yard penalty.

depth: An ample number of players available for or capable of playing a position or positions. A team with depth is less vulnerable to an injury to (or a poor performance) by one or more key players.

depth chart: A coach's chart that lists and ranks the available players for each position on a team.

diamond defense: The center part of a 3-4 defense, consisting of the nose guard, the two interior linebackers, and the free safety.

dime defense: A prevent defense that employs six defensive backs. A nickel defense uses one extra back, a dime, two extra backs.

dive: An offensive play in which the ballcarrier lunges headfirst into, under, or over the line in order to gain a short distance (as when lacking a yard or less to make a first down or score a touchdown).

diveback: The fullback or up back in the I formation.

dog: see *red dog*.

1. double: To double-cover.

2. double: Double coverage.

double-cover: 1. To cover a receiver with two defensive players, either simultaneously or using zones. In the latter case, when a receiver is double-covered, the field is divided into two defensive zones, with the cornerback responsible for preventing a short pass, and the safety for preventing a long pass. also *double*. 2. To join with a teammate in guarding a receiver. also *double*.

double coverage: The covering of a receiver by two defensive players. also *double*. see *double-cover*.

double-double zone defense: Double zone coverage on both sides of the field. see *double-cover*.

double motion: 1. A change or reverse in direction by a man in motion. 2. An obsolete offensive formation with two men in motion. Now an infraction of the rules, illegal motion, resulting in a 5-yard penalty.

double reverse: An offensive play in which a back running laterally toward one sideline hands off to a teammate running in the opposite direction, who in turn hands off to another teammate running laterally in the original direction of the play.

double-slot formation: An offensive formation that employs two slotbacks, one lined up in the slot between (and behind) the tackle and tight end, and the other lined up in the slot between (and behind) the other tackle and split end.

double-team: 1. To block an opponent with two players. 2. To join with a teammate in blocking an opponent.

double wing: An offensive formation employing an unbalanced line in which the ball is snapped directly to the tailback, positioned 4 to 5 yards behind the center, with the fullback about a yard in front and just to the side of him on the strong side. The remaining backs (the quarterback and a halfback) are positioned as wingbacks, just behind and outside of the two ends, with the quarterback playing on the weak side. Though tried as early as 1911 at Carlisle Indian School by Glenn S. "Pop" Warner, the double wing was not popular until Warner's Stanford team used the formation to defeat Army in 1928. The double wing was the basis for modern spread formations such as the shotgun.

1. down: 1. No longer in play, not able to be advanced, dead. (nullified the runback, and marked the ball down at the 20-yard line) 2. No longer able to advance the ball because of having touched the ground with a part of the body other than hands or feet after being touched by an opponent. (he is down at the 2-yard line)

2. down: 1. To cause the ball to be dead intentionally by touching it or one knee to the ground. 2. To tackle the ballcarrier. (caught from behind and downed at the 12-yard line)

3. down: 1. A play or period of action that starts when the ball is put into play with a snap (for a scrimmage down) or a

FOOTBALL (AMERICAN)

free kick (for a free kick down), and that ends when the ball is dead. see **dead ball.** 2. One of a series of four chances allotted to the offensive team to score or to advance the ball 10 yards in order to retain possession. Downs were introduced in 1882 and originally called for the offense to gain 5 yards in three downs to retain possession. Rules increasing the distance to gain to 10 yards and the number of downs to four were introduced in 1906 and 1912.

down-and-in: see *in.*

down-and-out: see *out.*

down box: A 5 to 6-foot rod, atop which is fastened a set of numbered cards (1 through 4) to indicate the down being played. At the start of each down, a member of the box and chain crew displays the appropriate numbered card and places the rod at the point indicated by the linesman along the sideline to mark the spot of the ball. also *down indicator, down marker, downs box.*

downfield: Toward the opposing team's goal line. also *upfield.*

downfield blocker: An offensive player, usually accompanying the ballcarrier, who makes blocks downfield away from the line of scrimmage or the start of a play.

downfield blocking: Blocking in an open field, away from the line of scrimmage or the start of a play. (got some good downfield blocking and went all the way for a touchdown)

down indicator: see *down box.*

down lineman: An interior lineman, one who normally assumes a crouching stance.

down marker: see *down box.*

downs box: see *down box.*

draw, draw play: An offensive play in which a quarterback, anticipating a pass rush, drops back as though passing to draw a rush, then hands off to a back who runs straight forward through the gap left by the onrushing defensive players. The first draw play was an accident, the result of a broken play involving Pro Football Hall of Famers Otto Graham and Marion Motley of the Cleveland Browns. In a pre-NFL merger game in the late 1940s, quarterback Graham, seeing that he was trapped by onrushing linemen on a pass play, in desperation handed off to full-

back Motley, who ran right by the rushers for a big gain. In the game films, coach Paul Brown noticed the alley up the middle through which Motley ran, and decided to employ the tactic as a designed play, dubbing it the "draw play."

drive: A series of plays which produces an advance toward the opposing team's goal line.

drive-block: To block an opponent in such a way as to drive him back, thereby clearing a space or path for the runner.

drop: 1. A quarterback's move back from the line of scrimmage to set up before throwing a pass. 2. A defensive player's move back from the line of scrimmage into a zone to defend against a pass. (would sometimes fake a blitz before making his drop to cover the zone)

drop back: To move straight back from the line of scrimmage with the ball to set up before throwing a pass. also *fade back.*

1. drop kick: A kick made by dropping the ball and kicking it just as or immediately after it touches the ground. In football's early days, the drop kick was a powerful weapon. The legendary Jim Thorpe could score a field goal with it from the 50-yard line. Though still legal for field goals, extra points, and free kicks, the technique virtually disappeared from football after the 1930s, when the shape of the ball was made less rounded. The pointed ends of a modern football make it difficult to get a true bounce. Among the last players to be known for the drop kick were 1939 Heisman Trophy winner Nile Kinnick of Iowa and Pro Football Hall of Famer Dutch Clark, who played for the Detroit Lions from 1934 to 1938. Ray "Scooter" MacLean made what is believed to be the last NFL drop kick in the 1941 championship game, scoring the final point for the Chicago Bears in their 37-9 victory over the New York Giants.

2. drop kick: To make a drop kick.

duck, duck ball: A poorly thrown pass that seems to hang in the air or float, making it easy to intercept. also *dying quail, floater.*

dump: 1. see *sack.* 2. see *dump off.*

dump off: To throw a short pass to a back when all primary receivers are covered, or to take advantage of an undefended area vacated by blitzing linebackers or defensive backs. also *dump.*

149

dying quail: see *duck, duck ball*.

eat the ball: To be tackled behind the line of scrimmage when an open receiver cannot be found for a pass. There are times when a quarterback must "eat the ball" rather than risk an interception.

eleven: A football team.

eligible receiver: Any player who is permitted by the rules to catch a forward pass. On the offensive team, only the backs and two ends are eligible receivers, unless a member of the defensive team touches or tips the ball, in which case, any member of the offensive team may legally catch it. All players on the defensive team are eligible receivers. A pass caught by an ineligible receiver behind the line of scrimmage results in the loss of a down. A pass caught by an ineligible receiver on or beyond the line of scrimmage results in the loss of 10 yards, or the loss of the down.

encroaching, encroachment: The illegal entry into the neutral zone (having a part of one's body on or over the line of scrimmage or free kick line) after the ball is ready for play up to the time it is put into play (snapped or kicked). The center on a scrimmage down and the holder and kicker on a free kick down are the only players permitted to be partially in the neutral zone before the ball is put into play. Encroachment results in a 5-yard penalty. compare *offside*.

end: 1. Either of two players positioned at the extremities of the offensive or defensive line. see *offensive end, defensive end*. 2. The position played by an end.

end around: A reverse in which a wide .receiver or tight end turns back through the offensive backfield for a handoff, and continues running around the opposite side of the line. Invented by Amos Alonzo Stagg.

end line: Either of two 160-foot lines, between and perpendicular to the sidelines, that mark the end boundaries of the playing area.

end run: An offensive play in which the ballcarrier runs around one end of the line.

●●An attempt to avoid someone or something. (did an end run around the autograph seekers by slipping out a side exit)

end zone: The 160-foot-wide by 30-foot-deep area at either end of the field bounded by the goal line, the end line, and the sidelines.

enforcement spot: see *spot of enforcement*.

exchange: see *snap*.

extra point: 1. A point scored by successfully placekicking or drop kicking the ball through the uprights, or by successfully running or passing the ball into the end zone on a "try for point" following a touchdown. From 1884 until 1897, when it was given its present one-point value, the extra point (then called the "goal from touchdown" or "goal after") counted for two points. Before 1884, it had been valued at four points, more than a touchdown, which then counted for two points. 2. Two points scored by running or passing the ball into the end zone on a "try for point" following a touchdown (an option in USFL, college, and high school play). also *PAT, point after, point after touchdown*.

face guard: see *face mask*.

face-guarding: The illegal obstruction or hindrance of a pass receiver by a defensive player who, turning his back to the ball, waves his arms in the receiver's face to interfere with his vision. Face-guarding is pass interference and results in a first down for the offensive team at the spot of the foul.

face mask: 1. A steel bumper or cage attached to the front of a helmet to protect the face, consisting of one or more horizontal bars around the front (and for linemen, one vertical bar in the middle). Invented in the 1950s by Cleveland Browns' coach Paul Brown. also *birdcage, cage, face guard, face protector*. 2. An infraction of the rules in which an opponent's face mask is grabbed, resulting in a 5-yard penalty, or a 15-yard penalty if the face mask is twisted or pulled.

face protector: see *face mask*.

fade back: see *drop back*.

1. **fair catch:** An unhindered catch of a ball kicked by the opposing team made by a player of the receiving team who signals his intention to the officials (by extending one arm at full length above the head and waving while the kick is in flight), and does not attempt to advance the ball after making the catch. In signalling for a fair catch, a receiver

forfeits his right to advance the ball in return for protection against being blocked or tackled immediately after catching the ball by an onrushing opponent, which could cause a fumble. The ball becomes dead when a fair catch is made, and is put into play at that spot by a scrimmage down or, optionally, by a free kick. If a fair catch is muffed, it is considered a loose ball as soon as it touches the ground, and may be recovered by either team.

2. fair catch: To make a fair catch of a kick. (a short kick that he will fair catch around the 40-yard line)

1. fake: 1. To feign an action (such as a move in a certain direction, pass, hand off, etc.) in order to momentarily deceive an opponent. (fakes a handoff, then completes a short pass to the tight end) also *juke.* 2. To momentarily deceive an opponent by a feigned move or action. (faked the free safety and went all the way for a touchdown). also *fake out, juke.*

2. fake: A feigned move or action that is intended to momentarily deceive an opponent. (got the cornerback going the wrong way with a fake to the outside) also *juke.*

fake out: To deceive an opponent with a fake. also *fake, juke.*

●●To deceive or fool someone. (faked her out by disguising his voice when he called)

false start: A rules infraction in which one or more offensive players move after assuming a set position before the ball is snapped, resulting in a 5-yard penalty. Any defensive encroachment or offside caused by a false start is nullified.

false trap: An influence, or deception play, in which a blocker pulls as though on a sweep or trap in order to cause the opposing defensive lineman to misread the play and follow the blockers, leaving his position vacant to be run through by the ballcarrier. also *sucker trap.*

field general: The quarterback.

field goal: A three-point score made by drop kicking or placekicking the ball between the goalposts over the crossbar from behind the line of scrimmage. In the late 1800s, a field goal was worth five points, and was assigned its present three-point value only after a rule change in 1909. The all-time record for the longest field goal in college play is 67 yards, set in 1977 by Texas kicker Russell Erxleben, equalled in the same year by Steve Little of Arkansas, and by Joe Williams of Wichita State in 1978. The all-time NFL record for the longest field goal is 63 yards, set in 1970 by then-New Orleans Saints kicker Tom Dempsey.

field judge: A football official who, at the snap, is positioned approximately 25 yards downfield near the middle of the field, and who is responsible for the ball, the tee, and the kicker on all free kicks, covering scrimmage kicks, passes, and runs into his area, timing the thirty-second count (twenty-five-seconds in college play) and the two-minute intermissions following the first and third quarters, and ruling with the back judge on conversions and field goals.

field position: The area where the ball is put into play by the offensive team, and its relative proximity to the goal line toward which the ball is being advanced. The closer the offensive team is to the opponent's goal line when the ball is put into play, the better the field position. (the interception and runback have given them good field position)

find: To complete a pass to a receiver. (found the tight end with a bullet over the middle) also *hit.*

fire out: To move off the line of scrimmage explosively the moment the ball is snapped. (the offensive line is really firing out and controlling play at the line of scrimmage)

first-and-ten: A first down.

first down: The first of a series of four downs in which the offensive team must attempt to score, or to advance ten yards in order to maintain possession of the ball for a new series of downs. also *first-and-ten.*

first string, first team: The players, or of and pertaining to the players, who regularly start or play in games, as opposed to those held in reserve or as substitutes. (made the first string in his rookie year)

●●The best or highest rated, or of or pertaining to the best or highest rated, of a team or group. (sent in the first string negotiators for the final round of talks)

first stringer: One who regularly plays on the first string or first team.

1. flag: 1. see *penalty flag.* 2. A pass pattern in which a receiver runs downfield then cuts diagonally toward the goal line marker or "flag" at the corner of the field. also *corner route.*

2. flag: To call a foul or infraction on a player. (nullified the runback when he was flagged for clipping)

flag football: A variation of football played between teams of usually six to nine players, and in which the ballcarrier can be "tackled" only by removing a flag or handkerchief hung from the waist or hip pocket. In flag football, all players are eligible to catch a forward pass, and the offensive team must score within four downs or lose possession of the ball. also *tail football.*

flag on the play: An instance of a flag being thrown because of a rules infraction or foul, a penalty.

●●An unforeseen problem which causes a change in plans. (right on schedule until a flat tire caused a flag on the play)

flagrant foul: A vicious act such as a slug or kick, a vicious clip, or a vicious grasping of the face mask, resulting in a 15-yard penalty, and often, the disqualification of the guilty player.

flak jacket: Special lightweight padding worn like a vest to protect the ribs. Adapted by designer Byron Donziz from the flak jackets worn by combat helicopter crews, the flak jacket was first used to protect the injured ribs of then-Houston Oilers quarterback Dan Pastorini.

1. flank: Either side or end of a formation. (a receiver out on the flank)

2. flank: To position oneself on the flank. (flanking on the strong side)

flanker: An old name for a wide receiver or an offensive player positioned wide of a formation, either on the line of scrimmage or a yard or more back (a flankerback). Amos Alonzo Stagg is believed to have introduced the use of a flanker (later called a split end) and a flankerback (a halfback positioned wide). In modern football, wide receivers line up in either position, depending on the play called.

flankerback: see *flanker.*

1. flare: A short pass to a back moving out toward the sideline in the backfield. Used as a safety valve when the quarterback is under pressure from a pass rush or blitz. also *swing, swing pass.*

2. flare: To release from a pass blocking assignment in the backfield and move toward the sideline for a pass. also *swing.*

flat: The area of the field to either side of a formation.

flat ball: A ball placed on its side (ends pointed toward the sidelines) for a placekick, instead of on one end, as on a tee.

flat pass: A pass made to a backfield player in the flat.

flea-flicker: A trick play that usually consists of a lateral followed by a pass, a handoff followed by a pass, or a pass followed by a lateral. Innovative 1920s Illinois coach Bob Zuppke is given credit for developing the first flea-flicker play (a pass followed by a lateral).

flex defense: A defensive strategy in which varying sets of two linemen drop back slightly just before the snap to protect against a run. The flex defense was developed in 1977 by Dallas Cowboys coach Tom Landry.

1. flip: A quick short pass.

2. flip: To make a quick short pass.

flip-flop: To exchange the positions of the safeties and/or linebackers before the ball is snapped in order to get the better tacklers on the strong side of the offensive formation. also *flop.*

floater: see *duck.*

flood a zone: To send more receivers into a zone than there are defenders to cover.

flop: see *flip-flop.*

fly, fly pattern: A pass pattern in which the receiver runs straight downfield at full speed. also *go.*

flying wedge: An early offensive formation in which blockers converged at full speed (from about 20 yards back) to form a moving wedge behind which the ballcarrier would follow, or be pulled or dragged along by his belt or special handles sewn onto his uniform. Invented in 1892 by Harvard coach L.H. Deland, the flying wedge and similar mass-momentum plays were soon in wide use, causing a number of deaths and serious injuries until they were finally outlawed in 1906.

football: 1. A game played between two teams of eleven players on a rectangular field 53-1/3 yards wide and 120 yards long (including a 10-yard deep end zone at each end of the field).

Points are scored by running with or passing an inflated ball (oval with pointed ends) into the opponent's end zone (a touchdown, six points), kicking the ball over a 10-foot-high, 23-foot, 4-inch-long horizontal bar (18 feet, 6 inches in the NFL) and between the 20-foot-high uprights (40 feet in the NFL) that together form a goal on the end boundary line of each end zone (if after a touchdown, an extra point, one point, any other time, a field goal, three points), running or passing the ball into the opponent's end zone on a try for point after a touchdown, two points (one point in the NFL), or tackling an opponent with the ball in his own end zone (a safety, two points). Defensive players are permitted to tackle the ballcarrier or the passer. Offensive players are permitted to protect the ballcarrier or the passer by using the body (not the hands) to block their opponents. Play starts (at the beginning of each half, and after each score) with one team kicking the ball to the other. The team in possession of the ball or offensive team (usually there are separate eleven-man offensive and defensive units on a team) has four scrimmage downs to score, or to advance the ball ten yards in order to maintain possession with another series of downs. Play on a scrimmage down is started from the line of scrimmage (the point at which the ballcarrier was tackled or went out of bounds) by one player (of the minimum seven offensive players positioned at the line of scrimmage) passing the ball back between his legs to a backfield player (usually the quarterback) who may run with the ball, pass it to another backfield player or to one of the two ends (players at either end of the offensive line), or hand the ball off to a teammate. Any player is permitted to run with the ball, but most often the ballcarrier is one of the four backfield players positioned 1 yard or more behind the line (usually a quarterback, fullback, and two halfbacks), and the linemen do the blocking. Defensive alignments vary, but most often there are four or five linemen (two ends, two tackles, and sometimes a middle guard), two or three linebackers positioned a yard or so behind the line, and four backfield players (two cornerbacks and two safeties). If the offensive team is unable to score or advance the ball 10 yards in the allotted four downs, or if a fumble is recovered or a pass intercepted by the opposing team, possession of the ball is lost, and the opposing team becomes the offensive team. When it seems unlikely that the ball can be advanced the necessary 10 yards in the allotted four downs, the offensive team may voluntarily give up possession of the ball by kicking or punting the ball (as far from its own goal line as possible). Rules infractions or fouls result in a loss of 5, 10, or 15 yards, or the loss or replay of the down. The game is divided into four fifteen-minute quarters (twelve-minute quarters in high school play) and the team with the highest score at the end of the fourth quarter wins. In the NFL, ties are decided in one or more fifteen-minute sudden-death overtime periods.
2. An inflated rubber bladder enclosed in a pebble-grained, leather case without corrugations of any kind. In the shape of a prolate spheroid (an oval with pointed ends), the ball is 11 to 11-1/4 inches long, and 21-1/4 to 21-1/2 inches in circumference around the middle, and weighs 14 to 15 ounces. Before the 1920s, when rule changes slimmed and streamlined it, the football was a blunt-nosed rugby-type ball. also *ball, pigskin.*
●●A "political football" is an issue that is figuratively tossed back and forth, and with which each side attempts to score points.
football knee: Cartilage and/or ligament damage to the knee that can result from the physical contact in football.

FOOTBALL

force: To turn a running play into the middle, or prevent it from getting outside.

force man: The defensive player (linebacker, cornerback, or strong safety) who is responsible for turning a sweep (or any running play to the outside) inside. (got outside after the lead blocker took out the force man)

formation: A specific offensive or defensive alignment at the beginning of a play, with players deployed in prearranged positions. also *set*.

40, forty: A 40-yard sprint used to measure the acceleration and speed of football players. (a lineman who can do a 4.5 forty)

forward lateral: An illegal lateral made in a forward direction beyond the line of scrimmage. A forward lateral is considered a forward pass from beyond the line of scrimmage, and results in a 5-yard penalty from the spot of the pass and the loss of the down.

forward pass: An offensive play in which the ball is thrown forward from behind the line of scrimmage to an eligible receiver (any backfield player or either of the two ends). Only one forward pass can be thrown on a down, and if the pass is incomplete, the ball is dead, and put into play for the next down at the previous line of scrimmage. The forward pass was made legal in 1906 as a part of a general movement to open up the game of football and cut down on the number of injuries. Both Wesleyan (vs. Yale) and Yale (vs. Harvard) are believed to have been among the first to use a forward pass in 1906. The pass came into national prominence in 1913 when Notre Dame upset a powerful Army team at West Point, 39-13, with quarterback Gus Dorais throwing to end Knute Rockne.

four-three defense: A defensive alignment that uses a four-man line (two tackles and two ends) and three linebackers. The four-three defense emerged in the NFL in the 1950s, and remained the standard defense for fifteen years, until the three-four began to gain popularity.

fourth down: The last of a series of four opportunities given to the offensive team to advance the ball a total of 10 yards.

free ball: see *loose ball*.

free-blocking zone: see *clipping zone*.

free kick: An unhindered kick (drop kick, placekick, or punt) made from or behind a restraining line (free kick line) beyond which no member of the kicking team may advance until the ball is kicked. The opposing team is under the same restriction at its own free kick line, located 10 yards in advance of the kicking team's line. The ball is put into play with a free kick (kickoff) made from the kicking team's 40-yard line (35-yard line in the NFL) at the start of each half, after a try for point, and after a successful field goal. A kickoff is usually made with a placekick. Punts are prohibited. When a safety is scored, the team scored upon puts the ball in play from the 20-yard line with a free kick (usually a punt). In the NFL, after a fair catch, the receiving team may elect to put the ball in play with a free kick from or behind the point where the free catch was made, as for a field goal.

free kick down: A down during which a free kick is made, as at the start of each half, after a try for point, after a successful field goal, after a safety, and, optionally in the NFL, after a fair catch. compare *scrimmage down*.

free kick line: Either of two imaginary restraining lines used during a free kick 10 yards apart, between and perpendicular to the sidelines, and beyond which the kicking and receiving teams may not advance until the ball is kicked. The kicking team's free kick line (from which the receiving team's line is measured) is set at the kicking team's 40-yard line (35-yard line in the NFL) for kickoffs, and at the 20-yard line after a safety (and for a free kick after a fair catch in the NFL, on or behind the spot of the catch).

free safety, free safetyman: 1. A defensive back usually positioned about 10 yards behind the line of scrimmage on the weak side. Normally the deepest

FREE SAFETY ●   STRONG SAFETY ●

LINEBACKERS

●   ●   ●   ●   ●
CB   CB

●   ●   ●   ●
END   TACKLE   END

FOUR-THREE DEFENSE

playing defender, the free safety covers the central area of the field against a long run or pass and is "free" to assist other defensive backs assigned to cover specific receivers. also *weak safety*. 2. The position played by a free safety. also *weak safety*.

front: The defensive line.

front four: The four defensive linemen in a four-man front.

front line: The players positioned on the line of scrimmage. also *line*.

fullback: 1. An offensive back usually positioned behind the quarterback (directly, in the T and I formations), and primarily responsible for blocking and carrying the ball, especially in short yardage situations. Fullbacks tend to be more powerful, if less elusive than other running backs. also *diveback, upback*. 2. The position played by a fullback. also *diveback, upback*.

full house: 1. Any offensive formation with all four backs in the backfield. 2. A full house T formation.

full house T formation: The basic T formation, utilizing all four backs. also *T, T formation, tight T*.

1. fumble: To drop or lose control and possession of the ball (as opposed to failing to gain control and possession of the ball on a pass or a kick). also *cough up the ball*. compare *muff*.

2. fumble: 1. The act of fumbling the ball. When the ball is fumbled, it becomes a loose or free ball, and any player recovering it may advance the ball. (the fumble in the first quarter was one of three critical turnovers) compare *muff*. 2. A ball that has been fumbled. (lunges to recover the fumble)

gadget, gadget play: A trick play, one that is deceptive and/or unusual. also *razzle-dazzle play*.

1. gain: To advance the ball a specified distance. (gained six yards with a run off tackle)

2. gain: The advancement of the ball or the distance a ball is advanced on a play. (ran a reverse for a long gain)

game ball: 1. One of the balls approved by the referee for use in a game. 2. A game ball that is awarded by the players to a teammate or coach for his contribution to a winning effort.

●●A figurative award given for excellence or a superior performance in some endeavor. (the chef should be voted the game ball for a feast like this)

game films: Sixteen-millimeter films of a game studied on special stop-motion and reversing projectors by the coaching staff and players of a team. To insure fairness, the NFL has strict rules governing the exchange of film by teams. Pro Football Hall of Fame coach Sid Gillman pioneered the use of game films in the late 1930s, when he was assistant coach of Denison College. Another Pro Football Hall of Fame coach, Paul Brown, was among the first to stress the use of game films in professional football.

game plan: The specific strategy and tactical schemes (both offensive and defensive) planned for a particular game or opponent.

●●A scheme or plan to achieve a particular goal.

gamer: A player whose performance in actual games always exceeds the ability he shows in practice.

games: The apparent changes (jitterbugging) and actual changes in alignments and rushing patterns (stunts, stacks, slants, etc.) employed by a defensive team on different plays to confuse the offense.

gang-tackle: To tackle a ballcarrier with two or more tacklers.

gap: An open space between linemen. also *daylight, hole*.

giveaway football: Sloppy play, characterized by fumbles, pass interceptions, and other mistakes.

go: see *fly*.

goal: 1. A wooden or metal structure centered on each end line consistng of a 23-foot, 4-inch (or in the NFL, 18-foot, 6-inch) long horizontal crossbar whose top face is 10 feet above the ground, with uprights at each end that extend vertically 10 feet above the crossbar (or 10 yards in the NFL). High school and college goals are usually H-shaped, with a two-post base. NFL goals are supported by a single standard, padded and slightly recessed from the plane of the goal and end line. also *uprights*. 2. The vertical plane extending indefinitely above the crossbar, between the goalposts or uprights. 3. Goal-to-go. (first and goal on the 3-yard line)

goal line: A line extending from sideline

to sideline 10 yards from and parallel to each end line, separating the end zone from the field of play, and over which the ball must be carried or passed to score a touchdown or a two-point conversion after a touchdown.

goal-line defense: The personnel and alignment used by the defensive team in a goal-line stand.

goal-line stand: An attempt by the defense to prevent, or an instance of preventing, the opposing team from scoring from near the goal line. also *goal stand*.

goal post, goalpost: Either of the two uprights that extend vertically from both sides of the crossbar, and mark the sides of the goal.

goal stand: A goal-line stand.

goal-to-go: A situation in which the opponent's goal line is closer than 10 yards from the line of scrimmage, the distance the ball would have to be advanced for a first down. (finally brought down at the 4-yard line, where it will be first down and goal-to-go) also *goal*.

go for it: To gamble and attempt to make the necessary yards for a first down instead of kicking the ball to the opposing team on fourth down. If the attempt is unsuccessful, the opposing team takes over possession of the ball in a usually more advantageous field position than if the ball had been kicked.

●●To pursue a desired goal or activity, regardless of the risk or consequences. (decided to go for it and quit her job to write full time)

go long: 1. To throw a long pass. (going long, looking for the bomb) 2. To run a deep pass pattern. (fakes to the inside and goes long)

grandstand quarterback: One who second-guesses the quarterback from the grandstands. also *curbstone coach*. compare *armchair quarterback, Monday morning quarterback*.

●●One who constantly second-guesses or offers advice about matters with which he is not concerned.

grasp and control rule: An NFL rule that empowers the referee to blow the ball dead and rule a sack when, in his judgment, the quarterback is within the "grasp and control" of a defensive player. The grasp and control rule was initiated in 1979 to help protect the quarterback from injury.

Green Gripper towel: A specially treated cloth (similar to baseball's pine tar towel) that is rubbed on players' hands to increase adhesion and make the ball stick to the hands of a receiver or defensive back. In 1981, the NFL outlawed the use of the Green Gripper towel, "stickum," and any other substance having qualities of slipperiness or adhesiveness.

grid: see *gridiron*.

gridder: A football player.

gridiron: 1. A football field. When the forward pass was legalized in 1906, the quarterback was required to be 5 yards behind the line of scrimmage and could move no more than 5 yards laterally in either direction before the

GOAL POST

pass was thrown. To facilitate this and help the officials watch for infractions, lines were marked the length of the field at 5-yard intervals between and parallel to the sidelines. These, combined with the yard lines at 5-yard intervals, gave the football field the appearance of a "grid" or gridiron. also *grid*. 2. The game or pertaining to the game of football. also *grid*.

grind out: To methodically gain short yardage with running plays through the line. (able to grind out another first down at the 35-yard line)

1. ground: Running plays or pertaining to running plays. (make up for their weakness in the air with a formidable ground attack)

2. ground: To deliberately throw the ball to the ground or out of bounds (away from any possible receiver) rather than be thrown for a loss behind the line of scrimmage. Intentional grounding is a foul that results in a penalty. also *unload*. see *intentional grounding*.

ground-gainer: A skilled ballcarrier, one who gains yards rushing.

guard: 1. Either of two offensive linemen usually positioned next to and on either side of the center, primarily responsible for pass blocking, drive-blocking to open holes for runs through the line, and pulling, whether for a trap or to lead a sweep. also *offensive guard*. compare *middle guard, nose guard*. 2. The position played by a guard.

Hail Mary: A low-percentage pass, one that would require a great deal of luck or the intercession of a "higher power" for completion. (won the game in the closing seconds with a spectacular end zone catch of a real Hail Mary) also *prayer*.

halfback: 1. An offensive backfield player who functions primarily as a receiver or ballcarrier. The number of halfbacks (more commonly called running backs) and their exact position varies with different offensive formations. 2. A cornerback. 3. The position played by a halfback.

halfback option: An offensive play in which a halfback with the ball has the option of carrying it, pitching it out to a teammate, or passing.

Hall of Fame: see *College Football Hall of Fame, Professional Football Hall of Fame*.

hand off: To give (hand-to-hand) the ball to a teammate. (hands off to the fullback on a draw play)

handoff: The act or an instance of giving or handing the ball to a teammate.

hang: 1. To stay up in the air a long time, as a kicked football. (gets off a booming punt that should hang long enough to be easily covered) 2. To kick a ball high enough so that it remains in the air for a long time. (hangs another towering punt)

hang time: The number of seconds between the time the ball is kicked and caught on a kickoff or punt. Along with accuracy and distance, hang time is used to evaluate the effectiveness of a kicker. A kick with a long hang time gives the defense an opportunity to get downfield in position to tackle the receiver, thereby narrowing the chances for a runback. The best punters try for a hang time of about five seconds.

hard-out: see *out*.

hashmarks: The field markings that indicate the inbounds lines at the yard lines. see *inbounds line*.

headhunter: A player known for excessive roughness or violence.

head linesman: see *linesman*.

head slap: An intentional clubbing blow to the side of an opponent's helmet. A personal foul that results in a 15-yard penalty and, if judged to be flagrant or vicious, the disqualification of the offending player. Legal throughout the 1970s, the head slap was an effective technique used by rushing defensive linemen.

hear footsteps: To anticipate and be momentarily distracted by an imminent hit or tackle by an approaching opponent. Often the cause of a hurried throw by the quarterback or a dropped catch by a receiver. (took his eye off the ball when he heard footsteps)

●●To be distracted from one's course of action by the fear of imminent danger. (might have invaded the smaller country had he not heard the footsteps of the international community)

heavy hitter: A player with the reputation of being a punishing blocker or tackler.

Heisman Trophy: The Heisman Memorial Trophy, an annual award given to the outstanding college football player of the year, as voted by sportswriters and former Heisman Trophy winners. The award for the player of the year was originated in 1935 by the Downtown Athletic Club of New York and given first to Chicago University halfback Jay Berwanger. The trophy received its present name in 1936, after the death of John Heisman, a College Hall of Famer who played at Brown University and Pennsylvania in the 1890s, before beginning a distinguished thirty-six-year coaching career. The first recipient of the Heisman Memorial Trophy was Yale All-America end Larry Kelley in 1936.

helmet: The protective covering for a player's head, comprised of a hard plastic outer shell with foam rubber and inflatable vinyl air cushions (connected by tubes to spread the load of an impact) individually fitted to conform to the size and shape of a player's head. The first leather helmets or "head harnesses" were worn around the turn of the century, primarily to protect the ears. In the mid-1930s, hard fiber composition crowns were introduced, and for the first time, players were able to use the helmet as a weapon. Plastic helmets were introduced in the late 1930s

HELMET

and used sporadically throughout the 1940s. After a number of injuries due to shattered plastic, leather and composition helmets regained popularity during the 1950s until new stronger plastic shells finally replaced them. Among the last holdouts, Chicago Bears end Dick Plasman was playing without a helmet as late as 1940. The NFL made helmets mandatory in 1943. In 1947, Los Angeles Ram halfback Fred Gehrke painted ram's horns on the team helmets, the first emblem or design ever to appear on a helmet in professional football.

hen's team: 1. A derogatory expression for a team with no blockers, or poor blocking. 2. An onside prevent defensive team, in which normal blockers are replaced by quicker backs and receivers, who have a better chance of reaching an onsides kick.

hideout play: Any of a number of variations of an outlawed play in which an offensive player who appears to be leaving the field (as with other players for whom substitutes have entered the game) lingers at the sidelines until the ball is snapped, then runs downfield for a pass. The Los Angeles Rams used a hideout play with some success until it was outlawed by the NFL in the early 1950s. also *dead man play, sleeper play.*

hike: To snap the ball to a back to begin play on a down. (will take on the nose guard the moment he hikes the ball) also *center, snap.*

1. hit: 1. To make contact with an opponent in blocking, especially by tackling. 2. To complete a pass to a receiver. (got on the scoreboard when he hit his wide receiver with a bomb) also *find.*

2. hit: The act or an instance of hitting. (stopped at the line of scrimmage with a tremendous hit by the middle linebacker)

hitch: A pass pattern in which the receiver runs straight downfield for a short distance, then abruptly turns to the outside for a quick pass.

hitch and go: A pass pattern in which the receiver runs straight downfield a short distance, fakes a hitch to the outside, then continues downfield at full speed.

hit the hole: To lunge into an open space in the line momentarily created by blockers.

hold: 1. To illegally grab, hook, grasp, or obstruct an opponent with the hands or arms. see *holding*. 2. To limit the yards gained by an opponent or opposing team. 3. To stop the opposing team from advancing or scoring. (could not hold them once they reached the 10-yard line)

holding: The act or an instance of illegally grabbing, hooking, grasping, or obstructing an opponent (other than the ballcarrier) with the hands or arms. Offensive holding results in a 15-yard penalty (10-yard penalty in the NFL). Defensive holding results in a 15-yard penalty (5-yard penalty in the NFL).

hole: A momentary gap or open space in the line cleared by blockers. also *daylight*.

1. hook: 1. To run a buttonhook pass pattern. 2. To move a defensive player to the side with a hook block.

2. hook: see *comeback*.

hook block: A block in which an offensive lineman steps to the side of a defensive player, then turns back to block him laterally, away from the ballcarrier.

hospital ball: A short pass lofted over the middle that forces a receiver to leap and catch it, leaving himself unprotected and vulnerable to injury from a hit by a defensive back.

1. huddle: A brief grouping of players between downs (usually in a small circle behind the line of scrimmage) in which signals and specific instructions for the next down are given by the quarterback or defensive captain. Amos Alonzo Stagg is credited with inventing the huddle.
●●A meeting to discuss a specific situation or plan of action. (should have a huddle before the next bargaining session)

2. huddle: To gather in a huddle with teammates before the next play in order to receive signals and instructions.
●●To meet in order to discuss a specific situation or plan of action. (huddled with her attorney to devise a strategy)

hurry-up offense: see *two-minute drill*.

I: The I formation.

I back: The tailback in an I formation.

I formation: An offensive formation in which the fullback and the tailback (running backs) are positioned in line behind the quarterback with the remaining back playing wide as a receiver. Coach Tom Nugent of Virginia Military Institute is credited with developing the I formation in the 1950s. see *power I*, *stack I*.

illegal motion: An infraction in which an offensive player other than one "man in motion" fails to come to a complete stop in a set position and remain motionless for one full second before the snap, or in the case of "backfield in motion," a backfield player is moving forward or more than one is moving laterally or backward at the snap. Illegal motion results in a 5-yard penalty. see *man in motion*.

in: 1. Into the end zone for a score. also *over*. 2. A pass pattern in which a receiver runs straight downfield, then cuts sharply to the inside (parallel to the line of scrimmage) for a pass. If the cut is made just a short distance from the scrimmage line, the pattern is sometimes called a short in. also *down-and-in*, *square-in*. compare *out*.

inbounds: Within the playing area, inside and not touching the boundary lines.

inbounds line, inbounds marker: Either of two imaginary lines extending the length of the playing field, 53 feet, 4 inches (or 70 feet, 9 inches in the NFL) in from and parallel to each sideline, and marked on the field at the yard lines by the hashmarks. When a ballcarrier is tackled in a side zone (the area of the field between the inbounds line and the nearest sideline) or a ballcarrier goes out of bounds over a sideline, or the ball is punted or fumbled out of bounds over a sideline, the ball is put into play at the intersection of the inbounds line and the yard line where the ball was dead or out of bounds. Inbounds lines (30 feet from each sideline) were experimented with in the first NFL playoff game in 1932, played indoors because of blizzard conditions (Chicago Bears 9, Portsmouth, Ohio, Spartans, 0). In 1933, the 30-foot inbounds lines were adopted for use in the NFL and in college play. Current specifications were

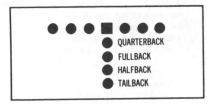

I FORMATION

159

adopted in 1947 and 1972 by the NCAA and NFL respectively. also *hashmarks.*

inbounds spot: The point at which the ball is put into play for a scrimmage down after it has been blown dead in a side zone or gone out of bounds, determined by the intersection of the inbounds line and the yard line where the ball was dead or out of bounds.

incomplete: Not caught or intercepted (as of a pass), and resulting in a dead ball. After an incomplete pass, the ball is put into play for the next down at the previous spot (the point from which the ball was put into play on the previous down).

incompletion: An instance of an incomplete pass.

ineligible receiver: An offensive player (any lineman between the two ends) who is not permitted to catch a forward pass, or to advance beyond the point where physical contact is broken with the opponent blocked from the initial line charge until the ball is thrown. If an ineligible receiver advances beyond this point before a pass is thrown (ineligible receiver downfield), the offensive team is charged with a 15-yard (10-yard in the NFL) penalty.

influence: An offensive tactic in which the linemen move at the snap in such a way as to deceive the defensive team, such as a blocker pulling as though on a sweep (causing the defensive lineman to misread the play and follow the blocker, leaving a gap through which the play is run), or dropping back as if pass blocking (so as to lure the defensive player across the line where he can be trapped).

in motion: Legally moving laterally or backward behind the line of scrimmage at the snap. After assuming a set position for one full second after the huddle or a shift, a single player may move or be in motion in a lateral or backward direction behind the line of scrimmage. see *man in motion.*

1. inside: 1. The middle area of the field, between the sidelines. also *middle.* compare *outside.* 2. The area of the line of scrimmage between the offensive tackles. Army's 1945 Heisman Trophy winning fullback, Felix "Doc" Blanchard, was nicknamed "Mr. Inside" (to halfback Glen Davis's "Mr. Outside") for

his ability to run through the inside. compare *outside.*

2. inside: To or toward the inside. (cut back inside for a gain of 4 yards) compare *outside.*

inside handoff: A handoff given to a running back who passes between the quarterback and the line of scrimmage.

instant replay: The televised repetition of a particular play or incident immediately after its completion by means of videotape. Often the replay is from several different angles and utilizes slow-motion. Using computers and advanced electronics, some stadiums and arenas are equipped to reproduce instant replays on scoreboard-sized screens. Although ABC Television pioneered the concept of replaying during a time out or break in the action, the instant replay was first used by CBS director Tony Verna on December 7, 1963, immediately after quarterback Rollie Stichweh plunged 2 yards for an Army touchdown against Navy. Ironically, it remained for NBC to give the technique its name. also *replay.*
●●Any kind of repetition or near duplication. (he is like an instant replay of his older brother)

intentional grounding: An infraction in which the passer, under a rush and unable to find an open receiver, deliberately throws the ball to the ground, into a player behind the line, or out of bounds to avoid being thrown for a loss. Intentional grounding results in a 5-yard penalty and the loss of the down. In the NFL, intentional grounding results in a 10-yard penalty and the loss of the down, or if the foul occurs more than 10 yards behind the line of scrimmage, the loss of the down at the spot of the foul, or a safety if the passer is in his end zone when he grounds the ball.

intercept: 1. To catch and control a pass meant for an opponent. 2. To have a pass one has thrown intercepted. (was intercepted only twice in the season)

interception: The act or an instance of a pass being intercepted, charged against the passer and credited to the defensive player making the interception in statistical records. Paul Krause of the Washington Redskins (1964-67) and the Minnesota Vikings (1968-69) holds the NFL career record for interceptions, eighty-one. The NFL record for the most interceptions in one season, fourteen, was set in 1952 by Dick "Night Train" Lane of the Los Angeles Rams. In 1943, Sammy Baugh of the Washington Redskins became the first NFL player to make four interceptions in one game.

interference: 1. The illegal obstruction or hindrance of an opponent who is trying to catch a pass or a kick. On a forward pass, receivers and defensive players have an equal right to the ball, and neither may interfere with the other's attempt to catch it. Offensive pass interference results in a 15-yard penalty from the "previous spot" and the loss of the down (or a 10-yard penalty in the NFL and USFL). Defensive pass interference results in an automatic first down at the spot of the foul (or in the USFL, a first down 15 yards ahead of the "previous spot" if unintentional, and a first down at the spot of the foul with a minimum 15-yard advance if intentional). On a kickoff, the kicking and receiving teams have an equal right to the ball after it travels 10 yards, but, as on a punt, no member of the receiving team may be prevented from catching it. Interference on a kick results in a 15-yard penalty from the spot of the foul. 2. Legal blocking or blockers, as in front of the ballcarrier. The first blocking rules permitting legal interference for the runner were sponsored by Walter Camp in 1884.

interior line: The part of an offensive or defensive line between the ends.

interior lineman: The center, guards, tackles, and middle or nose guard, all players positioned in the interior line.

iso: see *isolated camera.*

isolated camera: A television camera used to record the actions of one player (such as a receiver) on a particular play, for possible use on an instant replay. also *iso.*

isolation block: A delayed block by a back on a defensive lineman left "isolated" or unblocked by an offensive lineman.

jam: 1. see *chuck.* 2. To use acts or words designed to distract, disconcert, or confuse the offensive team at the snap. Jamming is considered unsportsmanlike conduct and results in a 15-yard penalty.

jitterbug: To jump in and out of the defensive line or exchange places with another defensive player just before the ball is snapped in order to confuse the offense and disguise actual rushing plans.

juice: see *vigorish.*

1. juke: 1. To fake a motion or movement in a certain direction in order to momentarily deceive an opponent. (tried to juke his way out of trouble just before he was hit) also *fake.* 2. To momentarily deceive an opponent by a fake. also *fake, fake out.*

2. juke: A simulated move or faked action that is intended to momentarily deceive an opponent. (got past the cornerback with a little juke after he turned the corner) also *fake.*

jump pass: A pass thrown at the peak of a jump.

kamikaze corps, kamikaze squad: see *suicide squad.*

keeper: An offensive play in which the quarterback keeps the ball and runs with it, often after faking a handoff. Pioneer football coach Amos Alonzo Stagg is credited with inventing the keeper.

1. key: A tipoff or indication of the opposing team's intentions (offensive or defensive) on a particular play.

2. key: To watch a particular opponent (where he looks, his position, or movement) as a clue to the intentions of the opposing team. (keys on the free safety to read the coverage)

key block: An important or pivotal block for a particular play, one without which the play would fail.

1. kick: 1. To propel the ball by hitting it with the foot. 2. To score by kicking. (kicked the extra point to tie the score) 3. To execute a kickout block on a defensive player, moving him to the outside, away from an inside run.

2. kick: The act or an instance of kicking the ball, as for a kickoff, a punt, a field goal, or a try for an extra point.

kicker: The player who kicks the ball.

kicking game: The execution and performance of a team's kickers (for kickoffs, punts, field goals, and extra points) and the players who make up the kicking team or teams.

kicking team: The members of a team who regularly play in kickoff, punt, field goal, and extra point situations.

kicking tee: A small, flexible plastic or rubber device used to prop up the ball on one end for a placekick. Legalized in 1948 (though solely for kickoffs in the NFL). also *tee*.

kick off: To put the ball in play with a kickoff.

•• To begin something. (Will kick off the festivities with a song

kickoff: A free kick (placekick) made from the kicking team's 40-yard line (or 35-yard line in the NFL) to put the ball in play at the start of each half, after an extra point attempt, and after a field goal. The kicking team may not advance past their free kick line (the line from where the kick is taken), nor may the receiving team advance past their free kick line 10 yards away, until the ball is kicked. On a kickoff, either team may recover the ball after it travels 10 yards, as long as no member of the receiving team is prevented from catching or recovering it.

kickoff return: The runback of a kickoff. Three players share the NFL record for the longest kickoff return, 106 yards; Al Carmichael of the Green Bay Packers (1956), Noland Smith of the Kansas City Chiefs (1967), and Roy Green of the St. Louis Cardinals (1979). The NFL career record for the highest average yardage on kickoff returns (30.56 yards) is held by Gale Sayers of the Chicago Bears (1965-71). The NFL record for the highest kickoff return average for a season (41.06 yards) was set in 1967 by Travis Williams of the Green Bay Packers. Williams also shares the NFL record for the most touchdowns scored in a season on kickoff returns (four, 1967) with Cecil Turner of the Chicago Bears (four, 1970).

kickout block: An offensive technique in which a defensive lineman is blocked toward the outside, as to clear a path for an inside run.

kill the clock: see *run out the clock*.

late hit: The act or an instance of diving or running into an opponent after he is down or out of play, or after the ball is dead. A late hit is considered unnecessary roughness and results in a 15-yard penalty.

1. lateral: A pass thrown (underhand or overhand) in any direction other than forward. Any player is eligible to catch a lateral, and more than one lateral may be thrown on a single down, but if a lateral is not caught, the ball remains in play and may be recovered by either team. Amos Alonzo Stagg is credited with inventing the lateral. also *backward pass, lateral pass*.

2. lateral: To make a lateral pass.

lateral pass: see *lateral*.

lead block: A block executed by a player who leads the ballcarrier or a play.

leg whip: To, while on the ground or falling, move or extend one's legs in order to trip an opponent. Leg whipping is a tripping foul and results in a 10-yard penalty.

1. letter: A school monogram to be worn on a sweater or jacket, awarded to students who are members of the school football team. Amos Alonzo Stagg invented the letter award, which is now given for participation in other sports and school activities.

••A figurative award, often given in jest. (has earned a letter in communication as captain of the gossip team)

2. letter: To earn a school letter in football, or another sport or school activity. (lettered in football and track in his senior year)

••To earn a figurative award, often in jest. (a fraternity man who lettered in beer-drinking and partying)

letterman: A student who is awarded a student letter for participation in athletic or other school activities.

line: 1. Short for the line of scrimmage. 2. The offensive or defensive linemen positioned at the line of scrimmage. At least seven players (usually a center, two guards, two tackles, and two ends) must line up on the offensive line. There are normally three to five players in a defensive line (defensive tackles and ends in a 4-man line, and a middle guard or nose guard for a 3- or 5-man line). also *front line*. 3. The positions played by linemen.

linebacker: 1. One of several defensive players usually positioned a yard or so behind the line, who are primarily responsible for backing up the defensive linemen on running plays, protecting against a short pass (as to a running back), or rushing the passer (as in a red dog blitz). also *backer-up*. 2. The position played by a linebacker. also *backer-up*.

line judge: A football official who, at the snap, is positioned even with the line of scrimmage on the opposite side of the field from the linesman, and who is responsible for the timing of the game and halftime intermission, for watching for encroachment or offsides, illegal motion or illegal shifts, an illegal pass from beyond the line of scrimmage, and for signalling the end of each quarter.

lineman: An offensive or defensive player who plays on the line.

line of scrimmage: An imaginary vertical plane (between and perpendicular to the sidelines) passing through the end of the ball nearest a team's own goal line when the ball is spotted for a down. Neither team may cross the line of scrimmage until the ball is snapped. The concept of the line of scrimmage or scrimmage line, guaranteeing unhindered possession of the ball to one team until the snap, is considered the single most important rule of football, making possible the use of prearranged plays and variable strategies. It was adopted by the intercollegiate rules committee in 1880 at the urging of Yale halfback Walter Camp, now regarded as the primary architect of American football. also *scrimmage line.*

linesman: A football official who, at the snap, is positioned even with the line of scrimmage on a sideline (switching to the other sideline for the second half), and who is responsible for supervising the box and chain crew, watching for encroachment and offsides and other action in and around the line, watching for the forward progress of the ball on his sideline, aiding the umpire in checking for ineligible linemen going downfield, and counting the offensive players on every play. also *head linesman.*

line surge: The forward movement of the offensive line at the snap of the ball on a running play. (easily made the first down behind a good line surge)

line-to-gain: see *necessary line.*

live ball: A ball that has been snapped or kicked and is in play, either under the control of a player or team, or "loose" or "free" and recoverable by either team. see *dead ball.*

locomotive: A mass cheer that, like a steam locomotive, starts slowly and increases in tempo. The locomotive was the first deliberate, rhythmic college cheer, and originated at a Princeton football game in 1871.

Lombardi Award: The Vince Lombardi Rotary Award, an annual award given to the outstanding college lineman of the year by the Rotary Club of Houston, Texas. Named after Pro Football Hall of Fame coach Vince Lombardi, whose Green Bay Packers won five NFL championships in the 1960s. The Lombardi Award was first given in 1970 to Ohio State All-American middle guard Jim Stillwagon.

long gainer: A play that makes a long gain.

look: The appearance of a certain alignment or the positioning of a key player or key players, used to determine (or to mask) a team's intentions on a play. (a sophisticated defense that moves constantly and gives the opposing quarterback a lot of different looks)

look-in: An offensive play in which the receiver runs diagonally across the middle for a quick pass.

look off: To deceive a defender or the defense by looking one way before throwing a pass to a different location. (looks off the linebacker, then completes a short pass over the middle)

loop: To circle around an adjacent defensive lineman at or just before the snap, as for a stunt. see *stunt.*

loose ball: A live ball that is not in the possession of any player, and that can be recovered by either team.

loss of down: The loss of the opportunity to repeat a down as a penalty or part of a penalty assessed for rules infractions such as intentional grounding, a second forward pass during a down, or a pass touched or caught by an ineligible receiver.

make the cut: To survive a cut or the elimination of unneeded or unsuitable players from a team or roster.

●●To be chosen, especially when others have been eliminated. (elated as she had made the cut and been offered a part in the play)

man, man coverage: see *man-for-man.*

man-for-man: A defensive coverage in which each receiver is guarded by one defensive player. also *man, man coverage, man-to-man.*

man in motion: The act or an instance of a single offensive backfield player, after assuming a set position for one full second after the huddle or a shift, moving in a lateral or backward direction behind the line of scrimmage at the snap. Putting a "man in motion" is one of the innovations of Amos Alonzo Stagg.

man-to-man: see *man-for-man.*

match-up: The confrontation between two specific opposing players who guard or play against each other in a game. (our wide receiver against their All-Pro cornerback is one of the most interesting match-ups in the game)

Maxwell Trophy: An annual award given to an outstanding college football player. Named after All-American lineman Robert Maxwell of Swarthmore, the award, originated by the Maxwell Football Club of Philadelphia, was first given in 1938 to Texas Christian quarterback Davey O'Brien.

measuring sticks: see *chain.*

middle: 1. The central area of the field, between the sidelines. also *inside.* 2. The middle of the line. (followed the big guard through the middle)

middle guard: A defensive lineman usually positioned in the middle of the line, opposite the offensive center, and between the defensive tackles, as on a three or five-man front. also *nose guard, nose man, nose tackle.* compare *guard.*

middle linebacker: The linebacker positioned behind the middle of the defensive line, often the defensive captain.

midfield stripe: The 50-yard line.

misdirection: An offensive tactic in which backfield players move in a particular direction at the snap in order to mislead or deceive the defense.

Monday morning quarterback: A football fan who criticizes or second-guesses a team's play after the fact. compare *armchair quarterback, grandstand quarterback.*

●●One who criticizes or second-guesses with the advantage of hindsight.

mousetrap: A trap block.

move list: A list containing the names of players taken off a team's active roster.

move off the ball: see *come off the ball.*

1. muff: To touch and fail to gain possession of a loose ball (such as a kick, pass, or fumble). compare *fumble.*

2. muff: The act or an instance of muffing a loose ball. compare *fumble.*

multiple foul: A situation in which two or more fouls are committed by the same team during the same down. If a multi-

ple foul occurs, only one penalty may be enforced. The captain of the offended team makes the choice.

multiple offense: An offense in which different kinds of plays are run from a single formation. Michigan State coach Biggie Munn, named Coach of the Year in 1952 by the American Football Coaches Association, is credited with popularizing the multiple offense.

naked reverse: A reverse in which all the blockers move in the original direction of the play (ideally, drawing the defense with them), leaving the ultimate ballcarrier (after the handoff) without blockers, but with an open field if the play is successful.

National Collegiate Athletic Association: The national organization that oversees, administers, and publishes rules for intercollegiate athletics. Formed in 1905 at a conference of colleges called by New York University Chancellor Henry MacCracken to decide whether to reform or abolish the game of football, the association was originally called the Intercollegiate Athletic Association of the United States. Renamed in 1910, the National Collegiate Athletic Association is headquartered in Shawnee Mission, Kansas, and presently oversees fifty-three national championships in twenty sports. also *NCAA.*

National Football Conference: One of the two conferences of the National Football League, the championship teams of which compete annually for the national championship in the Super Bowl, and from which individual players are selected to compete in the annual AFC-NFC Pro Bowl. The NFC is made up of three divisions: the Eastern Division, which is comprised of the Philadelphia Eagles, the Dallas Cowboys, the Washington Redskins, the St. Louis Cardinals, and the New York Giants, the Central Division, which is comprised of the Minnesota Vikings, the Detroit Lions, the Chicago Bears, the Tampa Bay Buccaneers, and the Green Bay Packers, and the Western Division, which is comprised of the Atlanta Falcons, the Los Angeles Rams, the San Francisco 49ers, and the New Orleans Saints. also *NFC.*

National Football League: The oldest and largest major professional football league in the United States. Established in 1920 as the American Professional Football Association, the National Football League (the name adopted in 1922) is comprised of two conferences, the American Football Conference and the National Football Conference, each of which is comprised of fourteen teams divided into three geographic divisions (Eastern Division, Central Division, and Western Division). Conference champions (determined by divisional playoffs) meet annually for the league championship in the Super Bowl. also *NFL*. see *American Football Conference, National Football Conference.*

National Football League Players Association: The sole and exclusive collective bargaining agent for players in the NFL. The present association was formed in 1970 by the combination of the American Football League Players Association and the old NFL Players Association, originated in 1956. also *NFLPA.*

NCAA: The National Collegiate Athletic Association.

necessary line: The yard line to which the offensive team must advance the ball within four downs in order to score or maintain possession of the ball for a new series of downs. Unless there is a penalty, the necessary line is ten yards in advance of the foremost point of the ball at the beginning of a series of downs. If the ten yards extend into the end zone, the goal line is the necessary line. also *line-to-gain.*

neutral zone: An imaginary area between the lines of scrimmage (one at either end of the football) on a scrimmage down or the free kick lines (10 yards apart) on a free kick down, extending from sideline to sideline parallel to the goal lines. Once the ball is spotted and the referee whistles play begin, no player from either team, except the snapper on a scrimmage down and the holder and kicker on a free kick down may enter the neutral zone until the ball has been snapped or kicked. The neutral zone was introduced in 1903 by former Harvard team captain Bert Walters. Previously, opposing linemen were separated only by an imaginary line through the center of the ball. The neutral zone virtually eliminated the time-consuming arguments on every down about who crossed the imaginary line.

NFC: The National Football Conference.
NFL: The National Football League.
NFLPA: The National Football League Players Association.
nickel back: The defensive back who replaces a linebacker when a nickel defense is employed.
nickel defense: A prevent defense in which five defensive backs are used, the extra back replacing a linebacker. The term nickel defense was coined by Pro Football Hall of Fame coach Clark Shaughnessy.
North-South runner: A ballcarrier who tends to run straight toward the opponent's goal line, rather than zigzagging back and forth across the field.
nose guard: see *middle guard.*
nose man: see *middle guard.*
nose tackle: see *middle guard.*
nutcracker: A contact drill in which ballcarriers are subjected to game-type hits, sometimes simultaneously or alternately by more than one player.
odd front, odd line: A four-man defensive line in an "over" or "under" shift, with one defensive tackle directly opposite the center. also *odd man front.* see *over, under.*
odd man front: see *odd front, odd line.*
off: Outside of a specified offensive lineman. (ran a slant off tackle)
offense: 1. The endeavor to advance the ball or score against the opposing team. (a great defensive team, but mediocre on offense) 2. The specific plan or formation used to advance the ball or score. 3. The offensive team or its members. also *offensive team, offensive unit.*
offensive: Pertaining to offense, or the playing of offense. (offensive play) (offensive game plan)
offensive end: 1. One of the two offensive players positioned at the ends of the offensive line, who are primarily responsible for blocking and receiving passes. In a typical unbalanced line, one offensive end (tight end) lines up just outside the offensive tackle, and the other (split end), is positioned on the line of scrimmage, ten yards or more wide of the other offensive tackle. also *end.* 2. The position played by an offensive end. also *end.*
offensive guard: see *guard.*
offensive tackle: 1. Either of two offensive

165

players positioned on the line of scrimmage outside of the offensive guards, and who are primarily responsible for pass blocking, drive-blocking to open holes for runs through the line, and pulling, whether for a trap or to lead a sweep. also *tackle*. 2. The position played by an offensive tackle. also *tackle*.

offensive team, offensive unit: The players on a team who regularly play offense. also *offense*.

official: Any of the four to seven officials who administer the rules of the game, and who are responsible for the timing and scoring of a football game. They are the referee, the umpire, the linesman, and the field judge (and in seven-man crews, also the line judge, back judge, and side judge).

official's time out: A time out called by the referee (and charged against neither team) when the ball is dead for the measurement of a possible first down, the repair of game or player equipment, an injury to a player or official, a conference for a rules interpretation, a change of team possession, and the notification of two minutes remaining for a half. also *referee's time out*.

offside, offsides: Illegally being beyond the line of scrimmage on a scrimmage down or the free kick line on a free kick down at the moment the ball is put into play (snapped or kicked). The center on a scrimmage down and the holder and kicker on a free kick down are the only players permitted to be partially in the neutral zone when the ball is put into play. Offsides results in a 5-yard penalty. compare *encroaching, encroachment*.

Oklahoma drill: see *nutcracker*.

old leather: One or more older or seasoned veteran players. An allusion to the old leather helmets and pads worn in earlier days. (a blend of talented rookies and old leather made them a championship team)

one-back formation, one-back offense: A T formation derivative in which only one back lines up behind the quarterback, with the others positioned as tight ends and/or wide receivers. also *ace formation, A formation, single-back offense*.

one-on-one: A situation in which a player is covering or covered by a single opponent.

••Any situation in which one individual is pitted against another, or interacts directly with another. (the principals resolved the misunderstanding in a one-on-one meeting)

on scholarship: Given under-the-table payments or placed on a team's official injured reserve list, though not injured. An illegal practice by a professional team in order to "protect" (keep other teams from signing) a player of potential future value while carrying the maximum number of players allotted on the active roster list. A team guilty of this practice ("stashing") is subject to a fine and further league disciplinary action.

onside: Legally positioned behind the line of scrimmage or free kick line when the ball is snapped or kicked.

onside kick: A kickoff in which the kicking team attempts to maintain possession of the ball by recovering the kick after it travels the required 10 yards. Because of the chance that the receiving team will recover the ball and have excellent field position, an onside kick is usually attempted only by a team that is behind near the end of a game. The onside kick was invented by pioneer coach Amos Alonzo Stagg. also *onsides kick*.

onside prevent defense: A tactic employed by the receiving team in anticipation of an onside kick on a kickoff, in which blockers who normally play on or close to the receiving team's free kick line are replaced by quicker backs and receivers, who have a better chance of reaching and recovering an onside kick. also *hen's team*.

onsides kick: see *onside kick*.

on the numbers: Chest-high, or on the chest. Numbers (first used on football jerseys by Washington and Jefferson College in 1908) make a good target for a tackle, a block, or a well-placed pass. (hit his wide receiver on the numbers with a perfect pass)

open: Unguarded by an opponent. (looking for an open receiver)

open field: The sparsely defended area of the field beyond the line of scrimmage, or away from the point of origin of a play. also *broken field*.

open field tackle: A tackle made in a sparsely defended area of the field.

option: 1. An offensive play in which the ballcarrier, after the play begins, has the option to run with the ball or pass. also *option play*. 2. Short for option clause. 3. Short for option year. see *option clause*.

FOOTBALL (AMERICAN)

option clause: A clause in professional players' contracts which gives a team the option for the services of a player for one additional year (option year) with an automatic raise (as per the NFL/NFLPA agreement) over the expired contract terms. The player may choose to play or to sit out during the option year, after which he becomes a free agent, or free to negotiate with other teams. also *option*.

option play: see *option*.

option year: see *option clause*.

out: A pass pattern in which a receiver runs straight downfield, then abruptly cuts to the outside (parallel to the line of scrimmage) for a pass. If the cut is made just a short distance from the scrimmage line, the pattern is sometimes called a quick out, hardout, or short out. also *down-and-out, square-out.* compare *in*.

Outland Trophy: An annual award given to the outstanding college interior lineman of the year as voted by the Football Writers Association of America. Named after All-American tackle John B. Outland, who played at Pennsylvania in the late 1890s, the Outland Trophy was first awarded to Notre Dame tackle George O'Connor in 1946.

outlet man: A receiver to whom a pass can be thrown if the primary receiver or receivers are covered and the quarterback is in danger from a pass rush.

out of bounds: Out of the playing area, on or over either of the sidelines or end lines, or touching someone (other than another player or an official) or something on or over the boundary lines.

1. outside: The area of the playing field near the sidelines, wide of the flanks of an offensive formation. Army's 1946 Heisman Trophy winning halfback, Glen Davis, was nicknamed "Mr. Outside" (to fullback Felix "Doc" Blanchard's "Mr. Inside") for his ability to run outside. compare *inside*.

2. outside: To or toward the outside. (trying to get outside and turn the corner) compare *inside*.

over: 1. Over the goal line for a score. (went over from the two-yard line) also *in*. 2. Short for overshift. compare *under*.

overshift: A defensive alignment in which all or some of the defensive linemen shift one position over toward the strong side of an unbalanced line (placing one tackle head-on the center) to disrupt blocking patterns, or to move big linemen to the expected point of attack. also *over*. compare *under, undershift*.

overtime: An extra fifteen-minute period of play to decide a game tied at the end of regulation play in the NFL. The period begins with a kickoff (decided by coin toss) and ends when one team scores, or when time runs out. In a regular season game, if neither team is able to score during the overtime period, the game ends as a tie. In a playoff or championship game, if neither team is able to score in the overtime period, fifteen-minute periods continue to be played (with two-minute intermissions in between) until one team scores. also *sudden death*.

pads: The various pieces of protective equipment worn to protect a player's shoulders, ribs, elbows, hips, thighs, and knees. Pads are usually constructed in layers, with a hard surface (such as molded plastic or combat-derived composite materials) on the outside and a foam or inflatable cushion layer underneath.

1. pass: The act or an instance of throwing the ball to a teammate. (scored with a short pass to the tight end) see *forward pass, lateral*.

2. pass: To throw the ball to a teammate, as in a forward pass, or a backward or lateral pass.

pass block: To protect the passer by blocking on a pass play.

passer: A player who attempts to throw a forward pass to a teammate.

passing down: A down in which the circumstances indicate the use of a pass to gain the yards necessary for a score of a first down (such as third and eight).

passing game: The use of the forward pass on offense. (hard to defense their passing game)

pass interference: see *interference*.

pass pattern: A planned route run by a pass receiver to be in a predetermined area or at a predetermined spot for a pass. also *pattern, route*.

pass play: A play in which a forward pass is attempted.

pass protection: Pass blocking, blocking to protect the passer. also *protection*.

pass receiver: An eligible receiver. One to

167

whom a pass is thrown, or for whom a pass is intended.

pass rush: An attempt to rush the passer by the defensive team. (had to hurry his throw to avoid the pass rush)

PAT: The point after touchdown. see *extra point.*

pattern: see *pass pattern.*

penalize: To charge or enforce a penalty against a team.

penalty: The loss of 5, 10, or 15 yards and/or the loss of a down (depending upon the nature and severity of the offense), imposed against a team guilty of a rules infraction or foul. Certain flagrant or violent fouls result in a disqualification penalty.

penalty flag, penalty marker: A weighted red or gold handerchief carried by football officials and thrown on the ground to signal an infraction or a foul. also *flag.*

penetration: 1. The movement by rushers through or past the opposing team's offensive line. 2. The advancement of the ball through the opposing team's defenses and to or toward its goal line.

personal foul: A foul in which a player strikes, kicks, knees, spears, trips, clips, charges into (as a kicker or passer), piles on, or grabs the face mask of an opponent, or commits other acts of unnecessary roughness or unsportsmanlike conduct, resulting in a 15-yard penalty and, if the foul is considered fla-

grant or violent, the disqualification of the guilty player.

picket, picket fence: A wall of blockers behind which the ballcarrier runs on a punt or kickoff return.

pick off: To intercept a pass intended for an opposing receiver. (picked off and run back to the 35-yard line)

pick up the blitz: To anticipate and adjust for a blitz by the defensive team.

pigskin: 1. A football. Actually a misnomer, as the only time a football was ever really close to a "pigskin" was back in the earliest days of soccer (from which American football is derived), when an inflated animal bladder was used as the ball. also *ball, football.* 2. Of or pertaining to football. (a pigskin festival)

piling on: The act of illegally jumping on a downed ballcarrier, or onto a "pile" of defensive players on a downed ballcarrier. Piling on results in a 15-yard penalty.

1. pinch: A defensive tactic in which a lineman positioned in the gap between two offensive blockers joins with an adjacent teammate in a charge against one offensive player in order to take that blocker out of the play and disrupt normal blocking plans. When big defensive tackles work a pinch on the center, the offensive guards and tackles are forced to move in, thereby shortening the pass rushing routes for the defensive ends. First tried by Pittsburgh Steelers defensive tackles "Mean" Joe Greene and Ernie Holmes in 1974, the technique was adopted as part of the Steelers' defensive strategy and soon copied by other teams in the NFL.

2. pinch: To execute a pinch against an offensive lineman. also *squeeze.*

pit: see *trenches.*

pitch out: To pass laterally toward the outside to a teammate behind the line of scrimmage.

pitchout: A lateral pass toward the outside made to a teammate behind the line of scrimmage.

1. placekick: A kick made while the ball is in a fixed position on the ground, on a kicking tee or held in position by a teammate. A placekick is normally used for kickoffs (at the start of each half, after an extra point attempt, and after a field goal) and for field goal and extra point attempts (a kicking tee may not be used for a field goal or extra point

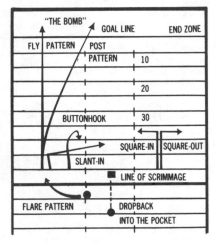

PASS PATTERNS

attempt in the NFL). Invented by Amos Alonzo Stagg.

2. placekick: 1. To execute a place-kick. 2. To score a field goal or extra point with a placekick.

placekicker: A placekicking specialist, or one who kicks a placekick.

platoon: Players who are put into and taken out of a game as a group or unit to play offense or defense. see *two-platoon system.*

play: 1. A specific and practiced plan of action for a down. (have gone into a prevent defense in anticipation of long pass play) 2. A down or the action that occurs during a down, from the moment the ball is snapped or kicked until the ball is dead. (will have time for one more play from scrimmage before the end of the quarter)

play-action fake: A fake handoff to a running back on a play-action pass. (freezes the linebacker with a play-action fake, then throws) also *play fake.*

play-action pass: An offensive pass play that is disguised to look like a running play, with a running back taking a fake handoff and following blockers as though carrying the ball. An effective tactic for deceiving linebackers (whose roles differ critically for a run and pass), the play-action pass was popularized in the NFL in the early 1950s (quarterback Bobby Layne and the Detroit Lions were among the foremost exponents of the tactic). It was originally called a "play number pass," the "number" being that of the specific running play the pass was to resemble. Later, this was shortened to "play pass" (still in use), and eventually became play-action pass. also *play pass.*

playbook: A player study guide that contains diagrams and notes regarding a team's plays and strategies.

play fake: see *play-action fake.*

play out one's option: To play for a team during an option year. see *option clause.*

play pass: see *play-action pass.*

pocket: An area several yards back from the line of scrimmage from which the quarterback passes, protected by blockers who drop back from the line of scrimmage to form a cuplike barrier. As rushing defenders are forced out and around the blockers, the quarterback is able to step up into the pocket to pass.

pocket passer: A quarterback who passes from a pocket, rather than rolling out or scrambling to pass.

point after, point after touchdown: see *extra point.*

point line: see *point spread.*

point spread: Betting parlance for an estimation by oddsmakers of the number of points by which one team is favored to beat another, given to provide a fair basis for wagering on teams of uneven strength. One who bets on the favored team collects and is said to "beat the spread" if the favored team wins by more than the point spread. One who bets on the underdog collects and beats the spread if the underdog wins, or loses by less than the point spread. The bet is considered a "push" and usually cancelled if the favored team wins by the same number of points indicated in the point spread. also *betting line, line, point line, price, spread.*

pop: 1. A hit, as a block or tackle. (the quarterback took a pretty good pop just as he was letting the ball go) 2. A short pass.

Pop Warner Football: A national organization that charters and oversees commercially sponsored football leagues for boys between the ages of seven and fifteen who compete in seven different divisions on the basis of age and weight. Founded as the Junior Football Conference in 1929 by Joseph J. Tomlin, the organization was renamed in 1934 after legendary coach and football innovator Glenn Scobey "Pop" Warner. Two-time Kansas All-American and Pro Football Hall of Famer Gale Sayers of the Chicago Bears is among the famous graduates of Pop Warner Football. National headquarters are located in Philadelphia, Pennsylvania.

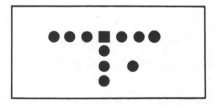

POWER I

possession: Control of the ball by a player or team.

possession football: see *ball control*.

post pattern: A pass pattern in which a receiver runs downfield near the sideline, then cuts inside toward the goalpost.

pour it on: To augment or concentrate a team's efforts in order to take advantage of a weak opponent, especially to run up a high score. Ironically, the man remembered as the greatest pour it on coach in the history of college football was John Heisman (of the Heisman Trophy), who once ran up a score of 222-0 against an overmatched opponent, still an American record.

power block: The act or an instance of drive-blocking, in which a defensive player is driven straight back or to the side to clear a path for a runner.

power I: A version of the I formation in which the fourth back lines up in the backfield beside the fullback rather than as a wide receiver. Developed and popularized by coach John McKay at the University of Southern California in the 1960s. see *I formation, stack I*.

power sweep: A running play in which both guards pull out of the line at the snap to lead a sweep around one end.

prayer: A low-percentage pass, one that would require a great deal of luck or the intercession of a "higher power" for completion. (in desperation sent up a prayer into the end zone) also *Hail Mary*.

prevent defense: A defensive formation that utilizes extra defensive backs (and/or extra linebackers) in order to protect against a long pass. Because of its vulnerability to a running play or short pass, a prevent defense is generally used only when the offensive team needs long yardage for a first down or for a score.

previous spot: The spot at which the ball was last put into play on a scrimmage down or a free kick down. Many penalties are enforced at (measured from) the previous spot. compare *succeeding spot*.

price: see *point spread*.

primary receiver: The first or intended receiver for a pass on a particular play.

Pro Bowl: An annual post-season exhibition game between all-star teams from the American Football Conference and the National Football Conference of the NFL. The original Pro Bowl was played in 1939 at Los Angeles between the NFL Champion New York Giants and a team of professional all-stars (won by the Giants 13-10). Suspended in 1942, the Pro Bowl was revived under a new format in 1951, matching the all-stars of the old American Conference and National Conference. The first AFC-NFC Pro Bowl was played in Los Angeles, California in 1971, and won by the NFC by a score of 27-6.

Pro Football Hall of Fame: The national institution that honors outstanding players, coaches, and contributors (administrators, owners, etc.) in professional football, located in Canton, Ohio, the site of the 1920 organizational meeting from which the National Football League evolved. A charter class of seventeen enshrinees was elected in 1963, the year the original complex was dedicated. New members of the Pro Football Hall of Fame are elected annually from the nominations of fans by a twenty-nine-member National Board of Selectors, made up of media representatives from each league city and the president of the Pro Football Writers Association. An affirmative vote of approximately 80 percent is needed for election.

pro set: Any of several variations of the T formation used in the NFL in which one back lines up as a wide receiver on one side of the formation, and the end on the other side is positioned as a split end. also *pro T*.

pro T: see *pro set*.

protection: see *pass protection*.

pull: see *pull out*.

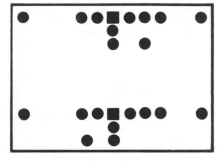

PRO SETS

pulling guard: An offensive guard who pulls back out of the line to lead the blocking for a running play toward the outside.

pull out: To pull back out of the line of scrimmage at the snap in order to lead a running play to the outside, or to trap block a defender. also *pull*.

1. pump: To fake a forward pass by cocking the arm and starting it forward, without releasing the ball. The quarterback will often "pump" the ball to freeze a defensive player, or make him commit in one direction before throwing elsewhere to the intended receiver.

2. pump: The act or an instance of faking a pass by pumping the passing arm. (freezes the linebackers with a little pump, then goes long to the wide receiver)

punishing runner: A powerful and bruising runner, one who takes a physical toll on tacklers throughout the course of a game. also *sledgehammer runner*.

1. punt: A kick in which the ball is held in front of the body, dropped, and kicked with the instep before it hits the ground. The longest punt in NFL history was 98 yards, made in 1969 by New York Jets kicker Steve O'Neal. Washington Redskins quarterback (1937-1952) Sammy Baugh holds the NFL career record for punting yardage, averaging 45.10 yards per punt. Baugh also holds the NFL one-season record, averaging 51.40 yards per punt in 1940.

2. punt: To make a punt. When a team is forced to relinquish possession of the ball (because of an inability to score or make the 10 yards necessary for a first down), the ball is punted to the opposing team, ideally, high in the air (to give the kicking team time to get downfield to tackle the receiver and prevent a runback) and as deep as possible in the opponent's position.

••To give up, to literally or figuratively retreat so as to cut one's losses in the face of an impossible situation. (decided he had better punt after his third motorcycle accident, and find a less risky hobby)

punter: A player who specializes in punting, or one who kicks a punt.

punt formation: An offensive formation from which the ball is punted. In a punt formation, the punter lines up 10 to 15 yards behind the line of scrimmage (or shifts into this position before the ball is snapped).

punt return: The runback of a punt. The NFL career record for the highest punt return average (13.16 yards) is held by Billy "White Shoes" Johnson of the Houston Oilers (1974-1980). The NFL record for the highest punt return average for a season (23 yards) was set in 1950 by Herb Rich of the Baltimore Colts. Jack Christiansen of the Detroit Lions (1951-58) holds the NFL career record for the most touchdowns scored on punt returns (eight). Christiansen also holds the one-season record (four, in 1951). Three NFL players have scored two touchdowns on punt returns in a game: Jack Christiansen of the Detroit Lions (twice in 1951), Dick Christy of the New York Titans (1961), and Rick Upchurch of the Denver Broncos (1976).

punt return specialist: A special teams player whose job it is to receive and run back punts, usually an evasive runner with great speed.

pursuit: The persistent movement of a defensive player toward the passer or ballcarrier, as from the opposite side of the formation, or after being delayed by a blocker.

push: Betting parlance for a bet that is neither won nor lost, but usually cancelled. When a favored team wins by the exact number of the point spread, the bet is considered a push.

put it up: To pass. (will have to put it up on third-and-eight) also *air it out*.

quarter: Any of four fifteen-minute time periods (twelve minutes in high school play) that make up a game. At the end of the first, second, and third quarters, the competing teams change goals. also *stanza*.

1. quarterback: 1. An offensive back usually positioned directly behind the center to receive the snap. The quarter-

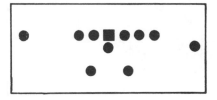

PRO OFFENSE

back runs a team's offense on the field, calling the signals to put the ball in play, then passing, running, or handing the ball off to a teammate. The quarterback was one of two positions created in 1880 (the other being the center) when the intercollegiate rules committee adopted the scrimmage concept with a center snap, urged by Yale halfback Walter Camp. The quarterback was not permitted to run with the ball until another rule change in 1910. also *field general, signal caller.* 2. The position played by a quarterback. also *field general, signal caller.*

•• A leader. (acted as quarterback on the outing because of his camping experience)

2. **quarterback:** To play the quarterback position.

•• To lead or direct an activity or group. (needed a strong President to quarterback the country)

quarterback draw: A draw play in which the quarterback, after dropping back as though to pass, runs straight forward through the onrushing defenders.

quarterback sneak: An offensive play for short yardage, in which the quarterback takes the snap and immediately runs over center. also *sneak.*

quick count: A shorter-than-usual sequence of signals called by the quarterback at the line of scrimmage to catch the defense off guard.

quick hitter: see *quick opener.*

quick kick: A surprise punt made on a down before fourth down and from a normal appearing pass or run formation. A quick kick is intended to catch the opposing team off guard, and to pin them deep in their own territory with little chance of a runback (because of the usual absence of a receiver in position to return the kick).

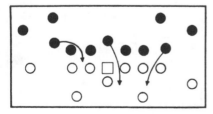

RED DOG

quick opener: An offensive play for short yardage in which a running back takes a quick handoff from the quarterback and plunges into a momentary hole in the line "opened" by blockers. also *quick hitter.*

quick out: see *out.*

quick release: The ability to set up and throw a pass quickly. (an accurate passer with a quick release)

quick slant: A quick opener in which the running back approaches the line from an angle.

razzle-dazzle play: A tricky and unconventional play (such as a double or triple reverse or a reverse and pass) intended to deceive or confuse the opposing team. also *gadget.*

read: To determine the intentions of an opposing player or team by observing keys such as the position or movement of an opponent or opponents. (read the blitz perfectly and dumped off to his running back for a first down)

receive: 1. To catch a pass or a punt. 2. To be the team to whom the ball is kicked. (won the toss and elected to receive)

receiver: 1. An offensive player who is eligible to catch a pass, to whom a pass is thrown, or who catches a pass. Don Hutson of the Green Bay Packers (1935-1945) was the first great receiver in the NFL, and the prototype for all those that followed. In only his second game as a professional, against the Chicago Bears, Hutson scored on an 83-yard touchdown pass from Arnie Herber. It was the first of ninety-nine touchdowns Hutson would score in his career, an NFL record. Hutson also scored a record seventeen touchdowns in 1942, a mark that was equalled in 1951 by Elroy "Crazylegs" Hirsch of the Los Angeles Rams and in 1961 by Bill Groman of the Houston Oilers. 2. A player who receives a kick, or who is designated to receive a kick.

receiving team: The team to whom the ball is kicked on a kickoff or a punt.

reception: 1. The act or an instance of catching a forward pass. 2. A caught pass, credited to a receiver's statistical records. Charley Taylor (1964-1975, 1977) holds the NFL career record for the most pass receptions, 649. Charley Hennigan of the Houston Oilers set the one-season record in 1964, with 101 receptions.

The one-game record was set by Los Angeles Rams receiver Tom Fears in 1950, when he made 18 receptions in a game against the Packers.

red dog: A pass rush or blitz by linebackers. During the 1949 season, New York Giants player Don "Red" Ettinger, normally an offensive guard, had to fill in at linebacker for a game. On third-and-long for the opposing team, Ettinger bolted from his position to rush the quarterback. The result was a sack and a loss of yards on the play. Asked about the manuever later, the red-headed Ettinger claimed he was "just doggin' the quarterback a little." Thus, the expression "red dog" was born. also *dog.* compare *blitz.*

red-dog: To rush the passer from a linebacker position. also *blitz.*

1. redshirt: A college student who practices but does not play with the school football team, either to rehabilitate an injury or to gain experience at a position without losing a season of playing time. The major sanctioning body for college athletics, the NCAA, permits an athlete to play any four seasons in a five-year span of eligibility. The name redshirt comes from the fact that such athletes historically wear red shirts on the practice field.
••The term is now also used in major college sports other than football.

2. redshirt: To practice, or have an athlete practice, as a redshirt while remaining off the varsity roster.

1. ref: The referee.

2. ref: To referee a game.

1. referee: The crew chief of all game officials, charged with the general oversight and control of a game. He is the final authority on the score, the number of a down, and on all matters not specifically delegated to other officials. On a scrimmage down, the referee is initially positioned behind the offensive backfield, to the right of a right-handed quarterback (or to the left of a left-handed quarterback). The referee is responsible for conducting the coin toss prior to the opening kickoff, explaining all fouls and their options to the team captains and indicating choices by the proper signal, administering all penalties, notifying the coach of a disqualified player, notifying the captain and

head coach when all allowable time outs have been used and at the two-minute warning, and raising and dropping one arm while sounding the whistle to signify the start of the twenty-five-second count (thirty seconds in the NFL) when the ball is ready for play.

2. referee: To act as the referee in a game.

referee's time out: see *official's time out.*

release: 1. The action of throwing a pass. see *quick release.* 2. To break off from one assignment (such as a block) to perform another.

remaining back: Either of the set backs who "remain" in the T formation while the other back is in motion or is positioned as a flanker.

replay: see *instant replay.*

1. return: To advance the ball after receiving a kick or intercepting a pass. also *run back.*

2. return: The advance of the ball by the player who receives a kick or intercepts a pass. (got to the outside for a 35-yard return on the kickoff) also *runback.*

reverse: An offensive play in which a back running laterally toward one sideline hands off to a teammate going the opposite way. The reverse was invented by Amos Alonzo Stagg and was used by him at Springfield College in Massachusetts as early as the 1890s.

ride the bench: To spend a lot of time on the bench rather than as a starter or regular player.
••To be unneeded or unused, particularly because of an inability to perform or function relative to others. (when the female lead recovered, the understudy went back to riding the bench)

ring one's bell: To stun, to cause one's ears to ring because of a blow or collision, as during a block or, tackle. (got the pass away, but took a pop that rang his bell)
••To stun by a blow or collision.

roll out: To move laterally behind the line of scrimmage after receiving the snap before passing, pitching out, or running with the ball. (rolls out to his right, fakes a pitchout, and cuts downfield to the 40-yard line for a first down) also *sprint out.*

rollout: An offensive maneuver in which the quarterback takes the snap and moves laterally behind the line of scrimmage before passing or running with the ball. also *sprintout.*

rotate: To move back into an adjacent zone according to a prearranged scheme of coverage to defend against a pass. see *rotation.*

rotation: The simultaneous movement of linebackers and defensive backs into adjacent zones to cover against a pass. In a rotation, linebackers retreat in one direction, the defensive backs in the other, thus appearing to "rotate" into position.

roughing the kicker: A personal foul in which a defensive player charges into the kicker on a punt, field goal, or extra point attempt (quick kicks and kicks following a fumble or an attempted pass or run are exempted). It is not roughing the kicker if the contact is incidental to and after blocking or deflecting the kick, the result of being blocked into the kicker, or the result of the kicker's momentum. Roughing the kicker results in a 15-yard penalty from the previous spot. In the NFL, a player can be charged with the less serious foul of running into (as opposed to roughing) the kicker, which results in a 5-yard penalty from the previous spot.

roughing the passer: A personal foul in which a defensive player charges into, blocks, or tackles the passer after it is clear that the ball has been thrown. Roughing the passer results in a 15-yard penalty from the previous spot.

route: see *pass pattern.*

roverback: A defensive back who also functions like a linebacker. Often in college football, the increased responsibilities of a roverback are assigned to a particularly skilled athlete in order to maximize his effect on defense.

Rozelle Rule: The original NFL rule governing compensation for free agents, in effect from 1962 to 1977. Named for NFL Commissioner Pete Rozelle, the controversial rule entitled a team losing the services of a player (a free agent who had played out his option) to another team mutually agreeable compensation (or compensation set by the commissioner) from the team signing the player. In 1977, the Rozelle Rule was replaced by a provision in the Basic Agreement between the NFL and the

NFLPA limiting free agent compensation.

rule blocking: The use of predetermined blocking assignments ("rules") for various contingencies. When a defensive alignment or shift precludes the normal blocking patterns for the play called, each blocker has rules to follow. Football innovator and coach Sid Gilman was among the first to develop a system of rule blocking, introducing it to the NFL in the mid-1950s.

1. run: To-advance the ball by carrying it rather than passing. (a big, strong team that likes to run right at you) also *carry, rush.*

2. run: An offensive play in which the ball is carried rather than passed. (not much success defending against the run) also *carry, running play, rush.*

run back: To return a kick or an intercepted pass.

runback: The return of a kick or an intercepted pass.

runner: The ballcarrier.

running back: An offensive back (halfback or fullback) who is used as a ballcarrier, blocker, and receiver. The term first came into use in the 1960s because of the different positions played by backs in pro football's multiple offensive sets, and, in 1970, replaced the more specific "halfback" and "fullback" as a matter of NFL policy.

running game: The use of the run on offense. (good blockers for a strong running game)

running play: A play in which the ball is advanced by running rather than passing. also *run, rush.*

run out the clock: To protect a lead near the end of a game by maintaining possession of the ball with conservative, time-consuming play, thereby denying the opposing team the opportunity to score and overcome the advantage. also *kill the clock.*

1. rush: 1. To advance the ball by running rather than passing; to run with the ball. Yardage gained by rushing is credited to the player and the team in statistical records. Jim Brown, running back from the Cleveland Browns (1957-1965) is the all-time NFL rushing champion, with a career record of 12,312 yards, averaging a record 5.22 yards per carry. Brown led the league in rushing for a record eight seasons, gaining 100 or more yards rushing in fifty-eight games, and scoring 106 touchdowns in his career (both NFL records). O.J. Simpson of the Buffalo Bills set the NFL record for the most yards gained by rushing in a single season in 1973, 2003 yards. Walter Payton of the Chicago Bears set the NFL record for a single game, rushing for 275 yards in a game against the Minnesota Vikings in 1977. also *carry, run.* **2.** To attempt to get through or past the offensive line to tackle the passer, kicker, or the ballcarrier, or to block a pass or kick.

2. rush: 1. The act or an instance of running with the ball. Rushes are credited to the player and the team in statistical records. also *carry, run.* **2.** The act or an instance of attempting to get through or past the offensive line to tackle the passer, kicker, or the ballcarrier or to block a pass or kick.

rusher: A defensive player who rushes.

1. sack: To break through or past the blockers and tackle the opposing quarterback in the offensive backfield before he can pass the ball. also *dump.*

2. sack: The act or an instance of sacking the opposing quarterback.

safety: 1. A two-point score awarded to the defensive team when an offensive player in control of the ball is downed or goes out of bounds on or behind his own goal line, or loses control of a ball which is downed or goes out of bounds on or behind the goal line (unless impetus to the player or ball comes from the defensive team), or when a foul is committed or an illegal pass is made behind the goal line by the offensive team. No safety is awarded if a player who receives a kick or intercepts a pass behind his goal line is downed or goes out of bounds, or downs the ball or fumbles it out of bounds, or if the momentum of the player intercepting the ball carries him back over the goal line and he is then tackled or driven out of bounds. After a safety, the ball is put into play with a free kick (usually a punt) by the team scored upon from their 20-yard line. compare *touchback.* 2. Either of two defensive backs usually positioned behind all other players, and primarily responsible for protecting against a

long run or pass. also *safetyman.* **3.** A player on the receiving team positioned deep to receive a kick. also *safetyman.* **4.** A safety blitz.

safety blitz: A blitz by one (usually the free safety) or both safeties. The safety blitz was first used by St. Louis Cardinals coach Frank "Pop" Ivy and free safety Larry Wilson in 1961. In the early 1960s, the Boston Patriots began to blitz not only the free safety, but the strong safety, an innovation that was soon copied in and wide use throughout football. also *safety.*

safetyman: see *safety.*

safety sack: A sack made by a blitzing safety.

safety valve: A short pass dumped off to a back in the flat when a quarterback cannot find an open receiver and is under pressure from a pass rush.

scatback: A tricky and elusive running back.

scissors: see *cross block.*

1. scramble: To move around behind the line of scrimmage eluding pass rushers when the pocket has been penetrated before passing or running. Some quarterbacks who are fast and mobile, and who have the ability to throw on the run, prefer to scramble rather than remain in the pocket. One of the most successful quarterbacks in football, Fran Tarkenton of the Minnesota Vikings and the New York Giants, was known for his inclination and ability to scramble. Tarkenton holds the NFL career records for the most passes completed (3686), the most yards gained (47,003), and the most touchdown passes (342).

2. scramble: The act or an instance of a quarterback scrambling.

scrambler: A quarterback who is known for his inclination and/or ability to scramble.

1. scrape: To "scrape off" or move from behind a defensive lineman at the snap in order to charge through a gap in the line. To stunt, as from a stacked position.

2. scrape: A linebacker's stunt around a lineman, often from a stacked position.

1. screen: A screen pass.

2. screen: To execute a screen pass.

screen pass: A pass thrown to a receiver in the flat (either a running back or a wide receiver who steps back) with a wall of blockers in front of him. Disguised to look like a long pass, a screen pass is particularly effective against a blitz or strong rush. also *screen*.

1. scrimmage: 1. An unofficial or practice game. 2. Pertaining to a scrimmage down. (pulled a muscle on the next play from scrimmage, and had to leave the game)

2. scrimmage: To engage in a scrimmage.

scrimmage down: A down that begins when the ball is put into play with a snap from the line of scrimmage and ends when the ball is dead. compare *free kick down*.

scrimmage kick: A kick made during a scrimmage down, such as a punt, field goal, or extra point attempt.

scrimmage line: see *line of scrimmage*.

seam: An undefended area between two zones of a zone defense. (hit him with a perfectly thrown pass in the seam)

secondary: 1. The players in the defensive backfield, the cornerbacks and safeties. 2. The area behind the defensive line and linebackers. (got into the secondary before he was finally brought down)

set: A formation, a specific offensive or defensive alignment at the beginning of a play.

set back: An offensive back positioned behind the quarterback, as in the T formation. also *remaining back*.

set up: To get into position in preparation for a pass.

shank: To miskick the ball on a punt, as with the ankle or off the side of the foot instead of the instep.

1. shift: 1. The simultaneous movement or change of position of two or more offensive players after assuming a set position. Legal once on each down as long as the shifting players assume a new set position and are motionless for

the required one full second before the snap. A shift is used, often in combination with a man in motion, to cause defensive imbalances and personnel mismatches or to distract or deceive the defenders. 2. The movement or change of position of one or more defensive players in anticipation of a certain kind of offensive play.

2. shift: To move to a new position as a part of an offensive or defensive shift.

shiver: A defensive lineman's technique in which the hands and forearms are thrust upward to stun an opposing lineman and deflect his block.

shoestring catch: A running catch (as of a pass) in which a player leans forward with his arms extended, grasping the ball just before it hits the ground.

shoestring tackle: A tackle in which the runner is able to be grasped only by the feet or one foot.

shootout: A high-scoring game.

shoot the gap: To rush through a space between offensive linemen toward the passer or ballcarrier.

short out: see *out*.

short side: The weak side of an unbalanced line, the "shorter" side with fewer linemen.

short yardage offense: A special offensive alignment employing extra players on the front line, used in situations where the ball must be advanced only a short distance in order to score or gain a first down.

shotgun offense: A spread formation primarily for passing in which the quarterback is positioned several yards behind the center to receive the snap, with the other backs lined up as slotbacks and flankers. Though a similar spread formation was used as early as 1920 by player-coach George Halas's Decatur Staleys (later the Chicago Bears), the shotgun was invented in 1960 by San Francisco 49ers' coach Red Hickey, and revived and popularized in 1975 by Tom Landry's Dallas Cowboys.

shoulder block: A block in which the opponent is hit with the shoulder.

shoulder pads: Padding that protects the collarbone and shoulder area of a player. Constructed with a hard outer surface (such as molded plastic or combat-derived composite materials) on top and a foam or inflatable cushion layer underneath.

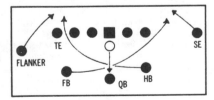

SHOTGUN

shovel pass: An underhand pass (with the arms swung as though "shovelling") often used for a pitchout or lateral.

1. sideline: 1. One of the two boundary lines on each side of the playing area between and perpendicular to the end lines. 2. The players' bench and surrounding area, from where the coach and coaching staff observe and send plays into a game. also *bench.* 3. see *sideline pattern, sideline route.*

2. sideline: To cause a player to be unable to play. (sidelined for three weeks with a pulled hamstring) also *bench.*

●●To prevent or remove one from active participation. (returned to work after being sidelined by the flu)

sideline pattern, sideline route: A pass pattern in which a receiver runs downfield then breaks toward the outside to catch a pass near the sideline. To gain time in the closing minutes of a game or a half, a receiver on a sideline route can step out of bounds to stop the clock. also *sideline.*

sidelines: The area next to either sideline, off the playing field.

●●Away from the action or activity, the point of view of an outsider or nonparticipant. (watched proudly from the sidelines as his son received the award)

sidewinder: see *soccer-style kicker.*

side zone: Either of two areas of the playing field between the inbounds lines and the sidelines. When the ball is blown dead or a ballcarrier is tackled in a side zone, the ball is put into play at the intersection of the inbounds line and the yard line where the ball was dead.

signal caller: A quarterback.

signals: 1. A coded series of words and numbers used in the huddle (or, when there is a change, at the line of scrimmage) by the quarterback or defensive captain to call for a specific play or alignment for the down about to be played. Offensive signals given by the quarterback also specify the precise timing of the snap. Gestures corresponding to the coded words and numbers are "wig-wagged" by coaches to send in signals from the sidelines. The use of signals originated in 1882 with the introduction of downs. Entire sentences at first, signals had, by 1885, been shortened to words and numbers.

2. A prearranged sequence of code words and numbers called out loud by the quarterback at the line of scrimmage to cue formation shifts and the snap from center. also *cadence, count, snap count.*

single-back offense: see *one-back formation.*

single wing: An offensive formation employing an unbalanced line in which the ball is snapped directly to the tailback, positioned 4 to 5 yards behind the center, or to the fullback, about a yard in front and just to the side of him on the strong side. The remaining two backs line up on the strong side, the quarterback as a blocking back behind the guard or tackle, and the other as a wingback behind and just outside the end. Invented by coach Glenn S. "Pop" Warner around 1906, the single wing was still being used successfully in the mid-1950s by UCLA, Arkansas, and the NFL Pittsburgh Steelers.

sit on a lead: To play conservatively so as to maintain possession of the ball and, thereby, protect a scoring advantage held.

six-man football: A variation of football with six players on a side, played, when possible, on a slightly smaller field (80 yards between goal lines, 40 yards wide, with 15-yard side zones) and special goals (crossbar 9 feet high, goalposts 25 feet apart). In six-man football, the offense must advance 15 yards instead of 10 in four downs, unless the ball is kicked or forward passed, it may not be advanced across the line of scrimmage until after a backward pass to a teammate (or "clear pass") is made by the receiver of the snap, all players (except the passer) are eligible to receive a pass, a field goal counts four points, a try for point counts two points if placekicked or drop kicked and one point if made by a pass or run, and the game is ended immedi-

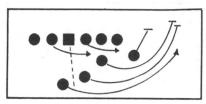

SINGLE WING OFFENSE

ately when one team is forty-five or more points ahead at the end of the first half, or when such a lead is secured during the second half.

sixty-minute player: 1. A player who is known for giving his full effort for an entire game. 2. A two-way player who plays on offense and defense. see *two-way player.*

skull session, skull practice: see *chalk talk.*

1. slant: 1. An offensive play in which the ballcarrier hits the line at an angle, such as off guard or off tackle. 2. A pass pattern in which a receiver runs diagonally across the middle of the field. also *slant-in.* 3. A planned charge at an angle to the left or right by a defensive lineman instead of straight ahead.

2. slant: 1. To angle into the line on a running play. 2. To charge to the left or right when rushing the ballcarrier or passer instead of straight ahead.

slant-in: see *slant.*

slasher: A ballcarrier who is known more for quick, powerful runs through the line than for outside speed or elusiveness.

sled: An apparatus that consists of a steel frame on skids with one or more large vertical pads attached to the front. As a training exercise, players practice blocking by contacting these pads with the arms and shoulders, forcing the sled straight back as it slides along the ground.

sledgehammer runner: see *punishing runner.*

sleeper play: see *hideout play.*

slingshot goalposts: The single-standard goalposts adopted by the NFL in 1967, as opposed to the H-shaped goals often used in high school and college games.

slot: The space or channel between (and extending behind) a tackle and an end in the offensive line.

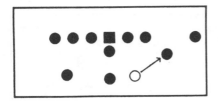

SLOT T FORMATION

slotback: A back positioned behind the space between a tackle and an end.

slot formation: A T formation in which one of the halfbacks or running backs is positioned in the slot between the tackle and split end. First popularized in the 1950s. also *slot T.*

slot T: see *slot formation.*

snakehips: An elusive or hard-to-tackle runner, one who "wriggles" away from tackles.

1. snap: 1. The method of putting the ball in play on a scrimmage down, in which the snapper (center), in one quick and continuous motion, passes or hands the ball backward between his legs from its position on the ground to a back behind him. The center snap and the scrimmage concept, football's cardinal and essential features, were adopted in 1880 by the intercollegiate rules committee led by Yale halfback Walter Camp. also *center snap, exchange.* 2. An instance of the center putting the ball in play by passing or handing it back through his legs. also *center snap, exchange.*

2. snap: To pass or hand the ball back between the legs to begin a scrimmage down. also *center, hike.*

snap count: see *signals.*

snapper: The center.

sneak: A quarterback sneak.

soccer-style kicker: A placekicker who uses the instep to propel the ball with a side approach (as one would kick a soccer ball) rather than the toe from straight back. In 1964, Pete Gogolak of Cornell University signed with the Buffalo Bills, becoming the first soccer-style kicker in professional football. Today, the majority of the placekickers in the NFL are soccer-style kickers. also *sidewinder.*

soft: Loose, a distance from the receiver one is guarding, as opposed to tight man-to-man coverage. (such a fast wide receiver that the cornerback has to play him soft)

solid play: A play that has no keys (such as a guard pulling to lead a running play, etc.) to tip off the defense.

1. spear: To deliberately drive the helmet into a player who is down, held by a teammate and going down, or obviously out of the play. A personal foul that results in a 15-yard penalty.

2. spear: An instance of spearing. see *spearing.*

spearing: A personal foul in which the helmet is deliberately driven into a player who is down, held by a teammate and going down, or obviously out of the play, resulting in a 15-yard penalty.

special team, specialty team: A squad of players (mainly reserves and substitutes) called into a game for one play in special circumstances. There are special teams for kickoffs, punts, field goals, and extra point attempts. see *suicide squad.*

1. spike: A ritual in which the ball is slammed to the ground and bounced in the end zone after scoring a touchdown, popularized in the 1970s.

2. spike: To slam the ball to the ground and bounce it in the end zone after scoring a touchdown.

spinner play: One of several variations of an offensive play from the single-wing formation in which the ball is snapped to the fullback, who either fakes or hands off to the other backs passing him as he "spins" in a full circle, sometimes keeping and carrying the ball himself.

spiral: 1. The smooth, even spin around the long axis of the ball on a well thrown or kicked pass or punt. Coach and football innovator Glenn S. "Pop" Warner was among the first to develop and teach the spiral pass and punt. 2. A pass or a punt in which the ball spins smoothly and evenly around its long axis.

split end: 1. An offensive player positioned on the line of scrimmage several yards outside the formation as a pass receiver. Originally known as a flanker, the split end is now most often called a wide receiver. also *spread end.* 2. The position played by a split end. also *spread end.*

split T: A variation of the T formation in which the line is spread out, with the tackles and ends lining up wider than usual. Coach Don Faurot of Missouri invented the split T in 1941, which was regularly used successfully by coach Bud Wilkinson's Oklahoma teams. also *spread T.*

split the seam: To pass into the middle of the unguarded area between two zones in a zone defense.

split the uprights: To make good on a field goal or extra point attempt by kicking the ball over the crossbar and between the uprights.

spot: To put the ball down where it is next to be put into play. (the referee spots the ball at the 30-yard line, where it will be first-and-ten)

spot foul: An offense that can (depending on specific circumstances) be penalized from the "spot" of the foul, where the official throws his flag down (as opposed to the "previous spot"). Clipping and defensive pass interference are two examples of spot fouls.

spot of enforcement: The point from which a distance penalty resulting from a foul is measured. Depending on specific circumstances, the spot of enforcement may be at the spot of the foul (such as for clipping or defensive pass interference), the spot from which the previous play began (previous spot), the spot where the ball will next be put into play (succeeding spot), or at the spot where the ball is dead. also *enforcement spot.*

spot pass: A pass that is thrown to a predetermined spot rather than to a receiver.

spotter: One who identifies players for the announcer on a radio or television broadcast of a game.

spread end: see *split end.*

spread formation: An offensive formation in which the backs are spread out (such as the double wing, shotgun, etc.).

spread T: see *split T.*

sprint out: see *roll out.*

sprintout: see *rollout.*

spying: To delay rushing, to hold back long enough to read the play. One of the first to employ the technique of spying was defensive tackle Eugene "Big Daddy" Lipscomb of the Los Angeles Rams (1953-56), Baltimore Colts (1957-1961), and the Pittsburgh Steelers.

square-in: see *in.*

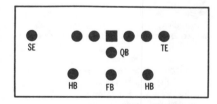

SPLIT T OFFENSE

square-out: see *out*.

squeeze: see *pinch*.

squib kick: A kickoff that is intentionally kicked low so as to bounce erratically along the ground and be difficult for the receiving team to handle.

1. stack: An offensive or defensive tactic in which players line up one behind another to disguise or delay recognition of the direction in which they will move (such as the intended path of a linebacker in a stack behind a lineman).

2. stack: To have one player line up behind another in a stack.

stack I: A variation of the I formation in which both running backs line up behind the fullback, creating a "stack" behind the quarterback.

stack the defense: To specially position defensive players in accordance with an opposing team's tendencies or strength, or to defend against a specific anticipated play.

stand one up: To block or tackle a charging opponent into a standing position, completely stopping his forward progress. (stood him up at the line of scrimmage)

stanza: A quarter.

stashing: An illegal practice in which a professional team "protects" (keeps other teams from signing) a potentially valuable player by under-the-table payments to the player, or by placing the player on the team's official injured reserve list, though not injured. A team found guilty of this practice in the NFL is subject to a fine and disciplinary action.

Statue of Liberty play: An old offensive play in which the back receiving the snap cocks his arm as though passing, but instead, the ball is taken from his hand by another back passing behind.

stick: To hit an opponent hard with a block or tackle.

sticks: see *chain*.

stickum: A once-legal sticky substance applied to the arms and hands of receivers and defensivebacks to increase adhesion and make the ball "stick" to the player. In 1981, the NFL outlawed the use of stickum and any other substance having qualities of slipperiness or adhesiveness.

stiff-arm: see *straight-arm*.

stone hands: An inability to catch a ball in flight, as a pass or a kick. (might have made a good receiver if he hadn't had stone hands)

1. straight-arm: To legally use the palm of the hand to ward off or hold at arms length a would-be tackler. also *stiff-arm*.

2. straight-arm: The act or an instance of straight-arming a would-be tackler. also *stiff-arm*.

stretch a zone: To pass to a receiver at the far edge of a defensive zone (such as deep to a fast receiver, or at the sideline).

stripe: Slang for a yard line. also *yard marker*.

strip the ball: To cause a fumble by knocking or taking the ball out of the ballcarrier's hands.

strong safety, strong safetyman: A defensive back positioned opposite the strong side of the offensive line, and primarily responsible for defending against a long run or pass. In man-for-man pass coverage, the strong safety usually covers the opposing tight end. also *tight safety, tight safetyman*.

strong side: The side of an unbalanced line on which the tight end is positioned.

strongside: Of or pertaining to the strong side. (stopped short of the first down by the strongside linebacker)

student body left: A power sweep to the left. see *student body right*.

student body right: A power sweep to the right. The expressions student body left and student body right came out of the coach John McKay era at the University of Southern California (1960-1975), when the USC offense ran the power sweep so successfully, with great running backs like Mike Garrett, O.J. Simpson, Anthony Davis, and Ricky Bell carrying the ball.

1. stunt: To exchange rushing routes with another defensive lineman by looping around him just before the ball is snapped.

2. stunt: The act or an instance of looping around a defensive lineman just before the ball is snapped to exchange rushing routes with him.

stutter step: A momentary change in rhythm or pace (and some times direction) while moving, or a feint in one direction with a quick step and return, in order to momentarily freeze or confuse an opponent.

stutter-step: To execute a stutter step.

1. submarine: To assume a low stance and duck under the block of an offensive lineman, thereby blunting his initial surge. A defensive tactic used to clog the intended path of the ballcarrier on a short yardage play.

2. submarine: The act or an instance of assuming a low stance and ducking under the block of an offensive lineman.

succeeding spot: The spot from which the ball is next to be put in play for a scrimmage down or free kick down. Some penalties, depending on specific circumstances, are enforced from the succeeding spot.

sucker play: An offensive play that is intended to specifically deceive and take advantage of one or more players on the defensive team.

sucker trap: see *false trap.*

sudden death: An extra fifteen-minute period of play to decide a playoff or championship game tied at the end of regulation play in the NFL. The period begins with a kickoff (decided by coin toss) and ends when one team scores, or when time runs out. If neither team is able to score in the overtime period, fifteen-minute periods continue to be played (with two-minute intermissions in between) until one team scores. Sudden death was first introduced by the NFL in 1941 to decide tied playoff games. Its use was expanded to championship games in 1947.

••A "sudden death" or tiebreaking period of play is now often used in other sports.

suicide squad: The special team for kickoffs and punts. Because of the higher-than-usual risk of injury from the full-speed head-on collisions that occur on kickoffs and punts, the special teams for these occasions are given names like the bomb squad, kamikaze corps, kamikaze squad, and suicide squad.

suit up: To dress (pads and team uniform) to play in a game. (first time he's suited up since his injury)

••To dress for a contest or an occasion. (suited up for the senior prom)

Super Bowl: The annual post-season game between AFC and NFC champions for the NFL championship. The first Super Bowl was played at Los Angeles in 1967, one year after the American Football League-National Football

League merger was announced. In Super Bowl I, the NFL Green Bay Packers defeated the Kansas City Chiefs of the AFL 35-10 (NFC and AFC conferences weren't formed until 1969).

1. sweep: An offensive play in which the ballcarrier runs outside around one end behind blockers.

2. sweep: To execute a sweep.

1. swing: Short for swing pass. see *flare.*

2. swing: see *flare.*

swing pass: see *flare.*

1. tackle: To seize and stop the forward progress of the ballcarrier, especially by knocking, pulling, or throwing him to the ground. also *bring down.*

2. tackle: 1. The act or an instance of tackling the ballcarrier. 2. Either of the two offensive or defensive tackles positioned on the line of scrimmage. see *offensive tackle, defensive tackle.* 3. The position played by a tackle. 4. A normal game of football in which tackling is permitted, as opposed to a game of touch football. (played his first game of tackle at the age of twelve)

tackling dummy: A heavy stuffed bag suspended from above and used to practice tackling. Pioneer coach Amos Alonzo Stagg invented the tackling dummy in 1889, when he was a student at Yale.

tailback: The deepest positioned offensive back in formations such as the I and the single wing.

tail football: see *flag football.*

Tartan Turf: A brand of artificial turf used in place of grass in some stadiums.

taxi: 1. To play on a team's taxi squad. (taxied for a year before he made the roster) 2. To assign a player to the team's taxi squad.

taxi squad: A squad of salaried reserve players who practice and scrimmage with a team, but do not suit up for games. Though the use of taxi squads was prohibited by the NFL in the early 1970s, the term is now applied to the four extra players allowed on NFL team rosters beginning in 1982 (forty-nine-man rosters with forty-five eligible to play each week). The taxi squad got its name from the late 1940s, Arthur McBride, the original owner of the Cleveland Browns (then still with the All-American Football Conference, rival to the NFL), used to employ some of his practice players as drivers for a taxi company he owned. also *cab squad.*

team area, team box: A marked area on the sidelines on both sides of the field for team benches, reserve players, coaches and trainers.

tear-away jersey: A special jersey often worn by backs and receivers that is designed to tear loose if grasped by an opponent, thereby freeing the ballcarrier.

TD: A touchdown.

1. tee: A kicking tee.

2. tee: see *tee up.*

tee up: To place the ball on a kicking tee. also *tee.*

T formation: An offensive formation in which the backs are arranged roughly in the shape of a T, with the quarterback positioned just behind the center to take the snap directly, and the fullback several yards straight back, in between and slightly behind the two halfbacks. The modern T formation, which ushered in an era of counter plays, players in motion, and forward passes to widely spaced ends and receivers, was developed in the late 1930s by Ralph Jones, coach of George Halas' Chicago Bears, and college coach Clark Shaughnessy. In 1940, in his first year as Stanford coach, Shaughnessy's team went undefeated employing the T, beating Nebraska 21-13 in the Rose Bowl. That same year, the Bears used the T in a 73-0 rout of the Washington Redskins in the NFL championship game. The T formation and its variations are still widely used in college and professional football. also *tight T.* compare *pro T, slot T, split T, wing T.*

thread the needle: To throw a perfectly placed pass between defenders.

three and out: A defensive team's motto and goal, to stop the opposing offensive team for three downs and force them to punt.

three-end offense: Any of the modern offensive formations which employ a tight end, split end, and a flanking back as a wide receiver, effectively three "ends." Although born in 1931 with Chicago Bears coach Ralph Jones's split end and man-in-motion, the modern three-end offense emerged in the late 1940s with the appearance of the position and role of the tight end.

three-four defense: A defensive alignment that uses a three-man line (a nose guard and two defensive ends) and four linebackers. The three-four defense was reported to have been used in 1922 by Georgetown University coach Maurice Dubofsky, though it was perfected and popularized by coach Bud Wilkinson at Oklahoma in the 1940s. College teams sometimes refer to the three-four as the "Oklahoma." Since Don Shula's Miami Dolphins went undefeated in 1972 using the three-four, the alignment has become a staple in the NFL.

three-man front: A three-man defensive line (a nose guard and two defensive ends), as in the three-four defense.

three-point stance: A crouching stance with the feet set 18 to 24 inches apart and staggered slightly, and the body leaning forward with one hand touching the ground. Linemen and some backs wait for the snap in a three-point stance.

throw a strike: To complete a pass, especially a perfectly thrown or accurately placed pass. (threw a strike into double coverage to make the first down)

throwball: A description of the wide-open passing game in the NFL made possible by rule changes in the late 1970s.

throw for a loss: To tackle the passer or ballcarrier behind the line of scrimmage for a loss of yardage. (couldn't find an open receiver and was thrown for a loss)

throw into traffic: To throw a pass to a receiver in the midst of defenders. Dangerous because of the high risk of an interception.

tight end: 1. An offensive lineman usually positioned at one end of the line of scrimmage within a yard or so of the tackle. The tight end is both a blocker and a pass receiver. 2. The position

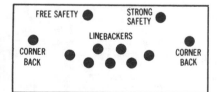

THREE-FOUR DEFENSE

played by a tight end. The position and role of the tight end emerged in the NFL in the late 1940s, making possible the modern three-end offense (tight end, split end, and a flanking back as a wide receiver).

tight safety, tight safetyman: see *strong safety*.

tight T: The basic T formation, called "tight" because of the small space between the linemen. compare *split T*.

time out: 1. A one and one-half-minute suspension of play requested by and charged to either team any time the ball is dead. Each team is allowed three time outs in each half. 2. A suspension of play by the referee. see *official's time out*.

●●A pause. (took a time out from his studies to watch the news)

total offense: A statistic which reflects the total net yards gained by rushing and passing by a player or team in a period of play, game, season, or (in a player's individual records) a career.

touch: 1. The end zone. (downed the ball in touch rather than attempt a runback) 2. Touch football.

touchback: A situation in which a ball kicked, punted, or passed by one team travels over the other team's goal line and is deliberately downed there by the other team, or goes out of bounds. After a touchback, the team into whose end zone the ball was kicked, punted, or passed puts the ball in play at its own 20-yard line. compare *safety*.

touchdown: A six-point score made by advancing the ball to a point on or behind the opposing team's goal line, whether by carrying it, passing it to a teammate, or recovering a loose ball there. Originally, a touchdown counted for less than an extra point (then called a "goal from touchdown" or "goal after"). In 1883, a touchdown was valued at two points, in 1884, four points (and the extra point was reduced from four points to two points), in 1897, five points (and the extra point reduced to one point), and finally, six points in 1910.

touch football: A variation of football played without protective pads, in which the ballcarrier is "downed" not by tackling, but by a defensive player touching him with both hands below the waist (or sometimes anywhere between the shoulders and knees). also *touch*.

1. trap: 1. see *trap block*. 2. see *trap play*.

2. trap: To execute a trap block against an opponent. also *trap block*.

trap block: An offensive blocking technique in which a rushing defender is allowed to charge through the offensive line, then is blocked from the side by a pulling guard or tackle (or occasionally, the center). also *mousetrap, trap*.

trap-block: To execute a trap block against an opponent. also *trap*.

trap play: A running play that depends on a trap block and is directed at the space vacated by the trapped defensive player. also *trap*.

trenches: The area around the line of scrimmage in which the offensive and defensive lines make contact and contend. (have taken control of the

PENALTY FLAG

OFFICIAL—TOUCHDOWN SIGNAL

trenches in the second half) also *pit.*

triple option: An offensive play designed to begin the same way on every down, in which the quarterback has three choices: he can hand off to the fullback for a run through the line, pitch the ball out to a halfback for a run to the outside, or keep the ball to run or pass it himself. Popular in college play, the triple option evolved out of the split T formation popularized in the 1940s.

triple-team: 1. To block or guard an opponent with three players simultaneously. 2. To join with two teammates to block or guard an opponent.

triple threat: A player who is able to run, pass, and kick the ball well.

••A person who is skilled in three areas of activity. (a triple threat who can sing, dance, and act)

triple wing: An offensive formation similar to the double wing, but with the fullback playing close behind and just outside the tight end, and the halfback on the weak side playing in the slot several yards back. also *trips.*

trips: see *triple wing.*

try: see *try for point.*

try for point: An attempt to score an additional point (or in high school, college, and USFL games, one or two additional points), by the scoring team after a touchdown. On a try for point, the scoring team is allowed one down at the 2-yard line (3-yard line in high school and college games) to successfully placekick or drop kick the ball through the uprights, or successfully run or pass the ball over the goal line for the additional point (or two additional points for a run or a pass in high school, college, and USFL games). also *try.* see *extra point.*

turf toe: A tear in the posterior capsule surrounding the joint that attaches the big toe to the foot (the first metatarsal

pharangeal joint). A painful injury caused by hyper-extending the joint when the back of the heel (of a player on his toes) is forced downward (as by an impact), bending the toe back. Called turf toe because of the frequency of the injury on the unyielding surface of artificial turf.

turn-in: A pass pattern in which the receiver turns in across the middle of the field after running downfield a short distance.

turn-out: A pass pattern in which the receiver turns out toward the sideline after running downfield a short distance.

turn over: To lose possession of the ball because of a misplay or an error.

turnover: The loss of possession of the ball by a team because of a misplay or an error. (fumbled the ball in the second half to give up another turnover)

turn the corner: To turn upfield after running laterally to the outside, as on a sweep or end run. (tackled before he could turn the corner)

two-minute drill: An offensive strategy in which several plays are called in one huddle in order to save time near the end of a half or a game (especially by a team which is tied or behind). Typically, two-minute drill plays feature passes thrown to receivers near a sideline so that the clock is stopped automatically with an incompletion, or by the receiver stepping out of bounds if the pass is complete. The first acknowledged master of the two-minute drill was quarterback Bobby Layne of coach Buddy Parker's Detroit Lions in the early 1950s. also *hurry-up offense, two-minute offense.*

two-minute offense: see *two-minute drill.*

two-minute warning: The referee's notification to the coach of each team that only two minutes remain in a half.

two-platoon system: The common practice of using separate groups or squads of players for offense and defense. Though a rule change made unlimited or free substitution possible in college play in 1941 (and 1943 in the NFL), the two-platoon system was first used by Michigan coach Fritz Crisler against Army in 1945. Its popularity spread until substitutions were severely limited by another rule change in 1953 (the NFL had ended free substitution in 1946). When unlimited substitution was restored by the NFL

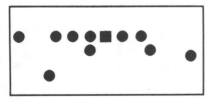

TRIPLE WING

in 1950 and the NCAA in 1958, the two-platoon system once again became popular.

two-way player: One who plays on offense and defense. The last real two-way player was Pro Football Hall of Famer Chuck Bednarik, who played both offense and defense for the Philadelphia Eagles in their 1960 NFL title drive. also *sixty-minute player.*

umpire: A football official who, at the snap, is positioned 4 to 6 yards behind the line of scrimmage in the defensive backfield, and who is responsible for supervising play at the line of scrimmage, assisting the referee in setting up the ball for the next play, and watching for ineligible linemen downfield on a pass play. Before a game, the umpire checks the players' equipment and any special bandages or pads worn.

unbalanced line: An offensive alignment in which there are more linemen on one side of the center than the other. The unbalanced line is credited to Amos Alonzo Stagg.

1. under: 1. Short for undershift. compare *over.* 2. Underneath, or under the coverage. (looped a little pass over the middle, under the coverage)

underneath: Short for an area or zone covered by defensive backs, to an undefended area between the line of scrimmage and the coverage. (will throw underneath to the tight end when his other receivers are double-covered) also *under.*

undershift: A defensive alignment in which all or some of the defensive linemen shift one position over toward the weak side of an unbalanced line (placing one tackle head-on the center) to disrupt blocking patterns, or to move big linemen to the expected point of attack. also *under.* compare *over, overshift.*

under the center: Positioned close to and directly behind the center, with the hands under him, ready to receive the ball.

United States Football League: A major professional football league that conducts an eighteen-week season from March through June, normally off season for football. Formed in 1982, the United States Football League (USFL) scheduled twelve teams to contest in

1983, the inaugural season, with three geographic divisions: the Atlantic Division (the Boston Breakers, the New Jersey Generals, the Philadelphia Stars, and the Washington Federals), the Central Division (the Birmingham Stallions, the Chicago Blitz, the Michigan Panthers, and the Tampa Bay Bandits), and the Pacific Division (the Arizona Wranglers, the Denver Gold, the Los Angeles Express, and the Oakland Invaders).

unload: 1. see *ground, intentional grounding.* 2. To inflict a particularly hard hit on an opponent with a block or tackle. (unloaded on the quarterback from the blind side)

unnecessary roughness: An illegal action such as kicking, striking, butting, or spearing an opponent, tackling or contacting the ballcarrier when he is clearly out of bounds, throwing the ballcarrier to the ground after the ball is dead, contacting a ballcarrier who falls or slips to the ground untouched and makes no attempt to advance (before or after the ball is dead), or running into or throwing the body against or on a player obviously out of the play (before or after the ball is dead). Unnecessary roughness results in a 15-yard penalty, and if the foul is judged to be flagrant,

UNDER THE CENTER

the disqualification of the guilty player.

unsportsmanlike conduct: An illegal act that is contrary to the principles of sportsmanship, such as the use of abusive or insulting language or gestures to opponents, teammates, or officials, hiding or substituting something in place of the ball, repeatedly baiting or distracting an opponent, giving unfair assistance to or accepting it from a teammate, or attempting to punch or kick an opponent even though no contact is made. Unsportsmanlike conduct results in a 15-yard penalty, and if the infraction is judged flagrant, the disqualification of the guilty player.

up back: 1. A blocking back positioned just behind the line on kicking plays. 2. The receiver or receivers positioned in front of the deep receivers on a kick. 3. The running back positioned just behind the quarterback in an I formation, sometimes called the diveback.

upfield: 1. Toward the opposing team's goal line. also *downfield.* 2. Back toward the area from which a play originates.

upright: One of the two goalposts that extend vertically from either side of the crossbar, and mark the sides of the goal.

uprights: 1. The two goalposts that extend vertically from either side of the crossbar (10 feet in high school and college, 30 feet in the NFL), and mark the sides of the goal. 2. The goal.

up top: Into the air, as with a pass or a pass play. (will be forced to go up top if he can't get his ground game going)

USFL: The United States Football League.

veer, veer ofense: An offense based on the triple option run from a modern three-end formation (with a tight end, split end, and a flanking back as a wide receiver).

vig: see *vigorish.*

vigorish: Betting parlance for the service

charge paid to a professional betting service or bookie when placing a bet, usually 10 percent of the bet. also *juice, vig.*

weak safety: A defensive back positioned across from the weak side of the offensive line. also *free safety, free safetyman.*

weak side: The side of an unbalanced line having fewer players (opposite the side on which the tight end is positioned). also *short side.*

weakside: Of or pertaining to the weak side.

wedge: A wedge-shaped alignment of blockers who form in front of the ballcarrier on kickoff returns, legal as long as the blockers neither link arms nor hold onto each other.

wide receiver: An offensive player positioned wide of a formation, as a split end or flanker, and who functions primarily as a pass receiver.

wind: Breath or the ability to breathe properly while taking part in a strenuous activity. (will have to train to improve his wind)

winded: Out of breath, unable to take in a sufficient amount of oxygen to sustain a strenuous physical activity.

wind sprint: One of a series of short sprints run at full speed with brief rest periods in between to build up a player's speed, wind, and endurance. Developed by Amos Alonzo Stagg.

wingback: 1. An offensive back positioned just outside and behind the end on the strong side of a single wing formation, and who functions primarily as a ballcarrier, pass receiver, and blocker. 2. Another name for the original flankerbacks. 3. The position played by a flankerback.

wing T formation: A variation of the T formation in which one halfback lines up on the flank as a wingback. Small-college coach Dave Nelson of Delaware is credited with inventing the wing T, popularized later by Forest Evashevski at Iowa.

wishbone, wishbone T: A variation of the T formation which utilizes an unbalanced line (with a split end and tight end), and in which the halfbacks are positioned to either side of and slightly behind the fullback (roughly forming the shape of a wishbone when viewed from

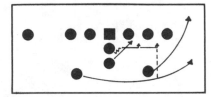

WISHBONE OFFENSE

above). Coach Darrell Royal's 1968 University of Texas team introduced the wishbone formation.

Xs and Os: 1. The two symbols used to represent a team and an opposing team in diagrams of offensive plays and defensive strategies. 2. Basics, the initial stages of teaching or learning offensive plays or defensive strategies. (would have gone back to the Xs and Os had he known they would execute so poorly)

Yale coverage: A defensive strategy against a pass that employs a zone defense deep, with each safety covering one half the field, and man-to-man coverage underneath.

yardage: The number of yards gained by a player or team in one play, a period of play in a game, a game, a season, or (in the case of an individual player) a career.

yardage chain: see *chain*.

yard line, yard marker: A marked or unmarked line and its vertical plane parallel to the end line. Yard lines extend across the field one yard apart and are named by the number of yards to the nearest goal line. also *stripe*.

zebra: An official, usually wearing the regulation black and white striped shirt.

1. zone: 1. An area of the field assigned to be covered by a particular defender or defenders in a zone coverage. 2. Short for zone coverage. (switched from man-to-man to a zone in the second half)

2. zone: To use zone coverage against an opponent. (will cover man-to-man short, and zone deep)

zone blocking: see *area blocking*.

zone coverage: A defensive strategy to protect against a pass in which specific areas or zones are assigned to defensive players, and any opponent entering the zone is guarded (as opposed to individual or man-to-man guarding). The fundamental principles of the zone defense, the rotation of the secondary, appeared in the NFL as early as the 1930s, when Earl "Curly" Lambeau's Green Bay Packers and Gus Dorais's Detroit Lions rotated the secondary toward George Halas's man-in-motion from the Chicago Bears' T formation. By the 1960s and 1970s, zone coverage had become the rule rather than the exception in the NFL. also *zone*.

GOLF

It is probable that the ancient Roman game *paganica*, in which a stuffed leather ball was knocked about the countryside by mallet-wielding players, was the progenitor of the various ball-and-club games developed in European countries. The basic elements of golf may also be related to the Roman game, but golf itself developed in Scotland.

Scottish shepherds made a game out of using a knotted staff or stick to knock a pebble (and later, a small ball) around on the tough grass between the heathery, wind-swept "links" or ridges of sand along the rugged coasts of Scotland. Friends and passers-by watched, then sampled the new game, and soon, fishermen, farmers, masons, and blacksmiths were also playing.

When St. Andrews University was founded in 1411, the game was already known throughout Scotland. The playing of golf had become so widespread by 1457 that the Scottish Parliament passed laws prohibiting the sport, which was said to be jeopardizing the national defense by seriously interfering with the practice of archery.

These laws were revoked in 1491, and near the end of the century, King James IV of Scotland himself became a devotee of the game. The Lord High Treasurer's accounts of 1502 and 1503 included payments for the king's "golf clubbis and ballis".

James IV's granddaughter, Mary, Queen of Scots, may have been the first woman golfer. When she returned to Scotland in 1560 from France, several young French boys, or *cadets*, came with her to serve as pages and porters. Whether or not these pages carried the Queen's clubs around when she played golf, golf club porters came to be known as caddies, an anglicized version of the French pronunciation "cahday".

In 1682, while in Edinburgh with the Scottish Parliament for his brother the king, the Duke of York (later James II, King of England, Scotland, and Ireland) and a local shoemaker, John "Far and Sure" Patersone, handily defeated two English noblemen in the first international foursome. The ball was made of leather, stuffed tightly with goose feathers. The players' golf clubs were hand carved from Scottish hardwoods, with crude and somewhat fragile heads and long, sturdy shafts, forcing golfers to play well away from the ball and use a flat or more horizontal swing. Some iron-headed clubs were in use, probably to cut down on breakage.

Though some claim that the Royal Blackheath Club was founded as early as 1608, and

188

the Royal Burgess Golfing Society of Edinburgh in 1735, the first documented golf club was the Honorable Company of Edinburgh Golfers, founded in 1744. In 1745, a tournament was played in Edinburgh for a silver club donated by the City Council, and won by John Rattray, an Edinburgh surgeon. Thirteen playing rules were drafted for the tournament. The same rules were adopted nine years later when the Royal and Ancient Golf Club of St. Andrews was founded in 1754. This organization, with its course in St. Andrews, was soon to become the governing body and the center of the sport of golf, as keeper of the official rules. Since 1952, that responsibility has been shared with the United States Golf Association.

The 1800s brought important changes in golf equipment. By 1810, varnish was being applied to wooden clubs to protect them from weather. In 1848, the revolutionary gutta-percha or "guttie" ball was introduced. Heavier and more perfectly round than the old feather-stuffed ball, the guttie could be driven farther (over 200 yards, vs. 175 yards maximum for the old ball), and could be bounced and actually rolled toward the hole. This quality when combined with the practice of mowing the greens closer around the hole, made the modern putt possible.

In 1860, the first tournament was staged at the Prestwick Course in Scotland, and won by pioneer professional, Willie Park, Sr. This competition would eventually be known as the British Open, not because both professionals and amateurs could compete, as they did from the second year on, but because after 1865, the tournament was "open" to any golfer who wanted to play, whether or not from around Prestwick.

The English were equally enamored of the game. In 1869, the Royal Liverpool Club was formed and a course laid out over a rabbit warren in Hoylake. It was at Hoylake that the first British Amateur Championship was played in 1885, won by A. F. MacFie. The Royal and Ancient Golf Club of St. Andrews accepted the management of both the British Open and Amateur Championships in 1919.

Golf was introduced into Australia as early as 1847 but did not gain widespread popularity until about 1895 when the Australian Golf Club in Sydney was revived.

In 1899, Coburn Haskell, an American from Cleveland, Ohio, produced the first modern golf ball, comprised of strips of rubber thread wound tightly around a rubber core, with a durable composite rubber covering. It was livelier and could be driven farther than the old guttie ball, and was much more resistant to cuts from iron clubs. Golfers, however, were reluctant to switch until 1901, when Alex "Sandy" Herd won the British Open, and Walter Travis, the US Amateur Championship, with the new ball.

The 1900 US Open was won by British golfing great, Harry Vardon. All athletes who profit by the use of their names to advertise products owe a debt to Vardon. Arguably the best golfer of his era, Vardon made the first-ever player endorsement, when Spalding introduced the Vardon line of golf clubs in 1901.

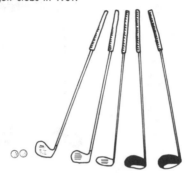

Harry Vardon, John Henry Taylor, and James Braid, known as the "great triumverate", and golfing great Edward "Ted" Ray epitomized Great Britain's dominance in golf since the late 1800s. When American-born amateur and former caddie Francis Ouimet won the US Open in 1913, defeating Vardon by five strokes, the tide began to turn.

In 1904, a golf competition was made part of the St. Louis Olympics and was won by George S. Lyon of Canada. Though judged to be a less-than-ideal Olympic sport and dropped thereafter, the fact that it was even tried indicated the growing popularity of the sport.

As the British pros had done in 1901, American professionals united in 1916 and formed the Professional Golfers Association (PGA). The first PGA Championship was held that year at the Siwanoy Country Club in Bronxville, New York and was won by James M. Barnes. Home-grown American golf stars such as amateurs Francis Ouimet and Charles Evens, Jr., and professionals such as Walter Hagen and Gene Sarazen began to emerge. Hagen's 1922 victory in the British Open (the first of four) clearly signalled the new prominence of the United States in international competition.

Stylish, witty, and a golfing friend of the Prince of Wales, Hagen raised the social status of the professional golfer and was the first pro to draw galleries of faithful fans. The sudden rise in national popularity of casual slacks and sport coats is attributed to Hagen's fashion influence, first with other golfers, then the general public. The trend is said to have started one day in the mid-1930s, when "The Haig" and the Prince of Wales neglected to change into their normal golf knickers, playing instead in slacks.

In 1922, Glenna Collett (Vare), after whom the LPGA Vare Trophy is named, won the first of a record six Women's Amateur Championships, and the United States team won the first Walker Cup international amateur competition. The following year, a twenty-one-year-old amateur from Georgia, Robert T. Jones, Jr., won the US Open. Bobby Jones would go on to become the game's greatest star. Jones won the British Open in 1926 and 1927, the US Amateur in 1924, 1925, 1927, and 1928, and the US Open again in 1926 and 1929. In 1930, Jones became the only golfer in history to score a Grand Slam, winning in that year the British Amateur Championship, the British Open, the US Amateur Championship, and the US Open. In 1981, Bobby Jones and Olympic champion and pioneer woman professional golfer, Mildred "Babe" Didrikson Zaharias became the first athletes honored by the US Postal Service with a commemorative stamp.

The first Ryder Cup international team competition for professionals was held in 1927 at the Worcester Country Club in Massachusetts, with the United States team defeating the team from Great Britain 9½ to 2½.

In 1934, the first Masters Tournament was held at the August National Golf Club, and won by Horton Smith. The Masters was soon considered one of golf's most prestigious tournaments, in which only the best golfers competed.

Entertainer and golfing enthusiast Bing Crosby put on the first-ever Celebrity Pro-Am match in 1937, at Rancho Santa Fe in Southern California. During World War II, Crosby and Bob Hope raised millions of dollars for war bonds, military relief, and recreation organizations by playing exhibition matches with Ben Hogan, Sam Snead, and other professionals all over the country.

After the war, major tournaments resumed, and other events were added to the pro Tour, all with ever-increasing purses. Women professionals, who had first organized in 1944 as the Women's Professional Golfers' Association, reorganized into the Ladies Professional Golfers' Association in 1950, with Patty Berg, Louise Suggs, Babe Didrikson, and others competing. In 1953 the USGA assumed the responsibility of conducting the Women's Open Championship, thereby putting all men's and women's national championships under the control of one sanctioning body. The previous year, the USGA had joined with the Royal and Ancient Golf Club of St. Andrews, Scotland, to issue the uniform code of playing rules observed throughout the world today.

During his administration, President Dwight D. Eisenhower's love for the game brought golf increased recognition. American television turned its spotlight on golf in the late 1950s with a weekly series, Shell's *Wonderful World of Golf*, hosted by Gene Sarazen and Jimmy Demaret. Tour events were televised with increasing frequency. Arnold Palmer was packing

the galleries (nicknamed "Arnie's Army") with his spectacular play and became the first professional golfer to have earned more than a million dollars in purses.

New professional stars emerged in the 1960s and 1970s, and the number of tour events increased yearly as golfers like South Africa's Gary Player, Jack "The Golden Bear" Nicklaus, (the all-time money winner as of 1981), Lee Trevino, Johnny Miller, and Tom Watson competed for higher and higher purses.

The Women's Tour also grew, producing players like Mickey Wright, Kathy Whitworth (the all-time money winner as of 1981), Judy T. Rankin (who, in 1976, became the first woman pro to win over $100,000 in a season), JoAnne Carner, Jane Blalock, Amy Alcott, and the popular Nancy Lopez. Australian Jan Stephenson was the first woman golfer to break the 200 for three rounds with an 18-under-par aggregate of 198.

By the early 1980s, Spain's Severiano Ballesteros, Isao Aoki and Mashishi and Tateo Ozaki of Japan, and Australia's David Graham had joined Roberto De Vincenzo of Argentina and others in making professional golf an international sport. American players like Jerry Pate, Bruce Lietzke, Tom Kite, Bill Rogers, Craig Stadler, and Calvin Peete added new excitement to the PGA Tour.

In addition to its popularity as a professional event, golf is now a major family participation sport. The modern trend toward efficient, low-maintenance golf courses should facilitate further growth, especially in places like China and Russia, where the first golf courses were being planned in the early 1980s.

1. **ace:** see *hole in one.*
2. **ace:** To make a hole in one. (aced the second hole)
1. **address:** To position oneself at the tee before hitting the ball. In a "hazard," a player is considered to have addressed the ball when he has taken his stance.

ADDRESS

2. **address:** 1. The act or action of addressing the ball. 2. The stance or position taken before hitting the ball.

advice: Any counsel or suggestion that could influence a player in determining his play, the choice of a club, or the method of making a stroke. A player may give advice to, or ask for advice from, only his partner or either of their caddies. Information on the Rules or Local Rules is not advice.

air-mail: To hit a long drive or shot.

air shot: see *whiff.*

albatross: see *double eagle.*

all flat: see *all square.*

all square: An even score after finishing a hole or a match. also *all flat, square.*

amateur: A golfer who plays the game as a nonrenumerative or nonprofit sport.

Amateur: see *U.S. Amateur Championship.*

Amateur Championship: see *U.S. Amateur Championship.*

Amateur Public Links Championship: An annual national championship open to individual amateur golfers and teams representing cities, played on a different public or municipal golf course each year. Nineteen-year-old Edmund R. Held of St. Louis won the first Amateur Public Links Championship in 1922. In 1923, the first Amateur Public Links Team Championship was won by Chicago.

American tournament: A match play tournament in which each competitor plays all the others, the winner being the player scoring the most victories. also *round robin tournament.*

angel raper: see *sky ball.*

approach: see *approach shot.*

approach cleek: An early iron-headed club, forerunner to the "mashie iron" or number 4 iron, and popular from the early to mid-1800s.

approach shot: 1. A shot hit onto the green from the fairway. also *approach.* 2. A long putt made with a putter. also *approach.*

apron: The grass encircling the putting green, cut somewhat longer than the green, but shorter than the fairway. also *collar, fringe, froghair.*

Around the World: A round of golf played with a score of eighty, an allusion to Jules Verne's *Around the World in Eighty Days.*

away: 1. The ball lying farthest from the cup on any hole. The player whose ball is away plays first. 2. The player whose ball is farthest from the hole.

baby a shot: To hit a ball (usually an approach shot) so feebly that it stops far short of its intended objective.

back door: The side or back rim of a hole. A ball is said to have gone in by the back door when it drops in at the side or around the back part of the hole.

back nine: The last nine holes on an eighteen-hole course. compare *front nine.*

backspin: A backward rotation given to a ball to make it rise sharply, then stop suddenly or roll backward upon landing. also *bite, stop.*

back stalls: see *back tees.*

backswing: The rotation of the body and backward and upward movement of the hands, arms, and club to a position from which the downward swing is initiated to contact the ball.

back tees: The back area of a teeing ground, usually reserved for expert or professional players. see *blue tees.*

baffing spoon: see *baffy.*

baffy: An obsolete term for a deeply pitched wooden club similar to a mod-

ern number 5 wood. So-called because the ground immediately behind the ball was "baffed" or struck. The term was popular until the numerical classifications for clubs were introduced in the 1920s. also *baffing spoon.*

ball: see *golf ball.*

ball at rest: A ball that has been struck during the course of play and has come to a standstill.

ball holed: A ball lying within the circumference of a hole, completely below the level of the lip of the hole.

ball in play: A ball on which a stroke has been made on the teeing ground. A ball remains in play until holed out, except when it is out of bounds, lost or lifted, or another ball has been substituted under an applicable Rule or Local Rule (the substituted ball becomes the ball in play).

ball lost: A ball that cannot be found or identified by the player after a five-minute search. A ball is also considered "lost" if another ball has been put into play under the Rules, or if the player has played a stroke with a provisional ball from a point nearer the hole than the place where the original ball is likely to be (the provisional ball becomes the ball in play).

BACKSWING

ball mark: 1. An identification mark put on a ball. 2. An indentation in the surface of a putting green caused by a ball landing.

ball marker: A small thumbpin-like plastic disc used to mark the spot on a putting green from which a ball is lifted.

banana ball: A ball that is sliced, traveling in a long arc (left-to-right for a right-handed golfer).

bandit: A high-handicap golfer who is able to play much better than his handicap indicates.

bango: see *bingo, bango, bungo.*

bare lie: A grassless patch of ground on which the ball comes to rest.

baseball grip: A grip in which a golf club is held similar to a baseball bat, with the hands meeting but not overlapping. also *ten-finger grip.* compare *interlocking grip, overlapping grip.*

bats: Slang for golf clubs. also *hammers, hickories, shooting irons, sticks, tools, weapons.*

beach: see *sand trap.*

belly it: To hit the ball poorly.

bend: To curve the ball around an object blocking one's passage to the green, as with a long iron or wood shot.

best-ball: A match in which the best individual score is used as a team's score on each hole. A best-ball match may also be a four-ball, or a match between one player and a side consisting of two or three partners.

billy goat course: A course that is laid out with many blind holes.

bingo: see *bingo, bango, bungo.*

bingo, bango, bungo: An informal game in which separate wagers are made on

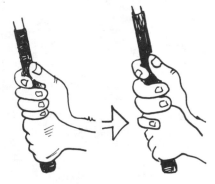

BASEBALL GRIP   OVERLAPPING GRIP

the first ball to reach the green (bingo), the closest ball to the pin (bango), and the first ball in the cup (bungo).

bird: Short for birdie.

bird dog: A particularly good caddie.

1. birdie: One stroke under par for a hole. The use of the expression "bird" for an extraordinary or unusual person or thing dates from the 1800s. There are conflicting accounts of exactly when the term was given its present golf meaning by two claimants, player A.H. "Ab" Smith and noted golf architect and historian A.W. Tillinghast. Both anecdotes place the origin around the turn of the century and tell of a particularly good shot (which led to a one-under-par hole) being called a "bird." Soon, "bird," then "birdie," came to mean a one-under-par hole. also *bird.*

2. birdie: To score a birdie. (birdied the fourth hole to pull even)

bisque: A handicap (of one or more strokes) deducted from a player's score at the player's option on one or more holes a round in match play, as long as the intention to use bisque on a hole is declared before play begins on that hole. A bisque may also be given in tennis and croquet, and was first used in the medieval game of court tennis. The term is of French origin, and connotes an advantage given.

bite: see *backspin.*

blacksmith: A player with a rough touch on the putting green.

bladesman: A particularly good putter. also *pool shark, undertaker.*

1. blast: To hit a ball out of a sand trap using an "explosion shot," in which the club (a sand wedge) digs into the sand behind the ball, driving the ball up and out with "explosive" force.

2. blast: The act or an instance of blasting the ball out of a sand trap. also *explosion shot.*

blaster: An old term for a sand iron or sand wedge.

blind bogey: see *kicker's tournament.*

blind green, blind hole: A hole in which the green or the hole is hidden from view when teeing off or making an approach shot.

block shot: A shot that goes off the club at an angle (to the right for a right-handed golfer), caused by hitting the ball with an open club face.

blow: 1. To suddenly begin to play badly,

as in a pressure situation. (was under par until he blew on the last three holes) also *blow up.* 2. To suddenly play badly and inflate one's score to a specified number. (blew to a seventy-six and dropped from the lead)

blowup: A sudden collapse in play, as in a pressure situation.

blow up: see *blow.*

blue darter: A ball hit in a straight line, a line drive.

blue plates: see *blue tees.*

blueprint: To execute a perfect shot. (blueprinted his tee shot and arrived at the green in two)

blue tees: The back area of a teeing ground, usually reserved for expert or professional players. The teeing ground is divided into three sections. The rear section, indicated by blue tee markers, is known as the "blue tees" and intended for professional use. The middle section, indicated by white tee markers, is known as the "middle tees" or "white tees" and intended for regulation play. The front section, indicated by red tee markers, is known as the "women's tees," "ladies' tees" or "red tees" and intended for women golfers. also *back stalls, back tees, blue plates, championship tees, tiger tees, tips.*

boge: Slang for *bogey.*

1. bogey: 1. A score of one over par on a hole. In Great Britain in the early 1890s, a "bogey" or "bogeyman" was a ghost or someone to be feared. When it became accepted practice at that time to rate golf holes to be played in a standard number of strokes, the fixed ground score (representing errorless play) became like another opponent. At the United Service Club in southern England, where all members held military rank, this mythical feared opponent was given the name "Colonel Bogey," shortened in popular use to "bogey." When the lively modern golf ball came into use in the late 1800s, the previously established "bogey" for a hole became too easy and soon in the United States the term came to mean one over "par." The British often still use the traditional meaning, referring to a par as a bogey. also *boge.* 2. The score an average golfer should be able to make under normal conditions on a particular course. In the United States, bogey is most frequently figured by taking an average of one stroke above par on each hole.

2. bogey: To score a bogey. (still managed to bogey the last hole after blasting out of the trap)

bogey sickness: An "ailment" caused by a particularly poor round by a professional player.

bold: The choice of a difficult and risky shot rather than a conservative shot. (decided to play bold and attempt to reach the green with one shot straight over the trees)

bolt a putt: To hit a putt so hard that it is still travelling fast when it drops into the hole.

bomb: see *boom.*

boom: To hit a ball exceptionally hard, propelling it like a cannon shot. also *bomb.*

1. borrow: The distance a putt will curve over a sloping section of green. also *break, fall.*

2. borrow: To bias a putt to the left or right to compensate for the slope of a green.

both cheeks in it: Hit with full power. (got both cheeks in it and drove the ball to the edge of the green)

bounce and squeeze course: A short, tightly laid out course where placement is more valuable than long-distance drives.

brag tags: Tournament tags left on a golf bag. also *scare tags.*

brassie: A name for a number 2 wood with a brass plate on the sole, popular until numerical classifications for clubs were introduced in the 1920s.

brassy: see *brassie.*

1. break: The curvature of a putt, as over a sloping section of green. also *borrow, fall.*

2. break: To curve or deviate from a straight line, as of a ball over a sloping section of green.

break par: To finish a round of golf with a score less than the designated par for the course.

brillo: A stubby section of rough near a green.

British Open: An annual seventy-two-hole stroke play competition, open to qualified professionals and amateurs. The first Open was played in 1860 at Prestwick, Scotland, and won by pioneer professional golfer Willie Park. That first contest was thirty-six holes, which remained the format until Harold H. Hilton won the first seventy-two-hole British Open in 1892. The competition was called the "Open" not because both amateurs and professionals could compete, as they did from the second year on, but because after 1865, the tournament was "open" to any golfer who wanted to play, whether or not from around Prestwick. In 1922, Walter Hagen became the first American to win the British Open.

buggy top: A two-over-par seven.

bumpy green: A putting green with an uneven surface. also *peanut brittle.*

bungo: see *bingo, bango, bungo.*

1. bunker: A grassless area causing a "hazard" on a golf course, usually a sand trap. The original bunkers were hollowed-out holes made by sheep to protect them from the wind on the seaside courses of Scotland. see *sand trap.*

2. bunker: To drive a ball into a bunker.

bunkered: To be in a bunker.

bunkering: The configuration of a course's bunkers.

bunker trap: see *bunker.*

1. bunt: To deliberately hit a short shot.

2. bunt: A deliberately hit short shot.

buzzard: Slang for an over par hole for professional players.

bye: 1. The position of a player who, assigned no opponent, automatically advances to the next round of a match. 2. The holes remaining to be played after the winning side has been determined in a round of match play. When a player's lead is greater than the remaining holes (as in the case of ten holes won with eight remaining), the remaining holes are not played. Often, however, the remaining holes are played as a separate match. Holes remaining after this match has been decided (as three remaining after five holes won by one player) are called a "bye bye." If the three remaining holes of that match are then played as a separate game, and two holes are won by a player, the remaining hole is a "bye bye bye." also *bye hole.*

bye bye: see *bye.*

bye bye bye: see *bye.*

bye hole: see *bye.*

cabbage pounder: A player who spends a lot of time in the rough.

1. caddie: One who carries a golfer's

clubs and assists him in accordance with the rules during play. From the French word *cadet,* (pronounced "cahday"), a young military officer, an apprentice. When Mary, Queen of Scots, the first woman golfer, returned to Scotland from France in 1560, several French youths accompanied her to serve as pages and porters. Whether these "cadets" carried the Queen's clubs around when she played, or whether those who did were just likened to the cadets, golf club porters came to be known as "caddies," anglicized from "cahday." The first caddie on record was Andrew Dickson, who carried clubs for the Duke of York (later James II, King of England, Scotland, and Ireland) in Edinburgh in 1681 and 1682. also *caddy, stretcher bearer.*

2. caddie: To act as a caddie. also *caddy.*

caddie cart: A small two-wheel pullcart to which a golfer attaches his bag of clubs. also *cart, golf cart, trolley.*

caddy: see *caddie.*

Callaway System: A method of determining handicaps for unhandicapped players in stroke play, devised by golf pro Lionel F. Callaway in the 1950s. Under the Callaway System, a player's handicap is determined after each round by deducting from his gross score for eighteen holes the scores of the worst individual holes during the first sixteen holes played. A special copyrighted table shows the number of "worst hole" scores to be deducted and the adjustments to be made, based on the player's gross score.

1. can: see *hole.*

2. can: see *hole out.*

1. card: Short for scorecard.

2. card: To make a specific score.

carpet: A particularly smooth putting green.

carry: The distance a ball travels from where it is struck to where it first lands.

cart: see *caddie cart.*

casting: A flaw in a player's swing in which the wrists are released prematurely at the top of the downswing, as though "casting" a fishing line.

casual water: A puddle or other accumulated water that is visible before or after the player takes his stance, and that is temporary in nature and not a regular water hazard. Casual water itself is not considered a "hazard." At a player's option, he may move the ball without penalty within one club-length of a point that is not nearer the hole, not in a hazard or on a putting green, and that avoids interference by the condition.

cat box: see *sand trap.*

championship tees: see *blue tees.*

character builder: A 6-foot putt.

charge: 1. To hit a putt hard at the hole. 2. To play aggressively and well on a given day, with one good score after another.

chief: The number 1 wood. also *driver.*

chili dip: To strike behind the ball, digging up a large piece of turf.

1. chip: see *chip shot.*

2. chip: To make a chip shot. also *pitch and run.*

chipper: The club used to make a chip shot, as a number 5, 6, or 7 iron.

chippie: A chip shot that is holed, especially one that wins a bet for the player in an informal game. compare *greenie, sandie.*

chip shot: A short approach shot in which the ball is lofted in a low arc onto the green and rolls toward the pin. also *chip, pitch and run, run up shot.*

choke down: 1. To play a shot with less than the full power of the club used by lowering the hands down the shaft and narrowing the stance. 2. To grip a club with the hands placed lower than normal on the shaft.

chowder: To play poorly, whether on one shot, a hole, or a round. (might have had a good round if he hadn't chowdered the last two holes)

circuit: A series of scheduled professional tournaments held in different locations throughout the season, and competed in by the same players. also *tour.*

cleek: 1. The number 4 wood (approximately the same loft as the number 1 or number 2 iron). 2. The number 1 iron (the least lofted iron club except for the putter). Gaelic for a bent piece of iron, the term cleek and the other names for different clubs were popular until the introduction of club classification by numbers in the 1920s.

clock: To hit the ball well, with full power.

closed stance: A stance in which the front foot is closer to the line of play of the ball than the rear foot when the ball is addressed. compare *open stance, square stance.*

club: 1. A long thin shaft with a grip at the top and a wooden or steel head at the bottom used to hit a golf ball. The three major types of clubs are woods: long shafts with thick wooden heads, used for shots from the tee and some long shots on the fairway; irons: shorter than woods with thin steel heads, used for fairway and approach shots; and putters: the shortest of the clubs with thin metal heads, used to tap the ball across the putting green and into the cup. Originally, woods and irons were identified by individual names, but since the 1920s, they have been numbered in order of increasing loft (the angle at which the club face is tipped back), woods, 1 through 5, and irons, 2 through 9. The pitching wedge and the sand wedge are usually unnumbered. These two specialty irons have the greatest degree of loft and cause the highest and shortest flight of the ball. A golfer is permitted to carry up to fourteen clubs, usually three or four woods, seven or eight irons, a pitching wedge, a sand wedge, and a putter. also *golf club.* 2. An organization or establishment that provides playing facilities and instructional programs for members and their guests. also *golf club.*

club face: see *face.*

club head: see *head.*

clubhouse: A building on the grounds of a golf club where members and guests can change clothing, relax, and socialize.

club player: A better-than-average weekend player.

club pro, club professional: The resident professional player at a golf club, usually responsible for overseeing all aspects of the club's golf activities, including instructional programs, course scheduling, directing club tournaments, and administering an in-house golf shop. Although club pros cannot spend the time to play regularly on tour, they are qualified to play in local Sectional events and eligible for the annual PGA Club Professional Championship. also *home pro.*

collar: see *apron.*

commercial job: A cautious putt that is holed for a win, as might be featured in a television commercial.

Committee: The group of members or officials in charge of the course or a competition.

concede: To award a holed ball to an opponent whose ball lies close to the hole without requiring him to actually make the shot. The conceded putt is scored as one stroke.

course: see *golf course.*

course rating: The evaluation of the playing difficulty of a course compared with other rated courses, expressed in strokes and decimal fractions of a stroke for the purpose of providing a uniform basis on which to compute handicaps. Performed by a Rating Committee of the golf association having jurisdiction, course rating is based on the "yardage rating" of a course with adjustments for the condition and length of fairway grass, wetness, the overall tightness of the course and width of the fairways, the amount and proximity of rough, out of bounds areas, and hazards, the design, size, and condition of the greens, ground slope, altitude, and prevailing winds. compare *par, yardage rating.*

cowboy: A reckless and erratic player.

cow pasture pool: The game of golf. also *pasture pool.*

cripple: A long slow putt that barely reaches the hole and topples in.

Cuban: A shot in which the ball is sliced, and veers toward the side of the player's dominant hand. also *fade, slice.*

cup: see *hole.*

cuppy lie: Small depressions in the turf where the ball is positioned.

Curtis Cup Match: A biennial international women's amateur competition, hosted alternately by the United States and the British Isles. The match features foursomes and singles competitions at match play between teams of eight players each. Named after Miss Harriet S. Curtis (Women's Amateur Champion in 1906) and Miss Margaret Curtis (Women's Amateur Champion in 1907, 1911, and 1912), who donated the trophy. The first Curtis Cup Match was played in 1932 at the Wentworth Golf Club, Wentworth, England, and was won by the United States team 5-1/2 to 3-1/2.

cut: 1. In tournament competition, the elimination of golfers whose scores exceed a set maximum after a specified period of play (usually two rounds). (only the second time he has not made the thirty-six-hole cut) 2. see *dimple.*

cut shot: A sliced high-arcing shot with strong backspin.

dead: A ball positioned so close to the hole that the next shot is a "dead certainty."

Declaration of Independence: A score of seventy-six for a round. also *play the trombone.*

delicatessan department: A situation that requires a finesse shot.

designated tournament: A tournament determined by a players' association as one required for top-ranked players.

deuce: 1. A score of two strokes on a hole. 2. The number 2 iron.

dew sweeper: 1. The first or among the first players on the course in the morning. 2. The first or among the first professionals to tee off in the morning during a tournament, often a rookie.

dimple: 1. One of the small impressions on the surface of a ball that reduce wind resistance on a ball as it flies through the air. There are approximately 300 dimples on the modern ball. In the 1890s, "pimpled" balls with bumps instead of dimples were tried to help the ball grab when landing, but were discontinued when it was found that they cut air speed. Spalding popularized the dimpled ball in 1907 when the Glory Dimple and Baby Dimple balls were introduced. 2. A crease in the surface of a golf ball made by a misaimed (too high) swing with an iron. also *cut, smile.*

ding-dong: see *ham 'n egg.*

direction post: A marker on the course that indicates the correct line of play to a hidden fairway or blind green.

divot: A piece of turf dislodged by the club during a stroke. also *rug.*

divot repair: The immediate replacement of dug up or displaced turf as per the rules of golf etiquette.

dogleg: A slight but abrupt change of direction in a fairway.

dog license: The British expression for a win in match play by seven and six (seven holes won with six left to play). From the traditional price of a dog license in Great Britain, seven and six (seven shillings and sixpence).

Dolly Parton: see *roller coaster.*

do or die: A "bold" or risky shot, fruitful if successful, but costly if missed.

dormie: Ahead of an opponent or team in match play by as many holes as remain to be played. From the French word *endormi*, meaning asleep, because a dormie player cannot lose even if he goes to sleep. also *dormy*.

dormy: see *dormie*.

double bogey: Two strokes over par for a hole.

double-bogey: To score a double bogey. (double-bogeyed the last hole)

double eagle: Three strokes under par for a hole. also *albatross*.

double press: A press or separate bet on the holes remaining on an initial press. see *press*.

double-press: To initiate a second press, a separate bet on the holes remaining on a press. see *press*.

down: 1. Behind, as by a number of strokes or holes. (started the back nine two holes down) 2. Having holed out. (took another two strokes to get down after hitting the green)

downswing: The downward and forward sweep of the arms, hands, and club, beginning at the top of the backswing and ending when the ball is contacted.

1. drain: see *hole*.

2. drain: To hole the ball. (drained it with one putt) see *hole out*.

1. draw: 1. The method by which pairings and order of play are decided in match play, the results to be published as a draw list or draw sheet. 2. The order of competitors' names as drawn and listed on a draw list or draw sheet. 3. A shot in which the player purposely hooks the ball. see *hook*. compare *Cuban, cut shot, fade, slice*.

2. draw: 1. To randomly pick the names of competitors in match play for a draw list or draw sheet. 2. To be paired with a particular opponent as a result of a draw. (drew a tough opponent for the first round) 3. To purposely hook the ball. (a difficult shot that required him to draw the ball to the left) also *pull*. see *hook*. compare *Cuban, fade, slice*.

draw list, draw sheet: An official roster of match play competitors, match-ups, and playing order based on the results of a draw.

dreadnought: A type of driver popular in the early 1900s, distinguishable by an oversized head.

1. drive: To hit the ball for distance, usually from the tee.

2. drive: A hard stroke hit from the tee toward the green.

drive and a kick: A short par-four hole.

drive for show, putt for dough: A popular axiom among professional golfers that indicates that, while driving may be more spectacular, getting the ball into the hole wins the money.

driver: A number 1 wood, used to drive the ball from the tee. also *chief*.

drive the green: To reach the putting green in one shot from the tee, especially on a hole where the par is more than three.

driving cleek: see *driving iron*.

driving iron: A number 1 iron; called a driving iron until numerical classifications for clubs were introduced in the 1920s. also *driving cleek, knife*.

driving range: A special area featuring marked distances where players can practice driving and other shots and take instruction.

1. drop: 1. To take a replacement for a lost ball or one in a water hazard, or to move a ball from an unplayable lie or ground under repair (under the Rules or Local Rules) by dropping it over one's shoulder while facing the hole so that it comes to rest no closer to the hole than where it originally lay, and within two club-lengths of where it first struck the ground. Dropping a ball often carries a one stroke penalty, depending on specific circumstances. 2. see *hole out*.

2. drop: The act of dropping the ball.

drown it: To hit the ball into water.

1. dub: An unskilled or inept player. Use of the slang term "dub" for a clumsy or bumbling person dates back to the mid-1880s in the United States.

2. dub: To hit the ball poorly. also *duff*.

duck hook: A low, sharply hooking shot.

duck-hook: To hit a low, sharply hooking shot. (duck-hooked his drive into the rough)

1. duff: A misplayed shot. also *fluff, foozle*.

2. duff: To misplay a shot. also *dub*.

duffer: An inexperienced, occasional golfer; one who is not particularly skillful.

dunk: To hole the ball. (dunked a 2-footer to win the hole) also *can, drain, drop, hole out, sink*.

1. eagle: Two strokes under par for a hole.

2. eagle: To make an eagle. (eagled the two last holes to win the round)

Egyptian Bermuda: see *sand trap*.

eight iron: An iron used to make approach shots to the green of 120 to 150 yards.

Known formerly as a lofter, lofting iron, and pitching niblick.

even par: A score of par for a hole or a round.

executive course, executive length course: A short (most often nine holes), less demanding course, usually designed to accommodate older players.

exempt player: A player whose past record makes him eligible to compete in a tournament without first qualifying. The American innovation of exempting proven performers began in 1920, when the first thirty-one PGA players to finish the U.S. Open were declared exempt from having to qualify for the PGA Championship.

explosion shot: see *blast*.

extra hole: see *sudden-death hole*.

face: The flat front surface of the head of a club with which the ball is struck. The angle at which the face is set regulates the amount of loft in a club. The higher the number of the club, the greater the angle and degree of loft. also *club face*.

1. **fade:** To purposely slice a ball. see *slice*. compare *draw, hook, pull*.

2. **fade:** A shot in which the ball is purposely sliced. see *slice*. compare *draw, hook*.

fairway: The specially prepared turf between the teeing ground and the green, excluding hazards.

fairway house: A house built close to a fairway on a golf course.

fall: see *borrow*.

fast green: A dry, fast-running green.

fastest foot in the South: Said of a player who often nudges the ball into a better lie in the rough.

1. **fat:** 1. Striking the ball low, sometimes digging up the turf behind the ball. also *heavy*. 2. Higher and shorter in distance than intended because of the club striking the ground behind the ball on a stroke, or striking the ball low. (hit it fat and ended up short of the green)

2. **fat:** The wide part of a putting green.

five iron: The iron used for approach shots to the green of approximately 160 yards. Formerly known as a mashie. also *nickel*.

five wood: The most lofted wood, sometimes used for getting out of difficult lies in the rough. Formerly known as a baffy, and a baffing spoon.

flagstick: A thin movable pole that is anchored upright in the cup, circular in cross-section, often bearing a numbered flag. also *pin, pole*.

flat iron, flat stick: A putter, a flat-faced iron with no loft.

flats: The lay-up area in front of the green.

flier: A high-trajectory shot with overspin that usually travels farther than desired.

flippy wrists: An inconsistency or weakness in putting.

fluff: see *duff*.

follow through: The continuation of the

swing after the club head makes contact with the ball.

foozle: see *duff.*

fore: The traditional vocal warning to golfers who might be playing ahead that a shot is about to be taken or that a ball is in flight. An Old English word meaning "in front."

forecaddie: A caddie employed by the Committee to be stationed ahead on the fairway in order to be able to indicate to players the position of balls on the course, considered an "outside agency."

forward press: A deliberate or involuntary slight movement of the body in a forward direction just before the backswing. also *press.*

four-ball: A match in which four players compete, with two on each side, and in which the better scorer between the two partners on one side is matched against the better scorer from the other side for each hole. Four-ball can be either match play or stroke play.

four iron: A long-range iron used for distances of approximately 170 to 180 yards. Formerly known as an approach cleek, and a mashie iron.

foursome: 1. A match in which four players compete, two to a side, with each side playing only one ball which the partners take turns hitting. also *Scotch foursome.* 2. A group of four players, two to a side, with each side playing only one ball which the players take turns hitting. In the United States and Canada, the term "foursome" is sometimes used inaccurately to describe a four-ball match, or simply to describe a group of four players, each playing his own ball and competing against the others. also *match foursome, Scotch foursome.*

four wood: A wooden club used for fairway shots of approximately 200 yards. Formerly known as a cleek.

free drop: A drop sometimes allowed by Local Rules when a ball lands in an unplayable lie and that does not incur a penalty stroke.

fresh air shot: see *whiff.*

fried egg: A ball that is buried in the sand.

fringe: see *apron.*

frisbee: A low, skulled shot.

froghair: see *apron.*

front nine: The first nine holes on an eight-

een-hole course. also *out nine.* compare *back nine.*

full stroke: A stroke in which the ball is hit "pure," with the sweet spot of the club head making contact with the ball.

fungo: One of a series of practice shots when not engaged in a match. From the baseball term for practice fly balls hit to players before a game with a special bat.

gallery: The fans and spectators at a golf tournament.

gamble hole: A hole laid out in such a way as to invite a bold or risky shot that would bring a considerable advantage if properly executed, but disastrous results if not.

gamesmanship: The science and/or practice of causing an opponent to experience confusion, anxiety, the loss of confidence or concentration by one's words and actions before and during a match. British golfer Steven Potter popularized the notion of gamesmanship in his 1947 book, *The Theory and Practice of Gamesmanship.*

gangsome: Slang for a group of more than four players.

gimme: A short putt that is conceded or given to an opponent.

Ginsberg: 1. A timid but successful putt, one that appears soft but is well-planned. 2. A free shot with a second ball sometimes permitted in informal play when a golfer's original ball is mishit, and that the player may then, at

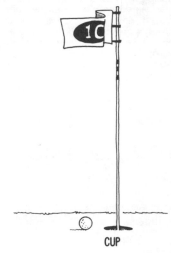

CUP

201

his option, choose to continue play with, rather than the original ball. compare *mulligan, Shapiro.*

gobble: An old name for a fast putt that drops into the hole, one that would have gone a long way past had it not been "gobbled" by the hole.

golf: A game in which one or more players (often groups of two to four), using several different clubs (up to fourteen) try to knock a small resilient ball into nine or eighteen holes in sequence, placed strategically over an outdoor course among hazards of sand, water, trees, and rough in the fewest possible number of strokes. When playing alone, a golfer competes against par (a specified number of strokes an expert golfer would need to complete a particular hole or course, based on the distance of the hole from the tee), or attempts to reduce his handicap (a specified number of strokes an amateur player is permitted to subtract from his score in order to be able to compete fairly against better players, determined by the golfer's past performance on a particular course). When more than one golfer plays, a round (usually eighteen holes) may be scored according to stroke play (the player with the lowest total number of strokes wins) or match play (strokes counted to determine a winner at each hole, with the winner of the most holes winning the round). A player may compete against all other players; against the best score of a partnered pair; with a partner against two other players, each playing a ball, with the lowest score for each hole winning that hole (four-ball); or with a partner against two other players, with each team playing alternate shots with a single ball (a foursome). Rules infractions can result in the addition of penalty strokes to a player's score or the loss of a hole in match play. There is still some question about the origin of the

word golf. It is now thought to be derived from the German *kolbe,* which, like the Dutch *kolf* and French *chole,* means club. All, in their earlier forms (*kolben,* the Icelandic *kolfr,* and Old High German *cholbo*), have been attributed by some etymologists to a hypothetic Gothic word *kulban,* meaning a knobbed stick. also *cow pasture pool, pasture pool.*

golf bag: A large bag designed to carry golf clubs and accessories, first used in the late 1800s. By the 1930s, golf bags had grown large and heavy, necessitating the invention of the two-wheel caddie cart. also *tool chest.*

golf ball: A spherically symmetrical ball consisting of a compressed solid rubber or liquid-filled rubber center wrapped tightly with rubber thread, and covered by a dimpled hard rubber composition, measuring not less than 1.680 inches in diameter and weighing not more than 1.620 ounces (USGA specifications) or measuring not less than 1.620 inches in diameter and weighing not more than 1.620 ounces (Royal and Ancient Golf Club of St. Andrews specifications). Strict guidelines also limit the liveliness, velocity, and distance (USGA only) specifications of a ball. In golf's earliest days, the ball was made of feathers stuffed as tightly as possible into a small bag of thin leather. Of varying quality and liveliness, the early ball could not be driven farther than a maximum of 175 yards. In 1848, the gutta-percha (or guttie) ball was introduced that could be driven over 200 yards. Perfectly round, the guttie, along with closely mowed greens, made the modern rolling putt possible. After noting the improvement in the flight stability of a marked or worn ball, indentations were first hand-hammered, then molded into the ball around 1880. In the 1890s, a pimpled ball was tried (with bumps rather than the normal 300 or more surface dimples on a modern ball) in the hopes that it would better grab the turf on landing. Instead, it was found that the bumps cut air speed. The modern rubber-cored, thread-wound golf ball was invented by American Coburn Haskell in 1899, but became popular only after it was used by Walter Travis to win the 1901 U.S. Amateur Championship, and by Alex "Sandy" Herd to

BALL ON THE FAIRWAY

win the 1901 British Open. also *ball.*

golf car: see *golf cart.*

golf cart: 1. A light battery-powered three- or four-wheel vehicle used to ride around the course, usually accommodating two golfers and their clubs. First popularized in the 1950s. also *golf car.* 2. A two-wheel pullcart to which a golf bag is attached. also *caddie cart, cart, trolley.*

golf club: see *club.*

golf course: A specially constructed and maintained course over which the game of golf is played, consisting of nine or eighteen holes, in most cases laid out 300 to 500 yards apart. Each hole consists of a teeing ground where the ball is put into play, a well-kept grass fairway, strategically placed natural or artificial hazards (such as a body of water or a sand trap), uncut areas of rough, and a well-trimmed area of short grass around the hole, a putting green. Most eighteen-hole golf courses are between 6300 and 7000 yards in total length, with an average tee-to-hole distance of 300 to 500 yards, though every hole and every golf course is unique. The most famous golf course in the world is the Old Course at St. Andrews in Scotland, home of the Royal and Ancient Golf Club of St. Andrews, founded in 1754. also *course, golf links, links.*

golf course architect: One who designs and supervises the construction of golf courses. The American Society of Golf Course Architects is headquartered in Chicago, Illinois.

golfdom: The realm and pertaining to the realm of golf and golfers.

golfer: One who plays golf.

golfing: The sport of golf or the action of playing it.

golf links: see *golf course.*

golf shoes: Leather shoes with sharp metal spikes for gripping the turf.

golf widow: The wife of a golfer who devotes most of his spare time to playing golf; one who has "lost" her husband to golf.

grain: The direction in which the grass grows on a putting green. (a short putt, but against the grain)

grand slam: A victory in the four major men's or women's golf tournaments (the United States Open, the British Open, the Masters, and the PGA Champion-

ship for men; the Women's Open Championship, the LPGA Championship, the Peter Jackson Classic, and the Nabisco-Dinah Shore for women) by one player in the same year. Only one player in history has won the men's grand slam, legendary amateur golfer Robert T. "Bobby" Jones of Atlanta, Georgia. Jones accomplished this remarkable feat in 1930, at which time the four major tournaments were the British Amateur, the British Open, the USGA Open, and the USGA Amateur. As professional golf gained dominance over amateur competition after World War II, the two amateur-only events were replaced by the Masters Tournament and PGA Championships as a part of the grand slam.

green: A smooth, closely shorn grass area surrounding the hole toward which the ball is played. Originally, "green" referred to the whole course, a meaning that survives in the term "greenkeeper" and the expression "through the green." also *putting green.*

green fee: A fee paid in order to play on a golf course. In the early days of the sport, golf courses were often located on a village green, and it became common practice to charge a fee to provide for their upkeep. also *greens fee.*

greenie: A shot that reaches the green (as from the tee on a par 3 hole) and lies closest to the pin, frequently the object of a bet in a casual game. compare *chippie, sandie.*

greenkeeper: The individual responsible for the preparation and maintenance of a golf course.

greens fee: see *green fee.*

greenside: At or adjacent to a putting green.

greensome foursome: A type of match in informal play in which all four players in

BALL IN THE ROUGH

a foursome drive a ball off the tee before each side selects one ball to continue playing the hole.

grip: 1. The manner in which a golf club is held. The three major grips used in golf are the overlapping grip or Vardon grip, the interlocking grip, and the ten-finger grip or baseball grip, differing mainly in the proximity of and relationship between the little finger of the bottom hand (right hand for a righthanded golfer) and the forefinger of the top hand. 2. The top part of the shaft of the golf club, covered with a rubber, leather, or leatherlike material to facilitate gripping by the hands. Regulations call for a grip to be substantially straight and plain, with channels, furrows, or molding for any part of the hands not permitted.

grooved swing: A well-practiced swing that can be repeated consistently, as though following a "groove."

gross score: The total number of strokes, before subtracting a handicap, taken to play a hole or a round. compare *net score.*

ground one's club: To place the club head on the ground behind the ball when addressing the ball. It is against the rules to ground a club when a ball is being played from a "hazard," resulting in the loss of the hole in match play, or two penalty strokes in stroke play.

gruesome: Slang for a mixed foursome. also *quarrelsome.*

hacker: A poor golfer.

Hall of Fame: see *LPGA Hall of Fame, PGA Hall of Fame, World Golf Hall of Fame.*

halve: To score an identical number of strokes on a hole or round as the opposing player or team in match play. (halved the first two holes before winning the next three)

hammers: Slang for golf clubs. also *bats, hickories, shooting irons, sticks, tools, weapons.*

ham 'n egg: To play well with a partner, either because of complementary skills or offsetting luck. also *ding-dong.*

handicap: A specified number of strokes an amateur player is permitted to subtract from his score in order to be able to compete fairly against better players, determined by the golfer's past performance on a particular course. A golfer's handicap is computed as 96

percent of the average differential between the course rating (not par) and the player's ten lowest rounds in the last twenty rounds played. A golfer's handicap may be subtracted in stroke play from his total score at the end of a round or at specific "stroke holes" noted on the scorecard. In match play, one or more strokes may be subtracted from the score at each hole or at specified holes. compare *plus handicap.*

handicapper: A golfer who has a specified handicap. (rounded out the foursome with a thirteen handicapper)

handicap stroke hole: see *stroke hole.*

hand mashie shot: A thrown ball.

hang: To stop rolling or be situated on sloping ground. (hung a chip shot just above the sand trap)

hanging lie: A ball resting on sloping ground.

hazard: An area of ground covered by sand (bunker) or water (water hazard, lateral water hazard), strategically placed in or adjacent to a fairway in order to present a special challenge to a golfer. A player is not permitted to ground his club behind a ball situated in a hazard. see *bunker, lateral water hazard, water hazard.*

head: The thickened part of a golf club at the end of the shaft, the "face" or front surface of which makes contact with the ball. also *club head.*

head up: A fault in a swing in which the head is raised and the eyes taken off the ball before it is hit, usually resulting in a poor stroke.

heavy: see *fat.*

heel: The part of the club attached to the shaft.

hello God: see *sky ball.*

hickories: Slang for golf clubs. The term comes from the fact that often golf club shafts were made of hickory before steel shafts were made legal in 1929. also *bats, hammers, shooting irons, sticks, tools, weapons.*

hit on the hat: see *top.*

hit on the screws: see *hit pure.*

hit pure: To make perfect contact with the ball, to hit the ball well. also *hit on the screws.*

hit the Chief: To use the number 1 wood or driver.

hit the deuce: To use the number 2 iron.

hit the nickel: To use the number 5 iron.

hockey it in: To sink a fairly good putt.

1. hole: 1. The small cavity into which the ball is played, 4-1/4 inches in diameter and at least 4 inches deep. also *can, cup, drain, pot, puttoon.* 2. A division (usually one of nine or eighteen) of a golf course, comprised of a tee, a fairway, and the putting green on which the hole is located.

2. hole: To drive or knock the ball into a hole. (holed it in three strokes to break par) see *hole out.*

holeable: A putt that appears to be reasonably easy for a golfer to sink.

hole high: A situation in which the ball stops even with the hole on one side or the other, such as in an approach shot. also *pin high.*

1. hole in one: A ball played from the tee into the hole in one stroke. also *ace, solitaire.*

2. hole in one: To hit a ball into the hole in one stroke from the tee. (took the lead on the eighteenth, which he holed in one) also *ace.*

hole out: To sink the ball into the cup. (took him four strokes to hole out) also *can, drain, drop, dunk, hole, sink.*

Hollywood handicap: A handicap that is based more on pride or vanity than on ability.

home hole: The final hole of a course or a round.

home pro: see *club pro.*

honor: The privilege of playing first from the teeing ground, decided by lot or draw on the first hole, and given to the winner of the previous hole thereafter.

hood the club: To lessen the loft of a club by addressing the ball so that it is positioned near the back foot, then diminishing the angle of the club face by advancing the hands so that they are forward of the ball at the moment of contact. also *shut the face.*

1. hook: A shot in which the ball is made to veer to the side opposite the dominant hand of the player. also *draw.* compare *Cuban, fade, slice.*

2. hook: To hit the ball in such a way as to cause it to veer to the side opposite the dominant hand of the player. also *draw, pull.* compare *Cuban, fade, slice.*

hooker: A player with a tendency to hook.

Hoover: A "sweeping" hook.

hosel: The socket in the head of a golf club into which the shaft is fitted.

hospital zone: The practice tee on a golf course.

1. hustle: To make or seek to make an unethical wager on a match, as by hiding one's true skill level or some advantage.

●●To unethically take advantage or seek to take advantage of someone by deception.

2. hustle: The act or an instance of hustling.

hustler: A player who makes money or attempts to make money by wagering on his matches, especially one who hides expertise or some advantage in order to attract less skilled opponents. One who seeks to make or win money by deception.

in: The last nine holes of an eighteen-hole course. (made par all the way in)

inchworm: A player who cheats a little bit every time he marks his ball on the green.

in jail: A ball mishit into trees, a bunker, or the rough.

in regulation: On the green in the prescribed number of strokes enabling the player to make par with two putts.

inside the leather: Close enough to the hole to be conceded. A reference to the common practice in informal play of conceding any ball closer to the cup than the length of the leather or rubber grip of a putter. also *in the leather.*

interlocking grip: A method of gripping a golf club in which the little finger of the lower hand (right hand for a right-handed golfer) interlocks with the forefinger of the top hand. compare *baseball grip, ten-finger grip, overlapping grip.*

in the clubhouse: A term used to describe a player who has completed his score.

in the leather: see *inside the leather.*

in to out: A swing in which the club is taken back and the downswing begun inside the line of flight, crossing to the outside of the line of flight as the ball is contacted.

Irish birdie: A score of one stroke under par for a hole, resulting from the use of a "mulligan." see *mulligan.*

iron: A club with a medium-length shaft and a relatively thin steel head, used to make shots from the fairway, the rough, and often from within a hazard. Though a number 1 iron or "driving iron" was once popular, irons are usually numbered from 2 through 9 in order of increasing loft (the angle at which the club face is tipped back). Two special and usually unnumbered irons, the pitching wedge and the sand wedge, have the greatest degree of loft and cause the highest and shortest flight of the ball. Though a putter is usually made of steel, it is not considered an iron.

jigger: A special thin, fin-faced iron club, used in the past for running up shots to the green.

jungle: In the rough. also *tiger country*.

junk man: An unstylish golfer who appears ineffectual off the tee and on the fairway, but always seems to arrive at the green in time to salvage a par or a bogey.

kickers' tournament: A competition for golfers with no established handicap in which participants choose a handicap that they estimate will bring their adjusted score for a round to within established parameters (such as between sixty-five and eighty). At the end of the

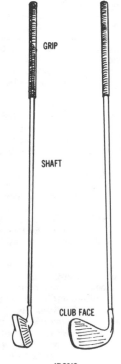

GRIP

SHAFT

CLUB FACE

IRONS

round, the player whose adjusted score matches or is closest to a number drawn by the Committee from within the established parameters wins. also *blind bogey*.

knife: see *one iron*.

knockout competition: An tournament in which players compete in pairs for a round of golf, the loser being eliminated from competition. The winner of each round moves to the next higher level to compete with other winners. At each level of play, the losers are "knocked out" of the tournament.

Ladies Professional Golf Association: The organization responsible for overseeing professional tournament golf for women. Founded in 1950, the Ladies Professional Golf Association is now headquartered in Houston, Texas, and is comprised of a Tournament Division and a Teaching Division. also *LPGA*.

ladies' tees: see *women's tees*.

lag up: see *lay up*.

1. lateral: see *shank*.

2. lateral: A shanked ball.

lateral water hazard: A water hazard running parallel or approximately parallel to the line of play. When a ball is hit into a lateral water hazard and is lost or unplayable, the player may, under penalty of one stroke, drop the ball (or a new ball) behind the hazard on a line formed by the hole and the point where the ball last crossed the margin of the hazard; play the ball (or a new ball) from the point where the original stroke was made; or drop the ball (or a new ball) outside the hazard within two club-lengths of the point where the ball last crossed the margin of the hazard or a point on the opposite margin of the hazard equidistant from the hole, so long as the ball comes to rest no nearer the hole than the point where the ball last crossed the margin of the hazard. Lateral water hazards are marked by short red stakes or by red lines.

lay up: To intentionally hit a ball short (as on a fairway or approach shot) to prevent it from going into a hazard. also *lag up*.

leaderboard: see *scoreboard*.

licorice sticks: Golf clubs with graphite shafts. also *soul poles*.

1. lie: 1. The position of a ball that has come to rest after a stroke. (not allowed to improve the lie) 2. The angle

at which the club head is attached to
the shaft.
2. **lie**: To occupy a location. (if hit proper-
ly, the ball will lie just outside the trap
at the edge of the green)
like as we lie: An old expression indicating
that the opposing sides have played the
same number of strokes at a hole.
line: The correct direction that a ball
should travel toward the green or hole.
For every shot, from the longest drive
to the shortest putt, there is a correct
line.
line up: To "read" or sight the line for
one's next shot.
links: A golf course. A Scottish word for
the rolling sandy coastal land that was
the site of many early golf courses. Pos-
sibly derived from the Old English word
hlinc, meaning a ridge of land. see *golf
course*.
linksman: A golfer.
lip: see *rim*.
lip out: see *rim*.
litter box: see *sand trap*.
Local Rules: Official rules that take into
consideration temporary and/or abnor-
mal conditions at a particular golf
course, published by the Committee.
1. **loft**: 1. The angle at which the face of a
club is slanted back (away from verti-
cal). Since the 1920s, golf clubs have
been numbered in order of increasing
loft (woods, 1 through 5, and irons, 2
through 9). Two usually unnumbered
irons, the pitching wedge and the sand
wedge, have the greatest degree of loft
and cause the highest and shortest flight
of the ball. 2. A stroke that causes the
ball to be lofted in an arc. 3. The height
of the arc of a lofted ball.
2. **loft**: To hit a ball in a high arc. (lofted
the ball over the water onto the green)
lofter: A number 8 iron, popularly called a
lofter until numerical classifications for
clubs were introduced in the 1920s. also
lofting iron, pitching niblick.
lofting iron: see *lofter*.
long game: The longer shots, as those
from the tee, or those made with
wooden clubs and low-number irons.
long iron: A low-lofted iron (such as a 1,
2, or 3 iron) for making long-distance
shots.
long knocker: A player who hits long
drives.
long steal: 1. A come-from-behind victory
in match play. 2. A long putt.

loop: Caddie slang for an eighteen-hole
round.
loose impediment: A natural object around
the ball or in the line of play that is
loose and movable and does not
adhere to the ball, such as a pebble or
stone not solidly embedded, an unroot-
ed leaf, twig, or branch, an insect, or
dung. Sand and loose soil are loose
impediments on the putting green, but
not elsewhere on the course. The play-
er may elect whether to consider snow
and ice a loose impediment or casual
water. Loose impediments may be
removed without penalty unless the ball
and the impediment are both in a
hazard.
lost ball: A ball remaining unlocated or
unidentified after a five-minute search;
or one given up as "lost" and replaced
by a new ball that is played, whether
or not a search is made for the original
ball; or one replaced by a "provisional
ball" that has been played from a point
nearer the hole than the place where
the original ball is likely to be (provi-
sional ball automatically becomes the
ball in play). When a ball is lost outside
a water hazard or is hit out of bounds,
a new ball may be played as near as
possible to the spot from which the
original ball was played with the addi-
tion of a penalty stroke to the player's
score for the hole. see *lateral water
hazard, provisional ball, water
hazard*.
LPGA:. The Ladies Professional Golf Asso-
ciation.
LPGA Championship: The LPGA's own
annual stroke play competition for
women professional golfers, one of the
four major tournaments that together
comprise the women's grand slam. The
first LPGA Championship was played in
1955 at the Orchard Ridge Country
Club in Fort Wayne, Indiana, and won
by Beverly Hanson.
LPGA Hall of Fame: The institution that
honors outstanding women professional
golfers. Originally a part of the
Women's Golf Hall of Fame founded in
Augusta, Georgia in 1950, the LPGA
Hall of Fame became a separate entity
in 1967, moving to one wing of the
World Golf Hall of Fame in Pinehurst,
North Carolina in 1977, and in 1982, to
its present location in Houston, Texas. In
order to be selected for membership in

the Hall of Fame, a woman must have been a member of the LPGA for ten consecutive years and have won thirty official Tour events including at least two different major championships, or thirty-five official Tour events including at least one major championship, or forty official Tour events. The first women to be elected to the LPGA Hall of Fame in 1951 were Patty Berg, Betty Jameson, Louise Suggs, and all-around athlete and Olympic champion Mildred "Babe" Didrikson Zaharias.

lumber city: A long course that requires many fairway wood shots.

magic wand: A favored club, with which a player experiences success, often a putter.

marker: 1. One who is appointed by the Committee to record a competitor's score in stroke play, sometimes a fellow competitor. 2. A small object (often a coin or a flat disc) left on the green to indicate the position of a golfer's ball when it must be lifted.

mashie: A number 5 iron, which at the end of the nineteenth century was the most lofted club in a normal set. The term "mashie" became less popular when numerical classifications for clubs were introduced in the 1920s. John Henry Taylor, five-time winner of the British Open (1894, 1895, 1900, 1909, 1913) was among the first to popularize the mashie, with which he developed an amazing mastery of the cut shot.

mashie-iron: A number 4 iron, popularly called a mashie-iron until numerical classifications for clubs were introduced in the 1920s. also *approach cleek.*

mashie-niblick: A number 7 iron, popularly called a mashie-niblick until numerical classifications for clubs were introduced in the 1920s.

Masters, Masters Tournament: An invitational open tournament held annually since 1934 (except in World War II years 1943-45) at the Augusta National Golf Club in Georgia. First won in 1934 by Horton Smith, the Masters got its name from the fact that the first competition was restricted to current and past tournament winners, and still ranks as one of the most prestigious events in the sport of golf.

match: A game of golf in which two or more players compete.

match foursome: see *foursome.*

match play: Play based on the number of holes won by an individual or a side in a round. Each hole is either won (fewer strokes), halved (an equal amount of strokes), or lost (more strokes), with the individual or side who wins the most holes winning the round. compare *medal play, stroke play.*

medalist: The low scorer in a stroke play qualifying round of a tournament.

medal play: see *stroke play.*

medium iron: see *mid-iron.*

member's bounce, member's kick: A favorable or lucky bounce.

merry: A British expression meaning too strong or too far, as of a putt. (the crucial putt was a bit merry)

middle iron: see *mid-iron.*

mid-iron: A medium-lofted iron for making medium distance shots, such as a number 4, 5, or 6 iron. also *medium iron, middle iron.*

mid-mashie: A number 3 iron, popularly called a mid-mashie until numerical classifications for clubs were introduced in the 1920s.

miniature golf: An informal putting game played over a small, specially constructed course (usually with a synthetic playing surface), consisting of a number of holes, each containing a series of strategically placed obstacles that the ball must travel through, over, under, or between in order to reach a tunnel, ramp, or channel that then advances the ball to the hole. The object of the game is to complete the course in the fewest number of strokes.

miss the green: To fail to reach the green in regulation. (missed the green, but scrambled to make par)

mixed foursome: A foursome made up of a man and a woman on each side. John Reid, one of the five founding members of the USGA in 1894, took part in the first reported mixed foursome in 1889 in Yonkers, New York. A mixed foursome is sometimes facetiously called a "gruesome" or "quarrelsome."

Mod-Sod: A brand of artificial turf made by Playfield Industries and used for synthetic tees and putting greens. First installed in 1980 at the PGA Tour's "Wee Links," a prototype low-maintenance six-hole course at the Walt Disney World Golf Resort in Florida.

moving day: The day following the thirty-six-hole cut in a professional tournament.

Mr. Aerosol: A name for a player who is a spray hitter.

mug hunter: see *sandbagger.*

mulligan: A free shot to compensate for a mishit ball, sometimes permitted in a casual game. Named after Canadian golfer David Mulligan. In the late 1920s, Mulligan, who provided transportation to the golf course for his regular foursome, was given a second ball after mishitting his drive off the first tee with hands still numb from driving over rough roads and a particularly bumpy bridge at the course entrance. also *Shapiro.*

Nabisco-Dinah Shore: An annual stroke play competition for women professional golfers, designated as one of the four major tournaments that together comprise the women's grand slam. Held at the Mission Hills Country Club in Rancho Mirage, California, the event (formerly the Colgate-Dinah Shore) was first won in 1972 by Jane Blalock.

nap: The physical characteristics of the surface of a putting green, as the length, thickness, and direction of growth.

Nassau, Nassau bet: A basis for betting in a casual game. Players make bets on the outcome of play on the first nine holes, on the second nine holes, and on the complete eighteen holes. Originally from a system of scoring in which one point was awarded to the winner of the first nine holes, one point to the winner of the second nine holes, and one point to the winner of the entire nineteen holes. Invented at the Nassau Country Club in Glen Cove, Long Island in New York at the turn of the century, reportedly to save face for local club members who, thereafter, were spared having to read newspaper accounts about losing team matches by more than three points.

National Golf Foundation: A nonprofit organization supported by the major manufacturers of golf equipment to promote the growth of the sport. Founded in 1936 by golf journal publishers Herb and Joe Graffis, the National Golf Foundation collects and publishes golf records and statistics, instructional programs, and educational materials about the planning and management of golf courses. The Foundation is headquartered in North Palm Beach, Florida.

National Open: The U.S. Open. also *open.*

NC: see *no card.*

neck: The thin part of a club head near the area where the shaft is attached. also *socket.*

net score: The total number of strokes taken to play a hole or a round after a player's handicap is deducted. compare *gross score.*

never up, never in: A golf axiom meaning that a ball that fails to reach the hole cannot possibly go in.

niblick: A number 9 iron. Four-time British Open winner Tom Morris Jr. (1868, 1869, 1870, 1872) popularized the use of the niblick for short pitch shots. The term "niblick" became less popular when numerical classifications for clubs were introduced in the 1920s.

nickel: A number 5 iron.

nine iron: An iron club with a high degree of loft, used for distances of approximately 120 yards. Formerly known as a niblick.

nineteenth hole: 1. The clubhouse bar. 2. An extra or "sudden-death hole" played to decide a match that ends up all square after eighteen holes. In such a case, the first hole is played again as the "nineteenth hole." see *sudden-death hole.*

no card: 1. No score for a round, marked NC on a scorecard. also *NC.* 2. A withdrawal from a tournament. also *NC, North Carolina.*

no deposit: see *out of bounds.*

nonreturnable: see *out of bounds.*

North Carolina: Slang among professional players for no card, or the withdrawal from a tournament. also *NC.*

nudging: The act or an instance of moving a ball to a better lie with the end of one's club, not allowed by the Rules of Golf, but sometimes permitted in informal play by local winter rules.

OB: Out of bounds. see *out of bounds.*

observer: One appointed by the Committee to assist a referee to decide questions of fact and to report to him any breach of a Rule or Local Rule.

obstruction: An artificial object that hinders normal play. Obstructions include anything built, placed, or left on the course, but does not include objects that define out of bounds (walls, fences, stakes, railings, etc.), artificially surfaced banks or beds in water hazards (including bridge supports on such a bank), and any construction declared by the Committee to be an integral part of the course. A movable obstruction may be moved if it interferes with the player's stance or intended area of his swing, or the ball may be lifted and dropped (not closer to the hole) away froi ၁ obstruction, without penalty.

odd: 1. One more stroke than used for a hole by one's opponent. 2. A handicap stroke deducted from the hole score of an opponent.

old man par: A slang expression for par, popularized by grand slam winner Bobby Jones, who claimed that during a match, he never played his opponent, but played against "old man par."

one iron: An old iron club with little loft, used to make shots of approximately 190 to 200 yards. Formerly known as a driving cleek or driving iron. also *knife.*

on the amateur side: Having missed a putt by underestimating the borrow or break of a ball over a sloping section of green. compare *on the professional side.*

on the professional side: Having missed a putt because of overestimating the borrow or break of a ball over a sloping section of green. compare *on the amateur side.*

on the dance floor: Having reached or on the putting green. The expression "on the dance floor" was popularized in the 1980s by Australian professional golfer and television commentator Bruce Devlin.

1. open: Enterable by both amateur and professional players.

2. open: A tournament that is open to both amateur and professional players, such as the U.S. Open.

Open: The U.S. Open. also *National Open.*

open stance: A stance in which the rear foot is closer to the line of play of the ball than the front foot when the ball is addressed. compare *closed stance, square stance.*

Oral Roberts: Slang among professionals for a shot mishit with the heel of a club, or a shot that is "well-heeled."

out: The first nine holes of an eighteen-hole course. (held the lead going out) compare *in.*

out nine: see *front nine.*

out of bounds: Ground on which play is prohibited, determined by the Committee, and marked by a fence, stakes, or a line on the ground. When a fence or stakes are used to define out of bounds, the boundary line is determined by the nearest inside edges of the fence posts or stakes. When a line is used to define out of bounds, the line itself is out of bounds. A ball is out of bounds when all of it lies out of bounds. When a ball is hit out of bounds, the stroke is replayed from as near as possible to the spot from which the original ball was played, and a penalty stroke is added to the player's score. also *no deposit, nonreturnable, OB.*

outside agency: Any person, being, or object that is not part of a match, or in stroke play, not part of a competitor's side (including any official appointed by the Committee). When a moving ball is stopped or deflected by an outside agency, it is considered a "rub of the green" and the ball is played as it lies, without penalty. When a ball lodges in a moving or animate outside agency, the player may drop a ball (or on the putting green, place a ball) as near as possible to the spot where the object was when the ball lodged in it, without penalty. A ball that is accidentally stopped or deflected by an opponent, his caddie, or equipment, may be played as it lies or cancelled and replayed from the spot where the ball previously lay.

overlapping grip: A method of gripping a golf club in which the little finger of the lower hand (right hand for a right-handed golfer) rests between the forefinger and middle finger of the top hand. also *Vardon grip.* compare *baseball grip, interlocking grip.*

overspin: see *topspin.*

1. par: 1. The number of strokes it would take an expert golfer to complete a particular hole (or course, when the individual hole pars are added together) under ordinary weather conditions. The par for a hole is computed on the basis of yardage (measuring from the middle of the tee area along the line of play planned by the course architect to the center of the green), allowing two strokes on the putting green. Yardage guidelines are provided by the USGA, who adopted the use of par in 1911. compare *course ratng, yardage rating.* 2. A golfer's score when it equals the par designation for a hole or a round. (finished the match with an even par seventy-four round)

●●Average (not feeling up to par today), or of a normal or expected quality or quantity (missed two questions on her driving test, which is about par for the course).

2. par: To make par, either on a hole or a round. (parred the last two holes of the front nine to take a two-stroke lead)

par in: To make par on the last nine holes of a golf course.

par out: To make par on the first nine holes of a golf course.

peanut brittle: A bumpy, uneven green.

penalty: 1. The assessment of one additional stroke (a penalty stroke) to a player's score for certain infractions, sometimes coupled with the necessity of replaying the ball or playing a new ball from the point where the original stroke was played (stroke and distance). 2. The assessment of two additional strokes (penalty strokes) to a player's score for a hole for a breach of the Rules of Golf in stroke play. 3. The loss of the hole in match play for a breach of the Rules of Golf. see *penalty stroke, stroke and distance.*

penalty stroke: 1. A stroke added to a player's score for a hole for hitting a ball twice during a stroke, improperly moving, lifting, or dropping a ball, for failing to mark a ball lifted from a putting green, for playing a second ball before informing the opponent and marker of the player's intention to hit a provisional ball, for a ball lost or out of bounds, for a ball resting in an unplayable lie, or for a ball resting in a water or lateral water hazard that cannot be played. 2. One or two strokes added to a player's score for a hole in stroke play for a breach of the Rules of Golf. compare *stroke and distance.*

Peter Jackson Classic: An annual Canadian stroke play competition for women professional golfers, one of the four major tournaments that together comprise the women's grand slam. The Peter Jackson Classic (formerly La Canadienne) was first played in 1973 at the Montreal Golf Club in Montreal, Quebec, and won by Jocelyne Bourassa.

PGA: The Professional Golfers' Association.

PGA Championship: An annual tournament sponsored by the PGA for touring professionals and the top twenty-five finishers in the PGA Club Professional Championship tournament. The first PGA Championship was played under match play rules in 1916 at the Siwanoy Country Club in Bronxville, New York, and won by James M. Barnes of England. Five-time winner Walter Hagen became the first American-born player to win the PGA Championship in 1921. Don Finsterwald was the first to win the tournament under stroke play when match play was discontinued in 1958.

PGA Club Professional Championship: An annual stroke play tournament sponsored by the PGA for club professionals (as opposed to touring professionals). The PGA Club Professional Championship was first won by Howell Frazer in 1968, and is now the largest seventy-two-hole stroke play championship in the world. The nine top finishers automatically earn a position on the International PGA Cup Match team, and the top twenty-five finishers are eligible to play in the PGA Championship.

PGA Hall of Fame: The Professional Golfers' Association honor roll of outstanding players (amateur and professional) and contributors to the sport of golf. New members are nominated annually and selected by a special Hall of Fame Selection Committee, which includes golf writers and others closely identified with the game. The PGA Hall of Fame was created in 1940, at which time the first twelve members were selected.

PGA Tour: The competitive arm of the PGA (a separate corporate entity since 1968, comprised of tournament players), directly responsible for the planning and organization of the series of major tournaments that make up the "tour." PGA Tour headquarters is at Ponte Vedra Beach, Florida.

Phillips Oil: Slang for a score of sixty-six for a round.

pick clean: To strike a ball high rather than swinging "down through the ball," imparting overspin, which causes the ball to roll rather than stop on landing (as on an approach shot).

pin: see *flagstick.*

pin high: see *hole high.*

1. pitch: A shot in which the ball is hit (usually with a wedge) in a high arc

211

with backspin to stop it from rolling when it lands on the green. also *pitch and stop, pitch shot.*

2. pitch: To hit the ball (usually with a wedge) in a high arc with backspin to stop it from rolling when it lands on the green.

pitch and putt course: 1. A small course laid out specifically to give a player practice with a wedge and a putter. 2. A short regulation course.

pitch and run: see *chip shot.*

pitch and stop: see *pitch.*

pitching niblick: see *lofter.*

pitching wedge: A high-loft (approximately fifty-five degrees) iron club used to pitch and sometimes chip the ball from close to the putting green. compare *sand wedge.*

pitch out: see *shank.*

pitchout: A shanked ball.

pitch shot: see *pitch.*

Pittsburgh Persimmon: A trade name for a particular steelie or all-metal "wood," facetiously named for the steel capital of the United States. Aerospace engineer John Zebelean is credited with developing the first successful stainless steel "wood," introduced in 1979 by the Taylor Company of California. Said by users to drive the ball farther and straighter than a normal wood, steel-headed clubs have become increasingly popular with professional and amateur golfers (over 12 million clubs were sold in 1982). The name "Pittsburgh Persimmon" was coined by Alan Cook, head professional at the Municipal Golf Course in San Clemente, California, and later patented with permission by the Taylor Company.

play: 1. To hit the ball with a club, to make a stroke. (has the honor and will play his ball first) 2. To direct a ball toward a target. (played a beautiful chip shot just short of the pin) 3. To be a longer or shorter distance from the tee because of a change in the exact location of the cup on the green. (the hole now plays shorter than at the beginning of the summer)

playable: Able to be hit or played, as of a lie.

playing the like: Playing the same stroke as one's opponent. compare *playing the odd.*

playing the odd: Playing one more stroke than one's opponent. compare *playing the like.*

play safe: To deliberately hit the ball short of the green or the hole to avoid possible trouble. (a hole on which all the amateurs play safe)

play the trombone: see *Declaration of Independence.*

play through: To continue play, moving ahead of a single player or a slower-paced match on the course with permission. Golf etiquette calls for a single player or a slow-paced match to stand aside and allow a match to pass or "play through."

plug ball: A ball that makes a small hole or indentation on landing and does not roll.

plus golfer: A better-than-scratch player, one with a plus handicap.

plus handicap: The number of artifical strokes a better-than-scratch player gives to adjust his scoring ability to the common level. compare *handicap.*

pocket the ball: see *rake it in.*

point tournament: see *Stableford.*

pole: see *flagstick.*

pool shark: see *bladesman.*

pot: see *hole.*

pot bunker: A deep, craterlike bunker with steep sides.

practice green: A putting green area constructed usually in close proximity to the clubhouse to allow golfers to practice putting away from the course's putting greens.

practice tee: A teeing area that is not a part of the regular course, used to practice tee shots. also *hospital zone.*

preferred lies: A provision sometimes included in Local Rules that allows a ball to be moved to a more advantageous lie under certain circumstances in informal play. Preferred lies or winter rules are sometimes invoked when severe weather either damages or makes unplayable certain parts of a course, or when other special or temporary conditions interfere with normal play.

1. press: 1. A bet made separate from any other bet on the remaining holes of a round. Once one or more holes of a press have been played, if yet another bet is made on holes that remain from that point, it is called a double press. 2. A forward press.

2. press: 1. To bet separate from any other bet on the remaining holes of a round. 2. To deliberately or involuntarily move a part of the body forward just at the beginning of a swing.

pro-am: A competition or tournament in which amateurs play with professionals.

Professional Golfers' Association: An organization dedicated to the growth and promotion of the sport of golf that tests and licenses local club and teaching professionals, provides three- to eight-year-long training programs for apprentices that emphasize practical business skills as well as playing and teaching, and ongoing educational, service, and junior golf programs. In addition, the Professional Golfers' Association produces some thirty tournaments per year, including the PGA Championships, the International Ryder Cup Matches, and the Club Professional Championship, the largest seventy-two-hole professional competition in the world. It also co-produces the World Series of Golf with the PGA Tour, a separate corporate entity since 1968, comprised of tournament players. Founded in 1916, the Professional Golfers' Association is now the largest working sports organization in the world, and is headquartered in Palm Beach Gardens, Florida. PGA Tour headquarters is at Ponte Vedra Beach, Florida.

provisional ball: A ball played from as near as possible to the spot where an original ball was played when the original ball is assumed to be out of bounds or lost (except for one that might be lost in a water hazard, for which a provisional ball may not be played). If the original ball is found, the provisional ball is abandoned, and play is continued with the original ball without penalty. If the original ball is out of bounds or cannot be found, the provisional ball becomes the ball in play, and one penalty stroke is added to the player's score.

pull: see *draw*.

punch shot: A shot that is deliberately hit low, as to provide additional control when hitting into the wind.

1. push: To hit the ball at an angle to the same side as the dominant hand of the player.

2. push: A stroke in which the ball is hit at an angle to the same side as the dominant hand of the player.

1. putt: A light stroke in which the ball is tapped while on the green or on the

edge of the green so as to roll along the surface of the grass toward the hole. The introduction of the perfectly round guttie ball in 1848 together with closely-cut greens made the modern rolling putt possible.

2. putt: To lightly tap the ball so as to make it roll toward the hole.

putter: 1. A short-shafted iron club with a flat face and no loft, used to tap a ball on the putting green toward the hole. When the perfectly round guttie ball replaced the old featherstuffed ball in 1848, Scotsman Allan Robertson, the pioneer professional golfer who reportedly never lost a match, introduced the use of the putting cleek on the green, the forerunner to the modern putter. Previously, wooden putters were used to jump rather than roll the old featherstuffed balls toward the hole. The minimal loft of the putting cleek allowed the ball to be chipped and rolled toward the pin. 2. One who is engaged in or skilled at putting. The first golfer to be known as a deadly putter was Willie Park Sr., four-time winner of the British Open (1860, 1863, 1866, and 1875).

putting green: see *green*.

puttoon: see *hole*.

quail-high: A description of a low drive or shot, resembling the flight of a quail.

quarrelsome: Slang for a mixed foursome. also *gruesome*.

quitting: A pulling back or hesitance on the downswing of a stroke rather than hitting "through the ball," usually resulting in a poor shot.

rabbit: 1. A touring professional not eligible for exempt status, thus having to "hop" from tournament to tournament in order to play in the qualifying rounds for tour events. This usage became archaic in 1983 when the PGA Tour was restricted to exempt players. 2. An uncomplimentary name for an indifferent golfer, alluding to such a player's timid nature and habit of aimlessly dashing around the course.

rake it in: To give up or withdraw from a tournament. also *pocket the ball*.

read the green: To analyze the slope and surface of a putting green before attempting a putt.

recovery: A stroke that successfully plays the ball out of either the rough or a sand trap.

recovery room: Slang among touring professionals for the scorer's tent at a tournament.

213

Red Grange: A score of seventy-seven for a round, alluding to the jersey number of the legendary football player Red Grange. also *Sunset Strip.*

red tees: see *women's tees.*

1. referee: An official appointed by the Committee to accompany players around the course and decide questions of fact and of golf law, and to act on any breach of a Rule or Local Rule, whether personally observed or reported to him by an official "observer."

2. referee: To act as referee for a match.

relief: The right to move a ball that lies in casual water, ground under repair, or in a hole, cast, or runway made by a burrowing animal, or one that is interfered with by an immovable obstruction without incurring a penalty stroke.

1. rim: The edge of the cup. also *lip.*

2. rim: To hit or roll around the rim of the cup with a ball without sinking it. also *lip, lip out.*

rim out: see *rim.*

roll: see *run.*

roller coaster: A putt over a particularly hilly green. also *Dolly Parton.*

rough: The rough ground or area of uncut grass immediately adjacent to and on either side of the fairway. (played it out of the rough to the edge of the green)

round: A complete circuit of the course, usually eighteen holes. A round was not always comprised of eighteen holes. That number came to be recognized as the standard number for a round because of the preeminence in golf of the St. Andrews course in Scotland. There, after subtracting four of the original holes in 1764, the game was played nine holes out, with the players turning around and playing the same nine holes in, completing one eighteen-hole "round." also *loop.*

roundhouse hook: A sweeping hook shot.

rub of the green: A situation in which a moving ball is accidentally stopped or deflected by an "outside agency." In such a case, the ball is played as it lies without penalty.

●●Luck or fate. (the accident was no one's fault, just a rub of the green)

rug: Slang for a divot.

1. run: The path followed and distance travelled upon landing by a ball hit into the air. also *roll.*

2. run: To hit the ball so that it rolls forward upon landing, as on an approach

shot. (unfortunately, ran the ball right past the hole, off the green)

run up shot: see *chip shot.*

Ryder Cup Matches: A biennial competition between professional teams from the United States and Great Britain (for whose team eligibility was expanded in 1979 to include British and European PGA members residing in Europe), featuring foursomes, four-ball, and singles matches, with the United States and Great Britain alternating as hosts. Named after British seed merchant Samuel A. Ryder, who donated the solid gold trophy bearing his name, the Ryder Cup Matches were first played in 1927 in Worcester, Massachusetts, and won by the United States team 9-1/2 to 2-1/2.

sandbagger: A player with an inflated or too-high handicap. also *mug hunter.*

sandblaster: see *sand wedge.*

sand bunker: see *sand trap.*

sandie: The basis for a bet in a casual game in which a player gets out of a sand trap and holes out in a total of two shots. also *sandy.* compare *greenie, chippie.*

sand iron: see *sand wedge.*

sand trap: A hazard consisting of a bare area or a depression filled with loose sand, usually located near or adjacent to the putting green. see *bunker.* also *beach, bunker, bunker trap, cat box, Egyptian Bermuda, litter box, sand bunker, trap, white face.*

sand wedge: A usually unnumbered iron club with pronounced loft (approximately fifty-five degrees), used to hit the ball out of sand. The base of the sand wedge is specially thickened into a flange, which digs into the sand behind and under the ball, and bumps the ball out with a cushion of sand. Clubmaker and golf great Gene Sarazen first produced this effect in the 1930s by altering the sole angle of an old flanged-sole sand club. also *sandblaster, sand iron.* compare *pitching wedge.*

sandy: see *sandie.*

1. sclaff: A misplayed stroke in which the club head bounces off the ground before making contact with the ball.

2. sclaff: To make a sclaff.

scoreboard: A display board, usually hand-operated, on which the current status, position, and scores of tournament leaders are posted during a competition. In 1981, the PGA Tour introduced a modular and portable electronic scoring and information system, consisting of one large leader-information board and up to twenty connected leader-status information boards to be placed at various locations around a course. also **leaderboard.**

scorecard: A card on which the score for each hole for one or more golfers is kept, and upon which "stroke holes" are listed where handicap strokes are to be applied. According to the Rules of Golf, in a stroke play competition, it is the responsibility of each player to check his scorecard for errors, and to make sure that both he and the "marker" have signed it before turning it in to the Committee. If a scorecard is not turned in, or if it is not properly signed, or if a lower score than was actually made is turned in, the player is disqualified. If a higher score than was actually made is turned in, the score must stand as returned. 1980 Vardon Trophy winner Lee Trevino was disqualified from the 1980 PGA Championship tournament for accidentally failing to sign his scorecard after the first round. The most famous case of a scorecard mistake occurred in the 1968 Masters Tournament, when Roberto DeVicenzo hurriedly signed an incorrect scorecard—one stroke higher than he actually scored—that cost him a tie and a chance to play off for the title. also **card.**

Scotch foursome: An American expression for a foursome. see **foursome.**

scramble: To recover or attempt to recover after a poor start on a hole, as to make par after failing to reach the green "in regulation."

scrambler: A player who seems always to be able to make a good score on a hole, even after an unimpressive start; one who makes the important or necessary shot under pressure, whether a critical approach shot, a recovery from the rough or a hazard, or a delicate or difficult putt. Walter Hagen, Gene Sarazen, Arnold Palmer, and Gary Player are among the golfing greats who have been known as scramblers.

scratch golfer, scratch player: A golfer with enough skill to play with no handicap.

Seniors: A class of competition for older players (over age fifty-five for amateurs, over age fifty for professionals). The first PGA Seniors' Championship was held in 1937 in Augusta, Georgia, and won by Jock Hutchison. The first USGA-sponsored Senior Amateur Championship was held in 1955 in Nashville, and won by fifty-six-year-old J. Wood Platt of Bethlehem, Pennsylvania.

seven iron: A high-lofted iron club used for approach shots to the green of approximately 140 yards. Formerly known as a mashie niblick.

shaft: The long, thin, cylindrical part of a golf club between the head and the grip.

shank: To mishit the ball with the heel of the club head, making it veer to one side. also **lateral, pitch out, socket.**

Shapiro: A mulligan with a Jewish name, a free shot with a second ball sometimes permitted in informal play when a golfer's original ball is mishit. Similar to a Ginsberg. However, like a mulligan, a Shapiro must continue to be played, even if it is mishit worse than the original ball.

sharpshooter: see **shotmaker.**

shoot: To make a particular score while playing. (shot an even-par seventy-one in the first round)

shooting gallery: Slang among professionals for an easy "birdie" course.

shooting irons: Slang for golf clubs. also **bats, hammers, hickories, sticks, tools, weapons.**

shoot scratch: To play with no handicap as professional players do.

short: Stopping before reaching the intended destination. (a well-aimed drive, right down the fairway, but short of the green)

short game: Of or pertaining to relatively short shots, such as approach shots or putts.

short iron: An iron with high loft and shorter shaft for short approach shots, such as a 7, 8 or 9 iron.

shot: A stroke in which the ball is hit. (a poor shot into the rough)

shotmaker: A player known for the ability to accurately place his shots. Tommy Bolt, winner of the U.S. Open in 1958 and the PGA Seniors' Championship in 1969, and five-time PGA Player of the Year (1967, 1972, 1973, 1975, and

1976) Jack Nicklaus are usually mentioned among the great shotmakers in the game of golf. also *sharpshooter*.

shotmaking: 1. The stroking of the ball to make a shot. 2. The making of accurately placed shots.

shut the face: see *hood the club*.

side: Two or more players who are partnered in a competition.

sidehiller: A putt that rolls or must roll across the face of a sloping green to reach the hole.

silent one: see *whiff*.

singles: A competition between two players.

sink: To hole the ball. (will win the match if she can sink this 6-foot putt) see *hole out*.

six iron: An iron club with medium loft used for approach shots to the green of approximately 150 yards. Formerly known as a spade mashie.

skull: see *top*.

skull shot: A ball that is topped or skulled.

sky: 1. To hit a ball almost straight up; a mishit. (fell behind when he skied his approach shot) 2. To intentionally loft a ball high into the air, as to clear a "hazard" or obstacle.

sky ball: A ball mishit almost straight up into the air. also *angel raper, hello God, up in Minnie's room*.

1. slice: To hit the ball in such a way as to cause it to veer to the side of the player's dominant hand. (sliced one into the rough) also *fade*. compare *draw, hook, pull*.

2. slice: A shot in which the ball is sliced, and veers toward the side of the player's dominant hand. also *Cuban, fade*.

slow green: A putting green with a soft or lush surface that inhibits the bounce or roll of a ball.

smile: see *dimple*.

1. smother: To hit down on the ball, causing it to roll a short distance on the ground.

2. smother: The act or an instance of smothering a ball.

snake: A long putt over a hilly green.

snowman: A score of eighty-eight for a round, because the figure 8 resembles a snowman.

1. socket: The thin part of a club head near the point where it joins the shaft. also *neck*.

2. socket: To shank a ball, hitting it on the socket of the club. see *shank*.

sole: The bottom of a club head.

solitaire: see *hole in one*.

spade mashie: A number 6 iron, popularly called a spade mashie until numerical classifications for clubs were introduced in the 1920s.

spoon: A number 3 wood, although, originally, all lofted clubs were known as spoons. The term "spoon" became less popular when numerical classifications for clubs were introduced in the 1920s.

square: see *all square*.

square stance: A stance in which the front foot and rear foot are positioned parallel to the line of play of the ball when addressed. compare *closed stance, open stance*.

1. stab: A short thrusting putting stroke.

2. stab: To make a short thrusting putting stroke.

Stableford: A type of stroke competition popular in Great Britain, in which play is against a fixed score (such as par) at each hole. Points are awarded in relation to par, with one point for a hole completed in one stroke over par, two

SLICE   HOOK

points for a hole done in par, three points for one under par, four points for two under par, and five points for a hole done in three under par. The winner is the player or side scoring the most points in a round. The scoring system for Stableford competitions, called "point tournaments" in the United States, was invented in 1932 by English surgeon and golfer Dr. Frank B. Stableford.

stadium golf: A concept of golf as a spectator sport, played on courses designed to provide spectators with accessible elevated vantage points for each hole and up-to-the-moment information about what is taking place on other parts of the course. The Tournament Players Club, opened in Jacksonville, Florida in 1981 as PGA Tour headquarters and the permanent site of the Tournament Players Championship, was the first golf course designed specially to accommodate "stadium golf."

steamy putt: A putt that has been hit too hard and rolls well past the hole.

steelie: Slang for a steel-headed "wood." see *Pittsburgh Persimmon.*

sticks: Slang for golf clubs. also *bats, hammers, hickories, shooting irons, tools, weapons.*

stick the pick: To stub the club head on the ground behind the ball before making contact on a chip or wedge shot, resulting in a mishit stroke.

stipulated round: A completed round of usually eighteen holes played in their correct sequence (unless the Committee authorizes fewer holes or a different sequence). To settle a tie in match play, the Committee may extend a stipulated round to as many holes as are required for a match to be won.

stone: To hit a ball that stops right next to the pin. (kept on stoning his putts after getting to the green in regulation)

stone dead: A ball that stops right next to the pin.

stop: see *backspin.*

stretcher bearer: Slang for a caddie.

string of birdies: Birdies (one stroke under par for a hole) on consecutive holes.

1. stroke: A swing or forward movement of the club that is intended to strike the ball, and that is charged to a player's score whether or not the ball is hit. (two strokes behind the leader on the sixteenth hole)

2. stroke: To swing and hit the ball with a club. (stroked one right down the middle of the fairway)

stroke and distance: A penalty in which a player is assessed one penalty stroke, and must play a new ball (or the original ball) from where the last stroke was made. A stroke and distance penalty is applied when a ball is lost or out of bounds, when a second ball is played before informing the opponent and marker of one's intention to play a provisional ball, and as one of the player's options when the ball rests in an unplayable lie, or in a water hazard or lateral water hazard. compare *penalty stroke.*

stroke hole: A hole on which a player applies a handicap stroke to hit gross score. The numerical order in which handicap strokes are allocated to specified holes of the course is usually shown on the scorecard. also *handicap stroke hole.*

stroke play: A competition in which the winner is the player who completes the stipulated round or rounds in the fewest strokes. Golf was always played at match play until the eighteenth century, when stroke play or "medal play" was first used in England for one-day competitions for the prize of a "medal." When the USGA conducted the first U.S. Amateur Championship in 1895, match play was still considered the standard method of play. The first U.S. Open was played the next day with thirty-six holes played in one day, reportedly so that the ten "professionals" who had entered wouldn't be away from their shops for too long. Stroke play flourished in the United States, and today, it is the method of play in most professional tournaments. compare *match play.*

stymie: A situation in which a player's ball rests between the cup and another ball (obstructing its path). The Rules of Golf were changed in 1951 to permit the interfering ball to be lifted in match play, and then replaced after the further ball has been played. In stroke play, the player whose ball is interfering may either lift or play the ball, at his option. There are conflicting ideas about the exact origin of the term, with some suggesting that "stymie" is from the Gaelic *stigh mi,* meaning "inside me," or the Dutch *stuit mij,* meaning "it stops me."

Others claim the term is derived from a similar English word, "styme," in use as early as 1300, as in the phrase "not to see a styme," meaning "not able to see at all," or in the golf application, not able to see around the interfering ball.

●●To be "stymied" is to be literally or figuratively blocked, stopped, or stumped. (stymied by the last question on the test)

sudden-death hole: An extension of the stipulated round by the Committee in match play, for the purpose of settling a tie after eighteen holes. Usually, as many sudden-death holes as necessary are played until the round is won by the first player to win a hole. The all-time record for the PGA is eleven sudden-death holes, in the 1949 Motor City Open, when Cary Middlecoff and Lloyd Mangrum were declared co-winners by mutual agreement. When the winner of a round is determined by a single sudden-death hole or "extra hole," the hole is sometimes called the nineteenth hole.

summer rules: A euphemism for normal play under the Rules of Golf, indicating that no preferred lies or winter rules provisions are in effect.

Sunday best: An excellent shot.

Sunset Strip: A score of seventy-seven for a round, an allusion to the 1950s television program, *77 Sunset Strip.* also *Red Grange.*

sweet sixteen: The group or flight of sixteen players who advance from a tour-nament qualifying round. (made the sweet sixteen for the big amateur tournament)

sweet spot: The central area of a club's face, optimum for making contact with the ball on a stroke.

swing weight: The characteristics of balance and weight that affect the feel and performance of a club as it is swung.

take away: The first hand movement taking the club back away from the ball at the beginning of the backswing.

take turf: To dig a divot or take a patch of turf when playing a shot.

teaching pro: A professional player who is primarily concerned with teaching golf to other players, as opposed to a touring professional. Most teaching pros are associated with a golf club, and often function as the club or home pro.

1. tee: 1. A small wooden or plastic peg, larger at the top end, upon which the ball is placed for the first shot on each hole. A New Jersey dentist, Dr. William Lowe, worried that his hands would be injured by constantly digging in the turf or sand to build a mound for a ball (the original tee), first marketed a wooden tee in the 1920s. 2. A mound of turf or sand used instead of a plastic or wooden peg, still legal, but not often used. Before the wooden tee became popular, teeing grounds were often equipped with a handy box of sand so that a golfer or caddie could make a small mound. 3. see *teeing ground.*

2. tee: To place a ball on a tee in preparation for a stroke. also *tee up.*

tee box: An old name for a teeing ground.

teeing area: see *teeing ground.*

teeing ground: The area from which the ball is teed and the first stroke is made for the hole to be played, a rectangle two club-lengths in depth, the front and sides of which are defined by the outside limits of two tee markers. A teeing ground is divided into three sections. The rear section, indicated by blue tee markers, is intended for professional use. The middle section, indicated by white tee markers, is intended for regulation play. The front section, indicated by red tee markers, is intended for women golfers. also *tee, tee box, teeing area.*

tee markers: Devices firmly attached to the ground that are used to define the tee-

TEE MARKER

TEEING AREA

ing ground from which play begins on each hole. Blue tee markers indicate the championship tees, white tee markers indicate the middle tees for regular play, and red tee markers indicate the ladies' tees.

tee off: To begin the play of a round of golf. (usually the first player to tee off in the morning)

●●To "tee off on" someone or something is to literally or figuratively hit, punch, or attack. (a scathing editorial which teed off on rising white collar crime)

tee peg: see *tee.*

tee shot: A shot played from the teeing ground, the stroke that begins play at each hole.

tee up: To place a ball on a tee in preparation for the first stroke of the hole to be played.

ten-finger grip: see *baseball grip.*

ten iron: A rarely-used special high-lofted iron club, replaced by the modern wedge.

Texas wedge: A putter, when used to play a ball that lies just off the edge of the green.

thread the needle: To make an excellent, straight shot.

three-ball: A match in which three golfers, each with his own ball, play against one another.

three iron: A slightly-lofted iron club used for distance shots of approximately 180 yards. Formerly known as an approach cleek or mid-mashie.

three-putt: To use three putts to hole a ball (rather than the two allowed for par). (three-putted for a bogey on the last hole)

three-putt territory: A difficult lie on the green, far away from the pin.

threesome: A match in which one plays against two, and each side plays one ball. Sometimes, the term "threesome" is inaccurately applied to a group of three golfers playing together.

●●Any group of three.

three wood: A wooden club used for fairway shots of approximately 220 yards. Formerly known as a spoon.

through the green: Any place on the course except the teeing ground and putting green of the hole being played and within a hazard.

throw it at the flag: To play a bold or risky shot at the pin.

throw-up zone: About six feet away from

the pin, close enough to put pressure on a player, but far enough away to be a difficult putt.

tiger: An expert or good player.

tiger country: Slang for the rough. also *jungle.*

tiger tees: see *blue tees.*

timber: A call given in jest when a ball is headed towards the trees.

tips: see *blue tees.*

toe: The tip or outer end of a club head.

tool chest: A golf bag.

tools: Golf clubs. also *bats, hammers, hickories, shooting irons, sticks, weapons.*

top: To strike a ball above the center or too high, causing the ball to roll or bounce along the ground, or imparting overspin, which results in a low flight and causes the ball to roll rather than stop on landing. also *hit on the hat, skull.*

topspin: A forward rotation (as imparted by skulling or topping) that causes the ball to move in a low flight, and to bounce and roll forward upon landing. also *overspin.*

Tour: see *PGA tour.*

Tour golfer, Tour player: A professional player who makes his or her living by playing on the PGA Tour or the LPGA Tour. also *touring pro, touring professional.*

touring pro, touring professional: see *Tour golfer, Tour player.*

Tournament Players Championship: The PGA's own major tournament, open to all designated players, winners of major PGA Tour co-sponsored or approved events during the previous year, the current British Open champion, and leaders in the PGA Tour official standings as necessary to complete the field. The first Tournament Players Championship was played in 1974 at the Atlanta Country Club in Atlanta, Georgia, and won by Jack Nicklaus. In 1981, the Tournament Players Championship moved to the site of its new permanent home (and headquarters of the PGA Tour) at the Tournament Players Club in Ponte Vedra Beach, Florida.

tour swing: A technically good swing, a swing that shows particularly good form, as might be expected from a professional on the Tour.

trap: see *sand trap.*

trapped: Bordered by sand traps. (an almost completely trapped green)

trap shot: A stroke made from inside a sand trap.

triple bogey: A score of three over par on a given hole.

triple-bogey: To score a triple bogey on a hole.

trolley: 1. A straight shot, as though on "rails." 2. British slang for a caddie cart. also *cart, golf cart.*

turn: The half-way point on an eighteen-hole course. From the early days of golf, at the famous St. Andrews course in Scotland, where, after four of the original holes were subtracted in 1764, the game was played nine holes out to the turn, with the same nine holes played in. Prior to 1764, the turn had been at eleven holes. (still leading at the turn)

twitch: A British expression for a "case of nerves" that causes a player to choke under pressure and miss a putt. also *yips.*

two iron: A long-range iron club used for distances of approximately 190 yards. Formerly known as a midiron. also *deuce.*

two wood: A wooden club used for long fairway shots of approximately 220 yards. Formerly known as a brassie.

twosome: Slang for a match between two players.

••Two people, a couple.

underclub: To use the wrong club (one with too much loft and not enough shaft), resulting in the ball landing short of the intended target. (didn't make the green in regulation because he underclubbed his fairway shot)

undertaker: A good or "lethal" putter, one who can "bury" the ball. also *bladesman, pool shark.*

United States Golf Association: The national governing body of golf in the United States. Formed in 1894 for the purpose of promoting and conserving the best interests and the true spirit of the game of golf, the United States Golf Association, or USGA, began work on a uniform code of rules in the 1920s, and in 1952, joined with the Royal and Ancient Golf Club of St. Andrews, Scotland to issue the Rules of Golf, in use throughout the world today. The USGA also developed and now maintains the national system of handicap-

ping, which allows players of different abilities to compete on relatively equal terms, and is responsible for testing and approving golf equipment and defining and maintaining the distinction between amateur and professional golfers. The USGA conducted its first national competitions in 1895, the U.S. Amateur, the U.S. Open, and Women's Amateur Championships. Today, the USGA conducts nine other national championships as well, including the Women's Open, Junior Amateur, Girls' Junior, Amateur Public Links, Women's Amateur Public Links, Senior Amateur, Senior Women's Amateur, Senior Open and Mid-Amateur Championships. The USGA also conducts international competitions such as the Walker Cup Match with the Royal and Ancient Golf Club of St. Andrews, Scotland, and the Curtis Cup Match with the British Ladies' Golf Union, and selects the U.S. teams for the World Amateur and Women's World Amateur Team Championships.

unplayable lie: A ball positioned so as to be impossible to play. Sometimes in informal play, Local Rules ("preferred lies" and "winter rules") allow a player to move a ball in an unplayable lie.

up: Ahead by a number of holes in match play. (two up at the end of nine holes)

up in Minnie's room: see *sky ball.*

U.S. Amateur Championship: The prestigious annual national tournament for amateur players, sponsored by the USGA. The first U.S. Amateur Championship was held in 1895 at the Newport Golf Club in Newport, Rhode Island, and won by Charles B. Macdonald, of the Chicago Golf Club. Francis Ouimet (1914, 1931), Robert T. "Bobby" Jones, Jr. (1924, 1925, 1927, 1928, 1930), Gene Littler (1953), Arnold Palmer (1954), Jack Nicklaus (1959, 1961), and Deane R. Beman (1960, 1963) are among those who won the Amateur Championship at match play. From 1965 through 1972, the format was changed to stroke play, reverting to match play in 1973. In 1981, Nathaniel Crosby won the U.S. Amateur Championship. Crosby's famous father, Bing Crosby, whose pioneer celebrity pro-amateur tournament did much to heighten the public appeal of golf, and particularly professional golf, is honored in the World Golf Hall of Fame as an outstanding contributor to the sport. also *amateur, amateur championship.*

use all the cup: To roll around the rim of a hole before dropping, as of a putt.

USGA: The United States Golf Association.

U.S. Open: The major annual national competition sponsored by the USGA, open to professionals and amateurs (with handicaps not exceeding two strokes) who are exempt or who have qualified in Local and Sectional Qualifying Championships. The first U.S. Open was held at the Newport (Rhode Island) Golf Club in 1895, and won by twenty-one-year-old Horace Rawlins. It was the first major tournament played at stroke play in the United States and was originally a thirty-six-hole, one-day competition. The Open was extended to seventy-two holes in 1898, played in four eighteen-hole daily rounds since 1965. The first amateur player to win the Open was Francis Ouimet in 1913, defeating British golfing greats Harry Vardon and Edward Ray. The record for the most victories in the U.S. Open is held by four men: Willie Anderson (1901, 1903, 1904, and 1905), Robert T. "Bobby" Jones, Jr. (1923, 1926, 1929, and 1930), Ben Hogan (1948, 1950, 1951, and 1953), and Jack Nicklaus (1962, 1967, 1972, and 1980). also *National Open, Open.*

Van Gogh it: To play an "artistic" round.

Vardon grip: The overlapping grip, first popularized by six-time British Open winner (1896, 1898, 1899, 1903, 1911, and 1914) Harry Vardon. see *overlapping grip.*

Vardon Trophy: The annual award given to the PGA member maintaining the finest playing average in events co-sponsored or designated by the PGA. The PGA Vardon Trophy, named in honor of the internationally famous British golfer, Harry Vardon, was placed in competition among American professionals in 1937 as a successor to the Henry E. Radix Trophy, which, prior to that time, had been awarded annually to the professional having the finest tournament record in play in this country. In 1937, the first winner was Harry Cooper. The Vardon Trophy has been won five times by Lee Trevino (1970, 1971, 1972, 1974, and 1980) and Billy Casper (1960, 1963, 1965, 1966, and 1968), four times by Sam Snead (1938, 1949, 1950, and 1955), and Arnold Palmer (1961, 1962, 1964, and 1967), and three times by Ben Hogan (1940, 1941, and 1948) and Tom Watson (1977, 1978, and 1979).

Vare Trophy: The annual LPGA award given to the woman professional player (with a minimum of seventy official rounds of tournament competition during the year) with the lowest scoring average at the end of each year, computed by dividing a player's total number of strokes in official LPGA tournaments by the number of official rounds she played during the year. The trophy was presented to the LPGA by Betty Jameson in 1952 in honor of the great American player Glenna Collett Vare. The Vare Trophy was first won in 1953 by Patty Berg, who played sixty-five rounds in an average of 75.00 strokes per round.

Volkswagen: An awkward or poor shot that turns out well; an unartistic but successful shot.

1. waggle: An intentional movement of the club back and forth behind the ball just before starting a swing, done to help break down tension in the hands, arms and legs.

2. waggle: The act or an instance of waggling before a stroke is made to relieve tension.

Walker Cup Match: A biennial international competition played between teams of ten male amateur golfers from the United States on the one side and from England, Scotland, Wales, Northern Ireland and Eire on the other, hosted alternately by the United States and Great Britain. The Walker Cup Match, so-dubbed by the press because the trophy (the International Challenge Trophy) was donated by George Herbert Walker (President of the USGA when the tournament was first discussed in 1920), is the oldest international golf competition. It was first played in 1922, with the United States team winning eight to four. Going into the 1980s, teams from Great Britain had won Walker Cup Matches only twice (1938 and 1971), tying once in 1965. The teams, selected by the USGA and the Royal and Ancient Golf Club of St. Andrews, Scotland, play four eighteen-hole foursomes in the morning and eight eighteen-hole singles in the afternoon on each of the two days of the competition.

water hazard: Any sea, lake, pond, river, ditch, surface drainage ditch, or other open water course except a "lateral water hazard" within the boundaries of a golf course, regardless of whether or not it contains water. When a ball is lost or unplayable in a water hazard, the player may, under penalty of one stroke, drop the ball (or a new ball) behind the hazard on a line formed by the hole and the point where the ball entered the hazard, or drop the ball (or a new ball) from the point where the original stroke was made. Water hazards are marked by short yellow stakes or by yellow lines.

weapons: Slang for golf clubs. also *bats, hammers, hickories, shooting irons, sticks, tools.*

weaver: Slang for a shot in which the ball is hit so straight toward the hole that it is said to "hide the flagstick," making it necessary for the player to "weave" from side to side in order to see the pole.

wedge: A usually unnumbered iron club with pronounced loft (approximately fifty-five degrees), used either to pitch and chip the ball from close to the putting green (a pitching wedge) or to hit the ball out of sand (a sand wedge).

Wee Links: A low-maintenance, six-hole course utilizing synthetic "Mod-Sod" tees and putting greens, first installed at the Walt Disney Golf Resort in Florida. The concept of "Wee Links" courses is to provide accessible low-cost training grounds for young players.

1. whiff: To swing and miss the ball completely, wasting a stroke. (fell behind at the beginning of the round when he whiffed on his first tee shot)

2. whiff: A swing of the club that does not make contact with the ball as intended. Though the ball is missed, the swing counts as a stroke on the golfer's score for the hole. also *air shot, fresh air shot, silent one.*

whiskey jerk, whiskey wrists: An "affliction" said to be suffered by poor putters.

white face: A sand trap, appearing somewhat like a white face amid the surrounding grass. see *sand trap.*

white knuckles: A slang expression for a shot that a player tries to hit with full power. (a long hole, requiring a white knuckles tee shot)

white tees: The middle section of a teeing ground, indicated by white tee markers, and intended for regulation play. also *middle tees.*

wind cheater: A low drive or shot under the wind.

windy: A comment or description of an air shot or whiff.

winter rules: A provision sometimes included in Local Rules that allows a ball to be moved to a more advantageous lie under certain circumstances in informal play. "Winter rules" or "preferred lies" are sometimes invoked when severe weather either damages or makes unplayable certain parts of a course, or when other special or temporary conditions interfere with normal play.

Women's Open Championship: An annual seventy-two-hole, four-day competition sponsored by the USGA that is open to exempt and qualified (in Sectional Qualifying Competitions) women professionals and amateurs with handicaps of not more than four strokes. The Open is one of the four major tournaments that together comprise the women's grand slam. The first Women's Open Championship was played in 1946 at the Spokane (Washington) Country Club, and won by golfing great Patty Berg (in match play that year only). The tournament was originally conducted by the then Women's Professional Golfers' Association from 1946 through 1948, and by the Ladies Professional Golf Association from 1949 through 1952. Two women have won the Women's Open Championship four times, Betsy Rawls (1951, 1953, 1957, and 1960) and Mickey Wright (1958, 1959, 1961, and 1964).

women's tees: The front section of a teeing ground, indicated by red tee markers, and usually reserved for women golfers. also *ladies' tees, red tees.*

Women's World Amateur Team Championship: An international amateur team championship for women, played biennially in conjunction with the World Amateur Team Championship in a different host country from one of three global zones; the Australasian Zone (Asia, Australia, New Zealand, and Oceania), the American Zone (North America, South America and Central America), and the European-African Zone. The Women's World Amateur

Team Championship is sponsored by the World Amateur Golf Council (comprised of representatives of national governing bodies of golf in nearly sixty countries) and is contested by three-woman teams over a four-day period. Competition is at stroke play, with the two best individual scores counted as a team's score each day. The winning team (with the lowest four-day score) is awarded the Espirito Santo Trophy, presented in 1964 by Mrs. Espirito Santo Silva of Portugal. The first Women's World Amateur Team Championship was instituted by the French Golf Federation on a suggestion by the USGA and won in 1964 by the French team at the St. Germain Golf Club, near Paris, France.

wood: 1. A long-shafted club with a large wooden head, for making long shots, as from the tee, fairway, and sometimes, the rough. Woods are numbered from one through five in order of increasing loft (the angle at which the club face is tipped back). In recent years, all-steel "woods" (with metal replacing the hardwood normally used in the heads) have been marketed. see *Pittsburgh Persimmon*. 2. A wood shot.

wood cover: A covering of leather or some other pliable material to protect the club heads of woods from knocking against other clubs. Wood covers were originally invented in 1916 by a Japanese golfer, Seiichi Takahata, later a leading figure in Japanese golf.

wood shot: A shot made with a wood. also *wood*.

workingman's par: A scrambling par, as of a par made after not reaching the green in regulation.

World Amateur Golf Council: An international amateur organization, comprised of representatives of national governing bodies of golf in nearly sixty countries, founded in 1958 to foster friendship and sportsmanship through the conduct of international team competitions. Based in Far Hills, New Jersey, the World Amateur Golf Council sponsors the World Amateur Team Championship and the Women's World Amateur Team Championship.

World Amateur Team Championship: An international amateur team championship for men, played biennially in conjunction with the Women's World Amateur Team Championship in a different host country from one of three global zones: the Australasian Zone (Asia, Australia, New Zealand, and Oceania), the American Zone (North America, South America, and Central America), and the European-African Zone. The World Amateur Team Championship is sponsored by the World Amateur Golf Council (comprised of representatives of national governing bodies of golf in nearly sixty countries) and is contested by four-man teams over four rounds of stroke play competing for the Eisenhower Trophy, named for former United States President and golfing enthusiast Dwight D. Eisenhower. Tied with the United States after four rounds, Australia won a playoff round to win the first World Amateur Team Championship, played in 1958 on the old course at St. Andrews, Scotland.

World Cup: An international competition of over seventy-two holes of stroke play between thirty-two two-man teams of professional players from among over fifty participating nations. Teams compete on the basis of total strokes, with a special award (the International Trophy) going to the player with the lowest individual score. The field is comprised of twenty-two exempt teams (based on five-year performance records) and ten teams that are selected in qualifying events in three geographical zones. Beginning with the 1982 World Cup, five special invitations for the individual competition were also extended to the current PGA Tour leading money-winner, the current British Open, Japanese Open, and Australian Open champions, and the national champion of the host nation. Originally founded by American scholar and industrialist, John Jay Hopkins, in 1953 as the Canada Cup, the competition was renamed the World Cup in 1965, and is sponsored by the commercially funded International Golf Association, headquartered in New York.

World Golf Hall of Fame: An institution that annually honors outstanding players and contributors to golf, and that also serves as a museum and shrine to the sport of golf. Located in Pinehurst, North Carolina, the World Golf Hall of Fame opened in 1974, when the first thirteen inductees were selected. Induc-

223

tees to the World Golf Hall of Fame are determined in two ways. Selection in the Pre-Modern category is accomplished by a panel of six members of the Golf Writers' Association of America and six members of the Hall of Fame. The Golf Writers' Association membership votes for the candidates in the Modern Era category. The LPGA Hall of Fame is housed within the World Golf Hall of Fame.

World Series of Golf: An international seventy-two-hole stroke play competition, played annually at the Firestone Country Club in Akron, Ohio. First won in 1976 by Jack Nicklaus (prior to 1976, the event was played as a four-man, thirty-six-hole exhibition), the World Series of Golf is open to the winner of the previous World Series, the previous Tournament Players Championship, the previous Masters Tournament, the previous U.S. Open, the previous British Open, the previous PGA Championship, the previous Canadian Open, the previous Western Open, the previous United States Amateur Championship (provided the player is still an amateur), the previous British Amateur Championship (provided the player is still an amateur), the

first two finishers in each of the four Season Championships within the PGA Tour, winners of two or more co-sponsored events on the PGA Tour in the previous year, the winner of the PGA National Club Pro Championship, the fifteen leaders on the PGA Tour official money list, and winners or leaders of the Order of Merit rating systems as follows: three each from the European and Japanese Orders of Merit, and two each from the South African, Australian and Asian Golf Circuit Orders of Merit.

yachtsman: A player who "tacks" toward the hole, from one side of the fairway to the other.

yardage marker: A permanent indicator of the starting point from which the length of each hole is measured, firmly attached to the ground at that point on each tee.

yardage rating: The evaluation of the playing difficulty of a course based on yardage alone. compare *course rating, par.*

yip: To mishit a putt, missing the hole as a consequence.

yips: A case of nerves causing a golfer to choke under pressure, missing an easy putt. also *twitch.*

RUGBY

Like soccer, rugby evolved from the crude "mob football" games of medieval England. Despite being periodically prohibited by royal decree, forms of football (as it was called initially because of being played on foot rather than on horseback) nevertheless survived the middle ages and the social upheaval of the Industrial Revolution to be reborn and "civilized" in English public schools in the early nineteenth century. Different versions of the game were played at Charterhouse, Westminster, Eton, Harrow, and Rugby, where in 1823, the incident widely believed to have been responsible for the name and form of modern rugby football occurred. In a twenty-a-side version of the type of football that had been popular at Rugby since at least 1817, a sixteen-year-old participant, William Webb Ellis, ignored the rules of the time (which allowed handling, but only to kick the ball) and evidently, upon gathering the ball, carried it over the opponent's goal line.

Whether or not this controversial act, now immortalized by a plaque at Rugby School, happened exactly in the time and manner recounted will never be known. Ellis, later a minister, died in 1872 before ever commenting on it, and there are no surviving eyewitness accounts. But contemporaries of his, among them the noted Rugby antiquarian Matthew Holbeche Bloxam (1805–88), were convinced of the story's accuracy and credit Ellis with introducing the game's distinctive feature. It is unarguable that running with the ball was later identified with the Ellis incident and Rugby as "that play at Rugby", "the Rugby game", and finally, just "rugby". In 1839, an old Rugbeian, Albert Pell, introduced the game at Cambridge, forming the first rugby club on record, though it would be another 33 years before rugby was officially recognized at the University. Appropriately, the oldest surviving code of rules is "The Laws Of Football As Played At Rugby School", framed in 1846.

By the mid-1850s, various forms of football were being played not only in schools, but by clubs as well. The inevitable split between those who favored Rugby's "handling game", with its rough play and "hacking" (legal shin-kicking and tripping), and those who preferred the less violent "dribbling game" finally occurred in 1863, when the latter group formed England's Football Association. Thereafter, the two games would be called "rugby" and "association football" (and soon, in the odd jargon of Oxford, "rugger" and "soccer").

In 1871, at the urging of the Blackheath and Richmond clubs, the Rugby Football Union (RFU) was formed and a unified code of Laws framed. The most important changes from the old Rugby School Laws were the elimination of hacking and tripping, and the simplification of "punting out" (eliminated entirely in 1883) of the in-goal area to determine the place for a "try at goal" (the only method of scoring points) after a "run-in". Within six weeks, the first international rugby match (still twenty-a-side) was played at Raeborn Place, Edinburgh, with Scotland defeating England in front of a crowd of 4,000 by 1 goal, both sides having scored a "try".

In 1872, Cambridge officially recognized the Rugby game, falling to the Oxford XX in the first intervarsity competition. The same year, British residents at Le Havre formed the first rugby club in France. Rugby had found its way to Australia as early as the 1860s, the oldest club, Sydney University, being formed in 1864. Two years later, the game was first played in New Zealand, where it was soon to thrive.

In 1875, at the fourth meeting between Oxford and Cambridge, teams were limited to fifteen-a-side, thereby opening up the game for running and passing (instead of the pro-longed mauls and rucks prevalent until then). The first fifteen-a-side international match was played in 1877. With both sides fielding eight-man forward packs, and two halfbacks, two three-quarters, and three fullbacks, England defeated Ireland 2 goals and 1 try to 0 at the Oval in a game described as "fast and brilliant from first to last".

The game continued to gain popularity throughout the 1800s, with rugby unions being formed in Scotland in 1873, Australia in 1875, Ireland in 1879, South Africa in 1889, and New Zealand in 1892.

The 1880s brought the novel use of three three-quarters by Scotland against Ireland in 1881, the development of the open game and passing by the halfbacks (by Oxford's Harry Vassall and Alan Rotherham between 1880 and 1883), the first overseas tour (New South Wales to New Zealand in 1882), and the formation of the International Rugby Football Board in 1886. By 1890 (when England joined), this body had moved to insure that one code of Laws governed all international matches.

In 1893, a controversy in England over whether or not players should be compensated for "broken time" (time away from their normal jobs) came to a head. Twenty-two northern clubs withdrew from the RFU to form the Northern Rugby Football Union, later to become the virtually "professional" Rugby Football League (RFL).

The new league prospered, and, to the dismay of RFU traditionalists, rules were changed to attempt to make the game faster and more interesting for both players and spectators. In 1897, all goals were valued at 2 points and the line-out was replaced by a free kick. Kicking directly into touch was made an infringement in 1902. Teams were limited to thirteen-a-side in 1906, and two years later, the "play-the-ball" rule was introduced (allowing a tackled player to release the ball and bring it into play again). Meanwhile, amateur rugby had been introduced to the Olympics in 1900, with the host country, France, winning the final.

In 1905, New Zealand's remarkable All Blacks toured England with their seven-man, 2-3-2 pack and wing forward or "rover", Dave Gallaher, winning 32 of 33 matches (losing only to Wales controversially when an apparent try was disallowed), and scoring 830 points to 39. While in England, the All Blacks attended some Northern Union games and watched with interest. Within two years, former All Black G. W. Smith led a team of Australians and New Zealanders on a successful English tour under Rugby League rules. This and reciprocal tours served to consolidate the professional game in England, as well as to introduce it abroad.

In 1907, a seven-team Rugby League began to operate in Australia. One year later, the first rugby league game was played in New Zealand. Both forms of rugby continued to gain popularity after World War I, with the amateur game taking hold in places as far away as Japan, Fiji, Romania, and Argentina. In 1924–25, a second All Blacks tour of England netted 30 wins in as many games played, the New Zealanders scoring 721 points, with only 112 against. South Africa's Springboks toured Britain for the third time in 1931–32. Employing a revolutionary 3-4-1 scrum formation and the relentless, accurate kicking of fly half Bennie Osler, the Springboks compiled a record of 23 victories, 1 loss and 2 draws. Their conservative, if successful tactics (called "ten-man rugby") were to have far-reaching effects on the game for many years.

In 1931, displeased with allegations of rough play and concealed professionalism in France, the RFU severed ties with the French federation. In 1933, France, together with Germany and Italy, formed FIRA (the Fédération Internationale de Rugby Amateur, or International Federation of Amateur Rugby) as the European equivalent to the International Rugby Football Board. A rugby league match was staged in Paris the same year, and soon the new game, "jeu à treize" (game to 13) flourished. No French amateur team was to play in England until the end of World War II, when a French Services team met a British Empire side at Richmond, paving the way for France to take part in the 1945–46 "Victory" internationals.

Amateur rugby has continued to grow as an international sport since the post-war years, with new international bodies governing Asian competition, and a much expanded FIRA presiding over European matches. On balance, Wales has been dominant in the British Isles, as has France in Europe and Japan in Asia. But in international competition, New Zealand and South Africa have been the powerhouses of modern rugby union. So, too, has Australia reigned in professional rugby. Remarkably, the Kangaroos' 1983 defeat by New Zealand was their first loss in seventeen Tests.

accidentally offside: Offside and unable to avoid making contact with the ball or the player carrying the ball. When a player is accidentally offside, play is allowed to continue unless the offside player's team gains an advantage. In such a case, a scrum is formed, with the ball being given to the nonoffending side. see *offside*.

acting halfback: In rugby league, either of two players (one from each side) who stand immediately behind the two opposing players taking part in a play-the-ball. The acting halfbacks are the only players permitted to be closer than 5 meters behind those involved in a play-the-ball, and must remain in this position until the ball has been played back. see *play-the-ball*.

advantage: Short for advantage rule.

advantage rule: A clause in the Laws of rugby which enables the referee to allow play to continue after a foul if a stoppage of play would take away an advantage (territorial or tactical) gained by the nonoffending side. The advantage rule does not apply when the ball or a player carrying it touches the referee, when the ball emerges from either end of the tunnel at a scrimmage (or scrummage) not having been played, or when a player is accidentally offside. also *advantage*.

against the head: From the opponents' put-in. In a scrum, when the ball is hooked back by the side not making the put-in, it is said to be won against the head, theoretically more difficult because the hooker on the side making the put-in has his head closer to the ball when it is put into play.

ankle tap: A tackle (often made as a last resort when an opponent is about to get away) in which a dive is made to make contact with the opponent's ankles in order to trip and bring him down.

Ashes, the: In rugby league, the symbolic prize awarded to the victorious side in any series of matches between national teams representing England and Australia. Patterned after the original cricket tradition begun in 1882. That year, Australia's humiliating Test match victory over England prompted a mock obituary in the *Sporting Times* mourning the death of English cricket. When an England team toured Australia the same year, an urn containing the actual burnt ashes of one of the stumps used in the Test series was presented to the English captain. Though the urn itself resides permanently in the MCC's Imperial Cricket Memorial Museum in London, The Ashes are said to be "held" by the winner of any England vs. Australia Test match. The tradition was borrowed by rugby league in 1908, when Australia's Kangaroos made the first tour of England.

Australian dispensation: In rugby union, the clause in the Laws that prohibits kicking directly into touch on the full except when inside one's own 22-meter line. Infractions result in a scrum being formed at the place from where the ball was kicked, with the put-in to the nonoffending side. Prior to 1968, when the International Board introduced this clause into the Laws, it was in force only in Australian domestic matches (along with several other rules and concessions) to make rugby union matches more attractive in the face of the severe competition provided by rugby league and Australian rules football.

back: Any of the seven players who do not take part in a scrum. Known collectively as the "back division" or "back line", the backs comprise a scrum half, a fly half, two center three-quarters, two wing three-quarters, and a fullback. also *back liner*.

back division: A collective name for the backs. also *back line*. see *back*.

back line: A collective name for the backs. also *back division*. see *back*.

back liner: see *back*.

back movement: The advancement of the ball by moving it along a line of backs in a running formation.

back pass: A pass made in a rearward direction.

back play: The performance of the backs in the course of one or more games.

back row: In rugby union, the three loose forwards; two wing forwards (blindside and open-side) and the number 8 (middle of the back). The name "back row" is derived from the position of these three players in the back row of the old standard 3-2-3 scrum formation.

back rower, back-row forward: Any of the three players in the back row (in the old standard 3-2-3 formation). also *loose forward*. see *back row*.

back-row play: In rugby union, the performance of the so-called "back row" in the course of one or more games, their ability to contain the opponent's backs, pick up loose balls, and help set up attacks. see *back play*.

back up: To move into a tactical position behind a teammate with the ball in order to be ready for a pass. also *support*.

bad ball: Bad service (unsafe rather than "quality" possession of the ball) to the backs from the forwards, as from a scrum, ruck, or line-out. A "hospital pass" back to the scrum half, one that is delayed long enough for opposing players to close in on him before the ball can be safely gathered is bad ball. compare *good ball*.

bad bounce: An unfavorable bounce that causes the ball to veer away from a player who is about to pick it up.

ball: An inflated rubber bladder enclosed in a leather or leather-like case, oval in shape (with pointed ends) and comprising four panels. A rugby union ball is 28-30 centimeters in length with a circumference of 58-62 centimeters, and must weigh between 400-440 grams. A rugby league ball is 27-29 centimeters in length with a circumference of 58-61 centimeters, and must weigh between 380-440 grams. The oval shape of early rugby balls was probably due to the shape of inflated pig bladders, replaced by rubber bladders in 1870. No mention was made of the size and shape of the ball in the Laws until 1892, when the RFU decreed that it should be oval in shape and assigned dimensions that, but for small changes making it slimmer and heavier in 1931, remain the same today. also *football*.

ball back: In rugby league, the formation of a scrum at the place from which the ball was kicked or touched after it has been kicked or bounced in a forward direction off a player into touch "on the full" (without first bouncing inbounds on the playing field).

banjoed: Players' slang for having been kicked in the groin.

barge: To illegally charge or bump an opponent. see *charge*.

barging: The act or an instance of illegally charging or bumping an opponent. see *charging*.

base of the scrum: Just behind the scrum, where the scrum half operates.

beat: To gain a momentary advantage over or get past an opponent, as with a fake, a feint, or a burst of speed. (sold the dummy to beat his man)

beef one's way through: To use one's size, strength, and momentum to break tackles and force one's way through opposing players. also *bullock*.

1. bend: To make a ball curve in flight by kicking it slightly off center. also *curl*, *swerve*.

2. bend: The curve in the direction of flight of a ball kicked slightly off center. also *curl*, *swerve*.

between the posts: In rugby league, midway between the goal posts, as for a dropout taken at the center of the goal line. see *dropout*.

bind: To tightly wrap one's arms around behind adjacent teammates (at or below the level of the armpits) in order to form a pack for a scrum or a ruck. In a scrum, the outside (loose-head) prop must either bind his opposing (tight-head) prop with his left arm inside the right arm of his opponent or place his left hand or forearm on his left thigh. The tight-head prop must bind with his right arm outside the left upper arm of his opposing loose-head prop. He may grip the jersey of the opposing tight-head prop with his right hand but must not pull downward. The middle forward in the front row (hooker) must bind to both flanking props (and they to him) either over or under the arms (in rugby league, the hooker must bind with his arms over those of the props). Players in the front row must stay bound while the ball is being put in and until it emerges from the scrum. All other players in a scrum must bind with at least one arm around a teammate. In a ruck, all players involved must bind a teammate with at least one arm. see *ruck*, *scrum*.

blind man swing: A surreptitious underhand blow delivered to an opponent in a scrum by a player hidden from the referee (often a flanker attempting to hit his opposing number). If such an offense is detected, the guilty player is cautioned or sent off (in rugby league, the player may also be temporarily suspended), and the nonoffending side is awarded a penalty kick.

blind side: The playing area on the side of a scrum, maul, ruck, or play-the-ball closest to the nearest touchline. compare *open side*.

blind-side: Of or pertaining to the blind side. (scored on a blind-side break) compare *open-side*.

blind-side wing forward: 1. In rugby union, the wing forward who plays on the blind side. The blind-side wing forward binds into a scrum behind his prop forward and alongside the second row on the blind side. compare *open-side wing forward*. 2. The position played by the wing forward on the blind side.

blow up: Players' slang meaning to, as a referee, whistle for a stoppage of play because of a foul or an infringement.

boots: The cleated shoes worn to play rugby. Rugby boots have either high-cut (for forwards) or low-cut (for backs) soft leather uppers with reinforced toes and tough plastic or composition soles into which six or eight replaceable studs are screwed. Studs (leather, rubber, aluminum, or approved plastic) must be circular, not more than 18 millimeters long, or less than 13 millimeters in diameter at the base, and 10 millimeters in diameter at the tip. The wearing of a single stud at the toe of a boot is prohibited. Rugby league rules state only that studs must be no less than 8 millimeters in diameter at the tip and, if metal, must have rounded edges.

box: In rugby union, the open space behind a scrum or line-out, between the scrum half and the fullback.

1. break: A sudden move that puts a player past or away from one or more opponents or into an open space, either to advance the ball or to set up a potential advance. also *breakaway*.

2. break: To suddenly move past or away from one or more opponents or into an open space, either to advance the ball or to set up a potential advance.

breakaway: 1. see *break*. 2. In rugby union, a wing forward, so-called because of the ease with which wing forwards can "break away" from their flanking positions in a scrum. also *flanker*, *flank forward*, *side row*. 3. The position played by a wing forward. also *flanker*, *flank forward*, *side row*.

bring down: 1. To tackle and bring an opponent carrying the ball to the ground. also *take down*. 2. To illegally trip or tackle an opponent who is not carrying the ball, a foul that results in a penalty kick for the nonoffending side. If, in the judgement of the referee, the foul is violent or dangerous, the guilty player may be cautioned or sent off (in rugby league, the player may also be temporarily suspended). also *take down*.

bullock: To use one's size, strength, and momentum to break tackles and "beef through" opposing players.

bullocker: Slang for a player known more for size and strength than intelligence, mobility, or flair.

1. cap: 1. A figurative award of merit (and in some countries, an actual tasseled cap) given to a player each time he participates as a member of a national team in international competition (in rugby league, a player must participate in two international Test matches to be eligible for a cap). From the nineteenth century custom of English public schools and universities awarding ornate tasseled caps for athletic accomplishments as sports were first organized and popularized. 2. A player who has been awarded an international cap. (a back row made up of three English caps) also *international*.

2. cap: To award a cap. (was first capped at the age of 22)

cauliflower ear: A deformity of the ear caused by repeated blows or mangling, not uncommon among longtime second row forwards who must bind with their heads between players in the front row of a scrum. Many forwards now wear scrum caps to protect their ears from this deformity.

1. caution: An official warning to a player guilty of a serious or deliberate offense against the Laws or the letter and spirit of the game, including obstruction, unfair play, misconduct, dangerous play, unsporting behavior, retaliation, and repeated infringements. After having received a caution, a player who commits another serious offense is sub-

CHARGE

ject to being sent off (or in rugby league, temporarily suspended or sent off).

2. caution: To issue an official warning to a player guilty of a serious or deliberate offense against the Laws or the letter and spirit of the game.

center: 1. Either of the two central three-quarter backs (left and right) who play between the fly half and wing three-quarter. also *center three-quarter*. 2. Either of the two positions played by the center three-quarter backs. also *center three-quarter*. 3. The center spot.

center line: The halfway line.

center spot: The spot marked at the middle of the halfway line from which kickoffs are made at the start of each half and after each goal. also *center*.

center three-quarter, center three-quarter back: see *center*.

chance: An opportunity to score. (scored on their first chance, a break up the middle)

change of pace: A sudden burst of speed, as to evade a tackle.

1. channel: In rugby union, any of the lanes between the players in the second row through which the ball can be heeled and directed after possession is won in a scrum.

2. channel: In rugby union, to, after having won possession of the ball in a scrum, heel and direct it back through one of the "channels" or lanes between the players in the second row.

1. charge: 1. To run into or make contact with an opposing player, legal only if contact is made with the shoulder (a "fair charge" or "shoulder charge") when contending for a ball within playing distance. see *charging*. 2. To, in an attempt to block a kick, suddenly rush toward the ball as it is kicked or about to be kicked by a player. On a kickoff, opposing players may not charge beyond the 10-meter line until the ball is kicked or the kick is retaken. On a kick at goal after a try, opposing players may not charge beyond the goal line until the kicker starts his approach or kick. If they do charge, the kick is retaken (unless the kick is successful) and opposing players are prohibited from charging. On a dropout, opposing players may not charge beyond the 22-meter line or the dropout is retaken. If opposing players charge for the sake of delaying or interfering with a dropout, a penalty kick is awarded. On a free kick, opposing players may not charge beyond a line parallel to the goal line 10 meters from the mark until the kicker starts his approach or kick. An infringement by opposing players results in the award of a penalty kick 10 meters in front of the mark or 5 meters from the goal line, whichever is nearer. see *dropout, free kick, kickoff.*

2. charge: 1. The act or an instance of running into or making contact with an opposing player. see *charging.* 2. The act or an instance of attempting to block a kick by suddenly rushing toward the ball as it is kicked or about to be kicked.

charge down: To fairly charge and block an opponent's kick with one's arms or body.

charging: The act or an instance of an illegal charge. Charging results in the award of a penalty kick at the place of the infringement. If, in the opinion of the referee, a probable try was interrupted, a penalty try can be awarded. If the infringement is deliberate, flagrant, dangerous, or repeated, the offending player is cautioned and can be sent off. In a line-out, contact (by a player involved in the line-out) with an opponent before the ball has been thrown in and has touched the ground or been touched by a player is charging and results in the award of a penalty kick 15 meters from the touchline on the line-of-touch. see *line-out, line-of-touch.*

1. chip: A short kick lofted over the heads of opposing players to teammates. also *chip kick.*

2. chip: To loft a short kick over the heads of opposing players to teammates.

chip kick: see *chip.*

clean pair of hands: Players' slang for the ability to catch the ball. (known as a great runner with a clean pair of hands)

clear: Momentarily in the open, with no opponents nearby. see *put clear.*

clearance kick: A kick made by defenders in order to regain lost ground, as by finding touch upfield.

collapse a scrum: To intentionally drop to the ground or pull down on either the jersey or body of the opposing forward in an attempt to gain an advantage by weakening or collapsing the scrum.

Because of the danger of injury from the collapse of a scrum, such actions result in the award of a penalty kick to the nonoffending side at the place of the infringement.

conversion: 1. The successful 2-point completion of a kick at goal after a try, the conversion of a try. see *convert a try.* 2. In rugby union, the successful 3-point completion of a penalty kick or a kick at goal in open play. see *drop goal, goal, penalty kick.* 3. In rugby league, the successful 2-point completion of a penalty kick or a kick at goal in open play (only 1 point is given for a drop goal in international matches). see *drop goal, goal, penalty kick.*

convert: 1. Short for convert a try. 2. In rugby union, to score a 3-point goal with a penalty kick or a kick at goal in open play. see *drop goal, goal, penalty kick.* 3. In rugby league, to score a 2-point goal with a penalty kick or a kick at goal in open play (only 1 point is given for a drop goal in international matches). see *drop goal, goal, penalty kick.*

convert a try: To score 2 points with a kick at goal after a try. To convert a try, the ball must be drop-kicked or place-kicked over the opponent's crossbar and between the goal posts (without first touching the ground or a teammate) from any point on the playing field on a line through the place where the try was scored.

corner flag: A small flag atop a post not less than 1.20 meters (1.25 meters in rugby league) high placed at each corner of the playing field at the convergence of the goal line and touchline. In rugby union only, four similar flags are placed at the point where the touch-in-goal lines and dead-ball lines converge.

corner flagging: The diagonal movement back across the field by players (roughly, toward one or the other of their own corner flags) in order to cover defensively when the opposing side wins possession in a scrum and is attacking.

corner post: A post (nonrigid in rugby league) not less than 1.20 meters (1.25 meters in rugby league) high surmounted by a small flag (corner flag), and placed at each corner of the playing field at the convergence of the goal line and touchline. The corner posts are in touch-in-goal.

cover: 1. To move into a defensive position so as to be able to prevent opponents from advancing the ball into an open or unguarded space, whether by running, passing, or kicking. 2. To mark an opposing player.

crash ball: A facetious name for straight-ahead, power running with the ball rather than any attempt at evading or deceiving tacklers.

crooked feed: An illegal, "not straight" put-in by a scrum half in which the ball is put into a scrum at an angle toward or closer to his teammates ("fed to his own feet") rather than down the middle line. A free kick is awarded at the place of the infringement to the nonoffending side. also *feed one's own feet.*

crossbar: The 3-meter high, 5.6-meter (5.5-meter in rugby league) long horizontal bar that extends between the two goal posts set on the goal line at each end of the playing field. For a goal to be scored, the ball must be kicked over the crossbar and between the goal posts. also *woodwork.*

1. cross kick: A kick in which the ball is punted high across the field from one side of the pitch to the other, either to a teammate, or for teammates to run on to. A cross kick is particularly useful when the player with the ball is trapped by opponents.

2. cross kick: To punt the ball high across the field from one side of the pitch to the other, either to a teammate, or for teammates to run on to.

curl: see *swerve.*

dangerous play: Any action by a player that, in the opinion of the referee, is dangerous or likely to cause injury to the player, a teammate, or an opponent. Dangerous play (stiff-arm

tackling, trampling, intentionally collapsing a scrum, etc.) results in the guilty player being cautioned or sent off (in rugby league, the player may also be temporarily suspended). In addition, depending on the type and location of the infringement and whether or not it prevented a probable try, a penalty kick or penalty try is awarded to the nonoffending side.

dead: Out of play, said of the ball. The ball is dead whenever the referee blows his whistle to signal a stoppage of play or when a conversion of a try is unsuccessful.

dead-ball line: The line marked parallel to the goal line at each end of the playing area, serving as the back boundary for the in-goal area. In rugby union, the dead-ball line is marked no more than 22 meters from the goal line. This distance was first mentioned (as 25 yards) in a clause added to the Laws in 1891. The following year, a new law defining the dead-ball line was introduced. In rugby league, the dead-ball line is marked 6–11 meters from the goal line.

differential penalty: A free kick (from which a goal cannot be scored directly) awarded for certain scrum, ruck, and line-out offenses that previously resulted in a penalty kick before a 1977 rule change. see *line-out, ruck, scrum.*

dismiss: see *send off.*

dismissal: The act or an instance of a player being ejected from a match, as for a serious foul or misconduct, or for repeated infringements after being cautioned (or in rugby league, after being temporarily suspended). see *send off.*

dive pass: A pass in which the passer dives headfirst toward the intended receiver parallel to the ground and thrusts the ball ahead. A dive pass is often made by a scrum half under pressure after the ball comes out of a scrum, or by a player being tackled. The dive pass was invented by South African Daniel H. Craven in the late 1920s, scrum half (and paired with fly half Bennie Osler) for the 1931–32 Springbok tour.

dive-pass: To execute a dive pass.

double scissors: A seldom seen offensive maneuver in which a player advancing diagonally toward one touchline with the ball hands or passes it back to a

CRASH BALL

teammate crossing behind him diagonally toward the opposite touchline, who in turn hands or passes it back to another teammate crossing diagonally behind him in the original direction of the play. compare *dummy scissors, scissors.*

1. draw: A tied match in which both teams finish with the same score. see *extra time.*

2. draw: To end a match with the score tied. see *extra time.*

1. dribble: To maneuver with or advance the ball along the ground by using the feet.

2. dribble: The act or an instance of dribbling.

1. drive: A determined effort that advances the ball toward the opponent's goal line.

2. drive: To, individually or with teammates, make a determined effort that advances the ball toward the opponent's goal line.

driving over the ball: The act or an instance of pushing collectively and forcing opponents back and away from the ball so as to be able to heel it to teammates, as by forwards in a ruck. compare *forward drive.*

1. drive for the line: A determined effort near the opponent's goal line to push the ball over for a try.

2. drive for the line: To, individually or with teammates, make a determined effort near the opponent's goal line to push the ball over for a try. also *go for the line.*

drop a goal: To score a goal with a ball that is dropkicked during open play. see *drop goal.*

drop goal: A goal scored in open play with a dropkick. In rugby union, a drop goal is worth 3 points. In rugby league, a drop goal is worth 2 points (1 point in international matches). also *dropped goal, drop shot, field goal.*

dropkick: A kick made by dropping the ball and kicking it the instant it rebounds. A dropkick may be used to score goals on penalty kicks (penalty goal), kicks at goal from the open field (drop goal), or to convert a try, or to advance the ball, kick for touch, or kick after a fair catch. A dropkick must be used for a dropout and after an unconverted try. also *half volley, pot.* see *convert a try, drop goal, dropout,*

kick for touch, penalty kick.

drop-kick: To make a dropkick. also *half-volley, pot.*

dropout: 1. In rugby union, a dropkick made by the defending side from on or behind the 22-meter line to restart play after an attacking player has propelled the ball over the dead-ball line or into touch-in-goal, after a defending player has touched the ball down in his in-goal area (when he has not wilfully propelled it over the goal line), or after an infringement or incident of foul play in the in-goal area by the attacking side. On a dropout, the kicking team must be behind the ball until it is kicked (or a scrum is formed at the middle of the 22-meter line), the ball must reach the 22-meter line (or the opposing team may have it dropped-out again or have a scrum formed there), and the opposing team must not charge over the 22-meter line (or the ball is dropped-out again or, if delay or interference is intended, a penalty kick is given). Until 1892, a dropout was known as a kick out. Because of the location of the kick (until metric measurements were recently standardized, it was from the 25-yard line), a dropout was also called a "25". see *line-out.* 2. In rugby league, a dropkick made by the defending side from the center of the 22-meter line to restart play after the ball goes dead in the in-goal area from a penalty kick, or a dropkick made by the defending side from the center of the goal line ("between the posts") after a defending player last touches the ball before it goes over the dead-ball line or into touch-in-goal, accidentally infringes in the in-goal area, touches the ball down or is tackled while in possession of the ball in the in-goal area, or kicks the ball into touch on the full from his in-goal area, or after the ball or a defending player in possession of the ball touches the referee, a touch-judge, or an encroaching spectator in the in-goal area and thereby play is irregularly affected, or after the ball bounces over the dead-ball line or into touch-in-goal from a kickoff without having touched a defending player. On a dropout, the kicking team must be behind the ball until it is kicked and may not touch it until it has traveled 10 meters in a forward direction. The ball must be kicked

233

in the prescribed manner, travel at least 10 meters in a forward direction, and not cross the touchline, touch-in-goal line, or dead-ball line. Opposing players must remain 10 meters from the line from which the kick is taken. Infractions result in a penalty kick for the nonoffending side, either at the center of the 22-meter line if the dropout is from there, or at the center of the line drawn parallel to and 10 meters from the goal line if the dropout is from between the posts.

drop-out: To make a dropout.

dropped goal: A drop goal. also *drop shot, field goal.*

drop shot: A drop goal. also *dropped goal, field goal.*

1. dummy: A fake or feint intended to momentarily deceive or wrong-foot an opponent. see *sell the dummy.*

2. dummy: To attempt a fake or feint in order to momentarily deceive or wrong-foot an opponent.

dummy scissors: An offensive play designed to look like a scissors maneuver in which a player advancing diagonally toward one touchline with the ball hands or passes it back to a teammate crossing behind him diagonally toward the opposite touchline. In a dummy scissors, however, the pass is merely faked to momentarily deceive the opponents. compare *scissors.*

early tackle: A tackle in which contact is made with a player before he is in possession of the ball. An early tackle results in a penalty kick at the place of the foul for the nonoffending side, and, if judged dangerous by the referee, the cautioning or sending off of the guilty player (in rugby league, the player may also be temporarily suspended). compare *late tackle.*

end: Either of the two halves of the field, from the halfway line to the goal line. (struggled to move the ball out of their own end)

equalize: To score a game-tying try or goal. also *knot.*

extra man: see *man over.*

extra time: 1. Playing time added to the end of a half to make up for time lost due to injuries or other delays. 2. Playing time added at the end of a drawn match in a knock-out competition authorized by the controlling body with jurisdiction.

fair catch: In rugby union, the act or an instance of a stationary player (with both feet on the ground) inside his 22-meter line cleanly catching the ball directly from a kick, knock-on, or throw-forward from an opposing player, and, at the same time, calling out "mark". A fair catch may be made even though the ball first touches a goal post or the crossbar, and may be made in the in-goal area. A free kick is awarded for a fair catch, to be taken by the player catching the ball. If, after one minute, he is unable to do so because of an injury, a scrum is formed at the place the catch is made, with his team putting in the ball. The scrum is formed 5 meters from the goal line on a line with the place of the fair catch if it is made in the in-goal area. The fair catch was defined first in the early Laws of Blackheath (1862) and Rugby School (1866), and by the RFU in 1871. also *mark.*

fall on the ball: To, in open play, momentarily fall on a loose ball in order to prevent the opposing team from gaining ground. If the player remains on or near the ball so as to obstruct possession by an opponent (first forbidden in 1892), or falls on a ball emerging from a scrum or ruck, a penalty kick is given to the nonoffending side.

1. feed: 1. A put-in. see *crooked feed.* 2. A handoff or pass of the ball back to a teammate or series of teammates, as after winning possession in and emerging from a scrum, ruck, or maul. see *maul, scrum, ruck.*

2. feed: 1. To put the ball in to a scrum. 2. To, as after winning possession in and emerging from a scrum, ruck, or maul, hand or pass the ball back to a teammate or series of teammates.

feed one's own feet: see *crooked feed.*

field goal: A drop goal. also *dropped goal, drop shot.*

fifteen: A rugby union side.

find touch: see *kick for touch.*

FIRA: The International Amateur Rugby Association (Fédération Internationale de Rugby Amateur), governing body for European amateur rugby. The Continental equivalent to the International Rugby Football Board, FIRA was formed in 1933 by France, Germany and Italy, and is headquartered in France.

first five-eighth: 1. In New Zealand, the name given to the fly half. also *fly half,* out half, outside half, standoff, standoff half, standoff halfback. see five-eighth. 2. In New Zealand, the position played by the fly half. also *fly half, out half, outside half, standoff, standoff half, standoff halfback.*

five-eighth: 1. In New Zealand, the name given to both the fly half (first five-eighth) and the inside center three-quarter (second five-eighth). The five-eighths were the creation of fly half Jimmy Duncan, captain of New Zealand's All Blacks in 1903. On a tour of Australia that year, Duncan moved his inside center closer to him at scrums and line-outs to work with him in plays, thus leading to the now common New Zealand designations of first and second five-eighths. 2. In Australian rugby league, the name given to the fly half. also *first five-eighth, fly half, out half, outside half, standoff, standoff half, standoff halfback.* 3. In Australian rugby league, the position played by the fly half. also *first five-eighth, fly half, out half, outside half, standoff, standoff half, standoff halfback.*

five-meter line: In rugby union, a line marked from touchline to touchline, 5 meters out from and parallel to each goal line. see *five-meter scrum.*

five-meter scrum: A scrum formed on the five-meter line when the place where the scrum normally would be formed is closer to the in-goal area (or in rugby league, when an attacking player in possession of the ball is held by one or more defenders in their in-goal area and is unable to ground the ball). A five-meter scrum is still often called a five-yard scrum, its name until metric markings were standardized in recent years.

five-yard scrum: see *five-meter scrum.*

flanker: 1. In rugby union, a wing forward. also *breakaway, side row.* 2. The position played by a wing forward. also *breakaway, side row.*

flat: Parallel to the goal lines. (able to break through when he caught the defense flat)

fly hack: A kick made when the ball is on the ground and loose, as to prevent opposing players from gaining possession or to advance the ball suddenly. In New Zealand, a fly hack is also called a speculator.

fly-hack: To execute a fly hack.

fly half: 1. The player who normally lines up behind a scrum between the scrum half and the three-quarters. also *first five-eighth, five-eighth, out half, outside half, standoff, standoff half, standoff halfback.* 2. The position played by the fly half. also *first five-eighth, five-eighth, out half, outside half, standoff, standoff half, standoff halfback.*

flying wedge: An offensive move occasionally employed when the ball is near the opponent's goal line in which a player either taps the ball to himself (as from a short penalty kick) or receives a short pass, then drives toward the line with his teammates binding onto either side of him in a "V" or "wedge". Because of the danger posed to defending players attempting to stop such a move, the flying wedge was banned in England in 1983 for school and junior rugby.

fly kick: The act or an instance of fly-kicking a ball.

fly-kick: To kick a ball in the air without catching it first.

football: 1. A name for rugby. also *rugby football, rugger.* 2. The ball used in rugby.

foot-up: The illegal raising of a foot before the ball has touched the ground on a put-in by a front row player in a scrum. This results in the awarding of a free kick (or in rugby league, a penalty kick) to the nonoffending side at the place of the infringement.

forward: 1. In rugby union, any of the eight players who bind together to form the pack for a scrum. These include two prop forwards, the hooker, two lock forwards, the number 8, and two wing forwards. 2. In rugby league, any of the six players who bind together to form the pack for a scrum. These include two prop forwards, the hooker, two second-row forwards, and a loose forward.

forward drive: The act or an instance of the forwards of one team pushing collectively in a scrum and forcing the opposing forwards back and away from the ball so as to be able to advance the ball and/or heel it back to teammates. also *forward rush, forward shove, push, shove.* compare *driving over the ball.*

forward game: In rugby union, a game dominated by the play of forwards and characterized by long, dull struggles between the packs in scrums, rucks, and mauls rather than open play with the backs running and passing. A forward game is more likely to be seen when the weather and field conditions are poor and the ball is difficult to handle.

forward pass: A pass made by the player with the ball in the direction of the opponent's dead-ball line. A forward pass is illegal and (depending upon whether it is unintentional or intentional) results in a scrum or a penalty kick at the place of the infringement, with the nonoffending side making the put-in or taking the kick. The forward pass or throw-forward, as it is known in the Laws, was forbidden even in the crude original forms of football. A description of the game from 1602 states, "It is prohibited to deal a foreball".

forward rush, forward shove: see *forward drive*.

1. foul: A serious infringement of the Laws that generally involves physical contact with an opponent. see *foul play*.

2. foul: 1. To commit a foul. 2. To commit a foul against a particular opponent. (fouled him with a stiff-arm tackle) see *foul play*.

foul play: Any action by a player that is contrary to the letter and spirit of the game, including obstruction, unfair play, misconduct, dangerous play, unsporting behavior, retaliation, and repeated infringements of the Laws. Depending upon the severity, circumstances, and location of the foul play, the guilty player is cautioned or sent off (in rugby league, the player may also

FOUL

be temporarily suspended), and the nonoffending side is awarded a penalty kick and (if the foul play prevented a probable try) a penalty try.

free kick: An unhindered kick given at the place of the infringement to the nonoffending side in the case of certain scrum, ruck, and line-out offenses, and from which a goal cannot be scored directly. In these cases, a free kick is a "differential penalty", given instead of a penalty kick prior to rule changes in 1977. In rugby union, a free kick is awarded for a fair catch. On a free kick, any kind of kick may be used, but the kicking team (except for the player holding a place kick) must remain behind the ball until it is kicked. An infraction results in a scrum being formed at the place of the kick, with the put-in being given to the nonoffending side. The opposing team must retire to or behind an imaginary line parallel to the goal lines and 10 meters from the place of the kick or to their own goal line if it lies within 10 meters from the place of the kick, and may not charge across this imaginary line before the kicker begins his run or kick. An infringement results in a penalty kick for the nonoffending side. see *fair catch, line-out, ruck, scrum*.

front five: In rugby union, the five players who made up the first and second rows of the pack in a scrum in the old 3-2-3 formation, the two prop forwards and the hooker (front row), and the two lock forwards (second row). see *3-2-3*.

front row: The three forwards who bind together to make up the front row of the pack in a scrum, the two prop forwards and the hooker.

fullback: 1. The player usually positioned closest to his own goal line, often the last line of defense. A fullback's responsibilities include tackling, falling on the ball, gathering high offensive kicks by the opposition, and clearing the ball when danger threatens. 2. The position played by a fullback.

full time: The end of regulation time for a match (two 40-minute halves), excluding injury or extra time. compare *no side*.

gain ground: To kick the ball upfield, either in the hope of recovering it on the playing field, or to find touch.

gain line: An imaginary line across the

field and parallel to the goal lines between the two teams at any point during a match. If the backs reach the gain line with the ball before the opposing team crosses it to dispossess them, they are said to have gained ground. If not, the opposing team is said to have gained ground.

gap: A momentary open space between defending players through which the ball can be advanced.

Garryowen, Garryowen up and under: An up and under kick, a punt lofted high in the air upfield for teammates to receive or follow up. The name is derived from a club noted for its use, the Garryowen RFC in Dooradoyle, County Limerick, Ireland.

give some stick: To play rough, especially to physically punish a particular opponent. A British expression applied to both rugby and soccer, and derived from horse racing and the jockey's use of a whip.

●● To verbally punish or abuse one or more persons. (gave the actor some stick about forgetting his lines)

goal: 1. The structure centered on each goal line consisting of a 5.6- (or in rugby league, 5.5-) meter horizontal crossbar whose top face is 3 meters above the ground, with uprights at either end that extend vertically at least 3.40 meters (or in rugby league, at least 4 meters) above the crossbar. To convert a try or score on any kind of a kick from the field, the ball must be kicked over the crossbar between the uprights. Goals supported by a single standard are permissible provided that the relevant dimensions are observed. Goals of the present dimensions were called for as early as 1866 in the Laws of Football at Rugby School. see *woodwork*. 2. Two points scored on a try conversion by drop-kicking or place-kicking the ball directly over the opponent's crossbar and between the uprights from any point on the playing field on a line through the place where the try was scored. see *try*. 3. Three points (2 points in rugby league) scored on a penalty kick by punting, drop-kicking, or place-kicking the ball directly over the opponent's crossbar and between the uprights from the place of an infringement. 4. Three points (2 points in rugby league) scored on a drop goal by drop-

kicking the ball directly over the opponent's crossbar and between the uprights from the open field. In rugby league international matches a drop goal counts for only 1 point.

goal kick: A kick at goal.

goal kicker: 1. A player who is proficient at or known for kicking goals. 2. A player who is regularly called on by his team to attempt to kick at goal.

goal line: The line marked parallel to the dead-ball line at each end of the field of play, extending the width of the field between the touchlines to serve as the front boundary of the in-goal area, and in the center of which is located the goal. The goal line is a part of the in-goal area, and a try can be scored if the ball is grounded on the line. also *line*, *try line*.

goal post: Either of two vertical poles or posts, 5.6 (or in rugby league, 5.5) meters apart and connected by the crossbar 3 meters from the ground, and which serve as the side of the goal. For a goal to be scored, the ball must be kicked over the crossbar and between the goal posts. also *post*, *upright*, *woodwork*.

go for a gap: To move the ball toward a momentary open space between defending players.

go for the line: see *drive for the line*.

good ball: Good service (clean, safe possession of the ball) to the backs from the forwards from a scrum, ruck, or line-out. also *quality possession*. compare *bad ball*, *quick ball*.

go the wrong way: To be wrong-footed or momentarily deceived and caused to move in the wrong direction by a fake or feint from an opponent.

Grand Slam: In rugby union, victory by one national team over the four others in the international tournament played by England, Ireland, Scotland, Wales and France. compare *Triple Crown*.

grind down: To, by means of individual or collective strength and relentless pressure, wear down an opponent or opponents in a match. Often, one or more forwards will grind down their opponents in the front row, thereby weakening the opposition's scrum.

ground: 1. A stadium or playing field and environs. A British term. also *grounds*. 2. A British term for a playing field. also *grounds*, *pitch*.

grounds: see *ground*.

ground the ball: To, while holding the ball in the hand (or hands) or arm (or arms), bring the ball into contact with the ground, or, while the ball is on the ground, to place the hand (or hands) or arm (or arms) on it with downward pressure, or fall on the ball with the front of the body (from waist to neck). A try is scored by grounding the ball in the opponent's in-goal area. A touchdown occurs when the ball is first grounded by a player in his in-goal area. see touchdown, try.

grubber: A punt that stays low, and skids or rolls end over end along the ground. From the worm-like larva of certain insects found in the ground. also *grub kick*.

grub kick: see *grubber*.

hack: To deliberately kick an opponent in the shins, forbidden by the Laws of rugby. see *hacking*.

hacking: The act or instance of deliberately kicking an opponent. Hacking results in the guilty player being cautioned or sent off (in rugby league, the player may also be temporarily suspended), and the awarding of a penalty kick to the nonoffending side at the place of the foul. A common occurrence in early forms of football, hacking was specifically prohibited in the 1871 Rugby Football Union Laws.

half: 1. Short for halfback. 2. Short for the position played by a halfback. 3. The interval between the two periods of play in a match. (led by seven at the half) 4. Either of the two halves of the field, from the halfway line to the goal line. (rarely were able to move the ball out of their own half) also *end*. 5. Either of the two forty-minute periods of play in a match. (scored two tries in the second half)

halfback: 1. Either of two players, the scrum half or the fly half. also *half*. see *fly half, scrum half*. 2. The position played by either the scrum half or fly half. also *half*. 3. In Australia and New Zealand, the scrum half. also *half, scrum halfback*. 4. The position played by the scrum half. also *half, scrum halfback*.

halfback pair: A collective name for the scrum half and fly half. also *pair of halfbacks*.

halfback play: The performance of the

scrum half and fly half in the course of one or more games.

half volley: A dropkick. also *pot*.

half-volley: To drop-kick the ball. also *pot*.

halfway line: A line marked across the center of the playing area (touchline to touchline) parallel to the goal lines. The center spot, from which kickoffs are taken, is marked in the middle of the halfway line. The term halfway line first appeared in the Laws in 1905. also *center line*.

handle: To touch, carry, strike, or propel the ball with any part of the hand. No player may handle the ball while it is in a scrum or a ruck, except in the act of obtaining a "push over" try or touchdown. An infringement results in a penalty kick for the nonoffending side at the place of the infringement.

hand off: To ward off a would-be tackler with the palm of the hand.

hand-off: The act or an instance of warding off a would-be tackler with the palm of the hand.

heavy pitch: A slow, soft playing surface, as one in which the turf is wet or not closely cut.

1. heel: To pass the ball backwards on the ground with the heel, as in a scrum, ruck, or play-the-ball. also *hook*. see *play-the-ball, ruck, scrum*.

2. heel: The act or an instance of passing the ball backwards on the ground, as in a scrum, ruck, or play-the-ball. see *play-the-ball, ruck, scrum*.

high tackle: A tackle aimed at the upper part of the body, often ineffective and, if judged dangerous by the referee, resulting in the cautioning or sending off of the guilty player (in rugby league, the player may also be temporarily suspended) and a penalty kick to the nonoffending side at the place of the foul.

holding: The obstruction of an opponent not in possession of the ball by grasping his body, illegal except in a scrum, ruck, or a maul. In a scrimmage or ruck, the dragging away of a player lying close to the ball is permitted. Otherwise, pulling any part of the clothing of an opponent is holding. An infringement results in a penalty kick for the nonoffending side at the place of the foul.

holding the ball: A deliberate hesitation

by the forwards in feeding the ball back to the scrum half in a scrum, often in the hope of drawing opposing forwards offside.

hook: 1. To, as the middle player in the front row ("hooker"), thrust the foot forward and win possession of the ball after it is put into a scrum. also *strike*. 2. To win possession of and pass the ball backwards on the ground with the foot, as in a scrum, ruck, or play-the-ball. also *heel*. see *play-the-ball, ruck, scrum*.

hooker: 1. The player positioned in the middle of the front row of a scrum, between the two prop forwards. The principal responsibility of the hooker is to win the ball on his team's put-in and heel it back to teammates. A proficient hooker is often able to win the ball on the opponent's put-in ("against the head"). Because of his unique and important responsibilities, the hooker (like the scrum half) is called a "specialist". 2. The position played by the hooker.

hospital pass: A pass made to a teammate who is in danger of being immediately hit by opposing tacklers. "Bad ball" to a scrum half can be an example of a hospital pass.

in: see *in and over*.

in and over: Over the goal line and in the in-goal area for a try. (put his head down and drove in and over for the try) also *in, over*.

in-goal: The rectangular area at each end of the playing field, extending from the goal line (a part of the in-goal area), back to the dead-ball line, and bounded on the sides by the touch-in-goal lines. In rugby union, the in-goal area is up to 22 meters deep, from goal line to dead-ball line. In rugby league, the in-goal area is from 6–11 meters deep.

injury time: Extra time added by the referee at the end of a half to make up for playing time lost because of an injury to one or more players.

inside center: 1. The center three-quarter usually positioned closest to the forwards and the fly half. also *second five-eighth*. 2. The position played by inside center. also *second five-eighth*.

intercept: To catch and control a pass meant for an opponent.

interception: The act or an instance of catching and controlling a pass meant for an opponent.

international: 1. In rugby union, a match between national teams. The first international rugby union match, albeit with twenty-a-side, was between Scotland and England in 1871, won by Scotland 1 goal to nil. The first fifteen-a-side international rugby union match took place in 1877 between England and Ireland, won by England two goals and 1 try to nil. also *representative match, Test, Test match*. 2. In rugby league, a match between national teams that is not given Test status, such as England vs. Wales. 3. A player who is a member of a national team. also *cap*.

International Board: 1. The International Rugby Football Board. 2. The International Rugby Football League Board.

International Rugby Football Board: The governing body of international rugby union for member nations Australia, France, England, Ireland, New Zealand, Scotland, and South Africa. Formed initially in 1884 by Scotland, Wales, and Ireland (England joined in 1890), the International Rugby Football Board is headquartered in Twickenham, England. also *International Board*.

International Rugby Football League Board: The governing body of international rugby league. Headquartered in Wetherby, West Yorkshire, England, the International Rugby Football League Board was formed in 1948. Member nations are Australia, England, France, New Zealand, and Papua New Guinea. also *International Board*.

in the loose: In open play, as opposed to in a "tight" scrum. compare *in the tight*.

in the tight: In a scrum or "tight" scrum, as opposed to in open play. compare *in the loose*.

into touch: Out of bounds, having touched or crossed over the touchline. see *touch*.

jeu à treize: The French expression for thirteen-a-side rugby league, literally "game to thirteen".

1. jink: A quick turn or change of direction, as to avoid an opposing tackler. From the World War II RAF expression for a move to evade the fire of an enemy plane in the air.

2. jink: To make a quick turn or change of direction, as to avoid an opposing tackler.

jumper: In rugby union, the player or any of the players designated to attempt to jump up and win the ball when the ball is thrown in at a line-out. see *line-out*.

keep the ball tight: Players' slang meaning to keep the ball in or close to a "tight" scrum.

kick for touch, kick to touch: To kick the ball into touch upfield, thereby gaining ground, a strategy particularly prevalent in rugby union, where the ball is put back into play with a line-out at the point where it crossed into touch. If, however, the ball is kicked into touch on the full from outside the kicker's 22-meter line, a scrum is formed (put-in to the opposing side) at the place from which the ball was kicked. This is the "Australian dispensation" introduced into the Laws in 1968, so-called because it had long been in force in Australian domestic matches to inhibit overused and dull kicking for touch. In rugby league, when the ball is kicked into touch, play is restarted with a scrum (put-in to the opposing side) 10 meters in from the point where the ball crossed into touch. If, however, the ball is kicked into touch on the full, the scrum is formed at the place from which the ball was kicked ("ball back"). If the ball

JUMPER

is kicked into touch from a penalty kick without touching any other player, play is restarted with a free kick (often a tap kick) 10 meters in from the point where the ball crossed into touch. The technique of kicking for touch was first perfected by Bennie Osler, the remarkably accurate kicking fly half for South Africa's Springboks on their successful 1931–32 tour of England. also *find touch*.

kickoff: 1. A place kick from the center of the halfway line at the start of each half or by the defending team after a goal has been scored. The ball must reach the 10-meter line, unless it is first touched by an opponent, or, at the opponent's option, it must be kicked off again or a scrum formed at the center (in rugby league, a penalty kick is awarded at the center to the opposing team). The kicker's team must be behind the ball until it is kicked or a scrum is formed at the center (in rugby league, a penalty kick is awarded at the center to the opposing team). The opposing team must remain behind the 10-meter line until the ball is kicked or the kick is taken over (in rugby league, a penalty kick is awarded at the center to the opposing team). If the ball is kicked directly into touch, touch-in-goal, or on or over the dead-ball line, the opposing team may accept the kick, have it kicked over, or have a scrum formed at the center (in rugby league, a penalty kick is awarded at the center to the opposing team). The earliest football games were started by throwing the ball up between the two sides. By the time the Laws of Football at Rugby School were written in 1846, this practice had been replaced by a kickoff. 2. In rugby union, a dropkick from the center of the halfway line by the defending team after an unconverted try, subject to the same restrictions of a kickoff made to start a half or after a goal.

•• Of or pertaining to the beginning of something, especially an introductory occurrence. (a controversial speech that was considered a kickoff to his election bid)

kick off: To execute a kickoff.

•• To begin something. (kicked off the evening's festivities with a song)

knock on: To make a knock-on.

knock-on: A ball that travels forward toward the opponent's dead-ball line after a player loses possession of it, strikes it with the hand or arm, or is struck on the hand or arm by it. If the knock-on is intentional, a penalty kick is awarded to the nonoffending side at the place of the infringement. If unintentional, a scrum is formed at the place of the infringement or, (in rugby union) if it occurs at a line-out, 15 meters from the touchline along the line-of-touch. The knock-on was specifically prohibited in the 1846 Laws of Football at Rugby School.

Knot: see *equalize.*

late tackle: A tackle in which contact is made after the player with the ball has handed or passed the ball to a teammate, or after he has already been tackled and brought down. A late tackle results in a penalty kick at the place of the foul for the nonoffending side, and, if judged dangerous by the referee, the cautioning or sending off of the guilty player (in rugby league, the player may also be temporarily suspended).

Laws: 1. The international rules of rugby union, controlled and interpreted by the International Rugby Football Board, the world-governing body of rugby union. Although codes of rules for mob football were published earlier at English schools (such as the Laws of Football as played at Rugby School, 1846, and the Cambridge University rules, 1848), the first modern rugby laws were framed in 1871, when the Rugby Football Union was formed. 2. The international rules of rugby league, controlled and interpreted by the International Rugby Football League Board. The first rugby league Laws differing from rugby union were framed in 1897.

lean on the scrum: 1. To ineffectually lean against rather than push or shove with the pack in a scrum, whether from fatigue, or in an attempt to be ready for a quick move away when the ball leaves the scrum. 2. To illegally use the weight of one's body and pull the jersey or body of the opposing forward downward in a scrum to gain an advantage. Because of the danger of injury from the collapse of a scrum, any such leaning or dragging down results in a penalty kick for the nonoffending side at the place of the infringement.

line: Short for goal line. also *try line.*

line-of-touch: In rugby union, an imaginary line on the playing field perpendicular to the touchline through the place where the ball is thrown in between the two files of players in a line-out. see *line-out.*

line-out: In rugby union, the method of restarting play when the ball is carried, knocked, or kicked into touch. If the ball goes directly into touch from a kickoff or dropout (and the kick is accepted), or from a kick made from beyond the kicking team's 22-meter line, the line-out takes place opposite the point from which the ball was kicked or at the place the ball went into touch, whichever is closer to the kicking team's goal line. A line-out is formed by at least two players (up to all eight forwards, as determined by the team throwing in) from each team lining up in single files perpendicular to the touchline where the ball is to be thrown in. With the first player in each file positioned 5 meters from the touchline, both sides wait to jump and contest for the ball when it is thrown in by a player from the team opposing that of the last player to touch the ball before it left the playing field. Until the ball is thrown in, each player in a line-out must stand no closer than 1 meter from his next teammate in the file, and no closer than 50 centimeters from his opponent in the opposite file. The ball must be thrown in on the line-of-touch, an imaginary line perpendicular to the touchline halfway between the two files. If it is not, the throw-in is awarded to the opposing team or a scrum is formed, at the opposing team's option. Any player participating in a line-out (those in the two files, the player throwing in and his immediate opponent, and one other player from each side who is positioned to receive the ball if it is knocked or passed back from the line-out) is offside if, before the ball has touched a player or the ground, he wilfully remains or advances beyond the line-of-touch (except to jump for the ball), or, after the ball has touched a player or the ground, while not carrying the ball, he advances in front of the ball (except in a tackle attempt), or, in a "peeling off" movement, he fails to keep moving close to the line-out until a ruck or maul is formed and he joins it or the line-out ends, or if, before the line-out ends, he moves more than 15 meters from the touchline (on a long throw-in players may do so once the ball is thrown). An infraction results in a penalty kick for the nonoffending side 15 meters from the touchline along the line-of-touch. Players not participating in a line-out are offside if, before the line-out is ended, they advance or remain in front of the "offside line", an imaginary line 10 meters behind the line-of-touch (or the goal line if it is closer to the line-of-touch) except in the case of a long throw-in. An infraction results in a penalty kick on the offending team's offside line opposite the place of the infringement, but not less than 15 meters from the touchline. see *short line, throw-in*.

linesman: Either of the two touch judges. also *line umpire*.

line umpire: A New Zealand term for a touch judge. also *linesman*.

line up flat: To defensively position the backs in a straight line out to the side of a scrum (rather than behind) in order to be ready for a tackle if possession is won by the opponents.

Liverpool kiss: Players' slang for a head-butt. A foul that, if intentional, results in the guilty player being cautioned or sent off (in rugby league, the player may also be temporarily suspended) and a penalty kick for the nonoffending side.

lock: Short for lock forward.

lock forward: 1. Either of the two forwards who bind into the second row of a scrum, just behind and on either side of the hooker, and in the modern 3-4-1 formation, between the two wing forwards. In the old 3-2-3 formation, these two players "locked" the pack together. also *lock*. see *second-row forward*. 2. The position played by either of the lock forwards. also *lock*. see *second-row forward*.

loop around: To, after having passed the ball to a teammate, circle behind him in order to be in position for a return pass and possibly, thereby, creating a man over situation. see *loop run*.

loop run: The act or an instance of, after having passed the ball to a teammate, circling behind or "looping around" a teammate in order to be in position for a return pass and possibly, thereby, cre-

ating a man over situation. The loop run is believed to have been invented before World War I by the great England and Huddersfield rugby league player, Harold Wagstaff.

loose arm: In rugby league, an infringement in which the hooker in one of the front rows of a scrum binds with only one arm, the other being "loose". This results in a penalty kick for the opposing side at the place of the infringement.

loose ball: A ball that is in play (other than in a scrum) but not in the possession of any player.

loose forward: 1. In rugby union, any of the back-row forwards (from the old standard 3-2-3 formation), the two wing forwards (blind-side and open-side) and the number 8 (middle of the back). These players are called "loose" forwards because they can quickly detach themselves from their perimeter positions once the ball leaves the scrum. also *back rower*. 2. In rugby league, the player who packs into the scrum behind the two second-row forwards. 3. The position played by the loose forward.

loose head: Short for loose-head prop.

loose-head prop: 1. The prop forward who binds into the end of the front row closest to the feed (across from and just outside the opposing tight-head prop) when his team puts the ball into a scrum. When the opposing team puts the ball in, the loose-head prop is farthest from the feed. also *loose head*. compare *tight-head prop*. 2. The position played by the loose-head prop. also *loose head*. compare *tight-head prop*.

loose maul: see *maul*.

loose play: In rugby union, play (especially by the forwards) that takes place during a maul (loose maul) or ruck (loose scrum). see *maul, ruck*.

loose scrum: see *ruck*.

lying deep: Offensively deployed deep behind a scrum in a staggered formation so as to have room to set up an attack. compare *lying shallow*.

lying on the ball: The illegal practice of remaining on or near the ball when it is on the ground so as to prevent or obstruct possession by an opponent, specifically forbidden in the Laws since 1892. Such an infringement results in a penalty kick for the nonoffending side.

lying shallow: Defensively deployed close behind or to the side of a scrum so as to be ready to make a tackle if the opponents gain possession. compare *lying deep.*

man down: see *man short.*

Man of the Match: An award given to the outstanding player in a match.

•• An award given figuratively or facetiously for an outstanding act or performance. (voted Man of the Match for remembering the umbrella)

man over: Having a momentary numerical advantage, said of a team that, at a given moment, has more players involved in an attack than there are defenders, whether because of a defensive mistake, or because of the clever use of a looping run or overlap by the attacking team. also *extra man.*

man short: Lacking one player on the field, said of a team after a player has been sent off or is unable to continue because of an injury. also *man down.*

1. mark: To guard an opponent. also *cover.*

2. mark: 1. The place where a free kick or penalty kick is awarded, or a scrum is formed. 2. In rugby union, a fair catch. 3. In rugby union, the exclamation called out by a player at the moment he makes a fair catch, thereby indicating the place from which his free kick will be made. 4. In rugby union, the place from which the free kick is taken when a fair catch is made.

1. maul: In rugby union, a struggle for possession of the ball when it is held by a player but has not touched the ground. A maul begins when one or more players from each team, on their feet and in physical contact, close around the player with the ball. A maul ends when the ball touches the ground, emerges from the maul, when a player carrying it emerges from the maul, or when a scrum is ordered (when the ball becomes unplayable and does not emerge after a reasonable amount of time, a scrum is formed, with the put-in made by the team moving forward prior to the stoppage of play). If the ball in a maul is on or over the goal line, the maul is ended. If a player jumps on top of another during a maul, a penalty kick is awarded to the nonoffending side at the place of the infringement. A player who joins a maul from his opponent's side, joins it in front of the ball, or does not join the maul but fails to retire behind the "offside line" (behind the hindmost teammate in the maul) without delay, or leaves the maul and fails to immediately rejoin it or retire behind the offside line, or advances beyond the offside line and does not join the maul, is offside. An infringement results in a penalty kick for the nonoffending side at the place of the infringement unless a line-out is in progress. In such a case, the penalty kick is taken 15 meters from the touchline along the "line-of-touch" (the line on which the ball is thrown in). also *loose maul.* compare *scrum, ruck.*

2. maul: To participate in a maul.

middle of the back: 1. In rugby union, the number 8 player, so-called from his position in the back row of a scrum in the original 3-2-3 formation. see *number 8.* 2. In rugby union, the position played by the number 8 player. see *number 8.*

mini rugby: An introductory form of rugby for primary school students. Though rules and measurements can be adjusted for different age groups, for ten-year olds and above, mini rugby is ideally played nine-a-side, with four forwards (a 2-2 pack formation) and five backs (a scrum half, a fly half, a center, a wing and a fullback) on a pitch of reduced size (approximately 65 meters long by 38 meters wide with 5-meter deep in-goal areas). When possible, small goals are used (goal posts 4.6 meters apart with a 2.6-meter high crossbar). In the most common variation, kicking directly into touch is forbidden (except from within 15 meters of one's own goal line), and line-outs are replaced with a scrum 10 meters in from touch. Now played in many countries, mini rugby was originated in the early 1970s by the Welsh Rugby Union under the guidance of famous Welsh coach, Ray Williams.

never pushed an ounce in his life: A derogatory expression, said of a forward who is considered lazy and who "leans" rather than pushes in a scrum.

nine-man rugby: In rugby union, a dull, conservative style of play that emphasizes the forward game and kicking for touch by the scrum half rather than passing and running by the backs.

This kind of "tight play", where the ball rarely gets far from the scrum unless it is being kicked is a recent version of the "ten-man rugby" first popularized in the 1930s.

no side: The end of a match. The referee has the power to declare no side before regulation time has expired if, in his opinion, the full time cannot for any reason be played. compare *full time.*

not straight: see *crooked feed.*

number 8: 1. In rugby union, the forward who binds into a scrum just behind and between the two lock forwards in the second row, named after the number worn on his jersey. also *middle of the back.* 2. In rugby union, the position played by the number 8. also *middle of the back.*

obstruction: The act or an instance of illegally hampering or impeding the movement of an opponent, resulting in the cautioning or sending off of the guilty player and a penalty kick for the nonoffending side at the place of the infringement. If the foul prevents a probable try, a penalty try is awarded.

official time: The actual time of a match, kept by the referee. In rugby league, the referee may delegate the job of keeping track of the official time to a timekeeper.

1. offside: 1. Being in front of the ball when it is kicked, touched, or being carried by a teammate. There is no penalty for being offside unless the offside player plays the ball, obstructs an opponent, or approaches or remains within 10 meters (in rugby league, 5 meters) of an opponent waiting to play the ball or the place where the ball pitches. An infringement results in a penalty kick for the nonoffending side at the spot of the infringement, or (in rugby union) at the nonoffending side's option, a scrimmage where the ball was last played by the offending side — or on a line with that place 5 meters from the goal line if the ball was last played in-goal. There is no penalty if an offside player is "accidentally offside", or does not interfere with, affect, or take part in play. The concept of offside (called "sneaking" at first) was born at the English public school, Eton in the late 1830s or early 1840s. Shortly thereafter, the name "offside" was first used at another public school, Cheltenham. The

1846 Rugby School Laws prohibited a player who was "off his side" from taking part in a play. see *accidentally offside, onside.* 2. see *line-out, maul, play-the-ball, scrum.*

2. offside: 1. The act or an instance of being offside. 2. The infraction which results when a player is offside.

offside line: 1. An imaginary line parallel to the goal lines through the hindmost foot of the players who are packed down in a scrum, and used to determine offside violations. see *scrum.* 2. In rugby union, an imaginary line through the hindmost foot of the players who are participating in a ruck or maul, and used to determine offside violations. see *maul, ruck.* 3. In rugby union, an imaginary line 10 meters behind the line-of-touch in a line-out and parallel to the goal lines, used to determine offside violations. If the goal line is closer than 10 meters from the line-of-touch, it then becomes the offside line. see *line-out.*

offside trap: An attempt, by some deliberately deceptive action, to lure the opposing team into an offside violation so as to gain an advantage from the penalty imposed. In a scrum, for instance, the scrum half can fake picking up the ball (as though it has been heeled to him) in the hope of drawing the opponents offside.

off the ball: Away from the ball. (kept the defenders guessing with good off the ball runs)

onside: 1. Being behind the ball when it is kicked, touched or carried by a teammate, and, therefore, not subject to a penalty for offside. An offside player can be made onside by retiring behind the player on his team playing or carrying the ball, or behind the place where the ball was last played. A player can be made onside by a teammate moving the ball in front of him, or by an opponent either running 5 meters with the ball or playing but not retaining the ball. see *offside.* 2. Being behind the offside line at a scrum, and, therefore, not subject to a penalty. see *scrum.* 3. In rugby union, being behind the offside line at a line-out, maul, or ruck, and, therefore, not subject to a penalty. see *line-out, maul, offside, ruck.*

on the full: In the air without having bounced after being played, as of a ball kicked directly into touch without first bouncing inbounds.

open game: A match in which the backs are brought into play and which features good running, passing, and kicking as opposed to a dull, conservative match with prolonged scrums (and in rugby union, rucks and mauls) and relentless kicking for touch.

open play: 1. Play in which the backs as well as forwards are involved in running and passing movements. Oxford University (and later England) players Harry Vassall and Alan Rotherham are credited with introducing the concept of open play in the early 1880s. 2. That play which takes place in the open field rather than in scrums, rucks, or mauls, and, therefore, play that involves running, passing, and kicking by the backs.

open side: The playing area on the side of a scrum, maul, ruck, line-out, or play-the-ball farthest away from the nearest touchline. compare *blind side.*

open-side: Of or pertaining to the open side. compare *blind-side.*

open-side wing forward: 1. In rugby union, the wing forward who plays on the open side. The open-side wing forward binds into a scrum outside and behind his prop forward alongside the second row on the open side. compare *blind-side wing forward.* 2. The position played by the wing forward on the open side.

opposing half: The half of the field defended by the opposing team. compare *own half.*

opposite number: The player who plays the same position on the opposing team, and who, traditionally, wears the same number.

order off: see *send off.*

out half: 1. An Irish term for fly half. also *first five-eighth, five-eighth, outside half, standoff, standoff half, standoff halfback.* 2. The position played by an out half. also *first five-eighth, five-eighth, fly half, outside half, standoff, standoff half, standoff halfback.*

outside center: 1. The center three-quarter usually positioned behind and wide of the inside center, and inside the wing three-quarter. 2. The position played by the outside center.

outside half: 1.A fly half. also *first five-eighth, five-eighth, out half, standoff, standoff half, standoff halfback.* 2. The

position played by an outside half. also *first five-eighth, five eighth, fly half, out half, standoff, standoff half, standoff halfback.*

outsides: In rugby union, the collective name for the halfbacks and three-quarter backs.

over: Over the goal line and in the in-goal area for a try. also *in, in and over.*

1. overlap: To unexpectedly join or rejoin an attack, thereby often creating a man over situation (more attackers than defenders). A player can overlap by moving forward from a defensive position or, after passing to a teammate, loop around him to be in position for another pass. see *loop run.*

2. overlap: The act or an instance of overlapping.

over the top: The act or an instance of illegally diving and/or rolling over a loose ball on the ground in order to delay or prevent an opponent from playing it. Going over the top results in a penalty kick for the nonoffending side at the place of the infringement.

own half: The half of the field defended by one's own team. compare *opposing half.*

pace: 1. The speed of a player. 2. The speed of the ball, as in a pass, etc. 3. The speed with which a game is played (whether by one or more players, or by one or both teams).

1. pack: The collective name for the forwards who bind into a scrum.

2. pack: see *pack down.*

pack down: To bind together with teammates to form a pack for a scrum. also *pack.*

pair of halfbacks: see *halfback pair.*

1. pass: To propel or throw the ball to a teammate, legal if in a lateral or backward direction.

2. pass: The act or an instance of propelling or throwing the ball to a teammate, legal if in a lateral or backward direction. see *forward pass.*

1. peel: In rugby union, a tactic in which the forwards of the team throwing in for a line-out leave their position at the moment the ball is thrown and run around the end of the line (parallel and close to it) in order to join the backs in a passing movement.

2. peel: see *peel off.*

peel off: To execute a peel. also *peel.*

penalize: To, as referee, award a penalty

kick against an offending player.

penalty: Short for penalty kick.

penalty goal: A goal scored from a penalty kick, worth 3 points (2 points in rugby league).

penalty kick: An unhindered punt, dropkick, or place kick given to the nonoffending side at the place of a foul and certain infringements, and from which a goal can be scored directly if the ball is kicked over the crossbar and between the goal posts. On a penalty kick, the kicker's team must remain behind the ball until it is kicked otherwise a scrum is formed at the place of the kick, with the put-in being given to the nonoffending side. The opposing team must retire behind an imaginary line parallel to the goal lines and 10 meters from the place of the kick or to their own goal line if it lies within 10 meters of the place of the kick, and must remain there motionless until the kick is taken. An infringement results in a penalty kick for the nonoffending side 10 meters in front of the original kicking place, or 5 meters from the goal line, whichever is closer. In rugby league, if the ball is kicked directly into touch from a penalty kick without touching another player, the kicking team restarts play with a free kick (often a tap kick) from 10 meters inside the place where the ball went into touch. The first penalty kick, then called a "fore kick by way of a penalty", was introduced by the RFU in 1882, though a goal could not be scored from it until 1886 (at which time it was known as a "free kick by way of a penalty"). The term penalty kick was first mentioned in the Laws in 1926. also *penalty*. see *short penalty*, *tap kick*.

penalty try: A try awarded to the nonoffending side when, in the judgement of the referee, a probable try was prevented by a foul (or if the try would have been scored in a more favorable position than where the ball was grounded). After a penalty try, the conversion attempt is taken from between the goal posts.

pitch: The rectangular playing area, up to 100 meters long from goal line to goal line and 69 meters wide (in rugby union) touchline to touchline, with an in-goal area at each end up to 22 meters deep, bounded on the sides by the touch-in-goal lines and on the ends by the dead-ball lines. Centered on each goal line is a goal consisting of a 5.6-meter horizontal crossbar whose top face is 3 meters above the ground, with uprights at either end that extend vertically at least 3.40 meters above the crossbar. Twenty-two meters from and parallel to each goal line, a line extends across the field from touchline to touchline, the 22-meter line. Five meters inside each touchline, a broken line is marked from goal line to goal line, the 5-meter line. Between the two 5-meter lines, a broken line is marked across the field 10 meters from either side of and parallel to the halfway line, the 10-meter line. Fifteen meters inside and parallel to both touchlines, short lines are marked intersecting the halfway line, the 10-meter lines, the 22-meter lines, and extending 5 meters into the playing field from each goal line. Flags mark the four corners where the touchlines and goal lines intersect, and the four corners where the dead-ball lines and touch-in-goal lines intersect. Flags erected a short distance outside each touchline mark the location of the 22-meter lines and the halfway line.

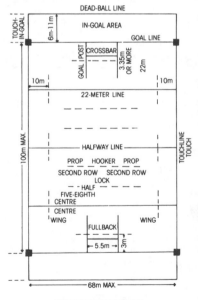

RUGBY LEAGUE PITCH

In rugby league, the maximum width of the field is 68 meters, there are no broken 5-meter lines marked inside the touchlines, the lines marked 10 meters inside and parallel to the touchlines intersect only the halfway line and 22-meter lines as broken lines, and broken 10-meter lines are marked in the middle of the field 10 meters out from and parallel to each 22-meter line as well as from the goal lines and halfway line. In addition, the in-goal area is less deep, extending back 6–11 meters from each goal line. Flags are erected only at the four corners where the touchlines and goal lines intersect. also *ground*, *grounds*.

place kick: A kick made with the ball stationary on the ground, whether or not held in position by a teammate. Kickoffs, conversion attempts, and penalty kicks are most often made with a place kick.

place-kick: To execute a place kick.

placer: One who holds the ball in a stationary position on the ground for a place kick.

play: To pick up, carry, or impart force or motion to the ball with some part of the body. (played it back to the fly half)

play off side: To make a move or fake that draws one or more opponents offside. (played him offside with a clever fake)

play on: A verbal signal to continue play, called out by the referee at a point when play could be stopped, such as after an infraction when the advantage is being applied.

play-the-ball: In rugby league, the method by which the ball is put into play after a tackle. The tackled player is released, stands and faces the opponent's goal, and, after dropping or placing the ball on the ground at his feet, kicks or heels it back to a teammate. One opponent is permitted to stand immediately in front of the tackled player. A teammate ("acting halfback") is permitted to stand directly behind these two players. All other players must be at least 5 meters away. When the players of one team have been tackled six consecutive times without the opponents touching the ball, the last player to be tackled must release the ball and place it on the ground. Play is then resumed by the nearest opposing player kicking the ball or heeling it to a teammate, and this play-the-ball does not count toward his team's permitted six tackles.

play the man not the ball: To illegally interfere with or tackle an opponent not in possession of the ball, a foul that can result in the cautioning or sending off of the guilty player (in rugby league, the player may also be temporarily suspended) and a penalty kick for the nonoffending side at the place of the foul.

possession: Control of the ball. (finally won possession after a prolonged scrum)

post: Short for goal post. also *upright*, *woodwork*.

1. pot: A New Zealand term for a dropkick. also *half volley*.

2. pot: A New Zealand term meaning to drop-kick the ball. also *half-volley*.

prop: 1. Short for prop forward. 2. A New Zealand expression for a sidestep.

prop forward: 1. One or the other of the two forwards who pack down on either

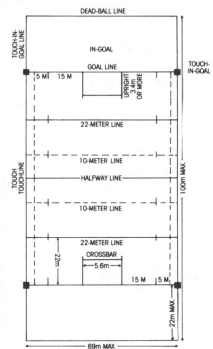

RUGBY UNION PITCH

side of the hooker in the front row of a scrum. also *prop*. see *loose-head prop, tight-head prop*. 2. The position played by either prop forward of a scrum. also *prop*. see *loose-head prop, tight-head prop*. 3. The position played by either prop forward. also *prop*.

pull offside: To, by means of a move or feint, lure one or more players of the opposing team into an offside violation. This is often done as a deliberate tactic (an "offside trap") to gain an advantage from the penalty imposed.

1. punt: A kick in which the ball is held in front of the body, dropped, and kicked with the instep before it hits the ground. A punt is most often used to gain ground or to kick for touch.

2. punt: To execute a punt.

1. push: To individually or collectively push against and drive opposing forwards back and away from the ball in a scrum. also *shove*.

2. push: The act or an instance of individually or collectively pushing against and driving opposing forwards back and away from the ball in a scrum. also *forward drive, forward rush, forward shove, shove*.

pushover try: In rugby union, a try scored by a determined push or forward drive in a scrum near the goal line.

put clear: To be caused to be momentarily in the open in possession of the ball with no opponents nearby, as by a pass, kick, maneuver or fake.

put in: To feed the ball into a scrum. When

PLACE KICK

a scrum is formed, a player (usually the scrum half) from the team not responsible for the stoppage of play (or, if unclear, from the forward-moving or attacking team) must, as soon as the two front rows have moved together, take a position 1 meter from the scrum midway between the two front rows to make the feed. Then, without delay, he must hold the ball in both hands by the ends halfway between the knees and ankles and thrust the ball forward in a single motion along a line through the middle of the scrum so that it first touches the ground immediately beyond the nearest prop forward. In rugby league, the ball is to be rolled along the ground. After the ball is put into the scrum, the scrum half must retire to a position behind the scrum. also *feed*.

put-in: The act or an instance of putting the ball into a scrum. also *feed*.

put the boot in: To intentionally kick an opponent who is on the ground, a foul which results in the cautioning or sending off of the guilty player (in rugby league, the player may also be temporarily suspended) and a penalty kick for the nonoffending side at the place of the foul.

quality possession: see *good ball*.

quick ball: Fast service in which the ball is not held in a scrum or ruck, but instead is immediately played back to the backs. Quick ball is not always "good ball", as is the case if the ball squirts out of a scrum before the scrum half has time to be in position to receive it.

quick throw-in: In rugby union, the act or an instance of throwing in the ball from touch without waiting for players to form a line-out. After the ball goes into touch, a quick throw-in is legal provided the ball that went into touch is used, it is handled only by the players, and it is thrown in correctly by a player from the proper team. see *throw-in*.

rate: 1. To estimate and consider the ability of a player or team. 2. To attribute a certain amount of skill or ability. A British expression. (our coach didn't rate him in spite of his reputation)

ref: Short for referee.

1. referee: The official in charge of a rugby match, assisted by two touch judges. The referee is responsible for enforcing the Laws of rugby, acting as timekeeper and recording all time lost because of injuries, deliberate time wasting by either team, starting and stopping play or terminating a match in emergency circumstances, calling and penalizing infractions or fouls by awarding scrums, free kicks, penalty kicks, and penalty tries, cautioning and, if necessary, sending off players guilty of serious, violent, or repeated fouls or infractions, awarding or disallowing tries and goals, and recording all tries, goals, and incidents of misconduct which warrant a caution or ejection. In rugby league, the referee may also temporarily suspend a player for a fixed five- or ten-minute period, and may delegate all match timekeeping responsibilities to a timekeeper. Originally, the arbiters of all disputes in a match were the opposing captains. Rugby's first officials (two to a match) were called umpires as early as the mid 1860s, but it wasn't until 1885 that their duties and those of a third official called a referee were clearly defined. The umpires were equipped with sticks to be raised in case of an appeal by the captains on a point of law and order, and the referee was given a whistle, but could grant an appeal only if an umpire raised his stick. By the early 1890s, the referee was empowered to make all judgements alone, and could send off a player for disputing his decision, while the umpires were becoming touch judges. also **ref**.

2. referee: To serve as referee. also **ref**.

replacement: In rugby union, a player who substitutes for an injured teammate during a match. Except in under-nineteen matches and special trial matches, a team may not use more than two replacements in a match, and then, only when the player to be replaced is, in the opinion of a doctor or the referee, too injured to continue playing. A player who has been replaced may not resume playing in the match. also *substitute*.

representative match: A match between teams representing nations (national teams). also *international*, *Test*, *Test match*.

retreating scrum: A scrum in which one team is being pushed back by the opposing pack.

reverse pass: A quick pass made back past the side of a player's body without turning.

RFL: The Rugby Football League.

RFU: The Rugby Football Union. also *RU*.

round-the-corner: A style of place kick in which the kicker approaches the ball in a curving arc from the side rather than from straight behind it. also *sidefoot*.

RU: The Rugby Football Union. also *RFU*.

1. ruck: In rugby union, a struggle by players from both teams for possession of the ball when it is loose on the ground, as when it has been dropped by a tackled player. In a ruck, two or more players from each team, in physical contact close around the ball in an attempt to gain possession by heeling the ball back to a teammate. Players involved in a ruck must bind with at least one arm around a teammate and may not return the ball into the ruck, handle the ball in the ruck (except to secure a try or touchdown), pick up the ball, wilfully jump on top of or collapse the ruck or fall or kneel in the ruck, or while lying on the ground interfere with the ball in or emerging from the ruck. An infringement results in a penalty kick for the nonoffending side at the place of the infringement. A player who joins a ruck from his opponent's side, joins it in front of the ball, or does not

REFEREE

249

join the ruck but fails to retire behind the "offside line" (behind the hindmost teammate in the ruck) without delay, or unbinds from the ruck and fails to immediately rejoin it behind the ball or retire behind the offside line, or advances beyond the offside line and does not join the ruck, is offside. An infringement results in a penalty kick for the nonoffending side at the place of the infringement unless a line-out is in progress. In such a case, the penalty kick is taken 15 meters from the touchline along the "line-of-touch" (the line on which the ball is thrown in). also *loose scrum.* compare *maul, scrum.*

2. ruck: To take part in a ruck.

rugby: 1. A game played between two teams of fifteen players (eight forwards and seven backs) on a rectangular field measuring approximately 69 meters wide by 100 meters long (not including an in-goal area approximately 22 meters deep at each end of the field). Points are scored by place-kicking or drop-kicking an inflated ball (oval with pointed ends) over a 3-meter high, 5.6-meter long horizontal bar and between the approximately 6.4-meter high uprights that together form an H-shaped goal on the boundary line (goal line) at each end of the field — a goal, worth 3 points, or by carrying or dribbling (with the feet) the ball over the opponent's goal line and then grounding it — a try, worth 4 points. After a try, the scoring team is given the opportunity to "convert the try" — score a 2-point goal with a free kick (an unhindered punt, dropkick, or place kick) from anywhere on the field on a line through the place where the try was scored. The ball is advanced toward the opponent's goal line by carrying, dribbling, or kicking it (a team may recover its own kicks). Only lateral or backward passing is permitted. The defending side is permitted to tackle the ballcarrier, who must then immediately release it and move away. The ball may then be played (heeled back) to a teammate by a player from either side, and thereafter, picked up and carried, passed, or kicked. A struggle by two or more players from each team for a loose ball on the ground is known as a ruck. A similar mass struggle for a ball held off the ground is known as a maul.

When the ball goes "into touch" (out of bounds), a "line-out" is formed to put the ball back into play. A player from the team opposing that of the last player to touch the ball before it went into touch throws it in from that place between two parallel lines of players (one line from each team) perpendicular to the "touchline" (sideline). Minor infractions result in the formation of a "scrum", a struggle for possession between two "packs" of forwards who push and shove against each other in an attempt to heel the ball back to teammates after it is "put in" on the ground between the opposing front rows. Fouls result in a penalty kick at the place of the foul (an unhindered dropkick or place kick from which a goal can be scored) and, if the foul prevented a probable try, the award of a "penalty try". In addition, the guilty player can be cautioned or sent off. Any player in front of a teammate with the ball or behind the hindmost teammate involved in a maul, ruck, or scrum, or, if not involved in a line-out, closer than 10 meters behind the middle of the line-out (on the side of his teammates), is offside and may not take part in any play. A ball that is not in possession and is tapped or knocked forward by the hand or arm (a "knock-on") may not be next played by the same player or by a teammate, but may result in a "fair catch" if caught by an opponent who calls out "mark". A free kick results. A referee controls a rugby match (two forty-minute periods of play), enforcing the Laws, calling and penalizing infringements and fouls, awarding scrums, penalty kicks, penalty tries, cautioning and sending off players, and awarding and disallowing goals and tries. He is assisted by two touch judges whose primary responsibility is to make rulings as to where the ball goes into touch and who last touched it. The name rugby comes from Rugby School in England, where in 1823, a sixteen-year-old student, William Webb Ellis, picked up the ball during a crude mob football match and, contrary to the rules of the time, carried it to the opponent's goal line. This controversial act soon became an accepted practice and was identified with the school as the "Rugby game". In 1871, the Rugby Union was formed and the first unified code of Laws was framed. also *rugby football, rugger.* compare *mini rugby, seven-a-side rugby, touch rugby.* 2. see *rugby league.*

rugby football: The game of rugby, whether rugby union or rugby league. also *football, rugger,*

Rugby Football League: The governing body of professional rugby in England. Because of the controversy in the 1890s over whether or not players should be compensated for time lost in their regular occupation while playing, many rugby clubs in northern England withdrew from the RFU in 1893 so as to be able to pay their players for this so-called "broken time". In 1895, twenty of these northern clubs banded together to form the Northern Rugby Football Union, which, by 1898, operated as a full professional league. In 1906, teams were limited to thirteen players on a side. The league was renamed the Rugby Football League in 1922, and is headquartered in Leeds, Yorkshire, England. also *RFL.*

Rugby Football Union: The governing body of amateur rugby in England in its original fifteen-a-side form, created in 1871. The Rugby Football Union is headquartered in Twickenham, Middlesex, England. also *RFU, RU.*

rugby league: An amateur or professional form of rugby with several important rule differences from rugby union. There are thirteen players (six forwards and seven backs) on a side. Rather than continuing play with a maul or a ruck after a tackle, the tackled player is permitted to release the ball, stand up, and heel it back to a teammate to begin another play five times in succession under the play-the-ball rule. On the sixth tackle, possession is lost and an opposing player then heels the ball back to a teammate. When the ball goes into touch, rather than resuming play with a line-out, a scrum is formed. When the ball goes into touch directly from a penalty kick, play is resumed with a free kick 10 meters inside that point. A goal from a penalty kick and a dropped goal are worth 2 points rather than 3 points (in international matches, a dropped goal is worth only 1 point). The in-goal area is only 6–11 meters deep in rugby league rather

than 22 meters. also *football, jeu à treize, rugby football, rugger.* see *rugby.*

rugby union: The original fifteen-a-side amateur version of rugby. also *football, rugby football, rugger.* see *rugby.*

rugger: 1. Oxford University slang for rugby, from the early 1890s. also *football, rugby football.* 2. A rugby player.

run on to: To catch up to a ball kicked or played into an open space by a teammate.

save the try but risk the penalty: An axiom describing a situation in which a defending player commits a foul in order to prevent a sure try by the opposing team, thereby risking a penalty try if the foul is seen by the referee.

scissors: An offensive maneuver in which a player advancing diagonally toward one touchline with the ball hands or passes it back to a teammate crossing behind him diagonally toward the opposite touchline. compare *dummy scissors.*

screen pass: A pass in which the ballcarrier turns away from defending players before passing so that the ball (and the exact moment and direction of release) is hidden or "screened".

screen the ball: 1. To turn away from defending players just before passing in order to hide or "screen" the ball (and thus, the exact moment and direction of release) from them. 2. To hold the ball on the opposite side of one's body (away from the tackler) when being tackled in order to protect the ball.

screw: To kick the ball in such a way as to make it spin evenly on its axis, thereby insuring stability and maximum distance for its flight.

screw kick: A kick in which the ball is made to spin evenly on its axis, thereby insuring stability and maximum distance for its flight.

1. scrimmage: A scrum. It is from the original meaning of the word scrimmage (a skirmish or confused struggle) that scrummage was derived. also *set scrum, tight, tight scrum.*

2. scrimmage: To take part in a scrum. also *scrum, scrum down.*

1. scrum: A method of restarting play after a minor infringement (and in rugby league, after the ball goes into touch) involving a struggle for possession of the ball in which the forwards of both teams assemble into tight formations ("packs") opposite each other. These packs then come together, the opposing three-man front rows bending forward and interlocking heads and shoulders to make a tunnel into which the ball is "put in" (delivered on the ground between the front rows) by a player from one of the teams (usually the scrum half, who then takes his place behind the pack) so that it can either be heeled back by one of the "hookers" (the players in the middle of the front row, between the two props) to his scrum half to begin a play, or moved forward at the feet of teammates in and behind the front row pushing in the scrum. The put-in is made by the team not responsible for the stoppage of play (or when not clear, by the attacking or forward-moving team). The prop closest to the put-in (loose-head prop) is from the same team. Players involved in a scrum must "bind" together with arms wrapped firmly around the bodies of at least one adjacent teammate (the hookers must bind with both props, and the tight-head prop must bind with the opposing loose-head prop) until the ball is put in. Front row players must keep both feet on the ground until the ball is put in, and no player may at any time raise both feet. While the ball is in the tunnel no player may handle it (except, in rugby union, to ground it for a try if the ball crosses the goal line) or play it with any part of the body but the lower leg or foot. No player may intentionally collapse a scrum, or fall or kneel inside of a scrum. Players who join the scrum from the opponent's side or place either foot in front of the ball while it is in the scrum are offside. Players not involved in the scrum must remain in back of the "offside line" (behind the hindmost teammate in the scrum) until the ball leaves the scrum. Infringements result in a penalty kick for the nonoffending side at the place of the infringement, and, if the infringement is repeated or dangerous, the guilty player is cautioned or sent off (in rugby league, the player may also be temporarily suspended). The word scrum is short for scrummage, and was first used around 1888. also *scrimmage, set scrum, tight, tight scrum*. see *put in, 3-4-1, 3-2-1, 3-2-3, wheel the scrum*.

2. scrum: To take part in a scrum. also *scrimmage, scrum down, scrummage*.

scrum cap: A harness-like cap with protective coverings for the ears, often worn by forwards (particularly lock forwards) to prevent damage from the mangling and prolonged rubbing of the ears that takes place when players are packed into a scrum.

scrum down: To take part in a scrum. also *scrimmage, scrum, scrummage*.

scrum half, scrum halfback: 1. The back responsible for putting the ball into a scrum, then receiving it when it has been "hooked" or heeled back through the pack. The scrum half is the link between the forwards and the backs, and the player who most often decides whether the ball should be kicked, passed or carried. Because of his unique and important responsibilities, the scrum half (like the "hooker") is called a specialist". 2. The position played by the scrum half.

1. scrummage: A scrum. The word scrummage, popularized in the 1880s, is a variant of scrimmage, meaning a skirmish or confused struggle. also *set scrum, tight, tight scrum*.

2. scrummage: To take part in a scrum. also *scrum, scrum down*.

scrummage on the move: Slang for a scrum in which one pack is dominant, effectively pushing the opposing side back.

scrummager: A forward player that takes part in scrums.

second five-eighth: 1. In New Zealand, the name given to the inside center three-quarter. also *inside center*. 2. In New Zealand, the position played by

SCRUM CAP

the inside center three-quarter. also *inside center.*

second phase, second-phase play: In rugby union, a ruck or maul that is the intended result of a strategy in which a player, after receiving the ball (first phase) in open play or from a scrum or line-out, deliberately runs into opposing tacklers. With opposing forwards committed in the ensuing ruck or maul, the hope is for quick, clean possession ("second-phase possession") by the team initiating the second-phase play before opposing backs have time to properly deploy defensively. Popularized in the 1960s, the concept of second-phase play (and, consequently, second-phase possession) is often brought into play several times in succession by a team.

second-phase possession: see *second phase, second-phase play.*

second row: 1. In rugby union, the two lock forwards and two wing forwards (or in the old 3-2-3 formation, the two lock forwards) who bind together to make up the second row of the pack in a scrum. 2. In rugby league, the two lock forwards who bind together to make up the second row of the pack in a scrum.

second-row forward: 1. In rugby league, either of the two lock forwards who bind together in the second row of the pack in a scrum. also *lock.* 2. In rugby league, the position played by either of the two lock forwards. also *lock.*

sell a dummy: To momentarily deceive or wrong-foot an opponent with a feint.

send off: To eject a player from a match, as for a serious foul or misconduct, or for repeated infringements after being cautioned (or in rugby league, after being temporarily suspended). When a player is sent off, the referee sends a written report of the incident to the official body with jurisdiction over the match. also *dismiss, order off.*

service: The passing of the ball back out of a scrum (by heeling) to the scrum half. Quick, safe service ("good ball") maximizes the chances of launching an effective attack.

set piece: 1. In rugby union, a scrum or line-out. 2. In rugby league, a scrum, or a planned set of moves when a match is restarted.

set scrum: A scrum. also *scrimmage, scrummage, tight scrum.*

seven-a-side rugby: A variation of rugby union utilizing seven players on a side (three forwards and four backs or two forwards and five backs). Seven-a-side rugby matches were first tried in Scotland in 1883, as Melrose RFC member, Edward Haig's crowd-pleasing answer to the club's financial troubles. Normally comprising two seven-minute halves, fast-moving seven-a-side rugby competitions are still popular in England. also *sevens.*

sevens: Seven-a-side rugby.

1. shield: To deliberately obstruct a defending player to prevent him from reaching the ballcarrier. This results in a penalty kick for the nonoffending side at the spot of the infringement.

2. shield: A player in the act of momentarily obstructing a defending player who might otherwise reach the ballcarrier, whether deliberately (penalty kick for the nonoffending side) or accidentally.

shinguards: see *shin pads.*

shin pads: Small protective pads for the shins worn under a player's socks, usually made of leather, or of a high density foam rubber or light plastic with a thin layer of foam rubber underneath. Shin pads were first used in soccer in 1874, and are normally the only protective pads worn by rugby players. also *shinguards.*

short line: A line-out in which only two or three players from each side line up to take part. The side with the throw-in may opt for this configuration, sometimes quickly throwing the ball past the line-out for teammates to gather.

short penalty: A penalty kick that is barely tapped forward, then picked up by the kicker to run with, kick, or start a passing movement. Before a change in the Laws in 1958, a penalty kick had to travel at least 5 meters. also *tap penalty.*

shove: see *forward drive.*

side: An English expression for a team. see *fifteen, thirteen.*

sidefoot: A place kick in which the kicker approaches the ball in a curving arc, striking it from behind and to the side rather than from directly behind the ball. also *round-the-corner.*

side-foot: To execute a sidefoot kick.

sideline: A touchline.

side row: see *breakaway*.

sidestep: To make a sudden step to the side in order to evade an opponent attempting a tackle. The expression was popularized in England near the turn of the century. also *prop*.

specialist: Either the hooker or the scrum half, whose responsibilities are unique and particularly important to a team. see *hooker, scrum half*.

speculator: see *fly hack*.

spoiling: The disruption of the opposing side's offensive play (as by quick tackling before a running or passing movement can begin), a defensive tactic.

standoff: Short for standoff half. also *first five-eighth, five-eighth, fly half, out half, outside half, standoff halfback*.

standoff half, standoff halfback: 1. A British term for fly half. also *first five-eighth, five-eighth, out half, outside half, standoff*. 2. The position played by the fly half. also *first five-eighth, five-eighth, out half, outside half, standoff*.

stiff-arm tackle: An illegal tackle in which the arm is swung or thrust out at the head of the ballcarrier, the aim being to physically punish as well as bring him down. A stiff-arm tackle is dangerous play and results in the cautioning or sending off of the guilty player (in rugby league, the player may also be temporarily suspended) and a penalty kick for the nonoffending side at the place of the foul.

1. strike: 1. To, as a hooker in a scrum, thrust the foot forward in an attempt to reach and gain possession of the ball when it is put in by the scrum half. also *hook*. 2. In rugby league, to, as the tackled player or the player marking him at a play-the-ball, thrust the foot forward in an attempt to win possession of the ball and kick or heel it when it is dropped or put down.

2. strike: 1. The act or an instance of a hooker in a scrum thrusting the foot forward in an attempt to reach and gain possession of the ball when it is put in by the scrum half. 2. In rugby league, the act or an instance of a tackled player or the player marking him at a play-the-ball thrusting the foot forward in an attempt to win possession of the ball and kick or heel it when it is dropped or put down.

strike against the head: The act or an instance of a hooker winning possession of the ball in a scrum from the opposing team's put-in, difficult because the hooker on the side making the put-in has his head closer to the ball when it is put into play. (a skilled hooker who managed three strikes against the head in the first half) compare *strike to the head*.

strike to the head: The act or an instance of a hooker winning possession of the ball in scrum from his team's put-in. compare *strike against the head*.

strip: A British expression for a team uniform.

strip the ball: To dispossess an opponent of the ball.

substitute: In rugby league, a player who replaces a teammate during a match. Rugby league rules permit the use of up to two substitutes at any time during a match, provided that they are identified as such to the referee before the match begins. A player who has been replaced by a substitute may not resume playing in the match. also *replacement*.

support: see *back up*.

1. swerve: To make a ball curve in flight by kicking it slightly off center so that it spins. also *bend, curl*.

2. swerve: The curve in the direction of flight of a ball kicked slightly off center. also *bend, curl*.

table: A British expression for a schedule of league standings.

1. tackle: To grasp (ideally around the legs) and hold an opponent carrying the ball in such a way as to bring him to the ground (in rugby league, a player in possession of the ball who is held upright by one or more opponents and unable to progress or to pass the ball is considered tackled). In rugby union, when a player is tackled, play is resumed with a ruck or maul (depending on whether or not the ball is touching the ground). In rugby league, when a player is tackled, play is resumed with a play-the-ball. If, in the judgement of the referee, the tackle is violent or dangerous, a penalty kick is awarded to the nonoffending side, and the guilty player may be cautioned or sent off (in rugby league, the player may also be temporarily suspended). also *bring down, take down*. see *maul, play-the-ball, ruck*.

2. tackle: The act or an instance of tackling a player carrying the ball.

take down: 1. To tackle and bring down an opposing player carrying the ball. 2. see *bring down.*

take some stick: To be the object of rough or violent play. A British expression applied to both rugby and soccer, and derived from horse racing and the jockey's use of a whip. To take some stick is the opposite of giving some stick, an expression popularized in the 1930s.

•• To be the object of verbal abuse. (took some stick for his sloppy appearance)

take the dummy: To be momentarily deceived or wrong-footed by the fake or feint of an opponent.

tap back: In rugby union, the act or an instance of tipping or knocking the ball back to a teammate from the throw-in at a line-out.

tap kick: A free kick that is barely tapped, then picked up by the kicker to run with, kick, or start a passing movement.

tap-kick: To execute a tap kick.

tap penalty: see *short penalty.*

temporary suspension: In rugby league, a fixed five- or ten-minute suspension of play for a player guilty of repeated infringements, or foul play or misconduct. A player temporarily suspended must immediately leave the playing field, and may not return until permitted by the referee at the end of the fixed time period.

ten-man rugby: In rugby union, a dull, conservative style of play that emphasizes the forward game and kicking for touch by the fly half soon after he gets the ball from the scrum half, rather than passing and running by the backs. Ten-man rugby was popularized by South Africa's Springboks on their successful tour of England in 1931 and 1932. With the powerful forward game of their then novel 3-4-1 formation and the relentless, accurate kicking (both for position and goals) of fly half Bennie · Osler, the Springboks won 23 of 26 matches, losing only once, with two draws.

ten-meter line: 1. In rugby union, either of two broken lines marked across the field between the 5-meter lines, parallel to and 10 meters from both sides of the halfway line. 2. In rugby league, any of the broken lines marked across the field parallel to and 10 meters in from the goal lines and the 22-meter lines, and 10 meters on either side of the halfway line. These lines ideally extend from touchline to touchline, but must be at least 15 meters in lengths. 3. In rugby league, any of the broken lines marked parallel to and 10 meters in from the touchlines, and intersecting with the 22-meter lines and the halfway line.

Test, Test match: A match between national teams. also *international, representative match.*

thirteen: A rugby league side.

three: Short for three-quarter. also *three q, three-quarter, three-quarter back.*

3-4-1: In rugby union, the formation most often used by forwards when packing down for a scrum, with three players (two props and the hooker) in the front row, four players (two wing forwards outside the two lock forwards) in the second row, and one player (the number 8) in the third row. The 3-4-1 formation was popularized in 1931 and 1932, when the South African Springbok team employed it on their remarkably successful tour of England, winning 23 of 26 matches (including the four internationals played), with one loss and two draws. By moving the two wing forwards up to the second row from their third row position in the old 3-2-3 formation, the Springbok pack was consistently able to wear down and physically dominate opponents in the scrum. compare *3-2-1, 3-2-3.*

three q: Short for three-quarter. also *three, three-quarter back.*

three-quarter, three-quarter back: 1. Any of the four players (two center three-quarters and two wing three-quarters) normally positioned between the halfbacks (or the scrum half, in rugby league) and the fullback. By the 1870s, rugby teams commonly employed ten forwards, two halfbacks, and three fullbacks. Near the end of that decade, a fullback was moved up to function as the first three-quarter back. By 1880, three three-quarters were commonly used. Cardiff of Wales is believed to have introduced the use of a fourth three-quarter around the mid-1880s. also *three, three q.* 2. The position played by any of the four three-quarters. also *three, three q.*

3-2-1: In rugby league, the formation normally used for a scrum, with three players (two prop forwards and the hooker) in the front row, two players (the lock forwards) in the second row, and one player (the loose forward) in the third row. This is the required formation unless a team is playing short-handed due to an injury, dismissal, or temporary suspension. In such cases, fewer players may take part in a scrum, as long as there are no more than seven backs. compare *3-4-1, 3-2-3.*

3-2-3: In rugby union, a scrum formation using three players (two prop forwards and the hooker) in the front row, two players (the lock forwards) in the second row, and three players (two wing forwards and the number 8) in the third row. Providing less power for pushing or shoving than the 3-4-1 formation that virtually replaced it in the 1930s, the 3-2-3 is seldom employed now unless the intention is to wheel the scrum. compare *3-4-1, 3-2-1.*

throw-forward: see *forward pass.*

throw in: In rugby union, to execute a throw-in at a line-out.

throw-in: In rugby union, the means by which the ball is put into play for a line-out. When a line-out is formed, a player on the team opposing that of the last to touch the ball in the playing area throws the ball in at right angles to the touchline (along the "line-of-touch") from the point at which the ball went into touch. The ball must travel at least 5 meters in the air along the line-of-touch before it touches the ground or is touched by a player, and the player throwing in must not put either foot in the playing area while doing so. An infringement results in the other side throwing in, or in the formation of a scrum 5 meters in from the touchline, at the option of the nonoffending side. The player throwing in may do so without waiting for a line-out to be formed (a "quick throw-in") if the ball that went into touch is used, if it has been handled by players only, and if it is thrown in correctly. Before changes in the Laws in 1905, the player throwing in had the option of bouncing the ball in (and, prior to 1892, walking it in and placing it on the ground), after which he could pick it up and pass, kick, or run with it. see *line-out.*

throw the ball about: To employ passing movements utilizing backs as well as the forwards.

tight: Short for tight scrum.

tight head: Short for tight-head prop.

tight-head prop: 1. The prop forward who binds into the end of the front row closest to the feed (across from and just inside the opposing loose-head prop) when the opposing team puts the ball into a scrum. also *tight head.* compare *loose-head prop.*

tight play: In rugby union, conservative play emphasizing the forward game and kicking for touch by the scrum half rather than passing and running by the backs. also *nine-man rugby.*

tight scrum: see *scrum.*

touch: 1. The out of bounds area along the sidelines (between the goal lines), including the touchlines. In the mid-1800s, before soccer and rugby were separated, the first rules for "football" governing a ball out of bounds on the sideline were adopted at the English public school, Cheltenham. These called for a throw-in (one-handed, and taken at right anlges to the line) to be taken by the first player to touch the ball after it crossed the sideline. Thus, out of bounds became the "touch area", later "touch", the sidelines became the "touchlines", with "touch-in-goal" and "touch-in-goal lines" following. 2. Short for touch rugby. also *touchball.*

touchball: see *touch rugby.*

touchdown: 1. The grounding of the ball by a defending player in his own in-goal area. After a touchdown, play is restarted with a dropout by the defending side from their 22-meter line (or in rugby league, from the center of their goal line). In rugby union, however, if a defending player carries or propels the ball into his own in-goal area before grounding it there, play is restarted with a scrum on the defending side's 5-meter line (put-in to the attacking side). 2. A common, if inaccurate term for a try. see *try.*

touch down: 1. To ground the ball in one's own in-goal area. see *touchdown.* 2. To ground the ball in the opponent's in-goal area. see *touchdown.*

touch-in-goal: The out of bounds area adjacent to both sides of the in-goal areas, including the touch-in-goal lines. see *touch.*

touch-in-goal line: One of the two boundary lines on each side of the in-goal areas, marked between and perpendicular to the goal lines and dead-ball lines. see *touch*.

touch judge: Either of two officials just outside the touchlines who assist the referee by indicating with a small flag when and where the ball goes into touch or touch-in-goal and the team which last touched it, making judgements about kicks at goal (when a penalty kick at goal or conversion of a try is attempted, one touch judge stands behind each post), and by alerting the referee when foul play or misconduct has escaped his notice. The present role and responsibilities of touch judges, formerly called umpires, evolved in the early 1890s. also *linesman, line umpire*. see *referee*.

touch kick: A kick intentionally directed into touch. see *kick for touch*.

touchline: One of the two boundary lines on each side of the playing field between and perpendicular to the goal lines. A ball or player touching the touchline is out of bounds. also *sideline*. see *line-out, kick for touch, touch*.

touch rugby: Any of several nontackling versions of rugby often played with nine (or fewer) players on a side, and usually not using goals, just shallow in-goal areas. These are divided into three equal parts between the sidelines, and scoring is achieved solely by grounding the ball in any of the three zones in the opponent's in-goal area (2 points for the outside zones, 3 points for the middle zone). Nine-a-side matches are normally divided into four fifteen-minute periods. In one common version of touch rugby, to begin play at the start of a period or resume play after a score, a player at the center of the halfway line passes the ball back between his legs (similar to the center snap in American football) to a teammate who then has the option to run with the ball, or to pass or knock it back to another teammate who may do likewise until an opponent touches the ballcarrier on the back with a hand (or sometimes two hands anywhere). This is considered a "tackle". The ballcarrier must then pass the ball within three strides (or two seconds). If the ballcarrier fails to com-

ply, or if the ball is passed or knocked in a forward direction, a free throw is awarded to the nonoffending team, to be taken with the ball resting on the ground, and all opposing players behind an imaginary line (parallel to the goal lines) 5 meters away. Some versions of the game limit the number of consecutive tackles permitted to a team before losing possession (like rugby league). When the ball crosses a sideline, a throw-in is awarded to the side opposite that of the last player to touch the ball in play, to be taken 5 meters inside of the point at which the ball crosses the sideline, with no player (from either side) closer than 5 meters from the sideline. If the ballcarrier is "touched" in the opponent's in-goal area before he can ground the ball for a score, the defending side is awarded a free throw at the 5-meter line. If the ballcarrier is "touched" in his own in-goal area, the attacking side is awarded a free throw at the 5-meter line. As in rugby, a match is presided over by a referee and two touch judges. Forms of touch rugby are often played as a less physical substitute for rugby in schools, or when the ground is unsuitably hard or rough, or as a practice game. also *touch, touchball*.

Triple Crown: In rugby union, a mythical award recognized in England, Ireland, Scotland and Wales, and given to any one of those countries that defeats the other three during a season. compare *Grand Slam*.

try: Four points scored by grounding the ball in the opponent's in-goal area. In rugby league, a try cannot be scored while the ball is in a scrum. In the first RFU Laws of 1871, the act of grounding the ball in the opponent's in-goal area was called a "run in", and did not count for points, but merely gave the attack-

TRY

257

ing side the opportunity to score points with a "try at goal" (kick at goal). The run in itself came to be known as a "try" around 1873, and by the early 1890s, was valued at 2 points. In 1894, the Laws were changed to award 3 points for a try, and again in 1971, when the present 4-point value was introduced. In common usage today, the word touchdown is often inaccurately substituted for try. see *penalty try, pushover try.*

try line: see *goal line.*

twenty-five: A now archaic term for a dropout, so-called because of the location of the kick. Until the recent standardization of metric measurements, this was the 25-yard line (now the 22-meter line).

twenty-two meter drop: A dropout from the 22-meter line. see *dropout.*

twenty-two meter line: Either of two lines drawn across the field 22 meters from and parallel to the goal lines. see *dropout, kickoff.*

up and under: A punt lofted high in the air upfield for teammates to receive or follow up. also *Garryowen, Garryowen up and under.*

upright: A goal post. also *post, woodwork.*

voluntary tackle: In rugby league, the act or an instance of deliberately inviting or waiting for a tackle, as by dropping to the ground when in possession of the ball, falling and deliberately remaining on a loose ball, or, when marking the tackled player at a play-the-ball, by making no effort strike for the ball as it is dropped, but rather diving behind the tackled player to fall on the ball as it is heeled. In such cases, a penalty kick is awarded to the nonoffending side at the place of the infringement.

wheel: Short for wheel the scrum.

wheel the scrum: To rotate the scrum once the ball is put in, a tactic sometimes employed by a pack, either defensively, to leave fewer options and little room to maneuver for opposing backs, or offensively, as when a side is attempting to advance the ball at their feet. also *wheel.*

wing: 1. Short for wing three-quarter. 2.

Short for the position of wing three-quarter.

wing forward: 1. In rugby union, either of the two forwards (blind-side and open-side) who pack into the ends of the second row (in the 3-4-1 formation) or third row (in the 3-2-3 formation) of a scrum. New Zealand's famous touring All Blacks of 1905 and 1906 (who won 32 of 33 matches in England and France) introduced a single "winging forward", the great Dave Gallaher. His then controversial role was to put the ball into scrums and afterwards, to act somewhat like a blocker for his scrum half. At other times, this "rover back" functioned as a three-quarter for overlaps. By the 1920s, wing forwards were used extensively to spoil the play of opposing scrum halfs and standoff halfs. Ironically, in 1932, New Zealand was the first country to require wing forwards to bind into scrums, thereby redefining the position they had helped to develop. also *breakaway, flanker, flank forward, side row.* 2. In rugby union, the position played by a wing forward. also *breakaway, flanker, flank forward, side row.*

wing three-quarter: 1. Either of the two back division players who normally play outside the two centers and near the touchlines. Wing three-quarters are usually among the fastest players on a side. also *wing.* 2. The position played by a wing three-quarter. also *wing.*

win the ball: To gain possession of the ball, especially in a scrum, line-out, maul, or ruck (and in rugby league, in a play-the-ball).

woodwork: Slang for the goal, especially the goal posts or crossbar.

work-rate: An English expression from soccer in the 1960s, meaning the amount of running a player or team does or is able to do or the amount of effort expended during a match.

work the scrum: To play in the position of scrum half, the player who normally feeds the ball into and takes the ball out of scrums.

wrong-foot: To, by means of a clever move or feint, momentarily catch a defender on the wrong foot and, thus, often be able to run past him.

SOCCER

Man has been "playing ball" since the first pebble was kicked along the ground, and in many early cultures, contests evolved in which a sphere was directed at, over, or through some kind of goal. Such ancestors to football, or soccer as it is known in Australia, the United States and Canada, were played centuries before Christ in the Orient and Europe, and surprisingly, date back as far as 1000 B.C. in the Americas.

Terra-cotta figurines of ball players from that period found in Xochipala in Guerrero, Mexico, are evidence of a game played in various forms by Indians all throughout Mesoamerica and the Caribbean Islands. Early in the sixteenth century, astonished Spanish conquistadores discovered the Aztec version of the game. Called *ullamaliztli*, it was played in a large walled court (*tlachtli*) in the shape of a short, broad capital "H", with vertical rings mounted as goals about ten feet off the ground, at the midpoint of the high sidewalls bordering the central section. Two teams of two or three players attempted to score points by propelling a solid rubber ball with the hip or knees against or over the low walls at each end of the court, or to end the game outright by putting the ball through one of the rings. In other versions, the ball was played with the head and feet. Reliefs from the Maya-Toltec era (960–1200 A.D.) depict the sacrifice of a player. It is believed that in certain contests, the losing players may have been killed as an offering to the rain gods.

Though the Spaniards ultimately demolished all the Aztec tlachtlis and prohibited the game because of its "heathen" religious aspects, they were fascinated by the rubber ball (Christopher Columbus had brought one to Europe in the late 1400s), and by the skill and dexterity of the players. In 1528, Indians brought to Spain by Hernan Cortes put on a demonstration at the court of Charles V.

Reports of warriors playing "football" games in China date back as far as the Spring and Autumn period (c.772–481 B.C.) and some believe that simple ball games may have been played as early as the Shang Dynasty (c.1766–1122 B.C.). *Tactics of the Warring States: The Tactics of the Qi Kingdom*, written about the period between 475 and 221 B.C., mentions that kicking a ball around was a favorite sport of the citizens of Linzi, the capital of Qi in Northeast China. The father of Liu Bang, founder and first emperor of the Han Dynasty (c.206 B.C.–220 A.D.) is said to have enjoyed the pastime. Records from the Western Han Dynasty (206 B.C.–24 A.D.) mention that famous Han generals Wei Qing (died 106 B.C.) and Huo

Qubing (died 117 B.C.) were enthusiasts of a competitive game played by soldiers using a leather-covered ball stuffed with feathers.

Inflated leather balls were introduced toward the end of the Tang Dynasty (618–907 A.D.) and large-scale football competitions were featured entertainments during the reign of Emperor Hui Zong (1082–1135). In these games, two teams of eleven players, wearing turbans and jackets of red silk for one side and black for the other and captained by a distinctively turbaned leader, attempted to kick a ball through a 20-inch hole in the upper part of a curtain hung in the middle of the playing area from a 30-foot high frame festooned with colorful streamers. The winners of a game were awarded such prizes as silver bowls and lengths of silk, while the captain of the losing team was whipped.

Football's European foundations were much less sophisticated than either the ancient Chinese or Mesoamerican examples. Among the earliest European ball games is one mentioned in Homer's Odyssey as being played by the Greeks in the twelfth century B.C. It is believed to be the Spartan game *episkyros*, or *epikoinos*, meaning "team game" which was played on a field with a center line, and in which players from two teams attempted to throw, push, kick, or wrestle a small ball past the opponent's goal line. A relief unearthed in Athens in 1922 shows six players engaged in such a game, with three on each side of a midline, one behind the other, somewhat suggesting the concept of defenders, midfielders, and forwards.

Julius Caesar himself is said to have enjoyed the rough-and-tumble Greek and Roman game of *harpastum*, in which players attempted to win possession of a small, hard, hair-stuffed ball from the opponents. Other ball games developed, predating the medieval Italian game *calcio*, in which an inflated ball was kicked between players, but it was harpastum that the Roman legions spread throughout Europe and Britain.

Within Britain itself, there are conflicting ideas about the exact origin of football. Most accounts center around Shrove Tuesday, including the centuries-old legend that the first football was the head of a captive Dane (or a dug-up Danish skull) kicked through the streets of Chester by a group of boys.

Glover's *History of Derby* mentions football contests played between church districts from 217, the year that local fighters are said to have vanquished a cohort of Roman legionnaires. It is alleged in Derby that the first Shrove Tuesday contest (and thus, the first soccer game) was a celebration of that battle. However records show that similar brawling contests in which a ball was kicked through the streets or over the countryside, occurred at about the same time in towns and villages throughout Britain. The memory of these early contests is still celebrated every Shrove Tuesday in Ashbourne, Derbyshire, in a ceremonial game played through the city streets between one side of the town and the other.

By the Middle Ages, the crude and often violent form of "mob football" (so called initially because it was played on foot rather than on horseback) had gained enough popularity in Britain to incur the displeasure of royalty and the church: In 1314, Edward II of England banned the game as a breach of the peace "forasmuch as there is a great noise in the city caused by hustling over large balls from which many evils might arise which God forbid". The pastime was seen by Edward III as no less than a threat to the security of the nation, taking thousands of young men away from archery and other martial training. In 1349, he too ordered the game suppressed, as did Richard II in 1389 in a statute which forbade "all playing at tenise, football, and other games". Henry IV, Henry VIII, and Queen Elizabeth all issued reinforcing prohibitions during their reigns, but interest in the game continued through the seventeenth century. Even Oliver Cromwell was an avid player, mentioning it frequently in his letters.

During the Industrial Revolution, former artisans, farmers, and merchants found less time for leisure activities such as football as their work conditions changed. By now, however, the game had become popular with the sons of the educated classes, and as the working man's interest waned, football flourished in the "civilized" atmosphere of England's public schools.

By the early nineteenth century, some form of football was being played at the best of these institutions, each school evolving its own style with various basic and sometimes conflicting playing rules. Charterhouse and Westminster played twenty men to a side and permitted no handling of the ball, while Harrow limited a team to eleven. Eton played its version of the game alongside a wall on a 120-yard long pitch which was only 6 yards wide (still played today as the traditional Eton Wall Game) and was first to recognize offside (called "sneaking"), though the actual term "offside" came later from Cheltenham, as did the first crossbar and throw-in from "touch".

In 1823, an incident occurred that would ultimately divide football into two distinctly different games. During a match at Rugby School (where the ball could be handled as long as the player didn't move his feet), one participant, William Webb Ellis, suddenly picked up the ball in frustration and carried it across the opponent's goal line. Although Ellis's act was controversial at the time, the practice soon became accepted and was identified with the school as the "Rugby game".

In 1848, in the first effort to arrive at a uniform code that would allow competition among schools, fourteen Cambridge University students, among them a Rugby graduate, finally agreed on rules that allowed handling, but no running with the ball, and prohibited kicking, tripping, or grabbing an opponent. Passing forward was allowed as long as three opponents were between the receiver and the goal. To score, the ball had to be kicked between two posts and under a connecting tape.

Football thrived with the new rules and was soon played outside of school by specially formed clubs. The first of these was created in the northern industrial city of Sheffield sometime in 1854, and, as Sheffield United, it remains today the oldest football club in existence. Some of the clubs that followed preferred a version of football dubbed "The Simplest Game", developed at Uppingham School, and still others the Rugby game.

In a historic series of meetings in 1863 between representatives of various local clubs at London's Freemason's Tavern, England's Football Association (FA) was born and, after long and heated arguments, a uniform set of rules was adopted that once and for all separated "rugby football" from the sport of "association football". Soon after, Charles Wreford-Brown, an Association committee member and player, was asked if he would like a game of "rugger", a nickname for rugby. "No, soccer", he replied, creating a similar word play on the abbreviation "assoc" for association football. Oddly, the term "soccer" would be widely used only later in the United States and Canada.

The 1863 rules were in fact just basic guidelines, but they did set the maximum dimensions for the pitch (200 yards by 100 yards) and goals (initially, two posts 8 feet apart, with no connecting tape), and specify the method of scoring (by kicking the ball through or over the space between the posts), offside rules (no player was to be closer to the opponent's goal than his teammate at the moment he kicked the ball), throw-in rules (at a right angle to the touch line, by any method), and initial regulations for kickoffs, free kicks, etc. They permitted catching the ball, and throwing or passing it if the ball was caught on the first bounce or with a "fair catch".

A specific playing code gradually evolved, and the game of "soccer" began to assume its eventual worldwide form. Handling the ball was abolished after 1866, and an upper limit for the goals was marked with tape. In 1867, the offside rule was changed back to the 1848 version, calling for three opposing players closer to the goal. Goal kicks were introduced in 1869, and in 1870, the number of players on a team was fixed at eleven, and separate playing rules were instituted for the goalkeepers. In 1872, corner kicks were introduced, as were umpires in 1874. Two innovations made their appearance in 1878: Floodlights were used to illuminate the first night game at Sheffield, and referees began using whistles when an infraction occurred.

Late in 1882, representatives of the English, Scottish, Welsh, and Irish Associations standardized the size of the ball, made crossbars mandatory, and agreed upon a version of the Scottish two-handed throw-in.

Though adjustments would continue for some time, the major laws of football were in place by 1891. By the early 1900s, the game that had been shaped in the British Isles had spread all through Europe and across the Atlantic to North and South America. England won the first Olympic Football competition in 1900, though a gold medal was not awarded until Canada won at the St. Louis Olympics in 1904. That same year, representatives from Belgium, France, Holland, Spain, Sweden, and Switzerland persuaded the English Football Association to join in forming the Federation of International Football Associations (FIFA) to govern what was already becoming a true world sport.

Football was brought to the United States some time in the early nineteenth century, long before the 1863 Football Association rules were framed, though surprised Pilgrims had watched American Indians in the New England area play a native game in the early 1600s called *pasuckquakkohowog*, meaning roughly, "gather to play football". In it, a small wooden or deerskin ball (about 2 inches in diameter) was kicked along the beach between goals set about a mile apart with a line marked halfway between them. Accounts say that teams ranged anywhere from thirty to over a thousand on each side when neighboring villages or tribes competed.

Though crude forms of football were played at Harvard and Yale Universities as early as the 1820s (sometimes as a means of hazing freshmen) and were subsequently banned at both schools in the 1830s, the first recorded soccer team in the United States was the Oneida Football Club of Boston.

In 1921, the American Soccer League was formed, the first professional soccer league in the Americas. Disbanded in 1933, the league was reorganized the following year and is still operating under the same name.

The sport continued to grow after World War I, and by the 1924 Paris Olympics, twenty-two nations were represented in the football competition. In 1930, the first World Cup tournament was hosted and won by Uruguay. Thirteen national teams participated, including the United States team (led by Hall of Famer Billy Gonsalves) and four European teams.

Football was becoming more popular, and international matches began to take on an added significance with national pride at stake. Nowhere was this more evident than at the World Cup. Italy won the second and third World Cups, the first at home in 1934, where Mussolini watched as the Italians crushed the United States team 7-1 in the opening round, and the second in Paris in 1938, as the dark clouds of war hung over Europe. The stars of soccer included the legendary Stanley Matthews, Spain's brilliant goalkeeper, Zamora, and the acrobatic Brazilian, Leonidas, who first showed his spectacular bicycle kick in Paris in 1938.

Uruguay won the 1950 World Cup, defeating Brazil in front of 220,000 spectators in Rio's Maracana Stadium. But the most stunning upset in international football occurred when England's first World Cup bid ended with a 1-0 loss to the United States. Haitian-born Joe Gaetjens headed in the game's only goal on a perfect cross from fellow Hall of Famer Walter Bahr.

The dominant club of the 1950s was undoubtedly Spain's Real Madrid, who won the first European Cup in 1956, and, with Argentine great Alfredo di Stephano and Puskas from Hungary, Real Madrid went on to win the next four.

The 1958 World Cup in Sweden was won by Brazil in a tournament that marked the debut

of the seventeen-year-old Brazilian "phenom", Pele.

Known as "The Black Pearl", "God of the Stadiums", or simply "El Rey", Pele reigned as the undisputed king of football and the most popular athlete in the world for over twenty years, scoring a record total of 1,251 goals in international or first division play (101 for Brazil, 1090 for Santos and 60 for the New York Cosmos), and 33 more in exhibition and All-Star games. He led Brazil to an unprecedented three World Cups, winning again in Chile in 1962, and in Mexico in 1970 (England won at home in 1966, the year Pele was carried off the field and unable to return after being brutally fouled in a game with Portugal). It is a tribute to his mastery that other great modern goalscorers, dribblers, and playmakers have been and continue to be measured against Pele, among them Portugal's Eusebio, George Best of Northern Ireland, Peru's Teofilo Cubillas, Franz Beckenbauer and Karl-Heinz Rummenigge of West Germany, Holland's Johan Cruyff, Kevin Keegan of Great Britain, Russia's Oleg Blokhin, Michel Platini of France, Italy's Paulo Rossi, Diego Maradona of Argentina, and Brazil's own Zico, known in that country as "The White Pele". Even defensive stars like England's Bobby Moore and goalkeeper Gordon Banks are often remembered by a particular effort against Pele.

Soccer in the 1960s fell into a negative, goal-stifling era in which mass defense was emphasized, with relentless man-to-man marking. The Italian *catenaccio* ("big chain" of defenders), with its extra back (*livero*) playing behind four fullbacks, served as the widely copied model for this style of play, epitomized by Italian coach Helenio Herrera's Inter-Milan team, winner of the European Cup in 1964 and 1965. Cup victories in 1967 by Scotland's attack-minded Glasgow Celtic, and in 1968 by Manchester United (with outstanding performances by George Best and Bobby Charlton) offered the first ray of hope.

Brazil's convincing win in the 1970 Mexico World Cup final over the conservative Italians marked the end of the defensive era. But it was Rinus Michel's energetic Ajax team from Holland, led by the brilliant Johan Cruyff, which introduced the first tactical innovation of football's new era, "total football" (or "total soccer"). European Cup winners in 1971, 1972, and 1973, Ajax employed a strategy in which players constantly exchanged positions during the course of play, moving freely between offense and defense as needed, as opposed to being restricted to a certain role or area of the field.

advantage: Short for advantage rule.

advantage rule: A clause in the rules of soccer which enables the referee to allow play to continue after a foul if a stoppage of play would take away an advantage held by the fouled player or his team. If the foul committed is serious or violent, the offending player may still be warned, cautioned, or ejected, even though the advantage rule is applied. also *advantage.*

air ball: A ball in flight, or in the air.

American Soccer League: The oldest professional soccer league in the United

States, headquartered in Bethlehem, Pennsylvania. Founded in 1934, the American Soccer League announced a six-team alignment in 1983, comprised of the Carolina Lightnin, the Dallas Americans, the Detroit Express, the Jacksonville Tea Men, the Oklahoma City Slickers, and the Pennsylvania Stoners. also *ASL*.

American Youth Soccer Organization: The largest youth soccer organization in the United States. Founded in 1964, the American Youth Soccer Organization conducts programs in twenty-eight states for boys and girls between the ages of five and eighteen. Special rules require balanced competition and specify that every player on a team must play at least one half of each game. The American Youth Soccer Organization is headquartered in Torrance, California. also *AYSO*.

area: The penalty area. also *box*.

ASL: The American Soccer League.

assistant referee: The official positioned by the side of the playing area of an indoor soccer game, who is primarily responsible for assisting the referee in the control of the game in accordance with the Laws. An assistant referee controls the bench and penalty box areas, indicates illegal substitutions and three-line violations, supervises the time-keeper, and keeps a written record of the game and time penalties.

association football: A British term for soccer, originally used to differentiate the kicking sport from rugby, also known as "football." The term refers to the type of football approved by the London Football Association, the first real governing body of soccer, founded in 1863. see *soccer*.

attacking zone: The part of the playing area in indoor soccer which contains the goal at which a team shoots, bounded by the nearest red line. compare *defensive zone, neutral zone*.

AYSO: The American Youth Soccer Organization.

back: A fullback or defender.

back four: The four fullbacks in a formation which uses four defensive players.

1. back heel: To kick the ball backward with the heel. (back heeled the ball to a trailing teammate)

2. back heel: The act or an instance of using the heel to make a backward pass.

back pass: A pass backward, made either with the heel or by rolling the ball with the bottom of the foot.

ball boy, ball girl: One of a number of boys or girls positioned around the perimeter of the playing area, responsible for retrieving the ball when it is kicked out of play.

banana kick: A kick in which the ball is hit off center to make it spin and thus curve or bend in flight (as around a wall of defenders) before dropping suddenly. Among the first to popularize the technique in the 1950s was the Brazilian Didi (Vvaldyr Pereira), whose special shot was called the *folha seca* (Portuguese for "dry leaf") because it dropped like a dry or dead leaf from a tree. Other internationals who have been known for the banana kick (a name popularized in Germany) are Eusebio of Portugal, Ireland's George Best, Bobby Collins of Scotland, England's Bobby Charlton, Franz Beckenbauer of Germany, and Brazil's incomparable Pele.

banjoed: Players' slang for having been kicked in the groin.

beat: 1. To gain a momentary advantage over an opponent, or to get past an opponent. (beat his man and sent a cross into the middle) 2. To score with

BICYCLE KICK

a shot past the goalkeeper. (beat the keeper with a little chip shot)

bench penalty: A penalty assessed in indoor soccer against a coach, trainer, or player on the bench for delaying the game or for ungentlemanly or violent conduct. A bench penalty results in a time penalty (the length of which depends on the nature and severity of the offense) to be served by a player designated by the coach and during which the offending side must play shorthanded. If the offense is severe, the offending coach, trainer, or player may be cautioned or ejected. After a bench penalty, play is restarted with a drop ball.

bend: To make the ball curve in flight by kicking it off center so that it spins. (bent the ball in by the far post) also *curl.*

bicycle, bicycle kick: An overhead kick in which a player leaps almost upside down to volley the ball with a scissors-like leg motion. When properly executed, the bicycle kick is a powerful shot and one of the most spectacular plays in soccer, whether used to score by a forward with his back to the goal, or to clear or even save the ball by a defender facing the goal. Most often associated with the legendary Brazilian player Pele, the bicycle kick was introduced in the 1930s by another Brazilian international, Leonidas da Silva, after whose nickname, "the Black Diamond," a candy bar was named. Because the leg motion is similar to that used in the horizontal scissors volley or scissors kick, the bicycle kick is sometimes referred to as a scissors kick. also *double kick, hitch kick, overhead volley, reverse kick.*

bite: To go for the ball in an attempt to

tackle it away from an opponent, to commit to tackling the ball. (will lay the ball off to the side as soon as a defender bites) also *challenge.*

blind-side run: An advance, unseen by defenders, by a player without the ball into an attacking space on the side of the field opposite that where the ball is.

block tackle: The act or an instance of blocking the ball with the foot or body at the moment an opponent attempts to kick it. also *front block tackle.*

1. blue card: A small blue card shown by the referee in MISL games to indicate that a player is being assessed a time penalty. see *time penalty.*

2. blue card: To show a blue card.

board: To illegally force or push an opponent into the boards which surround the playing area in indoor soccer. (injured his knee when he was boarded) see *boarding.*

boarding: The act or an instance of illegally forcing or pushing an opponent into the boards surrounding the playing area in indoor soccer. Boarding results in a direct free kick for the offended team and, if the infraction is serious, a two-minute penalty for the offending player.

boards: The 4-foot-high wooden wall which surrounds and forms the perimeter of the playing area in indoor soccer. Attached to the top of the boards (except in front of the players' benches) is an unbreakable glass screen to protect spectators from the ball. also *dasher boards, perimeter wall, woodwork.*

book: To issue a yellow card (or less frequently, a red card) to a player for a serious foul or unsportsmanlike conduct, and to record the name of the guilty player or players. All serious fouls and instances of unsportsmanlike conduct are reported by the referee to the league or sanctioning body for possible further disciplinary action should the guilty player repeat such offenses in future games. see *caution, ejection.*

booking: The act or an instance of issuing a yellow card (or less frequently, a red card) to a player guilty of a serious foul or unsportsmanlike conduct.

boots: The traditional name for cleated soccer shoes. Soccer boots normally have low-cut soft leather uppers (sometimes padded slightly to protect the Achilles tendon) with tough plastic or

BOOTS

composition soles and one of three types of cleats or studs, depending upon the playing surface. For thick grass and/or wet or muddy ground, boots with six (or occasionally eight) screw-in replaceable studs (not more than 3/4 of an inch long, nor less than 1/2 inch in diameter) are used. Such studs are made of leather, rubber, aluminum, or plastic, and must be solid. For normal grass or dry or hard ground, boots with ten or more molded cleats (3/8 of an inch minimum diameter) on the sole are used. For artificial turf, boots with many small (approximately 1/4 inch in diameter and 1/4 inch long) molded rubber cleats are used.

bounce ball: see *drop ball*.

box: 1. Slang for the penalty area. (sent a crossing pass into the box) also *area*. 2. Short for the penalty box in indoor soccer. also *sin bin*.

bring down: To cause an opponent to trip or fall down, as with an illegal or late tackle. A foul which results in a direct free kick by the opposing team at the spot of the offense, or if committed by a defender in his penalty area, a penalty kick. In indoor soccer, the offending player may also be assessed a two-minute time penalty. If, in the opinion of the referee, the foul is serious or violent, the offending player may be cautioned (an automatic two-minute time penalty in indoor soccer) or sent off (an automatic five-minute time penalty in indoor soccer, to be served by the ejected player's substitute). also *take down*.

bring the ball down: To trap and control an air ball until it reaches the ground so that it can be dribbled, passed, or shot. (brought the ball down, turned, and chipped it over the diving goalkeeper)

build up: The process of incorporating a number of players into the launching and supporting of an attack. A player who intercepts the ball at midfield will often pass back or laterally in order to allow time for a proper build up for an attack.

bully: A scramble by players from both teams to control a loose ball, especially in front of the goal.

by-line: The goal line. also *endline*.

capped: Having participated as a member of a national team in international matches. (capped six times before he reached the age of twenty) see *caps*.

caps: A term of merit awarded to players who participate as members of a national team in international matches. From the custom in some countries of giving a ceremonial tassled cap to each player for every international match.

1. card: To show a yellow card. see *caution*.

2. card: A yellow card. see *caution*.

catch the defense flat: To momentarily catch the opposing defenders lined up laterally across the field, with no one trailing behind to guard against a through pass. (caught the defense flat and quickly put the ball through into the area for the center forward) also *catch the defense square*.

catch the defense square: see *catch the defense flat*.

catenaccio: A system of play first popularized in Italy in the 1950s and 1960s, utilizing a *livero* or "free man" to cover any place behind a line of three or four fullbacks. Primarily a defensive system, the catenaccio (Italian for "big chain" of defenders) was adapted from the Swiss *verrou* or "bolt" system pioneered in 1931 by Karl Rappan, a former Austrian international player who coached the Servette-Geneva team in Switzerland. In 1947, in order to counter the scoring threat of some of the wealthier Italian first division teams, Nereo Rocco, manager of a small club, Triestina, used the deeply positioned back from the defensive mode of the *verrou* system to anchor his catenaccio. After Triestina's impressive climb from last place to second at the end of the season, other Italian clubs adopted the system, among them, Helenio Herrera's Inter-Milan, European Cup winners in 1964 and 1965. The catenaccio dominated Italian soccer for almost twenty years and served as the prototype for soccer's goal-stifling era of mass defense and relentless man-to-man marking.

1. caution: An official warning to a player guilty of a serious offense such as a deliberate or dangerous foul, persistent infringement of the Laws, dissent, dangerous play (at the option of the referee), entry to or exit from the field without permission, deliberate time wasting, infractions during a penalty kick, intentionally moving a corner flag, upright, or crossbar, ungentlemanly conduct, or in indoor soccer, to a player who is assessed a two-minute penalty more than once in a game for a penal offense. A player who receives a caution is automatically assessed a two-minute penalty in indoor soccer. also *card, yellow card.*

2. caution: To show the yellow card and issue an official caution. also *book, card, yellow card.*

1. center: To kick or play the ball toward attacking players in the center of the field, such as into the penalty area in front of the goal, from the side or sideline area. also *cross.*

2. center: A ball which is centered. also *cross.*

center back: 1. The central defender (or, less frequently, either of two central defenders). Normally positioned directly in front of the goal, the center back is responsible for man-to-man coverage of the opposing center forward and must be strong enough and tall enough to beat opponents on the ground and in the air. The center back was created in 1925 to counter the new-found freedom of forwards because of the change in the offside rule that year (only two, instead of three, defensive players had to be between an offensive player and the goal line when the ball was played). Herbert Chapman's Arsenal team featured a center back when he introduced the W-M formation, in which the old center half was moved back between the two fullbacks. Because of this, and the then-popular custom of numbering positions rather than players, the new central defender was still called a "center half" or "center halfback" (and remains so today for some British traditionalists). Arsenal's first center back was Jack Butler, but he was soon replaced by Herbie Roberts, a tall and able policeman who served as a prototype for all those who followed. also *center full, center fullback, policeman, stopper.* 2. The position played by a center back. (still called "center half" or "center halfback" by some British traditionalists). also *center full, center fullback, policeman, stopper.*

center circle: A circle with a 10-yard radius (10-foot radius in indoor soccer) marked around the actual center of the playing field and bisected by the halfway line. A kickoff is taken from the spot (center spot) in the middle of the center circle at the beginning of each half and overtime period and after each goal. On a kickoff, no player from the defending team may enter the center circle until the ball has been played. also *kickoff circle.*

center forward: 1. The central attacking player on the forward line, normally the player positioned closest to the opponent's goal. The center forward must be skilled enough on the ground to be able to turn and shoot with either foot when being closely marked, and good enough in the air to head in balls crossed into the area from the wings. also *spearhead, striker.* 2. The position played by a center forward. also *spearhead, striker.*

center full: see *center back.*

center fullback: see *center back.*

center half, center halfback: 1. The central midfield player in any formation with three midfielders. The center half has both offensive and defensive responsibilities (the extent of which vary with different formations and styles of play), and must be able to pressure opposing forwards and midfielders in the central portion of the field, to drop back to help out when the defense is outnumbered in the penalty area, and to serve as a link between the defense and offense, bringing the ball forward and distributing it to attacking players, as well as backing up and supporting an attack in progress. see *pyramid.* 2. The position in the midfield played by a center half. see *pyramid.* 3. The central defensive player.

center line: The halfway line, especially in indoor soccer. see *halfway line.*

center spot: The spot marked at the middle of the halfway line within the center circle, and from which kickoffs are made at the start of each half or overtime period and after each goal.

1. challenge: To confront an opposing player with the ball and attempt to tackle it away from him. also *bite.*

2. challenge: The act or an instance of challenging an opponent.

chance: An opportunity to score or shoot at the goal.

change: To pass the ball from one side of

the field to a teammate on the other side. also *switch.*

change on the fly: To substitute a player or players in indoor soccer while the game is in progress rather than waiting for a stoppage in play. A legal tactic as long as the player or players substituted for arrive at the bench (off the field or in contact with the sideboard in the bench area) before the replacement or replacements enter the field of play. When an infraction occurs (too many men on the ice), the offending player or players are assessed a two-minute penalty, and the opposing team is awarded an indirect free kick from where the ball was when play was stopped.

1. charge: To run into or make contact with an opposing player, legal only if contact is made with the shoulder (a "fair charge" or "shoulder charge") when contending for a ball within playing distance (3 to 4 feet). see *charging.*

2. charge: The act or an instance of running into or making contact with an opposing player. see *charging.*

charging: The act or an instance of an illegal charge. If the charge is made from behind the opponent (unless the opponent is deliberately obstructing) or made in a violent or dangerous manner, a direct free kick is awarded to the offended side from the place where the infraction occurred, or a penalty kick is awarded to the offended team if the infraction is committed by a defending player inside the penalty area. In indoor soccer, the offending player may also be assessed a two-minute time penalty. If, in the opinion of the referee, the foul is particularly serious or violent, the offending player may be cautioned (an automatic two-minute time penalty in indoor soccer) or sent off (an automatic five-minute time penalty in indoor soccer, to be served by the ejected player's substitute). If a fair charge is made with the shoulder when the ball is not within playing distance, or if no attempt is being made to play the ball, or if the goalkeeper is illegally charged, an indirect free kick is awarded to the offended team at the place where the infraction occurred.

chest: To trap and control an air ball with the chest. (chested the ball down to his thigh, gave it a little bounce, then turned and volleyed it into the net)

chest trap: The act or an instance of stopping and controlling an air ball with the chest. compare *foot trap, head trap, sole trap, sweep trap, thigh trap.*

1. chip: To kick under and lift the ball off the ground into a high lobbing arc, usually for a short distance (such as over one or more defenders). also *flight, loft.* compare *lob.*

2. chip: A pass or a shot which is lofted or chipped. (a set play which called for him to run onto a little chip over the wall) compare *lob.*

chippy: Unnecessarily rough, as of one or more fouls, the play of one or more individuals or a team, or of a game in general. (cautioned for a particularly chippy foul)

chop: see *hack.*

clear: To kick or head the ball away from in front of the goal, out of danger. (gave up the goal when his defenders failed to clear the ball)

clearance: The act or an instance of clearing the ball.

clear off the line: To clear a ball out of danger just before it entirely crosses the goal line.

close down: 1. To thwart or successfully defend against an opposing player or team, whether by aggressive individual marking or teamwork and strategy. (able to close down their center forward) 2. To defensively seal off an area of the field.

combination passes, combination play: A series of short, low passes between two or more players to advance the ball toward the opponent's goal. Combination play was introduced in the early 1970s by Queen's Park of Scotland, replacing the traditional English dribbling game and revolutionizing soccer.

convert a corner: To score a goal from a corner kick.

convert a penalty: To score a goal from a penalty kick.

Copa Libertadores: An annual tournament to determine the top club team in South America. The competition is open to the league champion and runner-up in all South American countries. The Copa Libertadores was first won in 1960 by Penarol of Uruguay.

corner: Short for corner kick.

corner area: The area within the corner kick arc marked inside each corner of the playing field. Corner kicks may be taken from anywhere within the corner area. also *quarter circle.*

corner flag: 1. A small flag atop a post not less than 5 feet high (and having a non-pointed top) placed at each corner of the playing field. The corner flag (including the post) may not be moved in order to take a corner kick. 2. A small flag atop a post raised 3 feet above the level of the perimeter wall in indoor soccer at each corner of the playing area, at the point where an undrawn extension of the goal area line meets the perimeter wall.

corner kick: 1. A direct free kick awarded to the attacking team when a defender is the last to touch a ball that crosses entirely over the goal line (outside the goal) out of play, taken from anywhere within the corner area on the side of the field on which the ball crossed the goal line. A corner kick is a dangerous scoring opportunity for the attacking team. Though a goal may be scored directly from a corner kick by "bending" the ball into the goal behind the goalkeeper (at one time a favorite technique of Irish soccer great George Best), the ball is usually lofted into the penalty area where it can be headed toward the goal by a teammate. Opposing players may be no closer than 10 yards from the ball until it is in play (travels the distance of its own circumference). The corner kick was first introduced in 1872 by the Football Association in England. also *corner.* compare *goal kick.* 2. A direct free kick awarded to the attacking team in indoor soccer when a defender is the last to touch a ball which leaves the playing area (passing over the perimeter wall between the corner flags in the zone), taken from the corner kick spot on the side of the goal on which the ball left the playing area. Opposing players may be no closer than 10 feet from the ball until it is in play (travels half the distance of its own circumference). also *corner.*

corner kick arc: The 1-yard radius quarter circle marked inside each corner of the playing field, enclosing the corner area from which corner kicks are taken. also *quarter circle.*

corner kick spot: A 19-inch dot marked at each corner of the playing area in indoor soccer at the intersection of the touchline and an undrawn extension of the goal area line. Corner kicks are taken from the corner kick spot. also *corner mark.*

corner mark: see *corner kick spot.*

cover: To take a defensive position behind a defending teammate, freeing him to challenge the player with the ball without fear of being beaten or of the player passing the ball through for an attacking teammate to run on to. A basic and essential tactic in soccer.

crease: The rectangular area marked in front of each goal in indoor soccer, measuring 16 feet wide (2 feet wider than the goal on each side) and 5 feet deep. The term is taken from hockey's similar "goal crease." also *goal area.*

create space: To cause the opponents to momentarily leave a strategic area of the field unguarded, such as by drawing defenders away with the ball, or with a dummy run or pass. (drew the defender out toward the wing, creating a space in the penalty area) also *make space.*

1. cross: To center the ball from the side or sideline area into the penalty area. also *center.*

2. cross: The act or an instance of centering the ball from the side or sideline area toward the middle of the field, especially in front of the opponent's goal. also *center.*

crossbar: The horizontal bar which marks the top of the goal, extending 8 yards between the goal posts 8 feet above the ground. First used at the Cheltenham public school in England, the crossbar was made obligatory by the Football Association in 1882. In indoor soccer, the crossbar extends 12 feet between the goal posts 6-1/2 feet above the ground.

curl: see *bend.*

cut down the angle: To move out from the goal line toward an attacking player with the ball so that he will be able to see less of the goal, and be forced to shoot from farther away. also *narrow the angle.*

cut the ball out: To tackle the ball away from an opponent.

dangerous play: Any action by a player which is dangerous or likely to cause injury to the player, a teammate, or an opponent. The most frequent instances of a dangerous play are kicking a ball near one or more other players which is high enough to normally head, or heading a ball near one or more other players which is low enough to normally kick. A dangerous play results in an indirect free kick by the opposing team from the spot of the offense.

dasher boards: see *boards.*

dead ball: 1. A ball that is out of play, such as when the ball crosses the goal line or a sideline or after a stoppage of play. 2. A ball placed anywhere within the playing area by the referee, such as for a kickoff or a direct or indirect kick. 3. A ball resting on the ground.

dead space: Areas of the playing field occupied by opposing players. compare *drop zone, space.*

defender: A fullback, one of the players on the back line whose main responsibility is to prevent the opposing team from scoring a goal. also *back.*

defense kick: see *goal kick.*

defensive zone: The part of the playing area in indoor soccer which contains the goal defended by a team, bounded by the nearest red line. compare *attacking zone, neutral zone.*

delay of game penalty: 1. An indirect free kick awarded to the opposing team when a player or players, in the opinion of the referee, indulge in tactics to hold up the game or waste time. 2. In indoor soccer, a two-minute penalty assessed to the goalkeeper (to be served by another player) when the ball is passed back into the defensive zone by a teammate from any other zone and is then handled by the goalkeeper (an indirect free kick is awarded to the opposing team from point of the infraction); or a two-minute penalty assessed to a player who intentionally kicks or heads the ball outside the playing area (an indirect free kick is awarded to the opposing team from the point of the infraction).

direct free kick: A free kick which is awarded to the opposing team at the point of the offense when a serious foul (such as pushing, holding or kicking an opponent) or infraction (such as intentionally handling the ball) is committed by a player, and from which a goal

may be scored directly against the offending team (should a ball be miskicked into a team's own goal, no goal results). When a direct free kick is taken, no opposing player may be closer than 10 yards from the ball (10 feet in indoor soccer) until it is played, unless the opposing player or players are standing on their own goal line between the goal posts. When a direct free kick is taken by a player from within his own penalty area, no opposing player may be inside the area or closer than 10 yards (10 feet in indoor soccer) until the ball is played. The ball must be stationary when a direct free kick is taken, and is in play when it has traveled the distance (or half the distance in indoor soccer) of its circumference (and is beyond the penalty area, if the kick is taken by a player from within his own area). The kicker may not play the ball a second time until it has been touched or played by another player. compare *indirect free kick.*

dissent: The act or an instance of vocally and persistently disagreeing with the decision of a referee, which can result in an indirect free kick being awarded to the opposing team from the point where the infraction occurred and in a yellow card (or in indoor soccer, a two-minute penalty) for the offending player.

dive: A faked or exaggerated fall to call the referee's attention to an alleged foul (such as at the time of a charge or tackle) in the hopes that a foul will be called against an opponent.

division: A group of competing teams at a specified level of play. In most countries, soccer competition is arranged by divisions, with the highest level being the "premiere" or "first" division, the next highest level being the "second" division, and so on. The English Football League, the first and prototype league for all that followed, added a second division in 1892. Each division is comprised of a given number of teams, with the highest finishers (usually two or three) of the previous season in each division below the first division moving up to the next higher division, and the last two or three finishers in each division suffering relegation to the division below for the next season. This automatic promotion system, pioneered by the Football League in 1899, provides incentive for teams in the lower divisions not only to win within their division, but to attempt to advance to a higher and more prestigious division, and for teams in the higher divisions to avoid relegation.

double minor: Two two-minute time penalties (minor penalties) assessed against a player (such as for unsportsmanlike conduct which does not warrant a caution) to be served consecutively. When a player is assessed a double minor and a goal is scored against his team during the first two-minute segment, the balance of the first segment is voided and the player remains in the penalty box for the second two-minute segment only. compare *major penalty, minor penalty.*

double pass: see *give-and-go.*

double kick: A bicycle kick.

drag the ball back: To suddenly move the ball closer with the foot, such as to protect it from an approaching defender.

1. dribble: To maneuver with or advance the ball using the feet to guide and control it with a series of light taps. (dribbled through the two fullbacks and shot)

2. dribble: The act or an instance of dribbling the ball.

dribbler: One who dribbles or is adept at dribbling the ball. Great Britain's beknighted winger, Sir Stanley Matthews (who played from the 1930s through the 1950s), Brazil's sensational winger of the 1950s, Garrincha (Manoel Francisco dos Santos), Ireland's magician with the ball, George Best (who burst into international prominence with Manchester United in the late 1960s and early 1970s), and, of course, Brazil's legendary Pele are regarded as some of soccer's greatest dribblers.

drop ball: A method of restarting play which has been stopped for a reason other than a foul (such as a serious injury, too many men on the field, or an outside influence) in which the referee drops the ball between two opposing players. The ball may not be touched or kicked by either player until it touches the ground. also *bounce ball, faceoff.*

dropkick: 1. A goalkeeper's technique in which the ball is dropped and kicked

just as it bounces up from the ground. 2. A half volley.

drop-kick: 1. To drop the ball and kick it just as it bounces up from the ground, legal for a goalkeeper when he is within the penalty area. 2. To half volley the ball.

drop pass: A pass in which the player in control of the ball, while moving forward, steps over the ball and rolls it, taps it (as with a back heel), or simply leaves it for a trailing teammate, and continues without breaking stride in the hopes of drawing away a defender.

drop zone: An area of the field unguarded by players of the opposing team, into which the ball is played to link up with an oncoming teammate.

dummy: A fake or feint intended to momentarily deceive an opponent. (went for the dummy and broke up the wall before the ball was kicked) see *sell the dummy.*

ejection: The expulsion of a player from a game for a serious or dangerous foul, persistent dissent, unsportsmanlike conduct, for a second caution during a game (or in indoor soccer, for his third two-minute time penalty for a penal offense), and which is signaled by the referee showing a red card to the guilty player. An ejected player may not be replaced by a substitute for the remainder of that game (except in indoor soccer, when the substitute must first serve a five-minute time penalty) and is usually suspended from playing in at least one future game. also *red card.*

eleven: A soccer team. (the most talented eleven in the country) also *side.*

encroach: To move closer to the ball than the 10-yard limit (10 feet in indoor soccer) on a kickoff, free kick, or corner kick (or on a kick-in in indoor soccer), to interfere with a throw-in or with the movement of a goalkeeper, or to enter the penalty area or move closer than the 10-yard limit (10 feet in indoor soccer) on a penalty kick. see *encroachment.*

encroachment: The act or an instance of encroaching, resulting in a caution for the guilty player and ejection if the infraction is repeated. In indoor soccer, encroachment results in a two-minute time penalty and a caution if the infraction is repeated.

end line: The goal line. also *by-line*.

equalize: To score a game-tying goal. (equalized in the final minute) also *knot*.

equalizer: A game-tying goal.

European Championship: The European Football Championship.

European Championship Clubs' Cup: A prestigious annual competition between the national champions of all European nations, commonly known as the European Cup. Proposed in 1954 by Gabriel Hanot, editor of the French sports paper *L'Equipe*, the European Cup was played first in 1956, with sixteen clubs participating. Real Madrid of Spain won the first European Cup, defeating Reims in the final played in Paris, France. With great foreign players such as Argentinian Alfredo di Stefano and Hungarian Ferenc Puskas, Real Madrid went on to win the next four European Cups (through 1960).

European Cup: The European Championship Clubs' Cup.

European Cup Winners' Cup: An annual tournament between cup winners from European nations (as opposed to national or league champions). The first competition was held in 1960, with Fiorentina of Italy winning in the final over Scotland's Glasgow Rangers.

European Football Championship: A quadrennial competition between national teams held midway between World Cup years. Originally called the European Nations Cup, the first European football Championship final was held in Paris in 1960, with Russia defeating Yugoslavia in extra time. also *European Championship*.

extra time: Playing time added to the end of a half to make up for delays because of injuries ("injury time"), a lost or difficult-to-recover ball or one in need of replacement, deliberate time-wasting by either team, or penalty kicks. The referee records all such delays to determine the amount of extra time to be added to each forty-five-minute half. The concept of extra time was introduced shortly after a controversial incident at the conclusion of a match in 1891 in England between Aston Villa and Stoke. With just over a minute left in the game, Stoke, down 1-0, was awarded a penalty shot. But Villa's wily goalkeeper grabbed the ball and kicked it as far as he could, over the

startled spectators and completely out of the playing grounds. Before it could be found and returned, the referee had whistled the end of the game.

face: Short for "face the goal" or "face the play," called out to teammates who have momentarily turned their backs on play, such as when players return after an unsuccessful attack or corner kick. "Face," then, is a warning to pay attention, so that the opposing team cannot gain a quick advantage when the ball is put back in play.

faceoff: Slang for a drop ball in indoor soccer. also *bounce ball*.

face off: To participate as one of the two players involved in a drop ball.

FA Cup: The Football Association Cup, the annual postseason elimination tournament and trophy for the championship of the British Football Association. The oldest continuous major sports competition, the FA Cup was the idea of British football (soccer) pioneer, Charles W. Alcock and was held first in 1872, with fifteen teams competing. In the first final, played in London before 2,000 spectators, the Wanderers defeated the favored Royal Engineers. The last amateur club to win the FA Cup was the Old Etonians in 1882. In 1894, Notts County defeated Bolton to become the first second division club to win the competition.

fair charge: A legal shoulder charge. see *charging, shoulder charge*.

far post: The goal post farthest from where the ball is being played. compare *near post*.

Federation Internationale de Football Association: The Federation of International Football Associations (FIFA), the international governing body of soccer. Founded in 1904, FIFA is headquartered in Zurich, Switzerland, with a membership of 154 nations.

field player: A player other than a goalkeeper.

FIFA: The Federation Internationale de Football Association.

fifty-fifty ball: A free ball in play that opposing players have an equal chance of controlling or playing. (an aggressive midfielder who wins most fifty-fifty balls)

1. finish: To shoot at the goal.

2. finish: A shot at the goal, as after a solo run, or after combination play approaching the goal.

finisher: One who shoots the goal. (looks awkward, but he's a great finisher)

1. **first time:** Played on the initial touch, without first trapping or controlling, as of a ball approaching on the ground or in the air. also *one touch.*

2. **first time:** Of or pertaining to a ball played on the initial touch, without trapping or controlling it first. (scored with a first time volley) also *one touch.*

fist: To punch a dangerous air ball away from the goal with the hand clenched, legal for a goalkeeper anywhere within the penalty area. (fisted the cross away to prevent a goal)

five-second rule: A rule in indoor soccer which prohibits a goalkeeper in full possession of the ball from delaying the release of the ball from his hands by more than five seconds. An infraction of the five-second rule results in the awarding of an indirect free kick to the opposing team from the place where the infraction occurred.

1. **flag:** A small, colored (usually bright yellow or red) flag on a short pole carried by linesmen and used to signal an offside, or the side entitled to a corner kick, goal kick, or throw-in when the ball leaves the playing area. (appealed to the linesman for the offside flag)

2. **flag:** To signify an offside by raising the flag. (flagged the offside to nullify the goal)

1. **flick:** 1. To pass or shoot the ball with the outside of the foot, quickly snapping the foot outward to propel the ball. (flicked the return pass into the goal first time) 2. To head the ball (usually a short distance) toward the goal or a teammate. also *nod.*

2. **flick:** A short pass or shot made by

DEFENDERS

MIDFIELD

FORWARDS

4-4-2

flicking the ball with the foot or head toward a teammate or the goal.

flick kick: A jabbing kick in which the ball is flicked with the outside of the foot. also *jab kick.*

flick on: To head an air ball in such a way as to keep it moving in or near its original direction. (flicked the ball on, just over the defender)

flick-on header: A header in which the ball is flicked on, in, or near its original direction.

flight: see *chip.*

football: 1. The international name for soccer. also *association football.* 2. A soccer ball.

footballer: A soccer player.

foot trap: A trap in which the foot is used to null and control a ball in the air, or a moving ball on the ground (such as with a sole trap or sweep trap). compare *chest trap, head trap, thigh trap.*

forward: A primarily attacking player on the front line. The center forward, strikers and/or wings are all considered forwards, as are the inside left and inside right in formations where these positions are utilized. Forwards are primarily responsible for maneuvering the ball close to the opponent's goal and taking shots. In some modern formations, all the forwards are called strikers. see *pyramid.*

1. **foul:** A violation of the rules which involves physical interference with an opponent (such as kicking, tripping, jumping at, charging, striking, spitting, holding, pushing and, in indoor soccer, boarding), intentionally handling the ball, dangerous play, or unsportsmanlike conduct, penalized by awarding a free kick to the opposing team (a direct free kick, indirect free kick, or penalty kick, depending on the location and severity of the foul) and assessing a yellow or red card (and in indoor soccer, a time penalty) to the offending player if the foul is considered serious or violent.

2. **foul:** 1. To commit a foul. 2. To commit a foul against a particular opponent. (fouled him when he took him down from behind)

4-4-2: A formation which employs four defenders, four midfielders, and two forwards. The 4-4-2 formation became popular in England in the 1970s, an outgrowth of the 4-3-3 formation first used by the victorious Brazilians at the 1962 World Cup in Chile, and then by the English national team, World Cup winners in 1966. compare *4-3-3, 4-2-4, pyramid, 3-4-3, W-M.*

4-3-3: A formation which employs four defenders, three midfielders, and three forwards. The 4-3-3 formation was introduced in 1962 by Brazil, World Cup winners that year in Chile, and used successfully again four years later at the 1966 World Cup by team manager Alf Francis's victorious English national team. compare *4-4-2, 4-2-4, pyramid, 3-4-3, W-M.*

4-2-4: A formation which employs four defenders, two midfielders, and four forwards. Though a somewhat similar system had been shown by the talented Hungarian team of the early 1950s, the 4-2-4 was introduced in 1958 at the World Cup in Sweden by the victorious Brazilian national team. compare *4-4-2, 4-3-3, pyramid, 3-4-3, W-M.*

freeback: see *sweeper.*

free kick: An unhindered placekick which is awarded to the opposing team at the point of the offense when a foul or infraction is committed by a player. When a free kick is taken, no opposing player may be closer than 10 yards from the ball (10 feet in indoor soccer) until it is played, unless the opposing player or players are standing on their own goal line between the goal posts. Depending upon the severity of the foul or infraction, a free kick may be either a direct free kick (from which a goal may be scored directly against the offending team) or an indirect free kick (from which a goal cannot be scored until the ball has first touched another player). In indoor soccer, a free kick must be taken within five seconds of the referee's signal. An infraction results in a two-minute time penalty for the kicker, and play is restarted with the original free kick. Free kicks were first introduced by the English Football Association in 1873. see *direct free kick, indirect free kick.*

friendly: A friendly match outside of regular league or international championship play. (will play a series of friendlies before their World Cup elimination matches)

front block tackle: see *block tackle.*

front man: see *target man.*

fullback: 1. A primarily defensive player on the back line who normally plays closest to the goal defended by his team. Fullbacks are primarily responsible for preventing opposing forwards from shooting at the goal, and for gaining possession of the ball, either to clear it away from the area in front of the goal, or to pass it to a teammate upfield. Depending on the style of play used, fullbacks may occasionally move forward to support or take part in an attack. also *back, defender.* see *overlap, pyramid.* 2. The position played by a fullback. see *pyramid.*

full time: The end of regulation time for a match, not including injury or extra time. A British expression.

funnel back: To, as a part of a deliberate strategy, fall back defensively in such a way as to "funnel" attacking opponents into a sealed-off central area.

get tight: see *mark up.*

ghost: To deliberately play in such a way as to go unnoticed by the opposing team (either momentarily, or for an extended period of time) in the hopes of being undefended at some critical point in a game or series of games.

give and go: To execute a give-and-go.

give-and-go: A play in which the player with the ball makes a short pass to a teammate, then breaks past a defender or defenders into an open space for a quick return pass. The give-and-go is one of the most effective and frequently used tactics in soccer. also *double pass, one-two, wall pass.*

give away a corner: To cause a corner kick to be awarded to the opposing team either deliberately or accidentally by being the last to touch the ball

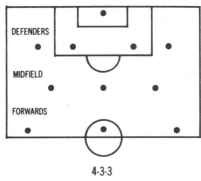

4-3-3

before it crosses out of play over one's own end line. When outnumbered or in danger in the penalty area (as when the goalkeeper is down or out of position), a defender will frequently kick or deflect the ball over the end line and "give away a corner" in order to give the defense time to regroup.

give some stick: To play rough, especially to physically punish a particular opponent. A British expression, applied both to rugby and soccer. compare *take some stick.*

●●To razz or give someone a hard time. (gave him some stick about showing up late)

goal: 1. The structure centered on each end line into which the ball must be played in order to score. A goal consists of a rectangular wood or metal (or other FIFA-approved material) frame, with two upright goal posts 24 feet apart, joined 8 feet above the ground by a horizontal crossbar. The goal posts and crossbar may be no more than 5 inches thick, and must be the same. A mesh net is attached to the goal posts and crossbar and the ground behind (back far enough to allow the goalkeeper room to maneuver) to completely enclose the top, back and sides of the structure. The first modern rules regulating goals were adopted at Cambridge in England in 1848, calling for two vertical posts with a string or tape stretched between them. In 1863, the English Football Association called for two posts 8 yards apart, adopting Cambridge's connecting tape in 1866. The crossbar, first used at Cheltenham public school, was made obligatory in 1882, with nets being added in 1891.

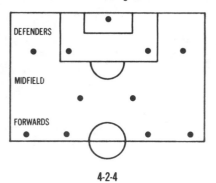

DEFENDERS

MIDFIELD

FORWARDS

4-2-4

also *net.* 2. The structure in the middle of the perimeter wall at each end of the playing area in indoor soccer, into which the ball must be played in order to score. A goal consists of a rectangular wood or metal (or other FIFA-approved material) frame, with two upright goal posts 12 feet apart, joined 6 feet, 6 inches above the ground by a horizontal crossbar. The goal posts and crossbar may be no more than 5 inches thick, and must be the same. A mesh net is attached to the goal posts and crossbar and the ground behind (to a suggested depth of 5 feet) to completely enclose the top, back and sides of the structure. also *net, nets.* 3. A point scored as a result of the ball being played (off of any part of the goalkeeper, or any part of a field player except for the arms and hands) completely over the goal line between the goal posts and under the crossbar. A goal is credited in the scoring records to the player who propels the ball into the opponent's goal. The legendary Pele is the greatest goal scorer in the history of soccer, netting an incredible 1,251 goals in first division or international competition in his 21-year career (1956-1977), not counting 33 goals scored in exhibition and All-Star games. Pele scored 1,090 goals for the Brazilian club, Santos, 101 goals for the national team of Brazil (14 in World Cup competition), and 60 goals for the New York Cosmos of the North American Soccer League. Giorgio Chinaglia, the NASL all-time goal scoring champion, set the single season record in 1978, scoring 34 goals in thirty games. In indoor soccer, the MISL all-time goal scoring champion, Steve Zungul of the New York Arrows, set the single season record in 1981-82, scoring 103 goals in forty games. also *marker, tally.*

goal area: A rectangular area marked in front of and centered on each goal, 20 yards wide and 6 yards deep (16 feet wide and 5 feet deep in indoor soccer), and from which goal kicks are taken. see *crease.*

goal area line: 1. A 20-foot line centered on each goal, marked 6 yards out from and parallel to the goal line, and serving as the front boundary of the goal area. 2. A 16-foot line centered on each goal in indoor soccer, marked 5 feet out from and parallel to the goal line, and serving as the front boundary of the goal area or crease. see *corner flag, corner kick spot.*

goal difference: A statistic which reflects the difference between the number of goals a team scores and the number of goals a team gives up during a particular period (as in a tournament or season).

goalie: Slang for a goalkeeper.

goal judge: Either of two officials positioned behind the goals in indoor soccer who decide whether or not the ball has passed wholly over the goal line for a goal, and who signify the scoring of a goal by switching on the red goal light (or by holding up a flag). The referee may overrule a goal judge's decision to allow or disallow a goal.

goalkeeper: 1. The defensive player normally positioned in front of the goal who is responsible for blocking shots and keeping the ball from going into the goal. The goalkeeper is the one player allowed to use his hands to catch or to deflect or punch the ball away, provided he is within the penalty area. He may not take more than four steps while holding, bouncing, or tossing the ball up in the air to himself, but may roll or dribble the ball, though it may then be contested for by opposing players. (In indoor soccer, the goalkeeper must release and distribute the ball within five seconds.) A goalkeeper must wear colors which distinguish him from the other players and the referee. The special rules which govern goalkeepers were introduced in 1870 by the English Football Association. also *goalie, keeper.* 2. The position played by a goalkeeper. also *goalie, keeper.*

goal kick: An indirect free kick awarded to the defensive team when an attacker is the last to touch a ball that crosses entirely over the goal line (or the perimeter wall between the corner flags in indoor soccer) outside the goal and out of play, taken from within the half of the goal area on the side of the field on which the ball left the playing area. A goal kick must clear the penalty area and may not be played again by the kicker until it has been touched by another player, nor may it be kicked into the goalkeeper's hands until it has first left the area. Opposing players must remain outside the penalty area until the kick is taken. The goal kick was introduced in 1869 by the English Football Association. compare *corner kick.*

goal light: A red light located behind the goals in indoor soccer, activated by the goal judge when a goal has been scored.

goal line: The boundary line marked at each end of the playing area, extending the width of the field between the touchlines, and in the center of which is located the goal (in indoor soccer, the goal line is marked only between the goal posts, with the perimeter wall between the corner flags marking the end boundary). When a ball crosses entirely over the vertical plane of the goal line between the goal posts and under the crossbar, a goal is scored. When a ball crosses entirely over the vertical plane of the goal line outside the goal (or the perimeter wall between the corner flags in indoor soccer), the result is a corner kick (if the ball was last touched by a defender) or a goal kick (if the ball was last touched by an attacker). also *by-line, end line.*

goal post, goalpost: Either of two square, rectangular, round, half-round or elliptical poles or posts, 24 feet apart (12 feet in indoor soccer) and connected by the crossbar 8 feet above the ground (6 feet, 6 inches in indoor soccer), and which serve as the side boundaries of the goal. also *post, upright.* see *goal.*

goals against: The total number of goals allowed by a goalkeeper or team within a specified time (such as a game, tournament, or season). In 1973, goalkeeper Bob Rigby (then of the Philadelphia Atoms) set the NASL record for the fewest goals against in a season, allowing only eight goals in 1,157 minutes played.

goals against average: The statistic reflecting the average number of goals allowed by a goalkeeper in one ninety-minute game, computed by multiplying the total number of goals against by ninety, then dividing by the total number of minutes played, usually carried two decimal places (a goalkeeper who has played a total of 2,880 minutes and given up forty-five goals has a goals against average of 1.41). Goalkeeper Bob Rigby holds the NASL record for the best goals against average for a season, 0.62 (Philadelphia Atoms, 1973).

good in the air: Adept at heading the ball.

graft: British slang for hard work and persistence on the playing field, especially in attempts to tackle and win the ball from opponents.

grafter: British slang for a player known for hard work and persistence on the playing field, especially in attempts to tackle and win the ball from opponents.

ground: 1. A stadium or playing field and environs. A British term. (aspires to play at Wembley, one of soccer's most hallowed grounds) also *grounds*. 2. A British term for a playing field. also *grounds, pitch*.

grounds: see *ground*.

hack: To kick an opponent, a foul which results in the awarding of a direct free kick to the offended team at the spot of the offense, or if within the penalty area of the defending team, a penalty kick. In indoor soccer, the offending player may also be assessed a two-minute time penalty. If, in the opinion of the referee, the foul is serious or violent, the offending player may be cautioned (an automatic two-minute time penalty in indoor soccer) or sent off (an automatic five-minute time penalty in indoor soccer, to be served by the ejected player's substitute). The prohibition of hacking in the first rules adopted by the English Football Association in 1863 was one of the provisions which separated soccer from rugby. also *chop*.

hacker: A derogatory name for a rough player, usually a defender, who often kicks or physically fouls opponents.

half: 1. Short for halfback. 2. The position played by a halfback. (a great playmaker at left half) 3. Either of the two halves of the field, from the midfield line to the goal line. (couldn't get the ball out of their own half) 4. Either of the two forty-five-minute periods of play in a game (plus any extra time added by the referee). 5. The end of the first forty-five-minute period of play in a game (plus any extra time added by the referee).

halfback: 1. A midfielder. see *pyramid*. 2. The position played by a halfback. see *pyramid*.

1. **half volley:** A powerful kick in which the ball is contacted just as it bounces up from the ground. also *dropkick*. compare *volley*.

2. **half volley:** To kick the ball just as it bounces up from the ground. (half volleyed the low cross for a goal) also *drop-kick*. compare *volley*.

halfway line: A line marked across the center of the playing area (touchline to touchline, or side perimeter wall to side perimeter wall in indoor soccer) parallel to the goal lines. The center spot, from which kickoffs are taken, and the surrounding center circle are marked in the middle of the halfway line. also *center line, midfield line*.

handball: The act or an instance of illegally handling the ball, a foul which results in the awarding of a direct free kick to the opposing team at the spot of the offense, and if the foul is committed by a defensive player (other than the goalkeeper) in his penalty area, a penalty kick. In indoor soccer, the offending player may also be assessed a two-minute time penalty. No handball is called if a goalkeeper handles the ball within his penalty area, if the player's hand is in a natural position and contact is unintentional, or if the player moves his hands in the path of the ball to protect his face or groin (or a woman to protect her breasts). also *hands*.

handle: To carry, strike, or propel the ball with any part of the hand or arm, a foul (except in the case of a goalkeeper within the penalty area). England's Football Association abolished the rugby-inspired fair catch and thus, handling, in 1870, permitting only goalkeepers to play the ball with the hands thereafter. see *handball*.

hands: see *handball*.

hat trick: Three goals by the same player in a single game. Though the expression is commonly used in connection with hockey, baseball, and horse racing, "hat trick" was originally from the game of cricket. In England in the late 1800s, a cap or hat was given to a "bowler" who took three "wickets" with successive deliveries. Soccer's greatest goal scorer, the legendary

Pele, scored ninety-three hat tricks in his remarkable twenty-one-year career (1956-1977).

head: To shoot, pass, or clear an air ball out of danger by propelling it with the head. Although there is evidence to show that the head was used in ancient Chinese and Mesoamerican "football" games, it is believed that a Lieutenant Sim of southern England's Royal Engineers team (FA Cup winners in 1875) was the first to use heading as an intentional tactic. also *flick, nod.*

header: A shot, pass or clearance which is propelled with the head. In a properly timed and executed header, contact is made with the forehead, and the ball may be accurately driven, using the neck muscles for power, or delicately lobbed toward the intended target.

head trap: A trap in which the head is used to null and control an air ball. compare *chest trap, foot trap, sole trap, sweep trap, thigh trap.*

heavy pitch: A slow, soft playing surface, as one in which the turf is wet or not closely cut.

heel kick: A backward pass made by stepping over the ball and kicking it with the heel.

Hermann Trophy: The annual award given to the outstanding college soccer player in America, as selected by college coaches, sports editors, and soccer writers. The equivalent to college football's Heisman Trophy, the Hermann Trophy was created in 1967 by soccer patron Robert Hermann of St. Louis, Missouri, owner of the former NASL St. Louis Stars. The Hermann Trophy was first awarded in 1967 to Don Markus of Long Island University in New York.

hitch kick: A bicycle kick.

hold: To illegally grab or grasp an opponent or the uniform of an opponent. Holding is a foul which results in the awarding of a direct free kick to the opposing team at the spot of the offense, or if the foul is committed by a defender in his penalty area, a penalty kick.

home: Into the goal for a score. (drove the equalizer home in extra time)

human pinball: A facetious name for indoor soccer because of the speed of the game and the way the ball is made to carom off the boards.

indirect free kick: A free kick which is awarded to the opposing team at the point of the offense when an infraction (such as a dangerous play, a fair charge when the ball is not within playing distance, obstruction, etc.) is committed by a player, or after a player is cautioned (as for illegally leaving or entering the field, dissent, or ungentlemanly conduct), and from which a goal cannot be scored until after the ball has been touched by another player. When an indirect free kick is taken, no opposing player may be closer than 10 yards from the ball (10 feet in indoor soccer) until it is played, unless the opposing player or players are standing on their own goal line between the goal posts. When an indirect free kick is taken by a player from within his own penalty area, no opposing player may be inside the area or closer than 10 yards (10 feet in indoor soccer) until the ball is played. The ball must be stationary when an indirect free kick is taken, and is in play when it has travelled the dis-

HEADER

tance (or half the distance in indoor soccer) of its circumference (and is beyond the penalty area, if the kick is taken by a player from within his own area). The kicker may not play the ball a second time until it has been touched or played by another player. compare *direct free kick*.

indoor soccer: A version of soccer played indoors on artificial turf between teams of six players (a goalkeeper and five field players) on a hockey-rinklike playing area approximately 200 feet long by 85 feet wide, and enclosed by an unbreakable glass-topped wall (to protect spectators) with 12-foot wide by 6-1/2-foot high goals centered on each end. The playing field is marked with goal and penalty areas, penalty spots, a center line and circle, four corner kick spots, and touchlines 3 feet from and parallel to the sideboards. Two red lines are marked 30 feet on either side of and parallel to the center line, dividing the playing area into three parts. Indoor soccer is played by international soccer rules with the following exceptions: a game is divided into four fifteen-minute quarters, and the clock is stopped when the referee blows his whistle to stop play or the ball goes out of play; unlimited substitution is allowed during a game, provided no more than six players a side are on the field at one time; kick-ins from the touchlines replace throw-ins when the ball goes out of bounds (over the sideboards);

corner kicks are taken from the corner kick spots; indirect free kicks are awarded to the opposing team when a ball is played in the air across the three lines (the center line and both red lines); on kickoffs, kick-ins, corner kicks, and all free kicks, opposing players must remain 10 feet from the ball until it is played; and two and five-minute time penalties are assessed for fouls, during which the guilty player must wait in a penalty box while his team plays short-handed (as in hockey). Though an indoor game with abbreviated teams was played in the United States as early as 1905 in New York's Madison Square Garden, professional indoor soccer (as played by the MISL) was the result of a popular series of exhibition games between NASL teams and the Soviet Union's Moscow Dynamo and Zenit-Leningrad in 1974. see *kick-in, Major Indoor Soccer League, North American Soccer League, three line pass.*

injury time: Extra time added by the referee at the end of a half to make up for playing time lost because of an injury to one or more players.

inside forward: Either of two attacking players (inside left or inside right) who normally play on the forward line between the wings and the center forward in the classic pyramid formation. see *pyramid.*

inside left, inside right: The inside forward on the left or right side of the field in

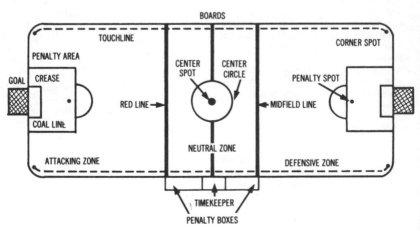

BOARDS

TOUCHLINE

PENALTY AREA

CORNER SPOT

GOAL | CREASE

CENTER SPOT

CENTER CIRCLE

PENALTY SPOT

RED LINE →

MIDFIELD LINE

GOAL LINE

ATTACKING ZONE

NEUTRAL ZONE

DEFENSIVE ZONE

TIMEKEEPER

PENALTY BOXES

the classic pyramid formation. see *pyramid.*

instep kick: A powerful kick in which the ball is struck with the shoelace area of the boot.

inswinger: A corner kick (or kick from the wing area near the end line) which bends or curves in toward the goal. compare *outswinger.*

interfere: To illegally obstruct or physically impede the play of an opponent, a foul which results in the awarding of an indirect free kick to the opposing team from the spot of the offense.

international: 1. A match between national teams. The first international soccer match was between Scottish and English select teams in 1972, a 0-0 draw in front of 4,000 spectators at the West of Scotland Cricket Club in Partick. 2. A player who is a member of a national team and takes part in international matches.

in to touch: Completely over the touchline and out of bounds. (couldn't get to the ball before it rolled in to touch) see *touch.*

jab kick: see *flick kick.*

jockeying: Strategically giving ground while marking the player with the ball in such a way as to lead him to a less dangerous or more securely defended area of the field. also *shepherding.*

juggle: To keep the ball in the air and under control by bouncing it with the feet, knees, or head.

keeper: Short for goalkeeper.

kick-in: The method of restarting play in indoor soccer when the ball goes out of bounds (passing completely over the perimeter wall) along either touchline. A kick-in is an indirect free kick awarded to the opposite team of the player who last touched the ball, and taken from the point where the ball crossed the touchline. A kick-in is the indoor equivalent to a throw-in. Ironically, in the 1860s and 1870s, some teams in the Sheffield area of northern England used a kick-in instead of a throw-in.

kickoff: The method of starting play at the beginning of a half (or a quarter in indoor soccer) and after a goal. A kickoff is a placekick taken from the center spot with the players positioned in their own half of the field. No opposing player may be closer than 10 yards

from the ball (10 feet in indoor soccer) until it has been kicked off. The ball must be kicked into the opposing half and is in play when it has traveled the distance (half the distance in indoor soccer) of its own circumference. The kicker may not play the ball a second time until it has been touched by another player. A goal cannot be scored directly from a kickoff. The rules which govern a kickoff were established in 1863 in England by the Football Association.

••Of or pertaining to the beginning of something, especially an introductory occurrence. (began the cruise with a kickoff party)

kick off: To execute a kickoff.

••To begin something. (will kick off the annual clearance sale with a full-page ad in the newspapers)

kickoff circle: The center circle.

kill a penalty: To use up the time one's team must play shorthanded while a teammate is in the penalty box without allowing a goal. A team attempting to kill a penalty emphasizes defense and deliberate, time-consuming ball control.

kill the ball: To null or trap and control a moving ball, especially an air ball.

knot: To tie the score of a game with a goal. (knotted the game with a header) also *equalize.*

late tackle: A sliding tackle made after the ball is clearly out of the defender's reach, and usually resulting in physical contact. A foul which results in a direct free kick by the opposing team at the spot of the offense, and if committed by a defender in his own penalty area, a penalty kick. In indoor soccer, the offending player may also be assessed a two-minute time penalty. If, in the opinion of the referee, the foul is serious or violent, the offending player may be cautioned (an automatic two-minute time penalty in indoor soccer) or sent off (an automatic five-minute time penalty in indoor soccer, to be served by the ejected player's substitute).

Laws: The international rules of soccer, controlled and interpreted by FIFA, the world-governing body of soccer. The Laws of soccer stem from the playing rules adopted in 1863 by England's Football Association, which in turn were heavily influenced by a code formulated in 1848 at Cambridge University.

libero: see *sweeper.*

linesman: Either of two officials just outside the touchlines who assist the referee by indicating offside violations and when and where the ball goes out of bounds and the team that last touched it by raising and pointing a small flag, and who call attention to fouls that might not have been seen by the referee. One linesman patrols each touchline in one half of the field, moving between the center line and the goal line as play dictates. A linesman's decision may be overruled by the referee. Linesmen replaced umpires and were given their present responsibilities in 1891, when the referee was moved to the field and given full control of the game by the Football Association in England.

linkman: 1. A midfielder, so-called because midfielders serve as a "link" between defensive and offensive players. 2. The position played by a linkman.

1. lob: 1. To kick a ball (stationary or moving on the ground or in the air) in a gentle high arc. compare *chip.* 2. To kick a ball in a gentle high arc over one or more players. (lobbed the diving keeper to score)

2. lob: The act or an instance of lobbing a ball. compare *chip.*

loft: see *chip.*

Major Indoor Soccer League: The youngest of the professional soccer leagues in the United States, and the only one to conduct its entire schedule indoors. Established in 1978, the Major Indoor Soccer League (MISL) began operating

with six teams for the 1978-79 season, with the New York Arrows defeating the Philadelphia Fever to become the first MISL champion. For the 1982-83 season, the MISL announced a forty-eight-game schedule (twenty-four home, twenty-four away), and an alignment comprised of fourteen teams split into two divisions: The Eastern Division, with the Baltimore Blast, the Buffalo Stallions, the Chicago Sting, the Cleveland Force, the Memphis Americans, the New York Arrows, and the Pittsburgh Spirit; and the Western Division, with the Golden Bay Earthquakes, the Kansas City Comets, the Los Angeles Lazers, the Phoenix Inferno, the San Diego Sockers, the St. Louis Steamers, and the Wichita Wings. The MISL league championship is decided in a best-of-five championship series between divisional playoff winners.

major penalty: A five-minute time penalty assessed against a player (or a coach, manager, or trainer on the bench) who receives a second caution during a game or is sent off (as for a serious or violent foul or abusive language). In such a case, the guilty player (or coach, manager, or trainer) must return immediately to the dressing room, and the five-minute time penalty is served by a designated substitute. The offending team must play shorthanded for the duration of a major penalty. compare *double minor, minor penalty.*

make space: see *create space.*

man advantage: A numerical advantage on the field in indoor soccer (as during a power play) when the opposing team has one or more players in the penalty box. compare *shorthanded.*

man-advantage goal: A power play goal. compare *shorthanded goal.*

man down: see *man short.*

man in the middle: Slang for the referee. also *ref.*

man short: Lacking one player on the field, usually because of an ejection. also *man down.*

mark: To guard an opponent. (closely marked for the entire game)

marker: 1. One who guards or is in the process of guarding an opponent. 2. A goal. (got his second marker with a diving header) also *tally.*

mark up: To guard an opponent, especially to move closer and guard an oppo-

CENTER BACK
OR CENTER HALF   GOALKEEPER

RIGHT BACK   LEFT BACK

MIDFIELDERS

CENTER FORWARD

RIGHT WING   LEFT WING

STRIKERS

3-4-3 OR W-M

nent. (allowed the winning goal because they failed to mark up on a corner kick) also *get tight*.

M formation: An attacking configuration (not to be confused with the defensive M of the more common W-M) in which two inside forwards play closest to the opposing goal, with three more forwards (attacking midfielders) playing further back, one in the center and one on each flank. Imaginary lines connecting them would appear like the letter M from above. compare *W formation, W-M*.

midfield: 1. The area in the middle of the field (roughly the central third) between the two goal lines. 2. The position played by a midfielder. also *half, halfback, linkman*. 3. The midfielders. (a strong, hard-working midfield)

midfielder: One of several players (the number varies with different formations) who function in the central part of the field, and whose responsibilities include moving the ball from the defensive area up to the forwards (and sometimes, depending on the style of play, supporting and participating in attacks), attempting to win the ball from opponents in the midfield, and falling back to help defend when the fullbacks are outnumbered in and around the penalty area. Usually, among a team's midfielders, different players emphasize the defending, playmaking, and attacking aspects of play. also *half, halfback, linkman*.

midfield line: The halfway line. also *center line*.

minor penalty: A two-minute time penalty in indoor soccer, assessed against a player (or bench personnel) guilty of an intentional penal or technical offense, or unsportsmanlike conduct. compare *double minor, major penalty*.

MISL: The Major Indoor Soccer League.

narrow the angle: see *cut down the angle*.

NASL: The North American Soccer League.

National Amateur Challenge Cup: The annual national competition for the "Amateur Cup," open to all amateur teams under the jurisdiction of the United States Soccer Federation. A knockout competition instituted in 1923, the National Amateur Challenge Cup was first won in 1924 by Fleisher Yarn F.C. of Philadelphia, Pennsylvania.

National Challenge Cup: The annual national competition for the "Open Cup," open to all amateur and professional teams under the jurisdiction of the United States Soccer Federation. The oldest soccer competition in the United States, the National Challenge Cup was first won in 1914 by the Brooklyn Field Club of Brooklyn, New York. also *National Open*.

National Open: The National Challenge Cup.

near post: The goal post nearest to where the ball is being played. compare *far post*.

1. net: 1. The hemp, jute, or nylon mesh netting attached to the goal posts and crossbar, and which covers the top, sides and back of a goal. see *goal*. 2. The goal. also *nets*.

2. net: To score a goal. (netted the equalizer in injury time)

nets: The goal. also *net*.

neutral zone: The central area of the playing field in indoor soccer, between the two red lines. compare *attacking zone, defensive zone*.

nod: see *flick*.

North American Soccer League: The premier professional soccer league in the United States and Canada. The North American Soccer League (NASL) was founded in 1968 when two one-year old professional soccer leagues merged, the United Soccer Association and the National Professional Soccer League. Seventeen teams participated in the NASL's initial season in 1968, with the Atlanta Chiefs emerging as the first league champions. For the 1983 season, in addition to the eleven regular league teams (the Golden Bay Earthquakes, the San Diego Sockers, the Seattle Sounders, the Vancouver Whitecaps, the Chicago Sting, the Montreal Manic, the New York Cosmos, the Toronto Blizzard, the Fort Lauderdale Strikers, the Tampa Bay Rowdies, and the Tulsa Roughnecks), the NASL and USSF announced the creation of an innovative new franchise, Team America, comprised exclusively of American players drawn from the NASL, MISL, and ASL. Based in Washington, D.C., Team America is functionally the nucleus of the United States national team and plays international matches as well as a full 30-game schedule against other NASL teams in competition for a playoff berth and the opportunity to play for the league championship in the Soccer Bowl.

nutmeg: To kick the ball through a defender's legs, then run past him to recover it and continue. Defenders consider being "nutmegged" a particularly humiliating way of being beaten by an opponent.

obstruct: To illegally hamper or impede the movement of an opponent (such as by stepping in front of an opponent or between an opponent and the ball when it is not within playing distance, or stepping in front of the goalkeeper to prevent him from putting the ball in play). see *obstruction.* compare *screen.*

obstruction: The act or an instance of illegally obstructing an opponent, a foul which results in the awarding of an indirect free kick to the opposing team at the spot of the offense.

official time: The actual time of a game, kept by the referee alone in all games played under international rules. In high school and college games, and in indoor soccer, a timekeeper keeps the official time.

off one's line: Away from the goal line and toward the shooter in order to narrow the angle, as of a goalkeeper. (came off his line quickly and made the save) see *cut down the angle, narrow the angle.*

1. offside: Being ahead of the ball in the opposing half of the field when there are less than two opponents (including the goalkeeper) nearer the goal at the moment the ball is played by a team-

mate, an infraction which results in the awarding of an indirect free kick to the opposing team at the spot of the infringement. An offside player is not penalized if, in the opinion of the referee, he is not interfering with the play or with an opponent, or not seeking to gain an advantage. Like most of the early rugby-soccer rules, the concept of offside, first called "sneaking," originated at one of England's public schools (Eton) in the mid-1800s, as did the name "offside" (Cheltenham). Initially, any player ahead of the ball when it was kicked anywhere on the field was offside. In the code adopted by the English Football Association in 1866, a player was offside if less than three defenders were nearer the goal when the ball was kicked. By the 1920s, the offense-stifling offside trap began to dominate the game. As a result, in 1925, the offside rule was changed to require only two defenders nearer the goal. In the following season, the number of goals increased by over 40 percent in the English Football League, but new tactics and formations (such as the W-M) were developed to both exploit and defend against the new freedom of attacking players. see *offside trap, W-M.*

2. offside: 1. The act or an instance of being offside. 2. The infraction which results when a player is offside.

offside trap: A defensive tactic in which one or more defenders move toward the halfway line to pull even with or pass one or more attacking players in an attempt to put them offside before a teammate plays the ball. The offside trap is an effective method of nullifying an attack, but risky because of the possibility of misjudging or mistiming, or of the referee and linesman not detecting the momentary offside. It was the development of the offside trap and its offense-stifling effect on the game which caused the offside rule to be changed in 1925, reducing the number of defensive players required to be between an attacking player and the goal from three to two.

offside violation: A three-line pass in indoor soccer. also *red line violation, three-line violation.*

off the ball: Away from the ball. (made the

OFFSIDE TRAP

goal possible with his off the ball running) compare *on the ball.*

1. **one touch**: Played first time. see *first time.*

2. **one touch**: Of or pertaining to a ball played first time. see *first time.*

one-two: A wall pass or give-and-go. also *double pass.*

on the ball: In possession or control of the ball, dribbling. compare *off the ball.*

on the turn: Turning to face or shoot at the goal, especially while being closely marked in the penalty area. (a strong center forward who is good on the turn)

open net: A goal left unguarded, as when a goalkeeper falls down, or is beaten or out of position, or when the goalkeeper has been pulled in indoor soccer.

opposing half: The half of the field that contains the goal defended by the opposing team. compare *own half.*

outlet pass: A quick pass from the goalkeeper or a defender to a teammate closer to the opposing team's goal, especially in indoor soccer to start an attack.

outside forward: 1. Either of two attacking players (outside left or outside right) who normally play near the touchlines in the classic pyramid formation. see *pyramid.* 2. The position played by an outside forward. see *pyramid.*

outside half: 1. Either of two midfielders who normally play on the flanks of a central halfback. see *pyramid.* 2. The position played by an outside half. see *pyramid.*

outside left, outside right: 1. The outside forward on the left or right side of the field. see *pyramid.* 2. The position played by an outside left or outside right. see *pyramid.*

outswinger: A corner kick (or kick from the wing area near the end line) that bends or curves out from the goal. compare *inswinger.*

overhead volley: A bicycle kick.

1. **overlap**: To move forward from a defensive position (with or without the ball) in order to take part in an attack.

2. **overlap**: The act or an instance of a defender overlapping.

over the top: A situation in which a player tackles over the ball in such a way as to kick or make physical contact with

an opponent's legs. A foul that results in a direct free kick for the opposing team at the spot of the offense, and if committed by a defender in his own penalty area, a penalty kick. In indoor soccer, the offending player may also be assessed a two-minute time penalty. If, in the opinion of the referee, the foul is serious or violent, the offending player may be cautioned (an automatic two-minute time penalty in indoor soccer) or sent off (a five-minute time penalty in indoor soccer, to be served by the ejected player's substitute).

overtime: One or more extra periods of play to decide a game tied at the end of regulation play. In the NASL, two seven and one-half minute sudden death periods are played, after which a shootout takes place if there is no winner. In the MISL, one fifteen-minute sudden death period is played, after which a shootout takes place if there is no winner. In college play, two ten-minute overtime periods may be played.

own goal: A goal that results when a member of the defending team accidentally knocks the ball into his own goal.

own half: In the half of the playing field that contains the goal defended by, one's team. compare *opposing half.*

pace: 1. The speed of a moving ball. 2. The speed with which a game is played (whether by one or more players, or by one or both teams).

1. **pass**: To kick, head, or deflect (first time) the ball toward a teammate, or toward a space into which a teammate is moving.

2. **pass**: The act or an instance of passing the ball.

penal offense: Any of nine offenses (ten in indoor soccer) which, if committed intentionally, result in a direct free kick or (if committed by a defender within his penalty area) a penalty kick for the opposing team. In indoor soccer, the offending player may also be assessed a two-minute time penalty. Penal offenses include kicking or attempting to kick an opponent, tripping or attempting to trip or throw an opponent down, jumping at an opponent, charging an opponent in a violent or dangerous manner, charging an opponent from behind (unless the opponent is obstructing), striking or attempting to strike an an opponent, or handling the ball (not applicable to the goalkeeper within his own penalty area). In indoor soccer, boarding (charging an opponent into the perimeter wall) is also a penal offense. A player is automatically cautioned for a second penal offense during a game in indoor soccer, and sent off for a third. compare *technical offense*.

penalty: 1. Short for penalty kick. also *spot kick*. 2. see *time penalty*.

penalty arc: The arc marked outside each penalty area with a 10-yard radius (10-foot radius in indoor soccer) from the penalty spot. At the time of a penalty kick, no player other than the kicker is allowed inside the penalty arc until the ball is kicked. The penalty arc was added in 1937 to help enforce the 10-yard rule on penalty kicks. also *restraining arc*.

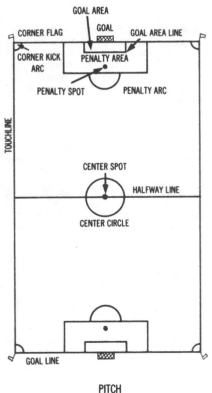

PITCH

penalty area: The rectangular area (44 yards wide by 18 yards deep, or in indoor soccer, 30 feet wide by 24 feet deep) marked in front of each goal, inside which the goalkeeper may handle the ball. A serious foul (any "penal offense") against an attacking player within the penalty area results in a penalty kick. The modern configuration for the penalty area was adopted in 1902 by the English Football Association. also *area, box*.

penalty box: Either of two enclosed areas (one for each team) within which a penalized player must remain for the duration of a time penalty in indoor soccer. Penalty boxes are located adjacent to the middle of the playing area across from the team benches, usually on either side of the area used by the timekeeper and assistant referee. also *box, sin bin*.

penalty box attendant: An official seated between the two penalty boxes in indoor soccer (sometimes one attendant is seated in each penalty box), who is responsible for the proper administration of time penalties in cooperation with the timekeeper.

penalty kick: A direct free kick taken from the penalty spot, awarded to the attacking team when a major foul (any "penal offense") is committed by a defender within the penalty area. When a penalty kick is taken, all players other than the kicker must remain outside the penalty area and at least 10 yards from the penalty mark (10 feet in indoor soccer), and the goalkeeper must stand (without moving his feet) on his own goal line, between the goal posts, until the ball is kicked. The ball must be kicked forward and may not be played a second time until it has been touched by another player. The penalty kick rule was adopted by the English Football Association in 1891, although the goalkeeper was not specifically prohibited from moving off his line until 1927. also *spot kick*.

penalty kick mark: The penalty spot.

penalty killer: Any player sent onto the field while one or more teammates are in the penalty box and the opposing team is on a power play. see *kill a penalty, power play*.

penalty mark: The penalty spot.

penalty spot: A spot in the penalty area marked 12 yards (8 yards in indoor soccer) out from the mid-point of the goal line, from which penalty kicks are taken. also *penalty kick mark, penalty mark, spot, 12-yard mark, 12-yard spot.* see *penalty kick.*

perimeter wall: see *boards.*

pitch: The traditional British name for the playing area, which must be rectangular and measure between 100 and 130 yards long by 50 to 100 yards (length must exceed width). also *ground, grounds.*

placekick: A kick taken when the ball has been placed on the ground, as for a kickoff, goal kick, corner kick, free kick, or penalty kick (and, in indoor soccer, a kick-in).

play on: A verbal signal to continue play, called out by the referee at a point when play could be stopped, such as after an infraction when the advantage is being applied.

play the ball: To cause the ball to move, stop or change directions with any part of the body. (played the ball back to the goalkeeper)

point: 1. The area on either side of the playing field close to the boards and just inside the red line of the attacking zone in indoor soccer. From the similar hockey usage. 2. The position of a player stationed at the point, especially on a power play.

policeman: 1. The central defender, a center back. see *center back.* 2. The position played by a center back.

post: 1. Short for goal post. 2. In indoor soccer, a position in or near the penalty area in front of the goal in the attacking zone, often occupied by a forward who acts as a targetman, receiving and relaying passes, and always a threat to turn and shoot. Similar to basketball's post position in the free throw lane, from where the term originates.

power play: A temporary numerical advantage on the playing field in indoor soccer while one or more members of the opposing team are serving time penalties. Because the opponents are outnumbered, a team on a power play has a greater opportunity to score a goal. also *man advantage.* compare *shorthanded.*

power play goal: A goal scored by a team on a power play. also *man-*

advantage goal. compare *shorthanded goal.*

professional foul: see *tactical foul.*

promotion: The automatic advancement to the next higher league division of the highest finishing teams (usually two or three) of the previous season in the division below. Conversely, the two or three lowest finishing teams in the higher divisions suffer relegation to the division below for the next season. Pioneered by the English Football League in 1899, the system of automatic promotion and relegation is now in use in many countries.

pull the ball back: To pass the ball from near the goal line on one side of the goal defended by the opponents back to a teammate in front of the goal. (was able to pull the ball back before it crossed the goal line)

pull the goalkeeper: To replace the goalkeeper with an extra field player in an attempt to score in the closing minutes of a game when behind by one or two goals. A desperate and risky tactic which is attempted by a team only when in control of the ball (should the opposing team gain control of the ball, an easy open net goal often results).

punch: To save, clear or deflect an air ball with a clenched fist. (punched away the centering pass before the striker could get to it) also *fist.*

punch save: A save made by punching an air ball out of danger.

1. punt: A goalkeeper's technique for kicking the ball a long distance, executed with an instep kick of a ball released from the hands.

2. punt: To execute a punt.

push: 1. To shove the ball forward (as for a short pass) with the inside of the foot. 2. To shove an opponent with the hands or arms. A foul which results in a direct free kick by the opposing team at the spot of the offense, or if committed by a defender in his penalty area, a penalty kick. In indoor soccer, the offending player may also be assessed a two-minute time penalty. If, in the opinion of the referee, the foul is serious or violent, the offending player may be cautioned (an automatic two-minute time penalty in indoor soccer) or sent off (an automatic five-minute time penalty in indoor soccer, to be served by the ejected player's substitute).

push off: To push or shove an opponent while jumping to contend for an air ball, considered a pushing foul. see *push.*

push out: To move away from the goal one is defending toward the midfield line in order to force opposing players to back up or be offside. also *push up.*

push pass: A short pass shoved or "pushed" forward with the inside of the foot.

push up: 1. see *push out.* 2. To move forward from a defensive position in order to take part in an attack.

pyramid: The original and classic tactical formation, in use from the 1880s until the W-M or 3-4-3 was introduced in 1925. Many position names originated from the pyramid formation, which used two defenders (fullbacks), three midfield players (halfbacks or halfs, including a center halfback or center half and two flanking wing halfbacks or wing halfs, sometimes called outside halfs) and five attacking players on the front line (forwards, including a center forward, two inside forwards on either side of him, the inside left and inside right, and two outside forwards, the outside left and outside right, or wings). The formation's name came from the pyramid or trianglelike appearance of the 2-3-5 configuration. compare *4-4-2, 4-3-3, 4-2-4, 3-4-3, W-M.*

quarter: One of four fifteen-minute periods of play in indoor soccer (or eighteen-minute periods in some high school leagues).

quarter circle: 1. The corner area. 2. The corner kick arc.

rate: 1. To estimate and consider the abili-

ty of a player or team. 2. To attribute a certain amount of skill or ability. A British expression. (supposed to be a good player, but the coach didn't rate him after the tryout)

1. red card: 1. A small red card displayed by the referee when a player is being sent off, or ejected from a game. 2. The ejection of a player from a game. (forced to play a man down after the red card) see *ejection.*

2. red card: To show a red card or eject a player from a game. (got red carded with twenty minutes left to play in the game) also *send off.*

red line: One of two red-colored lines marked across the playing area (and vertically to the top of the perimeter walls) in indoor soccer, 30 feet on either side of and parallel to the center line. The red lines divide the playing area into the attacking, defensive, and neutral zones, and are used to determine three-line violations. see *attacking zone, defensive zone, neutral zone, three-line violation.*

red line violation: see *three-line violation.*

1. ref: Short for referee. also *man in the middle.*

2. ref: To serve as the referee. also *referee, run the middle.*

1. referee: The official (or either of two officials in MISL indoor soccer) in charge of a match, assisted by two linesmen (or in indoor soccer, an assistant referee). The referee is responsible for enforcing the Laws of soccer, acting as timekeeper and recording all time lost because of injuries, a lost or not easily recovered ball, deliberate time wasting by either team, or a penalty kick to be added as extra time at the end of the period (in indoor, college, and high school soccer, the referee works in conjunction with an official timekeeper), starting and stopping play or terminating a game because of the elements, spectator interference, or an emergency, calling and penalizing infractions or fouls by awarding direct, indirect, and penalty kicks (and in indoor soccer, time penalties), cautioning and, if necessary, ejecting players guilty of serious, ungentlemanly, or violent misconduct, awarding or disallowing goals, and recording all goals and incidents of misconduct which warrant a caution or ejection. Originally, two

2-3-5 OR PYRAMID

umpires (one furnished by each team) officiated from the touchlines. In 1871, a neutral referee was added to settle disputes between the umpires, whose method of stopping play was the waving of handkerchiefs until 1878, when whistles were used for the first time in a game between Nottingham Forest and Sheffield Norfolk. In 1891, the umpires were changed to linesmen, and the referee was moved to the field and given control of the game, although until 1894, he could only give a decision if appealed to. also **man in the middle, ref.**

2. referee: To serve as the referee. also **ref, run the middle.**

referee's crease: The area within a semicircle with a 10-foot radius marked at the middle of the playing field against the perimeter wall in front of the timekeeper in indoor soccer. No player is permitted inside the referee's crease while the referee reports a time penalty to the official timekeeper. An infraction results in the assessment of a two-minute penalty to the guilty player, and if continued or repeated, a caution.

relegation: The automatic demotion to the next lower league division of the lowest finishing teams (usually two or three) of the previous season in the division above. see **promotion.**

1. restart: To resume play after a stoppage, as with a drop ball or free kick.

2. restart: The act or an instance of resuming play after a stoppage, as with a drop ball or a free kick.

restraining arc: The penalty arc.

reverse kick: A bicycle kick.

ride a tackle: To maintain control of the ball in spite of a tackle.

run: A clever or opportunistic advance (with or without the ball) to a position near the opponent's goal, as a blindside run into the penalty area for a through pass, or a dribble through several defenders.

run on to: To catch up to a lead pass or a ball played into an open space by a teammate. (ran on to a little chip over the wall)

run the line: To serve as a linesman. compare **run the middle.**

run the middle: To serve as the referee. compare **run the line.**

1. save: To prevent a goal by catching, blocking, deflecting, or clearing the ball out of danger before it crosses the goal line.

2. save: The act or an instance of making a save.

scissors kick: 1. A scissors volley. 2. see **bicycle kick.**

scissors volley: 1. A leaping horizontal volley in which a scissorslike leg motion is used to kick the ball. A spectacular and powerful shot when properly executed. also **scissors kick.** 2. see **bicycle kick.**

screen: To interpose the body between the ball and a defender, legal as long as the ball is being played (as opposed to just obstructing the opponent). also **shield.**

sell the dummy: To momentarily deceive an opponent with a fake or feint. (sold the dummy and broke into the penalty area alone)

send off: To eject a player from a game, as for a serious or violent foul, foul language or gestures, or for persistent misconduct after having received a caution. also **red card.** see **ejection.**

Senior Bowl: The Senior Bowl Soccer Classic, an annual East-West all-star game for outstanding players in their senior year of college, sponsored by the Intercollegiate Soccer Association of America (ISAA). Thirty-two participants are chosen after recommendation by their respective coach or athletic director by the ISAA National Selection Committee. The Senior Bowl was initiated in 1972 by Wayne Sunderland, then president of the ISAA.

service: Passes sent into the penalty area for strikers, such as centering passes or crosses.

set piece, set-piece play: A prearranged team strategy with specific assignments for certain players, such as for drop ball, free kick, corner kick and throw-in (or in indoor soccer, kick-in) situations.

1. shadow: To closely mark a particular opponent throughout a game. also **shadow mark.**

2. shadow: A defender assigned to closely mark a particular opponent throughout a game.

shadow mark: To shadow an opponent.

shepherding: see **jockeying.**

shield: To screen the ball with the body, legal as long as the ball is being played (as opposed to just obstructing the opponent).

shinguards: Small protective pads for the shins, worn under a player's socks, usually constructed of a high-density foam rubber or light plastic with a thin layer of foam rubber underneath. Shinguards were introduced in 1874, and are normally the only protective pads worn by soccer players.

shoot: To kick, head, or deflect (first time) the ball toward the goal in an attempt to score.

shootout: The method used in the NASL and MISL to decide the outcome of a game that is tied at the end of overtime. Beginning with the visiting team and alternating after each attempt, five players from each side individually challenge the opposing goalkeeper. Starting from a spot in the center of the field 35 yards from the goal line (or in the MISL, starting from the center of the nearest red line), at a signal from the referee, each player has five seconds to dribble and shoot (in the NASL, only one shot may be taken; in the MISL, any number of shots may be taken within the five seconds). There are no restrictions on the movement of the goalkeeper once the five-second period begins. The match is decided and attempts are ended when one team achieves an insurmountable advantage (such as scoring on the first three attempts while the opponents miss their first three). If the teams remain tied after five attempts each, alternate players continue to shoot until one team scores more times than the other in an equal number of attempts. Only those players who were playing at the end of overtime are eligible to participate in the shootout (except in the MISL, where all players dressed for the game are eligible), and no player may shoot twice until all eligible teammates have made one attempt. In the MISL, any foul committed by the goalkeeper outside of the penalty area results in a penalty kick. The shootout was pioneered by the North American Soccer League in 1977.

shorthanded: Outnumbered on the playing field due to one or more teammates serving penalties in the penalty box. see *kill a penalty*. compare *man advantage, power play*.

shorthanded goal: A goal scored by a team that has one or two less players

on the field than the opponents, due to penalties being served. compare *man-advantage goal, power play goal*.

1. shoulder charge: To use the shoulder to lean or push against the shoulder of an opponent while contending for a ball, legal as long as the ball is within playing distance (3 to 4 feet). see *charging*.

2. shoulder charge: The act or an instance of leaning or pushing with the shoulder against the shoulder of an opponent while contending for a ball, legal (a fair charge) as long as the ball is within playing distance (3 to 4 feet). see *charging*.

show the ball: To tempt a defender to challenge or tackle by displaying the ball in a seemingly vulnerable position. A favorite tactic of great dribblers such as England's now beknighted Sir Stanley Matthews, Garrincha of the Brazilian national team in the 1950s, and Ireland's George Best, to lure a defender into committing to a course of action.

side block tackle: The act or an instance of blocking the ball with the foot from the side at the moment an opponent attempts to kick it.

side-foot: To pass or shoot the ball with the side of the foot.

sideline: Either of the two side boundaries of the playing area, more commonly known as the touchlines. see *touchline*.

sitter: An easy goal, or the opportunity for an easy goal (as close in front of an open goal).

sin bin: Slang for the penalty box in indoor soccer. also *box*.

sky: To miskick a ball in such a way as to direct it much higher than intended, as over the goal.

1. slide tackle: To execute a slide tackle.

2. slide tackle: The act or an instance of sliding into the ball feetfirst (as a base runner slides in baseball) in order to dislodge or kick the ball away from an opponent. A slide tackle can be executed from the front, rear, or side, and is legal even though contact is made that causes the opponent to trip or fall, as long as the ball is played first and the contact with the opponent is the result of a natural follow through (and not violent or intentional). also *sliding tackle*.

sliding tackle: A slide tackle.

slot: 1. To kick the ball into the goal, especially with a shot that travels along a narrow, ideal path or "slot" (as between defenders or just outside the reach of the goalkeeper). (slots the ball just inside the post for a goal) 2. An imaginary area in front of the goal inside the penalty area in indoor soccer. From hockey.

soccer: A game played between two teams of eleven players on a rectangular field measuring 100 to 130 yards long by 50 to 100 yards wide (length must exceed width) and having a 24-foot-wide by 8-foot-high net-draped goal at each end. The object of the game is to propel an inflated ball into the goal defended by the opposing team. A team is comprised of a goalkeeper, usually positioned just in front of the goal, and varying numbers of defenders, midfield players, and forwards, depending upon the formation and system of play used. The ball is most often kicked, but may be propelled with the head or any part of the body except the hands and arms. Only the goalkeeper is permitted to catch or play the ball with the hands, and then only when he is within the penalty area, a rectangular area 44 yards wide and 18 yards deep marked in front of the goal. Players are not permitted to kick, trip, jump at, charge (except for shoulder-to-shoulder contact when contending for a ball within playing distance), strike, hold or push an opponent. Such fouls, if intentionally committed, result in a direct free kick (an unhindered placekick from which a goal may be scored directly) for the opposing team at the point of the offense, or if the foul is committed by a defender in his own penalty area, a penalty kick (an unhindered placekick directly at the goal, from a point 12 yards in front of the center of the goal line, during which the goalkeeper must remain on the goal line, without moving his feet, until the ball is kicked). For unintentional fouls and other infractions, an indirect free kick (an unhindered placekick from which a goal may not be scored until the ball touches another player) is awarded to the opposing team from the spot of the offense. At the beginning of a period of play and

SLIDE TACKLE

after each goal, play is started by a kickoff (an unhindered placekick into the opponent's half of the field from the center of the midfield line). When the ball crosses over the touchline, it is put into play by the team opposing that of the last player to touch it with a throw-in. When the ball crosses over the goal line (outside the goal) last touched by the defending team, it is put into play by the attacking team with a corner kick (a direct free kick taken from the corner on the side of the field the ball crossed over the goal line). When the ball crosses over the goal line (outside the goal) last touched by the attacking team, it is put into play by the defending team with a goal kick (an indirect free kick taken from the goal area). Soccer is played in two forty-five-minute halves (or in high school play, two thirty-five-minute halves or four eighteen-minute quarters) and play is continuous, stopping only in the case of a serious injury, a lost ball, or deliberate time-wasting by either team (in college soccer, play is also stopped after a goal and for a penalty kick; in high school soccer, play is also stopped after a goal and to administer a caution, warning, or ejection). Two substitutions are allowed during a game (unlimited substitution in high school soccer, unlimited substitution from among five designated substitutes in college soccer). The international name for soccer, association football, came from England's Football Association, formed in 1863 to separate soccer from the other football game, rugby. Association committee member and amateur player Charles Wreford-Brown is reported to have created the term "soccer" as a word play on the abbreviation "assoc." When asked at Oxford if he would like a game of "rugger" (rugby), he facetiously replied, "no, soccer." In countries other than the United States and Canada, the game is still known as association football, or football. see *indoor soccer*.

soccer ball: An inflated (9 to 10-1/2 pounds per square inch) leather or approved simulated leather-covered sphere with a circumference of 27 to 28 inches, and weighing 14 to 16 ounces at the start of a match. The size of the ball was fixed at a meeting in 1882 of representatives of the English, Scottish, Welsh, and Irish Football Associations. English football pioneer and mid-1920s Arsenal manager Herbert Chapman is credited with introducing the white soccer ball.

Soccer Bowl: The annual post-season game between Divisional Playoff winners for the North American Soccer League championship. Although the first NASL championship game was played in 1968 (won by the Atlanta Chiefs, led by player-coach Phil Woosnam—later NASL Commissioner), the name Soccer Bowl was first used in 1975, when the Tampa Bay Rowdies defeated the Portland Timber 2-0.

Soccer Hall of Fame: The honor roll of outstanding players and administrators who have made a contribution to American soccer. The Hall of Fame was originated by the Oldtimers' Soccer Association of Philadelphia in 1950, and by mutual agreement, taken under the guardianship of the United States Soccer Federation in 1953. Final selections for membership are made by the Soccer Hall of Fame Committee (former USSF presidents) from nominations made by affiliated state associations, the North American Soccer League, the Major Indoor Soccer League, the American Soccer League, the National Soccer Coaches Association, a special Veterans' Committee, and various intercollegiate groups.

sole trap: A trap made with the sole of the shoe, wedging the ball against the ground. compare *chest trap, head trap, sweep trap, thigh trap*.

SWEEPER

space: An open or unguarded area of the playing field that can be exploited by the attacking team.

spearhead: see *center forward*.

spot: Short for penalty spot.

spot kick: A penalty kick.

spread the defense: An offensive strategy in which attacking players attempt to draw defenders away from the middle of the penalty area toward the flanks.

1. square: 1. Laterally or directly to the side, roughly parallel to the goal line. (played the ball square into the middle) 2. Lined up laterally, roughly parallel to the goal line.

2. square: To pass the ball square.

square ball, square pass: A pass that is played square.

step over the ball: To attempt to momentarily deceive a defender by shifting the body as if to move one way with the ball, but instead, stepping over it, then quickly moving the ball in the opposite direction.

stopper: 1. The center back, originally, the player assigned to "stop" the opposing center forward in the W-M formation popularized in England by football pioneer Herbert Chapman's Arsenal team in 1925. 2. The position played by a center back.

striker: 1. The center forward 2. The position played by a center forward. 3. A forward.

strip: A team uniform. A British expression.

sweep: To play as a sweeper.

sweeper: 1. A roaming defender normally positioned just behind or in front of the back line, where he can move laterally across the field to cover or help out the other defenders. The origin of the sweeper dates back to 1931, when the Servette-Geneva team of Switzerland, coached by Karl Rappan, introduced the Swiss *verrou* or " bolt," so called because the deeply positioned back in the defensive mode of the system was likened to a boltlock against opponents. In 1947, Nereo Rocco, coach of a struggling Italian first division team, Triestina, introduced the *catenaccio* ("big chain" of defenders) anchored by a *livero*, a permanent deep fullback inspired by Rappan's earlier system. Eventually, the Italian "free man" became the *libero* and "sweeper" or "freeback" in Spanish and English-speaking countries, and by the 1966 World Cup, most teams employed a sweeper. A sweeper's role can be primarily defensive like that of hard-tackling Nobby Stiles of England's victorious 1966 World Cup team, or creative and offense-inspiring, like those created by Franz Beckenbauer and Carlos Alberto (later, both players for the New York Cosmos). also *freeback, libero, sweeper back*. 2. The position played by a sweeper. also *freeback, libero, sweeper back*.

sweeper back: 1. A sweeper. also *freeback, libero*.

sweep trap: A technique in which a moving ball is trapped against the ground with a sole trap, but immediately rolled in a desired direction with the bottom of the foot rather than stopped. compare *chest trap, head trap, thigh trap*.

switch: To pass the ball from one side of the field to a teammate on the other side. also *change*.

table: A British expression for a schedule of league standings. (a good team, currently third in the table)

1. tackle: To use the feet to block, dislodge or win control of the ball from an opponent. see *block tackle, slide tackle*.

2. tackle: The act or an instance of blocking, dislodging, or winning control of the ball from an opponent. (took the ball away with a perfect tackle). see *block tackle, slide tackle*.

tackle through the ball: To tackle with such speed or power that physical contact with the opponent's legs is assured after the ball is played, most often resulting in a fall, and sometimes, injury to the opponent. A foul, if intentional, that results in a direct free kick by the opposing team at the spot of the offense or, if committed by a defender in his penalty area, a penalty kick. In indoor soccer, the offending player may also be assessed a two-minute time penalty. If, in the opinion of the referee, the foul is serious or violent, the offending player may be cautioned (an automatic two-minute time penalty in indoor soccer) or sent off (an automatic five-minute time penalty in indoor soccer, to be served by the ejected player's substitute).

tactical foul: An intentional foul committed when the consequences of the foul are less damaging than if play is allowed to continue, as in the case of bringing down an attacker who is about to break through into the penalty area when the goal is unguarded because the keeper is down or out of position. By the time the resulting direct free kick is taken, the goalkeeper and a wall of defenders can be in position. Always questionable in terms of sportsmanship, the tactical foul was used in its most blatant and violent form to intimidate and injure key players like Brazil's Pele in the 1966 World Cup finals in England. also *professional foul.*

take down: see *bring down.*

take one's number: To note the jersey number or identity of a player who intentionally fouls or is unnecessarily rough so as to be able to retaliate later in the game (when the referee isn't looking). A common practice among professional players, although against the rules.

take some stick: To be the object of rough play, especially to be kicked. A British expression applied both to rugby and soccer. compare *give some stick.*

●●To be razzed or given a hard time. (took some stick about his political views)

1. tally: To score a goal. (tallied with a header to knot the game)

2. tally: A goal. also *marker.*

targetman: 1. The central striker positioned close to the opponent's goal to receive long or centering passes in order to relay the ball to other attacking teammates, or to turn and shoot. also *frontman.* 2. A centrally positioned midfielder to whom outlet passes are directed for distribution to attacking teammates. also *frontman.*

technical offense: An infraction of the rules or foul which does not involve physical contact in indoor soccer, such as playing the ball twice on a kickoff, kick-in, free kick or goal kick before it is touched by another player (outside the penalty area on a goal kick), an illegal substitution, a three-line violation, delaying the game, hitting the superstructure of the arena with the ball, penalty kick violations, and violations of the restrictions placed on goalkeepers. A technical offense results in a two-minute time penalty which does not count in the accumulation of total time

TACKLE

penalties for the purposes of ejection, unless a caution is administered for ungentlemanly conduct for persistent infringement of the laws. compare *penal offense.*

thigh trap: A trap in which an air ball is stopped and controlled on the thigh. compare *chest trap, foot trap, head trap, sole trap, sweep trap.*

3-4-3: see *W-M.*

three-line pass: see *three-line violation.*

three-line violation: A violation in which a ball is passed across three lines (the two red lines and the center line) in the air, toward the opponent's goal line, without touching another player or the perimeter wall. When a three-line violation is committed, an indirect free kick is awarded to the opposing team at the point where the ball crossed the first line. When a team is playing shorthanded by two players, a three-line violation by any player on that team except the goalkeeper is not penalized (at no time may a goalkeeper throw, punch, punt, or drop-kick over the three lines). also *offside violation, red line violation, three-line pass.*

through: Into an open space between the last line of defenders and the goalkeeper.

through ball, through pass: A ball passed into an open space between the last line of defenders and the goalkeeper for an attacking teammate to run on to. (caught the defense square with a beautiful through pass)

throw-in: The method by which the ball is put back into play when it crosses entirely over a touchline, taken from out of bounds at that point by the team opposing that of the last player to touch the ball before it leaves the playing field. At the moment a throw-in is taken, the thrower must be facing the field from no more than one meter away and have part of both feet on or outside the touchline and on the ground (the ball may not be thrown while running). A throw-in must be made with both hands moving simultaneously with equal force, and the ball must be delivered from behind and over the thrower's head. There is no offside nor can a goal be scored directly from a throw-in (a goal kick results if the ball is thrown into the opponent's goal). An

opponent may stand on the touchline in front of the thrower, but no attempt may be made to distract or impede him (an infraction results in a caution for the guilty player). Like many of soccer's rules, the concept of a throw-in from the touchline originated in the mid-1800s at one of England's public schools, Cheltenham, though it was delivered one-handed at right angles to the line, and by the first player to touch the ball out of bounds (thus, "touch" and "touchline"). By 1877, the throw-in was allowed to be taken in any direction by the team opposing the last player to touch the ball. The Scots favored a two-handed throw-in, and, at a meeting in 1882 of the English, Scottish, Welsh, and Irish Football Associations, it became the agreed method, largely because of England and Notts County cricket and football player, William Gunn, who could throw the ball one-handed 60 yards in the air, farther than most of his contemporaries could kick it. Other rule changes followed in 1920 (no offside), 1925 (both feet on the ground), and 1931 (throw-in to the opposing team for an illegal throw). In recent years, the long throw-in has

THIGH TRAP

295

emerged as an offensive weapon, with the ability of some players to deliver a centering pass-like throw from the touchline into the penalty area. compare *kick-in*.

throw in: To put the ball in play with a throw-in.

timekeeper: 1. The official responsible for keeping the time of a game and supervising the serving of time penalties under the jurisdiction of the referee in indoor soccer. The timekeeper is situated in an area adjacent to the playing field at the center line, between the penalty boxes. 2. The official responsible for keeping the time of a game in conjunction with the referee in high school and college soccer (one timer to be provided by each school).

time out: A one-minute interruption in play allowed to each team once during each half in indoor soccer, to be taken only at a normal stoppage of play when that team is in possession of the ball or when the ball is in full possession of the goalkeeper. No time outs are permitted in an overtime period.

THROW-IN

296

time penalty: A two-minute or five-minute penalty (or two consecutive two-minute penalties) assessed against a player or bench personnel for certain fouls and rule infractions in indoor soccer. For the duration of a time penalty, the guilty player (or a designated substitute in the case of an ejection or a penalty assessed a goalkeeper or bench personnel) must remain within the penalty box, and his team must play short-handed. see *double minor, major penalty, minor penalty*.

toe-kick: To miskick the ball with the toe instead of the instep.

toe kick: The act or an instance of miskicking the ball with the toe instead of the instep.

toe-poke: To push or poke the ball with a toe.

toe poke: The act of toe-poking the ball.

total football, total soccer: The name coined for the style of play developed by Rinus Michels's energetic Ajax team from Holland, European Cup winners in 1971, 1972, and 1973, and popularized by Holland (coached by Michels) at the 1974 World Cup finals in Germany. Total football or total soccer is a system in which the movement of players is constant and fluid, with few restrictions placed on any one position. Forwards exchange with midfielders, dropping all the way back to their penalty area when needed, and defenders frequently move forward to attack, confident that their defensive responsibilities will be taken up by teammates. Total football requires a high level of technical skills from all the players (not just the forwards), tremendous fitness, and equally important, understanding and teamwork. The 1974 Dutch side had all these, with gifted players like Ruud Krol, Wim Suurbier, Wim van Hanegem, Rob Rensenbrink, Johnnie Rep, Wim Rijsbergen, Johan Neeskens, and the brilliant Johan Cruyff. Playing the most exciting and creative soccer in the tournament, Holland defeated Uruguay, Sweden, Argentina, East Germany, and Brazil without giving up a goal, before losing 2-1 in the final to Helmut Schoen's West German team, who practiced their own, more disciplined, if less inspirational, form of total football.

touch: The out of bounds area along the sidelines, up to but not including the touchlines. The first rules governing a ball out of bounds on the sideline were adopted in the mid-1800s at the English public school, Cheltenham, and called for a throw-in to be taken by the first player who touched the ball after it crossed the sideline. Thus, out of bounds became the "touch area," later "touch," and the sidelines became the "touchlines."

touchline: 1. One of the two boundary lines on each side of the playing area between and perpendicular to the goal lines. A ball is not out of bounds until it has wholly crossed a touchline. also *sideline.* see *throw-in, touch.* 2. One of two broken lines (6-inch segments separated by one-inch spaces) marked 3 feet from and parallel to the side perimeter walls between the corner marks in indoor soccer, and from which kick-ins are taken. see *kick-in.*

1. trap: To stop and control a ball moving on the ground or in the air, as with the head, chest, leg, or foot. also *kill the ball.*

2. trap: The act or an instance of trapping a ball.

turn a defender: To make a defender turn one way with a fake, then quickly take the ball around him the other way. (was able to sell the dummy and turn the defender to break into the area)

12-yard mark, 12-yard spot: The penalty spot.

UEFA Cup: The Union of European Football Associations Cup, an annual competition played over five rounds of home-and-away pairings, in which the winner is determined by aggregate score (if a tie results, away goals count double). Sixty-four teams participate, selected from among the runners-up to league champions in European countries. The number of teams a country can enter is determined by points accrued in the competition over a five-year period. The competition began in 1955 as the Inter-Cities Fairs Cup, and was open only to cities staging international trade fairs. The first tournament took three years to complete, with FC Barcelona defeating a London side assembled with players from several teams. The Fairs Cup became known as the "Fouls Cup" because of unfortunate incidents of rough play and violence in the first years. In 1971, the competition

was taken over by the Union of European Football Associations, and the first UEFA Cup was won by Tottenham Hotspur. Because of the number of games played by the many entrants, the UEFA Cup is considered a good barometer of the relative strength of the European leagues.

United States Soccer Federation: The national governing body of soccer in the United States, an affiliate member of the Federation Internationale de Football Association. The United States Soccer Federation is responsible for conducting regional and national youth, amateur, and open competitions, and for the development and sponsorship of the various national teams (Youth Team, Olympic Team, and the National Team). Founded in 1913, the United States Soccer Federation is headquartered in New York. also *USSF.*

unmarked: Not guarded by a defender. (ghosted through unmarked)

unsighted: Blocked or unable to see, as of a goalkeeper. A British expression. (unsighted for the second goal)

upright: A goal post. also *post.*

USSF: The United States Soccer Federation.

1. volley: A powerful kick in which an air ball is kicked first time, without trapping or controlling it first. compare *half volley.*

2. volley: To execute a volley. compare *half volley.*

wall: A number of defenders (usually three or more) standing side-by-side to act as a human barrier in order to block a part of the goal when a free kick is awarded to the opposing team near the defenders' goal, legal as long as the wall is formed no closer than the minimum 10 yards.

wall pass: A give-and-go. The teammate who makes the return pass acts as a "wall" off which the first player bounces the ball, as though passing it to himself. also *double pass, one-two.*

W formation: The attacking half (three forwards, two midfielders) of the W-M formation. see *W-M.*

wing: 1. Either of two attacking players (left wing and right wing) who normally play on the outside or flanks of the front line. also *outside forward, outside left, outside right, winger.* see *pyramid.* 2. The position played by a wing. also *outside forward, outside left, outside right, winger.* see *pyramid.* 3. The area of the playing field close to the touchlines.

winger: see *wing.*

wing half: 1. Either of two midfielders who normally play on the flanks of a central midfielder in the classic pyramid formation. also *outside half, wing halfback.* see *pyramid.* 2. The position played by a wing half. also *outside half, wing halfback.* see *pyramid.*

wing halfback: see *wing half.*

win a corner: To be awarded a corner kick in the opposing half because the defending team, by an accidental deflection or an intentional play, last touches the ball before it crosses entirely over the goal line outside the goal. compare *give away a corner.*

win the ball: To gain possession of the ball by taking it away from an opponent, intercepting a pass or cross played to an opponent, first reaching and controlling a loose ball, or by playing it off an opponent in such a way as to win a corner kick or throw-in. (a good tackler who can also win the ball in the air)

withdrawn forward: An attacking player who normally operates from a central position behind the forward line. In modern formations, a withdrawn forward is considered an attacking midfielder, but the first withdrawn forwards were nominally center forwards, moved back to draw the opposing center back out of position. At Wembley in 1953, Hungary used a withdrawn forward to hand England its first defeat ever at home. With the English stopper Harry Johnston confused and drawn out of position to cover the withdrawn Hungarian center forward, Nandor Kidegkuti, Hungary's gifted strikers Sandor Kocsis and Ferenc Puskas were able to break through repeatedly in front of the English net. The result was a lopsided 6-3 win for Hungary.

W-M: A formation which employs three defenders, four midfielders, and three forwards. The W-M (so called because imaginary lines connecting the two front midfielders and three forwards would appear from above like the letter W, and similar lines between the two rear midfielders and three defenders, like an M) resulted from the 1925 change in the offside rule, reducing the number of defenders required to be between an attacking player without the ball and the goal from three to two. With the offside trap made more difficult and risky by the new rule, scoring opportunities increased greatly (the number of goals scored in the English Football League rose by over 40 percent in the first year of the change). To counter this, English football pioneer Herbert Chapman, just made manager of Arsenal, together with inside forward Charlie Buchan, devised the W-M, in which the old attacking center half was repo-

VOLLEY

sitioned between the two regular full-backs to become a center back or stopper, and the two inside forwards moved back to the midfield. The W-M was an immediate success and became the standard of soccer in England (and, consequently, much of the world) for twenty years. also *3-4-3.* compare *4-4-2, 4-3-3, 4-2-4, pyramid.*

woodwork: 1. Slang for the goal posts or crossbar. (caromed in off the woodwork) 2. Slang for the boards in indoor soccer.

work-rate: A term applied to the amount of running a player or team does or is able to do during a game. The expression originated in England in the mid-1960s, when a high work-rate became a basic tenet of English soccer. (known more for his work-rate than skill)

world-class: Having sufficient skill or merit to be able to compete at the highest level of international competition. (will get their first look at the new acquisition, a world-class midfielder)
••Being of the highest caliber. (feasted on a world-class meal)

World Club Championship, World Club Cup: An annual competition between winners of the European Cup (European Championship Clubs' Cup) and the South American Copa Libertadores. The World Club Cup (originally called the Intercontinental Cup) was first held in 1960, with Real Madrid of Spain defeating Penarol of Uruguay.

World Cup: The prestigious quadrennial competition between teams representing 24 countries from among the over 150 member nations of FIFA. With the host country and defending World Cup champion automatically qualified, the remaining twenty-two finalists are determined by qualifying rounds played within five geographical elimination groups; Europe, South America, CONCACAF (North and Central America and the Caribbean Zone), Africa, and Asia/Oceania. Through the efforts of FIFA president Jules Rimet, after whom the original World Cup trophy was named, the first competition was hosted and won by Uruguay in 1930. In 1970 in Mexico, Brazil, led by the incomparable Pele, won the World Cup for an unprecedented third time. The Jules Rimet trophy was retired and given permanently to Brazil. The present trophy, the FIFA World Cup (which cannot be won outright), was first presented to winner West Germany at the 1974 competition. It is estimated that over 1-1/2 billion people (roughly one-third of the world's population) watched the telecast of the 1982 World Cup Final (Italy 3, West Germany 1), the largest television audience ever to watch a sporting event.

1. **yellow card:** 1. A small yellow card displayed by the referee when a player is cautioned. see *caution.* 2. A caution, the act or an instance of a player being cautioned. see *caution.*

2. **yellow card:** To show a yellow card; to caution a player. (got yellow carded for arguing with the referee) also *book, card.* see *caution.*

TENNIS

Though some basic elements of tennis have been borrowed from early Arab, Greek, and Roman pastimes involving a bat or racket and a ball, the modern game of tennis is a direct descendant of a game that became popular in France in the Middle Ages. As its name *jeu de paume*, literally "game of the palm" or "ballgame" suggests, this was originally a hand game in which a small, tightly bound cloth or leather-stuffed ball was hit back and forth over an obstruction (later a net) and around the walls and cloisters of outdoor courtyards within twelfth-century monasteries. French clerics were certainly the first enthusiasts of the sport of court tennis. In Northern France, the Archbishop of Rouen became so alarmed by his priests' preoccupation with the game that he banned the playing of it in 1245. There is even evidence of a specially built indoor court fifteen years earlier in central France, owned by a Peter Garnier in Poitiers.

By the fourteenth century, royalty had taken a particular interest in the game, which had already spread to England and many parts of Europe. Louis X of France is said to have died in 1316 from a chill contracted by drinking cold water after a tennis match.

Now being played with small paddles or *battoirs* instead of bare or gloved hands, court tennis had gained enough popularity by the late 1300s to make its first appearances in Western literature, both in Chaucer's *Troylus and Creseda* ("but canstow playen racket to and fro . . ."), and in Donato Velluti's lines about invading French knights playing the game in his *Chronicles of Florence* ("at this time was the beginning in these parts of playing at tenes"). This was the earliest mention of any form of the world "tennis", which is believed to have come from the French *tenez*, meaning "take heed" or "play".

The first rules of court tennis were written in France in 1592 by Forbet, and published in 1599. In 1632, these rules were expanded and republished under the title *Le Jeu de la Paume* by Forbet's countryman, Charles Hulpeau. They describe a complex, scientific game that remains much the same today (as court tennis in the United States or real tennis in Great Britain) as it was in the days of Henry VIII.

The seventeenth century brought court tennis across the seas to the New World, even as its popularity began to decline in England and France. England's civil war during the reign of Charles I virtually brought an end to the sport, as did the French Revolution in that country in the eighteenth century. Though there were revivals in the nineteenth century when, once again, royalty and the gentry embraced the game, court tennis would never again be a popular sport.

Although court tennis had been played outdoors within walled courtyards and reports tell of some kind of "field tennis" played on a close-cut grass field in Battersea Fields near Ranelagh in 1767, no successful outdoor version of grass tennis was possible until the mid-1800s when a rubber ball was invented that would bounce on a surface other than flag-stones.

In 1858, Major Harry Gem and Jean-Baptiste Perera marked out a tennis court on grass in Edgbaston (Birmingham, England) and played the first recorded "lawn tennis" game with the rackets, net, and court markings of court tennis. In 1872, Major Gem founded the Leamington Lawn Tennis Club, the first outdoor tennis club.

An English army major and court tennis player, Walter Clopton Wingfield, first tried the outdoor game at a lawn party at his Lansdowne House in London in 1869. In 1874, Major Wingfield patented a version of the game, marketing a set including balls, racquets, a net, and an instruction booklet. Claiming that tennis came from an ancient Greek sport, Wingfield called his game "sphairistike", which was soon contracted to "sticky" and finally replaced by "lawn tennis".

A popular and commercial success, Wingfield's game featured a strange 60-foot-long, hourglass-shaped court, 30 feet wide at the baselines and 21 feet wide at the 4-foot, 8-inch-high net. Oddly, service was from a small diamond marked in the middle of one side of the court only, and delivered to a service court which was between the service line and the baseline.

A more stimulating game than croquet, and the only other outdoor sport that could be played by men and women, the "new" tennis quickly gained popularity. In 1875, the Marylebone Cricket Club, England's accepted governing body of court tennis and rackets, published a unified code of rules.

Wingfield's hourglass-shaped court was retained, though widened at the slightly higher net and lengthened to its present 78 feet. The service court extended 26 feet from the net, rather than being marked from the baseline. Only the server could score, keeping the serve until losing a rally. Scoring was derived from rackets, with a game being fifteen points.

In 1875, in order to increase diminishing revenues, the All England Croquet Club expanded to include tennis at the urging of one of its founders, Henry Jones. Facing another financial difficulty in 1877, the club (now named the All England Croquet and Lawn Tennis Club) decided to sponsor an all-comers tennis tournament, the first Wimbledon Champion-ship. Wimbledon remains today the most important, as well as the oldest, competition in tennis. Jones, who suggested the event, also participated in framing the rules for it, most of which were adopted around the world and remain virtually the same today.

Among Jones's contributions was the change from rackets scoring back to the "clock" system originally used in court tennis, with the four points being fifteen, thirty, forty-five (which is now shortened to forty), and game. The Wimbledon court was rectangular with the same outer dimensions as the modern singles court, though the net was 5 feet high at the posts and 3 feet, 3 inches at the middle.

An accomplished cricket player, Spencer W. Gore, introducing his somewhat controversial volley shot, won the first Wimbledon, a men's singles event only. The first men's doubles championship was held in Scotland in 1878, and the first women's singles championship, the following year in Ireland. The first "open" competition (in which other than club members could participate) in the United States was staged in 1880 at the Staten Island Croquet and Baseball Club, with O. E. Woodhouse, a British player who is believed to have introduced the smash, winning the "Championship of America".

In 1878 the Melbourne Cricket Club laid the first asphalt tennis court in Australia. However, it took a while for tennis to catch on. The Australian championships were inaugurated in 1905, not long after the Lawn Tennis Association of Australasia (later Australia) was formed.

In 1881, the United States National Lawn Tennis Association (later the USTA) was formed, becoming the world's first national governing body of tennis. That same year, the new organization adopted the All England Club's Wimbledon rules and staged the first official United States Championships at the Newport Casino in Newport, Rhode Island. Richard Sears won the singles championship in straight sets, the first of his remarkable seven singles titles. Though the inaugural men's doubles event was won by Clarence Clark and Fred Taylor, Sears went on to take the next six doubles championships. Meanwhile, in England, the Renshaw twins, William and Ernest, had introduced their aggressive and exciting style of play that would popularize tennis as a spectator sport and dominate Wimbledon for a decade. From 1880 to 1890, the Renshaws won eight singles titles (losing in the finals on two other occasions) and seven doubles titles.

The first United States National Men's Inter-Collegiate Championships were held in 1883, with the autumn leg won by Harvard's Howard Taylor and the spring leg by teammate Joseph Clark. The same year, Clark and his brother Clarence, with the permission of current United States doubles champions Dwight and Sears, journeyed to England to represent the United States against the British team of Reggie and Laurie Doherty in the first international tennis match. The Dohertys won and, in 1884, added fuel to the growing rivalry between tennis enthusiasts in the United States and Great Britian by defeating Dwight and Sears in the semifinals of Wimbledon's first men's doubles championship. The same year, Maud Watson, the nineteen-year-old daughter of an English vicar, defeated her older sister Lilian to become the first ever Wimbledon women's singles champion.

The first women's singles championship in the United States was staged in 1887 at the Philadelphia Cricket Club and won by Ellen Hansell. The USNLTA was reluctant to sponsor an official women's championship until 1889, but then recognized the two previous events retroactively. When the first modern Olympics were held in Athens in 1896, a tennis competition was included. J. P. Boland won the gold medal in men's singles.

In 1900, American player Dwight Davis donated the International Tennis Challenge Trophy for the first team competition between nations, known thereafter as the Davis Cup, the most prestigious international tennis competition. Behind the big serve of team captain Davis and the particularly baffling American twist and reverse twist serves introduced by teammates Holcombe Ward and Malcolm Whiteman respectively, the Americans soundly defeated the British team in the first tournament. In 1903, Britain won the Davis Cup with a two-man team of the incredible Doherty brothers, Reggie and Laurie, who from 1897 to 1906 won nine Wimbledon singles and doubles titles. In 1902, they won the United States doubles championship, and in 1903, Laurie Doherty became the first foreigner to win the United States singles title.

By the early 1900s, tennis had become a true international sport. Six nations entered the Davis Cup in 1905, won by Great Britain, and for the first time, an overseas player won a Wimbledon Championship when American May Sutton (ironically, born in Great Britain) took the women's singles title. The same year, the first Australian Championships were staged, with R. W. Heath winning in singles and T. Tachell and R. Lycett taking the doubles event.

The dominant players of the time were William Larned, who matched Dick Sear's record, winning the United States singles championship seven times, the last in 1911 when he was thirty-eight; Australian lefthander Norman Brookes, the first overseas player to win the Wimbledon's men's singles championship in 1907; New Zealand great Tony Wilding, four-time Wimbledon singles and doubles champion; and Maurice McLoughlin (the "California

Comet"), the two-time United States singles and three-time doubles champion, whose blistering serve at Wimbledon in 1913 was the first to be called a "cannonball".

In Paris in 1913, with representatives present from Australia, Austria, Belgium, the British Isles, Denmark, France, Germany, Holland, Russia, South Africa, Sweden, and Switzerland, the International Lawn Tennis Federation was founded.

Three of the greatest players of all time quickly established the popularity of tennis after the war: the magnetic and almost invincible Frenchwoman, Suzanne Lenglen; and two Americans, Helen Wills (later Moody), Lenglen's equally dominant successor, and the incomparable William Tatem Tilden II.

Lenglen burst into the tennis world at Wimbledon at the age of twenty in 1919, wearing a revealing calf-length dress with short sleeves at a time when women played only in high-necked, long-sleeved, ankle-length dresses with petticoats. Sipping brandy between sets, she stunned seven-time singles champion Dorothea Lambert Chambers in the final round, taking the title in what is now regarded as one of the classic matches in tennis. An emotional player with exceptional athletic ability and accuracy, Lenglen won both the singles and doubles titles at Wimbledon every year between 1919 and 1925 (except when illness forced a withdrawal in 1924) and proved to be tennis's greatest draw card. In 1926, Lenglen became the first true tennis professional and toured the United States under the management of sports entrepreneur C. C. Pyle.

Wills was entirely different from Lenglen, both in personality and style. Nicknamed "Little Miss Poker Face", Wills showed little emotion, basing her game on power and tactics rather than speed and mobility. She won the United States singles championships seven times and the Wimbledon singles title a record eight times in nine tries. Lenglen defeated Wills the only time they met, at a much celebrated match in Cannes in 1926, but Wills's supporters are quick to point out that at nineteen, she had not yet reached her peak, and that a year later, the game might have had a different result. From 1927 through to 1932, Wills won seven United States and five Wimbledon singles championships without losing a single set.

Bill Tilden first won the United States and Wimbledon singles championships when he was twenty-seven in 1920. A tall and graceful athlete, Tilden was the master of all strokes, as well as a brilliant tactician, competitor, and showman. He dominated tennis from 1920 through to 1926 and was practically unbeatable. Tilden won more Davis Cup matches for a record eleven years, and his record of sixteen consecutive singles match wins still stands. He won his second Wimbledon singles championship in 1930 at the age of thirty-seven, and finally turned pro in 1931 after years of feuding with the USLTA about his amateur standing. Tilden gave credibility to professional tennis, and in partnership with promoter Bill O'Brien, launched the first men's pro tour in 1932 and 1933.

New amateur stars emerged in the 1930s, among them the twenty-one-year-old American, Ellsworth Vines, who, with his 121 mile-per-hour cannonball, scored a phenomenal thirty service aces in the singles finals to win at Wimbledon in 1932; three-time United States and Wimbledon singles champion Fred Perry, considered England's greatest player; American Donald Budge, who, in 1938, became the first player ever to win the four major championships in one year, namely the United States, Australian, French, and Wimbledon Championships, a feat known thereafter as the "Grand Slam"; and American Bobby Riggs, the 1939 United States and Wimbledon singles winner. Typical of the crafty Riggs, he reportedly took English bookies for over $100,000 by betting he would win the singles, doubles, and mixed doubles events. He did, becoming the only man other than Budge to win a Wimbledon "triple". Starting with Vines in 1934, all these players followed Tilden's example and turned professional by the start of World War II, breathing new life into the young pro tour. Though the United States Championships continued uninterrupted through the 1940s, international play ceased until after the war.

In tournament play, American players dominated the 1940s behind the "big game" of Robert Falkenburg, Jack Kramer, Ted Schroeder, and Pancho Gonzales. American women were equally strong, winning every singles and doubles title in the United States, French, and Wimbledon championships, as well as the Wightman Cup for almost a decade after the war.

Australia's victory in the 1950 Davis Cup, led by Frank Sedgman, signaled a changing of the guard in men's tennis. Australian players, among them Sedgman, Ken Rosewall, Lew Hoad, Roy Emerson, Neale Fraser, Fred Stolle, and Rod Laver, were to take most of the major championships for nearly two decades and win fourteen of the next seventeen Davis Cup matches, losing only to United States teams led by Tony Trabert and Vic Seixas in 1954, Alex Olmeda in 1958, and Dennis Ralston in 1963.

The 1950s and 1960s produced some of the game's great women players, such as America's Maureen "Little Mo" Connolly, who, in 1953, became the first woman to score a Grand Slam, and whose brilliant career was cut short in 1954 by a leg injury when she was hit by a truck while riding a horse; Althea Gibson, two-time United States and Wimbledon champion and winner of eleven major titles, also the first black player to win a major championship; Maria Bueno of Brazil, winner of twenty Big Four titles and regarded as one of the game's great stylists; Australian, Margaret Court, holder of the all-time record for the most Big Four singles (twenty-four) and overall (sixty-two) titles, and who achieved the Grand Slam in 1970; and the incomparable Billie Jean King from America, second only to Court in overall Big Four titles (thirty-eight) and winner of more Wimbledon Championships (twenty) than any player in history.

By the late 1960s, tennis was at a crossroads. New stars were emerging from all over the world, including Australia's John Newcombe and Tony Roche, South Africa's Cliff Drysdale, Manuel Santana of Spain, Holland's Tom Okker, Jan Kodes from Czechoslovakia, Romania's Ilie Nastase, and Americans Arthur Ashe and Stan Smith, but more and more of the best players were becoming professionals. The problem was that the best tournaments were still amateur, or allegedly so. In fact, since the 1920s, ever increasing amounts of under-the-table money had been paid at major tournaments, giving rise to the characterization of tennis amateurs as "shamateurs". Finally, the ILTF relented, and, in 1968, the modern era of "open tennis" arrived. Professionals as well as amateurs could now compete in major tournaments.

Tennis was at last a big-time, big-money sport, and, in the 1970s and 1980s, millions of new enthusiasts watched on television as new superstars Jimmy Connors, Guillermo Vilas, Bjorn Borg, John McEnroe, Jose Luis Clerc, and Ivan Lendl rose to prominence. Due in no

small part to the efforts of Billie Jean King (including her widely publicized "Battle of the Sexes" victory over fifty-seven-year-old Bobby Riggs in 1973, watched in person by a record crowd of 30,472 and by over 50 million on American national television), women's professional tennis also flourished, showcasing the talents of players like Evonne Goolagong, Virginia Wade, Chris Evert, Martina Navratilova, and Tracy Austin. Austin, who in 1977 at the age of fourteen became the youngest player ever to compete at Wimbledon, was the first of a succession of female pro prodigies who followed in the 1980s.

1. **ace:** An unreturnable serve that the receiver is unable to hit, or a point won with such a serve. From the Latin and later the French *as* meaning a single spot or "one" in dice games, then card games, then tennis and other games. Originally, an ace could be any single winning stroke, but by 1800, popular use narrowed the meaning to an unreturnable serve. also *ace on service, service ace.*

2. **ace:** To serve an ace. (aced him at match point to take the singles trophy)

•• To get the better of, as by a decisive move or action. (kicked hard and aced him at the finish line)

ace on service: see *ace.*

ad: Short for advantage.

ad court: Short for advantage court.

ad in: Short for advantage in.

ad out: Short for advantage out.

advantage: 1. A point won by a player after deuce. If the same player wins the next point, he wins the game; if he loses the next point, the score returns to deuce. From the French *avant* meaning "ahead." also *ad, vantage.* 2. The score for a point won by a player after deuce. (advantage Smith) also *ad, vantage.*

advantage court: The receiver's left service court, into which the ball is served from the baseline behind the server's left court on an advantage point. also *ad court, backhand court, left-hander's court, second court.* compare *deuce court, first court, forehand court, right court.*

advantage in: The server's advantage. also *ad in, advantage server.* compare *ad out, advantage out, advantage receiver.*

advantage out: The receiver's advantage. also *ad out, advantage receiver.* compare *ad in, advantage in, advantage server.*

advantage receiver: see *advantage out.*

advantage server: see *advantage in.*

advantage set: A set tied after ten games. In order to win the set, one side must win two consecutive games. This principle was introduced at the 1878 Wimbledon Championships and stood until only recently. In 1967 at the Newport Casino Invitational, Dick Leach and Dick Dell defeated Tom Mozur and Len Schloss in what is believed to be the longest advantage set ever played in a major tournament, ending finally at forty-nine games to forty-seven. To prevent such marathon events, tiebreakers and sudden death began to come into use after 1970 as a way of ending tied sets. also *deuce set, games-all.*

alert position: The position assumed by a player waiting for a serve or a return. also *anticipatory position, readiness position, waiting position.*

all: Each; apiece, as for an equal number of points in a game or games in a set. compare *games-all.*

all-around play: Both a good ground game and a good net game. compare *all-court game.*

all-court game: The ability to play all kinds of strokes from anywhere on the court. compare *all-around play.*

all-court player: A player with the ability to play all kinds of strokes from any part of the court.

alley: Either of the two 4-1/2-foot-wide areas on the sides of the singles court that are used to make the court wider for doubles play and that are out of bounds in singles play. The use of the term "alley" was popularized in America and taken from the sport of bowling. From the French *alee,* meaning "walkway." also *tramline, tramlines.*

American formation: see *Australian formation.*

American twist: A serve in which topspin is imparted with an upward and outward motion of the racket as the ball is struck, causing it to bounce high and to the receiver's left (with a right-handed server) when it hits the ground. The American twist first came to prominence at the 1900 Davis Cup competition in Boston, when Holcombe Ward of the victorious American team bewildered his British opponents with the technique. also *kicker, kick serve, twist.* compare *reverse twist.*

1. angle: To hit the ball diagonally across the court.

2. angle: A stroke hit diagonally across the court.

angle game: A style of play which emphasizes short angle crosscourt shots which land in the forecourt or midcourt near the sideline.

anticipatory position: see *alert position.*

approach shot: A hard, forcing shot usually hit from the midcourt deep into the opponent's court after which a player moves to the net. A well-placed approach shot puts the opponent on the defensive and allows a player to move in to position to attempt to win the point with a volley.

around the post: A stroke hit from the area wide of the court which does not pass over the net, but lands fairly in the opposing court. A rare occurrence, but

legal even if the ball is low enough to be stopped by the the net.

Association of Tennis Professionals: A service organization for male professional tennis players. Founded in 1972, the Association of Tennis Professionals (ATP) functions as the representative of touring professionals in matters regarding tournament play and provides a computer ranking service (based on performance) for all professional players. To qualify for membership in the Association of Tennis Professionals, a player must be ranked among the top 200 players in the world according to the ATP computer. see *computer rankings.*

ATP: The Association of Tennis Professionals.

attacking game: A strategy in which a player attempts to keep the opponent off balance and on the defensive, as by aggressive net play utilizing the volley and smash.

attack the net: To move toward the net in order to be in position to volley or kill the ball for a winner. (likes to serve and attack the net) also *rush the net, take the net.*

Australian Championships: One of the Big Four or Grand Slam tournaments, along with the French, United States, and Wimbledon Championships. The Australian Championships were first held in 1905, with Rodney Heath winning the men's singles and Tom Tachell and Randolph Lycett winning the men's doubles event. Women first competed in 1922, with Mal Molesworth winning the first women's singles, Esna Boyd and M. Mountain the first women's doubles, and Esna Boyd and John Hawkes the first mixed doubles event. The Australian Championships became open to both amateurs and professionals in 1968. Since 1980, the Australian Championships for men and women have been held separately. also *Australian Open.*

Australian doubles: see *Australian formation.*

Australian formation: An unorthodox doubles formation in which the server's partner stands on the same side of the court as (or directly in front of) the server. In Australia, the formation is known as the "American formation." also *Australian doubles, I formation, tandem formation.*

BACKHAND

Australian Open: The Australian Championships.

backboard: A wall against which the ball is hit for practice, usually marked with a net-high horizontal line.

backcourt: The area of the court from the service line to the baseline, between the sidelines. also *deep court, no-man's land.* compare *forecourt, midcourt.*

1. backhand: A stroke hit from the side of the body opposite the racket hand, with the playing arm extended across the body. The term "backhand" refers to having the back of the racket hand toward the net when the ball is hit. Among the first exponents of the backhand was 1902-1906 Wimbledon and 1903 United States singles champion H. L. "Laurie" Doherty of England, but the player credited with changing the backhand from a defensive stroke into an attacking stroke was 1938 Grand Slam winner Don Budge, who is reputed to have had the greatest backhand in the history of tennis. compare *forehand, overhead.*

2. backhand: Of or pertaining to a stroke hit from the side of the body opposite the racket hand and made with the playing arm extended across the body. compare *forehand, overhead.*

3. backhand: To hit a backhand stroke.

backhand court: The left service court, on the backhand side for most (right-handed) receivers. see *advantage court.*

backhand grip: A method of holding the racket for a backhand stroke in which, with the racket held across the body (strings square to the net), the V between the thumb and forefinger is placed over the near bevel on top of the handle, and the thumb wrapped around extended diagonally across or straight up the back surface of the handle. also *Eastern backhand grip.* see *Continental grip, two-handed backhanded grip, Western grip.*

back room: see *runback.*

backspin: see *underspin.*

backstop: The fence or obstruction behind the ends of a court to keep the ball from rolling away.

backswing: The taking back of a racket just before a stroke is made.

1. bagel: Slang for a set won in six straight games. Coined in the early 1970s by popular American professional Eddie

Dibbs, who likened the loser's score, a zero, to a bagel. also *bagel job; love set.*

2. bagel: To win a set in six straight games.

bagel job: see *bagel.*

ball boy, ball girl: A boy or a girl who keeps the playing area clear by retrieving balls for the players during a tournament or match.

band: The canvas strip attached to the top of the net.

baseball grip: An unorthodox method of holding the racket for a two-handed forehand, in which the dominant hand is placed on the racket handle just above the other hand, as in gripping a baseball bat. see *two-handed player.* compare *chopper grip, Continental grip, Eastern grip, shake-hands grip, service grip, Western grip.*

baseline: Either of the end boundary lines or back lines of a court, extending between the sidelines, and behind which a player stands to serve.

baseline game: 1. A style of play in which ground strokes are played from near the baseline, with the player seldom moving to the net. The 1925 Wimbledon singles champion, Jean-Rene ("the Alligator") Lacoste, one of France's legendary "Four Musketeers," was the last great exponent of the baseline game. compare *net game.* 2. Ground strokes played from near the

BALL BOYS

baseline. compare *net game, net play.*

baseline judge: Either of two linesmen or lineswomen responsible for watching the baseline and calling when a ball goes out of play, positioned on a line with the baselines on the same side of the court as the umpire. also *baselinesman.*

baseliner: A player who stays near the baseline to play groundstrokes, seldom moving to the net. The 1925 Wimbledon singles champion, Jean-Rene ("the Alligator") Lacoste, one of France's legendary "Four Musketeers," was the last great baseliner. compare *net rusher, power player, retriever, shotmaker, touch player.*

baselinesman: see *baseline judge.*

beaten by the ball: Arriving too late to be able to make a good stroke, being passed or almost passed.

1. **Big Four:** The four "Grand Slam" events: the Australian Championships, the French Championships, the Wimbledon Championships, and the United States Championships. The countries sponsoring these championships were the most powerful or "Big Four" of tennis, whose supremacy at the Davis Cup was unchallenged until 1974, 1975, and 1976, when the competition was won by South Africa, Sweden, and Italy, respectively. see *Grand Slam.*

2. **Big Four:** Of or pertaining to the four "Grand Slam" events: the Australian Championships, the French Championships, the Wimbledon Championships, and the United States Championships. (will only play in Big Four events this year) also *Grand Slam.*

big game: A style of play which emphasizes a powerful serve and aggressive net play. Though the birth of the "big game" or "serve-and-volley" game is most often associated with the post-World War II American Davis Cup teams featuring Jack Kramer, Ted Schroeder, and Pancho Gonzalez, the same style of play was demonstrated as early as the 1914 Davis Cup Challenge Round between Maurice McLoughlin, the "California Comet," and Australian Norman Brookes, and later in 1932, by United States and Wimbledon Champion Ellsworth Vines. also *power game, power tennis.*

big serve: A powerful serve. also *cannonball.*

big server: A player with a powerful serve. also *fireballer.*

Big W: Slang for Wimbledon, the site of the British National Championships.

bisque: A bonus or handicap occasionally given in a friendly or informal game. As in golf, a bisque may be taken at any time during a game. Originally from the medieval game of court tennis.

blanket the net: To play at the net. (likes to blanket the net after his serve)

1. **blitz:** 1. A succession of quick, powerful shots to keep an opponent on the defensive. 2. A game with four straight points. also *love game.*

2. **blitz:** 1. To make a succession of quick, powerful shots to keep an opponent off balance. 2. To win a game with four straight points.

blocked ball: A ball returned with the racket held stationary, often resulting in a stop volley. see *stop volley.*

body shot: A serve or stroke hit directly at or close to an opponent, often resulting in a weak or clumsy return.

1. **break:** To win a game against the server. To be "broken" means to lose the game one is serving. (will lose the set if he is broken again) also *break service.*

2. **break:** 1. A service break. 2. see *kick.*

break back: To, immediately after being broken, break the opponent's serve on the next game.

break point: 1. A situation in which the next point to be played could result in a service break for the receiver if the point is won by the receiver. A break point score can be love-40, 15-40, 30-40, or ad out. (forced the game to break point before losing to the server) 2. The point which caused a service break.

break service: see *break.*

British National Championships: The Wimbledon Championships.

bullet: A hard-hit ball.

butt: The end of the racket handle.

bye: The right to, having been assigned no opponent, automatically advance to the next round of a competition without playing a match. Byes are necessary in the first round in order to achieve the correct number of players in the second when the number of entries in a draw is not exactly two, four, eight, sixteen, thirty-two, sixty-four, or a higher power of two.

The number of byes necessary in the first round can be determined by subtracting the number of entries from the next higher power of two. If, for example, there are twenty-seven entries, there will be five byes in the first round (thirty-two is the next higher power to two; thirty-two minus twenty-seven equals five). In some major competitions, byes are used to insure that seeded players or nations are not eliminated by each other in early rounds. The term "bye" comes from the Old English *bi*, meaning "near to," and probably derives from the fact that a player who has drawn a bye is left to stand by (or "near to" the competition) until the next round is played. also *walk-in*. see *draw, seed*.

l. call: To make and/or announce an official ruling or judgment on a play. (called a foot fault on the server)

2. call: 1. A ruling or judgment made by an official. 2. The score at any given time during a match.

cannonball: An extremely fast serve. The term was coined at Wimbledon in 1913 to describe the serve of Californian Maurice McLoughlin, nicknamed the "California Comet." Other players who were noted for a cannonball serve were the great Bill Tilden, 1932 Wimbledon champion Ellsworth Vines (who scored a remarkable thirty aces in the final round with his 121 mph serve), Pancho Gonzales (118 mph), and English professional Michael Sangster (154 mph). In the 1970s and early 1980s, left-hander Roscoe Tanner became known for having the fastest serve in tennis, clocked at over 155 mph. also *big serve*.

1. carry: To intentionally hold or carry a ball in play on the racket. An infraction which results in the loss of the point.

2. carry: The act or an instance of intentionally holding or carrying a ball in play on the racket. An infraction which results in the loss of the point.

center court: The main court in any tennis arena. After Wimbledon's famous Centre Court in England.

●●At the center of attention. (stood there arguing at center court, right in the middle of the dance floor)

center line: see *center service line*.

center line judge: Either of two linesmen or lineswomen, responsible for watching the center line on serves in tournament play and calling when a ball lands outside the service court. Center line judges are positioned in line with the center service lines behind the baselines.

center mark: A line (4 inches long and 2 inches wide) extending inward from and perpendicular to the baseline at its midpoint. A player serving must stay behind the baseline and between an imaginary extension of the center mark and the sideline on the side from which the serve is taken.

center service line: A line parallel to the sidelines which extends from the middle of the net to the midpoint of the service line, separating and serving as a boundary for the left and right service courts. also *center line, half-court line*.

center strap, center strop: A 2-inch-wide piece of canvas that runs down the middle of the net and is anchored to the court on some surfaces to secure the bottom of the net and to keep the top of the net at the proper height.

Centre Court: The hallowed main court at Wimbledon, used only for the Wimbledon Championships (with the exception of one professional tournament in 1967) since the 1936 Davis Cup Challenge Round. Opened in 1922, the Centre Court seats just under 12,000, with standing room for almost 3,000 additional spectators.

chair umpire: see *umpire*.

chalk: 1. The powdered white substance used to mark the lines on some tennis surfaces. In arguing about a ball called out by a line judge, players often claim to have "seen chalk," in reference to the puff of white dust raised when a ball hits a chalk-marked line. 2. A boundary line.

changeover: The one-minute period after every odd game in a set, during which players refresh themselves and change to opposite sides of the net. Players also change sides after the end of each set, unless the number of games played in a set is even, in which case the change is made at the end of the first game of the next set.

cheat: To move toward one side of the court in anticipation of a stroke.

1. chip: see *dink*.

2. chip: To execute a chip. see *dink*.

1. chop: 1. A slicing stroke in which a pronounced underspin is imparted to the ball (bottom of the ball rotates in the direction of flight) made by striking or "chopping" down with the racket and causing the ball to skid low, stop, or even recoil slightly, depending on the type and condition of the playing surface and the amount of underspin applied. compare *chip, cut, cut shot, cut stroke, dink, slice.* 2. Underspin. (a lot of chop on the ball) also *backspin, reverse spin.* compare *curl, cut, overspin, sidespin, topspin, twist.*

2. **chop:** To hit a ball with a "chopping" downward stroke (racket face open) in order to impart underspin. compare *chip, cut, dink, slice, undercut.*

chopper grip: The Continental grip. also *English grip, service grip.*

circuit: A scheduled series of professional tournaments. also *tour.*

clay: 1. The natural clay or claylike material used to form the surface of a clay court. see *clay court.* 2. Short for clay court. (prefers the clay for her baseline game) 3. Slang for a tennis court. (soft-spoken in person, but a fierce competitor on the clay)

clay court: A tennis court with a surface constructed on any of a number of kinds of natural clay or claylike loose material bound together by watering and rolling. Clay courts have a firm, smooth surface, are slower than grass, and favor touch players, retrievers, and baseliners, rather than power players. Among the earliest clay courts was one built in the late 1890s at the Hotel Beau in Cannes. In 1909, a new kind of court made from a blend of burned and finely crushed clay was built in Leicestershire, England, at the home of Commander Hillyard, R. N., captain of the English Tennis Team. It was inspired by the crushed and rolled termite ant-heap courts Hillyard had played on while touring South Africa. Because of the constant maintenance they require, clay courts have become less popular in recent years, although the French National Championships are still played on clay. In most of the world, a clay court is considered a hard court (in the United States, hard court refers only to concrete and asphalt surfaces). also *clay.*

clean winner: A winning stroke that is untouched by the opponent. also *placement.*

close: To move close to the net in doubles play to be in position to volley.

closed grip: A grip that makes the racket face tilt downward toward the ground, as with the Western grip. compare *open grip.*

closed racket, closed racket face: A racket held so that the racket face is tilted downward toward the ground. compare *flat racket, flat racket face, open racket, open racket face.*

club player: An individual who plays at one or more clubs rather than on a professional tour. Also commonly used as a somewhat pejorative reference to a player of less-than-professional skill.

computer rankings: Any of three computer rating systems (ATP, Nixdorf, and WTA) for professional players. Based on performance over a twelve-month period, computer rankings are issued periodically to determine tournament entries and seedings worldwide. ATP computer rankings are based on the performance of male players in Grand Prix tournaments (excluding the Volvo Masters). Nixdorf computer rankings are based on the performance of male players in Grand Prix tournaments (including the Volvo Masters), WCT tournaments, and major international team competitions (Davis Cup, ATP Team Championship, World Team Cup). WTA computer rankings are based on the performance of women players in WTA-approved tournaments.

concrete court: A tennis court with a surface constructed of a porous or nonporous mixture of concrete. Concrete provides a smooth, hard, and relatively fast surface, one that provides a firm foothold and favors power players rather than touch players, retrievers, or baseliners. Porous concrete courts require virtually no maintenance and have enjoyed increasing popularity since their introduction in the mid-1950s. The first concrete tennis court was constructed in 1879 in Santa Monica, California. compare *clay court, grass court, synthetic court.*

Continental grip: One of the two most popular methods of grasping the racket, in which, with the racket pointed at the net and held parallel to the ground (short strings pointing up and down), the palm of the hand rests near the top of the handle, with the V formed by the thumb and index finger (of a right-handed player) over the left bevel, leaving the racket face slightly open. Though difficult for beginners, the Continental grip is used by most high-level players for the serve and overhead volley and can be used for the backhand. Originally used in England in the early 1900s (and called the English grip), the grip soon became popular throughout "continental" Europe, where the low-bounce clay courts favored its open racket face, as did England's grass courts. also *chopper grip, service grip.* compare *baseball grip, Eastern grip, shake-hands grip, Western grip.*

court: 1. The rectangular playing area for the sport of tennis, 78 feet long by 27 feet wide for singles play (36 feet wide for doubles play) divided across the middle by a net, 3 feet high at the center, suspended from 3-foot, 6-inch-high posts, the centers of which are 3 feet outside the court on each side. Service lines, which extend between the singles sidelines, are marked 21 feet from each side of the net and parallel to it. On each side of the net, the space bounded by the service line and singles sidelines is divided into two equal parts called the service courts by the center service line, marked halfway between and parallel to the sidelines. A 4-inch-long perpendicular line, the center mark, extends into the court from the middle of each end boundary line or baseline. The center service line and the center mark are 2 inches wide. All other lines must be between 1 inch and 2 inches in width, except the baseline which may be 4 inches in width. All measurements are made to the outside of the lines. The playing surface of a court may be made of grass, clay, or claylike materials, concrete or asphalt, wood, or of synthetic materials, and, in championship play, must extend a minimum of 21 feet behind each baseline and 12 feet outside of the sidelines. The Marylebone Cricket Club's 1875 code of rules for lawn tennis called for an hourglass-shaped court that was wider at the "baseline" than at the net, as had been suggested by tennis pioneer Walter Clopton Wingfield. Regulations stipulating a rectangular court were adopted for the inaugural Wimbledon Championship in 1877. The word "court" comes from the old French *cort* (derived from the Latin *cohors*), meaning a yard or enclosure. also *tennis court.* see *fast court, hard court, slow court.* 2. The playing area and environs, including adjacent stands and backstops or side barriers. 3. Short for service court. also *service box.*

courtside: The area or seating area immediately adjacent to the perimeter of a tennis court.

cover: 1. To move into or be in position to return an opponent's shot. 2. To close the racket face or turn it downward in

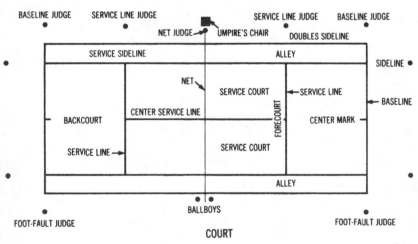

COURT

order to impart topspin to the ball.

covered court: An English expression for an indoor court, usually with a wood or synthetic playing surface. Though tennis had been played indoors for some time, specially designed "covered courts" with wood floors began to be constructed in Scandinavian countries at the turn of the century. In recent years, large inflatable plastic coverings which can be taken down in warm weather have become popular in Scandinavia and other cold winter locations.

1. **crosscourt:** Diagonally across the court. (volleyed crosscourt for a winner)

2. **crosscourt:** To or toward the diagonally opposite court. (ended the rally with a crosscourt backhand)

curl: see *cut.*

1. **cut:** 1. see *cut stroke.* 2. The amount of spin on a ball resulting from a cut stroke (usually a combination of underspin and sidespin). also *curl.* compare *backspin, chop, overspin, reverse spin, sidespin, topspin, twist, underspin.*

2. **cut:** To hit the ball with a short slicing motion and an open racket face. compare *chip, chop, dink, slice, undercut.*

cut shot: see *cut stroke.*

cut stroke: A stroke in which underspin and sidespin are imparted to the ball with a short slicing motion as the open racket face "cuts" under and inside or outside of the ball to make contact. The cut stroke was a refinement of early slicing strokes used in the forerunner of modern tennis, court tennis. In 1920 at Wimbledon, all-time tennis great Bill Tilden used a devastating cut stroke to defeat the defending champion, Australian Gerald Patterson, in the final. also *cut, cut shot.* compare *chip, chop, dink, slice.*

daisy cutter: A stroke in which the ball skids along the ground or bounces very low when it lands. A difficult shot to return unless it can be volleyed.

Davis Cup: An annual international tournament contested by two or three-man national teams (plus alternates) for singles and doubles competition. A total of sixteen teams compete for the Davis Cup, the twelve top teams from the previous tournament (seeded on the basis of results), and the winners of four zonal competitions held during the year. The Davis Cup (named after its donor,

Dwight F. Davis of St. Louis) was first offered in 1900 at the initial International Lawn Tennis Championship, played at the Longwood Cricket Club in Boston. A team from the British Isles was the only challenger in the first competition, which was won handily by the American team comprised of Dwight Davis, Holcombe Ward, and American champion M.D. Whitman. The tournament became a true international competition at Wembley in 1904, when Belgium and France first took part (ironically, the United States did not field a team that year).

dead: Slang for out of play, as for a ball which has bounced out of bounds, bounced twice on the court, hit the net, or which has been "killed" on a winning stroke.

dead rubber: A match that remains to be played in a team competition when one side already has a winning lead (such as 3-0 or 3-1 in the Davis Cup).

deep: Far into the backcourt near the baseline. (caught her offguard with a deep lob) compare *long, short, wide.*

deep court: The backcourt.

1. **default:** The failure of a player or side to take part in or complete a game, set, or match, resulting in a walkover, an automatic victory for the opponent.

2. **default:** To lose a game, set, or match because of failure to take part in or complete it.

defensive lob: A ball hit high in the air so as to give a player enough time to properly position himself for the next stroke. compare *offensive lob.*

defensive volley: A return that can only be made by a volley, usually in desperation from below the level of the net. also *low volley.* compare *high volley, offensive volley.*

delivery: A serve.

designated tournament, designation: One of twelve tournaments (including Grand Slam events) in which a professional player must take part in one year in order to participate in the Volvo Grand Prix competition and Masters tournament. Designations are chosen by a special committee of the Men's International Professional Tennis Council from a list of preferences made up by each player according to guidelines established by the player's performance in the previous Masters tournament or ATP computer ranking. A player who fails to participate in a designated tournament is subject to an action that may include fines, designation to additional Grand Prix tournaments, loss of bonus points in the Grand Prix bonus pool, and ineligibility to participate in the Masters competition.

deuce: 1. A tie in a game after six points have been played (each side having a score of forty). At deuce, one side must score two consecutive points to win the game. The point scored after deuce is called advantage (either to the server or receiver). If the side with the advantage scores the next point, that side wins that game; if the opposing side wins the point, the score reverts to deuce, and does so indefinitely until one side wins two consecutive points. Deuce, from the French tennis expression *a deux de jeu*, meaning "at two to play" (or that two points must be won), was introduced in the rules adopted in 1875 by the Marylebone Cricket Club, then the governing body of cricket, tennis, and rackets. At the time, rackets scoring was used, with the first side to reach fifteen winning, unless the score was 14-all ("deuce"), in which case two consecutive points were necessary to win. 2. A tie after ten games of play in a set (five games for each side). To win the set, one side must win two consecutive games.

deuce court: The receiver's right service court, into which the ball is served (from the baseline behind the server's right court) whenever the score is deuce. see *first court.*

deuce set: see *advantage set.*

die: To not bounce or scarcely bounce, as of a ball with underspin. (hit in the forecourt and died)

1. dink: A softly sliced return intended to fall between the net and the service line in front of an opponent. also *chip, softie.* compare *chop, cut, cut shot, cut stroke, slice.*

2. dink: 1. To execute a dink. also *chip.* compare *chop, cut, slice, undercut.* 2. To hit a dink against a particular opponent. (dinked him to keep him off balance)

double-fault: To commit two consecutive faults while serving from the same court, resulting in the loss of the point. see *fault.*

double fault: The act or an instance of committing two consecutive faults while serving from the same court, resulting in the loss of the point. see *fault.*

DINK

double-fisted player: see *two-handed player*.

double-handed player: see *two-handed player*.

double hit: The act or an instance of striking the ball twice during the same stroke. If done intentionally, an infraction that results in the loss of the point.

doubles: A game between teams of two players or "pairs," played on a court slightly wider than in singles, utilizing the two 4-1/2-foot alleys and baseline extensions normally marked outside the sidelines of a singles court. Rules for doubles play specify that service is alternated between the pairs with all four players serving in turn, and that the players receiving service must receive from the same court throughout a set (the order of service or the court from which either partner receives may be changed at the end of each set). All other rules of singles play apply to doubles. Doubles is categorized into men's doubles, women's doubles, and mixed doubles. The first recorded doubles championship (men's doubles) was held in Scotland in 1878.

doubles court: The 78-foot-long by 36-foot-wide rectangular playing area for doubles. A doubles court is slightly wider than that used for singles, and includes the two 4-1/2-foot alleys and baseline extensions normally marked outside the sidelines of a singles court. The portions of the singles sidelines that lie between the service lines are called the service sidelines on a doubles court.

doubles sideline: One of the two side boundaries for a doubles court, drawn 4-1/2 feet outside the singles sidelines and extending between the baselines.

double-strung racket: A racket strung with two sets of vertical (long) strings and only five or six widely spaced cross strings, wrapped at the junctions with various bracing materials (among them, a plastic tubing known as spaghetti, the source of the racket's other name, the spaghetti racket). A West German, Werner Fisher, invented the double-strung racket, which was used in several major tournaments in 1977 with startling results. The extremely low-tensioned strings virtually catapulted the ball off the racket, at the same time imparting an unnatural amount of topspin. Within the year, the double-strung racket was banned by the ITF.

down the line: Parallel and close to the sideline.

down the T: Down the middle of the court along the center service line, which forms a "T" where it intersects with the service line.

1. draw: 1. The method by which match-ups and the playing order of a tournament are determined. Except for seeded players who are scheduled before the draw, the names of entered players are drawn blindly from a hat or container and placed in the order drawn on a draw sheet that indicates match-ups. see *seed*. 2. The arrangement in the order drawn of match-ups on a draw sheet.

2. draw: 1. To randomly pick the names of players entered in a tournament to determine match-ups and playing order for a draw sheet. 2. To be matched against a particular opponent or be assigned a particular position in the schedule or a draw.

draw sheet: An official schedule of the match-ups and playing order for a tournament based on the results of a draw.

1. drive: A hard groundstroke (forehand or backhand), hit either flat or with topspin, usually from near the baseline. The drive is the most frequently used shot in tennis.

2. drive: To hit a drive with the forehand or backhand.

drive volley: A hard volleying stroke played from the backcourt in the manner of a drive.

drop: Short for drop shot.

drop shot: A softly hit forehand or backhand stroke (usually hit with underspin) in which the ball barely clears the net and "drops." A drop shot is used to catch a retreating or deep-playing opponent off guard, or to pull an opponent out of position for a subsequent passing shot or lob. also *drop*.

drop the ball: To execute a drop shot.

drop volley: A drop shot hit on the volley.

early ball: 1. A volley made by rushing the net, rather than waiting for the ball to arrive. 2. A half volley.

Eastern backhand grip: see *backhand grip*.

Eastern grip: The most popular method of holding a racket for the forehand drive, in which the player "shakes hands" with the racket (held on edge), resting the palm on the back side of the handle, with the fingers and thumb closed naturally around it. With the Eastern grip (so-called because it was first used by East Coast American players), the racket face is neither open nor closed, but flat or vertical. also *shake-hands grip.* compare *baseball grip, chopper grip, Continental grip, service grip, Western grip.*

elbow: A slang term for a case of nerves suffered by a player at a crucial point in a match. Possibly an allusion to tightening or contracting the elbow and, thereby, restricting the swing when feeling stress. (fighting the elbow at match point)

end: Either of the two halves of a court occupied by one player or a side.

English grip: see *Continental grip.*

error: A mishit and failed attempt to make a return, resulting in the loss of the point. see *forced error, unforced error.*

face: The flat surface formed by the strings on either side of a racket. also *strings.*

fall: To bounce twice without being returned, as of a shot.

fast court: A court with a surface that allows the ball to skid, promoting a fast, low bounce. Fast courts favor a big serve and serve-and-volley game, and, consequently, are preferred by power players. Grass, wood, smooth concrete and asphalt, and most synthetic surfaces tend to make fast courts (the bounce and speed characteristics of synthetic surfaces can be varied). compare *slow court.*

1. fault: The failure to complete a legal serve, either by serving into the net or beyond the boundaries of the proper service court, swinging at and missing the ball altogether, or by serving from a position other than behind the baseline and between an imaginary extension of the center line and the proper side sideline. One fault is allowed for each serve, but two faults on a serve result in a lost point. The term "fault" comes from the Old French *faute*, meaning "mistake." see *double fault, foot fault.*

2. fault: To commit a fault while serving.

Federation Cup: An international tournament played annually between national teams and consisting of singles and doubles competition for women. Compar-

able to the Davis Cup for men, the Federation Cup competition was first held at the Queen's Club in London in 1963, where the United States team of Billie Jean King Moffitt (later King) and Darlene Hard defeated the Australian team of Margaret Court and Lesley Bowrey.

fifteen: The first point scored in a game for either player or side. see *point.*

fireballer: A player with a cannonball serve. also *big server.*

first court: The receiver's right service court. Called "first court" because each game begins with a serve delivered from the baseline behind the server's right court to the receiver's right court. also *deuce court, forehand court, right court.* compare *ad court, advantage court, backhand court, left court, left-hander's court, second court.*

first serve: The first service delivery of a point, usually the server's hardest and best serve. If a fault is made on the first serve, the second delivery is usually made more carefully in order to prevent a second fault and the loss of the point. compare *second serve.*

flat: Fast and straight with little or no spin, as of a stroke or serve.

flat racket, flat racket face: A racket held so that the racket face is vertical or perpendicular to the ground. also *square racket, square racket face.* compare *closed racket, closed racket face, open racket, open racket face.*

1. foot fault: A fault committed by the server in which a serve is delivered while walking or running, or from a position other than behind the baseline and between an imaginary extension of

EASTERN GRIP

the center line and the proper sideline. Stepping on or over the baseline before making contact with the ball is the most common foot fault. A second foot fault on a serve or a foot fault that follows any other kind of fault results in a lost point. see *fault, double fault.*

2. foot fault: To commit a foot fault while serving.

foot-fault judge: The official responsible for calling foot faults, positioned on a line with the server's baseline on the side of the court opposite the baseline judge. see *foot fault.*

force: To apply pressure by putting an opponent on the defensive, off balance, or out of position with one or more shots.

forced error: An error or point lost by a player because of a good shot made by the opponent (rather than because of a mistake). compare *unforced error.*

forcing shot: A shot that puts an opponent on the defensive off balance or out of position for the next shot.

forecourt: The area between the service line and the net, between the sidelines. compare *backcourt, midcourt.*

1. forehand: A stroke hit from the same side of the body as the racket hand, with the palm of the hand facing the direction of movement. compare *backhand, overhead.*

2. forehand: Of or pertaining to a stroke

FOREHAND

hit from the same side of the body as the racket hand, with the palm facing the direction of movement. (won the point with a forehand volley) compare *backhand, overhead.*

forehand court: The right service court, on the forehand side for most (right-handed) receivers. see *deuce court.*

forehand grip: Any of several methods of holding the racket for a forehand stroke. Forehand grips include the Eastern grip, the Continental grip, or chopper grip, the Western grip, and the two-handed baseball grip. see *baseball grip, chopper grip, Continental grip, Eastern grip, English grip, Western grip.*

forty: The third point made in a game by a player or side. When both players or sides reach forty, it is called deuce. see *deuce, point.*

French Championships: The French International Championships, an international tournament held annually at the Stade Roland Garros, one of the prestigious "Big Four" or "Grand Slam" events, and considered the unofficial world championships on clay courts. The French Championships were first held in 1891 and open only to French citizens. That year, the men's singles competition was won by J. Briggs, with B. Desjoyau and Legrand winning in doubles. Women's singles was added in 1897 and won by Cecelia Masson. In 1925, mixed and women's doubles were played, and for the first time, the tournament was opened to non-French citizens. The competition was dominated by French players, however, with two of the famous "Four Musketeers" winning the men's singles (Jean-Rene Lacoste, the "Alligator") and doubles (Lacoste and Jean Borotra, the "Bounding Basque") and a third, Jacques Brugnan, teamed with one of the game's all-time great woman players, Suzanne Lenglen, won the mixed doubles. Lenglen also won the women's singles and, with Diddi Vlasto, the women's doubles. also *French Open.*

French Open: see *French Championships.*

gallery: 1. The area for spectators at the sides and ends of a court. In the medieval game of court tennis, the indoor ancestor of modern tennis, galleries were netted openings in the side wall on one side of the court, and a ball played into them figured in the scoring. 2. The spectators at a match.

gallery play: 1. A showy or elaborate shot made for the benefit of the spectators. 2. A sensational get or shot.

game: 1. A single contest throughout which one player or side serves, and that ends when either player or side scores four points if the opponent has scored two points or less, or when either player or side scores two consecutive points if both have scored three points (deuce). compare *match, rubber, set, tie.* 2. The final or game-winning point, as the fourth point scored by either player or side when the opponent has scored two points or less, or the second consecutive point scored by either player or side after both have scored three points (deuce). see *game-set, game-set-match.*

game point: The point that, if won by the leading player or side, wins a game. compare *match point, set point.*

games-all: see *advantage set.*

game-set: The game-winning point in a set-winning game. compare *game-set-match.*

game-set-match: The game-winning point in a game that wins a set that wins a match. compare *game-set.*

garbage: A lob, dink, or other softly hit shot.

get: A successful return of a difficult shot. (saved the point with an incredible get on the low volley) also *retrieve.*

Ginny Circuit: A series of eight or more professional tournaments for new or developing women players, with a year-end championship tournament for the winner and runnerup in each event. Effectively a minor league for the Virginia Slims World Championship Series.

Grand Master: A former major championship winner over forty-five years old who participates in the professional Grand Masters tournament circuit. see *Grand Masters.*

Grand Masters: A professional tournament circuit for players over forty-five years old who have won a major championship. The Grand Masters circuit was inaugurated by Cincinnati businessman Al Bunis in 1973.

Grand Prix: see *Volvo Grand Prix.*

1. Grand Slam: The winning of the four major tennis championships in one year (the United States, French, Australian,

and Wimbledon Championships). The expression "Grand Slam" was coined by American Don Budge after he became the first to accomplish this rare feat in 1938. Only three other players have won the Grand Slam: Maureen "Little Mo" Connolly of the United States in 1953, and Australians Rod Laver in 1962 and 1969 and Margaret Court in 1970. In 1951, Frank Sedgman and Ken McGregor of Australia achieved the first Grand Slam in doubles.

2. Grand Slam: Of or pertaining to the four major tennis championships (the United States, French, Australian, and Wimbledon Championships). Australia's Margaret Court won more Grand Slam titles than any player in tennis history (sixty-two, including singles, doubles, and mixed doubles championships). Fellow Australian, Roy Emerson, holds the men's record with twenty-eight Grand Slam titles (twelve singles, sixteen doubles). also *Big Four.*

grass: Short for grass court. (has been unbeatable on grass).

grass court: A tennis court with a grass surface, which, unless damp or soft, usually provides a relatively fast surface which favors power players rather than touch players, retrievers, or baseliners. The first tennis courts were laid out on the lawns of Victorian England (hence, the name "lawn tennis"), with the oldest on record dating back to 1858 at Edgbaston, near Birmingham. Because of the amount of maintenance required for grass courts, alternative surfaces were already in use by the 1900s. Today, grass courts are comparatively rare. The oldest and most famous competition in tennis, however, is still played on the grass courts at Wimbledon. also *grass.* compare *clay court, concrete court, synthetic court.*

groove: To repeat a stroke with little effort because of practice and familiarity. (will try to move his opponent around so that he can't groove his returns)

ground game: A style of play which emphasizes groundstrokes.

groundie: Slang for a groundstroke.

groundstroke: A stroke made by hitting the ball after it has bounced (as a forehand or backhand drive). Groundstrokes are hit from the backcourt or behind the baseline. also *groundie*. compare *volley*.

hack: To make an awkward or poor swing at the ball.

hacker: An ordinary or, by professional standards, poor player. Popularized by 1966 United States Championships winner Fred Stolle of Australia, who humorously referred to himself as an "old hacker" after his victory from an unseeded position.

half court: The service court.

half-court line: The center service line. also *center line*.

1. half volley: A stroke in which the ball is hit just as it bounces up from the ground. also *early ball, pickup shot*. compare *volley*.

2. half volley: To hit the ball just as it bounces up from the ground. compare *volley*.

Hall of Fame: The International Tennis Hall of Fame.

hard court: 1. In the United States, a concrete or asphalt surface court (or a rarely seen wood surface court). 2. In Europe, Australia, and most of the world, a concrete, asphalt, or clay surface court (or a rarely seen wood surface court).

Har-Tru: A particular brand of synthetic clay surface popularized in the United States in the mid-1970s.

heavy ball: A ball that travels through the air at great speed and drops suddenly because of topspin. (doesn't look strong, but hits a surprisingly heavy ball)

high volley: see *offensive volley*.

hold one's serve: To win a game one is serving. (held her serve again to take the set) also *hold service*. compare *break, break service*.

hold service: see *hold one's serve*.

I formation: see *Australian formation*.

impervious surface: A smooth, non-porous playing surface such as sealed concrete or asphalt. A relatively inexpensive, virtually no-maintenance surface popularized in the United States (particularly on the West Coast) after World War II. compare *pervious surface*.

International Tennis Federation: The world governing body of tennis and guardian of the official rules of tennis. The International Tennis Federation (ITF) now recognizes twelve official tennis championships (including the four Grand Slam competitions), authorizes all major professional tournaments, and organizes and manages the Davis Cup and Federation Cup International Team Championships. Founded in 1913 as the International Lawn Tennis Federation, with thirteen affiliated nations (the United States joined in 1924), the ITF is headquartered in London, England.

International Tennis Hall of Fame: The institution that honors all-time tennis greats and outstanding contributors to the game. From 1954 when it was founded, through 1974, only American players were enshrined in the National Lawn Tennis Hall of Fame. In 1975, the present name was adopted and British tennis great Fred Perry became the first foreigner to be inducted. The International Tennis Hall of Fame is located at the Newport Casino in Newport, Rhode Island. also *Hall of Fame*.

ITF: The International Tennis Federation.

jag: To hit the ball in any manner necessary to get it over the net, regardless of style or form. Australian slang.

jam: To serve or drive the ball directly toward or close to an opponent in order to force a weak or clumsy return.

kick: The bounce of a hit ball, or the speed, height, or change of direction of a hit ball as it bounces off the ground, especially from a cut or twist stroke. also *break*.

kicker: An American twist serve.

kick serve: An American twist serve.

1. kill: To slam the ball past the opponent or to a place on the court from which it cannot be returned, most often with an overhead. (killed the lob for a winner) also *put away, slam, smash*.

2. kill: A kill shot.

kill shot: A slammed shot that is virtually unreturnable. (ended the long rally with a kill shot) also *kill, put-away, slam, smash*.

lawn tennis: The traditional name for tennis, adopted in England in the late 1850s to separate the new game (played on grass) from the older court tennis.

left court: The service court to the left of the center service line on the server's side of the net, and the service court diagonally opposite it (the receiver's left service court). see *advantage court*.

left-hander's court: The left service court. Called "left-hander's court" because it is on the usually favored (forehand) side for left-handers. see *advantage court.*

let: 1. A serve which hits the top of the net before landing in the proper service court. When this occurs, the serve does not count and is replayed. also *let cord, net.* 2. The signal or call by a net judge or umpire indicating that an otherwise legal serve has hit the top of the net and must be retaken. also *net.* 3. A stroke which does not count and must be replayed, as when a serve is delivered before the receiver is ready, when a linesman's decision is doubted, disputed, or reversed by the umpire, or when play is interrupted (as by an animal running through the court, etc.). When a let occurs, the whole point is replayed (including both services, unless the let involves the second serve itself, in which case only the second serve is retaken). 4. The signal or call by an umpire when a stroke does not count and must be replayed.

let cord: see *let.*

line ball: A ball that lands on or touches a line and is, therefore, good. also *liner.*

line judge: see *linesman, lineswoman.*

liner: A line ball.

linesman, lineswoman: One of ten officials in championship play who judge whether or not the ball is good (whether or not it has landed in or out of the court). Each linesman or lineswoman is responsible for one boundary line on his or her side of the net. Three are positioned behind the baselines in line with the sidelines (sideline judges) and the center line (center line judges). Two are positioned parallel to the sideline (on the umpire's side of the court) on each side of the net, in line with the service line (service line judges) and the baseline (baseline judges). The judgment of a linesman or a lineswoman may be appealed to and overturned by the umpire. also *line judge, line umpire.*

line umpire: see *linesman, lineswoman.*

lingering death: A form of tie-breaker officially approved by the ITF in 1976 which may be invoked if a set is tied after twelve or sixteen games. One additional game is played, with the winner being the first player or side to reach seven points, provided there is a two-point margin. Often called the "twelve-point tie-breaker," but "lingering death" is more appropriate because

of the possibility of a drawn out game if the score reaches 6-6. compare *sudden death.*

1. lob: A stroke in which the ball is hit into a high arc either to allow a player time to get back into position (defensive lob), or to loop the ball over an opponent at the net (offensive lob). Wimbledon winner (1878) P. Frank Hadow introduced the lob. see *defensive lob, offensive lob.*

2. lob: 1. To hit the ball into a high arc. 2. To hit a lob over a particular opponent. (lobbed him as he rushed the net)

long: Out because of landing behind the service line on a serve or behind the baseline on a stroke, resulting in a lost point (or on a first serve, a fault). compare *deep, short, wide.*

love: A score of zero for a player or side. A popular theory holds that "love" is a corruption of the French *l'oeuf,* meaning "egg," because of the resemblance of an egg to a zero. It is more probable that the present use equates "love" with "nothing," as in the expression "a labor of love," meaning a task performed for nothing (but love).

love game: A game in which the losing player or side scores no points. also *blitz.*

love set: A set in which the losing player or side fails to win a game. also *bagel, bagel job.* 2. A set in which the winning player or side wins six straight games (regardless of whether the opponent wins one or more games). A British usage.

low volley: see *defensive volley.*

Masters: see *Volvo Masters.*

match: A contest between two players or sides, usually decided over the best of

three sets, or over one set in informal play. Men's singles and doubles matches are decided over the best of five sets in major tournaments and championship play. also *rubber.*

match point: 1. A point that, if won by the player or side leading, will decide the match in favor of that player or side. compare *game point, set point.* 2. A situation in which the leading player or side can win a match by winning the next point. compare *game point, set point.*

Men's International Professional Tennis Council: The governing body of men's professional tennis, with nine members representing players, the International Tennis Federation, and tournament directors. Formed in 1974 by the ATP and ITF, and expanded a year later to include tournament directors, the Men's International Professional Tennis Council administers the Grand Prix circuit and is responsible for matters regarding tournament applications, scheduling, player conduct, and conditions of play. also *MIPTC, Pro Council.*

midcourt: The part of the court near the service line. compare *backcourt, forecourt.*

MIPTC: The Men's International Professional Tennis Council.

mixed doubles: Doubles competition between teams comprised of one male and one female. The first recorded mixed doubles championship event was played in 1879 at the Irish Championships.

1. net: 1. The webbed barrier stretched across the middle of the court over which the ball is hit. The net is suspended from a cord or metal cable from two 3-1/2-foot-high posts (the center of which are located 3 feet outside the sidelines) and slopes to a height of 3 feet at the center, held taut by a center strap, a 2-inch-wide piece of canvas that runs down the middle of the net and is anchored to the court. A 2 to 2-1/2-inch-wide tape band covers the cord or metal cable at the top of the net. English tennis pioneer Walter Clopton Wingfield's 1874 rules called for the net to be 4 feet, 8 inches high at the center, attached to 7-foot-high posts on either side of the court, then 21 feet wide. The 1875 Marylebone Cricket Club rules widened the court to 24 feet

and made the net 5 feet high at the posts and 4 feet at the center. At the first Wimbledon Championships in 1877, 4-foot, 9-inch posts were used to support a net that measured 3 feet, 3 inches high at the center. The net posts were lowered to 4 feet in 1880, and to the present height in 1882. 2. see *let.*

2. net: To hit the ball into the net, resulting in the loss of the point. (netted what should have been an easy return)

net cord: 1. A shot that hits the top of the net then drops into the opponent's court. 2. The cord or metal cable that supports a net.

net-cord judge: see *net judge.*

net game: 1. A style of play in which a player stays close to the net whenever possible in order to volley the ball. compare *baseline game.* 2. Strokes (usually volleys) played from the forecourt close to the net. also *net play.* compare *baseline game.*

net judge: An official seated at one end of the net (below the umpire's chair) who is responsible for detecting and calling lets on a serve. When the ball is being served the net judge rests a hand on top of the net in order to be able to feel whether the ball hits the net. If a let is called, the serve is retaken. also *net-cord judge.*

netman: Slang for a tennis player.

net man: The partner in doubles who plays close to the net while his teammate serves.

net play: see *net game.*

net rusher: A player who regularly attacks the net after serving and whenever possible during a rally to be in position to volley. compare *baseliner, power player, retriever, shotmaker, touch player.*

no-ad: A method of scoring pioneered by tennis innovator Jimmy Van Alen in which the traditional love, fifteen, thirty, forty are replaced with one, two, three, four. Deuce is eliminated, the first player or side to reach four wins (when the score is tied at 3-3, the receiver is given the choice of courts for game point). No-ad scoring is presently used by Team Tennis. also *VASSS.*

no-man's land: Slang for the backcourt, or between the service line and the baseline. Called no-man's land because players standing there are usually too far forward to play groundstrokes and too far back from the net for offensive volleys, and frequently are forced to make awkward shots when the ball bounces at or near their feet. also *deep court.*

not up: Not playable. Called when a player hits the ball just as or after it bounces for the second time, or half volleys the ball down to the ground from where it then bounces over the net. The net judge (or the offending player if there are no officials) usually makes the call, which results in the loss of the point.

offensive lob: A lob hit deep into the backcourt, over the head of an opponent at the net. In 1878, P. Frank Hadow introduced the offensive lob to defeat the volleying of Spencer W. Gore at Wimbledon for the singles championship. compare *defensive lob.*

offensive volley: A volley that is made (usually from above the level of the net) in order to catch the opponent off guard by means of speed or placement. also *high volley.* compare *defensive volley, low volley.*

open: For both amateurs and professionals, as of a tournament. In the early days of tennis, professionals were always barred from competing. At that time, "open" meant that a competition was not restricted to the members of a club or the residents of a certain city, state, or country. The first such "open" on record was the inaugural Wimbledon Championship in 1877. The first "open" tournament in the modern sense of the word was the 1968 British Hard Court Championships, in which Ken Rosewall defeated Rod Laver in men's singles and Virginia Wade defeated Winnie Shaw to win the women's singles title. All major championship tournaments are now open competitions.

open grip: A grip that makes the racket face tilt upwards toward the sky, as with the chopper or Continental grip. compare *closed grip.*

open racket, open racket face: A racket held so that the racket face is tilted upwards toward the sky. compare *closed racket, closed racket face, flat racket, flat racket face.*

open up the court: 1. To draw an opponent away from a part of the court which is then left unguarded for the next shot. (opened up the backcourt with a little chip just over the net) 2. To

move to one part of the court and thus, leave another area unguarded.

overdrive: To hit the ball too hard and drive it over the opponent's baseline, resulting in the loss of the point.

1. overhead: A stroke (most often a smash) hit from above the head, much like a serve. Among the early players noted for the overhead were Maurice McLoughlin, the "California Comet," whose cannonball serves and overheads stunned the 1913 Wimbledon spectators, and 1932 Wimbledon singles champion Ellsworth Vines, also feared for his serves and overheads. compare *backhand, forehand.*

2. overhead: Of or pertaining to a stroke hit over the head, as of a smash or volley. (ended the rally with an overhead smash) compare *backhand, forehand.*

overspin: see *topspin.*

1. pace: The speed of a hit ball. A British term used first in billiards, cricket, and football (soccer), and derived from the Latin *passus,* meaning "rate of movement."

2. pace: To hit the ball at a controlled speed. (a highly paced first serve)

pair: A doubles team.

partner: A teammate on a doubles team.

1. pass: A passing shot.

2. pass: To make a passing shot against a particular opponent.

passing shot: A ball driven past and beyond the reach of an opponent in the forecourt or midcourt area. also *pass, pass shot.*

pass shot: A passing shot.

pervious surface: A porous court surface that permits water to filter through. compare *impervious surface.*

pickup shot: A half volley.

place: To hit a ball so that it goes precisely where intended. (fooled him with a well-placed drop shot)

placement: 1. A perfectly placed shot that the opponent cannot reach, a clean winner. 2. The placing of a shot or shots.

1. poach: To cross in front of a doubles partner to volley a ball that would normally be played by the partner. An aggressive tactic that can backfire if the volley is returned to the part of the court left undefended by the poaching player. The term "poach" is from the Old French *pochier,* meaning originally

321

"to put into a bag" and, in later usage, "to trespass" or "to steal." Poaching was used first by male partners in mixed doubles matches in the late 1870s.

2. poach: The act or an instance of poaching. (angled the winner with a courageous poach)

point: The basic scoring unit, with a game being won by the first player or side to win four points, unless both sides reach three points ("deuce") after which the game is won by the first to win two consecutive points. In the traditional method of scoring tennis, the first point is "fifteen," the second, "thirty," the third, "forty," and the fourth, "game" (except after "deuce," after which the first point won by either side is "advantage," and the second consecutive point, "game"). Scoring by fifteens ("forty") was shortened from "forty-five") began in the Middle Ages with the original French indoor tennis game, *jeu de paume* which was sixty points divided into four parts of fifteen. This was probably due to the medieval importance of the sexagesimal system, prevalent in weights and measures, money, and, of course, time (sixty seconds in a minute, sixty minutes in an hour). When lawn tennis was first played in 1858, variations of rackets scoring were used, and this practice was maintained in the 1874 rules published by tennis pioneer Major Walter Clopton Wingfield and in the first official rules published a year later by the Marylebone Cricket Club. Finally, in 1877, at the urging of cofounder Henry Jones, the All England Croquet and Lawn Tennis Club initiated the clock system for the inaugural Wimbledon Championship; fifteen (minutes) for the first point, thirty (minutes) for the second, forty-five (minutes)—later changed to forty, possibly because it was easier to say or to hear when called out—for the third, and game at one hour. see *VASSS*.

point penalty: A penalty of one point assessed by the umpire against a player for conduct violations such as delaying the game, throwing or kicking the racket or ball, verbal or physical abuse, or obscenities. Pioneered by the men's professional Grand Prix circuit in 1976, the penalty point provision allows the umpire to assess penalties of a point or a game, depending on the gravity or frequency of violations.

post: One of the 3-1/2 foot uprights that support the net.

power game: see *big game*.

power player: A player whose style of play emphasizes a big serve and powerful strokes, together with aggressive net play. Though the term was coined much later, the first great power player was 1912 United States Championships singles winner Maurice McLoughlin. The 1932 Wimbledon singles champion, Ellsworth Vines, was another early example, but the term "power player" is most often associated with America's post-World War II Davis Cup teams which featured Jack Kramer, Ted Schroeder, and Pancho Gonzalez. compare *baseliner, net rusher, retriever, shotmaker, touch player*.

power tennis: see *big game*.

Pro Council: The Men's International Professional Tennis Council.

puddler: Slang for a player who regularly chips shots just over the net, forcing opponents to stoop forward to retrieve them, as from a puddle.

put away: To hit a kill shot. (was able to

RACKET

put away his opponent's defensive lob) also *kill, slam, smash.*

put-away: A kill shot. also *kill, slam, smash.*

racket: The implement with which the ball is struck, an oval frame strung with crossing gut (lamb intestines) or nylon strings, and a long, straight handle. Modern racket frames may be constructed of wood, steel, aluminum, fiberglass or graphite. There are no rules that govern the exact size or shape of a racket, but most are between 25 and 27 inches long and weigh between 12-1/2 and 16-1/2 ounces. The word "racket" is from the Arabic *rahah,* meaning "palm of the hand" and was probably brought back to France from the Crusades. In the medieval French version of tennis, the palm of the hand itself was used to hit the ball, thus the name *jeu de paume,* literally "play of palm." Gloves and crude wooden paddles followed, and early in the sixteenth century, small strung *racquettes* were introduced. Larger rackets with a longer handle became popular in the eighteenth century, and by the late 1800s, the racket had evolved into the basic size and configuration that remains the standard today, although after steel rackets were introduced in 1967, other new frame materials such as aluminum, fiberglass, and graphite began to find favor. In 1976, rackets with "oversized" heads appeared. With approximately the same weight and balance as conventional models, these revolutionary rackets have twice the hitting area.

1. rally: An exchange of shots by opponents until one side fails to make a good return.

2. rally: 1. To engage in a rally. (rallied from the backcourt until he could move to the net) 2. To warm up before a game by exchanging practice strokes with one's opponent.

readiness position: see *alert position.*

receiver: The player to whom the ball is served. compare *server.*

1. referee: The official in charge of a tournament. Though not involved with the actual conduct of individual matches, the referee may be asked to come to the court in order to interpret a rule.

2. referee: To act as a referee for a tournament.

1. retrieve: To return a shot that is diffi-

cult to handle or reach. (had to get back in position after retrieving the lob)

2. retrieve: The act or an instance of returning a shot that is difficult to handle or reach. also *get.*

retriever: A player who emphasizes a defensive style of play, relying on the ability to retrieve whatever strokes are played by the opponent, rather than aggressive tactics like serve-and-volley. compare *baseliner, net rusher, power player, shotmaker, touch player.*

1. return: To hit a ball played by an opponent back over the net.

2. return: The act or an instance of hitting a ball played by an opponent back over the net.

reverse spin: see *underspin.*

reverse twist: An unorthodox serve in which topspin is imparted with an upward and inward motion of the racket as the ball is struck, causing it to bounce high and to the receiver's right side when it hits the ground. Malcolm D. Whitman introduced the reverse twist to the tennis world at the 1900 Davis Cup competition in Boston, where the unconventional and awkward delivery bewildered his British opponents and played an important part in the American team's victory. compare *American twist.*

right court: The service court to the right of the center service line on the server's side of the net, and the service court diagonally opposite it (the receiver's right service court). see *first court.*

round: A stage in an elimination tournament consisting of a series of matches, the winners of which advance to the next stage.

round robin: A tournament in which every player or side meets every other player or side in turn, with the final standings determined by the overall won-lost records. Originally, a "round robin" was a written complaint with the names of its signers arranged in a circle to disguise the order in which they signed.

rubber: A British expression for match.

run around the backhand: To avoid one's backhand, to position oneself or move so as to insure a stroke will be played on one's forehand side.

runback: The area at either end of the court between the baseline and the backstop. also *back room.*

run down: To run after and return a shot

hit to another part of the court. (ran down the crosscourt drive to save the point)

run out a set: To win all of the remaining games in a set.

rush the net: see *attack the net.*

second court: The receiver's left service court. Called "second court" because the ball is delivered from the baseline behind the server's left court to the receiver's left court on the second service turn in a game. see *advantage court.*

second serve: A serve made after a fault has been declared on the first serve. Usually a more conservative delivery, with more emphasis given to placement than power to prevent a second fault and the loss of the point. compare *first serve.*

1. seed: 1. To schedule top players within a draw to insure that they won't meet before the later rounds of a tournament. In major tournaments, professional players are seeded according to computer rankings and performance records. Some seeding was first tried at Wimbledon in 1924, with the singles events being completely seeded in 1927. From the Old English *saed,* meaning in agriculture "to separate or select from a group." 2. To rank players for a tournament. A seeded player is a player who is ranked.

2. seed: A player who has been seeded in a tournament. (will face the top seed in the final)

1. serve: 1. To put the ball in play with a serve. Derived from the Old French *servir,* meaning "to work as a servant" and originally, the Latin *servus,* meaning "slave." In the medieval game of court tennis, the serve was merely a convenient way of starting a rally, and often the ball was served by someone other than a player, as by a servant. 2. To act as the server for a particular game. (will serve the first game)

2. serve: 1. The method or act of putting the ball in play at the beginning of each point. In a serve, the ball is thrown into the air and hit (usually with an overhead stroke) over the net into the service court diagonally opposite the server (beginning with the right court and alternating with each point). To deliver a serve, the server must stand with both feet at rest behind the baseline in back

SERVICE

of the proper service court between an imaginary extension of the center line and the sideline (inside sideline for singles, outside for doubles). The ball must be thrown into the air and struck before it hits the ground (a player with one arm may project the ball into the air with the racket). The server may not walk or run, nor touch any area with either foot outside the prescribed area until the ball is struck ("foot fault"). If the rules of service are broken on a serve, or if the serve fails to reach the proper service court on the first delivery ("first serve"), a fault is declared and the server is given a second opportunity ("second serve"). If a fault occurs on the second serve, the point is lost. If an otherwise legal serve hits the top of the net before landing in the proper service court, or if a serve is delivered before the receiver is ready, a let is called, and the serve is retaken (regardless of whether it occurs on the first or second serve). Only one player serves in a game. In singles, players alternate as the server throughout the games of a match. In doubles, service is alternated between the pairs with all four players serving in turn, and with the receivers receiving from the same court throughout a set. (The order of service or the court from which either partner receives may be changed at the end of each set.) also *delivery, service.* 2. The turn or right of a player or side to serve. (will spin the racket to determine whose serve it is) also *service.* 3. A stroke made with a service. (aced him with a hard, flat serve) also *delivery, service.*

serve-and-volley: A style of play in which the server rushes the net after each serve in order to be in position to volley. also *serve-volley.*

serve and volley: To rush the net after serving, to play a serve-and-volley style of game.

server: The player who serves or whose turn it is to serve.

serve-volley: see *serve-and-volley.*

service: see *serve.*

service ace: see *ace.*

service box: Slang for a service court.

service break: The act or an instance of a player winning a game against the server. also *break.*

service court: Either of two 13-1/2-foot-wide by 21-foot-deep rectangular areas on each side of the court, bounded by the net, the service sideline, the service line and the center line (which separates them). In order to be legal, a serve must be delivered into the proper service court. also *court, service box.* see *left court, right court.*

service grip: The Continental grip. also *chopper grip, English grip.*

service line: The line on either side of the court that extends between the singles sidelines parallel to and 21 feet from the net, and which marks the rear boundary of the two service courts. The service line was originally drawn 26 feet from the net for the first Wimbledon Championship in 1877, and was changed to the present 21 feet for the 1880 event.

service line judge: Either of two linesmen or lineswomen responsible for watching the service line on serves in tournament play and calling when a ball lands outside the proper service court. Service line judges are positioned on a line with the service lines on the same side of the court as the umpire.

service sideline: The portion of the singles sideline that lies between the net and the service line, and that marks the outside boundary of the service court.

service winner: A serve that the receiver hits but is unable to return. compare *ace, ace on service, service ace.*

set: 1. The next to highest scoring unit, a group of games that is won by the first player or side to win at least six games with a two-game margin, or by a tie-breaker. "Set" is from the Old French *sette* meaning "sequence." see *tie-breaker.* compare *game, match, rubber, tie.* 2. The next to highest scoring unit, a group of games that is won by the first player or side to win thirty-one points in a tournament using VASSS single point scoring, or if the score is tied at 30-30, the first to win a tie-breaker. see *tie-breaker, VASSS.*

set point: 1. A point that, if won by the player or side leading, will decide the set in favor of that player or side. compare *game point, match point.* 2. A situation in which the leading player or side can win a set by winning the next point. compare *game point, match point.*

setter: A match with a specified number of sets. (will play a three-setter)

setup: A soft shot, often a high lob hit to the forecourt, that can be easily put away. also *sitter.*

shake-hands grip: The Eastern grip.

short: In the front part of the forecourt near the net. (dinked the ball short) compare *deep, long, wide.*

short ball: A ball hit short to the forecourt, especially when the opponent is playing deep.

shot: The act or an instance of hitting the ball toward the opposing court with the racket. also *stroke.*

shotmaker: A player whose style of play emphasizes placement and a variety of accurate rather than powerful strokes. also *touch player.* compare *baseliner, net rusher, power player.*

sideline: A side boundary, either for the singles court or the doubles court, extending between the baselines (27 feet apart for singles, 36 feet apart for doubles). Between the net and the service line, the singles sidelines serve as the side boundaries of the service courts ("service sidelines").

sideline judge: Any of four linesmen or lineswomen (two at each end of the court) who are responsible for watching the sidelines in tournament play and calling when a ball lands outside the court. Sideline judges are positioned in line with the sidelines behind the baselines.

sidespin: Spin around a vertical or near vertical axis imparted to the ball by brushing the racket face across the ball at the moment of contact, as with a slicing or cutting stroke. Sidespin causes the ball to curve in flight and to bounce or break to the side on landing (which side depends on the direction of the spin). compare *backspin, chop, curl, overspin, reverse spin, topspin, twist, underspin.*

singles: A game or match between two players, played on a singles court that does not utilize the two 4-1/2-foot alleys and baseline extensions normally marked outside the sidelines for doubles play. The first men's singles championship tournament was at Wimbledon in 1877, and won by S.W. Gore. The first women's singles championship was held in Ireland in 1879, and won by May Langrishe.

singles court: The 78-foot-long by 27-foot-wide rectangular playing area for singles, not including the two 4-1/2-foot alleys and baseline extensions normally marked outside the sidelines of a singles court. The present outside dimensions for a singles court were adopted in 1877 by the All England Croquet and Lawn Tennis Club for the inaugural Wimbledon Championship.

singles sideline: One of the two side boundaries for a singles court, 27 feet apart and extending between the baselines. Between the service lines, the singles sidelines are the side boundaries of the service courts (service sidelines).

sissy game: A derisive description of a game or a style of play characterized by soft lobs, slices, and weak groundstrokes, and by a lack of hard shots and aggressive play.

sitter: see *setup.*

1. slam: A smash.

2. slam: To execute a smash.

1. slice: 1. A stroke in which underspin and sidespin are imparted to the ball by hitting under and across it with an open racket face. With a slice, the ball curves in flight and bounces low and to the side on landing (which side depends on the direction of the sidespin). "Slice" is from the Old French *esclice* meaning "splinter." 2. Short for slice serve.

2. slice: 1. To hit a ball with a slicing motion of the racket to impart underspin and sidespin. 2. To hit or serve a slice.

slice serve: A serve hit with a slicing motion to impart underspin and sidespin. A slice serve curves in flight and bounces low and to the side (which side depends on the direction of the sidespin), and is often used for a second serve. also *slice.*

slowball: To use soft shots such as lobs, chips, slices, and drop shots against an opponent. (changed his tactics and slowballed him in the second game)

slow court: A court with a surface that produces a high bounce, such as clay or claylike surfaces. Slow courts favor shotmakers and touch players rather than serve-and-volley or power players. compare *fast court.*

slow court game: 1. A style of play that emphasizes lobs, sliced and chipped strokes, and a strong and steady baseline game. 2. The lobs, chips, slices, drop shots, and accurate groundstrokes that are most effective on a slow court.

1. smash: A hard overhead stroke in which the ball is hit down at the opposing court, often for a winner. It is believed that Englishman O.E. Woodhouse, winner of the title "Champion of America" at the first open tournament in the United States held at the Staten Island Cricket and Baseball Club in 1880, introduced the smash. also *kill, kill shot, put-away, slam.*

2. smash: To execute a smash. also *kill, put away, slam.*

softie: A dink. also *chip.*

spaghetti racket: see *double-strung racket.*

1. spin: Rotation imparted to the ball to affect its line of flight and the way it bounces. see *sidespin, topspin, underspin.*

2. spin: To hit a shot with spin on the ball. (spun her return crosscourt)

spin it in: To deliver a serve with spin (as a slice serve) rather than trying to hit it hard.

square racket, square racket face: see *flat racket, flat racket face.*

steelie: Slang for a steel frame racket. The steel racket was introduced in 1967 by Wilson Sporting Goods from a design by former French tennis great Rene Lacoste. Used at the United States Championships at Forest Hills that year by women's singles winner Billie Jean King among others, the steel frame racket was the first of a succession of revolutionary racket designs featuring new materials such as aluminum, fiber glass, and graphite.

stop volley: A soft volley in which the ball drops just over the net, used when the opponent is in the backcourt.

straight sets: Without losing a set, consecutive victories. (won the match in straight sets)

1. string: One of the nylon or gut (lamb intestines) cords that are woven in the head of a racket to provide a hitting surface.

2. string: To put strings in a racket, to weave and properly tension the strings in the head of a racket.

strings: The flat hitting surface. also *face.*

stroke: 1. A swing of the racket that is intended to hit the ball. (a slicing stroke) 2. A shot that results from hitting the ball with the racket.

sudden death: A tie-breaker of a specified length that may be invoked if a set is tied after twelve or sixteen games. One form, pioneered by tennis scoring innovator Jimmy Van Alen, is the nine-point sudden death, in which a single extra game is played, with the first player or side to reach five points winning. Another is the thirteen-point sudden death, in which the winner is the first player or side to reach seven points in the extra game. compare *lingering death.*

Supreme Court: A particular brand of synthetic carpet playing surface used in many professional indoor tournaments.

sweet spot: The optimum hitting area in the middle of the racket face, variable according to the size and design of the racket head and the gauge and tension of the strings. An enlarged sweet spot is the main advantage of the rackets with "oversized" heads introduced in 1976.

take the net: see *attack the net.*

tandem formation: see *Australian formation.*

tape: 1. The 2 to 2-1/2-inch-wide band of tape (usually canvas) that covers the net cord at the top of the net. 2. Slang for a boundary line because of the occasional use of tape to mark the boundary lines on clay courts. also *chalk.*

team tennis: A tennis competition between teams of players (usually two men and two women), with a match consisting of single sets in men's singles, women's singles, men's doubles, women's doubles, and mixed doubles. The winner of the match is the side that wins the most games.

Team Tennis: A one-month series of professional matches between teams of four players (two men and two women) consisting of single sets in men's singles, women's singles, men's doubles, women's doubles, and mixed doubles. No-ad scoring is used, and a tied set is decided by a nine-point tie-breaker, or, if the game decides the match, by a thirteen-point tie-breaker. A reorganization of the World Team Tennis circuit of the mid-1970s, Team Tennis began operating in 1981 with four teams and increased to eight teams in 1982. Headed by tennis entrepreneur Larry King, Team Tennis scheduled a twelve-team circuit for the 1983 season. see *no-ad, tie-breaker.*

tennis: A game between two players

(singles) or two teams of two players (doubles) played on a rectangular court (78 feet long by 27 feet wide for singles, or 36 feet wide for doubles), and in which players in each half of the court, using strung rackets, hit a small inflated felt-covered rubber ball over a net across the middle of the court until one side wins a point by hitting a stroke that lands within the opponent's court and cannot be returned. On each point play begins with a serve, a stroke hit from a stationary position behind the baseline in which the ball is thrown into the air and hit to the diagonally opposite service court. If the serve fails to land in the proper service court, or if any of the rules of service are broken, a fault is declared and the server is given another chance to serve. A second fault (double fault) results in the loss of the point. One player serves each game with service alternating between players in successive games (in doubles, service alternates between sides with all four players serving in turn). The first player or side to reach four points (traditionally called "fifteen," "thirty," "forty," and "game," or in no-ad scoring, "one," "two," "three," and "four") wins a game, provided there is a two-point margin. If each side reaches three points ("deuce"), the first side to score two consecutive points thereafter wins the game (in no-ad scoring, deuce is eliminated, and a 3-3 tie is decided by the next point). Groups of games are arranged in sets, with the first player or side to win six games winning the set, providing there is a two-game margin. If a set is tied after twelve games, extra games are played until one side or the other wins by a two-game margin (or the set is decided by a single tie-breaker game). A match is decided on the basis of the best of three sets, or in men's singles and doubles events in major tournaments, the best of five sets (or if the VASSS single point scoring system is used, on the basis of total points won, with the first side to win thirty-one points the winner, or if the score is 30-30, the side that wins a tie-breaker). Though a number of theories have been put forward regarding the origin of the word "tennis," some alluding to the ancient Greek game of *phennis* or a reported Roman game *teniludius*, or to the single early mention of a *tenes* game in western literature in the fourteenth century *Chronicles of Florence* by Italy's Donato Velluti, the most popular belief is that the French *tenez*, meaning roughly "take heed," was called out at the beginning of a game, and eventually came to represent the game. also *lawn tennis*.

tennis ball: A pressurized rubber sphere between 2-1/2 and 2-5/8 inches in diameter and weighing between 2 and 2-1/16 ounces, covered with a nap of wool and nylon (usually white or yellow). Though specific regulations govern the bounce and compression characteristics to insure a certain amount of uniformity, differences exist between the balls used in Europe and the United States. The American ball has more pressure, favoring the power game more than the softer European ball. In critical tournament play, the nap thickness of the ball varies according to the court surface in use, with hard courts calling for a thick nap, grass, a thin nap, and clay, in between. Early court tennis balls were made of thin leather or cloth stuffed with feathers, hair, or meal. Later, cloth centers were used, tightly bound with string and covered with flannel. The invention of a rubber ball (which would bounce on grass) made lawn tennis possible in the nineteenth century. The first regulations for a tennis ball were adopted in 1877 for the inaugural Wimbledon Championship and called for a ball between 2-1/4 and 2-5/8 inches in diameter and weighing between 1-1/4 and 1-1/2 ounces. In 1924, the first stitchless ball with cemented seams appeared. The result was an increase in speed and a lessening of the effects of spin. A pressure increase in 1931 was the last major change in the ball.

tennis court: see *court*.

tennis elbow: Pain and inflammation in the tendons around the elbow, the result of the excessive twisting motions of the hand and the jars and strains sustained while playing tennis.

thirty: The second point made in a game by a player or side. see *point*.

throat: The thin part of a racket between the head and handle.

tie: A British and European expression for a

team match between countries (such as the Davis Cup and Federation Cup). compare *game, match, rubber, set.*

tie-break: A tie-breaker.

tie-breaker: One of several methods of ending a set tied after twelve or sixteen games by playing one extra game instead of the traditional deuce or advantage set. Tie-breakers are either sudden death, in which the extra game ends with a sudden death point when the score is 4-4 in a nine-point sudden death or 6-6 in a thirteen-point sudden death, or lingering death, in which the extra game is extended until one side wins by a margin of two points. also *tie-break.* see *lingering death, sudden death.*

top: To impart topspin to the ball on a stroke.

top seed: The player judged by a tournament committee to be the favorite to win a tournament based on performance records and computer rankings and scheduled within the draw so as not to meet other favorites until the later rounds of the competition.

topspin: Forward spin around a horizontal axis imparted to the ball by brushing the racket face upward and over the ball at the moment of contact. Topspin causes the ball to drop deceptively and bounce high on landing. also *overspin.* compare *backspin, chop, curl, reverse spin, sidespin, twist, underspin.*

touch: Subtle and precise control in the placement of strokes. (may have lost a step with age, but he still has great touch)

touch player: A player whose style of play emphasizes precise control, placement, and a variety of accurate rather than powerful strokes. also *shotmaker.* compare *baseliner, net rusher, power player.*

tour: A scheduled series of professional tournaments. also *circuit.*

tramline, tramlines: British slang for alley. see *alley.*

triple: The winning of the singles, doubles, and mixed doubles events at a tournament.

twist: The combination of topspin and sidespin imparted to a ball, as with an American twist or reverse twist serve. Twist causes the ball to drop sharply and bounce high and to one side on landing (which side depends on the direction of the sidespin). compare *backspin, chop, curl, overspin, reverse spin, sidespin, topspin, underspin.*

two-handed backhand: A backhand stroke in which the racket hand is positioned normally with the other hand placed above it on the handle in a forehand grip. The strength and control of the backhand are improved with the two-handed shot, but reach and mobility may be somewhat restricted. Vivian B. McGrath, 1937 Australian men's singles champion, was the first world-class player to use a two-handed backhand.

two-handed player: A player who grips the racket with two hands to make forehand or backhand strokes, or both. Though two-handed players can be more vulnerable to angles and passing shots due to restricted reach and mobility, strength and control are considerably improved on the two-hand side. The first successful two-handed player was Australian Vivian B. McGrath, who defeated his countryman John Bromwich, another exponent of the two-hand technique, to become the 1937 Australian men's singles champion. McGrath, Bromwich, and fellow Australian Geoff Brown all played their backhand as a two-handed stroke, but in the post-World War II years, a two-handed forehand was first seen with the rise to prominence of popular Pancho Segura of Ecuador. In the 1970s, the two-handed technique was spotlighted again with the emergence of Jimmy Connors and Chris Evert (later Lloyd). also *double-fisted player, double-handed player.*

1. **umpire:** The official in charge of a match, positioned in a raised chair at one end of the net. The umpire keeps and calls out the score and is the final arbiter on questions of fact and judgment. An umpire may reverse the decision of a linesman or judge on appeal and is empowered to default a player for bad conduct. (In men's Grand Prix events, the umpire may also impose point penalties for rules infractions.) The first umpire was used at the inaugural Wimbledon Championship in 1877. To give him an overview of the match, the umpire's chair was placed on top of a table, the origin of today's raised chair. also *chair umpire.*

2. umpire: To act as an umpire for a match.

underspin: Backward rotation around a horizontal axis (bottom of the ball rotates in the direction of flight) imparted to a ball by brushing the racket face downward and under the ball at the moment of contact, as with a chop. Underspin slows the flight of a ball and can cause it to skid low, stop, or even recoil slightly on landing, depending on the type and condition of the playing surface and the amount of underspin applied. also *chop, backspin, reverse spin.* compare *curl, overspin, topspin, twist.*

unforced error: A point lost because of a mistake (such as hitting the ball out, or into the net) rather than a good shot by the opponent. compare *forced error.*

United States Championships: An international tournament held annually at the USTA National Tennis Center in Flushing Meadow Park, New York, one of the prestigious "Big Four" or "Grand Slam" events. The first United States Championships were held on the grass courts of the Newport Casino in Newport, Rhode Island, in 1881, with Richard D. Sears winning the men's singles competition in straight sets, and C.M. Clark and F.W. Taylor winning the men's doubles title. From 1915 through 1920, the Championships were held at the West Side Tennis Club in Forest Hills, New York. After three years at the Germantown Cricket Club in Philadelphia, the event was moved back to Forest Hills, where it stayed until moving to its present location in 1978. The first United States women's singles championship was held in 1887 at the Philadelphia Cricket Club and won by Miss Ellen Hansell. Miss Ellen Roosevelt and Miss Grace W. Roosevelt won the first women's doubles championship in 1890. The first mixed doubles championship was won by C. Hobart and Miss M.E. Cahill in 1892. All five events have been played at one location since the first open tournament in 1968. also *United States Open, United States Open Championships.*

United States Open, United States Open Championships: The United States Championships.

United States Tennis Association: The national governing body for amateur tennis in the United States. Formed in 1881, the then United States National Lawn Tennis Association was the world's first national governing body for tennis. In 1920, the word "national" was dropped from the name, and in 1924, the United States body became a member of the International Tennis Federation (then called the International Lawn Tennis Federation). In 1975, the name was officially changed to the United States Tennis Association (USTA). The USTA has conducted the United States Championships (which became the United States Open in 1968) since 1881.

up and back: A popular doubles strategy in which one partner plays close to the net while the other plays in the backcourt.

USTA: The United States Tennis Association.

Van Alen Streamlined Scoring System: see *VASSS.*

vantage: see *advantage.*

VASSS: The Van Alen Streamlined Scoring System. Any of several simplified methods of scoring pioneered by tennis innovator Jimmy Van Alen, all of which eliminate the provision of deuce in a game or set (advantage set), and therefore, prevent the marathon matches that sometimes occur with traditional scoring methods. Van Alen's no-ad system substitutes "zero," "one," "two," "three," and "four" for the more complicated "love," "fifteen," "thirty," "forty," and "game," with the winner being the first player or side to win four points. His sudden death nine-point tie-breaker replaces advantage sets with a single game, the winner of which is the first player or side to reach five. Under Van Alen's tournament scoring system, the first player or side to reach thirty-one points wins the set, with a tie-breaker to settle a 30-30 tie. see *no-ad, sudden death, tie-breaker.*

Virginia Slims World Championships: The season-ending championship tournament for the top twelve singles and six doubles finishers of the Virginia Slims World Championship Series. Along with Wimbledon and the United States Open, the Virginia Slims World Championships ranks as one of the three most important professional tournaments for women players.

Virginia Slims World Championship Series: A women's professional tennis series that links the most prestigious tennis tournaments (including the Grand Slam events) in a year-long worldwide circuit on which players earn points as well as prize money for their performance in each event. These points go toward a spot in the Virginia Slims World Championships (held at the end of the season) and toward a share in a bonus pool of prize money, distributed among the circuit's leading point-winning singles and doubles players at the conclusion of the series. To be eligible for the bonus pool, a player must agree to play in at least eleven WTA-approved major tournaments, not including Grand Slam events. The Virginia Slims World Championship Series is administered by the Women's International Professional Tennis Council. see *Virginia Slims World Championships.*

1. volley: A stroke in which the ball is hit in the air before it bounces. The word "volley" is from the Middle French *volee,* meaning "flight," and originally, the Latin *volare,* meaning "to fly." The volley was introduced in the finals of the inaugural Wimbledon Championship in 1877 by singles winner Spencer W. Gore. Other early volley exponents were 1881 United States singles champion Richard Sears, England's famous Renshaw twins of the 1880s, William and Ernest, and 1907 Wimbledon singles champion, the Australian left-hander, Norman Brooks. see *early ball.* compare *half volley, pickup shot.*

2. volley: To hit a ball in the air before it bounces. compare *half volley.*

Volvo Grand Prix: A men's professional tennis circuit that links the most prestigious tennis tournaments in a year-long worldwide circuit on which players earn points as well as prize money for their performance in each event. These points go toward a spot in the year-end Volvo Masters and toward a share in a bonus pool of prize money, distributed among the circuit's leading point-winning singles and doubles players at the conclusion of the Grand Prix year. To be eligible to compete in the Grand Prix, a player must agree to play in twelve designated tournaments during the year in the highest classification of tournament for which his ranking makes

him eligible. The four Grand Slam events make up the first or highest classification group, followed in descending order by the Super Series tournaments and Regular Series tournaments, which differ in the amount of prize money offered. Now administrated by the Men's International Professional Tennis Council, the Grand Prix circuit was initiated in 1970 through the efforts of former tennis great Jack Kramer. see *computer rankings, designated tournament, designations, Volvo Masters.*

Volvo Masters: The championship tournament of the Volvo Grand Prix circuit, played annually at Madison Square Garden in New York between the circuit's eight top singles players and the four top doubles teams. The first Masters Tournament, then called the Grand Prix Masters, was played in 1970 in Tokyo, with Stan Smith winning both the singles championship and, teamed with Ken Rosewall, the doubles title. also *Masters.*

waiting position: see *alert position.*

walk-in: see *bye.*

walkover: 1. A game, set, or match in which a winner is declared because the opponent defaults. 2. Slang for a particularly one-sided game, set, or match.

WCT: World Championship Tennis. A year-long worldwide series of twenty men's professional tournaments, divided into seasonal circuits of fall, winter, and spring, each concluding with an eight-man championship final. Players earn points as well as prize money for their performance in each WCT event, and for the United States, French, and Wimbledon Championships. These points go toward a spot in the season-ending WCT finals in Dallas in May, and toward a share of a bonus pool distributed there. In 1980, WCT introduced a new player rating system (Nixdorf computer ranking) and a new tournament format to begin the following year, in which the seasonal circuits are replaced by three separate "surface" circuits (hard court, clay court, and indoor carpet surfaces), each concluding with its own championship. A combination of twelve-tournament winners, high points scorers, and exempted ranked past winners meet in Dallas for the annual WCT Finals (first won by Ken Rosewall,

1971). WCT also sponsors the annual Tournament of Champions at Forest Hills in New York, open to all winners of major tournaments (first won by Harold Solomon, 1977). WCT was founded in 1967 by sports entrepreneurs Lamar Hunt and Dave Dickson (the latter was bought shortly therafter by WCT president Al Hill, Jr.) see *computer rankings*.

Western grip: A not often used method of holding a racket in which the player, with the racket held on edge, rests the palm of the hand near the bottom side of the handle. With the Western grip (so called because it was developed on California's lively concrete tennis courts), the racket face is closed, making the grip suitable for high volleys and high-bouncing groundstrokes. Some early exponents of the Western grip simply turned the racket over for a backhand stroke rather than making the necessary large change in grips, but in recent years, some players have used the Western grip as one half of a two-handed grip for backhand strokes. compare *chopper grip, Continental grip, Eastern grip, English grip, service grip*.

wide: Out because of landing beyond the service sideline on a serve or beyond the sideline on a stroke, resulting in a lost point (or on a first serve, a fault). compare *deep, long, short*.

Wightman Cup: An annual women's competition between the United States and Great Britain, consisting of five singles and two doubles matches. The trophy, actually inscribed the "Women's Lawn Tennis Team Championship between Great Britain and the United States," was donated by and later named for United States tennis great Mrs. Hazel Hotchkiss Wightman, who captained the winning side in the first event in 1923.

wild card: A player included in the draw (and sometimes seeded) at the sole discretion of the tournament committee rather than on the basis of a qualifying competition or computer rankings.

Wimbledon: 1. The All England Club in Church Road, Wimbledon, England, home of the Wimbledon Championships, the oldest and most famous competition in tennis. The original Wimbledon, abandoned for the present

facilities in 1922, was also the site of the first recorded international match in 1883 when C.M. and J.S. Clark (with permission from the United States doubles champions at that time, James Dwight and Richard Sears) represented the United States and were defeated by England's famous Renshaw twins, William and Ernest. 2. The Wimbledon Championships.

Wimbledon Championships: An international tournament held annually at the All England Club in Church Road, Wimbledon, England, one of the prestigious "Big Four" or "Grand Slam" events, and the oldest and most famous competition in tennis. The first Wimbledon Championship, for which many of the basic rules of modern tennis were drafted, was held in 1877, with S.W. Gore winning the only event, men's singles. Men's doubles were added in 1879 (won by L.R. Erskine and H.F. Lawford), women's singles in 1884 (won by Miss M. Watson) and women's doubles (won by Mrs. R.J. McNair and Miss D.P. Boothby) and mixed doubles (won by H. Crisp and Mrs. C.O. Tuckey) in 1913. Wimbledon became an "open" competition in 1968. also *British National Championships, Wimbledon*.

winner: A shot that wins a point, a winning stroke.

WIPTC: The Women's International Professional Tennis Council.

Women's International Professional Tennis Council: The governing body of women's professional tennis, comprised of representatives of players, the International Tennis Federation, the Women's Tennis Association, and tournament directors. Formed in 1975, the Women's International Professional Tennis Council is responsible for matters regarding tournament applications, scheduling, player conduct, and conditions of play. also *WIPTC*.

Women's Tennis Association: A service organization for women professional tennis players. Founded in 1973 through the efforts of first president Billie Jean King, the Women's Tennis Association (WTA) functions as the representative of touring professionals in matters regarding tournament play and provides a computer ranking service (based on performance) for professional players.

wood shot: A shot accidentally hit with the frame of the racket.

wristy: Having a lot of spin, as of a stroke or serve.

wrong-foot: To hit a shot to one side of an opponent who is leaning or moving in the opposite direction, or on the "wrong foot." (wrong-footed him to take the last point)

WTA: The Women's Tennis Association.

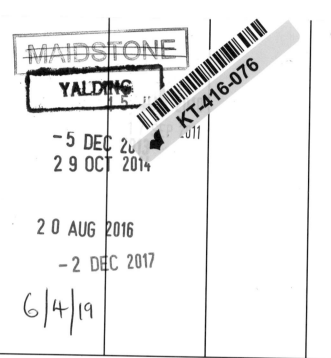

THE SPANIARD'S DAUGHTER

'I had just turned fifteen when I stole my first baby…'

Juliana Rodriguez is being raised to be a lady by her guardians Richard and Catherine Worledge, but both her name and the strawberry birthmark Catherine insists she keeps covered reveal the truth about her parentage. Even Juliana has heard the gossip, and yearns to know more of her past. Then, on the eve of her fifteenth birthday, she discovers a baby in the scullery destined for the haphazard care of a supposed wet-nurse. It seems that Catherine is the go-between in this illicit business, and it is then that Juliana takes the first step on a dangerous path: she steals her first child…

THE SPANIARD'S DAUGHTER

THE SPANIARD'S DAUGHTER

by

Melanie Gifford

Magna Large Print Books
Long Preston, North Yorkshire,
BD23 4ND, England.

British Library Cataloguing in Publication Data.

Gifford, Melanie
    The Spaniard's daughter.

    A catalogue record of this book is
    available from the British Library

    ISBN   978-0-7505-2655-5

First published in Great Britain 2006 by Piatkus Books Ltd.

Magna Large Print is an imprint of Library Magna Books Ltd.

Printed and bound in Great Britain by
T.J. (International) Ltd., Cornwall, PL28 8RW

To Gillian, Emma and Ben with thanks.

Chapter One

I had just turned fifteen when I stole my first baby. This was no dark concocted plot on my part. I wasn't much of a schemer, not then. I fell into it the way you might stumble over a pothole in the street. My life had already been thundering to some sort of crisis. It was like watching a cannon fuse burn down. You either tried to snuff it out with your fingers or stood back and waited for the explosion.

Juliana Rodriguez. An olive-kissed name for an orphaned bastard child. Yet my hair was not the glossy, jet-black of the Spaniard but red, a deep burnished copper that sometimes lightened to gold in the hottest days of summer. Some of my guardians' friends remarked that I had a cat's aspect – high cheekbones with a wide, tucked-up smile.

People told stories about me all the time. I knew this, but I'd yet to catch anyone in the act. Sometimes I got close. A pause when I entered the room, a snatch of breath. Conversations were sliced up and folded away. I witnessed it in the street, the coffee house and the apothecary where Catherine bought those foul-smelling potions to soothe her feet. I doubted anyone *knew* very much, but an absence of facts only served to oil busy tongues.

At the time I was naïve enough to think that

what they said didn't matter. Gossips were full of the war against the rebels in the Americas. Men were leaving by the shipload. Women wailed as if their husbands were already lost, or tumbled gratefully into the beds of their lovers. No one, I hoped, would notice me amid the chaos.

A stupid notion, on reflection.

Fifteen. Almost a woman. My guardians, Richard and Catherine Worledge, had decided to hold a birthday party in my honour at their town house in Wexborough. Or rather Catherine had decided and Richard, sensibly, agreed. The house was typical of the style of buildings that were sprouting like a rash across the town. Built from a soft, golden sandstone it had just the right number of windows, a pediment above the polished front door and marble steps spreading down into the street. I thought it resembled a slab of not-so-fresh butter sitting on a cobbled dish. It was astonishing, when I remarked on this to Catherine, how her face could deepen to scarlet then pale again in the space of a breath.

'Have you any idea how much that house cost?' her thin, bite-you mouth demanded. I replied that, whatever the cost, it still looked like a butter house to me. She didn't talk for the rest of the day and, unrepentant, I ended up taking supper in the kitchen. It seemed stupid that she should empty her purse on a certain type of building just because someone else had declared it fashionable. It wasn't like a dress that you could wear for a night then throw away after use. But that was Catherine for you.

The party was well underway and I hadn't put

12

a foot out of my bedchamber. Mrs Deever, Catherine's housekeeper, had toiled for three hours turning me into a French poppet. I fidgeted while she smothered me in a velvet gown, pulled a choker roughly around my neck and plastered my chin with thick, sticky cream.

'To hide your birthmark,' she explained. 'Hold still. I've chafed my knuckles once already trying to button up your stays.'

'I have to breathe don't I? Any more powder and I'll choke.'

'You'll just have to put up with it. You know that mark frightens the children.'

'I didn't invite them. They don't care whether it's my birthday so long as there's enough cake to stuff in their mouths.'

'Your mama says to cover it and cover it I will.'

'She's not my mama.'

A sharp tap on my face with the back of her hand. My teeth clipped the end of my tongue. Needles stabbed into my mouth. Deever waited, testing my willingness to defy her. Better take a slap now, I thought, than have her going off whining to Catherine, who seemed to keep a mental tally of all my supposed misdemeanours. Once I'd notched up a certain amount I'd feel the sharp side of her temper. The servants snitched on me every chance they got.

I let the old hag finish dressing me. Both feet were crammed into satin slippers and her skinny fingers tugged a wig down firmly over my red hair.

'Better,' she declared. 'Everyone will think so.'

I barely recognised the white-faced ghost

staring back at me from the looking glass. Deever ushered me out of the room and downstairs to the noisy carnival below. The hired quintet had struck up a merry tune. Guests performed a gavotte on the dining-room carpet. Festivities had spread from room to room, spilling into the hall and filling each alcove with laughter. Catherine, in a wig so tall she had to duck under doorways, passed me among her friends. I felt like an exotic trinket purchased for a guinea at a fly-blown foreign market. Visitors admired me the way they might a fine horse or a remarkable painting. People grinned and pinched my cheeks. I half expected one of them to examine my teeth.

'This one will wed a banker or merchant,' Catherine said, laughing, 'or catch the eye of some country squire.'

When she was finished with me I let go of my lopsided smile and stood quietly beside the parlour hearth. I curtsied at all the gaudy peacocks and did not speak unless spoken to. Later, Catherine put me with the children before returning to her guests. I tried to play party games. I sat infants on my lap or chased them around the room, these giggling bundles of chaos. Older girls had little time for me. They lost themselves in petty conversation while the minutes ticked down, talking and talking without actually *saying* anything. Others clustered their chairs near the open door and cast distracted glances into the hall, hoping to hook a handsome face.

My friends were picked, like a gown, a pair of slippers or a lace-trimmed nightshift. We did the rounds of one another's houses, moved like cards in a game of Hazard. I was at that in-between age, bored with childhood trinkets yet not old enough to be allowed a serious opinion. Sometimes I just wanted to smoke, get drunk or fall fumbling into a man's lap like loose women were said to do. The last time I was too rebellious Catherine punished me herself. That night in my distress I wet the bed, which put me in trouble with the servants who had to strip the linen and clean the mattress. I had often been called wilful but in reality thought myself a terrible coward.

Until I heard about the baby.

For nearly two hours I'd played the happy birthday girl and beneath the smile I felt like an exhausted dog. Finally, a harassed-looking maid wandered in carrying a tray of cakes. I caught her wrist.

'Look after the children.'

'Got work of my own to do,' she said, squirming free of my grasp. 'I ain't a nursemaid besides.'

'It's only for a while. I'll make sure you get something from the dining table. A few sweetmeats perhaps, or some party favours. There might be sixpences inside.'

'I'll get into trouble if I'm away from the kitchen too long,' she protested, but there was no conviction in it.

I escaped into the dining room. Long tables had been set up against the walls. Evening sunshine soaked the room in a dim, brassy light. Guests crowded around me. A drink, sherry from the smell of it, slopped over my arm.

Blake, sharp in his head footman's livery, stood over the remains of the buffet. It had taken cook all morning to prepare. The sweetmeats and cheeses had been ravaged, the cakes reduced to crumbs. Blake's eyes widened when he spotted me. Creases appeared in his pinned-on face. His tongue ran along the edge of his teeth.

Birthday trinkets were spread out on the table beneath the window. Guests wandered in, lifted, compared, speculated on who had bought what and how much it cost. Every corner was filled with chattering faces. I felt a pinch on my forearm. One of Catherine's friends leered at me. Her lips were a scarlet gash filled with a jumble of teeth. She muttered something, but the wine had gone to her mouth and I couldn't make sense of the slurred muddle. When I didn't answer she scowled and tottered off in search of a more sympathetic ear.

This was the very cream of Wexborough society. Beached seafarers, retired soldiers and petty politicians – all those who had escaped the war along with wives, mistresses and husband-hunting daughters. Most didn't even notice me. They passed my life between them as if it was a morsel from the buffet table. Each mouth took a bite.

'Richard fought with a business partner because of her, did you know that?' The speaker paused long enough to suck on a sculpted pipe. 'They traded blows on the lawn at the rear of the house. Richard is no brawler or I'm sure he would have killed the fellow, who at any rate was never invited to the house again.'

His companion wafted a feather-trimmed fan in front of her chin. 'The girl is very comely, would be a perfect angel if not for that mark.'

16

'Yes,' her friend agreed, 'if not for that mark.'

Richard had caught us in the back parlour. I'd been lured inside with the promise of a new game 'all the way from India' that his colleague wanted to show me. He was a crude, thick-set man with spades for hands. It wasn't the 'game' that had upset me the most but my guardian, returning afterwards from the garden with his nose bloodied and dirt streaking his silk shirt. He called me a strumpet and cuffed my cheek. Catherine had to get Blake to escort him upstairs. I cried for an hour.

That was when I first learned how dangerous beauty could be, but I wasn't aware of what might be achieved with this power until much later. I didn't spend much time pouting into mirrors. All I ever saw was 'the mark', the cherry-red smear running from the corner of my mouth to my chin. Not much of a thing compared to a harelip or a face scoured by the pox. I took a good teasing over it, until some bored child at a tea party screamed that I was a witch and had been drinking blood. That got all the darlings into a lather and Catherine took me home in embarrassed disgrace. I spent an hour trying to scrub the blemish off and gave myself a bad rash that stung for a week. The mark ran in my family. Catherine reminded me of that whenever she was in a bad mood. It seemed the only time I ever learned anything about myself was at the whim of her temper.

I fled the dining room. I couldn't fumble anything off the tables with Blake brooding over everything. The maid was going to have to wait.

The study beckoned, a refuge packed with

shelves of leather-bound books, though Richard always complained that he couldn't find a decent bookseller. I adored the written word and the places those words took me. Together we travelled the world and through those pages I met long-dead explorers, warriors and adventurers. It was as if I'd been allowed to enter their lives and share something wonderful.

When Richard was out on business or squandering Catherine's money at one of his gambling clubs, I spent hours curled up in his leather chair with a volume open on my lap. On good days the sun threw streamers of light across the mahogany desk. If my luck held I'd find a newspaper, neatly folded. Or one of Catherine's society magazines that Richard occasionally flicked through. When I closed the study door, the Butter House and all its simmering troubles were gone.

Now the door hung open. Richard was perched on the edge of his desk, idly flicking pipe ash on to the carpet. 'Another of my vessels has been requisitioned to take troops to the war,' he declared, gesturing with his brandy glass, 'which in any case we seem in danger of losing. Understand that I attach no blame to the King. Parliament is full of wastrels set on plundering other people's fortunes. Thievery, I call it.'

His friends pursed their lips and nodded. Their hunting dogs' eyes ranged over his books, the family portraits, the silver ornaments littering his desk. Richard was oblivious to this. His voice, taut with passion, carried above the discordant twang of the spinet that someone was trying to play in the music room next door. 'It's no longer a kind world to men whose business is the sea,' he finished.

I met a real sailor once, a grizzled old man with a chipped clay pipe in his mouth and a head full of stories. Catherine had taken me to Richard's offices at the docks. Richard wasn't there and I was obliged to wait outside while Catherine fetched the key from his clerk so she could retrieve some letters. While she fumbled around in the clutter the sailor, who was perched on a crate by the quayside, delighted me by seemingly producing a farthing from my ear. He showed me the scars on his back where he'd felt the lash and bade me touch his hands, which were like old leather after years of blistering work. I could almost smell the faraway places he had been to and imagined tropical winds breezing through his white, thinning hair.

Not like Richard, whose feet never left shore. Richard only ever smelled of brandy and tobacco, mixed with a whiff of the Italian cologne his vessels sometimes brought in. Catherine suffered his indiscretions with a tight smile. Sometimes when she glanced at him across the dinner table, or in the parlour in front of the evening fire, her eyes seemed to darken.

'The business which you claim to care for yet seldom manage because you are too drunk, or too fond of the card table, is mine,' she reminded him once, sewing needle puncturing the fine lace of her sampler in an ugly, erratic pattern. 'You only came into my fortune because your father had sufficient wit to find a fat-pursed spinster to marry his dullard son. My papa only agreed because he wanted me wed before he died. You would not have taken me to the altar otherwise.'

Richard's clothes were always too garish and the earnest expression etched on to his face made him look a buffoon. Despite his affection I felt like a debt he was obliged to pay off piece by piece. Yet if not for him, Catherine would've packed me off a long time ago.

I slipped away from the study door. I was tired and my belly hurt. I hadn't eaten a proper meal since supper the night before. The party might clatter on long into the night. I sent a maid to ask cook for a hot drink to settle me. She went off, scowling.

I retreated to my room. The party wouldn't suffer for my absence. A fresh coverlet had been spread over the bed and a candle flickered in its holder on the dresser. I opened both windows and peered into the deepening gloom. The sun had dipped into the not-quite-night of mid-summer. The air was warm, like a gust of heat from the kitchen hearth.

I flumped fully clothed on to the bed and waited for my drink. Footsteps creaked along the passage. I sat up, smiling.

Edward Blake slipped into the room with a friendliness that did not fit him and gently closed the door. The stench of sour wine lurked in his grin.

'Got a sore belly have we? Well, I know a trick that'll put it right.'

Thick fingers fluttered towards my bodice. His nails were polished. They brushed against the embroidered velvet. I edged away. Just enough to

20

put half an inch of muggy air between us. His grin slipped a little.

'Now,' he said softly, but with thorns spiking every word. 'No need to go behaving like that. Not when I'm trying to help you.'

'You shouldn't be in here, Blake.'

'I was Mister Blake last I heard.'

'Mister Blake then.'

'What about you, Miss Juliana? Why are you hiding in here like a frightened rabbit? You should be downstairs enchanting all your fine guests. Mrs Worledge will wonder where you are. If she asks me, what shall I tell her? What do I say? I'm head of the staff. If you go down sick it'll look bad for me.'

'My belly's only sore because I was starved to fit inside this frippery of a gown, besides, Deever says she's in charge.'

The grin tightened. 'No use trying to play the wily politician. I watched you leave the dining room and I saw you running up the stairs.'

'Don't touch me.'

'I only want to rub a bit of warmth into you, Miss Juliana, to settle that poorly stomach.'

'I'll lock the door next time.'

'You haven't got a key.'

'I'll put a chair against it.'

'What, and barricade yourself against poor Ed Blake who only wants to provide a bit of relief?' He shook his head. 'You're a bad 'un. Just like your papa. They stretched his neck. Who's to know what will become of you.'

'What do you know about my father?'

Blake didn't answer. With that jackal's smile, he

21

ran his fingers down the front of my gown. Sounds drifted along the hallway like voices in a fog. I tried to say something else but the words stuck in my throat. He leaned forward. His breath whispered over my face.

A sharp rap and the door swung open. A maid stood framed in the light from the passage, steaming posset in her hand. Blake hauled her back outside. Hot milk slopped on to the carpet. He slammed the door. Through the wood I heard him growling like a dog and the maid bursting into tears.

I held my breath. He did not come back. Five minutes I waited, then ten. I couldn't stand it any longer.

Downstairs the party droned on. Someone was yelling. A glass was knocked over in a flurry of exclamations. I stumbled through the house. The hem of my gown dragged on the floor. The wig felt hot and itchy. Some of the pins had come loose and it kept slipping. Nobody seemed to notice me. Only one refuge remained and I made for it now.

The back parlour was an odd, out-of-the-way place built from the remains of an old washhouse that once stood on the site. It lay at the end of a narrow, crook-leg passage ill served by daylight. Richard once thought he might use the room to store his documents but it was too chilly in winter and a chore to reach. These days it served as a graveyard for Catherine's whims. Monstrous dragons, bought when everything Chinese was the fashion, stood guard over a pile of rugs. Old paintings, obliged to surrender their wall space, lay stacked in a heap beside the bare hearth.

Mismatched tables and chairs dotted the carpet.

I fumbled through the gloom and squeezed behind the dragons. The rugs made a soft bed and I settled down with my back against the wall. Not a squeak from that tiresome party invaded this quiet place. I drew my legs up under me. Half an hour, no longer, then I ought to rescue the maid from my abandoned charges. She'd be fair spitting by now and would want something better than a couple of sweetmeats for her trouble.

I rubbed my eyes, trying to push Blake out of my head. He stuck to Catherine like a terrier and knew I wouldn't snitch on him. I'd decide what to do about the situation later. Despite my posset ending up spilled over the upstairs landing my belly had settled down to the odd gurgle. A ladleful of broth from the kitchen would fix that.

Outside, through the thin curtains, the last of the day's light leaked from the sky. Everything in the room blurred into shadows. A link boy's torch bobbed past the window and was gone.

The door whispered open. Catherine breezed into the parlour, candlestick gripped in one hand. She wasn't laughing any more. She set the candle on a card table and seated herself in the armchair beside the dead fire. A tall woman followed and perched on the high-backed chair opposite. Much of her face was pressed into a lace handkerchief, but not enough to hide the long, hooked nose or the brown mole sprouting beneath her left eye. It was Mrs Sorrell, a spindly creature with a demeanour like sour milk pudding. She often partnered Catherine at Hazard. Air wheezed out of her lungs. She was close to tears.

23

I pressed myself against the wall and peeked between the dragons' porcelain haunches. Catherine's voice was calm but firm.

'Did you bring the baby here?'

Mrs Sorrell snorted into her handkerchief. 'I had to. Philip will not tolerate it in the house.'

'Very well. I will make arrangements, though Richard must not know. Is it a boy or a girl?'

'A boy.'

'I see. Little wonder Philip will have naught to do with it. To have such a cuckoo in the nest must be an enormous blow to his pride. Bad enough that Jane is his only child. How is the girl?'

'The surgeon was with her throughout the labour. He tells me Jane is weak though will recover. Philip will not speak to her. He was black with anger the moment he learned of the brat festering in her belly and is now threatening to cast her into the street.'

'When did he discover Jane was with child?'

'Not until very late in her time. The girl was always thin. She could likely carry a whole litter and scarce put an inch on around the waist. She always insisted on wearing billowy cotton gowns around the house. We put it down to fancy and thought no more of it.'

Mrs Sorrell dropped the crumpled kerchief on the table and leaned back against the chair. 'I won't have that thing in my house, Catherine. Philip has locked Jane in her room. She can bawl the walls down and it won't make a whit of a difference. Our entire family has its hopes pinned on a good marriage for that girl and I can't let anything ruin it. Certainly not some wastrel's bastard.'

'Do you know who sired the infant?'

'Adam Fairchild.'

'Oh.'

'What difference does it make? The father could be a bishop or a dockside beggar and the result would be the same. Understand that we are only thinking of Jane. Her position and future happiness. Philip would rather disown her than suffer disgrace. This misadventure could be the ruin of us.'

'Fairchild will not accept the baby as his own?'

A shake of the head. 'He has painted Jane as a cheap whore. Philip can do nothing. Fairchild's friends are too numerous and too powerful and, in any case, he has gone to France for the season. It's no use. The child will have to go. We have no place for it.'

'Where did you bring it? Not to my front door I trust?'

'No, no. I did as your message bade me and had my coachman take it to the kitchen. A shilling tucked into his palm will ensure his discretion. Your maid was waiting for him and took the child. It has been given something to stop it bawling. I have no wish to see it again. It would be best if it had never been born.'

My guardian nodded as if the two women were merely discussing the whims of the weather. 'I think you ought to return home, Alice. If anyone enquires tell them you have a headache.'

'We are beholden to you, Catherine. My family's gratitude can prove extensive.'

'We will say nothing more of this. In the meantime see to Jane. She will get over the child.

Philip will forgive her and your household will be at peace. Now if you will pardon me, I have neglected my own guests. Our little package will be safe where it is for an hour or so.'

Mrs Sorrell tucked her handkerchief into her sleeve. 'Your scullery maid is reliable?'

Catherine collected the candlestick and led her guest to the door. 'She knows better than to do anything witless.'

The women slid out of the parlour as quietly as they had entered. The door closed with a soft click. The smell of burnt wax lingered in the air. I waited a few minutes then edged out from behind the dragons. I'd not thought much of babies. Just pink faces that were sick a lot and cried most of the time. One, birthed badly, had killed Catherine's sister. That, so the gossips said, put Catherine off having children of her own for good and Richard had no word on the matter.

I left the room and headed for the kitchen. 'You've a nose for trouble,' Catherine once told me. 'It runs in the family.' Yet I had no scheme or plan of any sort. I didn't think, first I will do this, then this and this. I stumbled along the passage, my ravaged belly forgotten. I'd never thought Catherine a kindly woman. But she'd been talking about getting rid of a baby. A *child*. It wasn't the same as throwing a scrap of rotten meat into the gutter for dogs to scrabble over.

A thin curtain of steam fogged the kitchen. I'd wandered in here often in the past, sometimes with special instructions from Catherine, other times out of idle fancy. I couldn't resist the warmth and rich smells of cooking food. Rarely

26

was it not full of noise and smoke, with huge iron pots hanging from cranes over the fire.

Maggie Burns was up to her elbows in grease from the mountain of dirty plates dumped in the washtub. Strands of limp brown hair hung loosely over her flushed cheeks. She was a parish girl who'd worked for us this past year. Her brow was knotted above tired eyes and she jumped when my shoes scraped on the tiles.

'Why aren't you at your party?' she asked irritably.

I checked for any sign of the cook. Her door was closed and, her work done for the night, she'd likely be asleep. She drank gin in the evening while Catherine turned a blind eye, because she got the best price for meat and her pastries were delicious. I pictured her squeezed into her over-stuffed armchair and snoring fit to crack the plaster.

'Where is the baby?' I demanded.

Maggie tucked her hair back under her cap with a greasy finger. 'What baby might that be?'

I shut the kitchen door and grabbed her arm. She yelped. 'The baby!' I pressed. 'Show me where it is.'

'Gerroff. I'm not fetching a beating on your account. Let me go or I'll yell.'

'Is that so? Shall I tell Mrs Worledge about the beef you've been filching from the pantry to sell to that ostler's lad? My bedchamber is right above the kitchen. Twice this week I've watched him slink out of the back door with a packet tucked into his coat. The mistress will have you thrown into the gutter. You'll have to beg or steal.

You'll eat stale bread and sleep with rats, and I will not care what becomes of you. I want the baby Mrs Sorrell's coachman brought to the back door. You took it out of his hands. I know it's here and I'll not ask you again.'

She stood in front of the sink, regarding me with those big, frog eyes. Water dripped from her hands on to the tiles. I could almost hear the thoughts clunking around inside her head. Then her gaze flicked towards the pantry.

I strode across the kitchen and yanked on the latch. Hinges squealed as I pulled the door wide and peered into the gloom.

'Fetch a candle.'

Maggie lit one and pressed it into my hand. The wavering light threw distorted shadows across the walls and ceiling. A draught slipped through a chipped windowpane. Sausages hung from hooks, along with onions and various dried spices. Earthenware jars glinted on the shelf and a sweet, cloying smell filled the cramped space.

Stepping inside, I peered past sacks of flour and boxes of fruit. Something shifted near the wainscoting and I tensed, half expecting to confront the glittering eyes of a rat. Instead the light fell across the pink face of a sleeping baby.

I stooped and held the candle closer. The child didn't stir. Its eyes, so small and yet so perfect I could count the hairs on each lash, were closed. An odd sensation fluttered in the bottom of my stomach. Here was a brand new mind, a new soul.

'Catherine,' I whispered, 'what have you done?'

My unease grew as I noticed the cheap basket in which it lay – an old, dirty thing a tinker might use to sell pegs at a local market. Coarse, stale-smelling linen swaddled the child. Yet Mrs Sorrell was a rich woman with a house that was considered one of the finest in Wexborough.

'What will happen to it?'

Maggie Burns fidgeted in the pantry doorway. 'The wet-nurse has been sent for. She will have the child away before dawn.'

'A wet-nurse?' I turned to look at her. 'It is to be cared for then?'

She pressed her hands against her cheeks and shook her head. 'The woman is bad with children. The baby will die within the week.'

'I don't understand.'

'Seldom does a newborn last more than a few days in the hands of Mrs Skegg. They wither like a bloom in want of water. If the poor mites don't starve then I've heard she puts them in her bed and rolls over them in the night so they suffocate. Then she pays a quack to say the child died of a fever. Saved many a titled family from disgrace, that woman has, and none of the gentry round here will say a word against her.'

I set the candle on a crate and picked up the sleeping child. The swaddling was warm in my hands. I could smell new skin, hear the whisper of soft breath. I'd never held a baby before. 'He's beautiful.'

'A pest is what he is, Miss Juliana. You mustn't go soft over him.'

'You wouldn't say that if he was your child.'

'I ain't got time for birthing brats.'

'I heard cook say you have two little brothers and a sister.'

Her gaze fell. 'Aye, that's true enough.'

'Fetch me a cloak.'

'I won't help you. You can snitch to Mrs Worledge about the beef all you like. There's worse things can happen than getting thrown into the street.'

'Fine, I'll get it myself.'

A homespun woollen cloak hung beside the back door. Cradling the baby in one arm I snatched the garment from its hook and wrapped it around myself with my free hand. It smelled of smoke and old grease.

'That belongs to cook,' the maid protested. 'She'll throw a fit.'

'I'm not venturing outside alone in this gown. People will think I'm a harlot. Now open the back door and be quiet about it.'

At first I thought she might refuse, but after a moment she unpegged the latch and eased the door open. The night whispered in. Candles spat and guttered. Maggie's eyes were wide with fright.

'Where are you going? If Mrs Worledge should come looking for you...'

'Close the door after me then go back to your dirty pots. I'll return soon.'

I stood on the back step and stared into the dark. Though I knew the town well enough, I'd never gone anywhere unescorted, even if it was only Richard's groom hanging on to my shadow. With the maid watching me I couldn't let my brave face crack now. I hurried into the lane running along the rear of the house. The rectangle of light flooding from the kitchen snuffed out as the door swung shut.

Chapter Two

The baby seemed to grow heavier in my arms as I hurried away from the Butter House, hugging the shadows every time a carriage clattered past. On the main road, orange torches bobbed in a welter of sparks. Summer was a curse upon the link boys, with so little dark in which to hook a customer. The short nights were also enemies of the cutpurse. The narrow alleys behind the fine houses made a fat nest for these leeches. Constables tried to clear them out, but they always came slinking back, blades and clubs greedy for another pocketful of someone else's coins.

I started to run, awkward in my billowing party dress. Cook's cheap cloak kept catching my ankles, threatening to spill me into the dirt. The baby shifted in my arms but didn't wake from its drugged sleep. Only a short distance to the docks. I could smell salt water on the air, hear the current pulling the ships against their ropes. I felt the thrill of spoiling Catherine's plans – of winning a trick over this ice-hearted woman. She'd be angry, and I'd be in trouble, but this was a child's life and any decent man or woman would do the same.

Wouldn't they?

Lanterns had been lit along the quayside, their light reflected in the rippling water. I paused and listened, hoping no one else was about at this hour. A dog barked somewhere nearby, like an old man coughing into his cup.

A breeze caught my face as I slipped around the corner of a warehouse and scampered past the barred doors of the traders' premises. There was the thick oak door of Richard's office, the shuttered windows glaring down at me like blank, wooden eyes. To my left, water lapped against the wooden pilings of the quay. Lights glimmered high up on the ships where the night watch tramped the decks, likely dreaming of bed and a mug of brandy. Planking creaked and dust swirled between the ropes.

Ahead stood a solitary bow-top caravan. Gypsies often came to the docks when the ships were in. They bought up damaged cargo and made what they would of it, turning out trinkets and making colourful clothes out of strips of cloth. I often spied their wagons when I accompanied Catherine to the office. A patch of common scrubland less than half a league beyond the town boundary stone provided good grazing for their ponies – the greys or skewbalds that pulled the caravans along the old drove tracks. Romany women haunted the harbour, selling dried flowers, herbs and wooden pegs.

I held my breath at the foot of the low wooden steps, trying to work out what I would say. Maggie Burns had a distant cousin who was a Romany and she was always prattling on about them. She seemed to find their odd way of life very exciting. I hoped that what she said was true.

Only one wagon, only one chance. Candlelight flickered behind thin muslin curtains. Music twanged softly, each note crisp and clear. A stringed instrument, an old lyre or perhaps a mandolin. Sailors brought some over from Italy and they were much in favour with travellers.

I must have made a sound. The music stopped. The caravan shifted on its leather springs and a figure became outlined against the candlelight. The half door whispered open and a gust of rich incense swirled about my head. A face appeared in the semi-darkness. Black plaited hair parted in the centre, a long nose, olive skin spiked with two piercing eyes. Her expression was thick with mistrust. I was a *giorgio,* an outsider.

'I have a little boy,' I blurted, unfolding the warm bundle from the cloak. 'I don't know if the stories about you are true or not, but he'll die if you don't help him. I've heard there's always use for a boy in a gypsy camp.'

I knew how it must have looked. I felt like a mummer in a bad play. The woman did not move from her place on the top step. 'This child, it is yours?' she asked in the clipped tongue of the Romany.

I swallowed hard and held the bundle out. 'Yes.'

Her skirts, stitched together from many colourful panels, rustled as her bare feet descended first one step, then two. 'You're not its mama. You could never give it up so easily if it were, no matter how badly you might want to save it. You don't know how it is to have life in your belly.'

She shook her head. 'I've had girls come to me, some younger than you, begging help for their little ones. Some want a charm or a blessing, others to run away with us. Always they bring

33

trouble in their wake. So tell me, *giorgio,* why should I take this baby and risk a rope around my neck if someone should come looking for it? Why shouldn't I just send you packing off into the night from where you came? You're not poor or desperate. There's no look on your face that speaks to me of trouble, of a household shamed or a papa threatening to kill you for birthing a bastard. You've lied to me once tonight. Who's to say you won't lie again?'

'No one knows I'm here,' I retorted. 'I did lie to you. I haven't birthed this child. I stole it from people who, rather than suffer disgrace, would see it die. There is no time and nowhere else to go. I'd pay you if I had money that was mine to give. I'll get down on my knees and beg if you want. But take the baby. Please.'

I was frightened, I had to admit it to myself I had no friends among the Romanies. This woman was tall and proud. She wore gold on her ears and fingers. I did not want to cross her. Get a gypsy blessing and prosper for life, the saying went, but a gypsy curse will make you shrivel and die.

'When he wakes he'll want feeding,' the woman said at last. 'I doubt he'll get anything from you. I can sweeten some goat's milk.'

She took the child from my arms, smoothed back the swaddling and studied his peaceful face.

'He's been dosed. Did you do it?'

'No.'

'Laudanum, I expect, but he'll be none the worse for it. You held him well. Perhaps there is something of a mother in you.'

She turned and slipped back inside the caravan,

closing the door behind her. Voices muttered within, then the music started up again, soft and lilting on the night air. In the morning the wagon would likely be gone.

I pulled the cloak tightly around my shoulders and made off through the muggy streets without looking back. When I arrived at the Butter House the kitchen door hung open. Inside, Catherine was waiting.

'You took the baby,' she said. 'You stole it.'

'What you planned was wrong,' I replied, as I had before and again before that. 'It was wrong.'

My throat was parched. A pitcher lay on the shelf by the hearth, pewter ladle protruding over the lip. I wanted to taste cool water, to go to my bed, sink into sleep and forget this dirty night. Accusations had been thrown at me until my ears hurt. The fire died and turned cold, candles burned down to their holders. Maggie Burns sat in the corner, white faced and crying.

I stood in the cook's cheap cloak and faced Catherine. She'd taken off the monstrous party wig. Her hair resembled frayed string hanging loosely around her ears and temples. She was still a young woman but the grey was starting to creep in. Crows' feet cracked the corners of her eyes.

'You will tell me where you have taken it,' she continued in that flinty voice.

'Madam, I will not.'

'You are a stupid girl. Stupid and selfish. Who is to say what damage you have done in your ignorance? Yet you stand there and defy me like some self-righteous hussy who's never had the benefit of a Christian home. You are an evil creature, and you have brought shame upon this household.'

I chuckled mirthlessly. 'How can I shame the likes of you?'

Maggie's hand flew to her mouth. Outwardly, Catherine's expression didn't change, but I saw a hardening in her eyes that I knew well enough. She glanced around the kitchen, at the heaps of dirty plates, the scraps of uneaten food. Empty bottles littered the floor. Some had toppled and spilled their dregs across the tiles.

She took a deep breath and curled both hands into fists. 'Come with me, Juliana.'

I followed Catherine out of the kitchen and down the hall to the lobby. The party had wound up, the guests returned home. A lady's satin slipper sat forlornly on the carpet amidst a dark patch of spilled wine. Catherine kicked it out of the way. Half-empty glasses were clustered on tables and lined up along the drawing-room mantelpiece. Stale smoke clogged the air, mixing with bittersweet perfumes into a horrible, cloying fug.

The study door lay open. Richard was slumped in his armchair, head cradled in his arms, caged by a crescent of empty bottles. Tobacco spillings littered the desk. Catherine barely spared him a glance.

The staircase seemed endless. I counted each step to the top landing. Servants hurried past, trying to tidy up before daybreak. Blake watched me from the bottom of the stairwell, a brass holder with half a dozen candles squeezed in his fist. He blew out each flame until his face faded into shadow. In the semi-darkness his eyes glittered like black diamonds.

Barely a scrap of breath remained in my lungs. My trip to the docks had exhausted me. Both feet hurt and my arms ached from holding the baby. The passage seemed to swim in front of my tired eyes, the candles fading into orange fireflies that sparked before my face.

Catherine stopped in front of the nursery and gestured me inside. She followed, closed and locked the door. What was passing through her mind? She could control her face the way a dock worker might call his pup to heel.

The nursery provoked no fondness. I couldn't recall ever playing there, or spending happy times under its plastered roof Gaily painted furniture was mostly hidden beneath thick canvas sheets. Dolls propped one another up at drunken angles on the shelves. The air was stale and flecked with dust.

A bulky wooden trunk sat on the floor beneath the window, its sides coloured with crescent moons. Catherine lifted the lid and took out a hickory tawse.

'Juliana,' she said, 'can you give me a reason why I shouldn't punish you?'

'I stopped you committing murder.'

Her knuckles whitened against the split wood. 'You must tell me where you have taken the baby. I am aware of your reasons for doing it and I don't doubt you thought they were right. But you are just a child and there are things you do not understand.'

I swallowed. My throat felt like tree bark. 'You

wanted it dead, I understood that. It wasn't even your child.'

'If word of this indiscretion gets out it could seriously damage us,' Catherine continued as if I hadn't spoken. 'We have gained important favours by helping good people dispose of their errors. A boy child would bring about a situation the Sorrells can ill afford. Tell me what you have done with it and I shall be lenient with you.'

'The baby is gone where you can't reach him. Split that stick across my spine if it pleases you, but I won't say any more.'

'How did you learn about it? At least your stubborn tongue can tell me that. If you've been listening to gossip...'

'I heard it out of your own mouth. You were speaking to that awful woman in the back parlour. I was trying to snatch a rest from the party.'

'I dislike it when people sneak around, Juliana.'

'You were doing the same.'

Her face coloured for the first time. The stick shivered between her fmgertips. 'You have your place in the world. Other people have theirs. That is the way of things and it is important you learn it. The baby was a ... mistake. Sometimes mistakes happen and we deal with them the best we can.'

'Was I a mistake?'

'You are a debt. One that can't be paid. As with all liabilities you leech us of our prosperity, more so than any of Richard's tawdry habits. I've spent years paying for your life. I own you as much as I own the horses in my stables.'

'You did not own the baby.'

'Yes I did. That child was given to me to do what was necessary. The wet-nurse turned up at the kitchen door while you were off on your little errand. I had to pay two guineas to be rid of her.'

Catherine dropped the stick on to the rug. 'Enough damage has been done. I won't make a martyr out of you. Pray that the child is not found. Everything you have done tonight could have repercussions.'

'How many other babies have arrived in the night?' I blurted. 'How many other families have you helped? What has been the cost in lives?'

I closed my eyes. The key turned in the lock and a draught wafted my face. When I dared look, Catherine had gone.

My room had been tidied, the bed remade. A fresh candle burned in the holder and a bag of primrose scented the air. A crisp nightshift was spread like a linen ghost across the coverlet.

I sat in front of the looking glass, nudged off my slippers and pulled the wig from my head, letting it drop to the floor in a flurry of white powder. I stared at my reflection. A pale face with drawn cheeks and dark crescents under both eyes stared back. I looked like an old woman.

A lace handkerchief plucked from the top drawer of the dresser wiped the paste from my cheeks. Rubbing hard around my mouth revealed my birthmark in all its lividness. I was sick of masks. Standing up, I tore the gown from my back and let it join the wig on the floor. The nightshift was warm against my skin. I padded barefoot to the open window and leaned out into the darkness. Thoughts about the baby flitted through my head. I imagined him growing up into a young man, good with horses perhaps, and a dusky Romany girl as his wife. Days on the road, nights around a gypsy camp fire with music and the rich scent of roasting hare.

'Be safe,' I whispered.

The sheets welcomed me with a clean embrace. I lay back on my pillows, savouring the comfort the soft mattress gave my aching bones. A moth fluttered across the ceiling, drawn to the flickering light. I yawned, blew out the candle, and surrendered to sleep.

But the night, it seemed, had other plans.

I was dragged from my rest by a figure standing over my bed. A burning taper made a yellow lantern of his face. He snuffed out the light. A draught wafted across my knees as he wrenched off the coverlet and tossed it into a corner.

The door. I had forgotten to bar the door.

I tried to call out. A hand clamped over my mouth. Blake brought his face within inches of mine. His breath was sweet with stolen claret.

'Got you this time, little miss,' he rumbled into my ear. 'Got you good and proper. I was outside the kitchen. Overheard your to-do with the scullery wench. I saw where you went, slipping into the night like a harlot from a lord's house with that little 'un in your arms. I followed you to the docks. It was easy to get away from the house for a bit. And I saw what you did.'

His other hand grasped my leg, the nails scratching the tender skin of my thigh. 'Sometimes you like to play the little lady,' he went on, 'but you're a canny slut and know when to open your mouth and when to keep it shut.'

His grip on my mouth loosened. I gasped for air. Terror and disgust nailed me to the mattress. Had it all been for nothing?

'If I scream they'll put you in gaol for sure,' I whispered, 'perhaps even hang you.'

He let out a low, rolling chuckle, like thunder rumbling over a distant range of hills. 'You ain't going to scream, little miss. Know why? Mrs Worledge has a mind to dismiss Maggie Burns, send her packing into the street without a reference. Perhaps I could persuade the mistress otherwise, perhaps not. Would you like to see the girl begging favours outside taverns? Maybe you don't care either way, but as for that little brat you stole...'

'No, don't tell Catherine where it is.'

I felt his triumph. He leaned over and kissed me gently on the forehead, the way a father might a beloved daughter. The hand holding my thigh slid up and plucked at the lining of my shift.

'Do we have a bargain, little miss?' he nuzzled into my ear. 'Two lives for your honour. A fair trade by any measure.'

'Don't hurt me.'

'No need to fret your pretty head. I've no mind to put a brat in your belly. Too many questions. Too much trouble. Your friend Blake just wants a fumble. Not much of a price to pay after what you've done tonight.'

His hands fell on me like a tumble of rocks. Lips pressed against mine. I fought not to choke. Images blurred through my panic-stricken mind.

41

I tried to think of the baby, but all I wanted was to shrivel and die. I felt each scratch, each bruise as it was jarred into my skin. He was cheapening me. And I was letting him do it.

When Blake was finished, when I was left snivelling on the sweat-soaked bed, he smoothed back my hair and pulled the shift down over my body. I felt like a deer after the hunt, lying torn on the grass with dogs licking the blood from my face.

'Not a word to Mrs Worledge,' he warned. 'Hear me, little miss? There's two sides to every bargain. Two.'

I said nothing as he slipped from my bed-chamber. After the doorknob clicked and his footfalls receded down the passage, I turned and buried my head in my pillow.

It could have been worse, I thought.

Blake served breakfast, strutting around the table in his green livery. I pushed food around on my plate with my fork. Catherine tried to make conversation, but the air between us was thicker than the butter on my toast and she quickly gave up. Possibly she mistook my silence for con-trition. At least she didn't press me about the baby again.

My body twinged. I'd put on a thick gown with a high neck and long, flowing sleeves to hide the bruises on my arms and upper chest. Catherine had eyed me curiously as I'd limped into the dining room. The day was set to be hot and already the sun was baking the busy streets outside. I mumbled something about wanting to stay indoors. She nodded and let the subject drop. Only later did I realise that she had no intention of letting me go anywhere.

Blake poured tea into my cup. I stared at his white-gloved hand as if it might bite but said 'Thank you,' in a polite voice and did not flinch when he brushed against my chair. He tried to slip me that oily smile. I reached for the cream, struggling not to spill it on the tablecloth.

I doubted that what I had given him – what he had taken – would be enough. My hatred of him had to be stronger than my fear or I'd never know another peaceful night in this house. He'd had what he wanted for now and I'd survived.

Blake often walked through this house as though he were its master. He demanded respect that wasn't his due and, when in the company of his betters, spoke in a cultivated voice that was so false it made me cringe. I never understood why Catherine retained his services. He was lazy, a brute to the maids and rude to tradesmen. Rumour suggested he'd performed an important favour for the family but no one could – or would – say what it was. Blake had power in this household but he wasn't going to enjoy those privileges for ever. Not while I lived.

Richard joined us afterwards in the front parlour. Groggy, shambling, his wig askew and shirt flapping out of his breeches. He'd slept late, the result of drinking enough brandy to put an ox into a stupor. He slumped into his armchair and propped his booted feet on the seat opposite. From the look of him he'd slept in his clothes, and a grizzle of dark stubble coloured his chin.

He peered around the room, eyes like two blood oranges. The house had a stale, used smell. 'My friends ... when did they leave?' he muttered.

Pride was not a word Richard understood, so it meant little to him when Catherine explained that his friends had left quietly after he'd collapsed across his desk. He tried to make a joke of it but quickly sensed the mood, which sobered him more than coffee or salts.

'I did not see much of you, Juliana,' he said. 'I gather there was something of a commotion in the kitchen.'

A twinge of alarm passed through me, but Catherine lied. She told him I'd gone outside and got carried away staring up at the night sky.

'You know what a dreamer she is,' Catherine said wryly. The 'commotion' was put down to some broken plates. A maid was being disciplined.

Richard reached over and squeezed my hand. His fingers felt limp and cold. 'That's Juliana,' he chuckled. 'Head's always full of fluff.'

'Will you go to the office today?' Catherine asked carefully.

Richard smiled and rubbed his eyes. 'Yes, yes of course. There are important matters to attend to.'

But he would be drunk again before noon.

I rose and brushed the creases out of my thick gown. 'I think I should like to go to the park, after all.'

Catherine did not look up from her lap, where a half-finished sampler sat in a tangle of coloured thread.

'You, my dear, shall not stray from this house.'

My incarceration lasted a week. During those long, sultry days I stayed out of the kitchen and as far away from Blake as the walls of the house would allow. Each night I listened for his footsteps in the passage, flinching at every creak as the bones of this large building settled. I couldn't sleep without the coverlet pulled over my head, and often woke, straining for air, in the small hours.

I had the parlour maid hunt out the key to my bedchamber and locked the door. Blake seemed to be biding his time, waiting for another, bigger bite of my particular apple.

Gradually my bruises healed. I glimpsed Maggie Burns a couple of times when she was sent up from the kitchen to collect dinner plates. She was waxen-faced and mostly stared at the floor. Once, she caught me watching her and turned away as if she'd been slapped.

Whispers followed me. They fluttered through walls, up and down stairs, into dark corners. Sidelong glances took bites out of my nerves.

There's Miss Juliana. The child stealer.

I wore circles in the carpet pile with my restless pacing. I haunted the maids, not wanting to find myself alone anywhere with Blake. They put a jolly face on my intrusions but it soon became irksome and Catherine told me to leave them alone. I was too afraid to go into the study by myself, rereading the few books I kept in my room until I knew them almost cover to cover. All day I was itchy, hot and irritable.

Catherine, at least, found something else to occupy her interest. A new circulating library and coffee house had opened up near the Corn

Exchange and she visited almost every day, often dressing elaborately for the occasion. All kinds of volumes came back stuffed into her reticule and I don't think she read a single one. Besides, there were more than enough books in Richard's study.

Of Richard himself, I saw very little. He was aware that something had happened between Catherine and myself, though he never remarked on it. He was away most days, leaving early in the morning and often not returning until well after dusk. Catherine and I spent many evenings facing one another across the dinner table, eating silently.

Catherine, for all her quiet manner, seemed very taken with herself. Her eyes were bright and lively. She would laugh to herself at odd times as though suddenly remembering something funny. She didn't seem to mind if Richard was out. I wondered if she had a beau, perhaps a gentleman she'd met at the coffee house. Whatever reason had brought about her change of mood, she chose not to tell me about it. I was happy enough with her good humour.

I had another reason to be thankful. Blake sometimes accompanied Richard during those long hours away from the house. When Richard dashed back home, Blake at his heels, to change his shirt or fetch papers from his study, it was hard to tell who was master and who was servant. Blake dressed so grandly, and swaggered about like a country squire.

Once, very late in the evening when I was too restless to sleep, I crept downstairs in search of some milk. A light shone from the open door of the study. Blake was inside, dressed in Richard's embroidered burgundy waistcoat and the riding jacket with the high collar. They were a poor fit; Blake was at least half a foot taller than his employer and thinner, but he sat like a lord in the leather armchair with a pipe in his mouth and a curl of blue smoke veiling his face. An open bottle of port stood on the desk. Manservants had been thrashed for less but I recalled the way Blake watched Richard. I forgot about my glass of milk, went back upstairs and locked my bedroom door.

Later in the week, Catherine relented and decided to take me with her to the circulating library. Thick, boiling clouds had rolled in from the sea, stacking up on top of one another like loose heaps of dirty cotton. The air cooled and carried specks of rain. Sharp gusts of wind rattled windows and whistled around the house.

Catherine bundled me into my best cloak, drawing the neck string tight. I felt like a ten-year-old. Outside, the town was a clamour of barking dogs and noisy traders. Carriages trundled past, lanterns rattling. I had to hurry to keep up with Catherine, whose long legs took her down the street in great, effortless strides. She clung to my hand the way she might a dog leash. Richard had taken the coach and Catherine refused to use the gig. It was old and creaked terribly, no matter how much grease the stable lad slapped on the axle. We could have hired chairs, but I was happy to walk with her. I enjoyed the fresh air and the tang of salt on the breeze blowing in from the harbour. I laughed as a street trader accidentally tipped over a slop bucket, causing passing ladies to squeal. I dodged potholes as we crossed the road, jumped cracks in the pavement and yelped with delight when the stagecoach rumbled past on its way to Bristol.

Catherine indulged my mood, and even paused to buy me a sweetmeat from a travelling vendor. It felt as if I'd been shut in that stuffy house for years. I was so glad to be outside I would've done anything to please her.

The new circulating library was housed in a former apothecary, the ghost of which lingered in the dated paintwork and Latin names inscribed above the doorframe. Shelves which had once held vials of powders were now laden with leather-bound volumes of all shapes and sizes. Pressing my face against the window I could see more inside, hundreds more, stacked in every corner. Tall paper towers reached towards the beamed roof and open boxes spilled their contents across the floor.

I fought to contain my excitement as Catherine opened the door and ushered me inside. A mixed scent of musty paper and hot, rich coffee filled my nostrils. A low archway opened into a room furnished with a dozen or so lace-covered tables dotted with newspapers. Patrons sat in high-backed chairs and sipped out of china cups. Some leafed through books or chatted quietly.

A lady and her daughter looked up when we entered. The girl was a smaller reflection of her mother. Same colour gown, identical bonnet a daffodil saucer perched at an angle on her plaited hair. I remembered her from my party. She'd sat near the door, her face slack with boredom, and refused to take part in any games. Her mother leaned over and whispered something in her ear. The girl smirked.

I longed for the books, but obediently followed Catherine's impatient tug on my arm as she shepherded me over to a low counter. Behind it stood a short, stocky man with tufts of white hair poking from the edges of his wig. He beamed at us.

'Good day, Mrs Worledge,' he declared, displaying a set of wooden teeth which protruded grotesquely over his bottom lip. 'Hot coffee and a good book provide the perfect remedy for inclement weather, is that not so?'

Catherine giggled like a milkmaid and mumbled something about how a twinge in cook's gimpy leg suggested it might brighten up later. Glancing at the darkening clouds outside, I thought cook would be as well to cut her leg off if that was the best forecast it could manage. But now the proprietor was peering across the counter at me.

'I see you have brought young Miss Worledge,' he gushed.

I stared at the sloppily tied cravat hugging his fat neck. 'I beg your pardon, sir,' I blurted, 'but my family name is Rodriguez.'

The whole coffee house caught its breath. In a corner, somebody laughed. Whispers rippled around the room and then settled back into the quiet drone of conversation.

Catherine muttered an apology, though I didn't see what she thought she had to be sorry for, and pulled me to a table beside a bay window. A serving girl brought coffee then returned holding a platter heaped with cakes.

I sipped my drink, relishing the strong flavour.

49

Much better than cook's watery tea. I picked up a cake and crammed it into my mouth. It was fresh and hot. Melting butter dribbled down my chin. I laughed at my reflection in the window.

My guardian said nothing. She wouldn't look at me. I was still conscious of other people's eyes darting our way, of the exchanged whispers. I poked my tongue out at one stony-faced lady who recoiled as if she'd been struck.

Catherine's face turned red above the rim of her coffee cup. She tried to read one of the news-papers but it was obvious she couldn't concentrate. Finally, she excused herself and disappeared into the back of the shop, presumably in search of a privy, or a secluded corner where she could cool her temper.

I lifted my cup to take another sip and became aware of someone standing over me, the girl who'd been chatting with her mother. She regarded me with wide blue eyes.

'My mama says you have tainted blood.'

I put down my coffee cup. 'What did you say?'

'Your blood is tainted. That stupid mark on your face proves it.'

I stared at her for a few moments, hot coffee rolling around inside my mouth. Then I did something that no one, myself included, expected.

I hit her.

Chapter Three

I don't know exactly what happened. It was as if my hands flew off the ends of my wrists before my brain had a chance to react. I remember feeling astonished at seeing my fingers in a flapping frenzy around her cheeks. The rest of my coffee tipped over her satin-bowed dress. She threw a screaming fit, grabbed a handful of my hair and hauled me out of my seat. I kicked her shins. She let go and I pushed her out of the way. She fell over another chair, caught the tablecloth on the way down and dragged everything on to the floor.

Catherine appeared, tight-faced, at my side. Sputtering apologies and cake crumbs to the girl's mother, she took hold of my arm and propelled me towards the door. My skin hurt where she pinched it and my eyes were watering because of what that strumpet had done to my hair. Out in the street, Catherine's expression warned me to keep quiet. No stroll back to the house this time. She summoned a chair and crammed us both inside. Her bony knees dug into my backside as the sedan jiggled along the road. The bearers were red-faced and puffing by the time they brought us to our front door. Catherine dismissed them without a tip, ignoring their sullen looks. Charity was the last thing on her mind. She didn't take me upstairs to the nursery but into the parlour. Right away I knew we were going to have one of *those* conversations.

'What an appalling scene,' she began. 'You disgraced me in front of everyone. First you were impertinent to Mr Ruddlewade. Then you start brawling like some street urchin with Mrs Parkhurst's daughter. I never know what you're thinking, Juliana. I cannot fathom your mind at all. Now we shall be the talk of the whole town.'

'The girl was rude,' I protested, 'and the coffee shop owner was wrong to call me Miss Worledge. What was I supposed to do?'

Catherine paced the carpet, clenching and unclenching her fingers. 'Worledge is your name and you'd best not forget it if you wish to lead a peaceful life in this house. Rodriguez is not suitable for the daughter of a respectable English shipping family.'

'I am not your daughter. Take away my name and I'll have nothing left.'

She halted. Livid red spots returned to her cheekbones and spread across her face. 'My husband brought you into this household. He saved you from the gutter and gave you a home. You had a criminal for a father and your mother was little better than a harlot, yet you sleep under my roof, sit at my table and take comfort at my hearth. How can you call that nothing?'

'You never talk about my parents. Whenever I ask, you order me to hold my tongue or go to my room. I can't mention it without scratching your temper.'

'Everything will be explained to you when you come of age. Believe me, you will wish you had never broached the subject. Think on that before

52

you spite me again in public. There is a limit even to Richard's charity.'

She wrenched open the door and stormed into the hall. I didn't want to cry, but my face cracked open like old dough. 'Why did you take me in if I'm such a burden?' I called after her.

'Why...?'

As thunderclouds boiled over Wexborough, so I weathered my own storm. Forbidden once again to leave the house, I tucked myself away in the back parlour with whatever books I managed to filch from Richard's study.

Catherine took her meals alone and stayed out of my way, which suited me. I'd had enough of her sour face and moods that changed from fair to foul depending on her whims.

Clouds hung in the sky like rolls of dirty sackcloth. Rain fell in sheets, hissing on window-panes and swamping the road outside. Thunder rumbled. Lightning cut the sky in two with bright spears.

I scampered into the empty dining room, which boasted the tallest window in the house, and watched as each flash painted the sky with fire. Street hawkers had been driven under cover. Shops barred their doors as rain turned gutters into fast-flowing rivers.

I was eager to throw open the window and scream into the clouds, to feel the thunder pummel my ears and taste the sweet rain on my lips. I wanted to dance in the downpour with my hair flapping around my cheeks. I was alive and I adored it. I relished the rush of blood in my ears, the feel of air sucked into my lungs, the tingling in my fingertips as if I had touched the very core of the storm. I felt as if nothing could hurt me.

The weather broke after two endless days, leaving the town looking washed and new. The air had lost its clammy feel. A warm breeze tickled in off the hills behind the town.

Catherine decided she couldn't stay away from her precious circulating library. The house was too quiet. Richard was away almost all the time now. Sometimes I heard him stumbling through the door in the small hours when the summer heat robbed me of sleep. Blake waited up for him, laughing whenever Richard bumped into something and sent it clattering to the floor. That laughter felt like a demon running its fingers down my spine.

Catherine pinned a bonnet to her hair and put on a fat pearl necklace. Against her pink skin, it resembled a row of gleaming teeth. She wore a light summer gown with a scandalously low neckline, trimmed with taffeta bows. Tight corsets gave her the waist of a girl ten years her junior. A coloured feather dangled from the brim of her hat.

She was like a child with a new scarf or fairing from the market. 'Fetch me a sedan,' she ordered a footman. When it arrived she was out the door in a breeze of rich cologne. I watched from the parlour window as she squeezed her petticoats into the chair and tapped on the door. The bearers set off, dodging puddles the returning sun hadn't yet managed to dry out.

I was sitting by the window when, less than an

hour later, she returned.

Anger pulled Catherine's cheeks as tight as drum skins. The chair had barely touched the pavement when she had the door open and was out, brushing aside the helping hand one of the bearers tried to offer her. She tore open her reticule and threw a handful of coins into the dirt before storming up the front steps. I heard her shoes clattering on the hall tiles followed by a muffled exclamation from the maid.

'Juliana!'

Catherine could always sniff me out when her temper was hot. I stood with my back pressed against the window as she blustered into the room. Her bonnet was torn off in a shower of pins and hurled into the corner.

'Everyone knows.' Each word was a barb dipped in poison. 'My reputation lies in tatters.'

She pulled off her gloves a finger at a time. Her mouth was a thin gash. 'They were all talking about me. My name was thrown around that coffee house as if I wasn't even there.'

She slapped the gloves on to the table. 'Do you know what is being said about me, Juliana? More to the point, my dear, darling girl, can you imagine what they think of you after that commotion the other day?'

They could call me the devil's daughter for all I cared. I just wanted to push myself through the glass and run up the street as fast as my trembling legs would take me. I didn't want to fight with Catherine again. I was sick of fighting.

Now the bows were coming off, torn from Catherine's bodice so that they littered the floor like dead butterflies. She ripped off her necklace. Pearls scattered across the rug. 'I warned you that you can't just behave any way you like, especially not in public. Mr Ruddlewade told me to my face that I was not to bring you to his establishment again. I was forced to pay for the damage you inflicted on his crockery. Right in front of those smirking women. "I will have my compensation now, madam," those were his very words, "or will be obliged to inform the magistrate".'

I couldn't hold my peace any longer. 'Why does it matter to you what those people think? They only care about themselves and their precious gossip.'

'That gossip could cost us dear,' she snapped back. 'Those women have husbands, Juliana. Men who have money invested in Richard's business. And what of me, if I cannot walk the street without stares and whispers following me like a pack of hounds? The whole town is probably aware of your little escapade. I don't dare show my face socially again.'

Catherine paused. Her breath rattled in her throat. She stared at the mess on the floor, then at her ruined gown, as if only just realising what she'd done.

'Promise me that you will heed every word of mine from now on and be obedient to my wishes without question.'

I shook my head. 'When you make that sort of promise, there always comes a time when you have to break it. Then you are sorry and you hate yourself.'

Catherine sighed. With that one sound I knew I

was lost.

'I want you out of my house.'

'It's Richard's house.'

Contempt replaced the fury in her eyes. 'Don't play the fool. It was never Richard's.'

That night Mr Worledge returned early. He'd contrived to win at cards and threw a scattering of coins across the dining-room table.

'Thought I'd try a hand or two before coming home.' He beamed. 'You should have seen the look on those rogues' faces when I trumped the lot of them. Told you good fortune would smile on me. It'll be a new bonnet for you, Catherine, or perhaps a brooch if you've a fancy.'

He leaned over. Brandy fumes wafted into my face. 'And how about a bunch of ribbons for your pretty head, eh, Juliana? Mustn't forget the other lady of the house.'

He fixed me with the bemused, foggy look that had squatted on his face so much of late. The pitiful collection of coins gleamed on the table-cloth. I thought of the I.O.U.s littering his study desk, made out to the very men he had so proudly taken a pittance from tonight, and I went on eating my dinner.

Much later in the night, Richard and Catherine had a storming row. A grumbling stomach had taken me to the kitchen in search of bread and hot milk. I listened at the parlour door as they yelled at one another like children quarrelling over a broken toy.

'The girl is no good,' Catherine declared. 'She has cast a shadow on this house from the day you

57

brought her over our threshold. Well, I have had enough. I will suffer that petulant, cherry-streaked face of hers no longer. If this is how she will meddle in my affairs now, what calamities has she in store for me in the future?'

Richard's voice: 'Girls at that difficult age are by nature precocious. It is the same for all parents of young ladies.'

'She's no lady. Did you see the way our male guests eyed her at the party? No, I don't suppose you did. You were too engaged in entertaining your drunken friends to notice much of anything. That girl was a trap for men from the day she bawled her way into this world.'

'Catherine...'

'Oh, what would you know of women, you farmer's sop? You would still be up to your knees in horseshit if I hadn't brought you into your fortune. If you are a man it is only because I have made you one. I will not have that harlot's daughter defy me in my own house as if she were my flesh and blood instead of some baggage you were tricked into taking as your own.'

The chink of a decanter. The gurgle of liquid poured into a glass.

'Indeed,' Richard continued, voice splintering, 'what kind of man am I with a wife who cannot bear me a child? I took Juliana partly because you wanted a daughter and we have strived to raise her as such. Yet you have chained her, heart and soul, and suffer despair because she does not think as you do.'

'I wanted a daughter, yes. Not some changeling who haunts my waking hours, makes me look a

58

fool in public and treats our good English name as if it was something despicable. She sleeps under our roof but never thinks of herself as one of us. Where does that leave your precious manhood, Richard, when your adoptive daughter would rather be laughed at in the street than permit herself to be called Worledge? No, she must go. She must learn to be a lady or I won't admit her into my home again.'

In the hallway and the lower rooms, the servants closed down the house for the night. Candles were snuffed, curtains drawn, fires damped down. Nobody spared me a glance, though I knew they were listening keenly. I wanted to shrink back into the powder-pink walls and let the shadows swallow me up.

'I shall send her abroad,' Catherine said now, 'with a governess to curb her surly moods and teach her the value of manners as well as respect for her betters. Juliana will have that time in which to redeem herself, or finish up in the gutter she seems so hell-bent on calling her own.'

'You can't send her away,' Richard countered. 'I promised him, Catherine. I gave my oath that I'd keep her under my roof and see she wanted for nothing.'

'What does it matter to you, a drunk who uses his time to waste my money?'

'I have my honour. If nothing else, I still have that.'

'Your honour lies at the bottom of a brandy bottle along with your wits. Leave the thinking to those that have a mind to do it. I am bound by no promise of yours, least of all one made to a convicted murderer. Think on that the next time you fudge a hand of cards.'

They argued some more, but Catherine had already bested him and Richard was merely trying to salvage pride. I slipped away from the door and started fumbling up the stairs to my bed. Catherine's words gnawed at my mind. I had nothing of my mother's. No picture or scrap of lace. No memory. Was it her red hair on my head, or my father's? Did I see through her eyes, or his? And the birthmark – whom did I have to thank for that?

Someone was watching me from the bottom of the stairwell. The candles in the hall had been extinguished, but a puddle of light splashed across the tiles from the open study door. I paused, nerves straining. I could hear him breathing, a rasping edge to each lungful of air. A tiny circle of orange glowed as he drew on a pipe, and fragrant smoke drifted past me towards the shadowed roof.

Instinctively I moved nearer to the wall. He chuckled and slipped back into the darkness, leaving a hint of cologne in the air. I recognised the sweet, fruity smell as one of Richard's favourites.

But Richard was still in the parlour arguing with his wife.

I scurried up the remaining stairs and along the passage to my bedchamber as fast as my flapping nightshift allowed. Once inside, I closed the door, fumbled for the key and turned it in the lock. My throat was dry and I felt sick. The stink of pipe smoke clung to me like leprosy. I wanted to throw my windows wide and suck in the night air, let it wash over me like a soothing balm. But all I could see was *his* face. I kept the casement fastened, pulled the curtains across the face of the moon and wriggled under my bedclothes.

I was to be gone from the house within the week. Richard would not look me in the eye or say a word in my defence. Deever oversaw the packing of my belongings into a pair of enormous, leather-clad trunks.

My new keeper was quickly engaged. On the day I was due to leave she turned up at the house in a gown the colour of ashes and a bonnet like an overcast sky. Even her face had the hue of dead flesh. Only her hair, which was the colour of rich mahogany, seemed in any way lively, though her expression when she greeted me was as unforgiving as her apparel.

'So this is the girl?' she said, eyeing me.

Mary Morgan was her name, and I was obliged to curtsy to her in front of the servants. Catherine ushered us both into the parlour, where I endured the coldest cup of tea that had ever wet my tongue. Miss Morgan coughed a great deal and smelled vaguely of garlic. She nibbled at her scone, wearing it down to the size of a pebble with her busy lips. Pleasantries were exchanged with Catherine in clipped sentences as though someone had taken shears and snipped away at each word. I kept stealing glances, trying to guess this dusty woman's age. Years of scowling had cut furrows into her forehead, yet she had the pink hands of a girl.

Catherine had booked our passage aboard a small packet boat called the *Lucky Maid*. The captain was one of Richard's men. I'd never met him, though knew he had a reputation for giving short shrift to passengers. Livestock and chattels were his business, not a pair of fragile women, but his vessel was bound for Belgium and there wouldn't be another for some days.

I was to share a cabin with Miss Morgan, into whose charge I was immediately placed. My luggage was already on its way to the docks. Richard had gone out and the servants had better things to do than see off the 'little viper' who was responsible for their mistress's foul moods.

Catherine lingered beside the front door. Was this goodbye or good riddance? My stomach was in knots at the thought of the journey ahead.

'Well?' she said. 'Have you nothing to say for yourself? No final words before you go? Making eloquent speeches was never a problem for you before, Juliana. Why so silent now?'

I drew my shawl tightly around my shoulders and climbed down the steps to the waiting gig. Summer was slipping away and the wind whistling down the street carried the first cool breath of autumn.

The *Lucky Maid* was a squat looking vessel of weathered timber. Eyeing her from the dockside, I wondered how anyone could dare venture out to sea on such a modest ship, let alone trade cargo in foreign ports. She sat low in the water like a featherless duck, the gaudy figurehead grinning down at me with chipped eyes. The harbour breeze was thick with the smell of sour fish and canvas. Men rolling barrels up the gangplank leered at me.

'Wait here,' Miss Morgan instructed. 'I will go and speak to the captain.'

As soon as she was out of sight I edged away from the quayside. Dock workers swarmed around stacks of barrels and crates, struggling to get them loaded. Pedlars hawked goods. Carts and carriages trundled past in endless succession. The rich rubbed shoulders with the lowly as both jostled to board vessels bound for places I'd only read about. A troop of soldiers marched past to the tune of drum and fife, looking grand in their scarlet uniforms. How many would lie dead before the war in America was over? Did the same thought cross their minds as they walked in perfect step beneath those fluttering banners?

I kept half an eye open for gypsy wagons, but they'd likely be at the other side of the harbour where ships were unloading. I arrived at Richard's offices. The door was locked, the windows shuttered. The building, once proud with a carved sign above the entrance, now looked drab and unwelcoming. Cream paint was beginning to flake off the walls. Moss had taken hold under the eaves and was spreading in a dark stain. On the upper floor the fastenings on a shutter had worked loose, letting it swing wide.

A tall hat bobbed through the crowds. Mr Littlejohn, Richard's business associate, hove into view. He was in an uncommon hurry for a man who was prone to falling asleep at his desk – something Richard had always joked about over dinner.

I checked to make sure Miss Morgan hadn't reappeared then went after him, dodging tradesmen and beggars. He stopped and turned at the sound of his name.

'Miss Juliana,' he declared, peering at me with his muddy eyes. 'A long time since I've had the pleasure of your company. Too long, I think.'

Some people are born old. I couldn't picture Mr Littlejohn as a boy. Age clung to him like a tight pair of breeches. He grinned mawkishly, baring fake teeth that stuck out over his bottom lip. The fingers and thumb of one hand danced along the end of his walking stick, beating out a restless tattoo.

'Richard has not been to the office?' It was more statement than question.

Mr Littlejohn removed his spectacles and rubbed them on the hem of his cotton waistcoat. 'It's been more than a month now. I have my hands full trying to keep the business afloat and our investors are losing patience. I don't know what concerns keep Mr Worledge away from his office, but if he does not minister to pressing affairs soon then my efforts shall have been wasted. I have tradesmen baying for my blood, excise men at the door and ship crews threatening mutiny. Yet my warnings go unheeded.'

He coughed. Spittle flew from his mouth. 'I can manage for a while longer, but there are important decisions that only Mr Worledge can make. When I receive instructions they are sent by letter and that man of his, Blake, keeps turning up and barking orders as if he was the one trying to put shillings in our employees' pockets.'

He took out a snuffbox, flipped the lid and took a generous pinch. After a moment he sneezed, shaking a cloud of powder from his wig.

'You must forgive me, Juliana,' he continued, eyes watering. 'I mustn't burden you with the problems of trade and commerce. A man forgets himself when matters weigh heavily on his mind. What brings you to the harbour today? You're not alone I take it?'

'I'm being sent abroad with a new governess. The trip is to better my education. To teach me to be a proper lady.'

'This is rather sudden.'

I nodded. 'We are travelling aboard the *Lucky Maid*. My new guardian is talking to the captain.'

'Sailors are a superstitious lot. Out on the ocean they will look for bad omens in everything. It might pay to be discreet.'

'Do you mean my birthmark?'

'Indeed, forgive my impertinence, but you may wish to powder your face.'

'Thank you for your concern, but I've been in hiding long enough.'

'Quite so. How long will you be gone?'

'I'm not sure. A year. Perhaps two.'

'A long time for a child to be away from home.'

'I'm hardly a child, Mr Littlejohn.'

'Even less so when you return. We must talk then, Juliana.' He tapped me on the shoulder with his cane. 'There are important matters to discuss which concern you and you alone.'

I was about to ask him what he meant when Miss Morgan billowed along the quay front in her coffin-clothes.

'I have to go,' I told Mr Littlejohn. 'I promise to speak to you when I come back.' I squeezed his arm and ran off to join my new guardian. She

65

glanced doubtfully at Richard's colleague but made no comment as she led me back to the *Lucky Maid*. Halfway up the gangplank I paused and looked back. Mr Littlejohn, once Richard's closest confidant, was scuttling back towards the harbour wall, holding his hat against the breeze. People put their heads together and laughed as he passed, though he was a well-known figure around the docks and there was no malice in it. A final look at the shuttered offices, then I fastened my cloak before climbing up the last part of the gangplank to where Miss Morgan waited.

Chapter Four

If the wind was brisk around the docks, it was howling on the open sea. Waves smacked against the planking of our ship, showering the deck in brittle spray. I'd never been on any kind of boat before and wasn't sure I liked the way the floor kept moving under my feet. Panic gripped me when the shoreline disappeared, swallowed up by the grey mist that even the strongest wind seemed unable to clear.

Miss Morgan refused to come out of the cramped cabin we shared. I often heard her retching into the basin at the side of her narrow bunk. I spent as much time on deck as I could. Once I'd come to terms with the heaving seas, I felt genuinely free for the first time in my life. Gulls screamed in my ears and wheeled like white kites above the masthead. The open air salted my tongue and the wind whipped my hair about my cheeks.

The ship's first mate clapped me on the shoulder and told me, winking, that I had good sea legs. 'Must have had a seafarer in your family,' he remarked, scratching at the puckered scar that seemed to split his face in two. 'You can always tell them that do. They take to boats the way fish take to water.'

Breakfast was taken with Captain Henry Lockhart, a sallow, bitter man who seemed to have taken up sailing as a result of ill fortune either in love or business. His cabin was a shrine to the life he had apparently once known, all gilt-edged books and silver tableware.

'Having women on board is a nuisance,' he declared, carving his meat into tiny squares. 'Some consider it bad luck to carry passengers on a merchant vessel. Can't say I'm superstitious myself, but Mrs Worledge must be in a hurry to get you to Belgium if she put you on my boat.'

What we knew of Lockhart we learned from the crew. Sailors it seemed were full of stories, each more fantastic than the last. I never knew if they believed their own yarns or were merely teasing us, but they lightened the journey and made Miss Morgan forget her queasy stomach. There had been times at the breakfast table when her face turned to buttermilk. She picked at her food while both the captain and myself ate heartily.

Time pressed heavily upon us. The fog chased us over the water and enveloped the ship in a clammy shroud. Nothing to see except a circle of featureless ocean around us and nothing to read except the Bible, which was the only book Miss Morgan had brought with her. I had been allowed none as they took up too much space in my luggage. My sense of freedom had evaporated. Instead of enjoying a great adventure, I spent hours curled up on my narrow cot, watching the lantern swing from its hook on the ceiling. Everything familiar was gone. My stomach turned in slow flips that had nothing to do with the swell of seawater against the *Lucky Maid's* hull. My entire world had been crammed into the trunks I'd brought from Wexborough. I felt neither brave nor clever, and there was no way off the boat. I gave in easily to tears, usually when Miss Morgan braved the deck to take some air. Often I wasn't even aware of the reason. Catherine's temper? Blake's unwelcome attentions? The worst aspects of the Butter House receded into a vague mental fug. I pined for my room, Richard's books, the park – everything about the noisy, clamorous town I'd left behind.

You've hardly been gone at all, I reasoned, yet in allowing myself to be sent away I had suffered a defeat. I felt shamed, guilty, a dozen other things. I *had* to be a bad person, surely, or none of this would have happened?

Sometime towards evening Miss Morgan overheard one of the sailors crack a ribald joke to his friend and she suddenly burst into laughter, her face as red as a field of poppies.

Settling down for the night in our cramped quarters, I asked her to tell me what she had heard. The mask fell back at once.

'Say your prayers then go to sleep,' she told me, 'tomorrow we will reach land and be off this wooden tomb. I am weary of the way it pitches like a carriage on a potholed road.'

But just before she blew out the candle, a smile crept back across her lips.

Rain was hammering down by the time *Lucky Maid* groaned into the crowded port and the crew made her fast against the quay. I leaned over the rail and viewed the grim scene before me. This dirty, grey place that stank of sewage and rotten fish, where buildings were crumbling and the locals went about dressed like beggars, had no place in the beautiful leather-bound books of Richard's study.

Miss Morgan and I exchanged glances. I'd heard she was well travelled but perhaps things had changed since she was last here. I was reluctant to leave the wooden planking of the *Lucky Maid's* deck. The crew was already beginning to unload the cargo. This was just another harbour, a place to work and then move on. They had not been banished.

A gloved hand slipped into my own and squeezed my fingers. Miss Morgan's face remained as stern as the flagstones of the dock. 'I will see if I can find a carriage,' she said, 'though forgive me if I come back with nothing better than a cabbage cart and an old donkey.'

My long exile began badly. For the first few days it would not stop raining and the bad roads frayed our nerves. It was a dull, colourless world we viewed from the window of our jostling carriage. We drove between fields that stretched for miles over flat land without a single hedge, populated by scarecrow people dressed in filthy rags who stared at us as we rattled past.

We slipped over the border into France. Though in an enemy country, we were regarded as a pair of harmless English fancies who would breeze away again like the wind that swept the south coast.

Everywhere, the poor, crippled and desperate littered the roads. There was no respect in their dirty faces, only a sullen animosity. Our coachman used his whip liberally to clear them from the lanes. Miss Morgan pulled down the blinds. 'Don't look at them,' she told me. 'There are many angry people in this part of the world, and anger can lead a man to forget his place.'

I settled back into my seat. I had already noticed how the rich lived in this country. We had passed their magnificent chateaux surrounded by gardens filled with fountains and flowers. Nowhere before had I witnessed such a vast gulf separating rich and poor.

The miles rolled on in a daze of jolting roads, cold days and restless nights spent in flea-ridden inns. Even the best of these seemed populated by tiny, tooth-laden demons intent on chewing our tender English flesh. In one memorable establishment the roof leaked, dripping water on my bed for hours on end. When I moved the leak seemed to move with me, until I gave up and woke the following morning with a damp nightshift and snivelling nose.

At the next place we stopped, the landlady's smile died on her lips and she flapped her hands in the air before slamming the door in our faces. Our coachman, Jacques, who had learned English from his sailor father, held a shouted conversation with her through a half-shuttered window.

'It is the red mark on *l'enfant*'s face,' he explained when he returned. 'She thinks the child has the plague and will not let her into the house.'

Miss Morgan and I spent that night in the coach while Jacques slept underneath with a pistol tucked into his coat. Thankfully it did not rain again.

And so it went on. One inn looked pleasant enough but harboured a barky little dog that never shut up, not once, all the time we were there. I hated the food, the water smelled and tasted strange, and I could not master the sing-song language no matter how patiently Miss Morgan tried to teach me. We visited crumbling castles and canals, took in some sagging French towns where tensions seemed to simmer beneath the shoddy façades. She told me of the country's history while I yawned and pined for the greener, friendlier fields of England.

Days turned into weeks and still my new guardian's cautious enthusiasm did not dampen. She called me Miss Rodriguez throughout, never Juliana. Only once did she address me as Miss Worledge.

'Don't call me that,' I growled. 'Don't you ever use that name, not in England, not here, not anywhere.'

The mistake was not repeated.

We had been advised to stay away from Paris. 'A hotbed of pestilence,' was how Miss Morgan described it, and I was told that we would not be visiting Spain, though I was given no reasons why. Instead we left Jacques at the coast and took a boat from Brittany southwards to Portugal, where Miss Morgan went down with some sort of ague in a Lisbon guest house, leaving me fretting for days with nothing but the view from the window and a simple-minded maid for company.

Then it was on the water again, through the Straits of Gibraltar and onwards to Marseilles. The land changed now as we delved deeper into Europe, from rolling vineyards to lofty mountain peaks. I took in opera in Vienna, chamber music in Salzburg and fell asleep in a museum in Prague. Weeks turned into months and the seasons paraded past in a succession of summer greens, autumn golds and crisp winter whites.

Every night after supper Miss Morgan sat down and took writing paper together with some quills from the small black valise that always accompanied our luggage. She set down word of our travels, and my progress, in her neat hand. I don't know how many of those painstaking epistles made it back to the shores of England, or whether any were received in return. We seemed to be on the move all the time, like leaves blowing in a restless autumn wind.

Finally, we travelled south again to Italy. Dark-skinned men pinched my skirts and made me feel like a queen while Miss Morgan blushed violets. We ate delicious food dripping with oils that brought spots out on my face. I could feel history instead of having it crammed into my head. A land of kind weather and ancient ruins. People with dancing hearts sang and squabbled in the space of a breath. Everyone talked with wild, excited gestures whenever anyone was willing to listen.

In Florence, we rented rooms in a three-storey house near the River Arno. The building was owned by a florid-faced dowager and her pregnant daughter, Elizabetta, who grinned at everything. Her belly was as enormous as her smile and she heaved it about as if it was a bundle of laundry. I hadn't thought it possible for a human body to swell to that size. Expectant ladies in Wexborough spent the last weeks of their confinement in the privacy of their chambers. They did not strip the linen from beds or hang out washing while humming tunes around a mouthful of pegs. The girl was not married but no one seemed to care, which was surprising in such a papist country. Any one of the half-dozen or so laughing, impudent young men who delivered goods to the back door could have put her with child. They all treated her with equal affection.

Every morning I had to wake up to that grin when Elizabetta waddled in to open the curtains. Thinking her insolent, I complained to her mother. In stuttering English, the dowager explained that her daughter was born grinning.

Deformed face muscles had frozen that smile on to her plump cheeks and she would take it to her grave.

'Men think she is good for anything. How can they take no for an answer when she is smiling at them all the time?'

Miss Morgan conducted my lessons on the terrace overlooking the river. Hours were spent learn-

73

ing Latin, which I picked up quickly, and Italian, which I didn't. A local instructor schooled me in dancing and social etiquette. Where the money for that came from I don't know. Miss Morgan paid it, with a po-face, out of her seemingly bottomless reticule. Wasted money, as my feet would not go where I wanted. I tripped, stumbled and fell flat on my behind. Just as well I couldn't understand my teacher's exasperated remarks when I trod on his toes or elbowed him in the midriff.

One afternoon I returned from sketching on the riverbank to find the house full of screams. I peered through an open door. Elizabetta was spread-eagled on an enormous bed, her thick legs splayed. The room stank of sweat and hot linen. A bald-headed man, stripped to the waist, squatted between her knees. I thought, what in God's name is going on? Did a secret brothel run within the ochre-coloured walls? The man offered encouragement. Blood smeared his chest. The dowager, who stood behind the chair, grasped her daughter's hands. Elizabetta heaved and spilled out something small and wrinkled. A thick sausage-like cord tied it to somewhere deep inside her. Spasms rippled along the girl's flaccid thighs. She groaned and heaved again.

The next thing I knew I was on my back in my bedchamber and Miss Morgan was applying wet linen to my forehead.

'Was I sick?' I whispered.

She nodded. 'You made quite a sight sprawled across the tiles. The dowager's son brought you upstairs.'

'They must think me a fool.'

'A little weak-kneed perhaps. In any case, Elizabetta is delighted with her baby daughter.'

'I'll never let a man touch me,' I declared.

'If the right man does the touching, you will want it with all your heart,' Miss Morgan replied.

I tilted my head to look at her, but she wrung out the linen and said nothing more.

Two streets away from the apartment, Miss Morgan discovered a small, tree-ringed park and took to walking there for half an hour each morning. Tired of listening to the baby's bawling, I asked my guardian if I might join her. To my horror, I found the place overrun with children.

'The park is a favourite haunt of mothers,' Miss Morgan informed me. 'Toddlers like to play on the lawns. This can be a dusty town. Grass draws them like water.'

After a few minutes strolling amid the trees, we took a bench by the fountain and talked for a while. Miss Morgan named all the plants, and commented on the architecture of the surrounding buildings. She would not tell me anything about herself, despite my gentle promptings. It was almost as if the sun couldn't penetrate the dull clothes she still wore. I noticed, however, that her gaze never strayed far from the children. Even on our route between the house and the park, she snatched thief-like glances at other people's babies.

Next morning, under the trees, a poppet-faced girl left behind a strip of lace, which had become snagged on one of the rose bushes. Miss Morgan worked it loose and tucked it into her sleeve.

Many times over the next few days I caught her with that strip in her hand, running her fingers over the material.

I was changing. In half a dozen months I had turned from a scampering child into a bundle of lank, swinging limbs.

Spots ravaged my face. As soon as one died another three took its place, usually somewhere horribly visible like the end of my nose or middle of my brow. My beautiful hair of deep burnished copper turned stringy and awkward despite hours of determined brushing.

'I need new clothes,' I told Miss Morgan, while struggling to squeeze into one of my old gowns. Everything was either too tight, too short or both. I was conscious of the way my body pushed against the material, of the shoes that felt like satin vices.

'You must have a new dress,' she agreed, appraising me. 'Something sensible and hard-wearing. I shall take you to the dressmaker's tomorrow.'

'You need something too.' Her grey dress was wearing at the elbows and the hem was frayed. A button was missing from the top of her bodice and another two were working loose. 'You'd look pretty in a blue gown with wide, white bows.'

Miss Morgan looked down at herself and her pale cheeks turned a shade of pink.

As promised she took me to a dress shop the following morning. The proprietor, a hawk-faced woman who spat English in a carving-knife hiss, stood by as Miss Morgan ordered a plain grey gown for herself and the most uninteresting jumble of cloth ever stitched by human hands for me. I suffered the indignity of being measured and tried not to flinch when the drab material was draped over my shoulders.

'I must slip out for a while,' Miss Morgan told me. 'Stay here. Don't wander.'

The second she was out the door I pulled off the sack she'd bought me and dropped it on to the floor. 'I'm not a beggar or milkmaid and I won't dress like either,' I declared.

The proprietor's eyes flicked over the discarded garment. 'What would the young lady suggest?'

Two women, sisters from the look of it, were standing near the window poring over some material. They were too engrossed to notice me. I pointed to the younger girl. 'I want to look like her.'

'Will cost extra. More than your friend has given me.'

I had an allowance set by; money Miss Morgan had provided which I'd never had cause to spend. 'I will pay you.' I tried to sound confident. 'And when I have chosen a gown for myself, we will pick something for my guardian. That grey thing she ordered belongs in a nunnery.'

I chose swiftly. A rose pink gown with a low, square neckline, fitted bodice and pagoda sleeves trimmed with taffeta bows. I decided to forsake a bonnet in favour of a square of gauze worn over a powdered wig. This, the dressmaker assured me, was very much in favour with well-to-do Italian ladies and sure to catch the eye of any gentleman.

For Miss Morgan we selected a pale blue gown with an embroidered bodice, sleeves and a looped skirt. The sort of thing the wife of an English vicar might wear for a tea party.

'Still, it is not the sort of garment I can imagine madam wearing, modest as it is,' my adviser remarked dryly. 'She does not seem the sort.'

'She is,' I assured her. 'She simply doesn't know it yet. Say nothing and deliver these to our apartments. It will be a surprise for her.'

I wriggled back into my old gown. When my guardian returned I waited innocently as the dressmaker informed her the garments would arrive in two days.

'Good,' Miss Morgan said. 'I have met the most charming English family. We have been invited to a party in celebration of their eldest son's birthday. The garments will arrive just in time.'

How nice, I thought.

The package was delivered at the end of the week. Miss Morgan threw a fit when she saw what I'd done, but she put on the blue dress and let me wear my new gown. She sat tight-lipped as we rode in a hired carriage to the party. The event was held in a large house near the centre of town, owned by a friend of Mr Thompson, the gentleman whose son's birthday we had come to celebrate. After a flurry of introductions, Mr Thompson made small talk with Miss Morgan. He complimented her on her dress and she blushed a deep scarlet, thanking him with the voice of a mouse.

At the dinner table, I sat and picked through my food. Boiled meat, vegetables, potatoes dripping with butter. None of the colourful Italian delicacies that had enslaved my stomach these past few weeks. Most of the other guests were English and they had a lot to say about themselves. Mr Thompson's eldest son was a swaggering nineteen-year-old who bragged as if he'd been born to it. He seemed to assume that one smile was enough to burst the heart of every girl in the room. I stared at the bits of food rolling around in his ever-working mouth and thought how the local men would laugh at his bluster.

The younger brother, a callow, lean-faced youth called Roderick, nudged me under the table. 'Come with me,' he whispered. The dancing had started and most of the guests had taken to the floor or were in the drawing room smoking or drinking port. I had been enjoying a glass of wine that was too large for my own good and felt light-headed. We slipped from the room and Roderick led me by the hand up a flight of stairs and then another until I stood with him, heart beating like sparrow's wings, on a darkened landing. Only a streak of moonlight through the window in the far wall lit our faces.

'This part of the house is not in use,' he whispered. 'No one ever comes here.'

'I will be missed,' I told him, pretending not to notice as his arms curled around my waist like warm-blooded snakes.

His face was only an inch from my own. Words whispered across my cheek. 'Not yet.'

In the peaceful gloom we exchanged breathless kisses. At first the bad memories rushed in. Blake's bruising fumbles. But Roderick's touch was soft and left my mouth tingling. He held me gently and I tasted bittersweet wine on his lips.

We remained like that for several moments, saying nothing while he drank me and I in turn became intoxicated by his warmth. But when his hand strayed towards my bodice I let go of him and stepped back.

'No, Roderick,' I said gently.

Confusion rippled across his face. I was afraid that everything would be spoiled but he smiled and took my hand again. We scampered back downstairs to the noise. Miss Morgan was lingering on the edge of the dance floor, clapping along to the music. On impulse, I grabbed her arm and hauled her into the middle of the floor.

'Dance with me,' I cried.

It was too late to resist. We were the oddest couple in the room, all feet and no grace, but Miss Morgan laughed and let her hair fall loose. When the hired quartet had finished playing, everyone applauded.

In the carriage home, Miss Mary hummed to herself while I sat clutching the posy of flowers Roderick had slipped into my hands. He told me his family was once more on the move, this time to Rome where his father had some business interests.

Nothing mattered for now. Miss Mary caught me watching her and smiled. She had drawn more than one admirer at the party and her eyes were full of secrets.

'Did you have a nice time, Juliana?' she purred.

I gazed at the flowers. 'Oh yes.'

Weeks merged into one another. We hardly noticed. Summer rolled around again and baked the streets with hot, golden sunshine. We travelled the country, enjoying beauty wherever we found it and discovering treasures in both likely and unlikely places. I could flirt with the local lads so outrageously that it was often I who turned their cheeks red. I had all the music, books and art I could want.

Miss Morgan wore ever more flattering dresses and kept her dark hair around her shoulders instead of scraping it up into ugly coils. A letter arrived for her during a month-long stay in Genoa. As soon as the messenger had gone, she scurried plum-checked to her room. She never told me who'd sent it but I guessed it was not Catherine.

Next day, while savouring the wares of a boisterous local market, she treated herself to a satin neck choker inlaid with a marble cameo.

'You must think me terribly vain,' she said apologetically.

I laughed and helped fasten it around her neck. 'Now you are fair game for any Italian prince.'

'Any man can be a prince,' she replied, 'as long as his heart is good, his love sincere and his head firm upon his shoulders.'

Soon the golden days had to end. My penance was over and England beckoned. We spent our last night on the terrace, listening to the sounds of the night as moths chased one another around the lanterns. In the distance, a man's voice raised in a lilting melody that tingled the nerves. I wonder if he sang to his lover, if he was saying goodbye.

'I shall miss this dear place,' Mary said. 'And you, Juliana. You most of all. You are not the creature Catherine painted you.'

I squeezed her hand. She gave a weary smile and closed her eyes. Light flickered across her eyelids. The distant song ended on a drawn-out note and the silence that replaced it seemed intense. We had become such friends over the days and weeks that it seemed the grey-faced woman I first met in Wexborough could not possibly have existed.

'I wonder if I shall ever wed,' I sighed, thinking back to Roderick and that moon-silvered landing. 'Did you ever come close?'

'Now there's a notion. I think one husband is enough in a lifetime.'

'You are married?' I gasped.

'I was, a long time ago when I was young, almost as young as you, Juliana. My father arranged the union and used up half his fortune to settle a good dowry on me. I was the last child in the family to be wed and I daresay Papa was keen to be rid of me. I was always a burden on his patience. My new husband only wanted money and an heir, but I loved him. I was an age to love anyone. My belly put paid to those fancies. I was barren, so my husband divorced me. It took a year and a ransom in lawyers' fees to do it. When the papers were signed I treated it like a death, wore black and mourned. In the end I became a governess to be near children, even if they were other women's children. It is an acceptable profession for one in my position and I do not have to rely too heavily on my father's charity. But all I ever wanted, and still want, is a child of my own. The ability to make life is the most precious gift a woman could possess.'

I swallowed hard. 'Do you know why Catherine sent me on this trip with you?'

She opened her eyes. 'I never question the motives of my employers. It is not my place.'

I shook my head. 'You more than anyone would understand.'

I stood on the quay in my pretty Italian shawl, a frown cracking my face as Mary busied herself checking the luggage. Our modest collection had grown in the course of our travels but I felt like throwing it all into the sea.

The weather, as if sensing our mood, rolled thick clouds across the sky. Specks of rain pecked my cheeks and a stiff breeze whirled around the harbour. A flurry of dust snatched my hair and filled my mouth with grit.

In a moment we would board the ship that would take us back to England. The *Sally Anne* was a merchant vessel that usually brought trade goods from the South Seas. It had been fitted with cannon to ward off the Corsairs that still plagued large areas of the Mediterranean, so the shipping agent had delighted in telling us. I found the idea of being boarded by a band of heathen cut-throats hopelessly romantic, but Mary soon toppled my fantasy.

'They would sell you into slavery, or hang you from a rope and set your hair alight,' she told me. 'Better to jump overboard than fall into the hands of those rogues.'

Our captain was a broad-shouldered Scot by the name of McDermott. He wore a beard the size of a bush and ran his crew like a team of horses. His deep voice boomed out curses and a hefty boot sought the rump of any seaman guilty of slacking.

As our baggage was taken on board the men kept stealing glances. One crossed himself after accidentally brushing against me. Mouths were full of whispers.

'Superstitious rabble,' McDermott said dismissively. 'They don't like that red smear on your face, lass. They should look at their own ugly faces. 'Twould make their mothers nervous.'

'I don't want to cause trouble.'

'Pay them no heed. You'll be treated well enough once we've put to sea.' He clapped me on the shoulder. I tried to smile but the sense of unease stayed with me and grew as the *Sally Anne* slipped its moorings and headed towards open water.

Someone kept watching me. A grizzled sailor with piercing green eyes and candle-wax hair cropped so close I could see the pink of his scalp. He did not cross himself, or turn to papist beads, or make the sign against the evil eye with his fingers. His gaze chained me to the deck, even as he worked. When he was perched in the rigging I could feel him looking down on me. When he scrambled below, I knew I was in his thoughts.

Less than a day out of port, the clouds broke apart and the wind died. All around us the sea was as flat as a blue china plate. Sails hung from the masts like empty canvas sacks. McDermott cursed the skies in some impossible dialect and sent out a rowboat to try to tow us into useful weather. The gentle dollop of oars dipping into water mingled with the creak of the towrope as we inched across the glossy millpond.

I turned away from the rail and there was the watcher, standing like a white-haired ghost I'd somehow conjured out of the decking. He marked me with that dagger gaze and his chapped lips peeled back from his teeth. He possessed the rough-cut countenance of an Englishman but when he spoke it was with the lilt of a Spaniard.

'That mark on your face,' he said. 'I've seen it before, dreaded it all my years on the sea. You're his daughter. No one but his kin could carry the stain.'

We were alone. He could put a blade to my throat and no one would know. I pursed my lips and tried to sound confident. 'I don't know what you mean,' I told him, hiding shaking hands in the folds of my skirts. 'It's just a birthmark.'

He shook his head. Corded veins stood out on his neck. A hand caught my chin. I tried to pull away but he held me firm, his finger tracing the red smear from the corner of my mouth to my jaw line. 'Nay, young lady. 'Tis far more than that. You're Manuel's. You bear the mark.'

I opened my mouth without any notion of what to say. Fear cut me to the pit of my belly. This was not some fanciful sailor's yarn spun to earn a coin from impressionable passengers. Something lurked in this man's face that warned me I was only a whisper away from learning some dreadful truth. I wasn't certain I wanted to hear it.

A hatch opened behind us and someone called. The sailor turned away. I stood knock-kneed as he clambered down the hatch to join his unseen shipmate. After it closed I remained beside the rail for a few more minutes, but he did not reappear.

When I felt calm enough, I went below. No luxury of a cabin this time but the sailors had rigged up a curtain in the corner of the hold. Hammocks stitched over and stuffed with canvas provided mattresses, while the first mate had lent us his bowl and looking glass. Dried fish, fruit and barrels of wine surrounded our makeshift quarters, as well as boxloads of expensive Italian drapery bound for the fashionable London shops. The smell was a little too potent for my nose but Mary seemed not to notice, or be troubled by it if she did. I found her sitting up on her pallet reading from a leather-bound book with a title written in Italian. Her lips worked soundlessly as she tried to improve her skills at the language. Thinking of England with its endless rain and sour-faced merchants only filled me with gloom.

Mary glanced up from the page when I sat down opposite, smiled and went back to her reading. I said nothing. I had a feeling my business with the watcher wasn't yet done.

Darkness fell over the water in a hushed blanket. Mary had fallen asleep early, lulled by a calm sea, which was much kinder to her queasy stomach. I paced the deck, cloak wrapped tight, watching insects circle the flickering lanterns. The boat hugged the shore, close enough for swarms to be drawn to the soft light.

Most of the crew was below apart from the pilot, the watch, and a small group of seamen rolling dice beside a guttering candle. A breeze of words carried on the night air. Someone chuckled when he had a lucky throw, followed by the envious curses of his fellows.

'What's your name?'

I flinched. The watcher peered at me through the gloom. His bare feet had made no sound on the wooden planking. 'What's your name?' he asked again. Rum sweetened his breath. The scent of salt and stale tobacco clung to his canvas breeches. 'Tell me what lie you live under.'

'Juliana Rodriguez,' I said in a little-girl voice.

His eyes widened. They glimmered like jet under the drifting stars. 'So he gave you his name? He must have been taken with you. Or perhaps it was your mother who charmed him.'

'I never knew my parents.'

He laughed softly. 'No surprise there. Few were acquainted with Manuel Rodriguez 'cept at the end of his sword and fewer still who lived to remember. The name Manuel the Bloody came from his scarlet mouth and his appetite for spilling other men's gizzards. He was a Spanish nobleman, robbed of his inheritance by the pretty young whore his father took to his bed. She bore his bastard and took Manuel's fortune, so the lad turned to plundering the shipping lanes. He raided holds, strung crews from their own mastheads and claimed the lives of any passengers, noble or commoner, that had the bad luck to be on board.'

He hawked and spat over the rail. 'No man could catch Manuel the Bloody. In the end, the Spanish king gave him a letter of marque to plunder foreign vessels legally, as a privateer. But the English sprung a trap and hanged him for piracy just the same, in a place called Antigua where he sometimes holed up to spend his booty. Many would dance on his grave.'

'Why are you telling me this?' I demanded. 'What do you want? Do you take pleasure in tormenting me with these gory tales of the past?'

He leaned forward so that his face was inches from mine. I matched his stare, though it chilled me to gaze into those bottomless eyes. 'Any man – or woman – has a right to know who they are and where they hail from. Maybe you have a destiny. What I tell you now might help you pick the right path. It's your due, nothing more.'

He straightened. I was trembling and it had nothing to do with the cool breeze wafting across the waters from the dark, huddled shore.

'I knew Manuel,' he continued. 'I served on one of his ships. For years I butchered for him. I helped spend his stolen gold, shared his harlots and drank myself into the gutter. And I dodged the noose for betraying him. Not that you have to believe me, mind, but the sea is my witness. Sometimes sleep doesn't come easily and I see that mark, bright even against Manuel's sun-beaten skin. I hear him laughing, telling me to settle my dues for turning him over to the English. That debt is now part-paid, and I'll wager every Spanish doubloon or English guinea I've stolen in my life that his blood is your blood, just as his mark is your mark.'

'Who was my mother?'

A hatch slapped open. Mary's sleepy head appeared. The sailor slipped into the shadows. Soft footfalls trailed across the deck.

'Juliana, what are you doing up here? I heard voices. Who were you talking to?'

I glanced over the rail. The black bulk of the

shoreline had faded into the distance. Around us, I felt the thick swell of the open sea. 'Just another seaman with a head full of stories.'

Next day the wind picked up. We had fair sailing all the way to England. When I returned to the Butter House, Catherine was waiting, and it was not long before I stole another child.

Chapter Five

'You look like a whore,' Catherine accused. 'You smell of cheap scent and too much wine. Where did you get that dress, and who smeared rouge on your face?'

I held my tongue and waited while she circled me like a hunting dog. Every so often she reached out to pluck at my bright Italian gown and her mouth curled. I forced myself not to flinch at the touch of her bony fingers. There was a great deal I wanted to say but this was not the right time.

It had proved an inauspicious homecoming. Our ship had docked without incident. A rented gig and pair had brought us and our dust-coated baggage from the harbour and deposited us outside the front door. The Butter House looked mostly unchanged, though the step was in need of a brickbat and the curtains were drawn.

Catherine herself admitted us. She hunched over as she walked. Her slippers whispered like dried leaves on the carpet. She seemed so small, or perhaps it was just that I had grown. Tired lines scored her gaunt face.

'Painted ladies, both of you,' she continued. 'Miss Morgan, your services were engaged on the strength of your reputation. I had hoped you would provide a steadying influence on Juliana. Prove to me that I was not mistaken.'

She sat us both down, in our travelling clothes, while our luggage lay unpacked in the hall. Mary was obliged to describe our trip in detail. Catherine hung on to every word. I was not allowed to interrupt. I wanted tea, or perhaps some water. I was permitted neither. When Mary was finished, sparing neither the truth nor my blushes, Catherine nodded as if nothing my guardian said had surprised her.

'It seems you omitted a great deal from your letters. Your father will hear of this.'

Mary folded her hands together and matched Catherine stare for stare. 'I am afraid, Mrs Worledge, that I have passed the stage where my father's attitudes are of any concern. Miss Rodriguez has learned a great deal during our travels abroad and behaved magnificently. You have every cause to feel proud.'

'Rodriguez is it? The girl has addled your wits. Leave my house before I have your bags thrown into the street. You can expect no further fee or reference. As for you,' she stabbed a finger at me, 'tidy yourself up then join me in the withdrawing room.'

Catherine shuffled off, leaving me in the parlour with Mary. I embraced her, not as a teacher, but a dear friend. She promised to write though we both suspected it was unlikely we would see one another again.

'I don't want any more of her money,' she said, spilling tears into a crumpled handkerchief. 'Be careful around that one, Juliana. Her mind is full of bitterness. Don't let it poison you.'

'Don't go back to wrapping yourself in those awful mourning clothes,' I countered. 'I should have made you leave them in Florence.'

She laughed a little, despite herself, then picked up her luggage and walked out the front door. A chair would take her to the coaching house, where she could catch a stage home. Only when the door closed did I begin to realise how much I would miss her.

My bed sported a new coverlet and a fresh pile of linen was stacked on the dresser. Both windows were thrown wide and a warm, late-summer breeze brought in the scent of roses from the gardens across the way. My luggage was already unpacked, the gowns hung neatly in the wardrobe, other garments folded and placed in drawers. I opened the top of the dresser and took out Miss Mary's parting gift: the Bible she had carried with her across Europe. I ran my fingers over the leather cover, worn smooth with handling.

I won't forget you.

Feeling hot and dirty from the journey, I began to undress. A hip bath had been brought from the kitchen and filled with steaming water. I slipped into the scented liquid, luxuriating in the way it soothed my tired flesh. I pampered myself until the water turned cold. After a brisk towelling, I rummaged in the dresser. I fancied a silk petticoat next to my clean skin and a light taffeta gown.

I frowned. Some of my underclothes were missing, the very best from Italy. I checked each drawer, the bottom of the wardrobe, even under the bed.

What had I done with them? I'd seen to the packing myself, since our Italian maid could not be trusted with the delicate silks. Exasperated, I threw on a robe, strode on to the landing and called for a maid. The girl who came running was a stranger, a loose-haired creature with crooked teeth.

'Who are you?' I demanded.

'Nancy, miss.'

'How long have you been here?'

'Nigh on six months.'

'What happened to our usual housemaid?'

'Don't rightly know, miss. I was a parish girl when the mistress took me on.'

'Some garments are missing from my luggage. Do you know what has become of them?'

'Mr Blake took care of the trunks. Told me to mind my business when I tried to help.'

Blake. That name still put shivers down my back. Too much to hope that he might have caught some terrible fever or been trampled by a runaway horse. Fate was never that kind.

'Where is Blake now?'

'If you please, miss, I think he's gone to join Mr Worledge in town.'

'And where in town might Mr Worledge be?' I pressed.

'Ain't my place to know or say, miss.'

Fuming, I let her go and made my way down-stairs. The house was gloomy and deathly quiet. I expected to find Catherine in the parlour, but it was empty. I checked the other rooms. No sign of her.

I frowned. Things were missing. Small things. Trinkets that Richard had brought from abroad, a couple of paintings, the bust that glowered from its pedestal beside the front door. Dust coated most of the furnishings.

Finding Maggie Burns still working in the kitchen was a relief. 'Mrs Worledge dismissed most of the servants,' she explained, 'and took on an orphan girl because she was cheap. Poor soul can't look after such a big house by herself. Mr Blake is rarely here and the stable lad has his hands full as it is. Still, the mistress doesn't seem to mind. Hardly anyone comes calling these days.'

'What about Mrs Deever?'

'Had a to-do with Mr Blake over who was in charge of the household. She complained to Mrs Worledge and was thrown into the street. I never thought I'd see that woman cry.'

Maggie stirred the pot of soup she had bubbling on the stove. She looked much older than I re-membered, with a streak of grey running through her fawn-coloured hair. The kitchen was a jumble of pots and pans, many in dire need of cleaning.

'Where is cook?' I asked.

'Her back gave out and now her son's looking after her in Chichester. Don't think he's too pleased about that seeing as he has a wife and brats of his own to feed. I look after the kitchens now.'

93

'Is there no one to help you?'

'The maid's clumsy and I don't care for her much. Was there anything else you wanted, miss?'

Catherine and I dined alone that evening. She pushed food into her mouth and chewed while her eyes appraised me. She had spent the afternoon in town and on her return we had sat in the withdrawing room while she tested me on my lessons. I spoke perfect Latin and managed a few lines in Italian without stumbling over the words. I quoted poetry and Greek philosophy, described the magnificent palaces of France, talked of paintings and sculpture. I said nothing about a white-haired sailor with piercing eyes who spoke of a pirate with a mark on his face the colour of blood.

'You have returned to England in good time,' Catherine remarked. 'We have been invited to a society ball at the new assembly rooms in Duke's Park. It will be a good opportunity to see how you conduct yourself. You have grown, Juliana. Many young men, I am sure, will take more than a passing interest. Try not to disgrace me.'

'How is Mr Worledge?' I asked. 'Will he greet me before I retire?'

Catherine flicked her hand. 'Richard is engaged in what he does best. You might see him within the hour or the week. In the meantime you will need a gown for the ball. Something respectable, not those harlot's rags you brought back from the Continent.'

'They are the height of fashion,' I protested.

Catherine waved her fork. 'I will not tolerate

94

anything frivolous. You are at a size now where one of my old gowns might fit.'

'I don't want one of your smelly old dresses.' I threw down my knife. It clattered on my plate and splashed gravy across the tablecloth. 'I want something of my own.'

I fled the table, knocking over my chair as I scurried out of the dining room and up the stairs. Catherine called after me but I covered my ears with my fists. When I reached my bedchamber I slammed the door and threw myself on to the bed. How stupid to think that things might have changed. Catherine was as sour as ever. She had brought out the gutter in me in no time at all. I wished I was back in Florence, amidst the flowers with a friend who listened and cared about what I thought and felt. I remembered Mr Thompson's young son, the kisses on the shadowed landing that sent the first quiver of love coursing through me. I desired that feeling again, wanted it to fill me and never go away. I despaired of spending another moment in this strange, dead house.

Morning found me in a contrite mood. I was eager for breakfast, so I let Catherine scold me before taking my place at the table.

'Why have you sold some of the things in the house, and dismissed most of the servants?' I asked, attention fixed on my plate.

She answered without looking up. 'Your education was costly, Juliana. It was necessary to make sacrifices. All the more reason for you to be grateful.'

Richard arrived home at noon the next day. I barely recognised the husk that stumbled into the hall, hat dripping with the rain that had fallen most of that morning. I greeted him alone. Catherine had grown a headache and taken to her bed for a nap. His eyes widened when he saw me. He opened his mouth to speak then paused as if he had forgotten my name.

'Juliana...' A hoarse whisper. 'Is that you?'

I curtsied and his thin mouth cracked into a smile. 'Welcome home,' he said. 'How long has it been? Let me see...'

His brow furrowed and I felt I could stand there for ever while he struggled to remember. He tried to say something else but fumbled the words.

'Over a year, sir,' I told him.

'Really? That long? Let me embrace you.' Arms circled my waist. Under his clothing I could feel bones. He shivered. A papery mannequin whose hair had dried to wisps. It hurt to look into his eyes. Watery and bloodshot, they could not seem to focus for more than a moment at a time. Grime encrusted the neck of his shirt, the cravat was badly tied and his shoes, once always polished until they gleamed, were scuffed and spattered with mud. He felt so fragile I feared he might snap in two. He straightened and gazed into my face, brushing a wayward strand of hair from my forehead and tucking it behind my ear.

'What a beautiful creature you have become,' he sighed.

Then the man I hated more than anyone else in the world stepped back into my life. Sharp as a pin in a fine coat and breeches, he made an entrance like the squire of a grand house returning to his property. On catching sight of me, he smiled a cat's smile and his tongue slipped across his lips. He said nothing, no word of greeting or deference, but his eyes flicked over me as if they were knives. Instead of taking Richard's hat and coat he threw his own over the balustrade and strode past me into the study. He helped himself to a glass of port while Richard struggled out of his own jacket. Having taken a leisurely sip, Blake rang for the maid. She came at a run and curtsied. He gestured towards Richard. The maid nodded and led him away. He mumbled to himself, one set of restless fingers entwined in the folds of his cravat. His other hand pulled a soiled kerchief from his pocket. Something fell out – a tattered, ink-stained paper. I waited until the maid had helped Richard upstairs then I picked up the note and smoothed it out. It looked like a page from a diary. The handwritten scrawl was barely legible and meandered over the page, but I managed to decipher the jumble of words.

It was an I.O.U. made out for a staggering amount of money. Richard's signature was scribbled on the bottom. I looked up to find Blake watching me. A moment later he closed the study door.

Later that afternoon Catherine took me into her bedchamber – a light, billowy place furnished with white lace and mahogany – and stood me in front of her tall looking glass. I was now her height, with a full figure and thankfully clear complexion. She opened her wardrobe and rummaged through her dresses. Some half dozen were selected, held up against me then laid across her bed. A couple of faded bonnets followed together with some gloves and whalebone stays.

'You may make use of these until I am able to obtain suitable replacements,' Catherine told me.

Dismayed, I stared at the jumble of garments. The bonnets were dusty, the gloves falling apart and the gowns ungainly monstrosities that would bury me beneath layers of crushed velvet. 'Miss Morgan paid a small fortune for my own gowns,' I muttered.

'Frivolous Italian fancies are not suitable for respectable English society,' Catherine answered, holding a muslin wrap up to the light. She nodded and added it to the pile.

'But I chose them myself.'

'Are there not enough harlots in this town without you wishing to parrot them? Now take off those gaudy rags. There is much to do today and I am short on patience.'

'I will not.'

Catherine blinked a couple of times. Quick as a cat, she grasped my bodice and tore the front of my dress open. Breath whooshed out of my lungs. Expensive silks ripped apart under her claws as though made of paper. Coloured bows were strewn across the carpet.

While I stood in my petticoats, Catherine picked a gown off the bed and thrust it under my face. 'Put it on,' she ordered, 'and do not argue with me again. I want you dressed decently for supper.'

I skulked back to my room like a scolded pup, Catherine's gown held tightly against my bared chest. Both wardrobe doors hung open and the inside was empty. I pulled open the drawers on my dresser. Everything was gone.

I slammed the drawers back into place and sank to my knees. Pain spread through my hands. I uncurled my fingers. My nails had dug sharp crescents into both palms.

I had no choice. I stood, pulled off the remnants of my ravaged gown and slid into the clothes Catherine had given me. The dress was an ungainly looking thing ideal for frumps and old women, not a girl who had returned from Europe wanting to light up the town. Two of the fastenings were broken and some of the embroidery had worked loose. I pinned everything together and regarded myself in the looking glass. I resembled a withered old maid.

I turned the mirror to the wall and went downstairs to the kitchen. I needed to talk to someone. Anyone. Maggie was nowhere to be seen, though steaming copper pots hissed angrily from their hooks above the hearth. The pantry door was open and I heard someone cough. I crept up and peeked around the doorframe.

Blake was squatting on a barrel, head bent, his back turned. I must have made a sound because he jerked to his feet. His cheeks were flushed, his eyes a livid blue. In his hand was one of my petticoats. It slid out of his grasp and on to the floor.

'Welcome home,' he said, before pushing past me. A moment later the kitchen door slammed.

Once I'd gathered my wits about me, I picked up the undergarment, took it into the kitchen and threw it on to the fire.

I was not safe from Blake yet.

Richard left the house again that evening. He stumbled down the front step and into a carriage, which immediately set off up the street. I watched from the door, wondering if I would see him again that night.

Blake remained behind. I heard him enter the study, then the clink of a decanter. A moment later, Catherine's slippers shuffled across the hall. The study door closed. A key turned in the lock.

I hurried into the parlour and stuck my head behind Catherine's writing desk. The Butter House had its tricks. Little twists of sound. Corners that gathered words like a vortex of autumn leaves and sent them spiralling around the masonry. This spot was a favourite eavesdropping haunt of mine, especially when I thought Richard and Catherine might be discussing me. I once had a nasty moment when Mrs Deever caught me on my knees with my ear pressed against the plaster. I mumbled something about dropping a hatpin.

'You'll likely find it there, I'm sure,' she'd declared.

'Would you care to help me look for it?'

'Church is the only place you'll see Ellie Deever on her knees.' And that had been the end of it.

It was a tight squeeze. Catherine's voice was low but carried clearly. 'More drink?' she admonished. 'You are becoming as bad as he. You would do well to keep a clear head and your wits about you. One cannot be complacent, even when dealing with fools.'

Blake's laughter rumbled through the stonework. 'If I dunked my head in a barrel of brandy and didn't surface for a week I still couldn't match the stomach of your beloved husband.'

'Never speak to me like that while in the house,' Catherine's voice hissed like hot coals in snow. 'I have warned you before. You are taking too many liberties. Learn patience.'

'Patience?' Blake's voice cracked. 'You enjoyed your comforts while I squatted in gaol with the rats. Even after my release the best you could do was let me become lackey to that fop. He took your business and squandered your money while I had to empty his pot and put his dinner in front of him every day.'

'Better that than the Tyburn gallows. Richard saved you from the hangman.'

'Aye, Catherine. For that reason alone I have not pressed a pillow over his drunken face, or scratched his throat with my razor.'

'Everything will turn out as it should. In the meantime you are too audacious with your airs and graces. People think it is a whim of Richard's to dandy you up and let you smoke his tobacco. But soon they will begin to wonder. Once the tongues start wagging there will be no stopping them.'

'It's your money, Catherine. Yours and mine.'

'Yes, money tied up in the shipping company. Father never suspected Richard would try to gamble away our lives. If he continues the banks will foreclose. You'd do well to remember that.'

'I ought to be the one with the fine carriage and the comfortable seat in the gentleman's club.'

Catherine laughed. 'You are no gentleman, nor

could any fortune mould you into one. Be grateful for what you have. It is infinitely preferable to the gutter.'

'You are a whore and a witch,' Blake retorted. 'Just like that redheaded foundling Worledge took under his wing.'

'Stay away from Juliana. She could still cause problems. Stealing that baby proved what she is capable of.'

'You think I'd hurt your little treasure pot?'

'I still don't like the way you look at her. No good can come of it. She is poison, that one. Whatever you do she will eventually turn it to her own purposes. Save your lechery for the bawdy house.'

They talked some more, shifting the conversation on to more trivial matters. When Catherine entered the parlour she found me in an armchair with my face in a book. 'What are you doing here?' she demanded, eyes narrowing.

'My bedchamber was too hot,' I replied with wide-eyed innocence. 'I came downstairs to read.'

She appraised me for a few moments, then her face relaxed. 'You move like a ghost sometimes, Juliana. One day your pitter-patterings around this house will land you in trouble.'

Supper that night was eaten in silence. Catherine and I sat at opposite ends of the table. Between us, a cluster of half-spent candles spat hot wax. Shadows leapt across the walls like living things.

Blake had apparently risen above such menial things as serving food. Instead the stable lad brought our dinner. His name, I learned, was William. He was an awkward, gawky lad with a missing tooth and an impudent smile. He tried to keep a straight face while serving my soup but I caught his eye and winked. His grin had me silently rejoicing. I was determined to find allies anywhere I could.

'Get me the key to Richard's bedchamber,' I instructed him the following morning.

'But miss, I've been told that no one's to go in there save Mr Worledge himself.'

'He is out for the day and possibly half the night as well,' I countered. 'His manservant is in the study helping himself to the port and Mrs Worledge is off buying a new hat for the ball. The maid has spare keys to all the rooms and she won't give any of them to me. She's too afraid of being punished. You, I suspect, will have better luck.'

Another gap-toothed grin. 'I just might.'

'Sixpence if you succeed.'

'You're on.'

I passed through to the kitchen and sent Maggie out to the pump, telling her I wanted a bath. She moaned that the stew would spoil if she wasn't there to keep an eye on it. I dug in my heels and made her take the biggest pail, knowing it would take an age to fill and that Maggie, who was a good two inches shorter than me, would struggle to haul it back across the yard.

Left to myself, I took the money jar out of the plate cupboard. I fished out a sixpence, tucked it into my sleeve then replaced the jar. These were petty funds kept for the occasional errand. Maggie never kept a note of its contents. She couldn't write, or count beyond her own ten fingers.

I slipped William the sixpence during afternoon

coffee. He pressed a brass key into my hand. I fingered the cool metal, eyeing Catherine as she bit into a sweetmeat. She had returned from town in a sour mood, unable to find any bonnet that took her fancy.

'The streets are filthy,' she complained, 'and my feet fit to drop off.'

She declared she would take a nap after coffee. I feigned sympathy and agreed it was a good idea. The moment she disappeared upstairs, I collared William and warned him to keep the maid occupied while I took my own liberties in Richard's room.

'Won't be a problem,' the lad boasted. 'I reckon Nancy has taken a shine to me. Daresay I could keep her in the washhouse for as long as need be.'

'You are too clever for your own good, William.'

He tipped me an insolent wink. 'Glad you see it that way, miss.'

Exiled from Catherine's bed, Richard kept his rooms at the opposite end of the passage. This corner of the house was a trap for the north winds that frequently blustered around the brickwork. Weak light seeped through a narrow window that overlooked the courtyard and stables beyond. A musty air of neglect hung over everything.

I fumbled the key out of my sleeve and pushed it into the lock. It turned with a click and the door swung open. A few paces into the room, my slipper knocked against something. It rumbled across the floorboards and fetched up against the foot of the dresser.

I stooped to take a closer look. An empty bottle.

I picked it up and sniffed the open neck, wincing at the odour of stale brandy. Other bottles, a great many bottles, lay strewn across the floor, piled on top of the trunk at the foot of the bed or gathering dust in crooked heaps in each corner of the room. A glass menagerie of greens and browns – even a broken-handled clay jug that a beggar might use to glug cheap spirits.

Careful where I put my feet, I moved deeper into the mess. The smell of alcohol clung to the furnishings. Loose bundles of clothing were tossed haphazardly over chairs or draped over the end of the bed.

No one's to go in there, William had said.

No one to change the bed linen or brush down the rugs. No maid slipping in early to throw open the windows and let in fresh air.

I opened the wardrobe and peered inside. Everything was in disarray. Mismatched garments were bundled together or lay where they had fallen. Shoes were crammed on to the shelf, some so tightly that the leather had been squashed into ugly shapes. Scraps of paper littered the cramped space. When I picked one up it flapped open like a dirty handkerchief. I spread it out against the wardrobe door, read it then picked up another. This one was torn from a tradesman's ledger book. The next was written on fine vellum bearing the crest of Richard's shipping company. Everything was scribed in his unsteady hand. All were I.O.U.s.

I searched his jackets, his waistcoats, even the pair of breeches poking out from under the bed. The pockets were stuffed to bulging with ink-smudged notes.

'Richard, what have you done?' I whispered.

I crammed the papers back into his pockets and, dodging the bottles littering the floor, turned my attention to the dresser. The mahogany top was lost under a layer of dust. Dirty plates and cutlery were caked with the decaying remnants of a meal. An ashtray brimmed with spent tobacco.

I pulled open the top drawer. More empty bottles. More I.O.U.s. The thick air of this filthy room clogged my throat. Richard was damned and there was no one to try to save him.

Except me.

Chapter Six

'Stop fidgeting, Juliana. We are almost there.'

'This dress is choking me,' I complained. 'It itches and smells like a horse blanket. No one will dance with me.'

'No one is likely to if your humour does not improve. Gentlemen are attracted to a smiling face, not the vanity of a pretty gown. Find some cheerfulness and the dances will follow.'

It had proved very difficult to smile at Catherine these past few days. I glared at her as she settled back in her seat. We had enjoyed a gentle journey through town, the rented carriage inching along the busy evening streets. Catherine had restored her features with the aid of thick powder and a rash of coloured patches. My birthmark was likewise buried. Her rented gown of crisp green velvet contrasted sharply with the drab sack in which I sat and suffered. What other treasure had disappeared from the Butter House to pay for this extravagance?

The Dovecote Assembly Rooms were housed in an imposing lump of a building funded by a merchant who made his fortune importing coffee. Stepping down from the carriage, I took in the warm sandstone and the rows of windows framed in white wood. Lanterns, resembling tiny coloured moons, lined the outer courtyard. Liveried footmen swung open the front doors as we approached. Catherine whisked me past their starched faces and into the muggy interior.

The sweltering press of bodies was intense from the lobby inwards. Everyone seemed to be drinking or talking. Pipe smoke clung to the ceiling in a blue fug. The gentle strains of music filtered through the hubbub, adding elegance to the chaos.

Catherine grasped my hand and herded me towards the end of the hall. She nodded and smiled greetings at strangers. My gown drew a few curious glances but there was far more eccentric fare to catch the eye. Monstrous head-dresses were topped with wax fruit or fleets of tiny wooden ships. Oversize bows looped across skirts, or hung from the back of gentlemen's wigs like huge velvet moths. It was a place of caricatures. Rouge-mouthed gargoyles with white painted faces, or satin-clad nymphs flitting among the throng, dispensing giggles like party favours. I anticipated meeting the hostess of this spectacle but Catherine seemed disinclined to seek her out. Did it even matter whose party it was?

We squeezed through an oval atrium papered with chattering dandies and into the main assembly room, a chamber filled with music and heady scents. Guttering candles were reflected a thousand fold in the chandeliers suspended above my head. Marble busts set into alcoves high in the walls added to the grandeur.

The floor was alive with dancing couples. Brisk melodies were thrummed out by an orchestra perched on a curved balcony above the entrance doors. Other guests clapped along to the melodies, or waited in hope of finding a partner.

Someone waved to Catherine from the far side of the room. 'A business matter,' she confided. 'Too pressing to let slip. Go and meet some of the other young ladies. No doubt they will be eager to make your acquaintance.'

Finding myself dumped amongst a gaggle of strangers left me feeling awkward. Catherine had already disappeared into the crowd. I cast about for a refuge. Refreshment tables had been laid out against the wall opposite the balcony. I picked out a path through the throng and made straight for the punch bowl. A serving wench in fancy dress poured me a generous cup. She was got up as old Queen Bess and looked quite sharp in a red wig and ruff. Two gulps and I was grinning like a simpleton. I let my gaze rove around the room, taking in the faces and letting their talk rumble around me. Much was said about the American war, a conflict that brought victory then defeat, then victory again, and seemed set to drag on for ever. Nothing had been gained. Good men were dying while other nations threw in their lot and the number of widows grew with the passing months.

Those who had returned from the battlefields spoke of how bravely they had fought. They described wounds just serious enough to earn a discharge home, and talked of heroism whilst other men nodded and scratched their chins. These sages were the dregs, the ones the war would not have. The old, the gout-ridden and the cowards who'd used up fortunes to buy their way out of duty.

Gossip travelled like a breeze through summer branches, whispering into every nook and alcove. It was very powerful, this tide of words. Every busy mouth found an eager ear. Names were tossed around and discarded. In five minutes I heard enough scandal to fill a book.

Two people in particular lay at the core of all this talk. Cecilia Fortescue and Adam Fairchild, the latter always mentioned with a slight catch of the breath as if the very words were poison. 'Who is this Mr Fairchild?' I asked the serving wench. 'Is he here tonight?'

The girl looked startled that I'd spoken to her. I smiled reassurance. Her eyes narrowed and she leaned across the table. 'There, by the door to the gentlemen's room. The fellow with the dark hair and no powder on his face.'

'He's as bad as they say?'

'Since you ask, miss, there isn't a gentleman here tonight who wouldn't like to see him dead.'

The notorious Adam Fairchild was holding court in a shadowed alcove beneath the gallery, surrounded by a gaggle of laughing women.

'He's ruined marriages and sired bastards by the score,' the girl continued. 'Pretty ladies are treated like cattle but would die for a smile from him.'

'You are making it up. I never knew a servant who didn't like to colour a good tale.'

She looked at the floor. 'As you like, miss. I was only telling you what most good people already know.'

I arched my neck to see above the bobbing heads. Fairchild stood no taller than most of his audience. He was not possessed of a strong build or countenance that would stop a heart beating. One might say that his nose was over-long, jutting over his top lip like a granite outcropping, or his eyes too close together. Black, curly hair clung to his scalp and tumbled reluctantly down the back of his neck where it was shackled by a velvet bow. A scar pinched his right cheek, lending his face a lopsided aspect that proved unsettling. When he smiled, which he did infrequently, his bloodless lips twitched as though the gesture was foreign to him.

But a few seconds staring at Adam Fairchild taught me that here was a man who did not rely on a pleasant face. He was possessed of a dark, brooding charisma that dominated the room. The sort of allure that could make a leader or devil of a man whatever his physical aspect. I could almost taste danger, sense the threat of a wolf let loose among lambs.

Despite myself, I felt stirrings inside me that I did not entirely dislike. I caught my breath as his charcoal eyes swept around the chamber, settling on me for only a moment before moving on. People seemed to wilt under that brittle gaze. My tongue dried in my throat. These feelings were different to those I had experienced with that boy in Florence, but every bit as powerful.

Someone pawed my sleeve. I dragged my eye away from Fairchild and faced Catherine. She was out of breath and red spots burned above her cheekbones. A man of indeterminate age stood at her side, regarding me with eyes like poached eggs.

'Juliana, I want you to meet someone,' Catherine gushed. 'This is Mr George Proudlove. His father is a clergyman and once ministered in our parish. George remembers you from early childhood and is keen to renew your acquaintance.'

'I was just a lad myself,' the newcomer confessed, 'though if I may say so, I have very fond memories of you.'

I took his measure, searching for any recollection and finding none. He had a curious flat face, a smudge of flesh for a nose and a demeanour that reminded me of a crumpled rug. An oversize cravat sprouted across the front of his shirt and spilled over the edges of his waistcoat. Unbidden, he took my hand and planted a kiss between the knuckles. His mouth felt like a fish freshly hooked from the river. I tried to pull away but he did not let go.

'I would consider it an honour if you would dance with me,' he continued, while Catherine watched us carefully.

'I don't dance.'

His fingers tightened. Pain flared through my hand. 'You are too modest.' He smiled and it was like a pit opening up in the ground. 'Your charming guardian tells me you have had lessons in Italy. It's not often that I am able to attend a ball in town. Even less that I should encounter such delightful company. I shan't take no for an answer.'

I glanced at Adam, but he was lost in his whimsies and Proudlove was already leading me on to the floor. Very well, I would give him a dance. A dance cost nothing.

The music started up and we worked through the first gavotte. Proudlove stumbled about the floor like a dog with three legs. I grimaced when the heel of his shoe landed squarely on my toes.

'You are uncommonly fetching,' he murmured into my ear as we applauded the orchestra.

'And you, sir, are disarmingly forward for a clergyman's son.'

He laughed as if I'd made a jest and waved a hand around the room. 'My parents frown on dancing and other such frivolities, but I am not of the cloth and therefore free to indulge myself more or less as I please. A generous tithe to his church ensures my father turns a blind eye. Another dance?'

I ached to be away, but he kept me on the floor for two more pieces. My head was ringing with his endless chatter, and the music was beginning to grate. In the end he let me go only because he claimed to have important matters to take care of. Stumbling back to the refreshment tables, I vowed to dance with every other man in the room rather than let Proudlove touch me again. Catherine thankfully was nowhere to be seen. Also absent was Adam Fairchild.

The maid had changed. A fat girl in an angel's outfit thrust a dish of hot tea into my hands. I savoured the drink, rolling its rich flavour around my tongue before swallowing. When I looked up from the dish, a young woman had joined me at the table. One look and I realised I had just met the notorious Cecilia Fortescue. Her sins had been laid bare by a hundred wagging tongues. A spirited, self-indulgent and very pregnant magistrate's daughter with a beguiling smile and eyes that seemed to fix on me whichever way her head turned. From what I'd overheard she was the scandal of the town, flaunting her swollen belly at all the fashionable parties just to spite her father, whose respectability she slighted at every opportunity. Cecilia often turned up uninvited and unaccompanied, but no one refused her entrance. The identity of the child's father was a secret she kept to herself like a sheathed sword.

At first I was treated with indifference but, sensing a kindred spirit, she quickly mellowed. I was fascinated with the way she treated all those disapproving faces with light-hearted contempt.

'Were you forced to wear that?' she said, eyeing my gown. 'I thought so. Some mothers insist on making identical poppets of their daughters.'

'Catherine Worledge is not my mother.'

'Old sour face? I'm not surprised. I could never imagine her putting up with the inconvenience of actually having a child.'

I spluttered into my teacup and dropped it on to the table. Cecilia watched me, grinning. I guessed she was very late into her term, at least eight months if my memory of Elizabetta in Florence served me right, and she carried herself as if proud of her condition. As she spoke, voice twittering like a nightingale's, she absently patted her rounded belly. Without warning she grasped my hand and laid it on the swelling.

'He is kicking,' she remarked gleefully. 'Can you feel it? I daresay he is dancing along to the music.'

I pulled my hand back as though it had been bitten. A curious fluttering sensation tickled the back of my throat.

'You get used to it soon enough,' Cecilia laughed. 'Have you ever handled a newborn baby?'

'Yes,' I replied. 'I have.'

She regarded me shrewdly and I wondered what, if anything, she knew about me. There was no time to reflect on it. Despite the scandal surrounding her, Cecilia did not want for dance partners. Time and again some nervous male plucked her out on to the dance floor. Men seemed to partner her to upset wives or sweethearts. Perhaps it was drunken bravado or they did it for a dare. She returned each time flushed and breathless, her eyes glinting.

'Did you see the look on Emma Branton's face when I had her husband in the gavotte,' she chuckled. 'Or the way Mary Smythe glared needles when her dullard of a fiancé couldn't stop talking to me at the end of the dance, then tried to steal a kiss.'

'Does it pleasure you to hurt people so?'

She tucked a loose hair back under her wig and smiled as though I was an ignorant child. 'Oh no, Juliana. They love to hate me. When they go home they will forget their own indiscretions and talk about what a flirt I was, and how I scandalised everyone by monopolising their husbands. They will pray for my soul and take to their beds with an easy conscience.'

'What about the child? Have you no thoughts for its welfare? All this dancing...'

But she only laughed and pecked my cheek before being whisked off by another eager partner. I also had my share of time on the floor, but only when Cecilia was already taken. Other than that, I found myself claimed by the old or ugly. Or meek little boys the other girls would not look at. No one to my knowledge succeeded in provoking jealousy from a loved one by dancing with me. If I could, I'd have ripped off Catherine's old gown and burned it on the spot.

When Cecilia returned at the interval she caught the look on my face. 'It's a dangerous game, Juliana,' she confided. 'It takes skill to humiliate our noble friends. One new to society mustn't scratch too deep, or she might find her claws drawn and clipped.'

'Is that a warning?'

'A little advice for the future.'

I didn't answer. Instead I went to fetch us both a drink. The smoky air had left my throat parched. Catherine was not visible anywhere in the room. Adam Fairchild, however, had returned wearing a change of clothes and carrying a silver-topped cane. His menage clustered about him once again. In the course of the evening, Cecilia had hardly affected to notice him. Now, as if reacting to some unspoken cue, they glanced at one another through a gap in the crowd. I caught it on my way back from the refreshment table with a glass of fruit punch in each hand. Their eyes locked for only a moment before returning to more immediate business. In that instance Cecilia spilled all her secrets.

I thrust the glasses into the hands of a startled footman, spilling punch over the front of his shirt. 'Anyone can become his doxy,' I told Cecilia. 'I will prove it to you.'

I elbowed my way between the guests and pushed into his grinning circle. I was his height and able to look him evenly in the eyes, though my throat felt full of rocks.

'Would you favour me with a dance, Mr Fairchild?' I cooed, using the most seductive voice I could muster. ''Twould be a shame to let such fine music go to waste.'

Someone tittered. Adam's dark eyes blinked and the corners crinkled into hundreds of tiny folds. There was something oddly loathsome about him. He was a dish with an undertaste, an apple with a worm lurking just beneath the glossy red flesh. But I willingly put my neck in the noose. I could not help myself. I was standing on the edge of the precipice and being pushed.

He flicked his gaze over me the way a butcher might pass a knife over a shank of meat. 'What an interesting dress.'

116

He pressed a wine glass to his lips and looked away. With a few words he had cut out my heart and thrown it to the dogs. His admirers laughed openly. I tried to leave the circle but stumbled over an outstretched foot. Recovering myself, I fled into the outer rooms, cheeks burning. I had tried to play the game and ended up a common fool.

I slunk to the entrance of a long, rectangular chamber. Smoke clouded the light from hundreds of guttering candles. The area was dotted with tables, each surrounded by men playing cards. Servants flitted expertly between them, serving drinks, lighting pipes. Beneath a set of tall, heavily curtained windows not more than a dozen paces from where I stood, I spotted Richard's ashen face. Beside him sat the grinning caricature that was George Proudlove.

I stepped forward. A footman's hand restrained me.

'You may not come in here, miss. 'Tis for gentlemen only. The ladies' parlour is further down the passage.'

'That man,' I indicated Richard, 'I need to speak to him.'

'Those guests have left instructions that they are not to be disturbed. I will be happy to convey a message once the game has ended. Now if you please...'

I wandered back down the hall, hunting for Catherine. I found her in an alcove with a boy half her age. She laughed like a merry young thing. Rouge smeared both cheeks and her wig sat at a drunken angle. The boy whispered something then nibbled on her ear. Catherine yelped in delight and slapped her thigh, sending her wedding ring tumbling from her scrawny finger. She didn't notice me though I stood within touching distance.

I stooped and picked up the ring. Catherine's foppish friend slid an arm around her waist. I weighed the cool metal in the palm of my hand, running the edge of my thumb along the inside. Something had been engraved there once, wearing down with the years.

Slipping the ring into my reticule, I weaved past revellers towards the front doors. I stood in the lee of the entrance, swallowing warm air in long, tearful gasps. I had come here to conquer and ended up the court fool. I debated whether to walk home. The carriage was not due to collect us for hours. Nearby, a link boy idled beside the boot scraper, his torch sputtering in the moth-speckled night. A stiff breeze whipped the treetops and clouds pondered overhead, underbellies turned silver by a low-slung moon. My imagination populated the darkness with robbers, no doubt lurking just beyond the rectangle of light spilling from the doorway behind me.

I turned back inside. I would wait in the hall until it was time to go home.

'There you are.' Cecilia appeared in a whisper of skirts. 'I thought you'd gone for good, and just when this party was really beginning to liven up.'

'Grown tired of being pampered by your men?' I mocked. 'Or are you saving yourself for a final bite of the apple?'

'Hmm, if not melodramatic then that was certainly poetic,' Cecilia observed. 'It's only natural that a kicked dog should want to snap back. Here, this will help divert you.'

From the bottom of her reticule came an engraved silver box. She prised open the lid. Inside was light brown powder. 'A potent brand of snuff,' she explained. 'Perfect for clearing an overburdened mind. Care to try some?'

'From an admirer?'

'Of course. I told him I was sick of flowers so he brought this. I was astonished at his initiative. I think of him whenever I sneeze.'

Cecilia took a pinch, spread it on the back of her hand and snorted it up each nostril. I followed suit.

'It is very strong,' she warned, 'and might take time to get accustomed to.'

I thought the top of my head was going to explode. I clutched my nose and doubled over. Tears streamed out of my eyes. I sneezed so hard I bit my tongue. Cecilia was beside herself with laughter, but then she sneezed too and that set me off again.

'Let's go back to the ballroom,' she said, struggling for composure, 'and see if we cannot tease a final dance or two out of those dullards before the night is over.'

The journey home found Catherine in a sober mood. Perhaps her dandy had found younger fare. Or the wine might be wearing off and her head was paying the price. Outside, thickening clouds had smothered the moon. The only light was the bobbing will-o'-the-wisps of the carriage lanterns.

Catherine's face was in shadow, but I could sense her watching me. Desperate to break the silence, I spoke first. 'I saw Richard.'

No reply. Paper rustled in the swaying darkness. Perhaps a note from her young beau, though she could not hope to read it.

'I saw Richard,' I said again. 'He was playing cards with a group of gentlemen. He looked very ill, but I was not allowed to see him.'

'You are mistaken,' Catherine responded, tongue as smooth as a viper's. 'Those rooms are always busy and full of smoke. It could have been anyone.'

'But...'

'It was not Richard.'

Her words grew jagged edges and her thin knuckles cracked as she pressed her fingers together. A full minute passed before she settled back against her seat.

'George Proudlove was very taken with you,' she said finally. 'He has asked if he may call. I have invited him over this Saturday.'

'I don't remember him.' The lie tripped off my tongue.

'He danced with you.'

'Many men danced with me, most of them badly. He was just another face.'

'A face with a good deal of privilege behind it. Mr Proudlove has a country house, extensive lands and a father in the clergy. You would do well to start thinking about your future, Juliana.'

I leaned across and pressed Catherine's wedding ring into the palm of her hand. 'And you would do well to consider your own.'

As soon as the carriage drew up outside the Butter House I clambered out and dashed inside. Scooping a candlestick from the hall table, I tripped up the stairs in a flurry of skirts, my shadow dancing in the bobbing light. Catherine had taken away the key to my bedchamber and Nancy was in and out as she pleased. But it was the only space in this mostly loveless house I could call my own.

Pulling up a stool, I sat in front of the dresser and regarded myself in the looking glass. My appraisal was honest and painful. What I saw staring back at me was a creature without life or spirit. Only in my eyes was there a spark, something that Catherine's old clothes could do nothing to disguise.

I pulled off the wig in a shower of white powder and wiped the paint from my cheeks. Beneath the dull mask was the girl who had so handsomely bloomed in the Italian sun. My skin had cleared, my hair was a rich copper and my eyes as bright as diamonds.

I wanted back the rouge and the fine Italian perfumes. Most of all I wanted a dress. A real dress, not some hand-me-down sack. And I determined to get it, whatever the cost. Never again would any man dismiss me with a glance or unkind word.

I smiled at myself in the polished looking glass, remembering Cecilia's swollen belly, the laughter we had shared.

But first there was Richard.

I wanted to save him but not because of love.

My motives were entirely selfish. I did not know how many secrets concerning my past were locked up in this house, but I felt sure that my position was safe only for as long as Richard lived. He spent much of his time indoors now, too ill or drunk to go anywhere. He rose late and, when he emerged from his bedchamber at all, chose to sit in the study surrounded by his books. There he drank bottle after bottle whilst Blake played the humble servant and brought in more whenever Richard called for it.

Then Blake disappeared for a while. Catherine continued her visits to the library and salons. I seized upon this brief opportunity, not realising that my most formidable enemy would prove to be Richard himself

I tried to help him. Swearing the maid to silence, I watered down the brandy, but Richard noticed and smashed the bottle against the study wall. He continued to drink as if filling his body with poison could somehow clear his mind, would help him make sense of his crumbling world. He squatted in his chair behind that huge mahogany desk, bills and I.O.U.s spread out in front of him. A dazed, almost amused look sat on his face, as if he did not understand what was happening to him or what to do about it. Talking achieved nothing but a slurred jumble of words. He neglected to change his clothes. Servants glanced at one another behind his back.

I never returned to the study in those terrible days. All its former magic had slipped down Richard's throat along with the port and brandy. A pall of tobacco smoke clung to the furnishings.

His illness spread through the house. I began to find more and more empty bottles. In the end I didn't even have to search before stumbling across them. I lined up a dozen on Richard's desk while he sat there, slack-jawed. He swore in his slurred tongue that he did not know where they had come from. I explained how I had found some in the hall outside his bedchamber, others in the privy or littering the path outside the back door.

'I do not know what you mean, Juliana. Pray stop haranguing me. I am very weary.'

Anger? I was too afraid for him, for myself, to be angry. I was losing the battle. He was slipping away from me like a thief in the night. He was almost always sick, retching for minutes on end, even when his belly was empty. Bile flecked his lips.

I asked Catherine to send for a surgeon, but she waved me away and went back to reading her letters. 'No one is to be summoned to this house without my approval,' she warned. 'Richard has shamed us enough. Do you understand, Juliana?'

I understood perfectly. Richard was killing himself, or being murdered, and there was nothing I could do to stop it. To stop them. He was falling into the pit and I was afraid. I became irritable and snapped at everyone. Exhaustion circled my eyes with dark rings. Next time I looked in the mirror I saw someone on the verge of being broken. The image frightened me, so I resorted to lies for protection. I wrote letters to Mary Morgan and Cecilia, and filled them full of happy thoughts even as tears blurred my tired eyes.

Catherine and I were like two feral cats edging

on one another's territory, ready to bare claws and fangs if either stepped over the mark. She was the mistress of the house, but we had learned how to prick each other. In that sense we were equals.

Over coffee, she turned the conversation to George Proudlove, mentioning him at every opportunity as though determined not to let him slip from my mind even for a minute. She watched me constantly. After a few days I found it hard to keep my temper. I even started to have bad dreams about the man, populating my nights with visions of his round, grinning face.

Letters arrived at the house, which Catherine zealously pushed into my hands. All the seals were broken, and they were all full of nonsense. Rambling paragraphs bored me with news of his estate, his parents, and admiration for me that, he declared, knew no bounds. He reiterated his desire to call and once enclosed a shiny guinea as 'a gesture of goodwill'. Did he think me a harlot?

'You must write back,' Catherine gushed, hovering around me like a bluebottle until I had read every last word of these tiresome missives. 'He is a good man from a fine family. You need to repay his kindness, Juliana.'

Later, I gave the guinea to William and instructed that any letters not from Mr Proudlove should be handed directly to me. Catherine was not to be told. He brought two, still sealed, and crumpled where he had stuffed them into his pocket. One was from Cecilia inviting me to tea. The other was from Mary Morgan. She was being courted by a widower called Ernest Pettit.

He'd had his eye on her for a while but Mary had been too smothered in her own gloom to notice.

'I am sure he will propose within the week,' she wrote, 'and an early wedding is likely. He has been making certain arrangements that he believes I do not know about. Such a sweet, naïve man! My only sorrow is that such a union would not be graced with children. Ernest's wife died in childbirth and the baby did not survive. However, we will find solace in our books and our mutual affection. I know that you will give us your blessing.'

It gladdened my heart that love should have found my friend after she had believed herself abandoned by it, gladness that turned bitter as I thought of the lies I would have to tell her in return. I did not want her to be concerned about me, or spoil her happiness with tales of my own misfortune. I pushed both letters under the rug and went to find Catherine. I wanted out of the house and was willing to make up any excuse. As it happened, she provided one for me.

'You have had another lovely letter from George,' she said, smiling at me from the parlour couch. 'He is in town on business and has asked to call. I have sent a messenger to his lodgings and anticipate his arrival a little after one o' clock. I expect you to receive him warmly.'

'You have no right to read my letters,' I told her. 'Whoever they are from.'

'Nonsense. As your guardian it is my duty and I shall continue to do so until you come of age.' She regarded me from beneath her thick eyelashes. 'Or you are married.'

She took some coins out of her purse and dropped them into my hand. 'You are spending too much time flapping around Richard. Go and buy yourself some fresh rouge to make yourself presentable to Mr Proudlove. And cover up that mark.'

Catherine offered the use of her carriage but I said I would walk or take a chair. I did not care for her driver watching my every move. In the street I hailed a sedan and gave the address Cecilia Fortescue had penned on her letter. It took me to the house she shared with her father, a lumbering block of a structure surrounded by stone walls and rumble-tumble gardens.

Cecilia's papa was a gruff, learned man with a stooped back and a ring of silver hair framing his face. He treated me with polite reserve at first, but I was at my charming best and he soon mellowed. Cecilia greeted me with a kiss and we sat in her parlour with two steaming dishes of tea. Whilst the clock on the mantelpiece dragged its hands through the hours, we exchanged gossip whilst avoiding the one subject that was close to both our hearts. More than once I felt she was working up to telling me something, but the maid would come in, or she'd lose her nerve, or something else would occur to distract her. When it had gone three o' clock I took my leave with a promise to visit again. As we embraced, the swell of her belly pressed against me and I fancied I could feel the child moving inside.

Catherine was in a terrible rage when I returned unrepentant and without the rouge she'd sent me out to buy. She wished all the ten plagues of Egypt upon my head for making poor George wait and then not turning up to greet him.

'He is not my friend, my beau or my kin,' I told her. 'I have no wish to see him today or any day. If you are so taken with George then why not wed him yourself since you seem so determined to become a widow.'

Dishes of cold tea littered the withdrawing room table and George's cologne hung in the air like a bad memory. The door hung open. In the hall, Nancy was on her knees trying to scrub the floor.

'George wants your hand in marriage,' Catherine told me flatly. 'He has agreed to settle a handsome sum on you.'

'More money with which to poison Richard?'

'That is his choice. Women can rarely interfere in male matters, less so when it involves their own husband.'

'So am I little better than a horse or pig a farmer might sell at the town market?'

'You will benefit the most from this. I can think of no better match for a daughter of mine.'

'Daughter? I am a member of your family only when it suits, Catherine. You have told me about George's house and lands often enough. What a rich pie to dip your finger into. Is this what you have been grooming me for, why you took me to the ball? To parade in front of him? How well you have planned it.'

Catherine didn't answer. She strolled over to the mantelpiece in a whisper of skirts and returned with a small, satin-covered box, which she held out to me. 'George wants you for his wife,' she repeated. 'Here, wear his ring. He planned to give it to you himself, but has grown weary of bending to your whims. The banns will be read and you will be Mrs Proudlove before the season is through. Do your duty by me, Juliana.'

'Is there no end to this?' I said quietly, staring at the box. 'You would have everything of Richard's and now you intend to meddle with my future. Very well, if George is to wed me then he must formally propose. I do not deal with a go-between; he must snare me himself. We shall see if he is man enough at least for that.'

Chapter Seven

I was helpless in the face of Richard's self-destruction. His creditors, tired of being fobbed off with excuses, sent messengers to our front door in ever-greater numbers. Most were content to leave with a few guineas and a promise of more, but one man brandished a fistful of I.O.U.s and threatened to see the magistrate if his dues were not settled in full. Blake, who was always on hand when there were debts to be paid, leaned forward and grumbled something in his ear. The man's face turned as white as fresh bread and he stumbled back down the steps. The I.O.U.s flurried out of his hands. Later they were torn up and fed to the kitchen fire.

The wine merchant, however, received prompt

payment and the following day arrived with a cartload of clinking bottles. I went out to meet him and, while petting his bony draught horse, begged him not to deliver any more. He laughed and told me it wouldn't make any difference.

'Can't stop a man drinking if he has a mind to,' the merchant explained. 'More'n enough taverns to keep 'im happy if he can't get none at home. I don't aim to let no alehouse or gentleman's club get any o' my business.'

When I was not looking out for Richard, I dodged George. I burned his letters and tore the heads off his flowers, littering the carpet with fractured blooms. He was in town for a week and took every opportunity to seek me out, wearing ever more outlandish clothes in his efforts to impress. Always the perfect gentleman in front of Catherine, he stammered and blustered when left alone with me.

'What does he want with me?' I asked, exasperated after one such visit.

'It is understandable that a single gentleman of some means would wish to call on an eligible young lady,' Catherine replied.

'I didn't ask to become the object of his affections.'

'Do you consider yourself so unique that you can pick and choose? Peasants do that and they breed like undisciplined curs.'

'George is pushing into my life as if he has a right to it. He grinds me down like a pebble on a bad tooth.'

Despite my attitude, he remained persistent. On Monday he left in a temper. On Tuesday he greeted me like an old friend. On Wednesday he found courage in the bottle. A few swigs of brandy and he blurted out all his plans. Catherine had given her consent. I would become George's harlot, only the word he used was 'wife'.

'You would make me very happy,' he slurred, fumbling his empty glass.

'What of my happiness?' I countered, 'or does that particular balance not enter into your accounts?'

He smiled, trying to put some charm into it. 'I would do everything within my power to ensure that happiness.'

'Then do not pester me with dead flowers, badly written letters or unwelcome proposals made over the rim of a brandy glass. With no choices I can never be happy, under this roof or yours.'

'Your guardian, Mrs Worledge, has said...'

'Richard Worledge is my guardian,' I corrected. 'Speak to him before you try to steal my life.'

On Thursday I overheard George talking with Catherine in the drawing room. They tossed my name back and forth as if playing a game of shuttlecock.

'This is becoming a bore, Catherine,' George said. 'Can't the girl be made to see sense? A good father would have beaten the reluctance out of her. I would be home with my dogs and she with my heir in her belly. I grow weary of playing games just to pander to her pride.'

'All part of the courtship game, George,' Catherine soothed. 'Be patient. Even a rock wears away with time.'

'Time is a commodity I cannot afford to squander, madam. I have stayed overlong in this wretched town already. Bring her to reason, or my patience will go the way of my temper. All I need is a legal consent and she is mine. Are you sure your husband cannot be made to sign? Is there no other way?'

Catherine laughed. 'You are too greedy to let Juliana go. While Richard lives she is under his protection. Drink may have befuddled his mind but he is all too aware of her worth.'

Silence fell between them. Then George grunted. 'Very well. I must conclude my business soon. Other matters demand my attention and my estate goes begging. I shall return a week today. I need not remind you, Catherine, that you also have a considerable investment in this enter-prise. It is in both our interests to succeed.'

I sought refuge with Cecilia. I called on her in secret while Catherine was at the library or the new literary circle she had joined. I never directly mentioned George Proudlove, though with her connections Cecilia must have known he was in town and spending a great deal of time at Catherine's house. But she was as circumspect with her own affairs as she was with mine.

'What will become of the child?' I kept asking. She always responded with a beguiling little cut of the lips and turned the conversation to something else. Cecilia was not a creature of this world. Watching her, seated on the parlour couch beside me with the sunlight turning strands of her hair into bright fingers, it was easy to believe that she was a ghost or a dream, which would

131

fade from sight with only a chuckle, like music tinkling on the wind, to remind me that she had ever been there. We gossiped, spun yarns, listened to each other's stories. But her secrets remained locked away in some inner place. Getting her to talk about Adam Fairchild was akin to drawing a nail out of a stout oak with your teeth.

On the third Saturday of the month I found Mr Fortescue waiting for me in the hallway. I'd tried a few hands of whist with Cecilia but the baby was pressing heavily and she'd retired for a nap. Everything she did required great effort and her rosy complexion had been replaced by a pallid, sickly look that reminded me too much of Richard.

'Don't fret so, Juliana,' she'd said, regarding me through puffy eyelids. 'It's just a touch of the vapours.'

She summoned the maid to help her upstairs. I saw myself out, but her papa stopped me at the front door.

'I would have words with you, Miss Rodriguez,' he said, tugging on his neck cloth. The ring finger of his left hand was missing, and his expression as he eyed me was unreadable. He sat me down in his oak-panelled study in a leather armchair that almost swallowed me whole. I waited while he poured himself a glass of brandy. He stared out of the window for a few moments, as if the answers to all the world's conundrums lay in the streets outside. Finally, he seated himself opposite me, his desk an expanse of polished wood between us, and spoke, steepling his fingers beneath his chin.

'You must tell her to get rid of it,' he began. 'I

will not have a bastard take my name and sit at my table.'

He paused. I didn't say anything. He swallowed a mouthful of brandy and slapped the glass down on the desk. 'For months I've watched her belly swell. I have had to suffer the derision of others while she pushes her way out of my affections. Do you know who the father is? No? Well, I doubt you would tell me even if you did. A gentleman would already have embraced his responsibilities. A man without honour is not worth knowing.'

He picked up a framed etching from the corner of his desk. A portrait of his wife, I guessed. Cecilia told me she'd caught some terrible sickness while in India and had taken weeks to die. All Mr Fortescue's money couldn't save her and he'd not ventured abroad since. Even now he stared at the etching as if he could will her back to life. Grief ploughed his face. I fancied that if I touched his cheek I would find it as cold and unyielding as iron.

'You are Cecilia's only genuine friend,' he continued, replacing the etching. 'Her peers are too concerned with their reputations to willingly become involved with her. I love my daughter but I am a pragmatic man. Someone has poked her for a marriage dowry, or to press me financially over the child. Either way, they want a cut of my fortune. I cannot permit that. It would open the door for every libertine in the county. I am not cruel, Miss Rodriguez, but she must dispose of the child. You must convince her.'

A clock chimed somewhere deep in the house.

Mr Fortescue checked his fob watch, made an adjustment then returned it to his waistcoat pocket.

'What if I was to take the baby?' I said.

He eyed me shrewdly and lit a pipe, filling the air above his head with rich blue smoke. 'How will you accomplish this? You are hardly at an age to legally adopt.'

'I know a respectable person in want of a child. You won't see or hear about it again.'

'You can assure me of that?'

'Yes.'

'And you wish payment in return?'

My fingers curled into fists. 'Not payment. A favour.'

'Pray continue.'

'I need a dress. Something Italian with an embroidered front and a sprinkling of bows. I have an important assignation and my guardian's household budget will not stretch to anything she considers frivolous.'

He nodded. My fingers relaxed.

I rode a sedan chair home with the smile of a witch painting my face. When I arrived at the Butter House, Maggie Burns was squatting on the front step bawling her eyes out. Behind her, the door hung open. The first fallen leaves of autumn gusted into the hall in a flurry of red and gold.

I stepped out of the chair, paid the bearers with a sum Mr Fortescue had given me and hurried over. 'Maggie, what's wrong?'

'Mr Worledge is dying,' she blubbed. 'He's been drinking all night. Bottle after bottle, and always screaming for more. William has gone to fetch the surgeon but I doubt he could get here in time even if he sprouted wings.'

She buried her face in her apron. I shook her. 'Where is Catherine?'

'Shut in her bedchamber with the door locked. She says there's naught to be done.'

I gritted my teeth and ran past her into the bowels of the house. A terrible sapping heat choked the study. The windows were shut tight and the fire stoked into a roaring, spitting demon with a bellyful of sparks. Richard's legs poked out from beneath his desk. He had fallen from his chair and lay with his shoulders propped against the polished globe that dominated the corner of the room. A vast world mapped out in faded reds and greens on which Richard had shown me the faraway places visited by his ships before he spun it into a blur of colour.

At first I thought he was dead. His eyes were open and fixed. Then I heard a drawn out sigh – a sound filled with pain. I knelt beside him. The carpet was a swamp of spilled drink, broken glass and bottle corks. Richard did not seem drunk. He had gone beyond that. He spoke as if his mind had been detached from his poisoned body the way a quack might lop off a gangrenous limb. He regarded me with a dreadful clarity, his eyes staring into my own with a child's innocence as if he could not fathom what he'd done to himself.

I was no doctor. I didn't know what part of him had broken, had finally given up under a swill of brandy. The life was slipping out of his body as if some devil had tapped into him and was draining his spirit away.

135

'I kept my promise.' Each word climbed painfully out of Richard's throat. 'You held on to your name.'

His lips broke apart in an agonised smile. 'The only thing in which Catherine failed to get her own way. She was sour for years because of it.'

'What promise? What vows have you made, Richard? And to whom?'

A coughing fit wracked his body. Blood flecked his chin. 'Manuel,' he wheezed. 'Your father, Juliana. God help me...'

I gripped his shoulders, my knuckles white against his green velvet jacket. 'Forget my father. I know about him. Who was my mother, Richard? Catherine is a soulless woman who will tear my life into pieces. You must help me. There is no one else.'

His face turned a dreadful pallor. A spasm coursed through his chest. He kicked out, splitting his shoe on the edge of the desk. He whispered two words as the last breath rattled out of his lungs.

'Littlejohn knows...'

I rose and backed away, staring down at his supine form. In the hearth, a log split open and spat a shower of yellow sparks into the chimney's black mouth.

A rustle of satin. Catherine filled the doorway. Pastry crumbs ringed her mouth.

'You let him die,' I accused.

'Did you try to help him up?' She stepped into the room. 'Did you run to fetch water? Hold his hand? Offer comfort?'

I looked away. 'You never loved him. Not from

the day you married or even before.'

'How could I? He was forced upon me, thrust into my life by a man greedy for a fat dowry and a wife for his doltish son. Richard was grateful that I never hated him. I felt too much pity for that.'

'Thrust upon you the way you would force George Proudlove on me?'

'Selfish as always, even as you kneel beside the man who succoured you. Make the best of it, Juliana. Worse things could happen to a young woman in your position. Marriage will bring respect and a roof over your head.'

'Provided I pander to my husband's whims?'

'Perhaps you will prove clever enough to turn things your way. Richard was never my master.' She eyed the body of her husband. 'Now don't you think you ought to find something to cover him up?'

Richard was buried with little fuss amidst the brambles and lop-sided tombstones of the town cemetery. He had no surviving relatives. A scattering of mourners coughed into their hand-kerchiefs. A persistent drizzle had fallen all morning, deadening the parson's voice.

I bawled most of the way through the brief cere-mony, despite Catherine pinching my arm. She'd borrowed a black dress from a widow friend because she did not want to spend money on a new mourning gown. I had to make do with more of her old clothes. A strip of black velvet knotted above my elbow was the only mark of respect permitted.

My tears dried abruptly. Mr Littlejohn stood on

the other side of the cemetery, mopping the drizzle from his brow with a crumpled handkerchief. He appeared shorter and thinner than I remembered. His clothes were a battered hodgepodge of fading colours and frayed cuffs. I tried to catch his eye but he stared at the open grave.

Muddy water was already swilling around Richard's coffin. The parson snapped his prayer book shut, a signal for the gravediggers to pick up their shovels. The mourners immediately started to drift away, some hurrying to their coaches as the clouds darkened further. A few stopped to offer Catherine their condolences. While she went through the act of the stricken widow I slipped away from her side and pursued Mr Littlejohn. He strode down the path towards the gate, coat flapping, tricorne pulled over his forehead. I caught up with him as he reached his hired sedan chair.

'Mr Littlejohn, I would speak with you, please.'

He shrugged me off, clambered inside and slammed the door. He made to signal the bearers with his cane, thought for a moment then leaned out. His nose twitched as though he could scent some terrible threat in the air, one that had nothing to do with the blackening clouds.

'It is not good for us to be seen together,' he warned. 'Come and see me at the shipping office. No, that'll likely be locked. Go to my residence in Brook Street. I will meet you there.'

He slumped back in his seat, tapped the roof of the carriage and was off, leaving me standing on the path with his calling card clutched in my hand.

'What business did you have with Richard's colleague?' Catherine demanded as our coach rumbled back into town.

I spluttered something about wanting to thank him for coming. 'Richard had so few real friends,' I added.

She eyed me carefully. I saw the questions, the poisonous thoughts brewing in the dark cauldron of her mind. 'Are you sure that is all? He seemed in an uncommon hurry to be gone.'

'I daresay he wanted out of the rain.'

'Stay away from that man. He is an old fool with a head full of nonsense. Mr Worledge involved him in the company as an act of kindness. He felt it his duty, a debt to an old acquaintance. I am under no such obligation.'

She was quiet for a few moments. 'From now on you are not to address me as "Catherine". I no longer consider it appropriate.'

'Yes, Mrs Worledge.'

She nodded. 'Many things will change now that Mr Worledge has died. His obligations were further reaching than you can imagine. Promises were also made that, as far as I am concerned, perished with him. We will discuss some of these later.'

That afternoon I watched as every scrap of Richard's existence was stripped from the Butter House. His clothes were given to the parish, his books crated and taken away to be sold. His private chambers were cleared and his bed shrouded beneath white sheets. Nancy scrubbed the floors and walls then burned sulphur so that even the scent of him was driven out.

Alone in his study, I gazed at the rows of empty bookshelves. The desk had been removed along with most of the other furnishings. My steps echoed on the bare floorboards. I was torn between a sense of loss for the only guardian I'd known, and an urge to seek out Mr Littlejohn. He claimed it wasn't safe to be seen with me. Safe for whom?

I dressed sombrely for dinner – really I had little choice – and made my way to the dining room as the last afternoon light faded into the blue-greys of evening. Blake was perched in Richard's chair, a glass of red wine by his hand and serving dishes spread out in front of him. He was peacock pretty in the finest velvet and satin. His dark, lank hair was swept back behind his head and secured with a large bow. A silk cravat tumbled down the front of his embroidered waistcoat.

I frowned. The fit was too good for Richard's clothes. Where had Blake obtained them? He lit a pipe and settled back in the chair. Catherine sat opposite. She smiled and dabbed her mouth with a napkin. Her gown was spotless, all sparkling whites and blues. Her teeth glimmered in the candlelight. She looked genuinely happy for the first time in years.

William took away their soup bowls. Blake waited until the boy returned with a platter of meat and a fresh bottle of wine. It was as though Richard's debts were so much waste paper, and all the precious items that had been sold to try to pay for them were of no consequence.

I was drawn into the flickering pool of light.

Gold glinted on Blake's finger. He wore Richard's wedding ring. His hands were a smooth, pale pink with neatly trimmed fingernails. Yet he handled his wine glass like a town bawd.

Catherine spotted me and laid her fork beside her plate. 'You are late. How long have you been standing there?'

My voice sounded small in the high-ceilinged room. 'I want to dine in the kitchen.'

'What?'

'I won't sit at the table. I'd sooner starve.'

Blake burst into laughter and had to push his napkin into his mouth to keep from choking. 'She'd rather eat with the servants, would she?' he said, recovering. 'Our company doesn't suit, then?'

'You *are* a servant,' I reminded him.

His mirth turned to anger in a wink. He made to rise from his chair but Catherine stilled him with a raised hand. 'Very well,' she told me. 'Perhaps a little time in the kitchen might teach you something about managing a household. A useful skill in a new wife. I'm sure George would agree.'

And, with a tilt of her head, I was dismissed.

Maggie Burns didn't utter a word of complaint when I appeared in her kitchen with a grumbling belly. She sat me on a stool, piled a trencher high with leftovers and left me to get on with it. Next day my bedchamber was left untidied. When I collared Nancy she squirmed out of my grasp.

'Let me go,' she howled. 'Mrs Worledge says you've to do it yourself.'

So I struggled upstairs with bundles of linen, made the bed, brushed down the rug and caught

141

a faceful of smoke when I tried to kindle the fire. Blisters quickly sprouted on hands that felt clumsy and awkward. The simplest tasks became a challenge.

Thankfully, William still ran errands for me. When I spoke to him his cheeks often turned radish red. He would find a stammer from somewhere, his blush deepening as his words fell over themselves in an effort to escape his mouth. Nancy's disgust was palpable.

Within the week, a gaggle of wintry-faced lawyers descended on the house, sporting old leather bags stuffed with papers for Catherine to sign. I couldn't eavesdrop as Nancy had been keeping an especially sharp eye on me these past couple of days, as if at any moment I might disappear into a closet with William. When Catherine saw the men to the door, a look of grim satisfaction sat on her face. I recalled the I.O.U.s and waited for an army of creditors to arrive and slice up the household, but no one came.

Blake was out most days, slipping from the house like a thief and not returning until dusk. Everyone was full of talk.

George Proudlove returned to Wexborough at the end of the week and promptly invited himself to dinner. He seemed in high spirits and greeted Catherine like an old friend. I was ordered to resume my place at the dining-room table.

When it came to eating and trying to talk at the same time, Mr Proudlove was an artiste. He had kind words for Nancy, and tipped William handsomely for the mere act of delivering the roast duckling. Unsurprisingly, it was left to Catherine to condemn me.

'You will wed Mr Proudlove at the end of the month,' she said. 'The ceremony will take place in his local church.'

George nodded eagerly whilst stuffing his mouth with carrots. He dropped his fork, grabbed my hand and crammed a ring on to my finger. The gem was as big as my knuckle but had a cheap look to it and the silver band pinched my flesh.

'There,' he declared. 'Now we are betrothed.'

I sat and let my dinner grow cold while they divided my life up like buccaneers sharing a trunk of booty. I could sense Catherine's triumph. After dinner, George signed the papers, sealing my future with ink and wax. He had bought me the way he might a horse at a market and there was nothing I could do about it.

At the end of George's visit, I was pushed towards the front door to bid him farewell. He paused on the step, the wind catching his coat and flapping it out like crow's wings. He leaned towards me and pressed his lips against my cheek. I recoiled. George was unfazed.

'A first kiss for the soon-to-be blushing bride,' he said. He buttoned up his coat, bid Catherine good fortune and let the night swallow him up. All that remained was the orange glow of smouldering tobacco where he'd emptied his pipe into the gutter, but his scent lingered on my skin.

Back inside the house, I tied on an apron and helped the servants clear the table, the very table at which I'd dined. After lugging a pile of plates down to the kitchen I rinsed my face in dishwater and rubbed it dry with a linen rag. No use. I could still smell him, and his ring wouldn't budge no matter how hard I tugged. Even smearing my finger with a dollop of fat from the turnspit failed to shift the cursed thing.

That's how I stood, by the leftover vegetables, squeezing back tears. I'd held them in so often lately I thought my insides must be swimming, that I'd start to leak through my nose and ears, perhaps the pores of my skin.

George might have my hand in marriage but he'd not stain his bed sheets with my blood. I'd wear his ring, but no heir of his would swell my womb.

I had no illusions about losing my virginity. Catherine had given me the 'wifely duties' talk and seemed dismayed that I wasn't as shocked as she thought I'd be. But I'd heard the parlour whispers among the older girls at the tea parties I'd attended. Cecilia Fortescue didn't get pregnant just by wishing a child inside her belly. Men became fathers by doing more than smiling at a girl in a comely way. I'd heard about blood and pain. I knew how horrible childbirth could be, that you 'might die'. But I'd listened to the other stories too and knew there were ways to stop it.

So who was to deprive George? William? No, his intentions were always good but his will power would crumble in front of Catherine. It would sour Nancy for good and ruin him, even if he had the wit to know that his manhood was meant for more than just piddling through.

Our coachman? He was an idle oaf with a foul temper. Rumour said a dose of the pox had nearly cost a kitchen maid her life when she grew too enamoured of him.

Over the next few days I appraised every man with a whore's eye. Finally, salvation arrived in the shape of a dirty-faced brute called Moses Cripps.

Chapter Eight

He turned up at the kitchen door with a bloody shank of beef thrown over one shoulder. Rain hammered down, but he wore nothing other than a rough pair of canvas breeches, a linen shirt open to the waist and scuffed leather sandals. He pushed into the kitchen warmth. Steam began rolling off his soaking clothes in lazy wisps that curled towards the ceiling.

I coughed on my breakfast and stared. Milk trickled from my open mouth. His arms were smeared with grease, his hair – long and raven black – lay slick against his skull. He threw the shank down on the kitchen table. Bone shattered. Lumps of gristle showered on to the floor.

'Here's your beef for the week, Maggie,' he rumbled. 'A good cut, just 'cause I'm so soft on you.' He looked more beast than man. A thatch of black hair sprouted across his chest and down to his navel, where it clustered at the waist of his breeches.

'Pagan out of his wits again?' Maggie asked from her place at the fire.

'He is that,' the visitor laughed. 'Won't see him out of his bed till Monday morn, I reckon. They've done keepin' his pew over at Queen's Church, seein' as how he never turns up for Sunday service.'

Pagan was the local flesher, an enormously fat, almost spherical man with a belly like a church bell and a thick beard smoking his chin. Since taking myself to the kitchen I'd caught a string of tales about this notorious drunkard. He employed a number of men to do his carting and carrying, freed criminals mostly so he could pay them less.

Footpad? Smuggler? Moses had the eyes of a hanged man. A smell, a heady mix of butchery and sweat clung to him like a shroud. He turned those eyes on me. 'Who's the wench?' he asked Maggie, wiping his hands on his breeches. 'A new maid? I thought that flint-eyed mistress of yours was keeping a tight purse these days?'

'Mind your mouth. Juliana was in Mr Worledge's charge.'

'So what's she doing in the kitchen eating off a wooden trencher? Not much of a lady if you ask me. My ma was buried in a better gown than that dusty old thing.'

I couldn't find a word of reply anywhere in my head. Suddenly he lunged towards me, teeth bared. I shrieked and scrabbled backwards off the bench. His laughter was like river water pouring over a lip of rock. I sat on the floor, fuming. Maggie laughed too. 'Come back day after next, Moses,' she said, wiping her eyes with the corner of her apron. 'Mrs Worledge wants a cut of ham and cook needs some bacon.'

'Got plenty o' bacon already,' he declared, squeezing the maid's behind. She squealed and batted at his thick arms until he let her go. She paid him with money out of her jar. Still laughing, he strode back out into the rain. A cart and dray horse waited in the street. Moses vaulted on to the driver's seat and kicked the animal into motion. He glanced back into the kitchen before the doorframe cut him from view. He wasn't looking at Maggie, but at me. The rain pummelled his skin, crisscrossing his chest with wet stripes.

I could have bludgeoned him to death with his own shank of beef for the way he'd dismissed me. I resented his familiarity with Maggie, his easy, rolling gait as though walking around the very world posed no great inconvenience, and his words which had run roughshod over us both. I thought of those muscles and stared at the lump of beef that lay, leaking blood and rainwater, on the kitchen table. I imagined him picking it up and tearing it to shreds with his bare hands.

Maggie closed the kitchen door and tried to straighten her mobcap. She regarded me for a few moments, her eyes round and shining. Her fingers fumbled on the cap. Perspiration spiked her face, though the fire had not yet been banked for the night's cooking.

'Mind yourself around Moses Cripps,' she laughed. 'It's only a bit of harmless mischief but he forgets his place sometimes.'

'Does he have a wife?'

'Aye, and she's a hard woman at that. Bear it in mind next time you fix your eyes on the crack of his shirt.'

That night I went to sleep with the smell of raw meat still in my nostrils. I awoke, tired and irritable, to find myself sent to the market with Maggie. We walked along thronging streets, skirting puddles and gutters brimming with refuse. The market was a squeeze. Everyone seemed to be yelling. I fidgeted while Maggie fussed over everything, discarding a parcel of flour then choosing another that to my eyes looked exactly the same. Nothing she saw was right, nothing quite good enough to grace the kitchen. When she was finally satisfied, her purchases barely covered the bottom of her basket and my feet were fit to drop off.

'It'll be a carriage for you when you wed Mr Proudlove,' she remarked as I hobbled along, desperately trying to avoid her swinging basket. I was too tired to think of any sensible reply and my belly was rumbling. It was already past noon. The rains of the past few days had lifted their wet skirts and gone elsewhere. Puddles shrivelled and the mud was baked into cracked flakes.

A carriage was waiting in the lane outside the stable yard when we arrived back at the Butter House. On top sat a po-faced coachman, stiff in a green coat.

'Hello, who's this?' Maggie remarked. 'I've not seen that carriage round these parts before.'

Entering the kitchen we discovered a lady's maid sitting at the table with tears smearing her face. 'Miss Rodriguez,' she said, getting up off the bench, 'you must come at once. Miss Cecilia's birthing has started, but the child is lying badly in the womb. The midwife says it is cursed and will not touch it. Mr Fortescue has sent for a surgeon but Miss Cecilia is asking for you. We are all afraid she will die.'

'I don't know anything about birthing children.'

'Please, miss, she needs a friend.'

So I found myself riding in a fine carriage much sooner than Maggie Burns or myself had anticipated. The driver ran the team at a cracking pace. However, when a couple of vegetable carts blocked the street the shouting match he had with their owners drew a jeering crowd. A good half-hour passed before we were underway again.

The maid's face was a pudding of tears. She took her sodden handkerchief away from her face long enough to tell me that her name was Emily. 'There had been birth pains before,' she blubbed, 'but they always came to nothing. The child was not due for another two weeks. Miss Cecilia doesn't know what to do. She lies in bed screaming fit to frighten the devil and spilling blood over the sheets.'

I grasped her wrists and tried to calm her down. 'Has anyone else called at the house? Mr Fairchild perhaps?'

She gawped. 'No, miss. None have called save the midwife.'

Mr Fortescue was waiting in the hall. 'The worst is over,' he told me.

'The surgeon arrived? He took care of her?'

He shook his head. 'Our usual surgeon was nowhere to be found. Ten guineas bought a quack who scratched like a dog and stank of gin. No reputable doctor would come, no matter what fee

I offered. They are all afraid of bringing scandal upon themselves, and their good names are apparently worth more than the life of my girl.'

'And the child?'

He sighed. 'It will live, whether through a miracle or a curse I cannot yet tell. My daughter has birthed a bastard boy with a thatch of dark hair and a chubby hand dipped into my fortune. What is it about these libertines that allows them to worm their way into young women's hearts with such ease? Not one possesses an ounce of decency. I loved Cecilia's mother. Loved her from the day we were first introduced. She was the only girl I courted. These rakes collect conquests they way some men display duelling scars. Honest daughters are made deaf to their fathers' concerns, and are blinded to these wastrels' lack of scruples. You can say to a girl: "Look at his bastards, look at the broken hearts – at the families' hearts", and off they'll go, at the flick of a whisker, to soil themselves at these creatures' hands. An irresistible poison, Miss Rodriguez; a foul brew from which they willingly sup. The more they have, the deeper they fall. Where is the sense in it?'

'Perhaps there is no sense to love.'

'Love has naught to do with it. This is wilful degradation. Cecilia is so moonstruck by this man she is incapable of making proper choices. Well, by God, I'll take the hook out of her mouth.'

'May I see Cecilia?'

He waved in the direction of the stairs. 'Yes, for whatever good it might do. The surgeon had to cut her to get the baby out, but she's of strong stock like her mother and will survive to shame me once again. Emily will take you to Cecilia's bedchamber. I cannot go in there.'

As I passed him, he laid a hand on my shoulder. 'We had a bargain, Miss Rodriguez. I trust you will remember it.'

Cecilia's bedchamber was a billowy temple of pale cream linen and lace-trimmed curtains. The windows were flung wide, permitting a breeze to waft about the room like a mischievous spirit.

'Please wait outside,' I instructed Emily. 'I wish to talk with Miss Fortescue alone.'

'But...'

'Do it.'

I thought she might try to defy me, but after a moment's thought she stepped back into the passage. A quick check ensured that she was not lingering by the keyhole then I secured the door and hurried over to the bed. Cecilia lay swaddled in a white eiderdown with a wet cloth pressed against her forehead. Sweat coated her face. Both eyes were closed and she seemed unaware of my presence. How tiny she looked, so fragile in this huge bed. The linen had been changed, but the air was coloured with smells. I sat beside her and found her hand. Her fingers curled around mine, the flesh clammy. Her eyes fluttered open and her gaze settled on me.

'Juliana.' Her voice cracked like twigs in a fire. 'Where is he? Why is he not here?'

I tried to summon a smile. It dried on my face. 'He is not coming. He was never coming. For all your wiles, you were foolish to believe otherwise.'

Cecilia's eyelids fluttered. I could not be sure she had heard me. Her breathing was harsh and the skin around her mouth pinched.

'A son. I have given him a son. If he could not love me then I hoped at least...'

She drifted off again into that semi-dark place where the hurt seek refuge. I released her hand and rose from the bed, absently wiping my fingers on my gown. Out in the hall, Emily was nowhere to be seen. I caught her coming back up the stairs.

'Where is the baby?' I demanded.

She halted on the steps. 'Cook took it into the kitchen to clean it. The doctor left right away, and Mr Fortescue won't come out of his study.'

'Has Cecilia held the child? Does he have a name?'

'No, miss. She wouldn't look at it. The doctor dosed her with laudanum and she's been asleep most of the time.'

'Very well, I'll see you get five shillings if you can keep your mouth shut. Bring the baby to the stable yard then forget you ever saw him.'

'I can't...'

'Cecilia doesn't want motherhood; anyone with half a wit can see that. This will not go hard on her. She knows her papa will forgive her and she can continue to live under his roof.'

I hurried downstairs and barged into Mr Fortescue's study. I demanded a hired carriage with a dependable coachman and a strong team of horses, plus expenses to cover additional costs. He had the sense not to ask questions, dropped a purse into my hand and sent a footman to the nearest coaching house. A post chaise and team rumbled into the yard barely half an hour later, just as sunset turned the sky molten gold. Emily pattered out of the kitchen door with a linen-wrapped bundle. I tucked the purse into her apron pocket, told her to split the contents with cook, and took the bundle into my arms. Emily turned to go but I called her back.

'Not a word of this to anyone,' I reminded her. 'No kitchen gossip or idle chitchat with the other servants.'

She curtsied. 'Yes, Miss Rodriguez.'

'Good. Now go and sit with Cecilia.' I laid the sleeping child on the seat inside the coach then climbed inside. I had no intention of looking at the child if I could help it. The shape, the feel, the smell was too familiar.

Thunder rumbled over the sea. A blanket of cloud rolled in from the west, dragging a storm towards the coast. The pretty sunset was drowned in a boiling mass of purples and greys. Metal-clad hooves sparked on the yard. The driver clutched his hat as a gust of wind swirled around the corner of the house.

I leaned out of the window and told him where I wanted to go.

'A two-hour drive at least, miss,' he replied. 'And that's only if we're blessed with clear roads.'

I glanced at the darkening sky. 'Hurry.'

Across town, traders packed up stalls and battened shutters. People scampered home, clinging to their bonnets while dogs barked into the rising wind. We stopped at the posting house near the end of the new turnpike. Another man climbed aboard armed with a gun. Muffled words were exchanged, a coarse laugh cut the gloom, then a whip cracked and the carriage lurched forward. An hour later and it was dark. Flickering coach lamps glowered like blinking eyes in the cool air, throwing distorted shadows across the trees now bordering the road.

The baby shifted in my arms. I prayed an empty belly wouldn't wake him up and start him bawling. I'd forgotten to ask Emily if cook had managed to find a wet nurse or put milk down his throat some other way. Holding him close, I kept whispering: 'Don't be afraid,' over and over. Outside, the night was a black cavern of swirling air. The carriage was buffeted on its leather springs. In the distance, lightning fired the sky, followed a few moments later by the low rumbling of the dragon's belly. In the dim light of the lamps, the trees were whipped up into a shivering fit.

I fiddled with the blind. Broken. On the roof, the coachmen shouted across at one another, the words stolen almost instantly from their mouths. Suddenly, the sky split apart with light. The carriage lurched sickeningly. A whip cracked, the world straightened. The coppery taste of blood filled my mouth where I had bitten my tongue.

Not one other soul did we meet on that long road. The storm increased in ferocity, as though the very elements of nature were coming after me to claim back what was taken. Only once did the baby open tiny, bleary eyes to look up at me from inside the folds of linen. He felt safe in my arms, I was sure of it, despite the howling gale outside. 'You won't be hurt, I promise,' I whispered, as the first of the rains began to fall.

Soft lights penetrated the murk as we clattered into the village of Afton Vale, leaking through shuttered windows and spilling from the mouth of a tavern. Lightning flickered, revealing a collection of dwellings clinging to the sides of a low hill. A church steeple poked a sharp finger into the tortured sky, weather vane spinning a mad dance on top of the spire.

I pushed open the door as the carriage halted and stumbled on to the verge. The wind sang about my ears in a wailing chorus of lost souls. It plucked the edges of my cloak with unseen fingers and slapped my hair about my face.

'Wait here,' I called up to the coachmen, their faces white moons in the storm light. One clambered down to settle the horses. I wrapped the baby in a fold of my cloak and hurried up the hill towards the church. A mud puddle sucked off one of my shoes and swallowed it greedily. My eyes were full of rain.

I struggled up a steep, narrow lane, houses crowding in on either side. My feet scrabbled on the slick cobbles. My lungs ached by the time I reached the lich-gate of the church. I paused to catch my breath before limping past the moss-blackened tombstones of the churchyard and into the clump of trees beyond.

The house was exactly as described. A former parsonage, modest though comfortable looking, with sagging eaves and ivy straggling up the front wall. I banged on the painted oak door. A chair scraped across floorboards. Then came a woman's voice, hesitant, enquiring.

155

'Who's there?'

The wind tore the words from my throat. 'Juliana. Juliana Rodriguez. Open the door.'

An iron bolt squealed and the door sighed open. She stood framed in candlelight, a hearty fire crackling in the hearth behind her. A flash of lightning lit up her face. She had filled out a little, her features losing many of the harsh lines that had always made her look so gaunt. Her hair was different too: all bunched on top of her head and dripping with ribbons. A hint of rouge warmed her cheeks and I picked up the sweet scent of cologne, even in the restless air of the porch.

'Hello Miss Mary,' I said, shifting the bundle in my arms.

Her face went through entire seasons of emotions. 'Come inside, come inside at once. What are you doing here? On a night like this?'

I stumbled into her parlour, dripping a trail of rainwater across the floor. Mary held out her arms to embrace me. I thrust the baby into her startled grasp.

'There, a child for you. The child you always wanted. Take care of your new son, Miss Mary.'

'It's Mrs Pettit now.' She unwrapped the linen bundle. Her jaw slackened when she spied the baby within. 'Juliana, what have you done?'

'Saved his life and given you something more valuable than a pretty dress. I have taken him from somewhere he wasn't wanted to somewhere I know he'll be loved. Look after him, please.'

'Has he no parents of his own? Did they not want him?'

Standing soaking in my dress, I told her the

whole of it. I did not sit down, or even pause for breath. She listened in that patient way of hers, head to one side, glancing occasionally down at the child as if unable to believe it lay in her arms. Years of frustration fell from her face when she stroked his smooth, white chin.

'What will I say to Ernest?' she asked when I had finished.

'He is your husband?'

'Yes, the wedding was very quick and simple. No relatives on either side, just a couple of villagers for witnesses.'

I tugged a handkerchief from my sleeve and wiped the rain off my face. 'Tell him what you will – that the child was a foundling left on your doorstep.'

She shook her head. 'He won't believe it. He knows how desperate I am.'

'He has no wish for a son? Someone to take his name?'

Mary gazed at the child. 'Every wish in the world. It is what he has always wanted, even though he will not put that desire into words out of respect for me. But I can read his heart. We could tell everyone that the child is a parish orphan. They would understand that.'

A draught shivered down my back and gusted around my ankles. It wheezed across the floor, sucked the smoke back out of the chimney and set the candles guttering in their holders. My wet clothes tightened their clammy grip on my body.

Mary beckoned. 'Warm yourself by the hearth, at least until the storm blows over. I have some milk to give the baby.'

I shook my head. 'A hired carriage is waiting. Close the door when I'm gone and forget you saw me tonight.'

'Things are still not well with you and Mrs Worledge?'

'No, not well. Best if you did not write for a while. Catherine likes to read my messages. So far I've managed to sneak letters past her but I can't tell how long my good fortune will hold.'

I noticed how naturally she held the child, how comfortable they were with one another. 'God bless you, Juliana,' she said, 'even though I don't know whether you're a devil or an angel.'

'I certainly need someone's blessing tonight.'

Slithering back down the hill, I found the coachmen sheltering in the lee of the tavern, supping hot broth fetched from the kitchen. 'Landlord reckons he has a nose for the weather,' the man with the gun told me. 'Says this storm will blow itself out within the hour.'

The carriage was turned and within minutes, Afton Vale was receding into the murk. I pushed my face into my hands and cried until my cheeks stung. I felt sick with nerves and utterly alone. A dry patch on my gown marked where I had held the child. I fingered the material while trying to weigh the rights and wrongs of what I had done. Outside the carriage, the storm rumbled further inland. The wind slackened and the thunder banged its heavenly drums over someone else's house, someone else's children. I whispered questions into the night but the darkness held no answers.

At the driver's insistence we pulled into a coaching inn. I could not begrudge it. Both men were soaked through, the horses badly in need of rest and fodder. I spent the remainder of the night on a straw bed. I would've gladly slept in a barrel for the sake of some peace.

Nevertheless, I had the men out of their beds at dawn and on the road again with barely a pause for breakfast. Arriving in town, I ordered them to drop me off two streets away from the Butter House and handed over the remainder of the money Mr Fortescue had given me. 'Not a word to anyone about last night's trip,' I warned.

Both men nodded. A click of the reins and the carriage rattled off. I dawdled on the way home, hoping Catherine hadn't missed me. I was oblivious to the busy throng of the street. Finally, I crept through the kitchen door and made my way through the house in a slither of still-damp petticoats.

Cecilia was waiting for me in the parlour.

'You took my baby,' she said, heavy weights hanging from each word.

She was seated in Catherine's armchair. Dark circles bruised both eyes and her thin lips were dry. Animosity glowered from her face.

'You should not be out of bed,' I told her. 'It is too soon.'

Her feet shifted beneath the thick cloak that swaddled her body, smaller now that the new life within had gone. 'Your stable lad let me in. Mrs Worledge is not here. Neither is her odious manservant. It seems you were not the only one with business in the night.'

I sat opposite and clasped my fingers together to stop them trembling. 'Did the maid tell you?'

'Yes, but only after I'd threatened her with the street.' She sighed bitterly. 'I don't suppose you will tell me where you took him?'

I shook my head. 'Leave him alone, Cecilia. You don't want him. Enjoy your parties then go and marry an earl or some fluff-headed fop. The baby has found a good home, I promise you that much. Your papa thought it would be for the best.'

'Papa has disinherited me more times than the sun has risen. He always forgives me, whatever my sins, because I am the only woman in his life, the only reminder of the wife he loved. Also, like all foolish men without a son and heir, he hopes my dowry will buy a respectable name. 'Twould make no difference if I lay with every thief and beggar in the south of England. A good match is favoured over any reputation, however scarlet. We all have reputations, don't we, Juliana?'

I felt my tongue turn to lead. A mirthless laugh fell out of Cecilia's mouth. 'We are alike in many ways, you and I. We don't enjoy being told what to do. We both want to shock, to indulge in whims that will outrage a society that in itself is full of outrageous people. It amused me to be associated with you, and I perceived you had a similar interest in me.'

'This is not a game, Cecilia. Or a whim to colour my standing in the eyes of stupid, arrogant people. I thought only of the baby. He's not something you can tuck away in a cupboard whenever you fancy attending a concert or masquerade.'

160

'He would have been looked after. I enquired about a nursemaid.'

'Your papa was determined he had to go. I could not stand by and see him become a parish boy or sold off to a sweep.'

'So you befriended me because you wanted my child? I suppose you have always wanted it, even though you might not have realised it at first. I noticed the way you kept looking at my belly while drinking tea on my couch. I could sense your mind asking questions, asking whether I had any love for my unborn child or, perhaps more importantly, the father.'

She closed her eyes for a moment. 'Yes, deny it as much as you like, I know of your desire. How does it feel to have your blood burn, to have someone constantly in your thoughts and not be able to push him out, even when you suffer for it?'

'I don't love anyone.'

'This has naught to do with love. I told you we had much in common, Juliana. So now I daresay I'm expected to forget all about the baby and go and make the proper match desired, provided anyone with a decent name will have me? Well, there are some things I cannot forget. I felt every second of that birth. I've never known pain like it. It seems as if a part of me has been torn out and can't be put back. Perhaps you would do well to remember that, child stealer.'

She coughed. Tremors shivered through her body like curtains rippling in a breeze. All her magic, all her charm, had gone, drained out like fine wine poured through the tap of a barrel. No longer the sylph, the coquettish young tease who held sway at parties, holding court amidst an assembly terrified of her social executions. She had lost her power.

I stood up. 'Let me see you out. I presume you have a chair or carriage waiting?'

Cecilia fumbled under her cloak and handed me a linen-wrapped package bound with string. 'Papa asked me to give you this. It seems you and he are better acquainted than I realised. He has good cause to feel pleased with you. I suppose I shall have to behave now there is no one to promise me the world.'

'Adam?'

'He brought me down further than he ever humbled you, Juliana. He has not replied to my letters. Messengers have been turned away at the door to his club or told he is not at home. He will never be at home. Not for me.'

'Yet you are still besotted with him?'

Cecilia didn't answer. She trod carefully to the door and put a hand on the knob. Then she turned. 'I hear you are to wed George Proudlove. Let us hope marriage proves kind to you. I thought you were my friend. It seems I was wrong about a great many things, but the greatest mistake you will make is believing you know how many times a man can hurt you before you are able to let him go.'

After Cecilia had left, Maggie Burns called down the passage from the kitchen. 'Your Miss Fortescue, she and the baby are hearty? Seems a mite soon to be up an about.'

I nodded. 'They are both well.'

162

'I daresay Mr Proudlove won't approve of you having friends such as her.'

I sighed and turned towards the stairs, Cecilia's package under my arm. 'On that account he has nothing to fear.'

I entered my bedchamber and closed the door. Satisfied that I would not be disturbed, I laid the package on the bed and tore at the string. The linen took an age to unravel. I was frantic with anticipation as the last of the wrapping unwound on to the floor. Revealed was an armful of velvet cut and stitched into one of the most alluring gowns my starved eyes had feasted on. I held it against me. A river of gorgeous material tumbled down to my feet. A queen. I would look like a queen.

I viewed my reflection in the looking glass. This was a garment to send the imagination flying. With it, there was nothing I could not achieve, no one I could not have if I set my mind to it.

'Fair bargain, Mr Fortescue,' I whispered. A smile cut across my lips as if slashed by the glinting blade of a buccaneer's sword. Tomorrow. Tomorrow was the day the meat carrier came.

I rested for the remainder of the afternoon and slept soundly that night. I rose with the sun and, yawning, laid out my new gown on the chair before starting to plan. I spun a cautious web, aware that I lacked the experience or sophistication to entice men as effectively as Cecilia. But my innocence could, in itself, prove my best weapon.

'A man likes nothing more than to deflower a maiden,' Cecilia once told me. 'Virginity is a challenge, and once claimed it is gone for ever. I swear most of the libertines who haunt Wexborough's assembly rooms keep a tally of their conquests, of the girls they have turned into women, and the wedding nights they have ruined when the groom discovers he was not first past the gate, as it were.'

The house was mine. Catherine had left word with William that she had gone to visit George at his estate and would not return for at least another day. Nancy, idle milkmaid that she was, malingered in bed and as a result Maggie was up to her ears in dirty linen. I sneaked into Catherine's bedchamber and plundered her dresser, determined to turn myself from a strawberry-faced doe to a royal consort. I filched her scent, dipped into her jewellery box and clouded my face with her powder. Dressing was difficult without help but my time in Florence had taught me a trick or two. A necklace for the final touch then I checked myself in the mirror, running my hands over velvet loops and bows, turning this way then that. No wig, I decided. I wanted him to see my hair, to run his fingers freely through it.

'How could any man resist you?' I declared.

How indeed?

The hands of the hall clock kissed noon. Maggie had gone to the washhouse with a cart groaning under mountains of laundry. That ought to keep her hands in water for two hours at best. William was cleaning out the stable and no tradesmen, save one, were expected at the door for the remainder of the day.

It was going to happen. It was *meant* to happen. I paced the kitchen, wringing my hands and stealing nervous glances out of the window. My ears strained for the lazy clop-clop of hooves on the packed gravel road. I would meet him here, in this grease-stained battlefield of copper pots and pans. The best terms a kitchen slut could offer.

Chapter Nine

Moses Cripps was not a man who bothered to knock on doors. He pushed his way into the kitchen with the same bare-chested crudity I'd witnessed a few days before. The door was left to swing on its hinges as he slapped a muslin package stained with fat on to the table top.

'Maggie, where are you?' he growled. 'I've a mind to squeeze your plump arse.'

He sniffed around the room, dark eyes taking in the empty hearth, the sacks of flour, and the vegetables strung from the rafters. Then his gaze settled on me. 'Why, if it isn't the little kitchen girl. For a minute I thought I'd stepped into a bawdy house. What brings you in here dressed like that?'

The folds of my new gown rustled as I crossed to the door and dropped the latch. 'Maggie has business elsewhere today.' I turned to face him, my back pressed against the hard oak. 'And I have some business with you.'

I knew how to stand, how to move my body and bring the heat into his cheeks. My instincts were

165

strong, my desire easily overpowering my fear. Hands on waist, hips thrust out, chin raised. Just like the harlots on Marlborough Street.

Cripps's voice rumbled at the back of his throat. His eyes glittered. 'You playin' games with me? Didn't anyone ever warn you that little girls ought not to toy with grown men?'

I swallowed. 'I am woman enough for you. If you think you are man enough for me.'

He towered over me. I was forced to stand on tiptoe just to meet his gaze. A smile bent his lips. He could bat me out of the way as easily as flicking a fly off the table top. 'Look at you, quivering like a rabbit with a ferret nipping at its tail. This ain't a parlour game. I don't want you running upstairs bawling to your mama just because I've ruffled your feathers. I get plenty of offers, from ladies as well as their maids. Why should I bother with a pup like you?'

'Because you will be my first.'

'So that's it?' Laughter rolled up his throat and spilled out of his mouth. I blushed, feeling all the more the child before this brute, and angry at my own weakness. Fumbling, I locked the kitchen door and tossed the key into a corner. One of us was a prisoner, but who had trapped whom? Palms sweating, I waited him out.

'How old are you?' he asked.

'Old enough to marry. Or take a lover if I choose.'

'Choice is one thing you ain't got. Not any more.' He bent towards me. My nostrils filled with his smell. He opened his mouth and ran his tongue across my eyebrow. A low moan escaped my throat.

'Aye,' he whispered, 'young as you are, you're woman enough.'

I kept touching myself in wonder. When I stood naked in front of my looking glass the little girl was gone for ever. The woman gazing out of the glass was confident, smiling. Already dark bruises were forming where Moses had handled me but these were the marks of passion and I would let them flower in their own way.

Behind me on the rug was a pitcher and ewer. I had washed my insides thoroughly. Perhaps that would be enough. Perhaps not. I folded up the Italian gown and slipped it under the foot of my bed. Then I fastened Catherine's scratchy old dress and glanced again at the figure in the mirror.

My body. All else having failed, my body would get me what I wanted.

Next day Catherine returned with a new bonnet and a gaggle of chattering friends. Talk over tea was all about the war and how the king's armies were being defeated by rebels in league with the French. The Americas were all but lost. I was brought into the parlour and paraded as George Proudlove's prospective bride. I had no idea who these people were or where Catherine had found them. She was full of plans for the wedding. I felt as if someone else entirely was getting married.

Released, I fled the room and spent the rest of the morning sulking at the kitchen window, watching next door's cat chase a few sluggardly birds around the square patch of garden. Later I sent William to the flesher's shop with a message for Moses Cripps to deliver more meat. I was still touched by the boy's enthusiasm to please me, despite having a sweetheart of his own.

During that endless afternoon, I invented every kind of excuse to stay in the kitchen, lingering by the back door long after William had returned from delivering his message. I offered to help Maggie but my heart wasn't in the work. Disgusted, she threw a dishcloth at my head and told me to keep out of her way. I strained my ears listening for the lazy clop of the butcher's horse, but apart from the excited squeals of children in the street, the day remained quiet.

Laughter filtered down the passage as Catherine's guests outstayed their welcome. Maggie was forced to go out to the washhouse with a large bundle of linen. Nancy was still in bed coughing her wits out. Left to myself, I found the kitchen oppressive. I glanced at the vegetables Maggie had asked me to cut before losing her temper, and thought I might still give it a try. I sensed her irritation wasn't only due to my clumsiness but so far she had avoided my careful promptings.

I needed to snatch some fresh air. Putting down the kitchen knife, I opened the back door and walked straight into Moses Cripps.

'Been waitin' for me?' he grinned darkly.

'Did you bring the meat?'

'Might have done. Does it matter?'

'I didn't hear your cart.'

'Don't need it for this sort of delivery. No fancy gown today?'

'I don't need that for this sort of service.'

He chuckled. 'That's my lass...'

I ran up the stairs to my bedchamber, intent on cleaning myself up before Maggie returned from the washhouse. The door hung ajar. I always closed it before going downstairs.

I crept inside. The room was gloomy, the curtains half drawn across the open window. The air was thick with tobacco smoke and the cloying scent of cologne. Someone was watching me from the shadows beside the bed. Blake. He sat, legs crossed, on the small armchair. He grinned, his teeth leaping out of his face like pearl daggers.

I fumbled back against the door and felt it close behind me. Stupid. I had not seen Blake since Catherine had returned and I'd assumed he was elsewhere on some business or other. To find him lurking in my room knocked the breath out of me. Instinctively my hands folded across my breasts.

The smile deepened. Nothing in the room appeared to have been disturbed. 'What are you doing here?' I demanded. 'You have no business coming into my bedchamber.'

He rose from the chair in a single, fluid movement, the velvet of his embroidered waistcoat whispering against his silk shirt. No one could mistake him for a footman now.

'On the contrary,' he purred. 'I have some pressing business with you, Miss Juliana.'

He held something in his hand, a hand laden with rings that glinted even in the dim light. A folded piece of writing paper. He waved it lazily in front of my face. 'This message is for you. The delivery boy was about to bring it to the front door. I was able to catch him. He swore the note was urgent and had to be given to you straightaway.' Blake shrugged. His feigned expression of ignorance painted a nightmare on his dark, crooked features. 'However, it seems you were busy.'

'Give me the message then get out.' I snatched at the paper but Blake flicked it out of my reach.

'There you go, playing the fool again.' He sounded bored, almost disappointed, though undercurrents rippled beneath his assured exterior. Before I could move, he seized my wrist, prised open my fingers and pressed the sheet of paper into my palm. He ran his other hand through my hair, nails scraping my scalp. Then he sniffed, nose twitching like a rat's. 'You smell of a rutting. Someone's had your skirts up, my pretty lass.'

'Let go,' I cried. 'Get off me. You'll never be as good a man as your master. Richard might have been a drunk, but at least he was a gentleman. You can wear his clothes, drink his port and smoke his tobacco but you belong in the gutter with the rest of the offal.'

His grip loosened. I pulled my hand away and backed to the far side of the room, glancing round for something I could use as a weapon. He was too strong for me, but perhaps I could startle him long enough to run.

'Whine all you like,' Blake jeered. 'You stink of lust, and with your wedding to George Proudlove not two weeks away. I care naught for your innocence or lack of it. You could bed the whole of Wexborough and Proudlove would still marry you. He takes whores with as much relish as he loses at cards. I'll wager you have the pox within a week of becoming his wife. If you haven't got it already.'

Blake grasped the doorknob, twisted it and pulled open the door. Then he was gone. I examined the letter he had thrust into my hands. The wax seal was broken and the page clumsily refolded. I smoothed it out and read the small, neat script.

Juliana, there is little time and I fear for my life. I have not heard from you since our encounter at the burial and it is vital that we speak. Hurry to my home and we will discuss matters there. Time is short.
Your servant, M Littlejohn.

I crumpled up the paper and tucked it into my sleeve. In the graveyard that day Mr Littlejohn's eyes had darted around as though expecting some unseen nemesis to leap out and confront him. For me, slipping out of the house was becoming more difficult. Catherine held me on a tight leash while she concocted her awful wedding plans. Flowers arrived from George, basketfuls of them – elaborate displays of lilies and white roses. My bedchamber resembled a garden gone wild. I starved the blooms of water, plucking a single flower from the wilting bunches to wear in my hair while Moses Cripps tupped me behind the oat sacks.

Meanwhile the dressmaker arrived to measure me for my wedding gown. I was also made to rehearse the ceremony with our own local parson and William standing in as the groom. Why did

George want me for a wife? Of all the prospective brides his position and privilege could have bought, why me? Catherine hadn't settled any kind of dowry as far as I was aware.

Gossip breezed through the servants. Glances were exchanged at the kitchen table, knowing looks passed from seat to seat like a flagon of bitter wine. Maggie had an idea, of course, and perhaps William also suspected the truth. The look he gave Moses one day when ordered to help unload the cart was as cold as a winter's gale.

Maggie grew sullen. Moses no longer flirted with her. He and I grew careless in our passion and Maggie caught us in the pantry, limbs locked together. She would not talk to me for hours afterwards. 'Don't get a bastard in your belly,' she said finally. 'Moses won't care. If you need a wise woman I can tell you where to go.'

Nothing passed beyond the kitchen door. No one was keen on George Proudlove. But whatever I did meant nothing as long as Blake pushed his way into my life as he pleased. He had gone to ground again, disappearing on one of his mysterious errands, but I kept expecting to find him grinning from some shadowed corner.

Still I was denied egress from the house. Catherine checked on me at least twice an hour, sometimes more. Though I had not seen George since being forced to dine with him that memorable evening, his family called. I was introduced to Mr Proudlove senior, an out-of-town parson crowed up in a black shovel hat, woollen hose, sturdy buckle shoes and a cloak still powdered with the dust of country lanes. A fat gold ring clutched the middle finger of his right hand.

'Show respect to Mr Proudlove,' Catherine instructed. I dipped a curtsy. I'd already been warned that he bore a facial injury but it was hard not to stare. A hole split the right side of the parson's face just below the cheekbone. Through it, gums glistened wetly, and a row of yellow teeth stood like jaundiced sentries. Breath wheezed in and out, turning his speech into a rasping drawl that sounded like pebbles rattling in a wooden bucket. The thought of his long, bony fingers touching me invoked a cold shudder.

I was presented to his dough-faced wife, Marjorie, and a clingy, wide-eyed girl called Charlotte. I thought she might be a niece or godchild, but learned that she was in fact their daughter. She looked about five years old.

Parson Proudlove perched on the end of the drawing-room sofa, thin legs clamped together. Grey eyes flitted across the furnishings as though trying to winkle sinners out of the woodwork. When offered refreshment, he declined tea and asked instead for brandy. William brought the bottle and the parson poured himself a generous measure, which he downed in a single gulp.

'The girl looks like a two-guinea trick out of a bawdy house,' he said, gesturing at me. 'George needs good breeding stock, a plain woman to teach him a little humility as well as the responsibility of raising an heir. Vanity has no place in a God-fearing household.'

Catherine pulled her lips into a smile. 'Juliana has been well educated. I invested a great deal in her tutelage.'

Proudlove flicked his hand. 'It does no good to stuff a woman's head full of nonsense. What use are fripperies so long as she can bear her husband healthy sons and run a household capably? And obedient – she must be obedient, one of the most important qualities in a wife.'

'You need not trouble yourself on that account,' Catherine purred. 'Juliana will do as she is bid.'

She glanced at me, her face a nest of threats. I bit back my tongue. They talked some more. I was not invited to sit down, or offered any tea. Parson Proudlove spoke directly to Catherine, pausing only to refill his brandy glass. For a clergyman he seemed overly ambitious, openly discussing his plans for rising through the church hierarchy. His wife nodded, then nodded again, continually stirring her tea as it grew cold.

I moved to the window and watched two noisy dogs chase each other around the street. Broken shadows fell across the huddled town buildings. Behind me, the parson droned on. I heard a forced laugh from Catherine followed by a nervous chuckle from Mrs Proudlove.

A tug on my skirts pulled me from my reverie. The little pale-faced girl stared up at me. I wondered if she ever smiled, if she even knew how to smile.

'Are you going to be my aunt?' she said, each word precisely formed by her tiny mouth. An intelligence beyond her years seemed to lurk behind those wide brown eyes.

'Yes,' I replied. 'It appears so.'

Charlotte leaned forward and whispered: 'Do

you believe in unicorns?'

I stroked the back of her small hand with my thumb. 'I am sure there are magical places filled with all sorts of wonderful creatures, places where people are always happy and nothing bad ever happens. But we can't always go to these places. We can only dream, and try to make the best of what we have here.'

I let go of her hand. 'Don't you have any friends or toys to play with? A favourite doll perhaps?'

'Papa says dolls are ungodly, and that the boys and girls in our village are the children of sinners.' She tilted her head to one side. Brown curls brushed her cheeks. 'Will you come to stay with us after you are married?'

I shook my head. 'I will have to go and live with your brother in his own house. Perhaps I will see you when we come to visit.'

A frown creased her forehead. I could sense the child-thoughts tumbling around behind her dark eyes. 'You won't stay with George,' she said. 'Not for long.'

Quiet settled over the Butter House. The Proudloves had left for their parish in Dinstock – a market village some twenty miles outside Wexborough. Catherine was upstairs enjoying an afternoon nap. I had business elsewhere.

The last time I saw William, he was squatting on an upended bucket rubbing oil into a carriage whip. Maggie was sorting out the larder. A rat had got in and she was determined to catch it. Nancy, threatened with a thrashing from Blake, had made a remarkable recovery and was cleaning out the dining-room hearth.

I had no money for a sedan chair and lacked the nerve to steal any more from Maggie's jar. I changed into a plain gown and bonnet, slipped out the front door and hurried along the street. With luck, people would think I was a maid chasing an errand. I didn't want to think about what might happen if I was spotted out of doors without permission. Catherine's naps were notoriously heavy but I'd already taken too many chances sneaking out of the house.

Torrential rain had carved ruts into the gravel road. Mud and refuse choked the gutters. I tried to watch where I put my feet, at the same time snatching glances at the clock on the front of the corn exchange. Brook Street lay midway between the Butter House and the harbour, a narrow thoroughfare ending in a square where the old customs and excise building once stood. It took half an hour of squeezing through busy streets before I arrived, exhausted but glad to be out of the Butter House's stuffy confines.

A long street of ill-matched buildings stretched in front of me. Chimney pots jostled for space on top of brick stacks, which looked ready to tumble at the first breath of wind. Stone-faced houses bore the scars of countless winters. Walls were pitted, gutters choked with weeds and old leaves.

I tightened Catherine's shawl around my shoulders. Seagulls wheeled overhead, raucous cries cutting the afternoon air. In the near distance I could hear the bustle of the harbour and the gentle shifting of water as the tide crept up the wooden pilings of the quay. Richard's office was nearby. I was heartsick at the thought of going anywhere near it. I was too frightened of running into Blake, too unsure of where he spent his time when off on one of his mysterious errands.

I found the house. Narrow, squeezed between a draper's shop and a coach house. Curtains were drawn across the windows and the green-painted front door was splashed with dirt from the street. I had knocked twice and was thinking of leaving when, through the wood, I heard a cough. Then a voice muttered something.

Bolts scraped in their brackets. A key was pushed into the lock and turned. The door opened a crack and a bleary eye peered out.

I had met Edith Littlejohn only half a dozen times during my childhood, but she was not the sort of woman one forgot easily. As well as a bellowing laugh and a potato face cracked with smiles, she was possessed of bright, shiver-me eyes that held you as she moved and spoke, gesturing with butterfly hands. Eyes in which a challenge lurked. A challenge not to find anything decent or beautiful in even the most ordinary things.

I had not admired her for her humour, which was as expansive as her generous girth, or her seemingly boundless patience, but for her ability to treat life's calamities with amused contempt. She put trivial problems in their rightful place and handled more serious matters with an optimism that inspired faith in everyone.

Edith strode through life whilst others scurried. She never pinched my cheek, patted my back or admonished me to be a good girl. She listened to everything I said as if I was a great philosopher or the wisest of sages. And in all the talking not once did she dismiss anything I said. Instead she taught me to see things differently, to try to look at things through someone else's eyes. Often my convictions – the childish truths that I held to be absolute – shifted. Life was no longer always a 'yes' or a 'no' but a 'maybe' and a 'perhaps'. Black and white blurred into greys, and then glorious colours. Everything came to be possessed of beauty in its own subtle yet wonderful way. Even in the most squalid of Wexborough's rubbish-choked back streets, she told me, children could be heard laughing.

Now Mrs Littlejohn's eyes were dull and blood-ringed with crying. Garments hung loosely from her shoulders. A handkerchief was pressed against her blotchy face, a face that looked as if it had cried for a lifetime, cried until the colour had been washed out. She regarded me vaguely, her other hand trembling as it fingered the streaks of grey infecting her black hair. I had stepped back without realising it.

'What's happened?'

She waved me inside. I followed her down a woodpanelled passage thick with the stench of soiled linen, food gone cold and rugs too long in want of a beating. It took a while for my eyes to adjust to the gloom. I found myself in a parlour filled to the seams with ornaments. Dozens of china-faced dolls peered down from their shelves with dark, glassy eyes.

'Sit down,' Mrs Littlejohn muttered. 'You shan't stay long, but I've not the strength to keep to my feet.' She slumped into a squat armchair while I perched on the couch opposite. A half-full glass of what looked like canary lay on the table beside her, alongside a plate littered with scraps of food. I shivered. Cold grey ashes spilled out of the fireplace. A heap of logs lay untouched in a wicker basket. Apart from Mrs Littlejohn's wheezing chest and my own rapid breathing, the house was a cavern of silence. On the mantelpiece above the dead fire, a clock sat with its hands frozen. 'I've been expecting you, Juliana. A pity you couldn't have come sooner.'

'Where is your husband? At the shipping office?'

She regarded me with those sore, tired eyes. 'Michael is dead, buried amongst beggars, whores and murderers. His body was stitched up in a canvas sack and dumped in an unmarked pauper's grave in a corner of the town cemetery. I couldn't see his face, couldn't say goodbye. Nothing remains of him.'

I was robbed of words. From their vantage point the dolls stared down impassively.

'I was told he had taken his own life,' she continued after a time. 'His body was found floating face down in the water beneath the quay. The boatmen who fished him out claimed they found an empty gin bottle in his jacket pocket. Barely out of the sea and he was buried in the ground. No church service for a suicide. Soon the accusations began. Michael was held to have mishandled Mr Worledge's accounts, embezzled funds, helped smugglers in return for a portion of the cargo – all sorts of nonsense.'

She wiped her cheeks. 'The magistrate said he

must have jumped off the quay. My husband had a weakness for fine tobacco and the odd hand of cards but he was no drinker. He hadn't the belly for it. Someone must have killed him. Stole his life the way Catherine Worledge stole everything Michael had worked for. Don't tell me you weren't aware of it, Juliana. Don't insult his memory.'

I gestured helplessly. 'Mr Littlejohn sent me a note to tell me he was in fear of his life. Apparently he had important information he wished to pass on to me, something about my past, but I couldn't get out of the house. Catherine would be furious if she discovered I was here. She tells me nothing, makes plans behind my back and treats me as a marriage chattel. I haven't put a foot inside the shipping office for nigh on two years.'

I covered my face with my hands and squeezed both eyes shut. I pictured Mr Littlejohn floating in the rubbish-choked waters of the harbour, his face eaten by fish.

'I was sorry to hear about Richard,' Edith said, leaning back in her chair. 'Some men aren't born to be strong. Odd how they seem to attract a certain type of wife.'

'I couldn't help him. I wasn't strong enough either.'

'Oh, settle down. Start crying and you will have me in tears again. Enough have been spilled in this house already. This has been a strain on everyone, what with Mr Worledge's drinking and Michael having to run the business virtually single-handed. Trade went from bad to worse. He had too much tied up in the company. When the books wouldn't balance the bank foreclosed.

Michael was already a broken man before his murder. A clever legal web means Catherine Worledge can sit untouched in her fine town house. She is welcome to it.'

I searched her face. 'Why would anyone want to kill your husband?'

Edith grasped the arms of the chair and pushed herself to her feet. I moved to help but she waved me away. 'This will only take a few moments.'

She rummaged behind a bookshelf stuffed with loose documents, ledgers and bundles of rolled-up parchments. 'If you want to hide a tree, put it in a forest, Michael once told me. Ah, here we are.' She returned with a bound sheaf of paper and dropped it on to the fireside table. My name was written in a barely legible scrawl across the top page.

'These papers have been a stain on our lives,' she continued, tapping the bundle with her middle finger. 'I can't remember how many times we argued over them – squabbled like two unruly children. Michael never once hinted at what they might contain, though he never kept any other secrets from me. Only his wish that they be handed over to you has prevented me from tossing them into the sea. A simple bundle, but weighed down with years of anguish. I give it to you out of cowardice. Destroying these papers would not be enough. Only when they are in your possession will I truly rid myself of the wretched things. Michael made me swear not to mention them to anyone. He considered himself partly responsible for you – agonised over your treatment at the Worledge house. I was too much the obedient wife to defy him.'

I stared at the package, at the clumsy knot in the string. 'What will happen to you? Why haven't any friends called? You can't sit here by yourself.'

'I am the widow of a bankrupt suicide. It is worse than harbouring a pestilence. Friendships that took a lifetime to build unravel in less than a day. I will lose my home and everything in it. The wolves must have their meat. Perhaps that's for the best. Every object, every corner of this house carries a memory of my husband.'

Edith tapped the bundle again. 'This has already driven someone to murder. You must get out of Catherine Worledge's house. Whatever it takes, whatever you have to do, leave as soon as you can.'

Chapter Ten

I hurried back through town, the sheaf of documents pressed against my chest. I was conscious of how light the package was, how fragile the knowledge contained within its pages. Mr Littlejohn had said, in his note, that the time had come to learn about my past. Could my life so easily be set down on a bundle of papers?

I skirted the market square and headed downhill, stumbling on the odd loose cobble. Leaving Mrs Littlejohn alone had proved upsetting.

'Don't fret over me,' she'd said, squeezing my hand. 'Michael lives while I hold his memory. No one can murder that.'

'What will happen to you? Where will you go?'

'I have a sister in Plymouth. A spinster with a decent house and a few guineas in the bank. I'll go and stay with her, try to build a new life for myself in the years that are left. Catherine Worledge and her lawyers can fight over the scraps I leave behind.'

A clock chimed the hour. I coaxed further effort from my aching legs. The tall chimneys of the Butter House poked up into the hazy afternoon. The package slipped and I clutched it tighter in my sweating palms. I'd had to fight the impulse to tear it open. The words inside could change my life if what Mr Littlejohn hinted at was true. But I couldn't risk anything in the open streets. Too many eyes and ears.

Outside the house, I checked Catherine's window. The curtains were still drawn. I was so intent on what I was doing that I didn't hear the rapid approach of footsteps. A rough push between my shoulder blades. I tumbled over in a flurry of skirts and my head smacked against the dirt. Pain exploded in my skull. The world filled with reds and yellows. I lay gasping like a landed fish, the package still in one piece beside me.

'There's payment for your services, whore,' a voice spat.

A small, flint-faced woman stood over me. Patched and faded garments hung from her wiry frame and leather-bound wooden clogs poked from beneath the frayed hem of her gown. Hatred simmered in her eyes.

'Who are you?' I coughed. 'What do you want?'

'Mary Cripps is my name, and I'm tellin' you to

183

leave my man alone. He can't get you out of his head, talks about you all the time as if you was something special.' She nudged me with the toe of her clog. 'I was the one he took to the parson, who bore his sons and shares his bed. I ain't giving up what little I got for the likes o' you.'

I dragged myself up on to my elbows. I was afraid she would hit me. The entire side of my face ached like a rotten tooth. The street was unusually quiet but I spotted the town constable hurrying towards us. I don't know if it was just coincidence or whether someone had alerted him. Mary Cripps caught sight of him too. She spat into the gutter beside me and scurried off.

The constable helped me up and thrust a handkerchief into my fingers. 'What happened, miss? Was that creature trying to rob you?'

'A misunderstanding. I don't want any fuss.'

'As you like, miss, but footpads are getting bolder in this district. War always brings the rats out of the gutters.'

I mumbled thanks and fled round the back of the house, praying that Catherine hadn't been awaked by the commotion and chanced to look out of her window. Maggie caught me at the kitchen door.

'An accident,' I muttered, shoving past her.

'Catfight more like,' she retorted, pursing her lips. 'That's quite an eye you've got there. You weren't supposed to leave the house.'

'Don't you have work to do?'

'I might, but that face needs sorting first. Your eye'll likely end up as black as a rotten apple. It's swelling up even as I watch. I can put a poultice on it, but for now you'd best go upstairs and see Mrs Worledge. She's awake and been calling for you this past quarter hour.'

'Do you know what she wants?'

Maggie shrugged. 'I don't reckon she's in a right mind to know anything.'

First I stopped by my bedchamber and, for want of a better place, shoved the bundle of documents beneath my pillow before hurrying along the passage to Catherine's room. She was still in bed, propped on a half-dozen pillows. Someone had opened the windows and curtains billowed out on soft currents of air. On the bedside table a laudanum bottle sat next to an empty sherry decanter.

Rouge smeared her face. It covered her hands, the pillows, the top of the bedspread. She grinned amidst the scarlet. It sliced her face open. She held out both arms and my first thought was: She's going to kill me. She's wanted to for years.

'You wished to see me, Mrs Worledge?'

She held out her arms. 'Come here and keep me company.'

I was pulled on to the mattress and cradled against her breast. Cool fingers stroked my forehead. She seemed not to notice my injured eye but instead held up a looking glass in front of her own face.

'Am I not becoming for a woman of my years?' she said, running a fingertip down the line of her jaw. 'Look, my cheeks are as pink as rosebuds.'

I didn't know what to say. Catherine held the mirror closer. She released me and pinched her painted skin. 'I must make sure I get enough meat. There is nothing better for enriching the

185

blood and putting the colour back into a lady's complexion. Too little and I might fall prey to some ill humour. I must send a message to the flesher's.'

I sat with her for a few more minutes but she said nothing else. Eventually she flopped back on to the pillows and was instantly asleep. I backed away from the bed and left the room as discreetly as I could. That put paid to any fears that Catherine might have observed me from her window. Whatever drunken vapours had taken hold of her, fate had granted me grace yet again. I returned to the kitchen so that Maggie could sort out my eye. I didn't mention Catherine. I sat twitching on a stool while some foul-smelling concoction was pasted to my tender flesh. The injury wasn't as grave as I'd first feared. Maggie handed me a herbal drink – mother's old recipe of course – and a strip of soaked linen to quell the throbbing.

I returned to my bedchamber and closed the door. My pillow lay on the rug. Mr Littlejohn's package was missing. I snatched up the pillow. Nothing beneath, nothing under the bed or on the table beside the dresser. The window was fastened, just as I'd left it, and my wardrobe doors closed.

My belly churned as I caught his scent: French cologne, stale tobacco, ruby port. The papers. He had my papers. He would notice that the binding was intact, know that I hadn't read the contents. Whatever secrets lay within were now his and likely Catherine's also. I started towards the door then hesitated, the pillow a crumpled feather bundle in my hands.

Perhaps to Catherine they were not secrets at all.

'Where'd you get that eye?' Moses demanded.

In the dim silence of the larder his fingers roved over my face. I flinched but his touch was as tender as a child's. He traced the outline of the bruise, his other hand cupping my chin.

'I fell and hit my head,' I told him.

'Aye, and I'm the next pope. Somebody's smacked you one, and I want to know who. Don't hold out on me.'

I pulled away. Blood thrummed in my temples. 'Blake. Mr Worledge's former manservant and now Catherine's lackey. He beats me if I do not grant him favours.'

'Favours?' Moses's eyes darkened. 'What favours are these? He been snatching at your petticoats, girl?'

I stared at my feet. 'He can do what he likes and I have no say in it. If he touches me again, I'll die.'

'No,' he said. 'Not you.'

I took a deep breath. 'I am also affianced to Mr George Proudlove, a country squire. The wedding will take place at the end of the month.'

Moses spat on the floor. 'You slut, why didn't you tell me this before? I could be hung in chains if we're caught.'

'I was forced into it. Are you going to turn coward on me?'

He grabbed me by the shoulders and shoved me against the cracked plaster wall. 'You'll belong to no one else, I swear. Let the cursed ceremony go ahead. Let this man steal your name. I'll take you in your wedding gown on the very day you utter your vows. I had you first and you'll always be mine. In the end you'll come back to me.'

'And Blake?'

Cripps released his grip and stormed out of the larder. A moment later the kitchen door slammed.

That evening I was once again instructed to take supper in the dining room. Catherine was at the head of the table; Blake sat opposite. I was perched in the middle, staring at the fruit bowl. The tablecloth was showered with half-chewed food as Blake shoved forkful after forkful of beef into his mouth. When he paused long enough to take a gulp of wine, a sly smile creased his mouth.

I nibbled my own meal with the manners of a mouse. When Blake leaned across the table – because he lacked the patience to wait for William to fetch the gravy – something fell out of his waistcoat pocket on to the buttered peas. Blake was very casual about fishing it out and wiping it clean with his napkin. A silver fob watch with a delicate flower pattern engraved on the case. Most unusual – the sort of thing a macaroni or similar eccentric might wear. Mr Littlejohn had possessed one like it. Blake caught my eye across the sputtering candles. We understood each other.

Afterwards, Catherine asked me to sit with her in the parlour and choose some hymns for the wedding. I feigned a headache and retired to the kitchen. No respite there, either.

'I know about Miss Cecilia's child,' Maggie Burns said.

'How?' I replied, genuinely startled. 'You rarely put a foot outside this kitchen.'

'I heard it from a marrow seller, who picked it up from a stable hand, and he got it from Mr Fortescue's cook. In this town everyone knows who you are and what your business is. You can't hide.'

The night wrapped dark hands about the house. An unseasonable chill drew cold fingers across the windows. William banked the fire and drew the curtains tight.

Before seeking the warmth of my bed, I took my courage in my hands and joined Catherine in the parlour. She was seated at her writing desk. Final invitations to the wedding littered the green vellum, addressed to people I didn't know. The ceremony was only a week away.

'I do not want Blake at my wedding,' I told her.

Catherine didn't look up. 'Mr Blake has proved indispensable to this family since Richard's death. Of course he will attend.'

'You may have elevated him to master of this house,' I persisted, 'but he does me no favours and I will not suffer his presence. Do this for me and I promise not to cross you again.'

She put town her quill and turned in her seat. 'Explain yourself.'

I swallowed. 'Blake is a brute. He frightens me. Invite him and you will have to drag me into that church and tear the marriage vows from my throat. I mean it, Catherine. You can force me to marry George but I will not countenance that usurper grinning at me from the pews.'

Catherine was silent for a second. Then she picked up the quill, bent her head and started scratching ink across paper again. 'Wedding nerves,' she said carefully. 'Fortunately Mr Blake is not disposed towards sentimental occasions and will think no ill of missing the ceremony. I shall instruct him to remain here.'

I curtsied. 'Thank you, Mrs Worledge.'

The week blurred into a frenzy of preparation. My few chattels were packed away and Catherine's old clothes cleared out of my wardrobe to make way for a new selection of garments, courtesy of my husband to be. Maggie wanted to give the cast-offs to the parish, but Catherine was appalled at the idea.

'Have beggars and wastrels strutting about in my dresses? I'd sooner see them burned,' she declared.

I sliced up the velvet confection Mr Fortescue had provided and fed it to the kitchen fire. I had no need of it now. The hook was firmly in the fish's mouth. Twice Moses Cripps arrived at the kitchen door and on both occasions I was ready, parading in my new dresses, always sure that my perfume was strong and my bodice a little too loose. I also ensured that one of the servants was also present.

'You, out,' Moses ordered Maggie when he found us picking at a basket of sweetmeats together.

'No, Maggie,' I purred. 'Stay. I enjoy your company.'

She looked from one of us to the other, uncertainty colouring her face. Moses, hands balled into fists, said nothing.

It rained on the morning of my wedding. A leaden sky turned my gown the colour of ashes. My hair was coiled beneath a wig, my face smothered in powder to hide my birthmark. I looked lovely. No denying it. Servants hovered around me like wasps around jam, goggling at my dress. I was unaccustomed to flattery and I would be a liar if I said I didn't enjoy the right sort of attention, but I did not want to look pretty. Not for George. I'd sooner go to the wedding dressed in old sacks. Catherine tried to appoint herself maid of honour but I talked her out of it, suggesting that she might put the younger girls to shame. She wore a monstrous wig packed with wilting blooms. Her eyes were glassy with laudanum.

Whilst waiting for the carriage I took a sip of wine, then another. I could not stand in front of a parson in my right mind and vow to love, honour and obey. When the ribbon-bedecked landau arrived, I sucked on a lemon to freshen my breath and tried not to totter up the step.

'You look a little peaky,' Catherine remarked. I told her it was nerves. A virgin's anxiety over her wedding night. Rain drummed on the landau's raised roof. People went about their business. Not many noticed a bride in a shadowed carriage, in the wet.

The journey seemed interminable. Catherine

kept a firm grip on my arm. Was that for support or to stop me running away? 'As you will not tolerate Mr Blake, who will give you away?' she said in my ear.

'You planned that he should do it?'

'Who else is there? William?'

'One of George's friends will suffice. He does have some, doesn't he?'

I was ushered into a strange church the way a criminal might be bundled through the prison gate. I was fool enough to think that I might be married by Nathaniel Proudlove, but George's estate edged into the neighbouring parish and this was the site he had chosen for our betrothal. Strangers filled the pews. Heads turned, eyes settled on me. No Marjorie, no little Charlotte with her face full of day dreams.

Catherine handed me over to some fellow in a scarlet army tunic, a smile curling her mouth. George waited at the end of the aisle. A bent, toothless parson stood beside him with a prayer book clutched in his hands. I appraised my husband-to-be with a clarity I had not enjoyed at our previous meetings. I noticed how short he was and realised I did not know his age. Though his cheeks were smooth, wrinkles lurked in the corners of his watery blue eyes. A fat belly strained against the silver buttons of his waistcoat and a wig, sharp as a raven's beak, perched on his head. I had never seen him without one, had no idea what colour his hair was, or whether he had any hair at all. He had chosen a yellow jacket that looked sickly next to my white gown, and the folds of his neck were buried beneath the frilly layers of his cravat. A sword hung from his waist, though I had not known him to be either soldier or seaman. Not once did he look at me throughout the entire ceremony. Behind me, women coughed, men shifted their feet and a baby bawled its heart out. George pressed a silk kerchief to his nose and grimaced.

The parson's voice droned on, countenancing me to be a good and obedient wife. I spoke when he told me to, repeated whatever words he uttered and felt a bite of metal as a second ring was pushed on to my finger. I took the vows that were to condemn me, whispering so the parson had to lean closer, and wincing at the stink of Madeira on his breath. I did it all. I did it because I wanted away from Catherine. I craved freedom from her plots and petty schemes, from under the workings of her blood-drenched hands. A small price in exchange.

A few final words then I was no longer Juliana Rodriguez but Mrs Proudlove. George's wife. His wet lips on my cheek sealed our pact and he took my arm to lead me back down the long aisle. Catherine's expression of triumph was at odds with her heavy black mourning gown. She was like a girl at a party.

Sitting behind her, like a cat with a mouthful of cream, was Adam Fairchild.

I stumbled. George caught me before I went sprawling. His grip on my arm was tighter than needed. I pulled my mouth into a smile, even though my stomach flipped over.

Who had invited him? Did he attend all society weddings, harvesting hearts like some dire reaper even as brides promised themselves to someone else? When did he arrive? Why hadn't I spotted him before?

I was glad to get out of the church. The grey clouds had broken apart, letting the weakening autumn sun cage the churchyard with beams of light. Jabbering women wet my cheeks with insincere kisses. Fingers plucked my dress, filched blooms from my corsage. I felt smothered.

'Who are you people?' I demanded. 'What are you doing at my wedding? I never invited you.'

'We don't need your invitation,' a girl in a lemon-coloured gown shot back.

'I was the one getting married.'

She laughed. 'Makes no difference.'

As if at a given signal, guests drained away like melt water. Reins snapped, gigs and coaches were turned and sent trundling down the road. Catherine stayed back, gossiping with a tardy cluster of women. I searched for my new husband. He was on the churchyard path, deep in conversation with Adam Fairchild. George kept fiddling with his cravat. His cheeks were a bright pink.

I tugged on Catherine's sleeve. 'My stays have come loose,' I fibbed. 'A minute inside the vestry and I shall have them fixed, if the parson will allow.'

'Very well, but be quick about it. Do not keep your husband waiting.'

I dipped an awkward curtsy and swished towards the vestry, skirts dragging on the grass. Drawing near, I heard George spit and bluster while Adam regarded him with a face like flint.

'I have married the wench. You will be paid, sir, and at a handsome rate of interest. A man's wedding is no occasion on which to come debt collecting.'

'See that you do pay, George,' Fairchild replied. 'There is much grumbling about you in town. Were it not for my intercession the dogs would already have been let loose. I suspect your integrity has been stretched even further than your pocket.'

George paled. To my horror he started dribbling. 'Yes... Yes, I am grateful, Fairchild, don't doubt it. But we must tarry awhile. The girl is not yet of age.'

'Any bank would gladly offer credit, given the circumstances.'

'Another loan? The estate is already...'

Adam spotted me and silenced George with a raised hand. 'Mrs Proudlove, should you not be with the ladies?'

I favoured them both with my sweetest smile. 'Mr Fairchild, I have been a bride barely ten minutes and already you would seek to draw my husband away from me.'

Adam relaxed. The makings of a smile fluttered across his lips. He bowed. 'I doubt I could coax any man away from your side for long, madam.'

'Nevertheless, it must be an important conversation.'

'Simply man's talk. Politics, property matters, that sort of thing. A bore for you, I'm sure.'

'Well, if you gentlemen will excuse me, I must go and thank the parson for the wonderful service.' I swept past them. Fortunately the vestry door wasn't locked. It was made of good English oak and once inside I closed it tight behind me. I was reasonably sure that neither Adam nor George believed I had heard anything of significance but I dared not stretch my luck.

I took a few deep breaths. No sign of the parson. A tall looking glass was set into the alcove opposite. Papery leaves crunched under my shoes, blown inside by autumn winds that were already colouring the trees in shades of red and gold.

I regarded my reflection. Flushed cheeks, visible even under the powder. Eyes a little tired looking. What had Fairchild been talking about? Why did George look so afraid?

A flicker of movement in the corner of the mirror. I turned, expecting to see the parson. Instead, Moses Cripps stepped out of the shadows. 'Quite the blushing bride, ain't you?' he growled.

'How did you get here?'

'Got a horse and cart, ain't I? That shire's a strong beast. Could haul me to London if it had a mind. Maggie Burns told me where you were getting wed. An easy journey. Nobody noticed me. I was just another tradesman on the road.'

'What do you want? You have no business at my wedding.'

'I've got plenty business.' He stepped in front of the door. 'I have as much right to be here as any man, more so than some.'

Cripps dominated the cramped vestry. His eyes cut into my skull. 'I saw everything from here. Stood and watched you promise your life away to that fop. So now you're a lady and can't be doing

196

with a common working man. Well, before long I reckon you'll ache to have me lying between your knees again.'

'You have no right...'

'But I do have a right, Miss Rodriguez, or is that Mrs Proudlove now? You and me had a bargain, remember? A covenant. And I've seen to my side of it.'

He took something out of his pocket and tossed it on to the table. It fell amid scattered prayer books and old sermons. A silver fob watch with an engraved case. 'Now it's time to keep your side,' he finished.

'What have you done?'

'What you wanted. He won't beat you again. Too much of a fancy for himself, that one. It's always a man's undoing.'

'Moses, tell me what's happened.'

'Easy enough. I followed him down to the harbour. He's always there after dark, stripping out some offices. Decided he wanted a piddle. Caught him behind some crates and, bang. Just another body in the water.'

'You weren't meant to kill him, just scare him off, perhaps give him a few bruises. You'll hang. We both will.'

'Anyone who beats a woman like that deserves the life knocked out of him. Don't try to say you didn't want him dead. Why else did you tell me? Why else parade that black eye? What man could hold his temper when faced with such a thing? Now give me what I came for.'

'No.'

Moses hooked his fingers over the front of my

gown and pulled. My bodice burst open like a seedpod.

'I could scream,' I warned. 'My husband is just outside the door.'

'You could but you won't.' He pushed me up against the table. His mouth was inches from my ear. 'You want me. Your tongue might spin lies to fool the devil, but your body gives you away.'

With the strength of a bull he ripped off my dress the way he might flick a moth from a candlelit wall. His big frame trembled. 'Now you've got no virgin's gown to hide behind. No harlot's slammerkin either.'

He pushed me to the floor and fell on top of me. My nails tore in to his neck as he split me open. I cried into the dust and dead leaves. My back ground against the stone tiles.

'Is this too much to ask?' he growled. 'I should tup you from now till doomsday for what I've done.'

The wig came off my head in a shower of pins. Moses buried his face in my hair. His tongue wriggled against my scalp and a low, animal noise issued from deep inside his chest. Fire built up inside me and seared through my veins. I stopped fighting him, stopped thinking, just gave myself up to the hot tide of pleasure. This was the stuff of deep, black sin.

Finally, he grunted and pushed me away. I lay supine on the floor, gazing up at him. My eyes took an age to focus. He fastened his breeches, making no move to help as I struggled, weak-kneed to my feet.

'Come away with me,' he said. 'I could give you

an honest life.'

'You have a spouse. Where's the honesty in that?'

'You can't refuse me.'

'Why? What are you going to do? Abduct me? Spirit me away somewhere and use me as you want? Am I nothing better than one of your shanks of meat?'

For a moment, Moses said nothing. I wondered if he'd understood. Then his face split into an ugly leer. 'As you like. I ain't got any more use for you. I've had all I want. Women are the same – all fine and headstrong until they get a taste of a man, then they're no different from any sixpenny tart plying her trade around Wexborough harbour. I can come back for you any time I want. You're my whore.'

I shrank away from him. Moses went on cramming his shirt into his waistband. I was being dismissed, tossed aside like a worn-out straw doll.

I shouted for help at the top of my voice. I shrieked until my lungs ached, then picked up the biggest prayer book I could find and hurled it through the vestry window. A jagged shower of stained glass exploded outwards. Shouts carried from the churchyard, followed by the sound of running feet.

Moses stared at me open-mouthed. The vestry door was flung open and men tumbled in, Adam Fairchild and George at their head.

'What in God's name…'

I jabbed a finger at Cripps. 'That animal tried to rape me.'

A whicker of steel and Adam had the tip of his

sword pressed against Moses' throat. 'It wasn't like that,' the meat carrier spluttered. 'The wench is lying to spare herself shame.'

I sobbed gustily, as fine an actress as any that had tripped out on to a stage. 'He delivers beef to Mrs Worledge's house. He has been trying to gain my favour for weeks and grew angry when I refused him. He followed me here, tore off my wedding gown and threatened to snap my neck if I tried to struggle. He has already confessed to murdering Mr Blake. He boasted about the crime right in front of me. I thought I was going to die.'

'Damn you,' Moses roared. 'You'll choke on your own lies.' He grunted as Adam jerked the sword tip. A trickle of blood ran down Cripps's neck and dripped on to his shirt.

'Another word from you,' Fairchild warned, 'and I shall carve out your throat.'

George took me by the shoulder and lifted my chin with his fingertips. His face was devoid of tenderness. 'Did this man poke you?'

I met his eyes. 'No, sir. I am as pure as God would require of any bride.'

He relaxed and let go of my chin. Moses roared again and lunged towards me, heedless of Fairchild's sword. Adam, taken by surprise, was knocked aside. Before Cripps could touch me, a pair of coachmen caught him by the arms. They were burly fellows, accustomed to handling difficult horses. They marched him, stumbling, towards the vestry door.

'There was something else, witch,' Moses bellowed. 'Something other than a fancy watch.

Blake had papers, important-looking papers. Pagan the flesher taught me to read a bit. I saw your name on them.'

He said more but by now he was outside and his words were swallowed up in a babble of curious voices. My belly felt as if it had been cast in lead.

Adam resheathed his sword. He picked up my dress and handed it to me. His voice was as smooth as milk. 'Apart from the damage to your gown, you say he did not touch you?'

'No,' I replied warily. 'I was able to draw your attention before he had a chance.'

He glanced at the shattered window. 'You certainly managed that. It seems strange, however, that you were able to slip his clutches long enough to do so. He is an uncommonly large fellow, yet moves as quick as a wink.'

'I bit him.'

'An ox of a man, in the heat of passion? I doubt he noticed. Did you see how those coachmen struggled to get him out the door?'

'What are you getting at, Fairchild?' George blustered. 'Are you questioning my wife's honesty?'

'I merely suggest that in the excitement the facts may have become juggled.'

I drew closer to George. 'My mind is not addled, sir. I managed to struggle free, as I told you. Count my injuries if you are still not satisfied. I like neither your manner nor your insinuations. You were keen enough to put your sword to his throat.'

Adam bowed. 'You are not on trial, my dear.'

Catherine appeared with a blanket from her

carriage and wrapped it around my shoulders. 'Cover yourself up, Juliana. You look shameful.'

I was ordered to wait in the vestry. A constable had been sent for. Adam took Catherine outside. George sat with his head in his hands. In the alcove, my reflection gazed out from the looking glass. My copper hair seemed to have turned the colour of dried blood.

Chapter Eleven

A great deal of that day's events have fallen out of my head, or been pushed, or cut out. A shocked mind's desperate efforts to save itself. Perhaps they are gone for good, no matter how much I try to pull them back. That might be for the best.

Yet other things remain vivid, as sharp in my memory as the moment they happened. Moses, his hands bound, yelling as he was bundled into the back of his own cart and driven away. Catherine screaming when informed of Blake's murder and rushing home to see if it was true. The parson fussing over me, laying a reassuring hand on my brow, my knee, or any other part of my body he thought might need succour.

I remember mouthing replies to seemingly endless questions, though I cannot recall what was asked or what I said in return. The parson's wife clothed me in a gown hurriedly fetched from her own wardrobe. The fit was poor but in my befuddled state I made no complaint. A surgeon was also summoned, a keen bloodletter whose remedy for any ill humour was to open a vein. I would not let him near me. This wasn't the first time I'd collected a few bruises.

Declared fit enough to travel, I was helped into George's carriage. We journeyed in silence alongside the turnpike road. My new husband would not look at me, choosing instead to sit and scowl out of the window. We stopped at a coaching inn as sunset painted the sky with streaks of fire.

George spent most of the night downstairs drinking with some friends who had ridden out from his gambling club. I was left in the care of the innkeeper's wife. She spent hours in an armchair soaking up the heat from my bedchamber fire.

Perhaps George was afraid I might try to climb out of the window, or the shock of the day would wear off and I'd throw a shrieking fit. The woman offered no help with my injuries, which had all subsided into one dull ache.

Eventually her fat head lolled on to her shoulder and she began wheezing like a pair of leaky bellows. I huddled myself for warmth and gazed around the narrow bedchamber, trying to salvage some hope out of the ruins of the past few hours.

The papers. Moses Cripps had found the papers. And I had watched him carted off.

At just after midnight according to the mantel clock, George stumbled into the room. He barked his shin on the edge of the door and cursed. The fat woman woke up and he sent her squealing from the chair.

Alone with my new husband, I managed to manoeuvre him on to the bed and, grunting, pulled off his boots whilst he leaned over the side of the mattress and retched. He stank of brandy. It reminded me too much of Richard. Getting the rest of George's clothes off proved impossible. I left him on top of the coverlet and climbed into bed. At some point during the dark hours he wriggled between the sheets, fumbled with his breeches and made me his wife. Afterwards he fell asleep with both legs sprawled across mine.

The following day, George sat over breakfast with a splitting head and an expression that could sour milk. 'I examined the sheets of our bed,' he said, forking trout into his mouth and swallowing. 'There was no blood.'

My own food congealed in my throat. 'I beg your pardon?'

'They were clean. This morning when you were taking air in the yard, I returned to our room. The maid had not yet changed the bed linen. There were no bloodstains.' He put down his fork. 'You were not a virgin when I came to you last night.'

'You were drunk,' I countered. 'You couldn't manage.'

'I know well enough what I could and couldn't do. You were no fresh little maid. Someone's broken you in, stolen what's mine by right.'

'In the vestry...'

'You claimed that fellow *tried* to have you. In God's name you said you were pure. That was your word. Pure. You've been tupped like a bitch in season. I could name you whore and throw you into the ditch.'

'Will you?'

He pushed back his chair, got up and walked away from the table.

'I had been attacked,' I called after him. 'I was hurt. What consideration did you give to that?'

I fingered my wedding ring and listened to the rain pounding on the carriage roof. The coach lurched on the rutted track. The driver spouted oaths above the steady pummelling as he fought to keep the horses in check. Beyond the window lay a washed-out world of grey. Flat fields stretched away under a lumpen sky, the soil dark and sodden.

I sat alone in my dry enclave. George had ridden ahead on a hired mare, his face petulant, his cloak flapping from his shoulders. He had tried to reason with me, tried to suggest that perhaps a fall from the saddle had resulted in the apparent loss of my maidenhead. 'Such an easy thing to happen,' he'd said, trying to keep his voice light.

'I don't go riding,' was my response.

So began my life as the wife of a country squire, taken from the town I knew to a sprawling estate. Locals spoke in a strange, rolling tongue. You could look for miles and not see another house, just acre upon acre of farmland rolling to distant wooded hills. My new home, Milton Manor, was a pillared block of buff-coloured sandstone. Much of its face was smothered in ivy, half-buried windows winking at me from within their green prison. Neat but unremarkable gardens

205

spread out from the gravel drive, flowerbeds slicing into the lawns like the spokes of a wheel. Behind the house and stables, a modest orchard of two dozen apple trees had thrown down a scattering of unpicked fruit to rot in the grass.

That first day, I was met at the door by the housekeeper who curtsied and addressed me as Mrs Proudlove, a name that stuck uncomfortably in the throat. The staff lined up in the marbled hallway to greet me. They bowed or curtsied as I passed along their rank, and I sensed their eyes on me. George was not present. I was informed that he had changed his clothes and was in the middle of a nap.

That night, on an immense bed in a high-ceilinged room, he claimed me again. I was squashed beneath his heavy, thrusting body. Sated, he rolled over and lay on his back, gasping. A sheen of perspiration coated his face. I waited, damp, wrung out.

Presently he slid off the bed and pulled on his breeches. 'You're a cold bitch,' he spat, scraping his hair into a tail behind his neck. 'I'll have an heir from you as my duty demands, but tupping a pig would give more pleasure.'

He slammed the door on his way out and did not return that night. I lay amidst the rumpled bedclothes and watched the last flickers of the dying fire play across the ceiling. My cheeks were damp but some time passed before I realised that I was crying.

George had visitors in the morning, local gentry who had come to offer congratulations and sniff out his new bride. Mostly they were polite, if curious, and guarded in what they said. Wives and daughters put their heads together and whispered.

Afterwards I took George to task over the matter. 'Those women who came to the house today,' I said. 'They were gossiping about me.'

'Country folk are a superstitious breed, whatever their station,' he replied without looking up from his newspaper. 'Some are put out by the mark on your face. 'Tis harmless nonsense and you would do best to ignore it.'

'Are you sure that is the only reason?'

'I am sure,' he said, taking a sip of port.

Half a hundred candles hissed and spat hot wax in an iron holder suspended from the ceiling. The bad weather had continued, turning the day into a twilight sludge.

'The man who attacked me at the church,' I continued after a moment. 'What will become of him?'

'As far as I know he was taken to Dunsgate gaol, where he shall no doubt be hung. The case is cut and dried. Your attendance at the assizes is unlikely to be required.' George glanced at me over the top of his paper. 'Some questions may arise but no one will doubt your word. I shall see to it.'

Later, George told me he was going riding. He kept an ageing nag, which he laughingly called a hunter, and spent a couple of hours each day plodding around the grounds. My husband was not a man of the land. Though his estate included some good grazing with extensive wheat fields and a modest amount of livestock, I quickly discovered it was other people's hard labour that kept things running. As for George himself, there was always another card game.

One morning, tired of staring listlessly out of one window after another, I offered to go walking with him. 'Just a stroll around the beech tree,' I suggested. 'I'd love to smell the autumn air.'

'I would hate to think of any further calamities befalling you,' he replied. I did not offer again.

Days merged into one another. It was hard to tell one week from the next. The manor was a cathedral of a place compared to my Wexborough home. Passages were endless, ceilings impossibly high. I had to ask directions to every room. Servants fluttered around like ghosts, not a flicker on their wooden faces. I wasn't allowed to do anything for myself. If I wanted coffee, it appeared on the table beside me. If I sneezed, a clean handkerchief was waved under my nose. I began to miss the warm times, helping Maggie Burns in the kitchen, or just delving into a pot of soup that I'd had a hand in making. I felt like a guest in a strange lodging house.

George never spent a whole night with me. Business took him away for days at a time, except that I knew his business was cards and his time spent at one of his town clubs. My experiences with Richard had taught me all the signs. On each occasion, George returned from these trips with a hard face and locked himself in the smoking room for hours, not seeing or talking to anyone.

During his absences, I spent hours by the parlour window sewing crude samplers with fingers that were never meant for needle and thread. I ached for a hot kitchen hearth. To the staff I was always 'madam' or 'Mrs Proudlove'. Never 'Juliana'. Never a friend.

No one of my acquaintance ever called to the house or wrote to me. From Catherine I heard absolutely nothing. I had no idea if Moses Cripps really had murdered Blake. Despite his crudity he hadn't struck me as a killer. George never broached the subject and I had no desire to submit myself to any more of his turnabout questions. It seemed as if our lives were severed from the rest of the world. Even Parson Proudlove never took the trouble to visit. I often thought of Charlotte and her unicorns, remembering those round, dark eyes.

'My father is much taken up with matters of the spirit,' George explained irritably when I remarked on the parson's absence. 'His is a large parish with an ever-wayward flock and he cannot spare the time to journey the breadth of the county for the sake of social niceties. He is getting on in years and coach travel seldom agrees with him.'

'Is that why he did not attend our wedding?'

George buried his face in a book.

Desperate for company, I followed my nose and slipped downstairs to the kitchen. I found none of the cosy familiarity that had made Maggie Burns's kitchen so endearing to a girl in the mood for toast and a tall yarn. A cavern of a room was divided along its length by a long oak table. A gaping, soot-ringed hearth yawned from the opposite wall. Above a pile of blood-red embers, a turnspit was cranked by a panting dog running endlessly in a wheel hung from the ceiling. Whitewashed walls, studded with hooks, cathedralled above me.

Servants sat clustered around the far end of the table. They gaped at me as I stood dithering in the doorway. The men were playing cards, a practice that George had forbidden among his staff. A minute of silence stretched out between us.

'Clumsy of you not to leave a lookout,' I said. 'Go on, finish your game.'

A sallow-skinned man seated at the end of the table picked up the cards and dealt them out. I recalled that he was Samuel, George's game-keeper. He had the better of his fellows judging by the heap of pennies beside him. He quickly stripped everyone of their remaining stakes then gathered the cards into a neat pile before tucking them into his jacket pocket.

'Is there something we can do for you, madam?'

'I am merely looking over my house. I thought there might be a back door to the stables through these kitchens.'

Samuel pushed himself away from the table and gestured me to follow him. I walked past the other servants and waited while he drew the bolts on an arched oak door. A slender man, tall, with long arms and an easy-going gait. Hair, so black it almost glittered, was scraped back into a tail behind his neck. Other, thicker hair sprouted from the backs of his hands.

'Going riding, madam?' he enquired as I

slipped past him into the yard. 'If so, you're hardly dressed for it.'

'Less of your insolence...' I began, turning back to face him, but the door had already closed behind me.

If I couldn't be a part of one world then I would force my way into the other. It was impossible to continue like this, a nothing person drifting in a strange house with a husband I hardly saw. So I wore my gowns, painted my face with fine French rouge and joined the giddy whirl that was country society – an endless round of tea parties and glittering balls.

George treated my new-found enthusiasm with suspicion but I was telling the truth when I explained that I was bored. If I was to be a squire's wife then I would play the part with conviction. What did it benefit me to sit at the window all day and stare out at the rose beds?

So he took me to his parties, reluctantly at first. I smiled at the proper times and exchanged pleasantries with strangers who warmed to me as I flattered and fawned my way through those darkening autumn nights.

Recalling all that Mary Morgan had taught me about ladylike behaviour, I joined the women in their parlours. Although curious, they were wary of this newcomer in their midst and questioned me, in polite roundabout ways, about my background. Of course everyone had heard of the wife George had brought out of town and talk soon turned to what had been fashionable in Wexborough when I was last there. I also proved to have a willing ear, which cracked the ice on their tongues in short order. Gossip poured out. It seemed there was nothing they would not tell me. A secret passed in confidence was safe for less than a minute before the whole gaggling herd knew about it. I simply repeated everything I heard, careful not to add anything of my own. No one seemed to notice and when I told someone the same story twice at two parties in the space of a week she laughed both times and declared it a scandal, though it was getting to be an old scandal by then. I was as much a subject of gossip as anyone else. A few people hinted that stories had wafted out of Wexborough as if blown on a bad wind. I wouldn't bite their baited hooks, so they tried other ways to unsettle me.

'The younger girls are afraid of you,' one hostess remarked. 'They think you will play cuckold with their husbands.'

I twitched my mouth into a semblance of a smile. 'I am a married woman, no thief of hearts.'

She slapped her fan into her palm. Her mouth was crammed with badly fitting porcelain teeth. She spat through each sentence. 'Marriage is a means by which women gain a well-fed belly and roof above their heads. You don't wear pretty jewels or ride in an expensive carriage by remaining a spinster. Matrimony allows men to put an acceptable face on their passions. It is a useful arrangement.'

'What about love?'

She laughed as if I had said something foolish. 'You are a wife yourself, my dear. You should know the answer to that one.'

Once he realised that I would not disgrace him, George was pleased with my rapid acceptance into the social fold. When it was our turn to entertain guests I became the perfect hostess. Visitors left the house complimenting George on his fine choice of a spouse.

'You are a good girl,' he told me in the aftermath of one such evening. 'I must say there were times when I thought you an awkward cuss but I am glad to see you settling into your role.'

I lowered my eyes and curtsied. 'I seek only to do you credit, sir.'

'See that you continue to do so.'

But George held other entertainments, gatherings to which I was not always invited. A small card circle visited the manor for his amusement, often involving a few members of the local gentry and, unusually, one or two of their women. These games of faro or whist were informal and the stakes never rose above a few shillings. If someone was unavailable I was asked to make up the numbers but I had no talent for the game. I fumbled the cards, missed my call or picked the wrong hand. My humble stake was plucked away from me in a matter of minutes.

'I should not let your wife play too often, George,' one of his friends smirked, 'lest she bankrupts you.'

'I don't find that remark amusing,' George replied, fingering his neck cloth.

'Really? You need a sense of humour given the way she handles the cards.'

Everyone laughed. My cheeks blushed roses. William Loxborough was my tormentor's name, a wine trader and owner of extensive farmlands bordering our own. I had encountered him at a couple of local tea parties where he had treated me with polite indifference. He was a squat man with a face that resembled a turnip freshly pulled from the soil. On his head sat a monstrous brown periwig that was at least a century out of fashion and he snorted fat portions of snuff from a silver box kept in his waistcoat pocket.

Accompanying him was a brace of giggling young women called Elspeth and Harriet, whom he loosely described as his nieces. I recognised them from my wedding, where they had chattered through the service. Loxborough regularly slapped their thighs or squeezed their plump behinds, chuckling through blackening teeth whenever one or the other squealed. George had invited them to stay the night and Loxborough decided to retire early. His 'nieces' took themselves into the parlour and plundered our sherry.

On retiring, I found that the maid had forgotten my nightly posset. I was halfway down the corridor when I heard giggling coming from Elspeth and Harriet's bedchamber. They'd neglected to close the door properly and my ear was drawn to the narrow crack.

I was eavesdropping like a common servant but this was my home. The girls were half drunk. I heard the chink of glass. They'd likely smuggled a decanter into the room.

'That girl is such an effort,' Harriet declared. 'Did you see the way she handled those cards? Why do you suppose George married her? She reminds me of the gypsy wench who brings the fish baskets each Friday. Do you suppose she has money?'

'She must do,' Elspeth replied, 'though I don't know if George has seen a whisker of it. All kinds of stories are circulating about her.'

'And as for that red streak on her face, you'd think she was poxed. Someone ought to put a horse's nosebag over her head.'

Both dissolved into giggles, then Elspeth asked: 'Will you see George later?'

'He asked me to come to his chamber at eleven, when plum-face is asleep. He keeps to his own bed, understandably. I have been promised sweetmeats and a night I shall not forget.'

'You'll end up nibbling on more than sweetmeats, I think. Supposing plum-face finds out?'

Laughter. 'Supposing she does?'

I huddled in the dark silence of my room until the clock in the downstairs hall struck the hour. I hadn't yet grown accustomed to the peace of the country. No barking dogs, drunks mouthing oaths or carts rattling past at all hours of the night. Sounds here were amplified. A creaking floorboard often jerked me into a clutching wakefulness.

Now, outside in the passage, the whisper of slippers, muted laughter and the sound of a door gently closing. I slipped out of bed, reached for the doorknob. My hand hesitated. I knew George slept with whores. It was something all gentlemen did, apparently. As his wife I was expected to accept the situation without complaint. But this was worse. I was being usurped under my own roof. I remembered the way William Loxborough had poked fun at me when I picked up too many cards, or put the wrong one down at the wrong time. Harriet and Elspeth, their eyes full of contempt as they flicked secret messages at one another behind their fans. And laughter, always more laughter for George's cloddish wife.

I swung my door open and flapped down the corridor in my nightshift, seeking the satisfaction of bursting into George's bedchamber and catching him, bare-buttocked, between Harriet's fat thighs. I'd scream 'Adulterer' and stir the entire household. All the servants, even in the furthest reaches of the manor, would hear me. I imagined parliament granting me a divorce. George would be shamed, his fortune leeched.

I got within five paces of his room when a hand caught my elbow. 'Where do you suppose you're going?' Elspeth purred.

She was in her dressing gown but lacked the gritty, puff-eyed look of the freshly wakened. Sherry tainted her breath. Her eyes glittered in the light from the candle sputtering in her hand. I had no idea where she'd sprung from.

'This is my house,' I said, shaking my arm free. 'I am not answerable to you as to what I do in it.'

I moved towards George's door but she slipped in front of me. 'You are not to go in there.'

'Get out of my way.'

She didn't budge. The hint of a smile passed across her mouth. 'Go back to bed. That is the best place for you.'

In a breath I felt I could curl my fingers around her neck and squeeze until her black heart burst.

Blood pounded in my ears. She waited me out. Pale breasts rose and fell beneath the smooth material of her dressing gown. No need to say any more. Confidence crawled over her face like a nest of ants. My fury lay in knowing that she was right, that I would do nothing – could do nothing. Physically, Elspeth was bigger than I was, though I believed I could fight like a cornered tomcat if it came to it. But the thought of finding George tupping that obnoxious slut made my belly squirm. Barging in would only bring a bucket load of trouble down on my head. I had put in too much effort chipping out a tenuous foothold in this slippery household. Elspeth, the smug bitch, knew it.

Like a scolded child, I returned to my room and did not emerge again for the rest of that long night. Loxborough and his party left early the following day with a promise to return in two weeks' time. There was no mistaking the look of triumph Harriet flashed me. Elspeth had told her everything, I supposed. I pictured them giggling about it over their morning coffee.

George was his usual self during lunch and only nodded when I said I felt unwell and wished to walk around the gardens. My stomach tumbled like a butter churn leaving me in no mood for a confrontation. The fresh air did little to cheer me up and my mind was a cauldron of black thoughts as I crossed the stable yard towards the kitchen. Perhaps a cup of hot milk would settle my belly.

As I reached the door, Samuel the gamekeeper stepped out, pulling his felt tricorne over his ears.

He acknowledged me with a nod and strode off in the direction of the gardens. I ran to catch up, struggling to match his long gait. 'Samuel, wait. I would have words with you.'

He halted and pulled off his hat. 'What might I do for you, Mrs Proudlove?'

I paused to catch my breath. 'You are not a local man,' I managed to say. 'Are you?'

'No, madam. I am from Newfoundland, though I have not seen my home in nigh on twenty years.'

'Where did you learn to play cards? You took the kitchen staff for a tidy sum.'

He immediately became cautious. 'I picked it up.'

'Do you cheat?'

He blinked a couple of times. 'A man has no call to cheat if he's clever enough. I don't call being clever cheating. Cards bought me my freedom and I owe them my life. I take care to use them right and they look after me.'

'Cards saved your life? I don't understand.'

He looked me up and down, though there was no disrespect in his manner. I sensed that he was debating whether to tell me any more. 'I daresay you wouldn't,' he said at last, 'but then you didn't spend two years rotting on a prison barge for a crime you didn't commit.'

'Crime?'

Samuel glanced at the sky. Gathering clouds heralded another afternoon of rain. 'You must forgive me, madam. I've prattled on too long.'

'Do you have a room in the main house?'

He eyed me curiously. 'I sleep in the game-keeper's cottage at the edge of the woods. Keep a better ear out for poachers that way. The estate used to be plagued with them until I took this post.'

'What do you do if you catch a poacher?'

'I break his leg.'

'That is barbaric.'

He shrugged. 'Better than packing him off to Dunsgate treadmill. Any man sent there for more than a year at a stretch often comes out in a sack and poaching in these parts carries a two-year sentence. Most of the county magistrates are landowners who don't take to having their game plundered, whether the thieves are starving or not. Some have laid gin traps that could lop a fellow's legs off. You won't hear many complaints about my methods.'

'This cottage of yours? Will you take me there?'

His expression hardened. 'Excuse me, madam?'

I laughed. I could not help it. He waited me out, eyes like flint beneath the brim of his tricorne. 'I've no mind to do something foolish in a garden hut with a gamekeeper more than twice my age,' I spluttered. 'There is something else I need. Something far more important.'

'May I ask what that might be?'

'Revenge.'

The gamekeeper's cottage was a stone box smothered in thick fingers of ivy. On the far side a row of trees stood like sentries, a vanguard for the woodland beyond. Good hunting country with plenty to tempt the poachers Samuel had mentioned. In summer this corner of the estate would be alive with lush greenery and buzzing insects. Now a carpet of dry blackening leaves rustled underfoot as Samuel led the way up a flagged path, pushed open the door and motioned me inside. I had to stoop to enter and wrinkled my nose at the deep, musty scent that hung beneath the beamed ceiling like an invisible fog. Half a dozen rabbit skins were strung from the rafters like executed felons. Canvas sacks bulging with secrets filled every corner. A hunting rifle mounted on pegs stood guard above a sooty fireplace and a coarse wooden table was littered with books.

I heard a scratching noise. Samuel noticed my expression. He reached under a bunk and drew out a brass cage.

I recoiled. 'A rat.'

'No, a ferret. Good for rabbiting.' The animal reared up against the bars, nose twitching as it regarded me with bright, button eyes.

'Revenge is a dark business,' Samuel continued, nudging the cage back under the bed with the edge of his boot. 'I don't know why you seek it, nor do I wish to. This job is all I have. If I lose it...'

I unclasped a pearl necklace from around my throat and dropped it on the bed. A wedding gift from one of George's wealthy friends. Samuel eyed it without comment. Gamekeeper or not, he would have some idea of its worth.

'I want to learn how to play cards,' I told him. 'Every trick you know.'

He nodded. 'I can show you, but you'll need a stiff face and a good eye to make it work.'

'I have two weeks in which to master the game.

Teach me and the necklace is yours. Can you do it?'

He tilted his head. 'How badly do you want to win?'

Day after day I sat in that tumbledown cottage while Samuel flicked cards one way and then another, calling up kings or knaves, hearts or diamonds seemingly at will. He was an easy man to warm to. Once he accepted that I was serious in my intentions, and that it wasn't some 'lady's whim', he seemed to relax.

'Get a feel for the game,' he told me with a wink. 'Sense when the hand is going your way or when it's turning against you. Don't hold the cards like slabs of wood but here, like this. They won't burn your fingers, only your pocket if you don't play wisely.'

'I can't know what the other players are holding,' I protested. 'Luck isn't something I can call to heel whenever it suits.'

'No, but you can read faces. It can take a man a lifetime to master himself, to give nothing away in either tone or gesture. Few manage it and those that do usually move on to better things than the card table.'

'Read faces?'

Samuel shrugged. 'Can't you tell when some-one is pleased or angry with you simply from the way they look?' He didn't wait for an answer. 'People give all sorts of things away. The key is to watch your opponent, not listen to what he's saying. Is he sweating? Does he look worried or triumphant? Are his eyes darting around even

221

though his face is a picture of confidence? Be discreet but watch for nervous habits – plucking at hair, rubbing thumb and forefinger together, reaching for a drink every few seconds even though the glass is empty. It doesn't matter what cards you hold. If you're afraid to take risks you can't win. Success hinges on pretending to have something you don't, something better than the other player. Twist his mind, punch holes in his resolve, make him believe with such certainty that he won't dare to try to match you. Don't trust to luck, she's too fickle. Make the cards work for you. Pride will keep your opponent in the game.'

Samuel held my fingers and showed me how to manipulate the cards in a way that would confuse and beguile the eye. He was a patient man; quiet, always evenly spoken. He cajoled where necessary and served up encouragement whenever I showed signs of mastering these tricky printed oblongs. Whilst he was out on his rounds, I sat in the parlour and practised until my fingertips turned numb. Needlework lay abandoned as I turned the cards again and again, wincing every time I fumbled or dropped one on the floor.

Going to the cottage was never a problem. Because the other servants liked and respected Samuel, they kept any gossip to themselves. George was always in Wexborough, or out riding, or napping in his study. He rarely visited my bedchamber and so far nothing stirred in my womb.

By the end of the first week I felt ready to try a proper game. Three times running I was beaten.

Samuel laughed when I discarded my best card and tried to play my worst. No malice lurked in his humour, but I cat-hissed and threw the cards on to the floor.

Samuel knelt and picked them up. He placed the deck on the table in front of me. 'It's not your ignorance of the game that will beat you,' he explained, 'but your temper.'

'You think this is just a game?'

'The rules are the same, whatever your reasons. So we'll start again, and this time you'll keep the cards on the table top where they belong.'

'Promise you won't laugh at me again.'

'Do something stupid and I'll laugh until my breeches split. It won't be any less than you deserve. Listen, learn, and don't make any more mistakes.'

'Tell me, Samuel, what did you do to warrant imprisonment, whether unfair or not?'

He fingered his jacket cuff. 'You have to realise that I'm from a proud family. It was with pride that I fought for the British against the French, though neither had any business waging war on my land. And it was a British general's wife who accused me of trying to violate her when I wouldn't pander to her fancies. All of this is common knowledge. I've made no secret of it.'

I said nothing. My heart was in my feet.

'In the barge I was surrounded by Frenchies,' he continued. 'Prisoners, all of them, and half starved or fever-stricken because of their wounds. I was afraid they'd try to throttle me in my sleep but I was no Englishman. Though none could speak a word of my tongue I made better friends there than I ever found in a line of red-coated soldiers.'

He cleared his throat. 'They carved model ships out of rat bones, using other bones as tools. Strands of hair fashioned the rigging. One man traded a boat with the turnkey. Got a deck of cards and taught me backstreet tricks. I'd managed to smuggle some gold aboard, stuffed it up my behind if you'll pardon me for saying so and used that to lure the barge master into a game. Staked my freedom against it. I won. I had to win. At first I thought he wouldn't let me go but what was one less prisoner? He could say I'd died and been thrown overboard. My country was a changed place and I a criminal, so I used the gold to buy passage to England. And now, proud that I was, I work as another man's servant. If I ever feel hard done by it, the cards don't let me forget. Now that's enough tales from me. Let's get back to the game.'

With each hour my abilities grew. One afternoon, amidst a downpour that had the cottage roof leaking like a piece of muslin, I gawped at the cards in front of me and realised that I had won.

He smiled, gathered up the deck and tucked it on to a shelf. 'You're ready,' he said.

I shook my head. 'Not quite.'

I had been finding out as much as I could about William Loxborough, this fellow who thought himself so high above others that he could insult another man's wife to his face and laugh about it afterwards. I invited the local scold, Mary Christ-

224

church, to come and take a glass of canary at the manor. Miserable Mary as she was known, whose face could sour milk and who would gladly sell her mother's soul for news of a good scandal. I poked in the dirt, stirred up the ashes of Loxborough's past and plied Mary with drink until her tongue damned him.

'He has a child on the way, did you know that?' she asked, coughing into her glass. 'He's gone and given Elizabeth Huxley, daughter of the local magistrate no less, a swollen belly. Her husband has been off fighting in America these past two years.'

'When is the baby due?' I asked, keeping my tone light.

''Twas due a week ago. The child is sitting awkwardly in the womb and the local quack fears it will be a difficult labour. I do not think the poor woman wants to live. Her papa has threatened to pack her off to a comfort home if she does not publicly name the father.'

I nodded. I had already learned that Loxborough had a reputation for chasing the wives of absent men.

'I think Lizzie fears her husband's anger more than anything,' Mary continued. 'She has threatened to smother the baby if Loxborough refuses to accept responsibility, yet he will not allow it be given over to the parish. I think he wants the poor mother dead.'

I plucked the top from the decanter. 'More canary?'

The moon stared brittle light on Loxborough's

coach as it rattled to a halt in front of the manor. George met them in the hallway. A breath of chilly air whispered through the open door. Something was brewing, like a dark concoction in a pot with the lid about to burst.

Loxborough greeted me with a hearty laugh. I tried not to flinch as Elspeth and Harriet pecked my cheek. I felt as if their kisses had branded me and the scent of their cologne turned my stomach. George was showered in their affections. He slid a hand around Harriet's waist and squeezed.

'Best not get too playful, George,' Loxborough chided. 'More than enough time for games later.' He regarded me. 'Is that not so, my dear?'

I dipped a curtsy and kept my eyes on the floor. 'I am looking forward to it.'

The two girls dissolved into giggles.

Dinner was mercifully brief. Everyone seemed keen to have it out of the way. Elspeth and Harriet kept glancing at me and nudging one another. Afterwards the men joined us in the parlour and talked a little business but their minds were on other things. 'What say we have a hand or two of cards to put us in good humour for the evening?' Loxborough said. 'And you, my dear Juliana, must join us again. The game would be so dull without you.'

Faces turned towards me, lips parted, teeth glimmering wetly in the soft light, eyes bright with anticipation.

'I would be delighted,' I said.

'Splendid. Simply splendid.' Loxborough rose from his armchair and exchanged a look with George. My heart was in my throat as I followed the others into the withdrawing room. A card table had already been set up, waiting like an executioner's block. I turned to Harriet, who had taken hold of my arm.

'Shall I begin?'

'Uncle always starts the game,' she retorted. 'Do not worry, Mrs Proudlove, your turn will come soon enough.'

'No, let her try,' Elspeth laughed. 'We can wait while she picks the cards up off the floor.'

I took my place at the table and fingered the deck. The cards felt cold, their edges knife blades ready to slice my pride into strips.

Treat them with respect, Samuel's voice said in my mind. Never forget.

I pretended to fudge the first hand. Everyone watched with quiet confidence, exchanging amused glances as I pushed more coppers into the centre of the green-topped table. Loxborough matched my stake, as did the others, and chuckled as he shoved an oversized pipe between his teeth. 'Let the entertainment begin,' he announced.

I won the first game in less than a minute and plucked his stake from under his bulbous nose. He stared, thunderstruck, at the empty space on the table where his money had lain, then dismissed me with a flick of the hand. 'Beginner's luck favours even you, m'dear. Enjoy your pennies while you have the chance, for a pittance is all you shall win from me tonight.'

I played again, glanced at each of my opponent's faces and placed two shillings on the table. Loxborough laughed uproariously. 'What's this? You want to up the stakes? George, your wife has lost her wits. A glimpse of good fortune and already she would have herself out of the game.'

He matched my stake. Others threw in their money. I won again and then again, upping the price each time. Suddenly no one was laughing any more.

'How high are you willing to go, Mr Loxborough?' I asked, leaning over the table and staring into his blood-tinged eyes. 'Shall I tell your friends that you were beaten by a woman who had barely touched a playing card as little as a month ago? I am sure the news will carry well around the ladies' parlours and perhaps the gentlemen's smoking rooms as well.'

'Juliana…' George warned.

'No, damn it,' Loxborough snapped. 'Let the wench play. I'll strip her of her paltry winnings and wipe the smugness of her face, watch and see if I don't.'

A flick of the cards proved him a liar. Shillings were replaced by sovereigns, followed by guineas. I emptied his purse, his jacket and the pockets of his satin breeches. I took the gold rings from his right hand and the fob watch out of his waistcoat. My pile of treasure increased as his face grew darker. Harriet's silver bracelet and cameo choker became mine before I put her out of the game for good and I relieved Elspeth of a gold brooch even as she begged me to let her keep it because it had belonged to her grandmama.

George sat, white faced, sipping glass after glass of port.

A cloud of blue tobacco smoke choked the air above his head. Twice he had tried to stop the game and both times Loxborough waved him away. Soon, only two of us faced each other across this green battleground. Discarded cards lay like dying soldiers. I could barely move for the pile of money and trinkets in front of me. Loxborough's eyes played Judas. I let him win five guineas then plucked them back in the very next turn. This sweating, heap of a man was mine to play with, his obnoxious nieces backdrops to his destruction.

'Another ten guineas,' I demanded, after winning again.

He scratched deep into his pockets then searched them a second time. Finally, he produced a crumpled wad of notepapers and asked for quill and inkpot, which George handed him. Painstakingly, he began to write an I.O.U. I snatched the paper out of his fingers and ripped it to pieces.

'I am not one of your gambling-house fops,' I told him. 'I don't want paper promises. Ten guineas are what you owe and I will have the coins in my hand now. Either that or winnings of my own choosing.'

He stared at me as though facing a demon that had prophesied his death. 'Well, it seems your wife has been leading us all a merry dance these past few weeks, George,' he said shakily. 'I wonder what other talents she keeps hidden.'

I rapped the surface of the table. Port slopped over the green baize. 'Talk to me. I am the one who has beaten you. Pay or suffer disgrace.'

He laid down the quill and tucked the notebook back into his jacket pocket. His fingers shook. In the hearth, a log burst apart in a shower of sparks.

On the couch, Harriet sobbed in her sister's arms. Elspeth glared at me as though she would see me burned at the stake. I matched her with a choice look of my own and she turned away.

'Very well,' Loxborough coughed. 'If my word as a gentleman does not suit, what winnings do you demand?'

'Your unborn bastard. The one you forced into Lizzie Huxley's womb.'

Chapter Twelve

'Your actions beggar belief.' George paced the parlour carpet, his boots threatening to wear a path in the thick pile. 'I introduce you to society and this is how you reward me, by humiliating a close friend and dragging my family name into disrepute.'

He paused to clatter among the decanters and pour himself a drink – a generous measure of brandy, though it was well before noon. 'I had high hopes for you, Juliana, especially as you seemed to be settling in. All this talk of wishing to become a dutiful wife – I have met many devious men at my club, men who would strip a fellow of his fortune with the same ease as they draw breath, but your capacity for deception would humble even them. Tell me where you learned to play cards like that. Have you always known and all these weeks of fudgery merely another deceit, another lie?'

He gulped his drink. Half dribbled down the front of his shirt. He wiped his mouth, banged down the glass and filled it again. 'Why'd you do it, eh Juliana? You've never met Elizabeth Huxley. Why give a ha'penny for what happens to her brat? It could be stillborn. Then where will all your tricks and contrivances have got you?'

I pushed myself deeper into the armchair. My eyes were full of grit, my brain begging for sleep. It had been a long night. Arguments, threats, banging doors and broken friendships. But I had won. Loxborough would not be back. His bastard child would be delivered into my arms the day it was born. I had picked up all my winnings from the table and thrown it in the face of her uncaring lover. 'Give this to Elizabeth Huxley,' I'd told him. 'Get her the best midwife you can find. Do that much for her.'

Loxborough left before daybreak, hauling his coachman out of his bed in the stables and forcing him, still in his nightshirt, on to the driver's seat. George went to see them off, trying to placate his precious friend's temper and at the same time console Harriet and Elspeth, who had turned into a pair of spitting cats. What would they say about plum-face now over the rims of their sherry glasses?

While George blustered around outside I slipped upstairs to my bedchamber and barred the door but he had not followed. Some hours later I crept into the withdrawing room to be told by a bleary-eyed housekeeper that my husband had gone riding. At least I knew that to be the truth. His riding clothes were damp from the early drizzle and smelled of horse. A crop was tucked into the leg of his boot.

'I was already aware of your penchant for other women's babies,' he continued. 'I bore the wagging tongues in the hope that I might turn you into a good wife. I can only assume you had other goals, namely to humble William and make a donkey out of me.'

I sat up straight in the chair. 'The same way you have allowed me to be humiliated? I know what you were up to last time, George, and it wasn't teaching that tart Harriet how to play whist. If you want me to start playing the decent wife then it's time you behaved like an honourable husband.'

George sat down then stood up again. He pulled the crop from his boot and slapped it against his palm. 'Harriet is a good friend.'

'How many other such friends are there? Have you already taken an entire gaggle of whores to your bed in the name of such friendship? You don't love me, George. You'd sooner spend a night between some strumpet's legs than waste a minute of tenderness on me.'

He jabbed the crop at me. 'Have a care not to test my patience, Juliana. Plans have been made for that baby. You cannot propose to bring it into my house.'

'What plans? By whom?'

He fumbled his brandy glass. It thumped on to the rug. 'What does it matter? I don't want it across my threshold. I won't hear of it.'

'Fine, as long as Loxborough honours his debt.'

'He is a gentleman.'

I laughed. 'If he was a gentleman he would have no debt to settle.'

George whipped the crop across my cheek. I screamed and banged my head against the back of the chair. My eyes watered with the pain. I put my hand to my face. Blood coated my fingers in a crimson glove.

'Learn your place,' George spat.

I sprang to my feet, grabbed an inkpot from the writing desk and hurled it. George was too startled to react. The pot caught him squarely in the chest, spattering his silk shirt with dark fluid. 'Don't you hit me,' I snarled. 'Don't you ever lift so much as a finger to me again or I swear I shall have a knife out of the kitchen and murder you in your bed. I am not some beast you can thrash at your leisure.'

He dabbed at the mess on his shirt with his handkerchief but only succeeded in spreading the stain. 'Vixen. I would have you dragged from the axle of my carriage if it was not for...'

He swallowed the words, gulped air and turned red about the cheeks.

'If it was not for what, George?' I prompted.

He dropped the blackened handkerchief and thumped out of the room, slamming the door behind him. A puddle of ink spread out from the spilled pot.

I pressed a square of lace against my injured cheek. 'If you will not tell me, then I shall find out.'

My husband left on horseback that afternoon, a travel bag buckled to the saddle. He did not tell me where he was going and refused to discuss anything else. I surmised from the housekeeper, as she put a fresh dressing on my cheek, that he intended to spend a few days in Wexborough and then ride on to Bristol. Everyone was aware that this was more than a simple domestic argument. Servants were always eavesdropping. Maggie Burns used to be a terror for gluing her ear to the parlour keyhole.

I wrapped a cloak around my shoulders and flushed Samuel out of his cottage. 'Can you drive the gig?' I asked him.

'Where might you want to go, madam?' he replied, wiping breadcrumbs and slivers of cheese from his mouth.

I slipped a shilling into his hand. 'Dunsgate gaol. Don't tell anyone.'

The prison was a former cattle barn that had been walled off from the road. It frowned from the slope of a boulder-studded hill on to the scattering of hovels that comprised Dunsgate village. The journey had taken a little over an hour. Sight of the gaol did nothing to quell the grumbling unease that had been stewing in my stomach. The moss-spattered stonework seemed to leech colour out of the surrounding land. Narrow windows had been punched into the walls at irregular intervals. As the gig laboured up the bumpy track I thought I saw a white face peering out at me.

Samuel halted the carriage outside the gate. 'Have a care, madam. This is a filthy place. The stench could knock down a horse.'

'You can wait here. I won't be long.'

'Good. I've no notion to find myself inside any kind of prison again, even as a visitor. But if you're not back out in twenty minutes, or I hear you yell, I'm coming in anyway.'

I thanked him and passed, shivering under a sweeping stone arch. How could men and women survive in such a place? In the muddy yard beyond, a turnkey waddled out of a wooden lean-to. He eyed my clothes and spat into the dirt. 'Are you lost, miss?'

I pulled my cloak tighter. 'Take me inside,' I threw sixpence at his feet. 'Now.'

He led me inside the barn and down a passage lined on either side with makeshift cells. Others had been built into the old hayloft above my head. 'Why is it so quiet? How many prisoners do you keep in this hole?'

The turnkey chuckled. 'Never a time when Dunsgate ain't full, miss. The walls have been reinforced. They're six feet thick in places. Swallows up sound. Snuffs it like a candle. No one but your cell mates will ever hear as much as a cough.' He caught my expression. 'Ain't so bad here, miss. It's cool in summer and I keep a big fire stoked in the winter months. Walls keep in the heat. Looks horrible, I know, but folk like to think that prisoners are suffering.'

I waved him on. Uneven flagstones scattered with straw caught my feet. At the back of the building was a cramped anteroom with a bench, squat desk and brazier. 'All right, miss,' the turnkey said. 'What can I do for you?'

I told him.

'Cripps? Moses Cripps?' The turnkey nodded. 'Aye, he's here, though there's talk of taking him to the public gallows at Tyburn. Magistrate reckons our hanging yard's not good enough. He attacked a girl on her own wedding day, though he says she wasn't worth the dirt he spread her out on.'

I arched an eyebrow. 'Let me talk to him.'

'I ain't allowed to let anyone see the prisoners.'

'Family must visit, surely?'

A loose-lipped grin revealed the blackened stumps of teeth. 'You family?'

I slapped coins on to the table. 'Here's two shillings that says I am.'

He scooped up the money and pocketed it. 'Sixpence a minute,' he said. 'That's how much time you've got. Fair bargain I'd say.'

'Very well, but I want to speak to him alone. Bring him here; I won't go near those cells. And no listening at the door.'

'Be it on your own head, miss, though I doubt you'll have much trouble from Moses Cripps.'

Keys jangled as the gaoler plodded to the door. I sat on the bench and waited.

'I knew you'd come running back to me,' Moses said. 'Though it ain't really me you want, is it?'

He looked leaner but still well muscled. A beard clung to his chin. Chains bound his wrists and ankles.

'Put some respect in your voice when you speak to me,' I said.

'What would be the point of that, seeing as you already have me where you want me?'

I took a deep breath. 'The papers,' I blurted.

'Where are the papers?'

A hollow laugh. 'Your precious bundle is safe. I reckoned you'd be after it soon enough.'

'I have influence now. I could buy you out of here, put you on a boat to Ireland. You'd never fear prison again.'

'Oh yes, a squire's wife, but you're still just a whore in a velvet gown. I'd sooner hang than skulk out of my own country at a harlot's behest.' He gestured at his surroundings. 'It's not as bad in here as you might suppose. Harry, the gaoler, is a decent man. Him and I have an understanding. I get clean straw, food in my belly and my clothes in the washtub once a week. You'll get your papers though. I've got a price right enough.'

'Name it.'

Metal chinked. In the torchlight, Moses's eyes were two black slugs. A grin split his face like a fissure opening in the earth. 'Maybe I'll let you stew awhile. Or I might get the rope before I decide to tell you. That would be justice of sorts.'

Before I could answer, the turnkey appeared to take Moses back to his cell. There was nothing I could do. I hadn't another farthing on me. When he returned I let him escort me to the gate.

'Get what you came for?' he asked.

I pulled off my gold wedding ring and dropped it into his palm. George would never notice. 'Don't let Cripps die.'

With George away from home and no friends calling, the hall seemed emptier than ever that week. I tried to catch up on my needlework, I read books or old newspapers. I took endless

237

walks around the gardens, sometimes in the pouring rain.

'You'll catch a fever, madam,' the housekeeper warned, when I struggled through the door one morning like a half-drowned puppy. 'Then it'll be bed and the doctor for you.'

I changed and spent the next hour in front of the parlour fire. A fair had come to the district and I had given most of the servants leave to go and enjoy themselves among the stalls, jugglers and dancing bears. Not so long ago the prospect of mummers and tumbling acrobats would have excited me. Now, after all those brash parties, I favoured solitude.

That Thursday, while the tents and wagons of the travelling troupe still speckled the common land with noise and colour, a baby was delivered to the kitchen door. Elizabeth's Huxley's daughter. My winnings.

'How is the mother, do you know?' I asked the coachman.

'She had a hard birth, but survived,' he said.

I summoned Samuel, who had no belly for the fair, and instructed him to find a home for the child amongst the travellers. 'I don't want to see it again, or touch it. Twice I've suffered when obliged to give someone else's baby away. I am the worst kind of thief.'

He scratched his ear. 'I don't understand. From what I heard, you won the child fairly.'

'I stole it, just like the others. But you wouldn't know about that, Samuel, unless you've been hearing other stories. I've stolen it as surely as if I'd snatched it from its mother's arms. Lizzie

Huxley had no choice, of course. The baby's irresponsible father and her own papa saw to that. But what if she spends the rest of her life chewed up with remorse? At least Loxborough was someone she could hate, somewhere to focus the pain. Now she has the agony of knowing that her child is alive but out of reach. What will it look like? When will it cut teeth, take its first steps? What are its fears, joys, hopes? Lizzie carried it in her womb, yet it will never know her. This is almost the same as murder, Samuel.'

'You are too hard on yourself.'

'You think so? Each act carries its own consequences. I can only weigh them to suit myself, to ensure I get the better of someone who has crossed me. I profit out of other people's misfortunes.'

'Then you would make a good banker.'

I laughed without mirth. 'My ledgers would be full of human lives and every account overdrawn. Who could balance my books or settle my debts? You think I've saved a life. All I've done is spited my husband and made more enemies. I daresay I ought to be glad. It's what I wanted.'

Samuel rode out with the baby that afternoon and returned empty handed two hours later. 'I found a family who were glad of the child,' he informed me. 'The man does tricks with horses, an honest-looking fellow who lost his own little girl to a fever barely three months ago. There's a wife and elder daughter to look after it and the fair's making good money. I explained that the baby had been orphaned, which is true in a sense, and everyone seemed happy enough.'

'Thank you, Samuel.'

He smiled. 'Thank *you*, Mrs Proudlove.'

George returned from town the next day, much earlier than expected. He'd barely shaken the rain from his cloak before summoning me to the withdrawing room. 'I want an heir,' he said without preamble. 'Whatever devilries you've been up to in order to prevent it must cease. You will discharge your wifely duties and provide me with a son. He will be named Nathaniel, after my father.'

I gawped at him. A child had been ordered the way he might tell cook to prepare a beef supper. 'I ... I am not a brood mare,' I stammered. 'As to whether any baby is a boy or girl, it is hardly in my hands.'

'A son,' George muttered, his jaw set. 'It must be a son. That mark on your mouth, does it run in your family?'

'I believe so.'

'Curse the devil that any brat of mine should be birthed which such a disfigurement. Can it not be removed somehow?'

'A brat, George? Is that what your child would be to you? Not a son or daughter?' I appraised his flushed cheeks, his frightened, glassy eyes, and realised what he was doing. 'You want to put a baby in my belly to silence me,' I accused, 'to force me to behave. You are afraid that word of what happened with Loxborough will slip out and you are looking for an excuse not to take me on social calls. Do those disgusting people mean so much to you that you intend to chain me with pregnancy? Or is there even more to it than that, George?'

He tore off his riding gloves and tossed them on to a chair. 'I am weary from my journey. Tomorrow night I will come to your bedchamber. Try to make yourself presentable.'

'No,' I quickly replied. 'It is my time of month.'

'You are lying,' he sneered. 'The maid checks your linen. I believe you are not due for another week. We will see if I cannot poke some of the coldness out of you.'

I supposed I was being unfair to George. Every married man had a right to a son. Yet all the next morning I behaved as a woman under a death sentence. What if I was barren? What if I couldn't give him what he wanted? I'd mostly taken care with Moses. A bit of fireside gossip with Maggie Burns had taught me how to do that but George had lain with me a few times and nothing had come of it. Perhaps he'd disown me, or have a bastard with a mistress and name that as his heir.

In the end, my mental wrangling was all for nothing. My husband broke his neck.

George had decided to go on a solitary canter around the grounds. He took a new chestnut mare Samuel had bought for him at the horse market and set off, with bottle and bread, to make a morning of it.

When it was past noon and he had not returned, Samuel and two stable hands went to look for him. His cooling body lay at the foot of the hedge he had tried to jump. The horse was cropping grass a few feet away.

241

Samuel broke the news to me as the men brought George's corpse into the parlour and withdrew, hats in hands. He was laid out on an old door that had been propped against the stable wall. A piece of canvas covered his face. Though Samuel tried to stop me, I snatched it away. I wanted to make sure that George was dead, know that it was not some cruel trick he had decided to play on me.

Death made a horrible spectacle of him. His neck was twisted at an angle and a smear of dried blood at the corner of his mouth parodied my birthmark. Mud caked his right cheek, his once immaculately tied hair had worked loose and become a tangled nest of dead leaves and grass. It was difficult to believe that this stiffening carcass had ever drawn a living breath.

I dropped the canvas back over his head. 'Put him in the ground as soon as you can,' I said.

Parson Proudlove arrived in a hired chaise to bury his son. After the ceremony he spared no words of kindness or comfort, merely nodded before climbing back into his carriage. The servants were all in tears. I was both touched and surprised at this expression of grief for such a bully of a man. Later I discovered that they had not been paid in two months.

Lawyers descended on the house like flies on carrion. Looking like so many vicars in their black coats, they had me sign a series of documents that meant nothing to my dizzy eyes. I did as they asked, if only to be rid of them, and held my peace while they addressed me as Mrs Proudlove throughout, giving emphasis to the name as if it was some sort of special title. Despite their respectful manner, my immediate future was made clear to me. I was to be tossed out on to the drive like a piece of old furniture.

After the lawyers had clattered off down the drive in their dark-panelled city carriages, creditors arrived in droves to tear up the estate. So many creditors I thought that George must be in debt to every man in the county. I could not see how there would be enough to pay them all.

'Your husband was too fond of cards, madam,' a banker from Wexborough informed me as he eyed the paintings lining the stairwell. 'A man ought not to play the tables lest he can afford to back up poor gamesmanship with proper security.'

A pair of labourers shuffled past carrying my chestnut writing desk. They manhandled it out of the front door and on to the back of a wagon, where it was covered with sacks and tied down with hemp. Everything movable in the house went likewise. By late afternoon a caravan of carts and dray horses had pulled most of my wealth down about my ears and spirited it off.

Amongst the throng of buzzards squawking over the remains of my marriage, I spotted a familiar face. 'Mr Fairchild,' I greeted him. 'Where there is a carcass, one inevitably finds a worm.'

He put down the silver candlestick he had been examining and peered at me through gilt-edged spectacles. They had no glass in them, I noted.

'Snappy little widow, aren't you?' he purred. 'I am here for my cut of the pie. Hold your temper and it might amuse me to leave you a bauble or two. The next time you beg a dance at least you'll look the part.'

I swallowed. 'How much did my husband owe you?'

He picked up a salver, squinted at it then dropped it on to a pile of other items. A man-servant bundled them into a canvas sack, which he hauled outside. Adam favoured me with a smile. Despite my anger, it had me quivering at the knees. 'George's debts ran much deeper than his losses at the card table. Money was not the only thing he was careless with.'

He cupped my chin in his fingers. His skin was cool and smooth. There was a time when I would have died for that touch. Instead I stepped away. His hand flopped back to his side. For a moment he looked disappointed, then the smile slipped back. 'I wonder if George really knew what he was doing when he married you. It's obvious that his death isn't going to break your heart.'

'And Cecilia Fortescue? What about her heart? Have you forgotten her as readily as you decided to abandon her child?'

'Cecilia has apparently lost her taste for parties.'

'So I should imagine.'

'She had no proof that I sired her brat. That was an act of fancy on her part. It was widely known she had a number of admirers.'

'I suspect, sir, that where you are concerned there is never any proof.'

'In business that would prove a virtue.'

'Is that how you regard people. As "business"? Was George "business"? Am I?'

'You've no right to talk about such matters,'

Adam said.

'I heard about the Loxborough bastard. The whole county knows. Ordinary lives never generate gossip. It's those of us with a sharp edge, who soar above the dull and common, that keep the tongues wagging.'

'Why *did* George marry me, Mr Fairchild? We both know it was not for love.'

He tugged a calling card from his waistcoat pocket and slipped it into my hand. 'Come to my club in Wexborough. Show that to the footman at the door and he will bring you to my private chambers.'

I tore the card in two and let the pieces fall to the floor. 'I am not your whore.'

The smile turned sour on Fairchild's lips. 'You may have cause to regret that remark.'

'I doubt it.'

'Indeed? A homeless, penniless widow standing proud on her dead husband's bankrupt estate? What an amusing notion.' He started to walk away, then turned as if just remembering something. 'Oh, bye the bye. That man who attacked you on your wedding day, what was his name again? Ah yes, Cripps. Word has it that the fellow escaped from Dunsgate gaol. Slipped right past the gaoler and made off in the middle of the night. I'd say those were the actions of a determined man, wouldn't you?'

He did not wait for a reply. Perhaps my expression told him all he needed. Moses was loose. A murderer. My lover.

I hurried upstairs, squeezing past half a dozen sweating workmen who were coaxing George's

245

four-poster across the landing. In my empty bedchamber, I fastened all the windows and locked the door before collapsing on to the bare floorboards. I remained huddled like that for the best part of an hour.

By the end of the week, my new life in the country was over. The house was gutted, the land sold off piecemeal, the servants dismissed.

The funeral passed in a blur. On my last Sabbath at the local church, people looked the other way when I took my place in the family pew. After the service, they hurried off.

'A terrible loss,' the vicar blurted. 'You must try to accept your new position with dignity. A sad affair, most sad.' He waddled off, shaking his head. Alone, I waited under the lich-gate as the first rains of the day began to fall.

I had lodgings at an inn, paid for with savings I'd managed to smuggle out of the manor. As soon as I returned I tore off my mourning dress and put on the only other luxury I'd been permitted to keep, a travelling gown in duck-egg blue. Powder went on my face, rouge on my cheeks. I packed a cloth bag with the handful of items that were all I had left in the entire world. Then I did the only thing I could.

I went back to Catherine.

I had already forgotten what a noisy, dirty place Wexborough could be. The market clamour and bustle of tradesmen mingled with the rattle of wagons going to and from the harbour. Children jostled me, street hawkers thrust wares under my face. My nose was thick with the scent of acrid smoke and rubbish.

The stagecoach had dropped me outside the corn exchange, a good half-mile from Catherine's house. I hadn't so much as a penny left to hire a sedan, so I'd hefted my bag and set off down the street. I was uneasy about turning up on Catherine's doorstep like a stray dog, so when I arrived I skirted around the side of the Butter House and into the yard, hoping to have a word with Maggie Burns before facing my former guardian.

Most of the rain clouds had been blown inland by a teeth-chattering wind gusting in from the sea. The sun was too weakened by the onset of winter to afford much warmth, yet no smoke swirled from the tall chimneystacks of the Butter House. My footsteps echoed on the cobbles. Stable doors hung open, hinges creaking in the wind. Inside, the horse stalls were empty, the straw swept up and lying in an unkempt pile in the corner. Harnesses had fallen from their hooks on the wall. There was no sign of William, no indication that a living soul had been here for days.

I returned to the yard. The water trough was rank and nearly empty. I skirted around it and checked the rear of the house. My bag lay where I had dropped it. Most of the upstairs curtains were drawn but a single bedroom window lay half-open, drapes shivering in the stiff breeze.

I scooped up my bag and made for the kitchen. The door was off the latch. I nudged it inwards with my foot. A stench of spoiled meat assaulted me. Pressing a handkerchief over my face, I stepped inside. 'Maggie? Maggie are you there?'

Nothing. I stepped around the table. It was littered with dirty plates, the mouldy remains of food. Pots were piled high in the washing tub. A stale odour hung over everything. I opened the inside door and hurried along the dark passage. The house was cold enough to prick my skin with goosebumps. I listened. Nothing. Not even the tick of a clock. Every door hung open, the rooms beyond swaddled in gloom. I checked each one, slipping like a ghost from parlour to drawing room to dining room in the space of two dozen frightened steps. Repeatedly jerking the bell sash achieved nothing.

I returned to the parlour and opened the curtains to let some light into this mausoleum. The windows were filthy. Thick dust shrouded most of the furniture though a few items, perversely, were sparkling clean as if polished only a moment before. I became aware too, of a curious symmetry about the place. Everything had been laid out in a careful pattern. Ornaments stood like sentries in an unbroken line along the mantelpiece. The armchairs and sofa were arranged in a perfect semi-circle. Even the rotting apples in the fruit bowl had been stacked according to size.

This house, whatever its faults, had always been a place more lived in than looked after. 'Comfortable,' was how Richard once described it, 'like an old pair of shoes you can slip your feet into without thinking about it.' Now every picture was straight, every cushion standing to attention.

I left the parlour and hurried into the front hall, shoes beating a tattoo on the patterned tiles. At the bottom of the stairs I halted, aware that someone watched me from the upper landing. With great deliberation, a figure began to walk down the staircase towards me.

Blake.

The hallway swirled in a blur of black and grey. I clutched the balustrade to prevent myself sprawling across the floor. It had all been a sham – a terrible lie. Blake was not dead. Moses had not killed him after all. He was coming to get me.

I recognised the cream hose with gold tassels. The black velvet breeches. His favourite embroidered waistcoat. I slumped to my knees as he stepped into the dim light seeping through the crescent window above the front door. I had no defence, no words with which to confront this horrible spectre.

But the face peering at me from beneath the brim of a velvet tricorne was Catherine's.

'Well, if it isn't the pretty wench,' the figure rasped. Catherine's voice, but low and horrible, with a knife twist to each word. The way Blake used to talk. She wore his blue satin solitaire which was two sizes two big and hung around her neck like a noose. Other garments hung from her in baggy folds. This close, she resembled a shrunken doll.

Without warning, her arms slithered around my neck and she crammed her lips against mine. Her mouth was a pit of dreadful tastes, of dirty teeth and bad food. I spat out her poisoned tongue and pushed myself away. Clawed fingers scrabbled at my bodice. 'Come now, pretty one,' she slurred. 'Why so coy? Here's Ed Blake with a sweet word to whisper in your ear.'

'You're not Blake. He's in the ground, rotting.'

I was dimly aware of someone thumping on the front door and voices shouting through the thick oak. The Catherine-thing advanced towards me. Like a petrified cat that's all hackles and spit, I backed away across the chequered tiles.

'What's this?' the Catherine-thing demanded, eyes glinting like badly cut sapphires. 'You have naught to fear from me. As gentle as a feather in the wind, I am.'

Hooked fingers reached out. I kicked out blindly. My flailing foot caught her knee and knocked the legs out from under her. She smacked on to the tiles, the tricorne spinning off her head and fetching up against the bottom stair. I crammed a fist into my mouth. She had cut her hair – shorn it almost to the skin in places. Patches of pink scalp mottled the back of her head.

The banging on the door increased. The voices grew more urgent. The Catherine-thing was getting up, blood gushing from her nose. I fumbled for the knob and prayed the front door wasn't locked. The brass twisted in my sweating palm and the door swung inwards. On the step stood Marjorie Proudlove, George's mother – and beside her, a pair of hefty-looking bailiffs. Without a word, the men brushed past me into the hall and took hold of the Catherine-thing. She was carried, screaming, into the street and bundled into a waiting carriage. A carriage that had no windows.

Marjorie helped me to my feet. The eyes in that doughy face were as hard as flint. 'You must come with me, Juliana,' she said. 'You must come now.'

Chapter Thirteen

'Her mind has gone,' Marjorie said, slamming the carriage door. 'It has been rotting for weeks, like an apple turning to brown pulp. I tried to catch you at the manor, to warn you not to come here. When I arrived, boards were already being nailed over the windows. I didn't expect you to leave so abruptly.'

I stared at my knotted fingers as the carriage rumbled out of Wexborough. 'Where are those men taking Catherine?'

Mrs Proudlove wiped her cheeks with a linen handkerchief 'Bedlam I expect. There'll be no curing her. I realised that yesterday when I called on her to talk about George.'

Catherine had been sitting in Richard's study, piles of torn-up bills littering the desk in front of her. 'She had spent hours ripping them into tiny pieces,' Marjorie continued. 'Paper lay everywhere – on the floor, the shelves, spilling out of her lap. I tried to speak to her, but she took a pair of scissors out of the drawer and began cutting off her hair. She called me a stupid old woman, a country clod and even,' Marjorie's cheeks flushed, 'a parson's cheap doxy.'

She pressed the handkerchief against her nose. 'I asked after the servants. Catherine told me they had all been dismissed, that she could run the house by herself. I don't think she'd eaten or

251

bathed for days. When I tried to take the scissors from her she lunged at me. Luckily her shin caught the corner of the table or those scissors would have ended up between my ribs. I ran from the house, my ears full of obscenities, and went directly to the magistrate. As it turned out there was no shortage of witnesses to testify to her growing lunacy.' Marjorie clasped my hand. 'It was provident that I returned when I did.'

I peered out of the window at the streets I had walked so hopefully less than an hour before. 'She thought she was Blake, Richard's dead man-servant. She wore his clothes, tried to talk in his voice. For a moment I even believed it was him.'

'Edward Blake was Catherine's brother, did you not know that?'

I turned my head and stared at her. 'No. How could I?'

'He was a thief and trickster bound for the gallows. Catherine spent a small fortune to buy his pardon and employed him as a footman. George told me about it on one of his rare visits to the parsonage. He was sodden with brandy and too eager with his tongue. I can readily believe it. Catherine Worledge always enjoyed mastery over men, even her own kin. I knew her as a wilful young woman who could spit and curse like a common tinker when someone crossed her. She loved Blake with a dark, twisted passion. Little wonder she lost her wits when told he was murdered.'

'Catherine made a servant of her own brother? A brother she loved?'

'It was not the love of a sister for her sibling, Juliana. This was something unnatural and heavy with sin. George laughed as he told me how Catherine used to take Blake into her bed when Richard was gambling or lying senseless with drink. They shared the same mind, the same black heart. Don't think ill of me for telling you this. You need to understand.'

I leaned back against the carriage seat and closed my eyes. Marjorie offered me salts but I shook my head. The sun ran fingers of light across my face. Soon, the bustle of town was replaced by the whisperings of open meadows and the creaking murmur of wooded lanes.

'Where are you taking me?'

'You married our son and are therefore our responsibility. You'll come to live with Nathaniel and myself in the parsonage at Dinstock. My husband is a pious man and intends to have you work for your keep but it will be honest work befitting a widow.'

'I was a squire's wife. You cannot expect me to become a scullery wench or a milkmaid.'

A snatch of breath. 'Pride is a sin. You must realise that you now have nothing in the world save what we, in God's good grace, provide. Raw knees are better than an empty belly, so treat Nathaniel with respect and accept his judgement with good countenance.'

I opened an eye. Marjorie was fumbling with something. A prayer book, the leather cover cracked and the pages well thumbed. Perspiration hung in a dewdrop from her top lip. 'You owe me nothing,' I said. 'I do not know exactly why George married me and since you did not see fit to attend either our wedding or his funeral

I can only suppose you cared as little for him as he did for me.'

Marjorie closed the book and dropped it into her lap. 'George? I cried for him, but it was like the loss of a distant cousin. He was never really my child. I lost him heart and soul before the first hair tufted his chin. The boy was always frivolous, always given over to whims and fancies. Notoriety was food and drink to him but he lacked the will to bend the world to any purpose. When I first saw you with that rich hair and the scarlet mark on your face, I believed he wanted an ornament, a flesh and blood trinket to show off at those godless parties. I would have tried to warn you but who listens to a parson's wife?'

I turned back to the window. 'I think he wanted me for something else. You know what that "something" is, but you won't tell me. You're too frightened. You've been afraid since the day I met you in Catherine's parlour and probably long before. Perhaps I'll never find out. As a Christian woman, I doubt your conscience grants you much peace.'

Marjorie didn't answer. She prised open her prayer book and buried her face in its pages. Did her husband beat her? No obvious marks coloured her face or neck. Of course that meant nothing.

Events had exhausted me. The rocking of the carriage brought on a dreamless sleep. I woke, stiff and riddled with cramp, as sunset burned the sky. We halted outside a low wooden gate almost smothered by a privet hedge. Beyond sat a drooping cottage made soft around the edges with ivy. Moss-speckled thatch hung from sagging gables. Square windows peeked out from ochre-painted stonework. A trellis supporting the bones of last summer's sweet peas clambered up one wall. In the near distance a brook gurgled over some rocks.

Marjorie stepped out, shaking her skirts. I followed her into the deepening dusk, trying to rub some life into my tired legs. An enormous cedar tree spread green arms across the pebble path that led to the cottage's front door.

'Very pretty,' I remarked, desperate to say something.

Marjorie glanced about her. 'These days I can't always give the garden the attention it deserves. Perhaps things will improve.'

Charlotte peered at us from a downstairs window. The intense frown, which had intrigued me in Wexborough, rippled across her forehead. I waved but she did not return the gesture. When we stepped inside, I heard feet slapping across the stone floor and a door closed somewhere at the back of the house.

Children could be jealous. Did Charlotte regard me as an interloper, a near-stranger breaking into her family circle? If so, could I win her over? I was not the most tactful person on earth and the child was clever. Would she regard any gift as a bribe?

My new bedchamber was little bigger than a cupboard, but much more welcoming than the palatial chambers of my former home. I regarded with bemusement the old dresser with a tarnished looking-glass mounted on top, the chipped silver oval throwing shattered reflections around the room. Instead of a four-poster, a single bed, sagging in the middle, hugged the wall opposite the door. A wardrobe with creaking doors took care of my few remaining possessions.

Well, it was better than being left destitute on the road. A window cut a bright oblong into the sloping ceiling. It looked out over the back of the house. Instead of sprawling, scissor-clipped lawns, thick woodland sprouted out of a dark loam floor. A flash of silver marked where the brook tumbled down a few feet of rock. Perhaps it held stickleback or trout. A square of coarse grass marked out a drying green and a log pile squatted under the eaves of an old stable.

'We live simply,' Marjorie informed me when I joined her in the kitchen half an hour later. 'No servants to pander to you here, only a village girl who scrubs the place twice a week and helps with one or two other chores. Earn your keep and I'll treat you as my own.'

'Where is Mr Proudlove?'

'Nathaniel is helping the parson of a neighbouring parish, who can't perform his duties on account of a belly upset. When my husband returns he'll want to meet you again, so you must make yourself presentable. No powder and no painting your cheeks with rouge.'

'Yes, Mrs Proudlove.'

'You must call me Marjorie, except when at church or in front of guests. Remember that you are Mrs Proudlove too.'

She waddled from the room and returned a few moments later with a black linen dress draped over her arm. 'Put this on,' she instructed. 'The fit looks good and it will serve for now.'

I stared at the garment. Another old dress. Another gown the colour of the grave. I made no move to take it from her. Marjorie caught my expression. 'You are in mourning for your husband,' she explained. 'The next few weeks will be hard. You will hear things, cruel things, from gossips who can't hold their tongues. George was known around these parts and not well liked. He had a good head for business once. His dealings made him his fortune; his excesses at the card table lost it. Gambling had a greater hold on his heart than I ever did and his ruin emptied more than just his own pocket. Some people will look for any reason to slight you. We must do what we can to lessen the injury. Please wear the dress, for Nathaniel's sake if not your own. He is very conscious of his position in the parish and hopes to better himself in the eyes of God and his peers.'

She was almost pleading with me. I took the dress. Marjorie beamed as if I was a favoured child. 'Supper is at eight,' she breezed. 'The clock on the landing will tell you the hour. Tomorrow I will take you into Dinstock. You will be happy here, Juliana, I know you will.'

I know you will, I mimicked after she had gone.

During the night, heavy rains washed the countryside. I spent hours trying to get comfortable. Water needled the windowpane, slithered down the roof slates, gurgled into the butt outside the back door. Sometime towards daybreak the weather eased up. The sun poked a bleary eye from between threads of cloud. The morning had a fresh, sharp taste and everything looked new.

Marjorie draped a muslin cloth over an enormous wicker basket and, humming a bright tune, led me through the front gate and into the lane. Charlotte had gone to the local miller's house to keep his daughter company. 'I need fresh bread,' Marjorie told me, 'and we must get you an apron to wear about the house.'

Her mood was infectious and I hummed along with her. As we skirted the ruts that dragged long, waterlogged trenches into the soil, I learned something of the local area and the people who were, ultimately, my masters.

'The land hereabouts is owned either by Matthew Jane or the church,' Marjorie explained. 'The Janes are a farming family and have roots in this part of the country that stretch back generations. Squire Jane, along with his wife Lady Elizabeth and daughter Emma, live at Dinstock Hall not three miles' walk from here. The house boasts one of the finest stables in England. Squire Matthew is a keen horseman and you'll spot him riding across the Downs most days of the week. Wheat and cattle, that's how he made his money. Honest money it is, too.'

My shoe sank into a puddle. I groaned. Marjorie seemed not to notice and ambled on, swinging that great basket back and forth. 'You may find you have something in common with young Emma,' she continued. 'She is a flighty girl and not keen on marriage, much to her father's vexation. But she has a good disposition and will snare herself a fine husband.'

'Perhaps she doesn't want to get married,' I suggested.

Marjorie laughed. 'All girls want to get married.'

Hedges on either side of the lane fell away and fields stretched for miles in every direction. Clusters of farm buildings sat like grey warts and an occasional tree spread wooden fingers to the sky. I had never seen so much empty space, even during my time at the manor. I watched breathless, as scudding clouds chased their own shadows across the earth.

'At harvest time all you could see was an ocean of wheat,' Marjorie said, 'as if God had gilded the soil. The men used to sing as they worked the fields. Plenty of jobs for everyone. People came from all the surrounding villages to work for Squire Matthew. Afterwards there was always a big end-of-summer fair with dancing and singing. Nothing sinful, mind.'

I tried to picture smiling field hands dancing in a smoky barn to the tune of a cheap fiddle. And lovers stealing into dark corners to exchange whispered secrets away from the noise and merriment. 'It sounds wonderful,' I remarked. 'Don't these things happen any more?'

'No, not any more.'

'What brought an end to it?'

But Marjorie was keeping that one to herself too. For a simple parson's wife she was a pot of secrets. Ahead, the lane broadened into Dinstock village. We stood aside to let a flock of sheep scurry past. A surly-faced drover in a smock and felt hat swished a stick above the backs of the bleating animals. He eyed me curiously as he passed.

Dinstock was a pigsty. No flagstones or cobbled roads. Muddy lanes were punctured with swollen puddles. A few looked fit to swallow a person whole. A ragtag collection of thatched cottages ran the length of the largest street. To the north, a market cross stood forlornly near the junction of two roads and, frowning over the scene, was a tavern called The Wheatsheaf. Stables dominated the opposite end of the village along with a smithy. Beyond, almost hidden by a copse of sycamore trees, lay a squat, grey-stoned church with a square tower. Parson Proudlove's church.

Marjorie wanted to visit the baker's so I asked if I could have a wander around the village. She nodded, already lost to the smell of the hot ovens. I crossed the street, avoiding the worst of the mud. A wagon lumbered past, dray horses snorting hot steam into the crisp, early winter air. I passed a dressmaker's, whitewashed walls streaked with ochre dirt. Next door was a wine merchant, then a flesher. Finally, to my delight, I discovered a small bookshop tucked away like an afterthought. This was the last thing I expected to find in a farming village, though I supposed it must supply the libraries of the better houses in the district. I pressed my nose against the glass and drank in the friendly sight of leather-bound volumes. Bibles and religious texts mostly but there were some essay collections and a little verse.

Another reflection joined mine in the window. Then another. I turned. A loose gathering of urchins took my measure as if I was a horse they were about to steal. They had approached with the stealth of thieves and did not utter a word between them. Though barefoot for the most part, one wore clogs, another a pair of scuffed leather sandals. Something in their eyes spoke of more than just curiosity.

I edged away from the window and hurried back along the street. The group followed, matching my pace. I stumbled, trying hard not to run. Other faces peered from cottage windows, adult faces.

The first pebble struck me on the shoulder, sending a flash of pain down the length of my arm. A second clipped me on the cheek. A third whisked past my right ear. Abandoning dignity, I hitched up my skirts and fled down that filthy road as fast as my frightened feet would take me. I splashed through puddles, lost a shoe to the mud and stubbed my toe against a half-buried rock. Muck spattered the hem of my black gown. Hair fell about my face in tangled coils.

'Strawberry mouth! Strawberry mouth!' my tormentors chanted, pelting me with stones and lumps of horseshit. An old woman eyed me from the door of her cottage as though I was a harlot being dragged through the streets from the back of the hurdle.

'Let me inside, please,' I begged.

'We don't want the likes of you here,' she replied coldly.

The door was slammed in my face.

I don't know where I found the strength to go on. I thought I would run myself right into the grave. The jeering gang pursued me all the way to the bakery. I tumbled into Marjorie and clung to her. Within seconds the children melted into hedges and gardens. Marjorie lifted up my head, checked my face and neck. 'You're going to bruise,' she said. 'No other harm done. Gypsies camp on the common ground for the winter and their children are fond of a bit of mischief. Nothing to be too concerned about.'

'It's not just the children,' I said. 'It's everyone.'

I tried to tell her about the faces at the windows, how the old woman had shut her cottage door in my face. Marjorie didn't seem to be listening. She took me back to where I had lost my shoe and fished it out of the mud whilst I kept stealing glances up and down the length of the street. 'I shouldn't have let you go off on your own,' she said. 'A black dress, that birthmark. You're a stranger. Locals are superstitious.'

As we made our way back to the parsonage, the wicker basket stuffed with eggs and fresh bread, I clung to her arm. In the kitchen, I washed my face and tried to shake dried mud from my gown. 'Why all these gypsies?' I asked. 'Where were the village children?'

Marjorie wiped her hands and emptied the basket. 'Most of them need to work in order to support their families. There's little time for games. It has been a hard year. The value of everything has fallen. Farmers are struggling. Do not take today's events to heart, Juliana. No one has much to smile about.'

I retired upstairs and shut myself in my room. Daylight eased into the grey muzziness of dusk. As the landing clock struck five, I heard a tap on my door. A girl, not much younger than me, entered holding a candle and a wooden trencher. A bite of supper, I was told. I guessed this was the villager who helped Marjorie around the house.

'Mrs Proudlove says you ain't feeling too well,' she said in a muddy country drawl. 'I've to make sure you get some hot broth inside you. I made it myself.'

I took the candle from her and held it up. A mat of black hair tumbled untidily around the girl's large ears. A nose you could hang a towel from sprouted from the middle of her face, and front teeth stuck over her lower lip. Her eyes, however, were a bright, rich blue. They fixed on my birthmark then flitted away.

'When is the parson due back? Do you know?'

She fumbled with the front of her apron. 'Day after tomorrow.'

I examined the trencher, which she had placed on top of the dresser. Wisps of steam curled up from the broth. The smell of cooked vegetables filled the room.

The girl coughed. 'Been crying have you, madam?'

'Get out,' I ordered.

A sharp tug on my coverlet dragged me from my troubled dreams. I opened sleepy eyes to find Charlotte peering down at me. Her face split into a toothy grin and a cluster of dried flowers appeared under my nose. I eased them aside and clambered out of bed. Early light leaked through cracks in the curtains. She perched on the edge of the mattress and watched as I threw on a robe and tried to brush some sense into my hair.

'I knew you would come to live with us,' she declared.

I fumbled with some pins. 'I hope we can be friends. You wouldn't mind that, would you?'

Her mouth pursed. 'Everyone is saying bad things about you.'

The hairpins fell on to the coverlet. I tried to return the brush to its place on the dresser and dropped it. Pulling up the stool, I sat beside Charlotte, fighting to keep my voice light.

'Oh? What sort of things?'

She rubbed her head with her tiny fingers and did not return my smile. 'They say you will put a hex on all the cattle, that the land will be spoiled and nothing will grow. They say you are the devil's daughter because you have his mark on your face. They are all afraid of you.'

I held her gently by the shoulders and looked down into her round face. 'The miller told you this?'

'I heard his wife say it. She was scared and crying. The miller told her not to be foolish but he was frightened too.'

I brushed away a strand of loose hair that had fallen across her forehead. 'Idle talk, Charlotte, that's all it is. Don't let it upset you. Close your ears.'

She let the posy of dried flowers fall on to the rug. 'I'll try.'

After breakfast had been eaten and cleared away, two visitors arrived at the gate.

'Squire Matthew and his daughter, Emma,

were out riding and have decided to come and meet you,' Marjorie announced. I put down the stocking which I'd blistered my fingers trying to stitch and let her usher me down the garden path. A black hunter and skewbald mare stood on the other side of the gate, snorting and pawing the grass verge. Astride the hunter sat a pickle of a man in a feathered tricorne and bowed wig. A bright yellow riding jacket glared above striped breeches and massive silver-tipped tassels adorned his boots.

In the other saddle was a handsome slip of a girl sharply dressed in a buff riding habit. Tight black curls were neatly ribboned beneath a tall hat. She eyed me coolly as her father propped a pair of tinted spectacles on the end of his long nose.

'By God, what's the matter with that girl?' he bellowed, fixing me with a hard stare. 'Has she split her lip? Put a bandage on it. Or perhaps a sack would serve better.'

Emma stifled a giggle. Marjorie shot me a sideways glance and dipped a curtsy. 'It's merely a birthmark, Squire Matthew. A touch of powder will cover it.'

'Indeed.' He leaned forward in the saddle. 'Well, her father must have been a curious-looking beggar, no doubt of that. Girl looks as though she's dribbled raspberry jam. What have you to say for yourself, child, or has that red stain turned you mute?'

'Powder will cover the mark, just as Mrs Proud-love explained,' I replied, 'though most people I encounter are not so offended by it.'

A palpable silence followed, then Squire Matthew exploded into laughter. 'By God, barely a minute at your gate and already the girl is spitting thorns.'

'She hails from Wexborough,' Marjorie spluttered, as if that explained everything.

'Wexborough, eh?' He pulled off his spectacles and slipped them into his jacket pocket. 'A den of thieves and harlots, by God. She'll have to learn to mellow that sharp tongue of hers. What say you, Emma? How'd you fancy a vixen like this to keep you company up at the Hall? Might get you out and about a bit more if you had her snapping at your heels.'

Emma's jaw tensed. Fingers shook where her gloved hands clutched the leather reins. 'Whatever you wish, Papa.'

'Whatever I wish indeed.' He chuckled and pinched her cheek. Emma winced. He turned away from her and exchanged a few more words of idle chat with Marjorie. Then he and his daughter took their leave, wheeled their horses and cantered off up the lane, Emma's mare keeping a few paces behind her father's hunter.

'You were a bit sharp with Squire Matthew,' Marjorie accused when were back in the kitchen. 'Why did you not show more respect?'

'He was rude and his daughter hates him. Anyone with half an eye could see it. And what is this about my keeping her company? Have you not better things for me to do than pamper some spoilt featherbrain? A week ago I was a squire's wife.'

Marjorie picked up a copper pot and ran her

finger around the inside of the rim. Satisfied that it was clean, she hooked it above the fireplace and lifted another from the pile by the washing tub. 'Emma is at a difficult time in her life. She doesn't often get the chance to meet girls her own age. Spending a few hours each week at Dinstock Hall will put you in good favour with the locals.'

'I will win their respect by myself,' I retorted. 'Is there anything you want from the village today, because I am going back? And I will suffer no nonsense, whether I have Squire Matthew's blessing or not.'

I was ready to argue but Marjorie was learning how to read my moods. 'Go to the bookseller and purchase a prayer book for yourself,' she said, 'for church tomorrow.'

'I have little to thank God for.'

'Nevertheless you will go.'

The weather turned mild. Mud dried, puddles shrank. I pattered down the lane, Marjorie's basket swinging at my hip. On the village outskirts I paused and kicked the grassy verge with the toe of my shoe. The rains had loosened the soil and it came away in thick, greasy lumps. I put the biggest of these in the basket and covered them with a checked cloth. Wiping my hands on the grass, I continued into Dinstock. I strolled past the shops and houses, meeting eye for eye any curious faces that peered out. Soon I heard bare feet scampering behind me, the furtive whispers and muffled giggles.

I walked on. The first stone thumped into my

spine between the shoulder blades, sending hot pain scorching across my back. I did not change pace but acted as if I was taking a leisurely walk in a town park.

The second missile struck the back of my leg. Thanks to my thick petticoats I barely felt it. However, I made as if to flee for my life and heard the triumphant whoop of my old tormentors.

At the last moment I spun around. The jeering gang of urchins almost ran into me. Jubilant cries died on their lips. Before they had broken stride I had the cloth off my basket and a good-sized divot in my hand. I hurled it at the tallest of the gang. It caught him squarely on the face, wrapping muddy fingers around his cheeks. He yelped like a scolded puppy and tried to back up but his feet ran out from underneath him and he landed on his rump. Mud dripped off his chin in thick dollops.

I did not wait to savour my success. I pelted those squealing little horrors with a rain of dirt. Some tried to return fire but I had their measure and caught them about the ears before they had time to loose any more missiles. I yelled like a madwoman. Muck covered the front of my dress. Within minutes the battle was won and I had sent my would-be assailants packing off to their mothers.

The bookseller threw a fit when I trailed mud across his shop, but he'd witnessed the battle from his window and could not be angry with me, no matter how hard he pretended. When I tried to brush the dirt from my gown and only made things worse, his face purpled with laughter. He let me have a prayer book for half price and when I went back out into the street I was ready for another fight. Not a soul anywhere except for a farmer standing by the market cross. He tugged his forelock and bid me good day. Amusement sat awkwardly on his face as if it had not known a home there for years. He would have something to talk about over supper.

I ran back up the lane, splashing through the remaining puddles and swinging the basket until my arm almost flew off. By the time I reached the parsonage, I was humming a silly childhood tune. In the kitchen, Marjorie was fussing over a brace of simmering pots packed with that evening's dinner.

'Glad you've found something to sing about at last,' she remarked over her shoulder. Then she noticed the state I was in and her own good mood turned to vapour. 'You look as if you've tipped end over elbow in a pigs' trough. Take off that filthy dress before you move another step and don't lay so much as a finger on my clean table.'

Laughing, I pulled off the gown, kicked my shoes into the corner and peeled off my wet stockings. Marjorie picked up the garments between her fingertips and tossed them out the back door. 'You can scrub those later. How did you manage to get in such a state?'

'Tripped and fell. I bought the prayer book though and it's not damaged.'

'Was there more trouble in the village?'

'No, no trouble. I doubt I'll have any again. Just a group of mischievous children, as you said.'

269

She wrapped a dry towel around me. 'Mr Proudlove is due back tonight. I want you as clean as an angel before you see him. The gown you brought from the manor will have to do. We can tie a strip of black cloth around the arm until something better can be found. Now go to your bedchamber and remember to brush the dirt out of your hair.'

An entire pitcher of water was needed to clean my hands, face and feet. The rattle of cutlery downstairs meant supper, so I threw on my blue gown and headed for the kitchen. Marjorie was already doling out potatoes from a copper pot. She seemed pleased with my efforts and asked me to fetch the rest of the vegetables from the stove. Through the window, I spied a black gig and mare standing idle in the lane. A scruffy young man in patched leather boots fussed around the horse. 'Has Mr Proudlove arrived?' I asked, accepting a carve of mutton. 'Will he take supper with us?'

'Nathaniel eats in the parlour. You are to go to him as soon as supper is finished and the clearing up done. Try not to be difficult, Juliana. He's had a busy day and is tired from the journey.'

The upstairs clock was striking seven when I was ready to meet my new guardian. We had previously spoken as social equals. How would he regard me now? I fingered the strip of black cloth Marjorie had fastened to my sleeve then knocked on the thick plank door. The parlour lay at the cottage's west side where the ochre stonework swelled into a bay window. It was the parson's private place and I had been warned not to go in uninvited.

A voice instructed me to enter. I had to stoop under the low doorframe. Heavy beams sprouted across the ceiling. A coarse sheepskin rug spread a woollen puddle over bare floorboards. An oak desk hugged the far wall and books were piled in an alcove next to the hearth, where a small fire spluttered. A candle burned on a table beneath the window, bending to the whims of each draught.

The parson sat in a high-backed leather chair studded with round metal buttons. He still wore his clerical garb and I was scrutinised from underneath a round-brimmed hat, which he had not troubled to remove.

'Look at me closely, child.' His voice was the bough of an old tree creaking in the wind. I blushed like a timid moppet as I met that unwavering gaze. His punctured face was as rugged as a limestone quarry. Tufts of steel grey hair clung to his temples. How like a predator he looked. When he breathed his teeth ground against one another.

'Ill fortune can befall any soul, rich or poor.' His eyes were twin sparks in the candlelight. 'You have had your share of bad luck, child. By God's grace you will be a better Christian for it. My dear wife believes it is our duty to keep you under this roof. While you dwell here I will expect both obedience and honest work, as is my due.'

'Yes, Mr Proudlove.' I curtsied. He gestured ambiguously.

'I shall determine suitable duties for you. Though Marjorie will likely keep you occupied around the house we have no need of a scullery maid and you are not qualified to act as a governess for Charlotte. She would gain nothing by having you flitting around her like a horsefly. In the meantime you are not to use our family name. Though we were related by law you are no blood kin. You will answer to "Miss Juliana". Do you understand?'

I curtsied again. My knees were beginning to ache from all this deference.

'Good. One more thing. I hold an important position within this parish. Visitors will call, often at unsociable hours. Mind your manners and your business. If I am entertaining guests, draw your curtains, put out your candle and stay in your room. Ignore whatever you might hear. This house is old and distorts sound. Remain obedient and you'll have no trouble. Now get up to bed. I will see you in church first thing tomorrow.'

He perched a pair of spectacles on the end of his nose and picked up the book that had been lying open on his lap. I slipped out of the parlour and closed the door. Disquiet gnawed at me, growing as I entered my bedchamber and threw back the coverlet on my bed.

Outside, a gathering wind began to whistle through the treetops. I paused whilst undressing and stood by the window, staring into the dark woods. Only the restless chuckling of the brook added its voice to the night.

'I will be happy,' I whispered.

Chapter Fourteen

The sun peeked a bloodshot eye over the trees. Frost cracked the muddy lane and haunted shadows with glistening white fingers. I struggled to keep pace with Marjorie and Charlotte on the mile walk to Dinstock church. My black gown, freshly scrubbed, felt unwieldy, and I had to curl my fingers to stop the borrowed gloves from slipping off. I scuffed my heels, earning a rebuke from Marjorie.

Needless to say, I was in no mood for walking. I had slept fitfully, tormented by terrible dreams. A cold breakfast hadn't helped. Charlotte, sensing she would have no play out of me today, ran up and down the grassy verges until Marjorie called her back. 'No tomfoolery on the Sabbath,' the child was told. 'Stay by me and behave more respectfully.'

Mr Proudlove had already gone ahead in the gig. His church was a sagging heap of grey stone held together by ivy and cracked mortar. It lurked behind a weather-beaten lich-gate and a cluster of crumbling gravestones. Grass, knee-high in places, hid names and dates. Nothing in this rambling building matched, neither the arched door at the front, the slate roof nor the stubby bell tower.

The inside smelled of pigeon droppings and stale candle wax. Rafters of light crisscrossed the air above the pews. Every seat was empty. Prayer books collected dust in a corner. The organ lid was down, the pipes silent. In the font the water had dried up. A scum of black dirt and dead flies coated the bottom of the marble bowl.

We took places at the front of the church. Parson Proudlove emerged from the vestry and began the service. His voice echoed around the bare walls. Marjorie's eyes never left her husband. I kept glancing back at the door, expecting other people to arrive soon, but not another soul entered. We sang hymns, mumbled prayers and uttered amens, our voices reedy in this dusty sepulchre.

After the service, I stood on the cinder path and sucked in lungfuls of fresh air. A coach waited outside the lichgate. The driver informed us that we were to go at once to Dinstock Hall, where Lady Elizabeth Jane wished to see us.

'Won't take long, ma'am,' he said. 'I'll have you back at the parsonage before your husband even notices you were gone.'

The coach was fast and held the road well. Marjorie pretended to be intent on the fields beyond the window but I was having none of that. 'Why was there no one else in the church? Was it a private service?'

'Dinstock people don't attend services.'

'Are they all papists? Is there another place of worship?'

'It is a matter for their own consciences.' She turned away from the window. 'One day you will tie your head in knots with all these questions.'

Dinstock Hall sat like a red-faced bawd on a swathe of grass sliced at the back by trees. Built in Tudor times, so Marjorie had said, it was smaller than George's manor but no less magnificent. We clattered up a gravel drive lined on both sides with poplar trees. Lady Elizabeth received us in her parlour. She was lank and fat bosomed. Paper patches spotted her cheeks.

'You there,' she addressed me. 'You with the blotchy face. Come closer so I can see you better.'

I stepped into a circle of sunlight. Lady Elizabeth pursed her lips and wafted a fan beneath her long nose. 'So you are the young widow who has caused such a stir in the village.'

'Yes, Lady Elizabeth.'

'You will address me as m'lady.'

'Yes, m'lady.'

She turned to Marjorie, who cast her eyes down as if she was a kitchen scrubber. 'A long way for your daughter to fall, Mrs Proudlove. Mistress of the manor to a village pup.'

I butted in. 'You are mistaken, m'lady. I am only her daughter-in-law. Rodriguez is my family name.'

We were forced to walk back to Dinstock. Marjorie would not talk to me, no matter how much I cajoled her. When Charlotte tried to speak she was shushed into silence. I bit back my temper and inwardly cursed my aching feet. Lady Elizabeth's outraged face was still clear in my mind.

At the parsonage I was denied lunch and

ordered to my room. Parson Proudlove arrived a little after noon and, after hearing what happened, immediately sent for me. He bolted the parlour door and drew the curtains. We faced each other in the gloom.

'You have disgraced me and shamed yourself,' he said. 'How dare you insult Lady Elizabeth.'

'How dare she insult me,' I retorted. 'Was I meant to stand and say nothing like a scolded child while she mocked me? My husband once owned land that stretched in every direction. I won't let some peahen of a woman tread on my pride. I have already had my fill of that family.'

I waited for him to say something. My breath came hard after that little speech. The parson did not reply. He stood and crossed to a narrow cupboard set into the wall beside the bookshelf. He opened the door and took out a polished stick made from some dark wood, perhaps hickory. He flicked it a couple of times. I heard a swish as it cut the air.

'What do you propose to do with that?' I demanded, backing towards the locked door.

Quick as a hawk that sights a pigeon, Proudlove snatched hold of my arm. Before I could utter another sound he bent me across the table in the bay window, sending the candlestick skating across the surface. My arm was pinned behind my back and my face rammed into the polished wood. His wiry, knotted limbs felt like iron. I yelped when he lifted my skirts and tore my petticoat open.

'No...' The word squeezed out of my mouth. A hiss of air and the first blow screamed white-hot

276

pain across my nerve endings. I bucked against the table. Proudlove's fingers pinched bruises into my arm as the stick struck a second time. Molten agony seared the length of my spine and into both legs.

As the stick came down again, the parson mouthed a litany of verses pulled from the pages of the Bible. Through the pain I heard his hoary voice rise in supplication to God, beseeching Him to save my damned soul. The stick cut into me a fourth time.

'Don't hit me again.' My voice was mangled, my face a puddle of sweat. 'I will do whatever you say. Please don't hit me again.'

I sensed the stick quivering in the air. Perhaps the next blow would knock me senseless, send my mind into a dark place where this man could not humiliate me any more. A second passed. Another. Footsteps crossed the floorboards and a lock clicked. I opened tear-soaked eyes. For a second, Catherine was standing in the doorway, knotted towel clenched in her hand. Her mouth was working, the words low and horrible, rasping like a sack dragged across dirt.

'You must be a good girl, Juliana. God punishes sinners. See that you behave, or your transgressions will be paid for in blood.'

The figure melted, the cream dress turning into a midnight black coat. Catherine's face sharpened. Skin wrinkled like paper turning to ashes in a hot fire. The parson stood in her place, no compassion anywhere in his stagnant eyes.

I dragged myself across the floor on my hands and knees. Proudlove stepped aside. I grabbed the doorframe, hauled myself to my feet, and stumbled out into the hall. The door closed behind me.

'I cannot go back to that church.' I winced as Marjorie applied a cloth steeped in hot, salty water to my raw behind.

'You must attend services and say your prayers,' she told me, 'or you can't live under our roof.'

'I will go somewhere else. A different parish.'

'You'll go nowhere of the sort.'

I jerked again as needles of pain stabbed into my tender muscles. 'That water is too hot. You are hurting me.'

'It's for your own good. Lie still and let me see to it, otherwise we shall be here half the night and I have Nathaniel's posset to make.'

I shifted on the bed. Spread-eagled with my skirts around my waist, I must have presented a ridiculous sight. I bit my bottom lip when Marjorie applied the cloth again. The beating hadn't drawn blood, but livid welts scored my rump. Despite my defiant tone, I felt anything but brave.

'Why did you tell Lady Elizabeth that your name was Rodriguez,' Marjorie asked, rinsing the cloth in fresh water.

'Because my name is the only thing I have left.' I wiped my sweat-soaked face on the coverlet. 'Though I didn't expect to have the skin flayed from my back for using it.'

'It's not wise to anger Nathaniel. He is under pressure from the church and has many parish duties that beg his attention. It is important to maintain good relations with the squire and his family.'

'They are not *my* family. Or my masters. Taking a stick to my rump won't change that.'

'Nathaniel is your father. It's his duty to chastise you.'

'He is no such thing. I doubt any parent would put a rod across a girl's back the way your husband did to me. Don't fret, Marjorie, I know better than to cross him again. I've had my skin thrashed for the last time. I will eat my food, say my prayers and go to bed when I'm told. The next time Lady Elizabeth slaps me with her tongue, I'll turn the other cheek. But I shall never call Parson Proudlove my father.'

Marjorie dumped the cloth in the pail, splashing water over the sides. She grabbed the handle and swung open my bedchamber door. 'Supper is at eight,' she reminded me. 'Make sure you are on time.'

'Yes, Mrs Proudlove.'

She paused on the doorway, looked as if she was about to say something, then thought better of it and tramped off down the stairs. Wincing, I eased my skirts back down over my behind. I'd likely sleep on my belly for a week.

Footsteps pattered across the landing. The door pushed in and there was Charlotte, looking at me with enquiring eyes. 'Sorry,' I told her. 'No games from me today.'

She scrambled to the bed, climbed on to the side of the mattress and pushed the damp hair off my forehead with her small hand. 'Did you really steal children?' she whispered.

I propped myself up on an elbow. This child had a knack for digging up awkward questions. 'Where did you hear that?'

'Sophie told me.'

Sophie was the miller's daughter. I nodded, unwilling to lie. 'Yes, it's true.'

'Why did you do it?'

'Because certain people wanted to hurt them. I took or sent them to places where they would be safe.'

The frown returned. 'Papa steals children too.'

I gaped at her. 'What did you say?'

'Papa steals children,' Charlotte repeated, 'and takes them to the Bad Place.'

I rolled on to my knees and climbed awkwardly off the bed. My throat had gone as dry as a stream bed in a six-week drought. 'What Bad Place?'

Her small face was a pot of storm clouds, her mouth flattened into a thin gash. I laid hands on her shoulders and summoned up a special smile but she did not return it. Such an expression was terrifying on a child.

'He takes them, boys mostly, and sometimes little girls like me. Babies too. He comes back with gold in his purse and a penny for me if I'm awake. He'll be angry if he knows I've told you.'

'Angry? How do you mean? Does he beat you? Does he hit you with his stick?' I was shaking her without realising it. Her face crumpled and she pulled out of my grasp. Just then her mother called upstairs. She fled the room, rubbing her shoulder. I cursed my clumsiness but a moment later her laughter burbled up from the kitchen.

Relief flooded through me.

I washed my face in the bowl of water on the dresser then brushed my hair. The pain in my backside had subsided to a dull throb but putting on a fresh petticoat still took effort.

Charlotte's words ran around inside my head. She was a fanciful child, given over to a colourful imagination but I couldn't dismiss that haunted look on her face. Something was happening in this sleepy part of the country. Something bad. And for all his piousness and his pretty cottage smothered in ivy, Parson Proudlove's black heart was at the centre of it.

The following day I was taken back to Dinstock Hall to apologise to Lady Elizabeth. She waited in her drawing room as I mouthed words of contrition then dismissed me with a flick of the hand. I limped into the parlour to join Emma. My backside, after a murderously uncomfortable night, had bruised the colour of a plum.

Marjorie, who had accompanied me on this pitiable errand, returned in the parson's gig, which had been loaned for the occasion. I spent the rest of the morning perched on the edge of the parlour couch with two cushions squeezed under my rump. Emma, ladylike in her own waspish way, asked no questions. I tried to keep her entertained but she was in a restless mood. She selected a volume at random from the oak bookcase sprawled against the far wall and handed it to me. I read the first couple of chapters quickly and fluently, however Emma's attention soon wandered. We spent most of the time trying to think of something to say. I answered her questions about Wexborough and she told me something of the country. But when I asked about her parents her face went slack. Only my changing the subject breached the long silence that threatened to follow. I was relieved when the Janes' coach drew up in front of the house to take me back to the parsonage. On the way out, Lady Elizabeth handed me a note for Parson Proudlove asking me to return on a regular basis.

So it was for the next few weeks, each visit more uncomfortable than the last. I was shown round the house, the gardens, the stables. I was allowed to pet Emma's mare, Brightwater, and she suggested that we ride together. It was the first time I had witnessed a spark of interest on her face. This was quickly snuffed when I confessed that I'd never been in the saddle and did not own a horse.

'Perhaps my groom can teach you?' she offered, but I could tell her heart was not in it. We retreated to the house again and tried card games but I was too good for her and she scattered them on the floor with an angry sweep of her hand.

Then she played the spinet. I sat and listened. I had no musical skills and wasn't much of a singer either. Sewing brought on a headache and when I tried painting, the mess I left on the canvas was matched only by the one on my gown. So most of the time we walked in silence or sat indoors if the weather turned foul.

Emma's lack of curiosity proved surprising. She asked only perfunctory questions, never probing very far. Whenever I tried to volunteer anything she appeared uninterested. Her parents were out most of the time on business or social engagements and, apart from the servants, we often had the house to ourselves. I would have poked my head into every nook, explored every hallway, climbed every staircase. But no, I had to remain in the parlour trying to think of a pastime we would both find tolerable.

At the parsonage I spent much of my time reading in my bedchamber. Sometimes I would walk in the woods behind the house, a dark place of shadows where trees crammed together in a cathedral of wood. Life teemed amidst the branches and on the soft forest floor. Owls, squirrels, rabbits. Once, a deer eyed me warily from the other side of the brook where it had paused to sip the clear waters.

At other times I helped around the house, dutifully attended that empty church each Sabbath and brushed the first of the winter's snow from the front path. Charlotte had been sent to stay with a cousin in Bristol for the season. I peeked into her box-sized bedroom, fingering her rag poppets or some of the other trinkets I knew she loved to play with.

One crisp morning, Parson Proudlove went into her room and gathered everything into a sack. He took a swatch of kindling from the hearth and built a fire outside the kitchen door, feeding it with logs from the woodpile. When the flames had caught, he emptied the sack on to the pyre and stood by as his daughter's toys and scrapbooks turned to ashes. He noticed me watching from the kitchen window and ordered me into the woods with a basket to fetch more kindling. Marjorie had gone into Dinstock and it was too early for the maid to arrive from the village.

I struggled deep into the woods on the hunt for suitable fuel. Stubborn patches of snow clung to the trees and a powder of frost made every stretch treacherous. When I returned two hours later the fire had reduced to a smoking, cindered ring. The empty sack lay beside it. Tiny, blackened faces stared out of the charred ruin. I nudged them with my foot. The porcelain heads were all that remained of Charlotte's dolls. From inside the cottage came the sound of someone weeping. I pushed open the door and stepped into the kitchen, stamping the cold out of my feet. Marjorie was seated at the table, her basket in front of her, the cover draped across the top. She stopped crying when she saw me and pounced on the kindling. 'The stove has gone out,' she said, trying to sound cheerful. 'We must get it going again else we shall all freeze.'

I didn't understand the significance of what I'd seen in the yard and wasn't willing to ask the parson. Perhaps he was clearing out before Charlotte returned from Bristol with a cartload of new things and Marjorie was just being sentimental. I did not press her on the matter. She was no friend or ally, no one I could confide in. She wanted to bend me too much to her way of thinking, almost as if she could not countenance anyone possessing a different view of the world than her own, or more accurately her husband's. I felt torn between fear of the parson, a desire to remain in her favour and a dull resentment at being pushed around like some serving wench with corn in my hair and mud between my toes.

Only in Charlotte, I believed, could I place a measure of trust, though more secrets than revelations lurked in those dark eyes. What had they seen? What had she heard in her tiny bedroom when sleep proved elusive?

'I have work for you,' the parson told me when I returned from my weekly visit to Dinstock Hall. 'Important work that I cannot spare the time to attend to. You will need to travel around the parish, for which I shall provide a carriage and driver, and be prepared to spend many hours in all weathers.'

He had been waiting in his parlour, perched on his armchair beside the hearth, a pipe stuck between his long teeth. A valise lay open on the floor. Inside were a Bible, prayer book and a thick sheaf of papers.

I curtsied and told him I would do whatever he pleased. The bite of his polished stick was too fresh in my memory. He explained that my coach would collect me at the gate tomorrow, just after daybreak. 'Be sure you are ready,' he warned. 'Many weeks of hard, Christian toil lie ahead.'

He outlined my duties, told me that I was to deliver clothes and food for the needy, collect tithes from local merchants, and hand over parish papers where appropriate. He gave me a list of hamlets and farms. 'Your driver is a local lad. He will know where to take you.'

'And my visits to Dinstock Hall?'

'Will continue.'

He grasped the arms of the chair and raised himself to his feet. I kept my head bowed. Looking the parson in the eye took more nerve than I could summon. 'Much of the work we do in the church is by necessity discreet,' he continued. 'Accept the wisdom of your betters and do not question matters that are none of your concern. Keep your attention on the work at hand. Get to know the parishioners, their families. The more we become aware of their needs, the better we will be able to serve them. Do your duty by me and I shall never have cause to punish you again. Do you understand?'

My voice was the squeak of a mouse. 'Yes, parson.'

His shadow passed away from me. I ached to sit down. Both legs had turned to water and I trembled so much I thought my teeth would shake out of their sockets. Parson Proudlove resumed his seat by the fire. Pipe smoke leaked from the hole in his cheek and curled around his face like dragon's breath. 'When you visit the farms, remember that birthing and dying are the day-to-day business of working folk. Sometimes I lose count of my flock. Keep a tally for me. I will need it when I give account to my superiors. You can do that, can't you?'

'Yes, parson.'

Released, and with no chores to do, I spent the remainder of the day alone among the trees. Eventually, driving rain penetrated the branches and had me running for the comfort of my bed. Daybreak caught me in a foul mood. I felt I had a lot to grumble about as I stamped my feet on the frost-cracked lane. I had slept fitfully again, poisoned by nightmares full of half-glimpsed faces that shifted in and out of focus.

My belly rumbled. Mrs Proudlove had barely put the kindling in the hearth when I'd padded into the kitchen, eyes gritty. The parson was already off on some business or other. Did he ever sleep? I pictured him stalking about his parlour in the dead of night with that one candle burning. Or perhaps other things kept him from his bed.

I blew into my hands and glanced at the leaden belly of the sky. More rain later, I suspected. I ached for bed and hot coffee. The pile of prayer books, old clothes and packets I was due to deliver today sat in neat bundles beside the gate. Marjorie had helped me out with them, puffing in the cold air.

A rumbling in the lane broke into my thoughts. I backed into the gate as a carriage hove into view. The driver, smothered beneath a heavy coat and scarf, gave a sharp whistle and brought the team of two to a halt. The coach was little better than a cart with a roof nailed on. It squatted on leather springs that squealed like trapped mice. Varnish flaked off the woodwork, the wheels looked as if they wanted to go off in separate directions and it had the damp mustiness of something that had mouldered under canvas for too many seasons. The pair of bays hauling it seemed sound enough, though they fidgeted as if ashamed to be caught between the shafts of such an ancient thing.

The driver let go of the reins and jumped down

from his perch. He was short compared to most men hereabouts and walked with a slight stoop. He plucked off his cap and revealed a mop of black curls clinging to the top of his skull. Pale skin was studded by thick eyebrows, an overlong nose and a pink half-moon for a mouth. From beneath heavy lids, two bright blue eyes regarded me with curious politeness.

'Good day,' he uttered in the local drawl. 'You are Miss Juliana? Prettyman is my name, Charles Prettyman.'

'You are my driver?' I said, as frosty as the ice-hard puddles dotting the lane.

'I am that. Let me get these things on board then we can be off.'

'In that?' I gestured at the carriage, which seemed to sag further on its springs even as I spoke. 'Do you suppose it will make it to the end of the lane without falling to pieces?'

Prettyman laughed, a rich, full sound that might have come from the lungs of a sturdy labourer. 'She'll take you to Scotland and back if you've a mind to go,' he declared, slapping the wooden panel with the palm of his hand. 'She's an old carriage but she's well built and can match the Wexborough stagecoach when the roads allow. Henry Colm over at Rosecroft Farm used it for years to cart his pigs around and they had no cause for complaint.'

'Pigs?' I stared at him aghast. 'I am to sit in a carriage that has had pigs in it?'

'I've washed it out for you. Colm bought himself a new wagon and sold this to Parson Proudlove. Parson got a bargain if you ask me. Here we go now. Would you mind getting the door for me?'

A piece of rope served as a handle. I jerked the door open whilst Prettyman started picking up the books. He only used one hand to load the carriage and kept the other tucked into his coat. 'Are you injured?' I asked, once he had stacked everything on to one of the wooden seats inside.

'No, miss. I've got a withered arm. No strength in it. I'd let you have a look but it's not so pretty. I was all right as a baby but the rest of me grew and the arm didn't. I mostly keep it covered, though I'm not one for grouching.'

'Wonderful,' I groaned. 'Not only do I have to sit with the stench of pigs but also I have to suffer a cripple to drive me.'

Coloured spots appeared above Prettyman's cheekbones. His eyes lost their bright edge. 'I'm as good a man as any, more so than some. No one in the county can handle a coach better and I'd be working for Squire Matthew Jane himself if I wasn't in debt to the church.'

'Anyone can brag. Children. Wet-faced boys. Just take me where I have to go.' I reached under my shawl, took out a sheet of paper and handed it to him. 'Here is a list of places we have to visit today.'

He stared at the paper. A flush spread across his whole face. 'I can't read. Nobody ever had time to teach me.'

'No, I suppose not.' I snatched the list out of his hand. 'Little use for reading if you spend your day shovelling dung out of a stable. Well, I'll make one thing clear, Charles Prettyman. I am

289

not here of my own choosing. All you have to do is drive this pig cart. Now help me inside then get back to your seat. A busy day lies ahead and we are already late.'

Muscles worked in his throat. He wrapped his scarf back around his face, hoisted me into the carriage, then clambered back on to his perch and clicked the horses forward. I leaned back on the hard wooden seat. The inside of the coach was scratched and bare but didn't smell of anything worse than old wood. My own carriage at last. A pig wagon.

The horses gathered speed. Prettyman could not have a more unlikely name, I reflected. He was as ugly as an old boot and spoke with the duncery of a tinker. I did not believe his boastful claims. A cripple working the stables at Dinstock Hall, in any capacity, beggared belief. Parson Proudlove must have considered it a fine jest to have such a fellow cart me around the country-side. A half-man to drive a broken-down coach. Well, I would play his game.

For four days I grit my teeth as we bumped down umpteen muddy lanes to hamlets with ridiculous names. Sour-faced locals stared at me with undisguised mistrust as I dumped the word of God on their doorstep or handed out clothes to replace their filthy rags, garments that would likely end up peddled at Dinstock market.

I suffered their sullen curiosity, the way they sometimes plucked at my mourning gown, tried to finger my red hair or fussed over my birth-mark, as if their own pox-raddled faces weren't bad enough. It was always the poorest farms we visited. Scrawny livestock scratched the dirt. Sagging thatched roofs, thick with moss, topped the tumbledown hovels in which these creatures lived. Speech was apparently beyond most of them. My missions of mercy were mostly greeted with silence or the occasional grunt.

I quickly came to hate the squalor. Faces were often scabbed with some god-awful festering that thrived on grubby flesh. Every place stank, either from the rubbish they burned in their hearths, the cow shit that plastered everything, or their own bodies. The only time anyone seemed to enjoy a wash was when obliged to step out into the rain. I hated them and they resented me. I heard the thunk of a rock against the carriage door after delivering a sack of potatoes to a starving family. Their own crop had shrivelled in the waterlogged fields because no one had the wit to drain the ground properly.

Prettyman kept an old pistol tucked into his belt. Not loaded, he assured me. 'This gun ain't fired a shot in nearly fifty years,' he explained, waving the relic in front of my face. 'But it'll put the fear of God into any who've a mind to forget their place.'

'Who are you to talk about place?' I snapped back. 'And don't point that thing at me again.'

By the end of the week the hem of my gown had frayed, along with my temper. I couldn't get the mud off my shoes or the shit from my hands. My clothes were permanently damp from wading through puddles or having to stand in the infernal drizzle that had bled out of the clouds these past few days.

Every night, after my rounds, the parson called me to his parlour. I stood in front of his armchair like a scolded child and related all the details of each visit. He listened, brows pinched, posing occasional questions, which I answered as honestly as I could.

'They accepted the clothes you offered?' he asked.

'I don't think anything was likely to be refused. Even toddlers' garments could be patched into something bigger.'

'Hmmm, no matter. A starving belly makes friends easily. You will gain their trust in time.'

It was with relief that I paid my weekly visit to Dinstock Hall. Clouds overhead had thickened. They hung over the landscape in slabs of grey, innards broiling with storms. The wind picked up as Prettyman took the coach along the exposed road towards the Hall. Gusts whooped across the fields and stripped twigs from the bare branches of the few trees lining our route. The canvas blinds flapped against the carriage windows, throwing chips of desiccated varnish over my skirts. Damp patches crept across the roof.

Eventually the drizzle turned to rain. Prettyman shouted something to the horses, voice muffled under the scarf. The carriage swayed in the wind, the wheels losing themselves in waterlogged ruts. Thunder grumbled in the distance.

By the time we pulled to a halt outside Dinstock Hall, the rain was scything across the lawns in vicious sheets. A footman appeared with a parasol, which was instantly snatched out of his hands by the wind and sent tumbling over the rose beds. I ran past him and shivered into the house. Emma greeted me in the hall, mouthing empty remarks about the state of the weather and my bedraggled appearance. She took me by the hand, her fingers warm against my chilled skin, and seated me in front of the parlour fire before ordering tea.

I was too miserable to notice the flush on her cheeks, or the way she danced around the room, hands fluttering like birds' wings. Her eyes kept wandering towards the door as she spoke in a voice that was a little higher than usual. She chattered non-stop about the latest fashions, the news from Bristol and London, in fact anything and everything. Her fingers drifted to her necklace or her earrings as if they were magical charms.

Emma had always been well dressed but today she'd chosen an especially fetching gown. Rouge tinted her cheeks with soft rosebuds. The parlour air was thick with her cologne. Jewel-studded rings formed glittering dewdrops on her hands.

I poured hot tea down my throat and sighed as its warmth spread through my belly. Emma could not sit still for more than five minutes and was soon at the window peering into the gloom. 'Is that your coach?'

I put down my teacup. 'I'm afraid so. It was the best the parson could find for me.'

'Your driver is standing in the pouring rain. He should go round to the kitchen. Cook will give him a stool by the fire and some hot broth. The wretch looks half-drowned.'

'The horses are skittish from the thunder,' I

replied. 'He must remain with the carriage and see they do not bolt.'

'Our stable lad can take care of your horses. There is plenty of room in the yard for the coach. I will send my footman back out to tell your driver.'

'There is no need...'

'I don't want that ugly thing in front of my house.'

Before I could splutter another word she pulled the bell sash and sent the servant out into the downpour. A minute later, my carriage rumbled away from the windows.

Emma returned to her place by the fire but still could not settle. Her eyes drifted to the door then the mantel clock, which showed a quarter past the hour. Her tea lay untouched in its cup.

'Do you want me to go?' I asked. 'It seems you have other things on your mind. Perhaps we can resume our pastimes another day?'

Emma flushed and pressed her hands to her cheeks. 'Forgive me. I must seem a terrible hostess but I cannot keep it a secret any longer.'

'Secret? Is it to do with hiding away my battered old carriage?'

She laughed too loudly and leaned forward in her chair. Her eyes were like a child's, bright with excitement. She glanced again at the clock. Now her voice was a whisper. 'I have a beau,' she confessed. 'Can you believe it?'

She caught the look on my face and giggled like a girl half her age. Her fingers scurried up and down the chair arm as if she had no control over them. 'He is the most divine fellow,' she declared, as if challenging me to disagree. 'A gentleman of fine talents and not inconsiderable wealth. I do believe I am in love. I know he loves me.'

I goggled at her. Now it was the turn of my tea to grow cold in its cup. I thought any man would have to be struck very hard about the head with a spade to fall for Emma Jane. 'He told you this?' I gulped.

'No, not directly, but men have a way of showing their feelings without putting them into words. 'Tis all part of the game. A gentleman would not be so forward as to declare his intentions outright, any more than a lady would bare her heart without first savouring the thrill of the chase. You will come to understand these things should you ever fall in love yourself.'

'Indeed?' I wondered what colour my face had turned. Emma favoured me with what I supposed was a kindly smile.

'I am sure it will happen before too long. Perhaps a prosperous farmer will catch your eye, or a merchant.'

'Emma, I am already a widow. Had you forgotten?'

Her eyes returned to the clock. I could have been talking to the rug for all the attention she paid me. I sat, jaw muscles clenched, whilst she described her new lover's carriage down to the last detail, even though she confessed to never having ridden in it, and his taste in clothes – surely the finest in all Europe. He was striking and debonair, a master gambler and an expert swordsman. When at last she had to pause to take a breath, I asked her where she had met this paragon of manliness. Emma explained that she had been introduced at a private ball in Wexborough. Her family had been invited through a colleague of her father's. Whilst he had slipped off to discuss politics with the gentlemen in the smoking room, the new light in his daughter's life chose that moment to put in an appearance.

'I could have danced with him until my feet dropped off,' she declared. 'The town women were staring at us, their faces sour with envy. I felt like a queen. It was the happiest night of my life and I never wanted it to end. Afterwards, he gained Papa's permission to call at the Manor. I would have died if it had been refused. All this week he has showered me with gifts, each delivered by his private messenger.'

I tried to shrug off the beginnings of a headache and sat patiently while she showed me the trinkets this mysterious lover had bestowed. Pretty baubles, sure enough, and expensive looking, but I did not care for anything. Not the gilt bracelet, or the porcelain figure of a stallion, or even the satin and ivory choker, though it looked beautiful on her and I said as much. These gifts had no sense, no order, as if they had been selected at random and packed off without thought.

I did not let Emma know what I was thinking. I doubted she'd listen. The place this 'love' had taken her lacked any door or window to the real world. I took the scone she offered and munched on it whilst she poured me a fresh cup of tea.

'What is your beau's name?' I asked, mouth a ring of crumbs. 'I attended many functions during my marriage to George Proudlove. Perhaps I have met him?'

She laughed. 'I doubt someone like you would have made the acquaintance of such a gentleman. In any case you *shall* meet him. I have decided. He is due within the hour.'

I mumbled excuses but Emma brushed them aside. The headache lingering at the back of my brow finally burst across my skull. I had no heart to argue. Emma droned on about the new dress she had bought to impress him and the picnics they planned to take by the river when winter finally thawed to spring. I mouthed a silent prayer of thanks, hypocrite that I was, when the sound of horses on the drive stopped her chatter. Emma squealed, clapped her hands and ran to the door, leaving me with a pot of empty tea and a plateful of broken cakes.

I rubbed sore eyes, wishing I could leave. The rain and the bumpy road now seemed preferable to this neat parlour with its gleaming ornaments and too-clean hearth. A man's voice rumbled in the hall, followed by Emma's shrill laughter. Footsteps approached the parlour. The door breezed inwards. The rich scent of cologne mixed with tobacco carried into the room.

I frowned. That cologne. I had smelled it before. I opened my eyes. Emma's new love stood before me, mud caking the soles of his boots and raindrops sprinkling his powdered wig like diamonds. He held out a gloved hand. Amusement shone in his eyes. 'Charmed,' he said in that cat-purr voice.

It was Adam Fairchild.

Chapter Fifteen

I don't know how long I stared at him. I was on my feet though unable to remember getting up from my chair. At some point I had knocked over my teacup and spread a brown stain across the carpet. In the background, Emma's out-of-focus face smiled and said something, though I couldn't hear what. Adam Fairchild and I regarded each other and nothing else in the room was real. His lips moved. 'A pleasure to meet you again.'

I was vaguely aware of Emma's smile faltering. She asked a question and Adam turned to speak to her, breaking the spell between us. 'I was an acquaintance of Mrs Proudlove's late husband,' he explained, 'and our paths crossed once or twice before that.'

Doubt lifted from Emma's face. Adam sprawled out on the sofa, planting his boots on the tea table. He lit a pipe with a taper from the fire and blew smoke rings into the air. Emma perched on the end of the couch, hands clasped in her lap, face like an eager dog expecting a reward after performing some trick or another.

I remained standing, unable to put myself to any purpose or conjure any sense out of my mouth. I might have spent the rest of the day like that if Lady Elizabeth hadn't breezed into the parlour in a cloud of perfume. She greeted Adam with a kiss as if he was a favoured child, then plucked me out of the room and along to her private chambers at the rear of the house. After closing the door, she yanked off her wig and tossed it on to the dresser. For one insane moment I thought her hair had come away too. Sunlight reflected off her bald, pink scalp. The skin was puckered with bug bites and old scabs.

'I've worn wigs since I was three years old,' she explained, catching my expression. 'When you spend all your time scratching like a tinker's cur it makes sense to lose your locks. So many lice inhabit that burdensome headdress I am surprised the thing does not jump off its stand and flee the room.'

I shot a look at the door. What were Adam and Emma doing? Were they talking about me?

'My cousin's hair fell out before she was forty,' Lady Elizabeth continued, seating herself on an embroidered divan. 'She refused to wear a wig. Eventually she refused to wear a dress and took to turning up at the house in hessian robes. Our gatekeeper mistook her for a tinker and, thinking she had come begging, refused her entry to the grounds. He was mortified on discovering the identity of this mysterious visitor.'

I glanced at the door again.

On the table beside the divan was a slim wooden box. Lady Elizabeth opened the lid and plucked out a long-stemmed clay pipe. She stuffed in a small wad of fresh tobacco and pushed the end between her teeth. She talked around it while coaxing a spark from her tinderbox. 'Don't look so shocked. I take snuff too. Why should men have all the pleasure in life, eh?' She patted the cushion beside her. 'Would you like to play cards, perhaps a hand or two of whist? I hear you are quite good.'

I shook my head. She took a long draw on her pipe, savouring the taste before releasing a cloud of blue smoke into the hot air. 'Mr Fairchild has taken lodging at Dinstock inn, and will remain in the district for the next month. You will curtail your visits unless summoned and remain discreet on the matter of their courtship.'

'She has known him barely two weeks and already you are calling it a courtship? You must be aware of this man's reputation?'

Lady Elizabeth tapped her pipe out on to the table.

'His exploits are familiar to every household in the county,' I persisted.

She sighed and glanced out of the window. The rain was still hammering down outside. 'He is a charming man, perfectly charming. Every gentleman of worth garners a reputation with the town gossips and scandal is usually born of jealousy, both among peers and members of the fair sex. If nothing else, bawdy behaviour is a symptom of exuberance and does not mean every male should be tarred as a libertine. Mr Fairchild's company is agreeable. Certainly he does not seem to be the lecher he is painted.'

A smile flitted across her lips. Her eyes took on a faraway look and she brushed her cheek with her fingers. She was thinking about him, the way I had thought about him for weeks after that first meeting at the Wexborough ball. Even now if I let my guard slip far enough, I could find myself thinking that way again. 'You are prepared to overlook his sins because he makes you forget you're not a girl any more,' I accused through clenched teeth. 'This is how he works, don't you realise that? He is using Emma for his own ends and putting you off the scent with sweet talk and idle compliments. While he has you distracted he will fill your daughter's womb with bastards and starve her of decency the way a leech sucks blood.'

Outside, a rip opened up in the clouds and threw sunlight across the floor. It carved Lady Elizabeth's face into light and shadow. 'Sit down,' she told me. 'Sit down you little fool before you hurt yourself.'

I panted like a dog after a fast chase and had squeezed both fists hard enough for my nails to cut my palms. I sat on the end of the divan.

'That is better,' she continued. 'There is bitterness on your face, plain for all to see. I accept that you have had some contact with Mr Fairchild but I do not wish to know what has passed between you. Whatever part he played in your life must remain in the past. You will not in any way compromise my daughter's happiness, do you understand? This is the second time you have crossed me, but I am prepared to overlook it. You are young and obviously hurt. I have known that pain myself and realise how it can twist one's thoughts.'

'I don't love Adam Fairchild.'

'No, of course you do not. And if I ever hear of you bringing his name into disrepute I will speak to Parson Proudlove and you will not be made welcome at Dinstock Hall again.'

I imagined the bite of that polished stick on my back and kept my mouth closed. The hall clock chimed the hour. A minute later I heard the parlour door open. Chuckling voices, words too soft to discern, drew claws across my imagination. I pictured Emma's love-soaked face, Adam's amused, slightly contemptuous charm. Then a pause, as if the entire house held its breath. In my tortured thoughts, he placed a kiss on her long fingers whilst she blushed and her head brimmed with dreams of marriage and children.

I rose from the divan and scurried to the door. Worse things than bitterness existed. Anger. Jealousy.

I thought Lady Elizabeth might try to follow me but she had confidence in her own power and her expression was warning enough. She refilled her pipe whilst I pulled open the door and gusted along the hall. Emma and Adam were standing by the open front door. Both turned to look at me as I clattered, cack-legged as any infant, across the tiles. How graceful Emma was, how elegant in her poise and mannerisms. Beside her, I felt a clumsy old widow. I tried to say something but my tongue made a hash of it. Emma giggled.

'My dear,' Adam addressed her, smile still playing across his lips, 'I fear I have left my gloves in the parlour. Would you be an angel and get them for me?'

She glanced at me then happily went to fetch them. Alone with Fairchild, I felt the air tighten around my throat. Every nerve in my body burned. 'Why?' I demanded. 'Why Emma Jane? What does she possess that you could want? You have taken and ruined richer, more amusing creatures than her. Why muddy your boots for an empty-headed country girl? What dark game are you playing?'

A nest of vipers hissed behind his teeth. 'A game you would dearly love to join in.' He leaned forward and, before I could or would stop him, brushed my lips with a kiss. I heard a strangled gasp. Emma stood in the parlour doorway, brown leather gloves gripped in her hand. Her face was the colour of ashes. She threw the gloves at Adam. He caught them, tipped his hat to both of us and strode out the front door in a gust of damp air. I watched as he clambered into his carriage, cloak flapping about his legs. A moment later the driver set the team galloping up the drive.

Emma's fingers closed like bony pincers around my arm. 'So, widow, you seek to become a rival under my own roof?'

I shrugged free. 'Fairchild is a womaniser who will kiss any pretty face he sees, whether that face is asking to be kissed or not. I did not invite his attention, nor was it welcome.'

'He is mine. Do not forget it.'

'Take him then and don't expect me to be around after he has left you broken-hearted and mewling for your mama.'

I stormed out of the house, dragging my shawl around my shoulders and cursing like a common thief. Prettyman was in the stable yard, seated inside my carriage, supping a mug of hot broth presumably begged from the kitchen. I yanked open the door. 'Out,' I commanded. 'Get back on the driver's seat.'

He climbed out and tipped the remains of his soup into the dirt. He left the mug on the kitchen step before climbing on to the carriage roof and picking up the reins. He did not utter a word, which suited me fine. I clambered inside and closed the door. 'Take me back to the parsonage,' I ordered, leaning out of the window. 'See if you can coax enough life from these nags to get there before the rain returns.'

Prettyman's face was pinched above his woollen scarf. He nodded and snapped the reins. I was flung back into my seat as the horses jerked forward. They took the drive at a fast canter. As we passed the front of the house I spied Emma watching from the parlour window. Neither of us waved. I suspected Adam knew what he was doing when he placed that serpent's kiss on my mouth.

Leather springs groaned as the carriage lurched into the waterlogged lane. I spotted a figure walking along the verge with three sizeable dogs straining on a leash. Swaddled in coats with a shovel hat crammed on his head, the figure stopped wrestling the animals long enough to look up. I recognised Squire Matthew. What was he doing outside the grounds of Dinstock Hall?

'Prettyman, stop the coach.' I banged on the roof until the carriage rattled to a halt. The moment I stepped out, the hounds were sniffing around my skirts. I tried not to wince when I felt their black button noses push into the folds. I was ignorant of dogs and did not know the breed, seeing them only as hairy bundles of fangs and scrabbling claws. One jumped up on its hind legs and slapped a warm, wet tongue across the back of my hand.

'Get back there,' Squire Matthew yelled, clipping the beast's ear with the end of the leash. It yelped and bounded out of the way. 'Back off I say.' Raindrops showered off his coat. He jerked the leash again. All three animals fell back, pawing the dirt around his boots. 'Rot my teeth, it's the young widow,' he declared. 'It gladdens me to see you, Miss Juliana, though that mourning sack makes you look like a sour old maid, let my legs turn putrid if that's not the truth.'

'Squire Matthew, I must speak to you.'

'Can't it wait for sweeter weather?'

'No.'

'Well, out with it, girl. These curs get lively when they want feeding.'

'That man who is calling on your daughter, you must not let him past your door. Forbid Emma to have any contact with him. Lady Elizabeth will not listen and Emma herself is too taken with the fellow to see any sense.'

He frowned. 'Adam Fairchild of Wexborough? Mighty impertinent of you, young widow, to dictate to me whom I can and cannot admit into my own home. What complaint could you have against him?'

'He is not all he seems.'

'Is that why you stopped that pile of wooden bones? To warn me that he is a rake and lecher? That he will wreck my daughter's happiness and bring her to ruin? That he would fritter away her possessions on drink, whores and card games?' He smiled at my look of astonishment. 'Climb back into your carriage and go home to the

305

parson and his wife. I'll finish walking my dogs and we shall forget we spoke today.'

The sky closed up and threw down a fresh flurry of rain. One of the dogs cocked a leg and piddled on the wheel of the coach. The others sat scratching on the wet grass. I tried to think of something else to say. Squire Matthew waited me out, his coat buttoned tight to the neck, his eyes regarding me from under his hat brim.

'You hate her so much that you would stand by and let this man destroy her?' I said finally.

He wiped his face and glanced at the sky. 'On the contrary, I love her dearly, but her lack of respect has become burdensome. Oh, she does as she's bid, I'll grant her that, but everyone has noticed the way she looks at me and heard the things she mutters when my back is turned. Rather than a daughter, I find myself lumbered with an intolerant scold who has no ear for anything I try to tell her. 'Twas only a matter of time before some purse-hunting rake hooked her by the heart. It may be a hard lesson she learns, but a lesson none the less.'

He gestured at the hounds. 'See these dogs, I love them like my own sons. One scrap of disobedience, however, and they feel the end of my boot. Now if you'll mind out, Miss Juliana, the beasts are itching for their kennels and I want some brandy inside me before this infernal weather has me down with a fever.'

The dogs immediately burst into a fresh chorus of barking. I jumped aside as a snarling maw lunged at my legs. Squire Matthew laughed and pulled the snapping creature away. I waited on the verge until he'd crossed the lane and turned into his drive, whistling and calling his hounds to heel.

I clambered back inside the coach and closed the door. Prettyman clicked the reins and sent us rumbling back towards the parsonage. Outside, swollen clouds blackened the horizon. Everything went dark.

At the cottage gate, Prettyman climbed down and opened the door. He waited in the downpour, felt hat knocked out of shape by the rain. I sat huddled on the end of the seat with both arms wrapped around my knees.

'I did not care for the way that man spoke to you,' he said, 'or the way he handled his dogs.'

I unfolded myself. 'He is the squire. He can do as he pleases and it is no concern of yours.'

'If he had allowed those animals to hurt you...'

'Then what would you have done? A cripple against a man with two good arms and three dogs spoiling for a fight? Your heroics would get you hung if the hounds did not carve your throat out first. Then who would drive this wreck around the countryside?' I did not wait for an answer but climbed out and pushed past him to the gate. I felt his gaze on my back all the way up the front path.

I lost count of the weeks as winter bit deeper into the land. On the bitterest mornings I awoke to find icicles hanging icy fangs from the window ledge. Sometimes the brook froze and I had to break the ice to draw water. On Christmas Eve our village help became afflicted with some malady that kept her at home. I found myself doing her work as well as running Parson Proudlove's errands.

From before daybreak until after dusk I laboured nonstop, grateful that I was too busy to even think. Half-dead with fatigue, I tumbled into bed each night and was instantly asleep. No nightmares. No Moses Cripps. I believed him gone, out of the county, overseas perhaps, and the documents with him. Better that way.

No summons arrived from Dinstock Hall, and Charlotte, I was told, would not be home until the following spring. Snow had blocked the Bristol road. 'The parsonage in winter is no place for a child,' Marjorie said. I carried out my chores with no complaint. Even the parson was satisfied enough to invest in a new shawl to keep me snug during those bitterly cold mornings.

Every day, Prettyman waited in the lane with the coach, never late, never grouching. Whichever way I looked at it, the carriage still resembled a battered collection of driftwood. During those mornings, with the frozen land resembling a cracked china plate, I delivered the sacks of food, threads of clothing or Bibles as required. I no longer cared if the locals scratched themselves or stank of piddle. Questions were always answered with blank stares so in the end I gave up asking.

'I will never understand these people,' I confessed to Prettyman in a moment of candour. 'They take our Bibles but refuse to attend the local church. Every Sabbath that place is like a tomb.'

'Bibles make good kindling,' he replied. 'As for

the church, look there after dark. You might see lights. Candles flickering in the dead of night when not a soul is awake. Everybody is scared. That place is tainted.'

'I don't understand.'

'Ask the parson. Or, if you've not the courage, try asking his wife. It'll take more than luck or persuasion to get a reply, I'll wager. Mrs Proudlove is like the rest of us, more frightened than a rabbit with its head in the snare.'

At the farms, I quelled resentment with the sheer frequency of my visits and the willing offer of hands, both my own and Prettyman's, whenever wood had to be fetched or fires stoked. Working evenings at the parsonage had given me a good touch in the kitchen and more than one flustered wife was grateful for my skills.

'You must not indulge these people,' Marjorie rebuked when I tried to beg an extra jar of preserves. 'They are always dirty and sickly and try to take advantage of our charity.'

I did not argue, but slipped out with a pot of treacle when her back was turned. I also saved some of that night's supper in a square of muslin hidden within the folds of my gown. Next day I took it to the widow who, I'd heard, lived in a squat, white-walled cottage further up the brook. Here, the water spilled in a large pool overhung with willow trees. Prettyman told me her husband had died in the fields, dropped dead under a hot sun with his face muscles twisted into a horrible grimace. But she had a son to look out for her, a strapping lad of thirteen who was already a man before his time. He sometimes brought fish to the table as well as rabbits poached from the woods on the other side of the stream.

'Squire Matthew doesn't much mind,' Prettyman explained. 'Turn a blind eye and you might get a bellyful of rabbit stew for your kindness.'

Betty Hendy was the widow's name. She was digging stones out of a vegetable patch and rose to her feet at the sound of the carriage. Wiping her hands on her apron, she waited whilst Prettyman reined in the team. I stepped out to meet her and immediately wanted to step back in again. For a moment we faced each other across a strip of lawn.

'What's the matter?' she said finally. 'Aren't you going to cover your eyes and run?'

A net of scars cut Betty Hendy's face into ragged squares. Old burns puckered her cheeks like patches of mouldy pastry. Most of her top lip was missing, her teeth a row of stumps squatting in her pink gums.

'No,' I replied. 'I am not going to run away.'

'You're that girl I was told might come calling. A widow like me.'

I nodded, taking in the small, neat garden. Beside a log pile a boy in white shirt and breeches eyed me. He was chopping wood with a handmade tool fashioned from a sliver of plough blade and a stout branch. He swung the implement above his head and brought it down on a chunk of wood, slicing it in two.

Widow Hendy untied her apron. 'You'd best come inside. I have lemonade, or a spit of ale if you've the stomach for something stronger.'

The front door opened on to a square, low-beamed parlour, sparsely furnished but clean and cosy. I was offered the best seat in the room – a polished oak chair with a tall back. After pouring two mugs of ale, Widow Hendy pulled up a stool for herself. 'You want to know why my face looks as it does,' she stated, surmising my thoughts. 'You're wondering if someone did this to me.'

I sipped the ale. I'd had it before on my trips around the farms and found the flat, bitter taste agreeable. I eyed the widow above the rim of the cup. Her hair was bunched up on top of her head in a knot of brassy curls, but a bare, poached-egg patch of scalp clung to the side of her skull. She fingered it absently. 'Nothing has grown here since the accident. The sun gets to it if the day is hot. Mostly I keep it covered.'

'The accident?'

Widow Hendy nodded. 'I suffer convulsions. Have done since I had Peter, my son. I threw a fit and fell face first on to the fire. Peter pulled me off but not before the flames did their work. No great loss. I was always a plain-faced wench. I've got worse scars.'

'You were lucky not to be blinded.'

'I daresay.' She took a long draught of ale. 'Throwing a fit in public is a humbling thing. You piss in your petticoats, choke on your own tongue, have everyone standing around gawping at you. I scared everyone near to death the first time it happened. People thought I was possessed. Not a day passes without my being petrified that I've passed whatever ails me on to Peter. I'm all right so long as he's here to mind me. He knows what to do.'

I took another sip of ale. The yeasty liquid slid easily down my throat. 'Have you no friends?'

Betty set her mug on the stone floor beside her chair. 'I used to go about with a towel over my head. "Ghost-face" the local children called me. That's when they weren't chucking stones. And then I thought: why should I hide? I've no cause to be ashamed of myself. So I walked into the taproom of the inn, and this after the Tuesday market when it was packed to the rafters. I strode right up to the bar, in front of everyone, and told Bill Wheedon, the landlord, to pour me a jug of ale. After he'd stood and stared at me for a minute or so, I asked again and put my money on the counter. I got my beer and took my time drinking it. I never had to buy any more after that. I can't have proper friendship so I've settled for respect. Now I don't hide any more, though I won't normally let strangers into my house.'

'Why did you invite me?'

'Because of that mark on your face. I reckon you know what it's like to be stared at.'

I handed her the packet I'd brought. 'Here are some preserves for you, compliments of the parish.'

'Hmm. Marjorie Proudlove makes these herself. She ought to go into business. 'Tis a more honest trade than being a parson's wife.'

I wanted to ask what she meant by that remark but Peter kept flitting in and out of the cottage. No matter how many jobs he had to do, he was always careful to stay near his mother. Chopping more wood, fetching water in two round-bellied pails, gutting a scrawny chicken – even when stoking the fire his eyes flitted across the room to where she sat and followed her as she crossed to the window or poured hot water from the kettle on its hook above the stove. His muscles were always tense, as if he was ready to pounce. Even whilst I sat with her, he did not relax but prowled catlike around Betty's modest parlour. When I spoke he did not look at me but at his mother, as if afraid something terrible would happen in the split second it took for his eyelids to drop into a blink then rise again. I began to wonder if he was mute but when Widow Hendy offered him a drink he said, 'No thank you' in a thin voice. Mostly though, he let his busy hands do the talking.

Betty was generous with her odd, half-chewed smiles. We joked and swapped stories. I let her treat Prettyman to a mug of ale. She had brewed the drink herself using bits gleaned from the fields when the harvest was finished. Parson Proudlove was never mentioned even when I handed over the clothes he wanted her to mend. I felt disinclined to talk about my guardian. Although I never said as much, I guessed that Betty knew I did not care for him.

'Peter is growing strong,' she remarked, glancing at her son. 'He has talked about starting a farm. My cottage isn't big enough to hold his dreams and he aches to feel his feet on the land. "I'll look after you, mama," he says to me. "I'll take a wife and you'll come and live with us. Together we'll run the farm, have bacon from our own pigs and bread from the wheat I'll grow."'

A shadow crossed her face. 'For all that, he is still a boy and does not realise how deeply into debt he would have to go.'

A tardy spring left the land gripped in a fist of cold all the following week. Parson Proudlove turned his ankle when he slipped on the icy church step and a surgeon was fetched from Wexborough to bind the limb. 'Local quack will bleed you white,' Proudlove flustered. 'If my throat was cut he'd open a vein in a bid to fix it.'

He retreated to his parlour. Marjorie and I helped him into his chair and made sure he had a blanket and bottle of brandy. He snapped at us like an irritable old hound and called for the trunk containing his books and papers, which he spread across his lap. We were ordered to leave and not return unless summoned by the brass hand bell he placed beside the chair.

The night spat out a stranger on to our doorstep. He had come on foot, stumbling along the rutted lane from Dinstock, his way lit by a bleached moon. Mrs Proudlove let him into the kitchen. He stood in front of the fire, blowing life back into his chilled hands. I was at the table finishing a dish of hot oatmeal. Was I supposed to say something? Greet him? Brew coffee? He didn't even glance at me. His face was a rock fall of deep lines and pox scars. A long nose stabbed the air above his thin lips and a tuft of greying beard clung to his chin. Mrs Proudlove went to inform her husband. I kept my eyes on my bowl. Logs cracked open in the hearth, puncturing the silence.

Marjorie returned and beckoned from the doorway. The visitor swept out of the kitchen. Despite the roaring fire, cold clung to his garments as though it had stained the coarse wool. He glanced at me before stooping beneath the door-frame, as if noticing me for the first time.

I finished the oatmeal and put down my spoon. Pleading a headache, I took to my bed. Marjorie gave me a posset and candle before returning to her needlework. She had been trying to persuade her tired fingers to mend a rip in the parson's coat. The needle strayed all over the material and the stitches would have to be unpicked in the morning, but she kept pushing the sliver of metal in and out, in and out. She did not look up when I bid her good night.

In the hall, a flickering strip of light bled from underneath the parlour door. I set the candle down and inched closer. After checking the kitchen door had closed behind me, I pressed an ear against the thick oak and strained to listen. The wood turned the voices beyond into mumbles and a metal flap on the other side of the keyhole thwarted curious eyes.

Frustrated, I picked up the posset and candle and climbed the stairs. Charlotte's room lay above the parlour. I slipped inside like a thief and blew out my light. Kneeling, I pulled back the rug and spread myself out on the floor, laying my head against the bare boards. My years at the Butter House had turned me into an expert eavesdropper. Now I could hear the crackle of the hearth, the rustle of paper and the bump of a chair. Voices ghosted into the room, filling the space with threats and curses.

'You will have to get the girl to do it.' The stranger's voice, spitting daggers. 'We won't stop now just because you can't keep your feet on your own church step. I don't have the men to spare and Ironjack needs the boy before the end of the week. We've lost enough money as it is, Nathaniel. I don't like an empty pocket.'

The clink of a glass, then Parson Proudlove spoke. His throat seemed full of old leather. 'I'll trust her to deliver sacks of potatoes to those beggars in my parish but my gold is a different matter. I've already had cause to put my stick across her back. Now she scrapes to me like a serving wench but her eyes say different. Get a man from the tavern to do it. Some will sell their wives for a shilling.'

'Aye, and flap their tongues to the justices for a crown. Won't look good to have a parson dancing from a gibbet. We need the girl. If things turn sour then she gets the blame. None in these parts would question her guilt.'

A door opened in the hall downstairs. Footsteps padded across the floor. I scrambled up, retrieved the dead candle and crept on to the landing. Marjorie was caught in the light spilling from the kitchen. Her face was lost in shadow but her head was tilted as if she was also trying to hear what was being said beyond that locked parlour door.

I tried to slip back into Charlotte's room. My foot stubbed against a protruding floorboard. I stumbled against the door. The candleholder tumbled out of my fingers and clattered on to the landing.

'Who's there?' Marjorie called up the stairs, voice twittering like a frightened sparrow. 'Juliana, is that you?'

I flattened my back against the wall. Marjorie shuffled along the passage, gown rustling like moth wings. The bottom step creaked. I could sense her peering into the gloom. I pressed harder against the cold stonework and closed my eyes. The silence of the night returned to the dark landing.

Marjorie waited for a few moments then made her way back along the hall. The kitchen door closed. Snatching up the candleholder, I hurried to my room and lay on the bed, not bothering to pull the curtains across the window. Voices whispered through the walls from the parlour. Too faint. The landing clock chimed then chimed again as the night ran its course. Below, the men continued talking.

I huddled against the bedpost with the coverlet drawn around my legs. The last of the season's frost drew patterns across the window. My breath plumed into the moonlit air.

At last the parlour door groaned open.

Daybreak found me hungry. Muscles ached, drums pounded inside my head. I hurried into the freezing kitchen and crammed some cold oatmeal down my throat before coaxing fresh life out of the embers of last night's fire. Marjorie appeared a few minutes later, puff-eyed and shrouded in her night attire. She placed a cup on the table in front of me. The dregs of my posset. 'I found this in Charlotte's room,' she said. 'What were you doing in there?'

I picked up my shoes and started scraping off the dried mud. 'I miss her. I was searching for a keepsake.'

'I miss her too, but I don't want you going in there again.'

I dropped my shoes on to the floor. 'Who was that man? The fellow who marched into this house last night as if he owned it? He eyed me as if I was a harlot, when he troubled to notice me at all.'

'He was a man of the cloth come to discuss parish matters with Nathaniel.'

'No vicar comes calling in the middle of the night, and no church business would keep him talking until cockcrow. He seemed more cut throat than cleric. I could not sleep for his rantings.'

Marjorie paled. 'What did you overhear?'

'Nothing. Just voices.'

'Did my husband not warn you to mind your business?'

'Yes, he did. I still have the marks on my back to remind me.'

'Then be sure to do as he says.'

She picked up the cup and tipped its contents into the slop bucket. 'Nathaniel has other work for you today. Go and see him.'

The parlour was a sour pit of stale pipe smoke and spilled brandy. In the hearth, the fire had choked on its own ashes. Dried soup crusted a bowl. Papers spilled off the table and littered the rug.

The parson waved me to a stool in front of his chair. He fingered his throat whilst I seated myself. His clothes were crumpled and dusted with pipe ash. He coughed as if the rotten air in the room was strangling him.

'No farm rounds for you today,' he began. 'This evening you will go to Eastleigh and fetch a lad whose parents have died. You must take him to his uncle, who is lodging at the Rose Inn. 'Tis a long journey across the length of my parish but there is no one else to look after the lad. Once you've delivered him return directly here, do you understand? Don't stop. Speak to no one on the way.'

'The Rose Inn?' Prettyman frowned. 'I've heard that name before. Many times. Why are we going there?'

'What you might have heard is of no concern to me,' I said, climbing into the coach. 'We are going because Parson Proudlove wishes it. I have no choice in the matter.'

Six miles outside Dinstock one of the horses threw a shoe. Prettyman cursed like a tinker as he clambered down from the driver's seat and fished the shoe out of the mud. He tried to knock it back on with his boot heel while the animal snorted and kicked. I sat on the carriage step, trying not to laugh. The shoe slipped out of his hand and he had to scrabble in the dirt for it. 'Get a move on, you oaf,' I called. 'I would like to get this business done and go home.'

The sun kissed the horizon and dark clouds brewed in the west. My behind ached from trying to keep its place on the seat whilst the bad road took its toll on my patience. My belly was grumbling too. I had nothing but a slice of cheese with which to pacify it.

'We need a smithy,' Prettyman said. 'This shoe will come off again within a few miles.'

'We will continue on our journey. You will have to fix the shoe as best you can. I cannot spare the time.'

'The animals will need to be fed and watered. There is a smithy in Morley, a village not two miles from here. Otherwise this horse could go lame.'

'Then make sure it does not, otherwise I will put you in the harness and you can haul the carriage. Now finish your work. I want to collect our charge before those clouds decide to split above our heads.'

Red circles cut into his cheeks. He held the horse's leg firm as he knocked the shoe back into place. The hammer head broke as the last nail went in. He threw the pieces into the ditch and wiped his hands on the side of his coat. Moisture glistened at the corners of his eyes as if the rains had come early and washed his face with their cold, relentless touch. 'Why don't you like me?'

My face was as harsh as the winter and my heart without a spark of warmth. 'I was a lady once. Even before I married George Proudlove I enjoyed a good roof over my head. You remind me too much of what I've become. In many ways I'm just as poor, just as crippled as you.'

I climbed back into the coach. 'You can be a lady again,' he whispered.

The storm sniffed us out like a hunting dog.

Thick curtains of rain swept along the road and pounded the carriage as if it was a ship on a wild ocean. I thrust my head out into the screaming wind. Hair slapped about my face. I screwed up my eyes and peered into the murk. There: a smudge of light within the grey. Eastleigh. Three miles short stood the crossroads where we were due to collect our charge. It was marked by a hand post that pointed splintered fingers to the four points of the compass.

At first I thought the place was deserted. Prettyman brought the horses to an untidy halt. A figure shifted beside the dyke and staggered to its feet, huddled against the driving rain. Prettyman had lit the carriage lamps. In their doleful light stood a boy of about ten, soaked through despite the heavy coat that shrouded him and shivering fit to crack his teeth. 'Is no one with you?' I shouted, my words snatched up and flung across the encroaching fields.

He shook his head and pulled the coat tight across his chest. I opened the carriage door. It took all my strength to stop it being wrenched out of my fingers. The boy walked like a drunken rooster, both feet sliding on the mud. Before Prettyman had a chance to come and help I caught the lad by the collar and hauled him inside. For the next few moments I battled with the door while the wind howled around my ears. It closed with a thump and I fell back on my seat in a flurry of raindrops. Prettyman immediately set the horses on the road to the Rose Inn.

The boy huddled in the corner with his arms wrapped around his legs, watching as I tried to tug some order back into my hair. He touched the corner of his mouth with one finger and traced a line to his chin. I managed a smile, though Lord knew it was hard. I had enough water down the front of my dress to give myself a bath and my ears were stinging with the cold. I rubbed my chin then held up a clean finger.

'A birthmark,' I told him. 'Nothing more.'

Six miles separated the Eastleigh crossroads from our destination and the boy said nothing, not a word, for the entire journey. Instead he sobbed into his thin fingers like an old man while his sodden clothes spread a puddle of dirty water across the floor. When offered a handkerchief he cringed and covered his head with both arms.

Outside, night swelled like an inkblot across the storm-cracked sky. Open farmland gave way to clusters of trees, branches whipped into a frenzy by the gale. Sometimes the boy ceased his bawling and stared out of the window at the darkening countryside. He'd be a fair-looking lad if all the crying hadn't made red sores of his eyes. Under the coat, his breeches and jacket were of a fine cut, and his hands were free of the calluses that marked the Dinstock farm men.

'Why don't you speak?' I prompted. 'You know I'm not going to hurt you. Even your name would be a start. It's not much to ask, is it?'

He went rigid with fright. I felt like shaking him, to knock a response out of those cold, puckered lips. Immediately I felt ashamed. This boy had lost his parents. He was an orphan like me. Little wonder he burrowed into the corner of the coach and tried to push the world away.

At some point I fell asleep, dragged under by sheer exhaustion. I awoke to darkness and an anxious silence. I sensed the boy staring at me from his corner, though it was too dark to see his face. Some time in the night the storm had died, the clouds squeezing out the last of their rain before moving on.

We had stopped. I poked my head out of the window. Prettyman was struggling with one of the horses, a lantern flickering at his feet. He heard me and looked up. Sweat streaked his brow. 'So you're awake,' he said. 'This animal has thrown its shoe again and this time I can't fix it back on. You should have listened to me. Now I'll have to walk the horses to the Rose Inn and hope I can get a shoe there.'

I yawned and rubbed my eyes. My body was a sack of aches and pains. I wanted hot soup and a warm bed. 'How far is it?'

He dropped the horse's leg, pocketed the broken shoe and wiped his hands on his coat. 'Can't be much more than a mile.' He glanced at the sky. 'It won't rain again tonight. If I can get the horse shod at the Rose you can be back in the parsonage before dawn. Best get back inside and see to the lad.'

I pulled down the blind and the carriage crawled forward. It seemed we had not been underway for more than ten minutes before we halted again. My patience in tatters, I opened the carriage door and jumped into the mud. I got soaked to my ankles for my trouble but I was too angry to care. I wanted this accursed journey fmished and that silent, staring boy in the hands of someone better able to care for him.

Prettyman was up front with the horses, lantern shielded behind his hat. He stared up the road at a cluster of lights and waved me to silence when I tried to speak. 'Can you hear it?' he asked, as I stood and fumed. 'That sound on the air. Like screaming, only worse.'

I listened. There it was, like a cat chorus only deeper and far more threatening. A mixture of voices, human and animal, carrying through the night. I forgot to be angry and I was sorry that I had left the carriage. 'Those lights,' I whispered, 'is that the Rose Inn?'

He nodded, his face a horrible pallor in a loose sliver of lantern light. 'Now I know why I've heard the name before, and what that sound is. I shouldn't have brought you here. Get back inside the coach and I'll take you home. We'll just have to suffer the horse going lame.'

'What is that noise? It is like the devil screaming.' I shivered, wishing I had brought a thicker shawl.

'Dogs, fighting to the death. Behind the inn is a killing pit. A circle of sand, or maybe sawdust. Animals are tossed in to battle it out. Sometimes when the bloodlust gets them they'll chew each other to pieces. The ground turns red with spilled blood. Sit at the front and a torn limb might hit you in the face. The beasts are bred to die in the ring. The place stinks like a flesher's stall.'

'Cockfighting took place each week at Wexborough market,' I pointed out. 'It drew a fair crowd.'

He snorted as if I was an ignorant child.

324

'Cockfighting's too clean for the sort of men that haunt the Rose. Why would your parson have dealings with such a place?'

'Should a man of the cloth not be found amongst sinners?' I countered. 'The boy is to be delivered to his uncle, nothing more.'

Prettyman strode back to the carriage. He held up the lantern, illuminating the interior. I ran after him and peered over his shoulder. The boy shrank further into his corner as if trying to burrow into the panelling. Both hands shielded his face.

'Look at him,' Prettyman growled. 'He's like a rabbit in a fox's jaws.' He put the lantern on the carriage floor and held out his good hand. 'Talk to me, lad. Tell me whom this uncle is you're going to meet.'

The youngster turned his face to the wood-work. 'Satisfied?' I demanded. 'Now you have upset him even more. How am I going to get him out of the carriage when he clings there like a tic on a cur's back?'

Prettyman picked up the lantern and held it in front of my face. 'For all your bluff and bluster, you're just as scared as he is. Let me take you home. I'll speak with the parson. This boy can't go anywhere.'

'Proudlove will thrash the skin from your back and throw you into the ditch. My guardian is not a man who listens well. I know that more than most.'

His eyes hardened. 'How do you know? Does he beat you? Tell me, Juliana. Has he taken his stick to you? Or worse?' I tried to push past him but he caught my arm and spun me around. 'Tell me.'

'Get off.' I pulled free. 'Don't ever touch me again. Drive the last mile or I shall walk. The boy goes with me even if I have to carry him.'

Prettyman climbed back onto the driver's perch. As soon as I was back inside he urged the stumbling horses up the lane. But the fight had not gone out of him yet. Some minutes later the coach clattered to a halt outside the Rose Inn. He caught me at the door as I stepped out. 'Let me go in with you,' he said. 'I'm a better man than I look. My good arm is strong and I can kick like a donkey. This is no time to turn proud on me. The Rose is no place for a woman. You can see that, surely?'

'You have to find a shoe for the horse, you said so yourself. Besides, the coach and team might get stolen. If the customers are spoiling for a fight you will only make matters worse. You're a cripple, whether you like it or not. Don't give anyone an excuse to make sport of you.'

I reached back inside the carriage and grasped the boy by the collar. Exhaustion had put him into a whimpering sleep and he was limp in my arms as I hauled him outside. The chill air brought him round and he remained sullenly obedient whilst I buttoned up his coat and led him towards the inn.

It was going to be another frosty night, the clouds having split apart to reveal the cold mercy of the stars. The air was pregnant with the sounds of barking dogs and yelling men. We both shivered. Glancing back over my shoulder I saw

Prettyman standing with the horses, the carriage whip gripped in his hand. Get a shoe, I mouthed, but if he noticed he didn't let on. I thought I'd smile to reassure him but there was no smile to be found inside me.

The Rose Inn presented a square, brooding face, light spilling out of its eyes and open mouth. I'd be two minutes, no more. I gritted my teeth and pulled the boy along. The door hung askew on its hinges like a drunkard. I banged my head on a low wooden beam. Cloying heat smothered me. Pipe smoke, thick as a fog, swirled between the dozen or so tables. Men sat drinking or gambling with dice, pausing only to lean over and spit on a packed earthen floor littered with dirty straw. Grease and tobacco stained the walls with long brown fingers and a huge fire coughed sparks from a fat stone hearth.

As I edged towards the bar, some men turned to eye me. Others were beyond seeing anything. They sprawled across tables, waxen faces lying in puddles of spilled drink and vomit. A woman giggled in a darkened corner, a coarse, guttural sound, followed by a man's drunken jeer. At the back of the room an open door led outside, presumably to the killing pit. This close, the noise was like a gaggle of howling demons.

Someone pawed my behind as I squirmed between the tables. I jerked away, knocking over a mug. A leering hulk of a man blocked my path, his face cut from ear to ear by a puckered white scar. A gap-toothed grin split his mouth open like a rotten apple. 'A shilling for you,' he growled. 'And two for the boy.'

'Let me through,' I demanded. 'I have business with the landlord. This boy must be delivered safely into his uncle's hands.'

'Uncle is it?' My tormenter snorted. 'I think you and I have other business to settle first.' He reached for my bodice. I braced myself, ready to stick a knee into his crotch. But a well-muscled arm batted his hand away. A thick voice rumbled through the noise and stink of the room.

'Leave her be. She's doing the parson's work. We've enough whores in here, enough even for you, Jimson. Go and see to your dogs. Leave this matter to me.'

Jimson grumbled under his breath, pulled a felt cap down over his matted hair and took himself outside. I turned to face a stout, bald-headed man with a moustache that curled in a hairy grin. A leather apron hung from his neck, stained with spilled ale, dollops of fat and dried blood. He scratched his ear and regarded me with quiet amusement. Despite coming to my rescue, no friendliness lived in his round, rheumy eyes. 'I'm the landlord,' he declared. 'Was I right in thinking the parson sent you?'

I pushed the boy forward. He'd pulled his head down into his coat collar as far as it would go. 'This is the lad from Eastleigh. I will leave him with you and be on my way. Are there any papers to sign?'

The landlord scooped up a bag from the counter and tossed it at me. It jingled when I caught it. 'There's your "papers". See the parson gets 'em.' He laughed and some of the men at the tables joined in. Ears burning, I picked my way back to the front door. Risking a last glance at the boy, I saw him fetch a cuff around the ear before being bundled through a curtain on the other side of the bar. Then the night embraced me. I ran towards the carriage. Behind the inn, the unseen fight intensified, as if a hundred snapping dogs were spilling their lives into the blood-soaked dirt of the killing pit.

Prettyman tried to catch me as I scrabbled for the door. I dodged his outstretched arm and threw myself into the comforting darkness of the coach. 'Take me home,' I ordered. 'Get me away from this filthy place.'

'I couldn't find a shoe. The stables were full of dog pens. The beasts are half starved.'

'I don't care. We'll just have to risk the horse.'

He hesitated, his boot on the mounting step. 'Where is the boy?'

'Where he belongs. Now get on the road.' Still he wouldn't move. 'Do it, Prettyman. A word from me to the parson and you'll never work or hold lodgings in this parish again.'

He reached up and tugged his forelock. 'Yes, Miss Juliana. Whatever you say.'

The door slammed. I sank back on to the seat, low sobs slipping out of my throat like blood oozing from a wound. The reins clicked and the carriage lurched forward, the shoeless horse trotting unevenly between the shafts. The sounds of savagery faded with each slow, painful mile.

About half an hour later the coach drew to a gentle halt. The bag I had collected at the inn felt heavy in my lap. I pulled open the drawstring and tipped it up. A welter of coins tumbled into the hollow of my gown.

The door opened. Prettyman's face appeared framed within a starlit rectangle of night. 'I need to know what happened back there,' he said. 'If some ill had befallen you it would be my head in the stocks.'

He held up the lantern, swallowing the stars in a yellow halo. I squinted at him, saw the blood drain from his haggard face as he stared at my lap. Gold glimmered in the folds of my dress.

'That child wasn't adopted,' he whispered, and I could be Judas himself for all the accusation in his words. 'He's been bought. And you made me take him to that godawful place. I hope the parson rewards you well.'

The door shook on its hinges as he slammed it on my stupid, sinning face.

'Charles...'

But he had already clambered back on to the driver's seat. A second later the carriage trundled forward again.

Chapter Sixteen

A hand pummelled my shoulder. 'Wake up, Juliana. Hurry and put some clothes on.'

The coverlet was pulled off the bed. Cold air swept across my legs. I opened a bleary eye. Marjorie's taut face hovered above me. 'What's wrong?' I mumbled.

Already she had my wardrobe door open and

was tossing garments on to the bed. 'Lady Elizabeth has taken ill. She asked for you. We are to go at once.'

I swung my legs over the edge of the mattress and rubbed sleep out of my eyes. The curtains had been thrown wide and the sun was a yellow eye stabbing me with daggers of light. 'What ails her? Can her surgeon not deal with it? I thought she paid a handsome fee for the ministrations of some local quack?'

In one deft movement, Marjorie snatched the hem of my shift and hauled it over my head. Despite the bright day outside my bedchamber was an ice pit. I dressed as quickly as I could, fingers struggling with some of the fastenings.

'At first they thought it was a fever, one of those seasonal things that has you sneezing into a handkerchief for a week,' Marjorie explained. 'But something has gone bad inside her. The doctor is at a loss. She has been desperately ill for hours and Squire Matthew fears for her life. With my husband away and the vicar of Eastleigh laid up with gout it falls on us to offer what spiritual succour we can.'

My clothes felt stale and clammy. I crammed my feet into a pair of shoes.

'The messenger from Dinstock Hall was sick with worry,' Marjorie continued. 'Squire Matthew is beside himself. Elizabeth is very dear to him.'

I combed the tugs out of my hair. The looking glass was turned to the wall. I did not care for the reflection it gave – a haggard peasant girl with tired red hair, gaunt, haunted face and bruised-looking eyes. My birthmark stood out in a livid

331

welt against my pale skin. With no rouge, I pinched my cheeks to bring the blood up and tied my lifeless hair with a scrap of ribbon.

We journeyed to Dinstock Hall in my old carriage driven by Charles Prettyman. I had no heart for this errand. Too many people in the surrounding farms were already sick to the gills for me to feel much sympathy for the squire's wife. Though I still made occasional visits to local smallholdings my duties had been restricted since the night of the Rose Inn. 'We have given all we can for the time being,' the parson said. He had been furious with Prettyman over the shoeless horse. As feared, the animal had gone lame and was useless for weeks afterwards. If not for his own injured leg, Proudlove would have taken his stick to my hapless driver. And it was my fault.

The parson was now on the mend. The local blacksmith had bound his leg and fashioned crutches for him to hobble around on. I made no more night-time visits to the Rose.

The bell tower of Dinstock church slipped past the carriage window. 'I can't imagine what Lady Elizabeth wants with you,' Marjorie remarked, examining her nails. 'You're hardly schooled in church matters.'

'Perhaps it is for Emma's sake,' I suggested.

'Emma has Mr Fairchild to look out for her. You haven't visited Dinstock Hall for some time. She'd be better served in the company of a man who loves her rather than a sour-faced widow.'

'Sometimes women need each other.'

'Mr Fairchild gives her all she needs.'

'I am sure you are right, Mrs Proudlove.'

I'd had my fill of Adam Fairchild. Marjorie slipped his name in to conversations as easily as she might comment on the weather. She talked about the happy couple over dinner, at the fireside, on the way to church. I was force fed stories of Fairchild's charm and gallantry, of how a country girl like Emma was lucky to land such a fine catch. When I mentioned that he was the scandal of Wexborough society my words were wasted in the air.

These days I saved my breath and let the paragon remain on his pedestal. Since leaving Dinstock Hall in near disgrace I had not set eyes on Fairchild. Talk was rife in the village – not the idle gossip of farmhands or milkmaids, but dark snatches of conversation whispered above gin mugs and behind bolted doors. Our maid was being courted by a cellar boy who worked at the inn and he liked to scare her with tales of what went on behind the Tudor façades of Dinstock Hall. Lazy as the girl often was, her tongue could never keep still. She passed on these rumours whilst I supped with her in the kitchen or we collected kindling from the woods.

'Miss Emma Jane has taken the devil himself to her bed,' she told me in the silence of the trees. 'He likes to hurt her, do unnatural things that ain't fit for a man and woman. Mary Clark, who delivers bread to Dinstock's kitchens, says she saw Miss Emma lying on a pile of straw in the stable like she was dead. Marks covered her face and neck, like one of the dogs had got her. 'Tis said that Fairchild fellow has bewitched Squire Matthew and Lady Elizabeth and that he won't stop his perversions until Miss Emma has split her womb birthing him a trough of bastards.'

'Your country superstitions sicken me,' I told her, gathering up some deadwood. She laughed, nudging twigs into a pile with her bare feet.

''Tis also said the more Mr Fairchild hurts Miss Jane, the more she likes it. I've heard he's ridden her like a mare across her own parlour carpet. He's tupped Lady Elizabeth too – took her whilst the squire was out and her daughter asleep in the room next door. I'm thinking there'll be bastards born on all sides at Dinstock Hall.'

'Don't think. You are not very good at it.' I picked up the last of the kindling and tramped back to the house. Behind me, the maid's mulish laughter echoed through the woods.

Outwardly, Dinstock Hall had not changed. The carriage halted at the front steps. No footman scuttled out to welcome us. Squire Matthew himself opened the door. The stink of grief hung around him, a tired, wasted smell that clung to his clothes. Loose skin sagged from his neck and jowls. 'Thank God you have come,' he said.

We kept silent as he led us to an upstairs bedroom. Lady Elizabeth lay in a sprawling four-poster, her small frame shrouded beneath an embroidered coverlet. The windows were shut tight, the curtains closed. A candle sputtered yellow light over her face.

'No servants,' Squire Matthew flustered. 'Lizzie won't allow anyone in except the surgeon and myself. But she keeps asking for the widow girl.'

Lady Elizabeth eyed us from within a mountain of white pillows. Her eyes were cold ashes staring out of a pinched mask. Lips split apart into a worn smile. She tried to lift a hand in greeting.

'Lie still, m'lady. This is a very delicate business.' A man in a sharp coat and white-ribboned wig leaned over her, his nose clutched by a pair of spectacles. He had opened a vein in her arm and was letting blood pour into a porcelain bowl. On a table beside the bed was a leather wallet glittering with metal scalpels and a tourniquet fashioned from a strip of linen.

Marjorie scurried to the other side of the bed and took Lady Elizabeth's free hand in her own. The surgeon secured the tourniquet and laid the bowl, brimming with crimson, next to the wallet.

'I am dying,' Lady Elizabeth whispered. 'Nothing this oaf can do will prevent it.'

Her voice was like a sigh on the wind. She did not move her head as she spoke, as if even that small effort was too much.

'A fever, m'lady, nothing more.' Marjorie clucked. 'This changeable weather has us all out of sorts. The winter was greedy. It didn't want to let go. Now we are left with headaches, sour bellies – all sorts of devilments. Rest and prayer will have you on your feet.'

The surgeon looked up and frowned. I dithered at the foot of the bed, trying not to gag at the fetid smell thickening the room. Every puff of air Lady Elizabeth exhaled carried the reek of decay.

'We have prayed for you,' Marjorie continued, stroking that flaccid hand. 'God will help.'

Lady Elizabeth gave a dry, bitter laugh. 'God was driven from this house months ago. We drove Him out with our avarice and let the devil take his place. Why should He return to help me now?'

'You don't mean that. The fever is talking through you.'

The hand was pulled free. 'You are a worthless fool, Marjorie. Let me speak to the widow girl. She has intelligence, a spark of fire, everything you lost as a girl. Get away from my bed.'

Stricken, Marjorie stumbled away from the four-poster. Lady Elizabeth beckoned me to her side and clasped my hand in her cold fingers. Four words were whispered into my ear.

'Emma is with child.'

She was in the parlour with her lover, her swelling womb pushing out the waist of her loosened gown. Hair hung in lank, greasy strands around her cheeks. She resembled a rug that someone had pegged up and beaten the life out of.

Fairchild was reading a newspaper. A half-empty glass of port lay on the table beside him. He folded the paper and consulted his pocket watch. 'Ah, a reluctant visitor,' he said, noticing me for the first time. 'How fares Lady Elizabeth?'

'She has fallen asleep,' I replied. 'The surgeon is still with her. Do you intend to marry Emma?'

His cheeks were powdered the colour of white marble, his mouth a scarlet gash that cut a tooth-ringed hole into his face. A bleeding heart had been painted below his temple. Gold and silver rings glinted on his fingers. A green velvet coat topped a pair of sharp riding breeches and soft leather boots gripped his calves. A dandy dressed for the hunt. 'Fetch me another fill of port,' he said. 'I have a thirst fit to crack my throat.'

'I am not your servant.'

Emma stood behind him. She leaned over and circled his neck in lace-wreathed arms and rested her cheek on the crown of his head. Adam regarded me with glittering shark's eyes.

'Port,' he repeated. 'Now.'

Marjorie found me sitting at the bottom of the staircase snorting tears into a handkerchief. I told her I was upset over Lady Elizabeth. 'Go home,' she instructed. 'I'll stay here with the squire and his family. Nothing more can be done for m'lady. You'll be sent for if she wakes and asks for you again.'

I dried my face and waited outside whilst Marjorie sent a footman to fetch my driver. In the lifetime it took for Prettyman to bring the coach around from the stable yard, I spied Fairchild and Emma watching from the parlour window. Her arms were still draped around him. She smiled at me then smothered his face in elaborate kisses.

'But I have a secret, Emma,' I whispered, as a sudden gust caught my hair and spun it into windmills of copper. 'I know your lover. I've heard the lies he's woven. You won't wear that smile for much longer. Not once you've seen what's behind those eyes.'

This house was sick. A poison had wormed its way under the doors and through the windows. It had knocked Lady Elizabeth off her feet and turned Squire Matthew into a flustered, finger-kneading ploughboy. No contagion this, but a malady of the heart, and it was burrowing into Emma.

The sun fled. Clouds rolled over the sky in a dark wave. Raindrops spat on the white gravel and smeared the tall windows of Dinstock Hall. A drumming of hooves and the carriage drew up. Prettyman scrambled from the roof, bad arm flapping at his side. 'Don't bother with the step,' I told him. I tried to hoist myself inside but my skirts caught on something and I stumbled back on to the drive. He made to catch me with his good hand but I shrugged him off.

'You've been crying again,' he said.

'Just take me home.' I pulled myself inside at the second try and slammed the door.

Rain. Another unrelenting downpour. I gazed dismally at the wet curtain swishing across the open fields. The carriage slid and bumped along the exposed lane. The horses seemed to be crawling. Each yard felt like a mile. I stood up and banged on the roof. 'Hurry up. I want to be home before I drown!'

'The road is treacherous,' Prettyman shouted back. 'The ruts have filled with water and I can't tell how deep they are. We could get bogged down, or one of the horses might catch a hoof in a pothole. They're struggling as it is.'

'Then I will get another horse. And perhaps another driver.'

Prettyman slapped the reins and our pace increased a notch. I plumped back down on the seat and folded my arms. He was a fool. An ignorant cripple who tried to put himself on equal terms with other men.

The carriage lurched. Springs groaning, it listed like a sinking ship. I thrust my head out of the window. Swirling mud was only inches from the bottom of the door. We had ground to a halt, the horses snorting as they pulled on their harnesses. Prettyman threw down the reins and jumped into the lane. He checked all around the carriage then splashed over to my window. 'We're buried to the axle. I warned you this could happen.'

I ignored the rebuke. 'Can you free us?'

His head slipped out of sight then reappeared. 'The axle itself looks good and I don't reckon the wheel's broken. If you climb on to the roof and work the reins with me pushing from the back then we might get her out.'

'I am not going to suffer a drenching just to save you a bit of work. There must be another way. You're the driver, think of something. It's what you are paid for.'

'I ain't paid a penny for what I do. Remember that next time you don't want to get your feet wet.' He checked the lane. Our route crossed a high point in the surrounding farmland. 'I can see a thicket of gorse about half a mile ahead. If I can break some off it'll go under the wheels and give better purchase. This mud is treacherous. I can't do any more until the rain's eased.' He glanced at the sky. 'The clouds are breaking up over to the west. This downpour won't last but the blackest cloud is right above us.'

As if to confirm his words, the rain intensified into a hammering sheet that beat against the carriage with a million tiny fists. Prettyman pulled open the door. A shower of freezing water shivered around my feet. He tried to climb inside. I caught him with my heel and shoved him back into the lane. 'You're not to come in here. Find another place to shelter. Go and crawl under one of the horses.'

He rubbed the top of his shin. I grabbed the door, ready to slam it. He reached back inside, grabbed my sleeve with his good hand and pulled. I tumbled out of the coach as if I weighed nothing and landed on the verge.

He's going to hit me, I thought. Self-control seemed to have fled Prettyman's face. His fingers curled into a taut fist. His teeth were bared, his neck muscles bunched like knotted rope. He tore off his hat and threw it into the mud with a savagery that made me flinch.

'I won't take you any further, Juliana Rodriguez, Mrs Proudlove or whatever you want to call yourself. Not another inch. Though it might cost me the only job I've ever had I'd sooner sleep in a barn and eat with pigs than stand your company another mile. You cut my peace to ribbons with your poisoned tongue.'

Rain plastered his black hair to his scalp and streamed down his face. He held his hand out as though pleading. 'What happened to make you so bitter, to give you such a hateful, twisted view of everyone? Nothing can pull a smile from your sour face. What dark things haunt you? How can I ever drive them away?'

My gown was already drenched, my own hair hung in tangled knots. I faced Charles Prettyman and wished him into his grave. 'I wanted love and

340

got hatred. I longed for kisses but received bruises. Instead of truth I was lied to, instead of being cherished I was abused. No one cares, cripple boy. Does that answer your question?'

'You won't let anyone care. You shut yourself up inside your head and spit at the world. I've never knowingly crossed you, yet you curse me to my face and trample over what little pride I have left. Did you expect me to thank you for that? Did you expect me to like you?' He shook his head. 'Something ails you that's beyond the help of any preacher or surgeon. I pity you.'

'Pity? From a servant?'

'Yes, a servant. Not a slave to hatred. You can walk back to the parsonage and if you drown or break your leg in a rut it's no longer any concern of mine. I'll unharness the horses and ride back with them. Someone can fetch the carriage once the rain's eased off.'

He walked away. His figure soon blurred in the downpour. His name was on my lips before I knew what I was doing and when he did not stop I said it again. My eyes were full of water. He paused, looked over his shoulder. Then he came running back. But when he reached out I pulled away. I could not bear his hand on me. Not yet.

'I don't know who I am,' I whimpered. 'Or where I come from. All I have is a name and a story told to me by a sailor that may or may not be true. Everyone wants me for their own ends as if I have no right to choose for myself what I want to do with my life. I am worse than a dog with a rope for a collar.'

'You've called me an oaf, a fool and a cripple,'

he said. 'That last part is true. I'm ignorant about a lot of things but that's different from being stupid. I've been foolhardy more times than I dare count. Sometimes I've made the right choices. Whatever happens, this is the life I've got and I don't moan about it.'

He hooked my sleeve with his finger. 'Come inside the carriage. You don't belong out here in the mud. The rain will stop soon and then I will take you home.'

'The parsonage is not my home. It's just a place where I live.'

'Better than nothing, Miss Juliana. For now.' He slid his good arm around my waist and lifted me back inside. I didn't protest when he climbed in after me and closed the door. Dirty water pooled on the floor. But the coach offered a haven out of the downpour. We could hear one another's breathing even through the ceaseless hammering on the roof.

I shivered like a petrified rabbit. My gown clung to me in a shroud. Charles tucked himself up against me and warmth seeped into my drenched skin. We both laughed at our dripping wet hair. From somewhere inside the folds of his coat he found a strip of clean linen and wiped my face while I sat like a child. He brushed my face with his fingers. I flinched again.

'No,' he whispered. 'I won't touch you that way, I promise.' He shifted on the bench. His leg pressed against mine. 'Are you scared because I want to be kind to you?' he continued. 'Afraid that my kindness will unbar some of those doors you've locked yourself behind? Maybe you need to let a bit of fresh air into your soul.'

'Listen to you,' I teased. 'A country sage in muddy boots.'

'My mama said I had to speak well or not at all.' He stroked my forehead, a gesture that would earn us both a beating if Parson Proudlove ever got to hear of it. 'There must be someone who knows about your past.'

I shivered again. 'There is.'

During the last days of Lady Elizabeth's life, I was called back to Dinstock Hall to help Marjorie attend her. Since my guardian had no authority over the Hall staff, she took to ordering me about. I fetched towels, water by the bucketful and took soiled linen down to the kitchens where it was boiled in a big metal tub.

The surgeon bled his patient white and filled her throat with vile concoctions. At night her bedchamber was filled with whispered prayers. She smelled of death. I covered my ears whilst she screamed for hours at a time. Her arms flailed as whatever badness was killing her ate up her insides. Squire Matthew hung around her bed with a face like a crumpled blanket, muttering, 'Oh dear, oh dear,' until the surgeon, in irritation, ordered him from the room.

Emma was not at her mother's bedside when she died. Adam Fairchild had taken her to a ball in Wexborough. She had bought a new gown for the occasion and had filched Lady Elizabeth's best necklace from her jewellery box.

Three days after the internment in the Jane family vault, I resumed my visits to the district farms and hamlets. Everyone was full of talk. They treated me as if they could scent death clinging to my skirts.

'You were at the house the night she died,' one farmer's wife said. 'You there and her daughter gone off with some rake. 'Tis not right.'

'I had no say in it.'

'I've heard Squire Matthew is a broken man,' the old clod persisted. 'The estate could be sold off and us along with it. The church has already put in an offer for the land. My husband's worked this farm all his life, as did his father before him. I've a right to be afraid.'

I gave her a sack of flour and some parish clothes, then left.

Last call of the day was to the Widow Hendy. I was in no hurry to return to the parsonage, especially as I had not seen the widow for some weeks. Charles Prettyman whistled a merry tune as he eased the carriage down the narrow track to her cottage. His good spirits lifted my gloom.

Spring had been forced into retreat by a cold north wind but no smoke drifted from the cottage chimney. Widow Hendy always favoured a generous hearth, even on the milder days and Peter more often than not would be outside chopping logs.

The garden was empty, the vegetable patch churned up, the seedlings trampled. Wheel tracks rutted across the square of lawn that was the only luxury the widow and her son had enjoyed.

Charles stopped whistling. A face peeked out from behind drawn curtains. I climbed out of the coach and picked my way across the garden.

Battered plants littered the grass. Hoof marks crisscrossed the path. Muddy footprints trailed back and forth from the front door. Careless damage wrought by men who had other things on their minds than looking out for a few vegetables. Broken glass yawned a jagged mouth from one of the window frames. The front step was a swamp of dried muck. I banged on the door. Charles had settled the horses and was already hurrying across the lawn.

The door groaned open. Betty Hendy's face was a broken mess of lank hair, tear-streaked cheeks and bloody eyes. A plum-coloured bruise hugged the left side of her face and her dress was ripped in several places. Even with the fresh air at my back I caught her stink and the parlour behind her looked cold and dusty, even with the curtains closed.

'What do you want?' she demanded, clutching her tattered bodice.

'Betty, what has happened? Were you robbed?'

'Robbed, yes I was robbed.'

'Where is Peter?'

She covered her face with her hands. 'My son is gone.'

'I should not have let you in. I should have shut the door in your face and put the bar across it. You live with that man, eat food from his table and sleep under his roof. You're as guilty as he is and I'd curse you to your face if I did not think it could mean more trouble for me.'

I shifted on the squat wooden stool. Widow Hendy paced the rug, anger and terror fighting for control of her face. Cold ashes had turned to powder in the hearth and a half-eaten plate of mouldy food drew the first of the season's flies. 'What trouble? You are talking in riddles, Betty. I am your friend.'

She rounded on me, finger stabbing the air. 'I don't want your friendship. I want Peter back and if you had a spit of influence over that devil you would not have let him steal my son away.'

She started walking again, wiping her mouth with her sleeve. 'Where were you when the men came with the parson at their head? Where were you when this mighty pillar of the church violated me, slapped my face and called me a slut before taking the only thing I had not been willing to give him?'

'The parson did this? But he is in Bristol on church business.'

Contempt dripped from her voice. 'You really are the innocent, ain't you? His cut-throats put a rock through my window because I tried to bar the door. Then he ploughed me the way a farmer turns over a field. I bit and scratched and kicked. All I got for my pains was a black eye. "Cause trouble and we'll have the rest of this hovel down about your ears," that's what I was told. I daresay I should be grateful they didn't all take turns with me.'

'Betty...'

'Proudlove ended up going to Bristol, right enough. A merchant lives up in Clifton, a man with no son of his own. He'll pay handsomely for a strong boy like Peter. I had to sign the papers – sign my son away. I'd no choice. I've not an ounce of courage or a strip of pride left. I can't go to the magistrate. Everything has been done legally. Who'd doubt the word of a parson against the likes of me?'

'He sold your son?'

'Sons, daughters, infants – he sells them all. But I never thought he'd touch a village child. "Ill-bred peasants" is what he calls us. Peter is strong with a good head on him. Too tempting for that whoreson.'

'Perhaps Peter will find a way to return home. He's bound to try.'

'If he does he'll be flogged and me along with him. Proudlove threatened to take his stick to me if I ever tried to fetch him back. You're scared of the parson too. It's on your face. You must have felt his anger, seen what he can do. I'm frightened. More frightened than I've ever been in my life.'

'My driver will light a fire and clean up your house.' I gestured at her torn dress. 'I've one or two garments left in the coach that might fit you.'

'Keep your leftover rags along with the rest of your charity. I used to spend the evenings with my son beside that hearth. No fire will burn there again.' I reached for her hand but she pulled away. 'Don't touch me.'

'Why, Betty?' I asked, knocked stupid by the things she had told me. 'Why did he do this to you? Why not just take the boy and go?'

Her eyes spat hatred. 'Because I am in debt to his church. This plot of land, the house, every-thing is his. He charges rents I can't pay and if I tried to move out his bailiffs would have my chattels sold and both of us in the debtors' prison.

347

I was only twenty-five years of age when I became a widow. My man was barely in the ground before Proudlove came debt collecting. He took me on my own bed, the bed I'd shared with my husband, while I was still wearing my mourning gown. I've been paying debts ever since.'

'Did your son know about this?'

'Of course not, otherwise he would've tried to do something stupid and got himself hung.' Her lips pulled back from her teeth. 'Perhaps Peter is better off where he is, where he won't see his mother's shame.'

On the way back to the parsonage I tapped on the roof and had Charles halt the coach. I climbed out to meet him as he jumped down from the driver's seat. 'Why do you work for Parson Proudlove?' I asked. 'A good, strong-witted coachman can surely find work elsewhere, bad arm or not. There's more able-bodied men have less skill with the reins and less chance of persuading a stubborn horse to pull a carriage out of a rut.'

'I have to work for him.' Charles took off his hat and mopped his forehead. 'I'm in debt to his church.'

'You are in debt to him?'

'That's right, near enough the whole county is.'

Mrs Proudlove was in the kitchen cutting vegetables. Through the open window came the maid's tuneless whistling and the swish of a broom on the back step. 'You're late,' Marjorie said, slicing a fat turnip in two.

I slipped off my shoes and placed them beside

the hearth. 'What happens to the children?'

'What children?'

'The ones that get taken away?'

'Away?'

'Yes, to the Rose Inn.'

She chopped the turnip into cubes and dropped them into a pot. 'The winters are always hard and sickness is rife. Many children are orphaned, in fine houses as well as the farms. Last year Mrs Yelland – daughter of a local parliamentarian, no less – took sick and withered like a bloom without water. She left two young sons. With no surviving relatives, a husband at sea for five years and a father in his grave for two, other homes had to be found for her children.'

The pan hissed as she hung it from the crane and pushed it over the fire. 'Sometimes whole families are buried in a single plot. The soil is barely turned on one unfortunate before another is laid to rest. These are harsh times, despite Nathaniel's good work. Now go and find a clean apron and help me with the dinner.'

I did not move from my place at the table. 'It seems that mothers don't have to die to lose their children.'

'Whatever do you mean?'

'Falling in debt to the church seems cause enough. Don't feign ignorance, Marjorie. Sons and daughters are sold like cattle. Peddled to wealthy merchants, ladies with barren wombs or titled men who cannot father an heir. 'Tis not God's work your husband is about but a trade in flesh. That is why he sent Charlotte away. She knew about the Bad Place, the Rose Inn, where the children are taken and sold on. I've carried the parson's blood money in my own hands.'

Marjorie slapped a side of beef down on the tabletop and began sawing with a knife. Sweat prickled her brow. She grunted like an old woman climbing a steep hill. 'Charlotte will return within the month, when the weather is kinder.'

'I doubt you'll see your daughter again, not while the parson runs his errands in the night.'

'He wouldn't harm Charlotte.'

'No, but he would sell her. You too if there was an extra shilling in it.'

A sound trickled out of the back of her throat. Hair caged her face in limp, greying strands as she bent over her work. The meat had been hewn into ragged strips. Not even a dog would find that mangled food fit to eat. I leaned over to see her face. Her mouth was carved into a grimace, the eyes shining.

'You have been listening to the gossip of farmers' wives,' she said. 'Those women are idle and dirty – too stupid to live any better than the scrawny animals they rear. They don't deserve to be mothers. Other women are more fit for the task.'

'You knew it was going on,' I accused. 'You have always known.'

The knife cut into the tabletop, gouging brittle splinters that showered on to the floor. Finally, the blade snapped. The edge sliced into her palm. 'See what you made me do,' she cried, dripping blood on to her apron.

'You did it to yourself. God knows what other harm you've done.'

'I did my duty by my husband, which is more

than you can say, you spiteful wretch. I want you out of this house. Pack your belongings and take yourself to the church stables. Nathaniel will deal with you when he returns.'

I fled the kitchen and ran upstairs. Working quickly, I spread my belongings out on the bed. More than my one small bag could carry. I chose what I thought was essential, stuffed the bag to bursting and fastened the straps.

Downstairs I paused in the hallway. I could hear Mrs Proudlove moving around in the kitchen. I opened the front door, spat on the knob, then slipped outside. The walk to Dinstock was the longest mile of my life. Charles was in the church stables, grooming the horses. He spotted me standing in the open doorway, scuffed bag in my hand. 'Mrs Proudlove turned me out,' I explained. 'I can't say I'm unhappy about it.'

He put down the brush and grinned. 'That tongue of yours never stops getting you into trouble. Well, you can stay with me if you want. No doubt the village scolds will have plenty to say but any bed is better than the ditch. But first there's something you need to know...'

Chapter Seventeen

'Someone has been asking for you in the village. He wouldn't give his name. I heard it from the wheelwright, Tom Bryant. He says the fellow was poking around the inn, a man with muscles like

351

knotted rope and scars around both wrists. He wanted to know where you lived. Tom said that as far as he knew you were still at the parsonage with Nathaniel Proudlove and his family.' Charles eyed me from beneath the brim of his hat. 'Any notion who this fellow is?'

'Perhaps it is one of George Proudlove's old creditors,' I replied. 'My husband left a debt far bigger than his fortune when he died but no doubt there are those who believe he did not entirely leave me penniless.'

Charles was silent for a moment. He led me along the cinder path that skirted Dinstock church to a low roofed stone hut that squatted by a rusted gate set into the wall. The building had a graveyard for a garden and a door of oak panelling stripped from a carriage. 'My palace,' Charles announced, taking out a heavy iron key and shoving it into the makeshift lock. ''Tis as old as the church, built from broken pieces of stone and leftover timber. Gravediggers used it for some years but they have cottages in the village now and there wasn't any sense in letting the place stand empty.'

He nudged the door open with his boot and gestured me inside. I had to stoop under the sagging lintel. It took a few moments for my eyes to adjust in the thin light seeping through the shuttered windows. A square room with a stove in the corner. A chipped wooden dresser, a bare stone floor and narrow bunk. Everything was makeshift but clean. A scent of dried herbs tinted the air.

Charles breezed in after me, lifted the bar on

the shutters and swung them open. Daylight pierced the murk. Slivers of old stained glass, along with a few bottle pieces, had been used to patch up the window. It mottled everything in hues of red, green and brown. 'I've a kettle and packet of coffee,' he said. 'Or if you prefer, a nip of ale is tucked away in the bottom drawer of the dresser. You can draw water from the butt beside the door. The baker gives me his leftover bread and I've laid rabbit snares in the strip of woodland that runs alongside the churchyard.'

He thumped the wall with his fist. 'Two feet thick. Stove only needs a couple of logs chucked in to keep this place hearty. Dinstock Hall it ain't but you can have all the peace you want. No one ever comes here, not nowadays.'

'What about the church?'

'The door's always locked and the parson has the key.'

'And the lights you mentioned?'

'I don't see them.'

'Why don't you see them?'

'I look the other way. I've been looking the other way for the past three years. Like I told you, I'm scared.'

I sat on the bed. The straw mattress shifted under my weight. 'You are not going to tup me, Charles Prettyman. I will make that clear now. I'll live under your roof but I won't share this strip of a bed.'

'You think I'd want to, do you? Think I've never had a woman before, that no one would be interested in a cripple?' He laughed. 'Ain't nothing wrong with me where it counts, as some have found to their joy.'

He tossed the door key on to the woollen bed blanket. 'I'll sleep in the stables. Should be warm enough now that spring is coming. The horses will keep me company.'

I fingered the key. 'I will have to face the parson.'

'He won't beat you, I promise.'

'You haven't felt that stick across your back.'

'That may be, but I won't stand by and let him hurt you again.'

'You are in debt. You said so yourself. He could have you thrown into gaol. How can you stand up to Proudlove if you are afraid of a few flickering lights in a church in the middle of the night? He's got you, Charles. Like he almost had me.'

Prettyman sat down on the bed beside me. His bad arm was tucked inside his coat and the other rested on his knee. 'Some might say I ought to be grateful to Proudlove. He took me in after my parents died and gave me what I have now in exchange for menial work.'

'That was very charitable of him.'

'Charity?' Prettyman laughed bitterly. 'He kept me only because I couldn't be sold on. Not even a sweep would take me as his boy. Now I am the parson's dog to fetch and bark as he sees fit. But I promised it wouldn't be for ever and that's a vow I aim to keep.'

I slipped my fingers into his hand, felt the hard flesh and rough edges of calluses. 'My father was hanged. I don't know who my mother was. Chances are that I am a bastard. I am no better than you, Charles. I know what it's like to be unwanted.'

'You're better than a queen,' he said, 'and prettier than an angel.'

I laughed and let go of his hand. 'An angel? Clothed in a homespun mourning gown with a cherry-coloured birthmark running down my chin? There are those who would call me a witch.'

'Are you?'

I wasn't sure if he was teasing me. He rose, donned his cap and lifted the door latch. 'Fresh kindling is in the box by the fire, the log pile is underneath the window and you'll find water in the jug on top of the dresser. I'll see if I can get a scrap of beef and some milk. This is no lady's parlour but it's yours for as long as you want it.'

'Here.' I handed back the door key. 'I won't lock you out of your own house. I trust you.'

He stared at the key then looked up, mouth tight. 'If that's so, why did you lie to me?'

'Lie?'

'Yes, when you said you didn't know anything about the stranger who's been asking about you in the village.'

'Why do you believe I wasn't telling the truth?'

'You wouldn't look at me, and your voice was all wrong. A child could've seen it.' He tossed the key back on to the bed. 'You don't trust me enough.'

A pounding on the door woke me from a troubled sleep. Dawn poked a bleary eye through a chink in the shutters. I shivered in the cool morning air.

The hammering continued. Urgent, demanding.

Yawning, I threw back my patched coverlet and padded barefoot across the stone floor to the window. Opening the shutter a fraction, I peered outside. A young woman stood at the door wearing a bonnet and shawl. Distress pinched her face.

I shoved my arms into an old overcoat and unlocked the door just as her fist rose to beat another tattoo on the wood. 'What do you want?' I demanded, rubbing the sleep out of my eyes. 'Charles Prettyman is not here. You will find him at the church stables, if he is not already out on the day's work.'

'Beg your pardon, madam, but it's you I'm after.'

I frowned. She looked familiar but a hundred such faces could be found around the county. Behind her, the last of the morning's mist seeped into the ground.

'I'm from Dinstock Hall,' she continued. 'I was Lady Elizabeth's maid. I'm here to tell you Miss Emma's baby is coming.'

'It can't be. Not so soon.'

The girl nodded. 'Two months before its time. Miss Emma was with child long before she told anyone. Turns out she was hiding the signs. Even though, the baby's still early.'

'Well, it is a matter for the surgeon or midwife, not me. Is Mr Fairchild not present?'

She grimaced. Dampness clung to her clothes with shivering, clammy hands. 'He's there, right enough, and I pity Miss Emma all the more for it. I remember you from your visits to the Hall. You were kind to her, tried to be friends when she hadn't a friend in the world.'

'That was a long time ago. I am not wanted now.'

'Please go anyway. The housekeeper will let you in.'

'What of Squire Matthew?'

'Off in Bristol. He doesn't care about his daughter. M'lady's death has broken him.'

'How am I to travel? Did you bring a carriage?'

'No, madam. Squire Matthew has the coach. Lady Elizabeth's gig has a broken axle and no one knows where Mr Fairchild's driver has gone.'

'So I am to trek three miles there and another three back?'

The maid shrugged. 'I'll walk with you, madam. It's all I can do.'

I arrived at the Hall muddied, footsore, and with a temper that could slice marble. The maid had jabbered incessantly into my ear until I'd threatened to throw her into the ditch. It was all 'Miss Emma' this and 'Miss Emma' that and 'isn't Mr Fairchild such a terrible fellow?'

The housekeeper met us at the front door and ushered us inside. 'Miss Emma has had a daughter,' she told me. 'An easy birth, praise God. The midwife has already left.'

'Where is Emma?' I asked. 'In her room?'

The housekeeper nodded. 'Mr Fairchild is with her. You may wait in the parlour until she is ready to see you.'

'No, I won't wait.' I kicked off my muddy shoes and ran up the stairs in my stockings before the flustered servant could gather her wits. Emma's bedchamber door stood ajar and Fairchild's voice purred within – calm, persuasive and utterly chilling.

I pressed my body against the wall and peeped through the crack. Emma was sitting up in her grand four-poster. Bedcovers were gathered around her legs in a knotted heap of soiled linen. She resembled a doll with most of the stuffing pulled out. Her pale, moon face was a pathetic picture of hope and trust. Poor, silly woman. She still believed that Adam would look after her, that he'd forsake everything for their bastard child, even as he stood at the foot of her bed and told her that he was leaving and wouldn't return. She asked if he would write. He chuckled. When she started to cry he laughed openly. She gestured at the crib beneath the window but he would not go near it.

Finally, Adam Fairchild walked out of Emma Jane's life as quickly and brutally as he'd pushed his way into it. He pulled open the door and strode right past me as if I wasn't there, Emma's parched voice calling after him. He descended the stairs two at a time, slapping his riding gloves into his open palm.

I stepped into the room. Emma's head was cradled in her arms. My shadow fell across her and she looked up, her eyes like shattered windows. 'Come to gloat?'

'I have better things to do.'

She wiped her nose with a damp kerchief. 'Why are you here then?'

'Lady Elizabeth's maid fetched me. She thought you might need a friend. I was the nearest thing she could find. A desperate choice.'

'You have every right to hate me.'

'You are too foolish to be hated. As foolish as every other empty-head Adam Fairchild has bedded from here to Wexborough and beyond.'

'I thought he loved me.'

'Did he ever say that? Did you once hear those words pass his lips? No, I thought not.'

'Have you come to take my baby?' She drew the tangled sheet over the tops of her white, swollen breasts. 'I've heard talk about you. Some say you stole newborns from women who did not deserve their children.'

'No, Emma. I will not touch your child. You must play the part of a mother with as much passion as you have played the fool. You will grow up at last, just as your father wanted.'

'I will get a nurse.'

I shook my head. 'No respectable wet-nurse or surgeon will tend you or your bastard. I'll wager the midwife was some wise woman lured out of the woods with the promise of a shilling.'

Emma's face turned grotesque with horror. 'But I don't know how to look after a baby.'

'You will have to learn.' I glanced at the crib. 'Listen, the child has started to cry. She's hungry. Better get used to those tears. Especially when she starts teething, when she falls over, and when her heart is broken for the first time. Think about what you will say when she asks where her father is, or for that matter, who he is.'

Emma pressed her fists against her forehead. 'I want to die.'

'You can't afford to die. Your daughter needs you. Do what's right for her. In the end you'll have her love if nothing else. More than I have ever known in my life.'

I turned away and made to leave the room. A pillow flew past my head and struck the wall. 'I hate you,' Emma cried. 'You are a witch. You are doing this out of spite because Adam came into my bed instead of yours. You wanted him as much as me, don't deny it. Yes, he's gone, but I have something of his that you'll never have, and you cannot bear it can you, child stealer?'

I slipped into the passage and closed the door behind me.

I was heartily footsore by the time I arrived at Dinstock church. Walking lopsidedly, I skirted the tombstones until I found the cinder path to Charles's hut. Peace had settled over the churchyard. I paused a moment to savour the simple pleasure of it. Ahead, the door to the gravediggers' hut stood ajar. Light glimmered in a hundred facets from behind the unshuttered window. Inside, I found a warm fire crackling in the hearth. The stone floor had been swept and my bed was made – the woollen blanket smoothed out and neatly turned over at the top. Bread and a round of cheese lay on a trencher on top of the dresser.

I smiled. Charles would be wondering where I'd gone. Perhaps he was looking for me even now. Even as that thought occurred to me a shadow filled the door. I turned, grinning widely. 'You make a good housekeeper, Charles, I...'

The smile fell off my mouth. A figure lumbered into the hut and closed the door. A smell of old sweat filled my nostrils. I felt all four walls draw in on me like the sides of a coffin.

'Greetings, my little kitchen queen,' said Moses Cripps. In the firelight I could see the twisted muscles of his arms, the hard gristle ringing his neck, and his chest, like rough bark, caught in the V of his open shirt. He had all the brutal savagery of an animal on the run.

'So you lost your husband.' He spoke with a loose, tooth-broken mouth that turned each word into a snake hiss. 'And now you have a new fancy man. You always were a sharp one. I followed him here. Then I waited, as I've waited these past months.'

'Where is Charles? Have you hurt him?'

'No, he's gone to see to his horses. I made sure before coming back here. Maybe he'll return, maybe he won't. Makes no difference either way.'

He stepped forward. I stepped back. 'They'll catch you,' I warned. 'You'll be hung for sure.'

Laughter burbled out of his throat. 'I'm bound for Ireland. Got a horse waiting and a boat to carry me across, once my business here is done.'

He flicked my dress with his forefinger. 'You've gone up and down in the world. Suffered a bit perhaps. But not like me. It took a while to track you down but I'm able to bide my time. Prison taught me that. It took away my dignity but I learned patience. I've hidden in barns and ditches, grubbing food out of pig troughs and running like a fox with dogs nipping at my heels. The winter nearly did me in. My fingers swelled with the cold but the thought of meeting you again, my pretty young betrayer, kept me alive.

You who wrecked my life just to save yourself a bit of shame.'

He plucked at his shirt. 'Like my clothes? Better than those prison rags.'

'Stolen I suppose?'

'Just like you to think that. I worked for a tinker to earn them. I was an honest man before I met you. I aim to be an honest man again.'

'After you've murdered me?'

'By God, you've a neck on you. Aren't you afraid at all?'

'Yes. Afraid for my life. I knew you were coming. I heard about the stranger asking after me in the village but I had no intention of running away. Better to be frightened now and get it done with than spend the rest of my days seeing your face in every corner, jumping at every shadow or squirming at every piece of gossip my imagination might link to you. I won't be hunted.'

He grinned again but something melancholy lay in his expression. 'I can live with Blake's death on my conscience because he was a bad 'un and got what was coming to him. I won't add your life to that tally, worthless as it may be. It'll be a new start for Moses Cripps.'

'So why did you come here?'

'To finish things properly.' He rummaged in the belt of his breeches and pulled out a sheaf of papers. The pages were soiled and the wax seal had flaked off so that only a red stain remained. But I recognised them at once.

'I know who you really are,' Moses said. 'I know everything about you. These have been in the safekeeping of a friend all the time I was imprisoned. Yes, even I, murderer and criminal that you made me, still have friends. This one learned his letters as a lad. Told me what's written here. It's quite a tale.' He dangled the papers in front of me. 'How badly do you want to learn the truth? How much does it mean to you?'

'What is your price?' I demanded. 'There *is* a price isn't there, behind all this teasing? If you're not here to kill me then say what you want and get out.'

'How much are you willing to give?'

I stared at the papers dangling a few inches in front of my face. Cripps was ready to snatch them away in a twitch. While he held that bundle, my life would always be in his hands.

'Everything,' I whispered.

He laid the documents on top of the dresser next to my uneaten supper. 'Still ready to sell the world in order to get what you want? Thank you for making it easy to let you go.' Cripps spat on the floor and left. The makeshift door shook in its frame as he slammed it. His footsteps crunched on the path then silenced to a whisper as he cut across the grass. I wrenched the door open again, squinting into the weakening afternoon light. But he was gone, disappeared into the churchyard as though the tombstones themselves had swallowed him up. Crows wheeled overhead, their raucous cries like laughter in my ears.

I stepped back inside and closed the door. The bundle of papers lay on the dresser where Cripps had left it. With shaking hands, I picked up the documents and sat on the end of the bed. I remembered how they had once looked – the paper crisp, the wax seal a vivid red against the cream-coloured sheets. In my haste, I broke a fingernail trying to snap the binding. Infuriated, I pulled the string off with my teeth. The bundle fell apart in my lap like a dropped egg. A stale, musty smell, like leaves rotting on the ground in early winter, clogged my nose. But I could see Mr Littlejohn's handwriting, remembered how he used to sit at that big oak desk in the shipping office, the surface a clutter of papers and ledgers, and enter the day's business. Each line flowed and looped so that the words seemed to be chattering to themselves. The sentences in front of me were faded, the writer's hand unsteady, but there was my name at the top of the first page.

'My dear Juliana,' it began.

Charles was in the stables when I tumbled in with the sun climbing up my back and the village yawning awake. He put down the bucket he was holding in his good hand and grinned. 'Sorry I couldn't see you last night,' he said. 'I got called out to help Francis Bryson with his dray. Damn thing got its leg caught in a gate. It's the only nag he's got to pull his milk cart and he can't afford it going lame. He sent his lass, Betsy, to tell you where I was. I take it from the look on your face that she did no such thing.'

I shook my head.

'Thought not,' he continued. 'She probably met a sweetheart on the lane. Damn girl's head is full of butterflies. Well, don't be too hard on me. There's no harm done and the beast will recover.'

'I had a visitor right enough but it certainly

wasn't Betsy Bryson. I need to talk to you, Charles.'

I related my encounter with Cripps. At some point Charles picked up a brush and started grooming one of the horses in long, hard strokes. The animal flicked its tail and snorted at the rough treatment.

'Moses Cripps gave me back my past,' I finished. 'The one thing I wanted more than anything else. I wrecked his life. He had every right to wring my neck if he chose.'

Charles put down the brush. 'Well, Juliana Rodriguez, it seems you have finally found what you were searching for. I hope it was all worth it.'

'You are my friend, the only real one I've ever had. Those papers Cripps left me won't change that.'

He picked up a blanket and threw it over the horse's back. 'I don't want to hear it. You've had fair use out of me and I shan't begrudge that. But friends trust one another. They don't cut the truth up into snippets and hand them out as they please. You know this Cripps fellow better than you've cared to admit. Escaped prisoners don't stalk a young woman for weeks just to hand over a bundle of papers.'

I didn't know what to say to that. Charles waited for a few moments then shrugged. 'You can stay in the hut as long as you want, or until the parson throws us both out. I promised he wouldn't beat you and I'll hold to that. I'll go on driving your carriage if I must but you shall not have anything more from me.'

'You are a stubborn fool,' I blurted, and was

sorry the moment the words were off my lips.

His expression was chipped out of flint. 'Aye, but even fools have pride.'

The night was mild but I held a blanket around me in a shroud whilst staring at the patterns made by the crackling flames. I could not let the fire die, despite the kind weather. I needed its comfort too much in this restless graveyard. Owls and other creatures of the night kept their homes and hunting grounds amidst the tombstones.

My mind was a cauldron of confusion and self-reproach. It robbed me of sleep as a thief might rob a traveller of his purse. My eyes were sore with crying. I could not guess the hour. Time seemed to crawl, prolonging my misery. From where I lay I could see the bundle of documents that I had left on a fold-down table beside the hearth. How easy it would be to slip out of bed and throw them on the fire, watch as the pages blackened and curled before bursting into orange flame. In the morning nothing would remain except ashes.

I sighed and sat up on the edge of the bed. Moses was gone. Even if I burned the papers I already knew the truth. In a way, I resented poor, murdered Mr Littlejohn for confirming all my suspicions, for spelling them out on those neatly written pages.

I wiped my eyes. 'Mother..' I whispered.

Sound was amplified in the night, carried on the spring air. Footsteps in the churchyard. They hesitated then crunched uncertainly towards the hut. I had left the shutters open in the hope that

Charles might see the firelight and come in to warm my heart, to forgive me, to embrace me and most of all understand.

I hurried to the window and peered through the glass. A figure, lit by a bobbing lantern that hung in the air like a ghost light, picked his way along the cinder path. Every few paces he halted and held up the lantern. I sensed him peering into the darkness, trying to follow the path's course as it wound between the broken monuments to death and decay.

It was not Charles. This man, wrapped up to the eyes in a cloak with a tricorne cocked on his head, was too tall. Prettyman could have bounded across the graves in the blackest of nights without the aid of any light. I waited, more curious than afraid, as the figure drew closer. He made no effort to conceal his movements. Here was no robber or rapist. I stifled a giggle as he stumbled on the half-buried stump of an ancient headstone. His cloak breezed open to reveal a coachman's liveried jacket. What brought another servant to my door at this deathly hour of the night? Not more trouble at Dinstock Hall, surely?

When he arrived, brushing the mulch from his coat, I was ready. The bottom drawer of the dresser had conjured up a threadbare cloak. I pulled this around my shoulders before slipping my bare feet into a pair of coachman's boots.

I opened the door on the first knock. The coachman started back in surprise. Confusion scrawled across his features. He held up the lamp to get a better look at me. 'You, wench,' he growled. 'I have come for Mistress Juliana. Is she somewhere in this hovel?'

'Nearer than you think,' I replied, 'and I'll have less of your impudence. Now what is so important that you have to drag me from my bed?'

He squinted. Dark spots pricked his cheeks. 'I beg your pardon, madam. I have brought a visitor from Dinstock Hall. The carriage is in the lane. I am to take you there at once.'

I frowned. Squire Matthew must have returned from Bristol. No doubt he'd be curious about Adam Fairchild. Visiting a disgraced widow in daylight hours was out of the question and he wouldn't want me at the Hall where Emma would get to hear of it.

'Very well,' I sighed, 'but let me carry the lantern. This is consecrated ground and you've blackened it with enough profanities. Follow me and try not to end up on your rump.'

I set off across the graveyard at a brisk pace, the coachman scuttling to keep up. Two bay mares stood snorting between the shafts of a chaise drawn up outside the lich-gate. The coachman was obviously keen to be away from this place and ushered me into the lane. He opened the carriage door and gestured at the dark interior. I handed back the lantern, wrapped the cloak tightly around me and clambered inside. The door closed with a soft 'click'.

I sensed movement, heard the rustle of blankets. 'Squire Matthew?' I whispered. 'You would have words with me?'

'Sit down, Juliana.'

I thumped on to the coach seat. The figure shifted. A face pushed into the soft bleed of light from the carriage lamps outside. Emma Jane's face, cold and bleak, her features drawn into an ugly visage. 'You must help me.'

Her voice was low and horrible. Old woman's words. Something was desperately wrong. The chill weight of fear pressed me back against the seat. 'What has happened? Why are you not at home with your daughter?'

She pressed her fingers against her cheeks. Tears gushed out of her eyes.

'My child is gone,' she said.

Chapter Eighteen

Emma's tears spread a damp patch across the front of my shift as I cradled her head. She wiped her face on the edge of a coach blanket. I waited while she gathered her thoughts. Some night creature scuttled through the grass bordering the lane.

'My child is gone,' she repeated. 'When Papa returned from Bristol, Parson Proudlove was waiting in the library. Whilst I slept, Papa paid the parson a hundred guineas to take my baby away. I didn't wake up for another three hours. A servant told me what happened. Papa was drunk out of his wits. No sense could be coaxed out of him. I came to you because you know where my child has been taken. I don't care what becomes of me. I can suffer your disgust and my father's contempt. You were right, my daughter is my life now.'

'What would you have me do?' My mind was in a whirl.

'Steal her. Fetch her back from that evil man who profits from his parson's garb. As for Adam Fairchild, I was a fool to think I loved him. I will never doubt your word again, Juliana, I swear.'

Easy for her to say, I thought, as if you can sacrifice everything for someone and then throw him out of your life. I doubted whether Fairchild would show his face at Dinstock Hall again but whether Emma pined or prospered as a result of that would depend on just how strong a character she was. Either way, the matter had been out of my hands for some time.

For now, it seemed as if I was back in the Butter House larder with a sleeping baby in my arms and a minute to decide its future. Emma spoke the truth. I knew where the baby would have been taken, at least for tonight.

'If I fetch it, where will you go? Return to the Hall and your father will merely hand the child back to the parson. Proudlove runs a trade in children and will spirit yours out of the county at the first opportunity.'

Emma sat up. 'Mama put aside a large sum for me in the event of her death. I daresay she always suspected Papa would buckle at the seams. Any ties that bound me to him were severed the moment he placed my child into Parson Proudlove's hands. I will lodge with some acquaintances I made in Brussels during my tour of the Continent a couple of years ago. The letter has already been drafted and I know they will not ask too many questions. It is the only future I can offer my child for now.'

'You will travel alone?'

Her dark hair was a shadow within shadows. 'My coachman will accompany me.'

'Have him take me to the edge of the common land, then go to the church stables where you will find my driver, Charles Prettyman. Wake him if need be and tell him I sent you. He will keep you safe until I return. I hope to have your child before daybreak.'

'Where are you going?'

'A place where someone like you doesn't belong. I could be risking my life for you, Emma. I hope you realise that.'

'What do you want in return? Money? Name your price.'

'I'll need cash for bribes, true, but I want no payment for myself. Nor do I want your friendship or gratitude. In fact, after this week I don't ever wish to see your face again. Now, let's make haste.'

The gypsy fires were burning high on the dark circle of the common. I was taken to the stone bridge spanning the boundary stream, the same one that chuckled so merrily past the back of the parsonage. Now its waters shimmered black and cold. Swollen with rain, they gushed around exposed rocks and splashed into flooded pools. In the distance, behind the caravans where the firelight could not reach, dogs barked above the wheezing melody of a hurdy gurdy.

'Shall I go with you, madam?' the coachman asked. 'A gypsy camp at night is no place for any man, let alone a young woman.'

I unhooked a lantern. 'People come to the gypsies after dark for favours they don't dare get when the sun is up. Find Miss Emma at the church stables and wait there with her.'

'I ought to wait for you.'

'This is not something you need get involved in any further. You will be of more use to Miss Emma. It is safer this way, for everyone.'

I stood by the bridge until the carriage was out of sight then took my courage in my hands and set off across the common, stumbling over clumps of wild grass and bracken. Half a dozen bow-topped caravans were spread in a loose semi-circle, the horses grazing a short distance away. Camp fires spat orange sparks into the deepening night, the smoke caught in a cauldron of hot air and sucked up into the blackness.

They sat beside the largest fire, the dark-skinned men and women. A pot suspended over the flames filled the air with the smell of cooking meat. Stew, probably made from rabbits poached off Squire Matthew's land, and potatoes hooked out of the earth whilst a farmer was having his fortune told. Or perhaps his eyes were turned by some lithe gypsy girl with a love potion in one hand and a blade to cut his purse in the other.

I showed them Emma's gold and explained what I wanted. They glanced at one another, speaking a silent language with their eyes. A nod was given and one of the women slipped away on silent feet to a caravan, returning with a bundle that she dropped on the grass.

Their leader, a big man who reeked of incense

and nameless herbal concoctions, nudged the bundle open with the toe of his leather shoe. 'You will become one of us now,' he said in an accent that called no county its home.

I put on the bright gypsy gown. I stripped my feet bare and rubbed cinders into my hair. When I saw my reflection in the bowels of the moonlit brook, I looked as wild as any Romany woman born on to an unforgiving road.

Pietre, the gypsy leader, took me to the fireside and examined my hands in the blazing light. 'You've done work,' he said, tracing the outlines of old blisters. 'Hard work.'

Fetching wood, scrubbing the parsonage floors, hauling bales of clothing into my old carriage. Yes, I had earned those marks. Pietre grinned and cuffed my shoulder when he caught the look on my face. The men with him laughed before drifting off into the fire-spiked darkness.

We took two wagons, filled them with muzzled dogs and laughing young women – the prettiest in the camp. Before we left I had my face painted. A swirl of pagan colours hid my birthmark. I sat next to Pietre on the driving seat of the leading caravan. Behind us, crammed into the cluttered interior, the Romanies immediately fell into a pin-drop silence. Even the three dogs, held in a pen on the floor between the gypsies' feet, caught the mood and subsided into a watchful stillness.

'We do business at the Rose once, sometimes twice a year,' Pietre quietly explained. 'Ironjack, the landlord, will likely try to sell me cheap on the dogs. I of course, will argue. I will point out what fine beasts they are and explain that the paltry sum he is offering is not worth my effort or the wear and tear on my wagons. It is a game we always play and it can go on for an hour or so. That should give you the time you need. There's never less than thirty or forty men in the taproom or killing circle any night of the week, but most will be too drunk to cause trouble, and my girls will keep them distracted. Ironjack himself is the one who always needs to be watched. Never touches a drop when the inn is open for business.'

The gypsy pursed his lips. 'I've had the better of him in the past – beat him at arm wrestling a few times and won shillings off him in a fistfight. But he's slippery – keeps an old hunting gun in an empty barrel behind the counter. If you get caught watch your back because, woman or not, Ironjack will put a lead ball between your shoulder blades.'

'I have promised you more money…'

Pietre shook his head. 'The Rose needs my dogs. Ironjack could get animals from elsewhere but not the winners I fetch. He owes me too many favours to bear a grudge. He'll wait until autumn when I return from Bristol with new animals smuggled in on the slave ships. Slave dogs are vicious killers. Not too bad to sell to a gypsy though.' He winked and clicked on the reins.

The wagons joined the high road as it rose above the sleeping village and cut a path across the moorland beyond. The bright moon made for easy driving and Pietre pushed the horses into a fast walk. Apart from the creak of wood punctured by an occasional snort from one of the dray animals, it remained a hushed procession that moved along the weary miles.

I tried to swallow down my growing unease. Pietre caught me mopping my face for the fifth time in as many minutes. He fumbled beneath the seat with his free hand and plopped a small earthenware jug into my lap. 'You're afraid,' he said. 'Can't let my dogs get the scent. Ironjack will notice too. A nervous lass always gets his lust up. Drink some of that, no more than two mouthfuls.'

I eased out the rag stopper, put the mouth of the jug to my lips and took two draughts of the warm liquid. My tongue recoiled at the mix of oil and spirits but I gulped it down. Replacing the stopper, I handed back the jug. 'What's in it?' I asked, spluttering.

'Courage mixed with a bit of gypsy magic. Tonight will seem like a dream to you. Your mind will dance a little but your body will stay sharp, your wits keen and your mouth silent.'

His silver tongue was persuasive. It sounded like a tale to pamper the ears of the gullible. But tonight, on the winding moonlit road with a breeze gusting over the moors and uncertain trials waiting ahead, I was prepared to believe in a little gypsy magic.

The Rose Inn sat like a fat spider in a web of light. Doors and windows were flung wide, noise spilling out of the open portals in a raucous tide. Laughter, oaths, a screeching dirge torn out of a badly tuned fiddle. And the dogs, always fighting, spilling their lives on to the stained sand of the killing pit.

My senses heightened by the gypsy brew, I smelled blood on the air, heard each snarl and snap of those vicious jaws. It set my veins on fire. Fear, excitement, the taste of violent death in the night. The animals behind me caught it and snarled, only to be silenced with a sharp word from Pietre. He drew the caravan to a halt in the yard. The second wagon rolled to a stop a few feet away. Someone loitering outside the tavern door shouted a greeting and ran over. Words were exchanged – rich-sounding gibberish in some foreign tongue. Pietre jumped off the driver's seat and slapped the fellow on the back. Then he waved towards us. The dogs and the women were brought out to murmurs of approval.

My feet weighed nothing, my head danced along with the music. I followed everyone inside the inn. Tables were shoved aside and the dogs' cages were placed in the middle of the floor for inspection. Ironjack stepped out from behind the counter. The same gore-encrusted apron was tied loosely around his waist. His chin was blue with stubble. 'You're two days early,' he told Pietre.

The gypsy shrugged and thrust an empty tankard into Ironjack's fingers. 'I'm leaving Dinstock. There's no more money to be had. The local land grubbers have all dried up. Give me a drink and let's do business. My tongue is like dried wood.'

Ironjack shook his head. 'I can't bid high, not tonight. My takings are poor. The fighting's not much better. I don't know what's got into those animals tonight.'

'So I take what I can get and come back with more beasts in the autumn. Tonight you get a bargain. Now give me some ale.'

Ironjack filled the tankard and the two men started haggling. The gypsy girls spread from man to man, lap to lap, kissing, teasing, caressing dirty faces and laughing as shillings dropped down the front of their bodices. The driver of the second caravan plucked the violin out of its owner's hands and started up a wild, ear-jangling tune. Pietre's own daughter clambered on to one of the tables, hoisted her skirts above her knees and began a lithe dance that had the drunken, leering rabble falling out of their chairs.

I glanced towards the curtained door behind the counter. Ironjack had not recognised me. I edged towards the gap in the bar. The room whirled. Smoky lights, jeers and laughter, the stench of vomit and alcohol tainted my senses with giggling demons. My head pounded, my throat tightened until I thought I would suffocate. Hands, always hands wherever I went. Groping, slapping. I grinned stupidly at everyone and pecked their cheeks with sweet gypsy kisses.

Ironjack crouched with his back to me. He baited the dogs, encouraging them to lunge at the bars of the cage. I allowed myself to be pulled into another ale-sodden lap. A face framed with matted whiskers swam in front of me. I nibbled at the scarred ear and laughed like a simpleton when breath, fouler than the deepest cesspit, blew lecherous promises into my face. I wriggled loose and cupped the chin of another purple-nosed drunkard. 'You. I like you better.'

This one was as ugly as the first but to a chorus of cheers I fell on him, smothering his cheeks with my mouth. My former admirer mouthed an oath and grabbed my legs. I kicked him away. He pulled my hair and I tumbled on to the floor. Bone crunched as a fist smacked into my assailant's face. Blood gouted from his nose. He responded with a boot to the other fellow's crotch. Both men fell in a writhing heap, limbs flailing, curses colouring the air. Drunken friends joined in. Jugs smashed, tables were overturned. The music stopped in mid-note.

And I was alone.

I crept around the edge of the counter and slipped through the frayed curtain into a narrow passage. I straightened and fumbled along the wall. The place smelled of stale piddle and rancid meat. I tripped over a huddled shape that groaned and shifted. Whoever it was muttered something unintelligible then settled back into a drunken stupor. I let out my breath and carried on.

So little time. Already Ironjack's voice was calling the rabble to order. A moment later the music started up again. I reached a dimly outlined door at the end of the passage. Behind it, a child was crying. I pressed my ear to the wood and thought I also heard laughter but I couldn't be sure.

Mouthing a prayer, I felt around for the latch, lifted it and pushed. The door swung inwards on well-oiled hinges. Beyond lay a cramped, low-ceilinged room bloated with ale barrels and sacks of animal feed. A stained blanket littered with crusts hugged a far corner. The floor was slippery with grease. Moonlight bled through the half-

378

shuttered window puncturing the opposite wall. On top of a pile of crates, a gasping lantern threw streaks of light across the plaster walls.

Three women sat on a makeshift bench in the middle of the room. Toothless witches straight from the pages of *Macbeth*. I ducked behind a row of barrels and peered through a chink. One of the trio spat on the floor and scratched herself. Another poured something down her throat from a cracked earthenware jug.

The baby girl was passed around like a gin bottle, each taking a turn to press her tiny mouth against one grubby tit and then the other. She wailed morosely, cheeks plum red with effort. The women handled her as they might a bundle of dirty linen. These were the kind of whores not even the lowliest brothels would take. Wet-nurses selling their milk for a penny a time. Wexborough was full of them.

Noise from the passage behind me. A groan followed by a curse. The woman holding the baby scratched and jerked her head. 'Sounds like old Merrow's come to,' she cackled. 'He'll be wanting more gin, otherwise he'll be back to pester us.'

'He thinks your tit's wasted on a baby,' one of her companions laughed. 'Sixpence for a suck is what he once offered me.'

'He ain't got no more 'n' tuppence to his name. Only way he'll ever get his paws on me is if he digs up my dead body and I hope I'm smothered in quicklime just to spite him. Wait now, and I'll go and see if I can shut him up. There's enough row already with this brat bawling its gums off.'

She hauled herself off the box and set the baby

down in a crate lined with tangled straw. After she'd disappeared into the passage, the other women continued drinking, gin slopping down their chins. I edged around the back of the barrels until a few feet separated me from the child. A shuttered window lay directly at my back.

The women looked strong. Old scars criss-crossed their cheeks, necks and arms. Surprise was on my side but I doubted I could overpower them both. Their companion would return within moments.

I fumbled along the top of the crate. My fingers curled around the base of the lantern. I picked it up and hurled it on to the floor, splitting open the cheap brass and setting the candle to the tinder-dry straw. The fire caught quickly, devouring this new-found fuel with hungry tongues of blue and orange. Fiery fingers spread out in a web of heat, locking the barrels in a searing embrace.

The women screamed. The jug fell out of their hands and smashed open. Gin added venom to the blaze. A burning carpet swept across the floor. Running to the window, I hauled open the shutters and tried the catch. It wouldn't budge. The frame had been painted closed, sealing the prison. In desperation I picked up a box of dog meat and hurled it at the glass. The window splintered outwards, showering the night with jagged shards of glass. I scooped up the baby and tucked it inside my gypsy shawl.

Footsteps pounded along the corridor. I kicked over the makeshift crib, adding more straw to the fire. Both women had retreated to a far corner and were beating at the flames with their bare arms.

I eased out of the window. Broken glass scratched my arms. A sliver cut through my scalp and I squealed in pain. Worse waited outside. My bare foot landed on a glittering lawn of broken glass, but the cool air was a blessing compared to the inferno I had created inside. I hauled my other leg over the sill just as Ironjack appeared in the doorway and stared at me over the top of the flames. Recognition coloured his features. Then rage. 'That's no gypsy,' he bellowed. 'It's her, the parson's foundling. He's double dealt us.'

I dared not try to find Pietre. I fled into the enfolding arms of the night, the baby pressed against my chest. Perhaps it caught my terror, because it wailed all the louder. Behind me, the inn flared like a beacon, its old walls succumbing to the surging flames.

Exhaustion weighted my limbs and my bleeding feet sent screams of pain up both legs. I sought a refuge amidst the maze of lanes leading away from the Rose Inn. Above the crackle of the fire I heard an angry mob baying for my blood. Then the vicious snarl of the dogs. The beasts would run me down in no time. If I hid they would sniff me out. The child would be just another piece of meat between their jaws.

I halted, gasping, in the road and tried to get my bearings. Ahead lay a black expanse of moor. To the right, water glimmered under a fugitive moon. A lake squatted like a silver shilling in the coarse grass. So be it. With my last ounce of strength and the dregs of my courage I would walk out into the cool, soothing waters. Better we both drown than let our blood be spilled on the dirt.

I opened my shawl and gazed at the tiny life nestling in my arms. She had quietened. Her round eyes peered up at me.

'I am so sorry,' I whispered. 'I hope your mother will forgive me.'

The stampede of horses, of wheels thundering down the lane. Not even enough time to lose myself in the bowels of the lake. I waited and hoped that death, whether under a wagon or at the blood-slavered jaws of fighting dogs, would be mercifully quick. But a coach hove into view from the opposite direction – out of the stomach of the black moor. Perched on the driver's seat was the unmistakable figure of Charles Prettyman.

Harnesses jangled as the carriage squealed to a halt. 'Juliana, get up here,' Charles yelled. I scrambled one-handed up the ladder and squeezed next to him on the wooden seat. Providence smiled on us. The lane here was wide enough to turn the carriage. We were soon galloping back the way we had come. Behind us, the inn was an orange welt on the horizon. A hot wind churned out of its burning innards and rained cinders around us.

'We won't get away.' The swirling air plucked the words from my mouth. 'A coach cannot outrun men on horseback.'

Charles leaned across and shouted into my ear. 'Dinstock wood lies ahead. 'Tis a rabbit warren of old drovers' roads and foresters' tracks. I spent my whole childhood exploring them. I know this area better than any man. Hold tight.'

The carriage lurched as he made a turn. Immediately the stars were lost above a canopy of branches. Charles ordered me to extinguish the lanterns. It was as if we had fallen into a black pit with sides we could not see. He pulled on the reins to slow the careening horses. 'Keep the child from bawling if you can,' he said. 'Those dogs won't give up easily and I want to put at least five miles between them and us.'

They chased us into the dawn but their hearts were not in it or their animals too weary. We clopped into Dinstock as the first blood-red fingers of the new day groped above the treetops.

'Why did you come after me?' I whispered. My throat was parched. A grey film of ash covered the coach roof and the backs of the horses. Falling embers had singed my hair in places. Charles looked like a ghost.

'That Jane girl warned me not to follow you,' he said, hands limp on the reins. 'When she told me you had set off after her child, I knew you were bound for the Rose. I would've left at once but the parson's wife turned up with young Charlotte. Mrs Proudlove's face was black and blue and the child was screaming. She begged me to take her to her cousin's house in Wexborough, claimed the devil had a hold of her husband and she feared for her life. I tried to explain that I had pressing business. She nigh went berserk, used curses I'd never heard before and set about me with her fists. In the end she collapsed in front of the stables. I had to get the Dinstock coachman to take her and the girl up to the Widow Hendy's. I'd have been after you sooner were it not for that.'

'Betty Hendy? Was that a good idea?'

His cheeks coloured. 'I've been keeping an eye on her. I lit the fire in her hearth, cleaned her house and made sure she had something to eat. Having someone else to look after for a bit will take her mind off her boy.'

'Well, it seems I wasn't the only one keeping secrets, Charles Prettyman. We owe you our lives, myself and the baby, but you may have damned yourself in coming to our aid. I saw where they kept the children at the Rose. I burned the place to the ground but not before Ironjack recognised me. Chances are he escaped the fire. Whilst others turned a blind eye to the goings on in this county, I have blundered in and learned enough to have them all hung in chains. They will want my life for it, I am sure, and yours too for helping me. The gypsies cannot help me now. I must go to the magistrate in Wexborough.'

Charles's face was grim. 'You'll do no such thing. Look at yourself, Juliana. You're half-dead with exhaustion.'

'I daren't go back to the cottage. Or to your hut. The parson is bound to learn what happened.'

'Once we have delivered the baby to its mother I will take you to a place where you can rest safely for a while. Five men could barely have managed what you did alone tonight.'

I was too tired to argue, or laugh at the ridiculous compliment. The baby had cried itself to sleep and my arms ached holding it. But I would not give it up and Charles knew better than to ask. We pulled up outside the church stables just as a distant cock started screeching at the dawn. I fought to keep my eyes open. Charles clambered down and hurried inside. When he returned, Emma was with him, running like a demented thing. I buried the baby in my shawl. I wanted to pick up the reins and snap the sweating horses into a gallop. I would leave Charles, leave Dinstock and all its sins behind me. I would flee until the horses dropped, then I would run on my bare, bleeding feet. I had nearly died for this child. It was mine as surely as if I had carried it in my own womb.

'Give her to me,' Emma squealed, clapping her hands as if applauding me, as if I was an actress in a travelling show who'd performed some pleasing drama. Two seconds of eternity passed. I sat without moving, staring down at her with more loathing than I had felt for any human being in my life. Uncertainty slipped across her face. The baby woke and started crying again.

'Juliana…' Charles said gently.

I passed the child down to the woman who had borne it. I would not call her a mother. It felt too much like some vital organ had been wrenched out of my body. I had no right, no right at all. But Emma would not have rubbed cinders in her hair and travelled with the Romanies. Pretty Emma, who spent her life wrapped in silk and muslin, would not have faced the flames, or the dogs, or the rage of the mob. If not for me she would have sat and wept, and let this precious child be taken away for ever.

'Bless you,' she smiled, nuzzling the baby's head against her face. Her coachman reached into his coat and tossed up another bag of jangling coins.

He had to leap aside when I threw it back. The bag burst and scattered coins across the packed dirt of the stable yard.

'Feed the child,' I said, 'then go to Belgium and don't come back.'

Charles drove the coach down a narrow track to a place where the brook formed a series of large pools overhung with trees. The crumbled remains of a mill, its waterwheel long ago plundered for wood, hugged the bank. A dense patch of woodland kept the area hidden from the road.

Charles made up a bed on the carriage seat and let me rest while he unhitched the horses and led them to the water's edge. He kicked off his boots and waded into one of the pools to tickle trout, which he did expertly with his good hand. Within half an hour two good-sized fish lay flapping on the bank.

He kindled a fire and built it in such a way that it gave off almost no smoke. While the trout were sizzling, he washed the ash and cinders from the carriage. The horses had drunk their fill and wandered off to crop the lush grass sprouting between the walls of the ruined mill. My breakfast was brought to me on the end of a stick and washed down with a flask of bitter ale.

Charles waited until I had licked the grease from my fingers and drained the flask. 'What'll you do now that you've changed both our lives for ever?' he asked.

'I will go to Wexborough and see the magistrate,' I repeated. 'Then I have affairs of my own to attend to. My papers ... oh!' Realisation,

386

followed by despair, hit me like a rock. 'I have left them in your cottage. I must fetch them before going to town.'

Charles put his feet up on the seat and settled back against the window. 'Yes, the papers. What's in them? What could be so important that even now sees you willing to risk more? I know you tried to tell me and I wouldn't listen. I'm listening now.'

'I do not wish to talk about it, not any more.'

'This is my business too. You've brought me along this road with you, Juliana Rodriguez. I want to know where we're going and what lies at the end.'

'I've involved you enough. I don't want to pull you in any further.'

'You didn't want to give Miss Jane her child back either but it was her right to take it, just as it's my right to demand a reason for not returning you to Parson Proudlove, as my duty requires.'

'You would not dare.'

Prettyman picked at his teeth with a fingernail. 'I'd dare. I'm only a humble, half-crippled coachman who does as his master bids. I was not recognised on the road last night and I didn't put the Rose Inn to the torch. If you want your papers, you'll need my help to do it.'

'So, now I have to pander to you? How many other people do I have to satisfy? I do more running around than a scullery wench.'

He sat up and clasped his hands as if in prayer. 'Is there still room for nothing but bitterness in your heart? You spit at life, yet you save the

387

children of strangers, of people whom you owe nothing. Why do it? Are you seeking glory? Or salvation?'

'I want those children to have a life, a right to their place in the world.'

'What about your place? Who are you really, Juliana? What made you the way you are?'

I pulled off the coat he had spread over me and sat opposite him. Our faces were only inches apart. 'Did Emma tell you about her lover, that same lover who went on to ruin her? Did she mention that she stood with her arms draped lovingly around his neck whilst he humiliated me? That child was worth much more than the purse of money her coachman tried to offer me. I daresay I was trying to prove a point. My father would have been proud.'

'Your father?'

'Oh yes. I have his blood in my veins, right enough.'

'Juliana, you're talking in riddles.'

I prised his hands apart and took hold of his fingers. 'Do you really want to learn about me, Charles? Very well. You can decide for yourself whether my past has turned me into what I am. It is quite a tale, full of romance and tragedy.'

'As long as it's the truth, I don't care.'

I squeezed his knuckles. 'I am the daughter of Manuel Rodriguez, an executed cut-throat who plagued the southern seas.'

Charles gawped. 'A *pirate?*'

I squeezed out a bitter smile. 'Officially he was no criminal. A letter of marque from the Spanish king gave him the right to plunder English ships, which he did so mercilessly, often butchering the crews and hanging their corpses from the rigging. Any women and children travelling as passengers were sold as slaves or concubines. One ship he raided carried the daughter of a wealthy merchant who had interests in the West Indies. She was sailing to join her father, in a place called Antigua, and her fiancé whom she planned to wed within the month. A renowned beauty respected for her wit as well as her looks, she warmed the heart of this butcher-seaman. He threatened to kill any of his men who mistreated her.'

I stared at my lap and the pink knot of my clasped fingers. 'Forgive me for asking, but are your parents still alive?'

'Sorry to say they're not. Fever claimed them both. Bowled them off their feet like a pair of wooden pins and put them in the ground in less than a week.'

'Did you know them well?'

'Here, look at this.' He reached into his shirt and pulled out a leather cord with a ring attached. A semi-precious stone was set in a lead band that moulded itself to the finger.

'I always wear this around my neck. I made it for my mother the year before she died. I was only eleven years old. When I was born my da wanted to wring my neck. Said he wouldn't suffer a cripple for a son. Ma warned him that if he tried it he'd have to throttle her too. He loved her, the old bastard, and so I lived.'

'I don't know what I can tell you about my mother. Was she fair or dark? Brown eyed or blue? Tall and thin or short with a rounded face?

No sketch or etching was included in the papers. I've no memory of her touch, her scent, or if she smiled when she saw me for the first time.'

'She gave you up?' Charles asked gently.

'It was her husband's wish. She probably had a notion what would happen to her if she were returned to her family – what would happen to me. The marriage would likely be annulled. I'd be branded a bastard and spirited off in the night. My mother saved me, and I never even knew her.'

'I take it this was the girl on the boat, the one who met the pirate?'

I nodded. 'A bargain was struck. She offered to become his wife if he spared the other passengers and crew. Manuel agreed. Though he could have taken her like any cheap whore, he recognised the treasure he had found. In any case, this fresh young girl, straight from England's green heart, was captivated by him in turn and became a willing spouse, turning her husband from murder.'

'Then what happened?'

'One of Manuel's men, who lived for blood and booty, was not happy with this new-found tenderness in his captain and betrayed him to the British. Manuel had suffered a death sentence on his head for many years. The authorities tricked him, hooked him and threw him in gaol. His wife was already big with child. A daughter was born while Manuel rotted in his cell awaiting execution, a little girl with her father's blood-red mark staining her mouth. Me.'

I swallowed. It felt like a pebble was stuck in my throat. 'My mother was to be returned to her family who had almost died of shame, for word of this bonding had spread quickly around the islands and beyond. I was never spoken of. A wet-nurse, or someone like that, would take me away. I would not be seen again.

'Manuel thought only of his child. He saw me just once, through the bars of his cell. A maid smuggled me in. The prison was also used as a storehouse for rum and other goods bound for England. A young man whose business was in shipping came to inspect the cargo. His name was Richard Worledge. Manuel watched as the young Englishman played cards with the clerks and cargo master. He had a fair hand for the game back then and quickly stripped them of their stakes. Manuel seized his chance. As soon as the Englishman was alone, Manuel offered a hidden cache of Spanish gold as his stake and challenged Richard to play.

'All night the cards turned, Manuel goading the English gentleman, pushing him into higher and higher stakes. Richard found himself owing a small fortune and without a farthing in his pocket. "Why should I consider myself in debt to a criminal," he said, "when you are due to be hanged?" But the Spaniard challenged his honour, dared him to default and still call himself a gentleman.

'"From the gallows I will tell everyone that you would not honour your dues," he warned. "Even as they put the rope around my neck I shall shout it to the crowds. Thousands will be there to see Manuel the Bloody executed. They shall all know of your disgrace."

'Richard bluffed and blustered but in the end Manuel forced a payment. I was the price. Rich-

391

ard was to take me to England and raise me as his own until the day I wed. Manuel made him swear to do so. "Give her what Christian name you will," he said, "but she is a Rodriguez and that part of her must not be taken away." The next day he was hanged.

'So there I was, a nothing child, raised not out of love but to honour a debt. Catherine, Richard's shrewish wife, discovered through his business associate that a large amount of Spanish money had been put in trust to me. I was forced to marry George Proudlove, the parson's son. George was an oaf in life and a fool at the card table. He owed money to some very dangerous people. I was his guarantee, even though I would not come into my inheritance until my twenty-first birthday. Not even a broken neck absolved my husband of his debts. His estate was plundered and I was taken in by the parson.'

Charles stroked my cheek. I did not move away. 'Have you found out what became of your mother?' he asked.

'Taken off to the madhouse. Her wits shattered along with her heart. Perhaps she is still alive. Perhaps some day I will find her.'

He cupped my chin and looked into my eyes. 'Those papers told you all this?'

'Enough for me to piece the rest together. Quite a tale, isn't it? Richard's colleague was always a shrewd man. Catherine and her incestuous lover would have come in for a big bite of my fortune. That was the bargain they struck with George. I was sold like a dray horse and Mr Littlejohn was murdered.'

I rested my head against Charles's shoulder and grasped his coat sleeve. It was his withered arm but he did not seem to mind. 'I have the knowledge about my past that I always craved. I have money, I have the evidence to bring Proudlove down. I ought to feel elated but I don't. I have looked inside myself and found nothing. All those people who have helped themselves to a part of my life – I think they have taken too much.'

He placed a kiss on the crown of my head. 'We'll get your papers,' he said gently, 'but now we must rest and wait until nightfall. They'll be looking for *you*, not your documents. Your past will be safe enough for the next few hours.'

'The children,' I sighed. 'All those children.'

His lips brushed my ear. 'I think it's time you had a child of your own, don't you?'

I pulled away. Heat rose in my cheeks. 'What do you mean? That was a foolish thing to say. Don't laugh at me.'

'It's what you want,' Charles said, grinning. 'It's what you've always wanted. I saw the look on your face when you held Miss Emma's baby, remember? You were wrong, Juliana Rodriguez, when you said no one ever loved you. I adored you from the moment you first tumbled into the lane in that black dress and started ordering me about like a peasant. I love you still and would gladly be a father to any child of yours if that was the only thing in the world that could make you truly happy.'

He touched my lips with his fingers. I kissed them, savoured their taste as if they were drenched in sweet wine. 'You are beautiful beyond words,'

Charles whispered, 'and I will spent the rest of my life fighting to win you.'

'Love me now,' I said, 'and the fight is already won.'

He shook like a frightened child but his touch was as gentle as a whisper. We held each other. I wanted nothing more than to see pleasure on his face and see my own delight reflected in his eyes. He gave instead of taking and I gave in return. When it was over we sat together, Charles with his good arm wrapped around me, and slipped off into a comforting sleep. We woke after sunset. Night enfolded the carriage in a soft black glove.

We slipped along the lane like a pair of brigands and ducked behind the hedge bordering the churchyard. Charles peeked over the top and declared the place deserted. He took my hand and helped me through a gap. We fetched up against one of the larger gravestones and waited. The church was a dark sepulchre of mossy stones, silent against the stars.

'Wait here while I check the hut,' Charles said. Before I could protest, he crossed the intervening space with the stealth of a poacher stalking game. His figure appeared briefly at the cottage door then he crouched to peer through a chink in the shutter. Satisfied, he slipped inside.

I set off across the churchyard. A few yards felt like a hundred miles. I imagined snarling dogs waiting to pounce, grizzled men with clubs, or Ironjack, face black with soot, rising from behind one of the stones with a pistol clutched in his hand and a shot bound for my heart. I stifled a squeal when a rat scurried out of my way. When

I stumbled through the hut's door, Charles was waiting for me. He'd lit a candle stub and his face was tense. 'Where did you say you hid those papers,' he whispered. 'I've looked where you've told me, but nothing's there.'

I fell to my knees and pulled open the bottom drawer of the dresser. Old clothes spilled out on to the floor. I scrabbled around inside but the documents were gone.

'Someone's been here,' Charles said, sniffing the air. 'Perhaps just one man, I can't say for sure.'

I rose to my feet. I could smell it too. A faint whiff of tobacco, a hint of ruby port hugging the stale air inside the hut. A familiar smell, teasing my nerves like a nagging ache that wouldn't go away.

The parson.

Chapter Nineteen

A light glimmered in the parlour window.

'D'you suppose he's there?' Charles whispered in the dark tunnel of the lane. 'The curtains are open, but I don't see anyone moving around.'

'The rat always returns to its hole,' I replied. 'With Ironjack and his company of cut-throats at large, Proudlove will likely want to lie low. I doubt any of that mob will dare to show their faces this close to the village.'

We waited half an hour to make sure but nothing stirred either in or around the silent house. 'He may be asleep,' I said at last, 'either in his armchair or upstairs in bed. He is an old man, for all his wiry strength. Sometimes he naps for hours.'

'I say we slip through the kitchen and take our chances,' Charles ventured. 'I'm not keen on the front door. It's too near the window. Besides, if we're caught we can always run back out into the woods. D'you know if the parson keeps a gun?'

I climbed out of the hedge and tugged the hood of my woollen cloak over my head. 'I never noticed any weapons, if you don't count his stick.'

'He's handy enough with that,' Charles admitted, 'but I learned a few tricks from a bare-knuckle fighter. Taught me how to use my good arm to do the work of two.'

'I would rather not meet him. Who knows what he might keep locked up somewhere.'

'Suppose he's out and the house is locked. I'll have to force a window.'

'The kitchen key is on a small ledge above the lintel.'

'That settles it then.' His hand sought my own and squeezed it. Together, we scurried across the garden into the shadow of the woods. The back door latch lifted on the first try and we crept into the empty kitchen. Stuffy, oppressive. Utterly quiet. The hall door hung open. The clock on the upstairs landing had stopped. I listened for sounds of life – breathing, snoring, floorboards creaking as someone crossed the room, or perhaps the squeak of leather as the parson shifted in his chair.

Nothing. Yet I was sure we were not alone. The parlour door, always closed when Proudlove was at home, hung ajar. Through the crack I spied his armchair. Unoccupied. The fire had crumbled into a pile of dead embers. Charles pushed the door wide. A brace of candles flickered on the table beneath the bay window. They had burnt down to stubs. No one was in the room, nor any sign that there had been for some hours.

'Take a look inside that trunk,' I whispered. 'I think it's where he keeps all his important papers.'

Charles crossed the parlour, pulled out the trunk and rattled the heavy padlock binding the lid. 'I'll have to drag this outside and get an axe to it.'

'There's one by the woodpile, but search the room first. I will check upstairs.' I turned to leave and was fetched by a pistol poked into my stomach. Adam Fairchild grinned, his face a mask of teeth glinting in the half-light. Behind him, the front door stood wide open.

'Back inside,' he ordered.

I backtracked into the parlour, not taking my eyes off the gun. Charles was fussing around the bookcase and did not realise something was amiss until I bumped into him. His face blanched when he set eyes on Fairchild.

'So, two rabbits caught in a snare,' Adam purred.

'No longer pretending to be a swordsman?' I enquired. 'Or a gentleman?'

'What have you done with the brat?'

'Oh?' I raised an eyebrow. 'You mean your newborn daughter?'

'A hundred guineas is what I mean,' he snarled. 'That's how much I was due for poking the Jane

397

bitch. Only half of what the parson would receive for selling the child on.'

'So you too are part of this trade in flesh?'

He moved further into the room, the pistol still aimed squarely at my belly. 'Well-bred babies fetch a tidy sum when our lords and ladies can't manage to make their own, or when it dies in the crib and they can't wait for another. But this particular child is missing, stolen by you I daresay, and the parson won't pay. Clearly he failed to keep you on a tight enough leash. Old Fortescue was prepared to pay two hundred guineas to be rid of the bastard I put in Cecilia's belly. A couple in Exeter would have bid another two hundred to take it. Instead you got a fancy gown and we were left with nothing. Not even marrying you off to that imbecile George Proudlove was enough to curb you.'

'You were paid to get women pregnant?' I was awestruck. 'I underestimated you, Adam. I thought you were driven by lust and a desire to notch up conquests. I had not thought you capable of such a scurrilous business arrangement. How many unmarried girls, how many wives of men fighting in America have you charmed into compromise, only to have Parson Proudlove conveniently arrive when there was a child to be rid of?'

'Mostly what we did was within the law,' Fairchild retorted. 'Papers were signed, or we had witnesses to say the babies died. There's not a courthouse or country assizes would send me to gaol. Did you get signatures when you stole babies? You're the thief, not I.'

'What about Catherine Worledge? Was she involved, or was she trying to imitate you? The baby I stole from her was going to be killed. I know that for a fact.'

Fairchild gestured vaguely with his free hand. 'Sometimes, if there is too much involved, too much risk of a scandal, other measures have to be taken.'

'Murder?'

'No. Correcting errors.'

'But you were the one putting their daughters with child.'

'I did not force them into bed. If their lack of morality opens up opportunities for sharp-minded businessmen to make a little profit, then who is to blame?'

'And George?'

'Wanted your fortune to pay off his debts. No need to look surprised, we all knew about your Spanish plunder. As your husband, everything you owned would become his. Catherine would fetch a healthy slice as a reward for putting you into his hands. We would stave off George's creditors until you came of age, with perhaps a child or two as security.'

'You would have taken my children?'

'So many little ones die before their first year. A little invention and you would have been none the wiser. Unfortunately, George seems to have proved somewhat deficient in that respect.'

'This is all too clever for you, Fairchild. You are nothing but a male harlot. All your talent lies in your breeches.'

'Your tongue will prove less sharp with a rope

around your neck. You were seen burning down the Rose Inn and making off with a child. One of those crimes alone would be enough to send you to the gallows.'

'The baby has gone abroad with her mother. You won't see either again.'

Fairchild shook his head. 'No matter. I am done with this business. You've stirred up too many hornets with your prodding for things to remain comfortable. Tell me where the parson keeps his money and his papers. I might decide to let you both make a run for it.'

'Proudlove will find you,' Charles broke in. 'His henchman, Ironjack, will feed you to his dogs.'

A smile played across Fairchild's mouth. 'I daresay you guessed what happened to old Littlejohn. Other men came too close to the truth, or became greedy and tried to take more than their share. The parson is a possessive man. As he sees it, you are his property but in betraying him you have lost your value. He will see you do penance. When it is finished, you will pray for the comfort of a hangman's noose. Turning king's evidence will save me. Proudlove can hang alongside you, 'tis your choice. You have lived with him, been inside this very room I don't doubt. Tell me where he keeps his papers.'

I spread my hands. 'I don't know. We came here tonight to recover my property. You are welcome to anything of his you find.'

His smile never faltered. 'You are a cunning vixen. I admire that. However my patience is not inexhaustible. Remain stubborn and I will kill the cripple.'

The pistol shifted and aimed at Charles's head. Fairchild cocked the hammer. A rash of sweat broke out on his face. His eyes were twin mirrors full of death.

A clap of thunder. A stench of hot gunpowder. Blood sprayed across the front of my cloak. I screamed. A trapdoor of wet flesh flapped open on Adam Fairchild's skull. The life had already gone out of his eyes before he crumpled on to the rug. He twitched once, twice, his hand still gripping the pistol, which miraculously had not discharged. The dregs of his final breath rattled in the back of his throat. Beside me, Charles cursed softly.

Another figure stood in the doorway. Death in a shovel hat, the night clinging to his black clerical garb. He tucked a smoking gun into his belt and cocked another with the ease of one accustomed to dispensing misery. 'My traitorous friend was correct in one respect,' Parson Proudlove said, nudging Fairchild's carcass with the edge of his foot. 'You are a clever witch. An element of risk was always involved in bringing you under my roof.'

Without taking his eyes off us, he swooped down, pulled off Adam's rings and pocketed them. An engraved snuffbox was plucked from a waistcoat pocket followed by a gold fob watch. Fairchild's purse was emptied on to the rug, the parson taking the sovereigns but leaving the rest to be swallowed up by the spreading pool of blood.

'Not content with murder?' I accused. 'Now you must rob the dead?'

401

To my horror, he slipped his tongue through the hole in his cheek and licked his jaw free of some irritation. 'I have taken back that which belongs to me. Even his garments are mine by rights. When a dray horse turns sour and the farmer must slaughter it, he will keep the harness, for what does it profit him to lose that as well?'

'I don't understand.'

'But my child, it was you who correctly surmised that Fairchild was not a gentleman. In fact, his father was a cooper spending a second year in a debtors' prison. The mother was a whore. I found Adam working in the same brothel, catering for patrons with special tastes. Such a charismatic lad. I clothed him, taught him to speak well, put the rings on his fingers and threw society at his feet. What well-bred filly could resist him?'

'Did you pick his women with care?' I spat. 'Did you wait until they were at their most vulnerable before sending in your lackey with his oily charm? Even their husbands, in debt and humiliated could do nothing after Fairchild had stripped them at the card table. Only now with a gun aimed at my head can I fully appreciate what you have done.'

'You are young and healthy,' the parson continued. 'I could squeeze a dozen children out of you. Such a waste.'

'So I am still to die, after escaping Fairchild's gun?'

'You are already dead. After setting fire to the Rose Inn, you fled into the night. You have not been seen since. Perhaps in the dark you wandered into the nearby lake and drowned. Or you blundered out on to the moors and fell to your death over an escarpment. At any rate you will never be seen again, you or your lover.'

'Ironjack will get you. He believes you tried to use me to turn a trick on him.'

'Any misunderstanding can be cleared up with enough money. I could build him a dozen pigsties like the Rose. Now,' he waved the pistol at the door, 'it is time to go to church and make your peace with God.'

We had no choice but to do as he wanted. He marched us down the lane to the stables. Charles and I stumbled along in silence. No carriage or horseman passed us. The parson was eerily sure-footed, as if moving through the dark was second nature to him. At the stable door, he ordered Charles to pick up a spade before shoving us both in the direction of the church. Once through the lich-gate, Proudlove gestured at a patch of weed-covered ground next to one of the older tomb-stones. 'Start digging,' he said. 'Make it a deep hole, deep enough for both of you.'

'I'll not dig my own grave,' Charles growled. 'You'd be as well to kill me here and now.'

'Don't try to be noble. There are many ways to die. Defy me and I'll shoot the wench's belly out. A slow, painful death, and I won't miss. I've been knocking the wings off sparrows since I was a boy.'

'What kind of clergyman are you?' I whispered. 'You wear the cloth whilst delighting in the works of the devil. If you like to inflict suffering, why not go with the army and vent your black passions in America? A battlefield is the place for a butcher, not a church.'

He laughed. A hideous expression on his mutilated face. 'For such a clever one you have the sense of a donkey at times. I fought in wars before your father spat you out of his loins. I was a mercenary prior to becoming a clergyman, back to the Seven Years' War and earlier. 'Twas not the pox that put this hole in my face but a French musket ball. With his own bayonet I gutted the man who tried to kill me. However, the ways of the church were to my liking. A parson's collar can open more doors than a scarlet uniform and who would question a cleric who wishes to travel the county visiting his flock?'

He gestured with the pistol. 'No more talking. You girl, get on your knees and help him dig. Use your hands.'

Footsteps crunched on the cinder path, the sound amplified in the still air. Proudlove snapped around. Marjorie stood on the path, burning torch in hand, her face a wrinkled grey blanket. 'No more killing, Nathaniel.' Her voice was barely more than a whisper. 'No more sin.'

'Ah, the prodigal wife returns to lecture me.'

An expression of terrible weariness hung in the folds of her face. 'I was not always your wife. I had pride once.'

'Go back to the house and shut the door,' Proudlove told her. 'Better still, crawl into your miserable bed and forget you saw anything tonight.'

'As I had to forget the day of my father's funeral? When you ripped the fastenings on my mourning gown and took me with tears of grief still wet on my cheeks?' She turned to me. 'When I found out I was carrying his bastard I wanted to die. I could not accuse him. He had weaselled his way into the minds and pockets of all the fine households and dispensed terror from the pulpit to bring common men to their knees. He needed a wife for respectability. What choice had I? The rest of my family would have disowned me for birthing a child out of wedlock. I faced ruin.'

Marjorie took a deep breath. 'I should've embraced the gutter with open arms. When George was born he wanted to sell him to a couple in Somerset and tell everyone that the child had died in his sleep. I swore that if he touched the boy I'd denounce him, no matter the consequences. Let me raise the lad myself, I said, and I'll hold my tongue. I will turn my eyes away and close my ears. That was the pact I made.'

She held up a strand of grey hair. 'Do you know how old I am, Juliana? Forty-eight years I've suffered on this earth, yet I have the look of a crone. His evil has sucked the life out of me.'

'You turned barren and it soured your temper,' Proudlove retorted. 'You made a martyr of yourself.'

'Birthing Charlotte tore me up inside. I could have no more children. After the surgeon told me, I cried for weeks. I couldn't bear to be touched. Nathaniel took his pleasure elsewhere, tumbling the farm girls because their fathers could not pay a tithe to the church. He keeps his money hidden in an altar to a God he has no respect for. His church is tainted with the cries of stolen children. He has desecrated the entire county.'

405

Proudlove paced up and down the path, pistol swinging. 'Don't shed any tears over that rabble. They are no better than flies. They proliferate without thinking of the consequences. Women have four, five, six brats in the knowledge that at least half shall die. Their foul wombs are breeding pens for hordes of hungry mouths. Throughout their lives they spread filth and disease. Even in death they blight the earth. Paupers' graves are scattered everywhere like boils.'

'Nathaniel, for years I've kept my peace. I played the pious wife, sitting quietly in that empty church each Sabbath while you laughed up your sleeve at the ignorance of your parishioners. Now you would murder these two for depriving you of a few sovereigns. It can't go on.'

'Then tell me, wife, what you propose to do about it.'

'Drive your gig to Eastleigh and tell the constable. He's an honest man who won't be bought with your liar's gold.'

Proudlove gestured at Charles and myself. 'Is this really what has turned you from a sheep into Judas? An orphan-widow and a crippled farmer's boy?'

'You sold Betty Hendy's son. That brute from the Rose, the one called Ironjack, came prowling around Dinstock. I saw him leave the tavern and caught him in the street. The fellow was burned about the head and babbling like an idiot. He told me you sold Peter Hendy to a merchant in Clifton. Ironjack planned to keep the money because you tricked him and put his inn to the torch.'

'Criminals spout nonsense the moment they

scent the gallows. Talk, talk, talk, as if making speeches could prevent their deaths. That sort will say anything to earn a few extra moments of life. They don't care whom they sully with their lies.'

Charles muttered something. The parson rounded on him. 'Did you say something, cripple-boy?'

'A light is burning in the church,' Charles said. 'It's getting bigger.'

A huge crash sounded from the building's east wall. The tall window exploded in a shower of glittering splinters. A tongue of flame thrust out of the shattered mouth. Melting lead spread gunmetal fingers across the blackening stone-work. We all stared as a tunnel of smoke spiralled into the sky. Strips of ash wafted on to the ground like dandelion seeds.

It seemed like the end of the world. Another window shattered, raining glass on to our heads. Instinctively we ducked, the parson shrouding himself in his black cloak. A shard sliced into my cheek. I felt warm blood slither down my neck. Another split Charles's good hand open. He stuffed it inside his coat, staring in horror at the blazing church.

We ran around to the front, the spade left abandoned by the tombs. A terrible sight greeted us. Beyond the open door, the church had become an inferno. Rivers of pitch entwined the pews like black ivy. Prayer books lay scattered on the floor, their innards gutted and ripped into white shreds. The pulpit was a tower of fire, the roof a sheet of orange flame. Rafters cracked and dropped blaz-ing splinters into the christening font.

'This is your doing, wife,' Proudlove roared. 'You and your ignorant friends will have to work all the harder to pay for it. I shall have it out of your blood if need be.'

He lunged towards her. Marjorie thrust out the torch and caught him on the side of the face. He howled like an injured cur and backed away, clutching his temple. I could smell singed hair. 'If you've robbed me...' he gasped.

'I have taken nothing,' Majorie said. 'Your hoard is still inside. Enough money for fifty churches. Lives can't be bought back, Nathaniel. Not for all the sovereigns in the country.'

A livid welt blackened the parson's head where she had branded him. Hatred simmered beneath his chiselled brows. He shoved Marjorie aside and ran into the furnace, a black, flapping figure like a huge crow. He managed to pull a brass-studded box from behind the burning pulpit and crammed it inside his cloak. Cinders rained from the ceiling. On the way out he lost his grip on the box. It smacked on to the floor and the lid burst open. A welter of coins rolled into the fire.

Marjorie blocked the door. He raised a fist to strike her. She shook her head. 'You can't kill us all.'

'I won't be hung,' he growled, 'not by a gaggle of peasants.'

Fire licked at the hem of his cloak. The pitch-sodden material blossomed into flame. He threw his arms wide and backed into the church. Through the colours of his own destruction, the parson's face melted like a wax candle. He screamed something, the words unintelligible.

His cloak was now a shroud of fire.

Charles leapt forward and pulled Marjorie away from the door. My senses swam with the mixed stench of burning pitch and wood. I prayed that I would pass out on the ash-caked grass, begged for darkness and relief. But I could not close my eyes, or cover my face and run.

The roof caved in and the fire swallowed itself up. Three of the church's walls collapsed in a rumbling cacophony of dust and shattered masonry. Smoke swirled around the gravestones, gritting our eyes. We fought not to choke on the scorched air. The sky had turned the colour of blood and everything was tainted.

Footsteps pounded up the lane. Men's voices cried out in alarm. Too late to do anything. Charles's arm slipped around me. I pushed myself deeper into the nest of his comfort. We slunk away, Marjorie in tow, and hid inside the hut whilst the church burned to the ground. Villagers stood in a loose circle, no one making any effort to quench the flames. Afterwards, when the morning sun revealed a blackened, smoking husk, Charles went to tell everyone that the parson was dead.

As if a spell had been broken, a rowdy mob of village men gathered outside the tavern. They streamed out of Dinstock by cart, on horseback or, if no other transport could be found, on foot. Returning at dusk – grim and unwilling to talk – they shut themselves behind their doors and drew the curtains across the windows.

Later, I heard that members of the parson's unholy gang had been rounded up as they tried to seek refuge in the countryside. Some were garrotted, others strung up from the nearest bough.

Ironjack was dragged, still babbling, from the barn in which he'd been hiding. The following morning a miller from Eastleigh found him lying face down beside the brook. His skull was caved in. A bloodied rock lay nearby.

For Marjorie's sake we slipped away to the Widow Hendy's. There was no telling what the mob might do to the parson's wife. She clung to Charlotte, quietly sobbing into the girl's hair. Meanwhile a spark had returned to Betty Hendy's eyes. She stoked the hearth, made coffee from a packet hidden under her bed and fussed and clucked around everyone.

That night, the parsonage was looted and put to the torch. An orange glow lit up the treetops. In the morning we made our way to the church stables. The parson's gig had been pulled to pieces and scattered across the cobbled yard. His charcoal mare was missing. The other horses, though badly frightened by the carnage, had not been touched.

We smuggled Marjorie out of the village in my old coach, Charlotte seated on her lap. My papers were tucked into her gown. Knowing where they were hidden, she had smuggled them out of the parsonage before coming to the church. After long hours on the road we arrived, bedraggled and exhausted, at her relatives' house in Wexborough. The family received us with great kindness and bid us stay as long as necessary. Whilst in town I settled my legal affairs and swore a statement for the magistrate. News of events in Dinstock was already beginning to filter through. The coffee houses were all buzzing with it, I was told.

On the way back, my hired chaise passed the Butter House. The windows were boarded up, the front door nailed shut. Weeds poked green heads between the cracks on the front step. The lawyers handling my inheritance had explained that the property was for sale at a bargain price but no one wanted the house of a madwoman.

Catherine was indeed committed to Bedlam. They kept her bound, as much to avoid her hurting herself as others. Each night she cried out for her dead brother. Her lover. Sometimes my name tumbled out of her mouth, though most of what she said no longer made much sense.

I came into my father's money but found I couldn't live easily with the trappings of wealth, or the kind of society it bought me into. Some declared that to look deep into my eyes was to see a hundred stories simmering away like a pot about to blow its lid. Others suggested that many scars lurked behind my tucked-up smile.

But my days of telling stories were done and my sleep no longer haunted by nightmares. My smiles were real enough. I had much to be glad about.

I knew what love meant now and held it dearer than any other treasure. Much of my new fortune rebuilt the lives of those the parson nearly destroyed. Dinstock received a new vicar, a humble, devout man who held services on the common land when the weather was kind. Sometimes the gypsies, when camped there, listened to his sermons.

The widow's son, Peter Hendy, was found bedraggled and hungry on the Bristol road. His would-be purchaser, getting wind of a scandal, had ordered his coachman to dump the boy on the outskirts of town. Peter had tramped miles, begging food and snatching nights in barns when the chance arose. Betty was transported with joy. It was a new beginning, and we all hoped more would follow.

Meanwhile the old church remained a charred ruin in the middle of the neglected graveyard. No one ever went there. In the days following the burning, a group of village men poked among the rubble. All they found were blackened coins and a brace of twisted candlesticks. Nobody wanted the money. Not even the poorest in the parish would touch it. A curse lay upon the place and mothers frightened unruly children with tales of the parson swooping through the night to snatch babies away.

They spoke too, of the child stealer, who brought Miss Jane's baby back from the Bad Place. With each telling the story grew. One child saved became ten, then a hundred.

But such tales were nonsense and would fade with time. I was content with what I had. I heard that Marjorie married a banker and moved to a fine house in Wexborough with her daughter. Charlotte was growing fast and would become a young woman to reckon with before long. Neither returned to the ruined parsonage. The bones of Adam Fairchild lay undisturbed.

Charles still travelled to Dinstock, usually on

business. He turned into quite the horse dealer, my husband, with a haggling skill and eye for a bargain that would put the Romanies to shame. We bought a smallholding five miles north of Eastleigh that boasted a modest but comfortable house, excellent stables and a few acres of good land. Our business prospered. Though Charles could squabble like a woman sometimes, we loved each other very deeply. I treasured every moment of my normal, ordinary life.

Spring was painting the land green again when I felt the first stirring of life within my womb. Our daughter, Mary, was born just before Christmas, a healthy, bawling child weighing all of seven pounds. Charles lifted her up and laughed as if he had cracked open the world and found it lined with gold.

I could never forget looking down on her face for the first time as she pressed against my breast. White, all white save for the dark lashes and tiny, rosebud lips. A tuft of coppery hair was my bequest, but those round, enquiring eyes could only have come from her father. Her skin was as pure as a fresh sheet of linen. She did not bear the red smear that had marked me out all my life. Manuel's legacy ended here. Charles's blood flowed in her veins as well as my own. She was a part of us both. Our child.

And no one would steal her away.

The publishers hope that this book has given you enjoyable reading. Large Print Books are especially designed to be as easy to see and hold as possible. If you wish a complete list of our books please ask at your local library or write directly to:

Magna Large Print Books
Magna House, Long Preston,
Skipton, North Yorkshire.
BD23 4ND

This Large Print Book for the partially sighted, who cannot read normal print, is published under the auspices of

THE ULVERSCROFT FOUNDATION